Jim Murray's

WHISKY BIBLE

2005

This 2005 edition of "Jim Murray's Whisky Bible", is dedicated
with pride and lifelong gratitude to: Andy Marshall,
Kevin Muscat (Andy Roberts, 42), Matt Lawrence,
Darren Ward, Robbie Ryan (Marvin Elliott, 56), Dennis Wise,
Paul Ifill (Peter Sweeney, 29), Tim Cahill, David Livermore,
Danny Dichio and Neil Harris, all of whom made the
Glenfiddich 1937 taste so much sweeter.

This edition published in 2004

10 9 8 7 6 5 4 3 2

The "Jim Murray's" logo and "the Whisky Bible" logo are trade marks of James
Murray and are used under licence

A CIP catalogue record for this book is available from the British Library

ISBN 1 84442 670 X

Printed in Singapore

Project Editor: Martin Corteel
Design & Project Art Direction: Darren Jordan
Production: Lisa French
Illustration: Bill Caldwell

Author's Note

I have used the spelling "whiskey" or "whisky" depending on how the individual
distillers prefer. All Scotch is "whisky". So is Canadian. All Irish, these days, is
"whiskey", though that was not always the case. In Kentucky, bourbon and rye
are spelt "whiskey", with the exception of the produce of the Early Times/Old
Forester Distillery and Maker's Mark which they bottle as "whisky". In Tennessee,
it is a 50–50 split: Dickel is "whisky", while Daniel's is "whiskey".

Jim Murray's

WHISKY BIBLE

~ 2005 ~

*The world's leading whisky guide from
the world's leading whisky authority*

CARLTON
BOOKS

Contents

Introduction 6
How to Read The Bible 7
Bible Thumping 9
Review of the Whisky Year 12
Jim Murray's Whisky Award Winners 2005 16

Scottish Malts 22

Aberfeldy 25
Aberlour 25
Allt-A-Bhainne 28
Ardbeg 28
Ardmore 35
Auchentoshan 36
Auchroisk 38
Aultmore 38
Balblair 39
Balmenach 40
The Balvenie 41
Banff 42
Ben Nevis 43
Benriach 44
Benrinnes 45
Benromach 46
Ben Wyvis 47
Bladnoch 47
Blair Athol 48
Bowmore 49
Braes of Glenlivet . 53
Brora 53
Bruichladdich 55
Bunnahabhain . . . 58
Caol Ila 60
Caperdonich 64
Cardhu 66
Clynelish 66
Coleburn 69
Convalmore 69
Cragganmore 70
Craigellachie 71
Dailuaine 71
Dallas Dhu 72
Dalmore 73
Dalwhinnie 74
Deanston 75
Dufftown 76
Edradour 77
Fettercairn 77
Glen Albyn 78
Glenallachie 78
Glenburgie 78

Glencadam 79
Glencraig 79
Glendronach 80
Glendullan 80
Glen Elgin 81
Glenesk 81
Glenfarclas 82
Glenfiddich 85
Glenflagler 87
Glen Garioch 88
Glenglassaugh 89
Glengoyne 89
Glen Grant 90
Glen Keith 93
Glenkinchie 94
The Glenlivet 94
Glenlochy 98
Glenlossie 99
Glen Mhor 100
Glenmorangie . . . 100
Glen Moray 103
Glen Ord 104
Glenrothes 105
Glen Scotia 107
Glen Spey 108
Glentauchers 108
Glenturret 109
Glenugie 110
Glenury Royal . . . 110
Highland Park 111
Imperial 116
Inchgower 116
Inverleven 117
Isle of Arran 117
Isle of Jura 118
Knockando 120
Knockdhu 120
Ladyburn 121
Lagavulin 121
Laphroaig 122
Linkwood 125
Littlemill 127
Loch Lomond . . . 128

Lochside 128
Longmorn 129
Macallan 131
Macduff 143
Mannochmore . . . 143
Millburn 144
Miltonduff 144
Mortlach 145
Mosstowie 147
North Port 147
Oban 148
Pittyvaich 148
Port Ellen 149
Pulteney 151
Rosebank 153
Royal Brackla 155
Royal Lochnagar . . 156
St Magdalene 157
Scapa 158
Speyburn 159
Speyside 159
Springbank 160
Strathisla 163
Strathmill 165
Talisker 166
Tamdhu 167
Tamnavulin 168
Teaninich 168
Tobermory 169
Tomatin 171
Tomintoul 171
Tormore 172
Tullibardine 172
Unspecified Singles
    Campbeltown . . 173
    Highland 173
    Island 175
    Islay 175
    Lowland 177
    Speyside 177
Vatted Malts 179
Mystery Malts . . . 187

Scottish Grain 188
Caledonian 190   Girvan 190
Cambus 190   Invergordon 190
Cameronbridge 190   North British 190
Dumbarton 190   North of Scotland 191

Scottish Blends 193

Irish Whiskey 224
Pure Pot Still 226   Single Grain 233
Single Malts 229   Blended 234

American Whiskey 240
American Single Malt 242   Wild Turkey 245
Clear Creek 242   **Bourbon Brands** 245
Edgefield 242   **Tennessee Whiskey** 262
St George 242   George Dickel 262
Bourbon Distilleries 243   Jack Daniel 262
Barton 243   Virginia Bourbon 262
Buffalo Trace 243   **Corn Whiskey** 263
Brown-Forman 244   **Rye; Single Malt** 263
Four Roses 244   Anchor Distillery 263
Heaven Hill 244   **Rye; Straight Rye** 265
Jim Beam 244   **Kentucky Whiskey** 267
Labrot & Graham 244   **American Whiskey Blend** 267
Maker's Mark 245

Japanese Whisky 268

Canadian Whisky 284
Canadian Single Malt 286   Okanagan Distillery 286
Glenora Distillery 286   **Canadian Blended Whisky** ... 286

European Whisky 290
Austria 291   Poland 295
Belgium 292   Spain 295
Bulgaria 292   Switzerland 295
France 292   Turkey 295
Germany 293   Wales 296

World Whiskies 297
Australia 298   New Zealand 301
Brazil 300   South Africa 302
India 301

whiskybible.com 303
Credits 304

List of Maps
Scottish Malts 22–23   United States 240–41
Speyside Malts 24   Japan 268–69
Scottish Grain 145   Canada 285, 286
Ireland 224–25

Introduction

As I sit here, the early June sun setting on some of the most beautiful non-distilling countryside in the world, only ten months have passed since I wrote the introduction to the first-ever *Jim Murray's Whisky Bible*. Ten, not twelve, because such has been the success of the Bible we have had to bring the printing forward by two months so copies can reach every corner of the globe by Christmas. The idea had been from August to August. Now it is June to June.

But fear not: you are not being short-changed. This edition offers an extra 700 or so tasting notes covering just about every whisky I could find launched between August 2003 and June 2004, (plus the Macallan and Karuizawa vintage ranges which also made spectacular tasting) taking the coverage to nearly 3,000 whiskies globally. And during editing we should be able to include a few midsummer – or winter, if southern hemisphere – bottlings as well. To further prove that the Bible is just that, we have bumped up the book by 50 pages ... at no extra cost to you.

I would like to thank the hundreds upon hundreds of people who have contacted me since *Jim Murray's Whisky Bible* was launched. I have been enormously touched and almost overwhelmed by your many complimentary words. Thank you.

I have managed to reply to most but some slipped through the net due to a rather spectacular computer failure, one that has hindered the launch of the accompanying website and also lost details of some people requesting signed copies. If I didn't respond to you, or send the books, my most sincere apologies. Please e-mail me again: I will be delighted to hear from you. Oh, and the website is on its way if not already with you by the time you read this. Its delay has been a source of irritation to me, but keep logging on to **www.whiskybible.com** and eventually we shall all be rewarded.

Of all the e-mails I received, amazingly only one was to complain. And that was because there were no colour pictures of labels. Which, I think, speaks volumes. And shows that it is very rare that people don't see the actual point of the Bible, which seems to have been enthusiastically welcomed by all aspects of the whisky world. *Jim Murray's Whisky Bible 2004* went into more than one printing and was emptied from warehouses within days of arriving. I was personally 3,000 copies short of fulfilling orders sent to me, such was the demand, and I apologise to those who were unable to get a copy.

Right: on to the 2005 edition ... By and large the quality of the new bottlings I have uncovered have been high: certainly higher than the previous year. This is possibly because most have come from independent bottlers who have now tuned into the fact that more and more whisky lovers prefer their whisky natural. The impassioned plea I made in last year's Bible for the dropping of caramel probably received the greatest number of endorsements among readers and I even received the odd communication from distillers admitting that they were now thinking of heading down that particular path. Result!

Because the Bible was put to bed two months earlier than originally planned my travelling was confined to Australia and New Zealand. Asia will have to wait until this coming year (2004/05), when I should also be embracing South America and possibly South Africa. The whisky universe just keeps on expanding ... .

Jim Murray
The Cricket Pavilion
Ockley
Surrey (June 2004)

How to Read The Bible

The whole point of this book is for the whisky lover – be he or she an experienced connoisseur or, better fun still, simply starting out on the long and joyous path of discovery – to have ready access to easy-to-understand information about as many whiskies as possible. And I mean a lot. Thousands.

This book does not quite include every whisky on the market ... just by far and away the vast majority. And those that have been missed this time round – either through accident, logistics or design – will appear in later editions once we can source a sample.

Whisky Scoring

The marking for this book is tailored to the consumer and scores run out just a little higher than I use for my own personal references. But such is the way it has been devised it has not affected my order of preference.

Each whisky is given a rating out of 100. Twenty-five marks are given to each of four factors: nose (**n**), taste (**t**), finish (**f**), balance and overall complexity (**b**). That means that 50% of the marks are given for flavour alone and 25% for the nose, often an overlooked part of the whisky equation. The area of balance and complexity covers all three previous factors and a usually hidden one besides:

Nose: this is simply the aroma. Often requires more than one inspection as hidden aromas can sometimes reveal themselves after time in the glass and increased contact with air. The nose very often tells much about a whisky, but – as we shall see – equally can be quite misleading.

Taste: this is the immediate arrival on the palate and involves the flavour profile up to, and including, the time it reaches maximum intensity and complexity.

Finish: often the least understood part of a tasting. This is the tail and flourish of the whisky's signature, often revealing the effects of ageing. The better whiskies tend to finish well and longer without too much oak excess.

Balance: This is the part it takes a little experience to appreciate but it can be mastered by anyone. For a whisky to work well on the nose and palate, it should not be too one-sided in its character. If you are looking for an older whisky, it should have evidence of oak, but not so much that all other flavours and aromas are drowned out. Likewise, a whisky matured or finished in a sherry butt must offer a lot more than just wine alone and the greatest Islay malts revel in depth and complexity beyond the smoky effects of peat.

Each whisky has been analysed by me without adding water or ice. I have taken each whisky as it was poured from the bottle and used no more than warming in the glass to extract and discover the character of the whisky. To have added water would have been pointless: it would have been an inconsistent factor as people, when pouring water, add different amounts at varying temperatures. The only constant with the whisky you and I taste will be when it has been poured directly from the glass.

Even if you and I taste the same whiskies at the same temperature and from identical glasses – and even share the same values in whisky – our scores may still be different. Because a factor that is built into my evaluation is drawn from expectation and experience. When I sample a whisky from a certain distillery at such-and-such an age or from this type of barrel or that, I would expect it to offer me certain qualities. It has taken me 25 years to acquire this knowledge (which I try to add to day by day!) and an enthusiast cannot be expected to learn it overnight. But, hopefully, *Jim Murray's Whisky Bible* will help...!

Score chart

Within the parentheses () is the overall score out of 100.

0–50	Nothing short of absolutely diabolical.
51–64	Nasty and well worth avoiding.
65–69	Very unimpressive indeed.
70–74	Usually drinkable but don't expect the earth to move.
75–79	Average and usually pleasant though sometimes flawed.
80–84	Good whisky worth trying.
85–89	Very good to excellent whiskies definitely worth buying.
90–93	Brilliant.
94–97	Superstar whiskies that give us all a reason to live.
98–100	Better than anything I've ever tasted!

Key to Abbreviations & Symbols

% Percentage strength of whisky measured as alcohol by volume. **b** Overall balance and complexity. **bott** Date of bottling. **db** Distillery bottling. In other words, an expression brought out by the owners of the distillery. **dist** Date of distillation or spirit first put into cask. **f** Finish. **n** Nose. **nc** Non-coloured. **ncf** Non-chill-filtered. **sc** Single cask. **t** Taste. ∴∴ New entry for 2005.

Finding Your Whisky

Worldwide Malts: Whiskies are listed alphabetically throughout the book. In the case of single malts, the distilleries run A–Z style with distillery bottlings appearing at the top of the list in order of age, starting with youngest first. After age comes vintage. After all the "official" distillery bottlings are listed, next come other bottlings, again in alphabetical order. Single malts without a distillery named (or perhaps named after a dead one) are given their own section, as are vatted malts.

Worldwide Blends: These are simply listed alphabetically, irrespective of which company produce them. So "Black Bottle" appears ahead of "White Horse" and Japanese blends begin with "Amber" and ends with "Za". In the case of brands being named after companies or individuals the first letter of the brand will dictate where it is listed. So William Grant, for instance, will be found under "W" for William rather "G" for Grant.

Bourbon/Rye: This is one of the most confusing types of whiskey to list because often the name of the brand bears no relation to the name of the distillery that made it. Also, brands may be sold from one company to another, or shortfalls in stock may see companies buying bourbons from another. For that reason all the brands have been listed alphabetically with the name of the bottling distiller being added at the end.

Irish Whiskey: There are four types of Irish whiskey: (i) pure pot still; (ii) single malt, (iii) single grain and (iv) blended. Some whiskies may have "pure pot still" on the label, but are actually single malts. So check both sections.

Bottle Information

Because there are no labels included in this book in order to save room I have tried to include all the relevant information you will find on the label to make identification of the brand straightforward. Where known I have included date of distillation and bottling – to day, month and year if known. Also the cask number for further recognition. At the end of the tasting notes I have included the strength and, if known, number of bottles released and in which markets. So NL will mean it is available in the Netherlands.

Bible Thumping Coveting Thy Neighbour's Malt

Many years ago I gave my first-ever tasting to an audience of over 100 people. It was at the Chelsea Hotel, Knightsbridge, and the one and only time I ever felt nervous as I began my talk about the eight assembled malts.

I needn't have worried. After a faltering first five minutes I hit my note-less stride and a long and warm ovation ended the good-humoured evening in front of an appreciative and increasingly sozzled crowd. For over twenty minutes afterwards people patiently waited to shake my hand and ask me questions.

Finally, the very last gentleman – a man well into his pension and by some way the oldest member of the audience – offered four fingers and a thumb in darkened, shrivelled skin, then a half-hearted hand-shake.

"Mr Murray," he addressed me in cut-glass English direct from a black-and-white film from the '40s. "Just after the last war I was in charge of sales for Johnnie Walker in the Far East. Singapore and all that kind of thing. There were no malts in those days, you know. No people like you standing up and describing all these smells and flavours. People just drunk blends and enjoyed them. Usually with ice and a dash of soda. Anyway, you are a busy man and you don't want to hear me rattle on. All I wanted to say to you is this: I have sat here for nearly three hours this evening, listened to all you have said and I can tell you I have never heard such a load of old bollocks in all my life...." And with that he turned on his well-healed shoes and made a dignified exit from the room.

Its possible that wonderful old gent has a relation just a few yards from my home. He is in his early 90s and was an established part of the Hong Kong scene before enduring a difficult period of incarceration after its fall during World War II. He is a dear friend to me and I am probably his only living friend in the area. He is fascinated by my work, but he admits he cannot understand a word of it. "You might as well be writing a book about brain surgery, it would make just as much sense. Whisky's whisky to me."

Both those noble and honest gentlemen have, in their own way, underlined an important aspect of the perception of whisky and thus played a telling role in my professional life. Not just by keeping things grounded, but also never allowing me to look away from what counts in whisky communication: that it is vital to be able to talk to anyone at whatever level when it comes to trying to get the best out of a spirit of sometimes unfathomable depth. Also, that it is imperative to respect the views of those who see things differently. And that there are those who do not want single malts or people how to explain to them how they might get more out of their glass. That if someone is to champion the cause for whisky then equally the fight must be made for every jewel in the spirit's crown.

This stance, then, more than partly explains my total frustration – sometimes anger – when it comes to the promoting of blended whisky. Yes, malts are fabulous.

Yes, they can intrigue and tease and play games. Yes, they often surprise you and sometimes seduce you. They are individual parts of a mosaic that takes a lifetime to interpret. And that mosaic is a blend. For there are people out there – and I mean in their millions worldwide – who simply adore blended whisky and don't buy the single malt story. If that is what they prefer, then that is their choice and they have as much right to be respected as single malt or straight bourbon lovers.

Which is why it is absolutely essential that blended whisky is treated on a par with malts. If one thing irritates me more than any other, it is the condescending way that blended whiskies are portrayed in magazine and newspaper articles. Whisky snobbery not only exists, but it is being openly promoted. To the extent that people who drink blends have now become apologists without even noticing. The fact they prefer to sit in a bar and savour a blend often makes them feel like whisky lepers: "Oh, I don't know much about whisky, I'm afraid. I just drink blends." Every year I hear a similar phrase countless times. And the fact that they have make excuses for their preference after years of brainwashing makes my blood boil.

Snob in a blender

On British television the only Scotch whisky adverts you are likely to see is for Bell's and Grouse, though the odd Glenfiddich moment is there for us. But even with Bell's the irritating wording sends a dangerous subliminal message: it mentions something about only the best malts being blended together. No mention of grain. Which, of course, tells only about 35% of the story.... and counters the point of the advert by insinuating that malts are better than blends.

Of late only Dewar's – obviously aware of the worth of such a magnificent blending heritage – is bringing on to market newly formulated blends. This last year's batch have been quite magnificent, which is in curious contrast to their range of malts which have been comparatively disappointing. But I will happily sacrifice those malts for the mercurial brilliance of a new blend. Because people are more likely to learn and understand whisky from a great blend than they will from any average single malt.

It is for that reason I always try and include blends in tastings and seminars. And there is another reason: organisers of malt whisky clubs don't like the idea and as often as not try to persuade me not to. The general message is: "Look, we're into malt whisky and don't do blends. Too downmarket, old boy. We've progressed from that."

Then when I talk to the audience I begin to wonder. Because it seems that an entire generation has passed blended whisky by. Often it started with fine wine and then moved on to single malts. Blends, perceived as something cheap for the masses and an altogether inferior product, never entered the equation. Which was quite different from that audience in Knightsbridge the best part of 15 years ago. Just about each and every one of them had been blend drinkers and now they were discovering the malts that were beginning to flood the market.

In the decade since, whole forests of paper has been used to tell people how great single malts are, which is fabulous news. Pity, though, the same resources have not gone into promoting blends. So now when talking to people at whisky events worldwide very few have ever received a Grant's or learn from Teacher's. Bailie Nicol Jarvie could be a firm of Edinburgh solicitors.

Worldwide, it appears an entire whisky-worshipping fraternity has passed blended whisky by. Or whiskey. How many connoisseurs had I met who would never touch a Jameson (well, until they read *Jim Murray's Whisky Bible 2004*), but were besotted with Redbreast? Japan boasts some of the most magnificently salivating whiskies you could pray for, most of them blends. But the Japanese perceive them as inferior to common-or-garden single malt Scotch, which they are anything but.

How do we change something that has become so deeply ingrained? For a start the patronising tones of certain whisky commentators could do with being turned down. Buyers and barkeepers should be taken to seminars to have explained to them that just maybe they are missing a trick. They could and should be at the vanguard of a revivalist – or revisionist – movement.

And, equally as important, the malt whisky lover should take some time out and go on a journey of discovery. Perhaps then I will be told less often how these people can't stand blends, when on gentle interrogation they admit they have tasted only one or two, and probably none in the last few years.

Meanwhile distillers and bottlers without taking their eye off the single malt revolution should have the conviction to put equal energy improving the vision of people who are willing to see if only they were shown. A start has been made with some distilleries being used as the homes to promote certain blends, though often the blending part is too simply glossed over. Whisky companies should be braver, editors less tunnel-visioned.

Never has the interest in whisky been greater. And there are millions of palates out there just waiting for an experience that, once, was the common joy to us all. Blends may be too easily perceived as an old man's drink, but that is no more than a fop to fashion. As I am sure the old gentleman of Knightsbridge might tell you if he is still alive, quality – and, in the case of some blends, genius – comfortably transcends time and age.

Review of the Whisky Year

Nosing is never easy when you are fighting for air. But it has been another busy, breathless 12 months. Not quite in the same league as the brain-exploding previous year when no week seemed to pass without news of some distillery about to be going somewhere, but whisky season 2003/04 has been one to keep everyone on their toes.

So, where do we start? Well, St David's Hall in Cardiff is as good a place as any. For there on March 1st 2004 – St. David's Day – Welsh whisky was officially brought back into the world. It had been a good hundred years since the last drops of Welsh were filled into bottle, a process discontinued at the Frangoch Distillery in Bala on account of its poor quality. It is unlikely that such a fate is to befall the **Penderyn Distillery** near Aberdare. But such is the financial demands of distillers, it is vital that they put whisky into the market place at the earliest opportunity, as The Welsh Whisky Company – Y Cwmni Wisgi Cymreig – discovered.

Some – myself included – feared that bottling as a three year old would simply put too much of a strain on a spirit lighter than the average malt on account of a convoluted distilling process that sees the spirit leave the still at a much higher than average strength (a staggering 92% abv, no less), and therefore cleaner than any other of the world's malts. However, consultant in charge Jim Swan has come up trumps with his clever usage of Madeira cakes which, combined with bourbon-cask maturation, gives a richness and depth that has so far afforded the most pleasant of surprises.

Cornish pride

Meanwhile England is set to have its first malt on the market in a few years time. But don't tell the Cornish. Cornwall is England's Celtic county with its own language and a powerful sense of independence from the remainder of the country. To them it is Cornish, not English, whisky. The fact they go about things differently in that part of the world was colourfully illustrated by how Cornish whisky came about in the first place. Normally new distillers contact breweries and come to some kind of arrangement so the fermentation is carried out by people who have the equipment, capacity and know-how. Which is what happens, for instance, with Penderyn, where the wash is made at the Brains Brewery in Cardiff, and in Tasmania where the ancient Cascade Brewery supplies a couple of distilleries down there; the practice is also carried out in areas as diverse at Portland, Oregon, and Switzerland.

However, it was the brewer at the 150-year-old, history-soaked St. Austell's brewery who came up with the idea of making whisky. To do so they contacted distinguished local cider and apple brandy makers **The Cornish Cyder Farm**. The idea appealed to them, so the wash was made in the brewery, transported to the Cyder Farm, and I watched a genuinely first-class spirit trip from a traditional copper pot still made by none other than Forsythe's of Rothes in the heart of Speyside. So far there are only about ten barrels of maturing English/Cornish malt spirit, but a high grade fruity malt is on its way.

On the subject of Speyside, no new stills were needed at **Benriach**, though one day they will be. Because Benriach, silenced by Chivas, is back producing after, as predicted in last year's Bible, being the first – and only Scotch whisky distillery – to change hands in the last year. The new owners are a company led by former Burn Stewart blender Billy Walker. Already plans are underway to bottle a number of versions, and in the Benriach section I have given tasting notes for the whiskies they had in mind to market. They include some tasty peaty numbers produced because Chivas has never owned an Islay distillery and needed stocks of peated malt for blending. Much as in the same way the **Knockdhu** distillery has made some heavily peated (35 ppm) malt for the Inverhouse blending lab. That was made in the early summer of 2004 and though it will be used for blending, a cask or two is likely to be put to one side for one-off bottlings.

A toast to absent friends

Returning, briefly to Benriach: I for one am delighted that the charming little distillery in the shadow of Longmorn is at last going to become a malt marketed with belief and passion. The old Chivas bottling was a pretty sorry affair, a 70cl essay in exactly how not to treat a Speysider with the malt's delicate charm pointlessly swamped under the unsympathetic weight of caramel. I am only sorry that a gentleman of a distiller Ian Grant who for years ate and breathed Benriach is no longer with us to share in its upturned fortune. I have never fully put on record my debt of gratitude to him when, in the late '80s he patiently helped teach me much about the inside secrets of distilling at a time when I had decided that I was going to make a career out of writing about it. Many an hour did he pour into my advanced education and never once did he complain. He was a whisky man of the old school, with the natural and dignified gentleness of an eight-year-old Benriach. I learned recently that he had passed away a couple of years back: my first pouring from a Billy Walker bottling shall be a toast. To Ian.

Remaining in Scotland, there was also some wonderful news from **Scapa**. That much neglected and under-rated Orkney distillery is at last receiving the attention from its owners, Allied, that it deserves. Scapa has wowed them in Duty Free for years, but despite its growing following (have you ever met anyone who has tasted Scapa and not been smitten?) the distillery was operated for only a few weeks each year and usually by staff from neighbouring Highland Park when the manager there had men to spare.

I know Allied received at least one firm offer for the distillery, and four other companies have at various times in the last two years contacted me regarding my views on a possible bid. Perhaps it was this wide interest in the distillery that helped Allied commit to restoring the distillery back to full production with the ghost of Ardbeg haunting them. Elsewhere, late 2003 saw both **Glencadam** and **Tullibardine** come back on stream soon after falling into the hands of new owners. At the latter distillery it is good to see John Black back in distillery management; it is a relief to see such an excellent distillery in such safe hands.

The pen is mightier

Now last year you may have read in the Bible my unease with Diageo's decision to re-launch **Cardhu** as a vatted malt at the same time that thousands of casks still bore its name as a single malt. The vatted Cardhu was the second to last whisky to be tasted for inclusion in *Jim Murray's Whisky Bible 2004* and I had little time to respond to the news other than with an uncomfortable gut reaction. Well, it appeared that my unhappiness was shared by not only whisky drinkers but the remainder of the industry, especially William Grant's who headed a spirited campaign that quite took aback Diageo. The end result was Diageo, after initially digging its claws in for the long haul, backing down and scrapping the new vatting, returning Cardhu to the world as a single malt and even giving back the distillery its Cardhu title after re-naming (or should that be re-renaming?) it Cardow. It was one of the sweetest victories for us traditionalists in living memory.

Even Diageo came out with a crumb of honour by holding their hands up and admitting they had made a mistake. It was the kind of episode that restored some belief in human – and yes, even corporate – nature.

That was not the only surprise to come from Scotland. Founder Jamie Walker has sold **Adelphie**, while a few thousand members of the Scotch Malt Whisky Society were left dumbfounded when this semi-institution of an independent club and bottler was bought by **Glenmorangie plc**. Some members were already up in arms that the Society had begun – horror of horrors – bottling Japanese malt and even bourbon. The fact that the Japanese malts were actually often superior to the vast majority of the Scottish malts was not enough to prevent resignations winging their way in to Leith. More followed with Glenmorangie's takeover. Personally, this is not something I find myself writing indignant letters about: I have no beef with who owns the Society. All that matters, surely, is that members are offered the same if not a better diversity of whiskies at a reasonable price and at varying ages. If, though, every other bottling is a Glen Moray or Glenmorangie then ink will flow. However, the chances of that happening are just about nil.

If these same people resigning from the Society only take their **Macallan** dark, then this has been a very distressing year for them indeed. Because the one thing I could never understand about Macallan – and had written and broadcast this view more than once – was their insistence that all their bottled malt output should be from sherry cask. I have come across enough ex-bourbon cask Macallan over the years to know what a charmer that can be and often thought that some of the best Macallan I had ever tasted was when I had vatted ex-bourbon and ex-sherry casks together in my lab. Macallan, like any company using sherry butts, are not immune to the threat of sulphur-tainted whisky being in the midst of their stocks. Recent bottlings have shown that some had leaked into the system, thus putting an even greater strain on their sherry-matured reserves. Ironically, one that had been spoiled by sulphur was Macallan's first attempt at using a mix of bourbon and sherry oak, the Elegancia.

Imagine my astonishment, then, when a series of new malts from the distillery arrived at my lab. It was the first brand that was specifically marketed as a vatting of bourbon and sherry casks and ranged from 8 to 30 years of age. The way they were spread, at 8, 10, 12, 15, 18, 21, 25 and 30 years gave an extraordinary and unique insight into the workings of Macallan and represent by far the best range of non-vintage whiskies to be launched by any one distillery for possibly the last decade. These are malts that get beneath the sherried veneer of the standard Macallan and in the 15 years old reveals an age when the complexity peaks almost to unbelievable effect.

Macallan may not thank me for saying this, but this compilation, the Fine Oak range, far better serves the distillery and consumer than the standard sherry-soaked 10, 12, 18 and 25-year-olds which portray the malt in a single light and have at times been slightly over-hyped by those who appear to think that there is no such thing as a sub-standard sherry butt. Even when these bottlings do hit top form and offer shimmering elan, they still cannot quite match the breadth, depth and sophistication of the Fine Oak range. Well, that's my firm view and I envisage many an hour's heated debate among Macallanophiles on that one... At the moment only the 10-year-old Fine Oak needs some attention, and that is probably only a matter of better sherry-cask selection. By the 2006 edition of the Whisky Bible it is likely be up there with its younger and older brothers. The remainder are simply jaw-droppingly good and are almost certainly going to be the focus of the biggest debate amongst whisky lovers for the next twelve months.

That's the good news from Macallan. The bad is that they had to admit that some of their ancient bottlings in their private collection are fakes having carried out sophisticated dating tests on them. This has come as no great surprise to those who us who discovered an almost certain fake "nineteenth century" Ardbeg on the loose in Sweden a year back. As soon as I opened the bottle I told the gathered press that I believed the owner had been "had". These fakes have nothing to do with Macallan's vintage malts dating back to 1926 but, rather, bottles of extraordinary antiquity. What I could never understand was why it was bottles from distilleries that had cult followings that kept turning up, when a century ago they were just another distillery. The repercussions in the auction houses will make interesting viewing over the next year.

Beyond Scotland, Europe has been busiest of all with two new types of whisky finding their way onto the shelves (see the European section).

Riding off into the sunset

It was a pretty quiet time in Kentucky but a big loss to the industry came with the death of larger-than-life Booker Noe. Booker was a descendent of the Beam family that set up Kentucky's now most heavily branded bourbon. His tales of old Kentucky life and distilling were legendary and he became a natural figurehead for the Jim Beam brands. But he was a big man who had suffered ill-health for a long while. Oddly, over 20 years, Booker and I had only ever spoken by phone. Our plans to one day meet have now been put back a few further more years.

Luckily, though, I will still be seeing two other whisky greats, blenders Lincoln Henderson and Barry Walsh, even though they have swapped their blending room passes for pension books. Linc had been the blender for Brown Forman for more years than he was willing to admit and had also helped my education with regard to bourbon and Tennessee whisky. While Linc was among a number of eminent bourbon blenders, Barry Walsh had become an institution in Ireland as the man behind all of Irish Distillers projects. His 16-year-old Bushmills will go down as a global great and his recent re-vamping of the standard Jameson blend confirmed his position among the top four or five blenders in the world. As well as two of the best in their trade, Linc and Barry are also among the funniest company and closest and kindest mates you could wish for. And when from time to time I criticised one of their creations between them they never once picked up the phone in a huff or uttered a sharp word or raised voice. Two great pros retired and the industry has suddenly become a poorer place.

Ending on a high note

Finally, congratulations are due to Hedley Wright and the rest of his Springbank squad who this year opened **Glengyle**, the first new Campbeltown distillery for over a century. Or should that be re-opened as it was a matter of Springbank distillery manager Frank McHardy meticulously planning the re-fitting of a distillery that closed in the 1920s. I remember three years ago Frank, eyes sparkling at what was in store, taking me around the shell of the building explaining what would go where and how it would all work. In March 2004 that became reality when J & A Mitchell officially opened the first new Scottish distillery of the twenty-first century. Frank, befitting his high reputation in the industry, delivered the goods.

On the day the ceremony took place I was chairing at the International Wine and Spirit Competition about 400 miles away in Ockley, Surrey. So a few weeks later I rang Springbank to offer my apologies in not attending. "That's all right," came the reply. "You weren't invited..."

Nearly 25 years ago I first visited Springbank and, as a peasant whisky drinker, asked if I could have a look-see. "F*** off!" came the reply from a burly guy who didn't even bother to look at me. For the opening of Glengyle it was strictly employees and contractors only. There was not a single whisky writer or newspapermen in sight: you can only admire and applaud when a distillery keeps so steadfastly to its traditions.... Now let's hope that Glengyle will produce a make even 75% as good as Springbank's. If so, a brilliant new distillery has been born.

Jim Murray's Whisky Bible Award Winners 2005

To save you reading nearly 3,000 whisky tasting notes one by one I have made life easy for you. Each year *Jim Murray's Whisky Bible* will announce a World Whisky of the Year selected from the winner of one of at least 18 categories. It is not only to help you. But it is to personally pay tribute to those who have created something exceptionally special in an already high quality industry.

As well as listing those that I believe have topped their particular tree we also have a roll of honour for all those elite brands which have scored 93 marks or above. During the research and writing of this book it has become apparent that the marking system has something of the Richter Scale about it: the higher the marks, the more pronounced it becomes. In other words, there may be little difference between whiskies marked at 69 and 71, but the gap between 89 and 91 becomes very large indeed.

With well over 2,750 whiskies evaluated for *Jim Murray's Whisky Bible*, it is obvious that the 123 whiskies making it to a score of 94 and above does represent the very highest peaks of the mountain range. Likewise the similar number on 93 itself represents the crème rather than double the crème.

For those of your wondering why, for instance, the masterful Old Malt Cask Ardbeg 1975 doesn't pick up a gong, it was bottled in 2000 and therefore doesn't represent a recent bottling – even though a few unclaimed bottles can still be found here and there.

It is a strange thing, this tasting whisky for a living. Every day you sample a whisky for the first time, or re-sample it for the umpteenth, and over the years you get a feel for the best distilleries. Perhaps, then, it is no surprise that those I consider the top three in the world, Ardbeg, Buffalo Trace and Wild Turkey are all Award Winners, yet curiously not always with the brands I expected to see running away with the prizes. Also I was disappointed to see neither the 10 years olds of Laphroaig and especially Talisker make it to the 93 mark, let alone win their category.

Two years back I would have been genuinely surprised to see Jameson top the bill for the Irish and an unsung distillery on the outskirts of Melbourne pick up the best small distillery award.

The question is what will *Jim Murray's Whisky Bible 2006* unearth? As this book amply demonstrates, absolutely nothing can be taken for granted as far as whisky is concerned ... except that true genius will always be celebrated within these pages.

Award Winners

2005 World Whisky of the Year
George T Stagg

Scotch Single Malt of the Year
Platinum Old and Rare Caperdonich Aged 36 Years

Best New Scotch Single Malt of the Year (single cask)
Platinum Old and Rare Caperdonich Aged 36 Years

Best New Scotch Single Malt of the Year (multiple casks)
The Macallan Fine Oak 15 Years Old

Best Single Malt of the Year 12 Years Old and Under
Glenmorangie 10 Years Old

Scotch Blended Whisky of the Year
William Grant's 21 Years Old

Scotch Blended Whisky of the Year (Aged)
William Grant's 21 Year Old

Scotch Blended Whisky of the Year (Standard)
Black Bottle

Best New Scotch Blended Whisky
Dewar's Signature

Best New Scotch Brand
Macallan Fine Oak

Bourbon of the Year
George T Stagg

Best Bourbon Aged 10 Years or Under
Wild Turkey Russell's Reserve Aged 10 Years

Rye Whisky of the Year
Sazerac Rye 18 Years Old

Irish Whiskey of the Year
Jameson

Japanese Whisky of the Year
Nikka Single Cask Coffey Grain Whisky 1991

Japanese Single Malt of the Year
Yoichi Nikka Single Cask Malt Whisky 1991

Japanese Blended Whisky of the Year
Suntory Special Reserve 10 Years Old

Canadian Whisky of the Years
Seagram's VO

Best Small Distillery Whisky of the Year
Bakery Hill Peated Cask Strength (cask No. 14)

European Mainland Whisky of the Year
Hessicher Whiskey (German bourbon-style whiskey)

The Rankings (97–93)

97

Scotch Single Malt
Old Malt Cask Ardbeg 1975 Aged 25
Years *(bottled Oct 00)*
Bourbon
George T. Stagg

96

Scotch Single Malt
Ardbeg 1976 Single Cask 2390
Ardbeg 1977
Ardbeg Committee Reserve
Ardbeg Provenance 1974
Old Malt Cask Ardbeg 25 Years Old
(dist 75, bottled May 01)
Platinum Old and Rare Caperdonich
Aged 36 Years
Hart Brothers Glen Grant Aged
29 Years
Isle of Jura Aged 36 Years
Duncan Taylor Longmorn 1978 Aged
25 Years
Blended Scotch
Ballantine's 17 Years Old
William Grant's 21 Year Old
Bourbon
Elijah Craig 12 Years Old
Wild Turkey Russell's Reserve Aged
10 Years
Straight Rye
Sazerac Rye 18 Years Old

95

Scotch Single Malt
Ardbeg 21 Years Old
The Dalmore 62 Years Old
Glenglassaugh 1973 Family Silver
Private Collection Glen Grant 1953
Highland Park Aged 18 Years
Scott's Selection Longmorn-
Glenlivet 1971
The Macallan 1949 (53 Years Old)
cask no.136
The Macallan 1970 (32 Years Old)
cask no.241
The Macallan Fine Oak 15 Years Old
Earl of Zetland Malt Tasting Club
Macallan 1975
The Macallan ESC IV
Cask Port Ellen 1980
Old Malt Cask Port Ellen Aged 25
Years dist Sept 78, bott Feb 04
Springbank Aged 35 Years

Talisker Aged 20 Years
Blended Scotch
Black Bottle
The Royal and Ancient 28 Years
Royal Salute 50 Years Old
Teacher's Highland Cream
William Lawson's Founder's Reserve
Aged 18 Years
Scotch Vatted Malt
Compass Box Juveniles
Irish Pure Pot Still
Midleton 1973 Pure Pot Still
Irish Single Malt
Knappogue Castle 1994
Blended Irish
Jameson
Bourbon
Daniel Stewart Aged 12 Years *(aka
Original Barrel Bourbon
Aged 12 Years)*
Old Bardstown Aged 10 Years
Estate Bottled
Japanese Single Malt
Hakushu 1984
Suntory Pure Malt Hakushu Aged
12 Years
Yoichi 20 Years Old
Yoichi Nikka Single Cask Malt
Whisky 1991
Japanese Vatted Malt
Pure Malt Black

94

Scotch Single Malt
Aberlour a'bunadh 12 Years Old
Stirling Silver Label
Old Malt Cask Ardbeg 1975 Aged
24 Years
Platinum Old and Rare Ardbeg Aged
29 Years dist 73
Platinum Old and Rare Cask Ardbeg
Aged 29 Years dist 75 bott 04
Cask Ardmore 1990 (Gordon &
MacPhail)
Ardmore 100th Anniversary 12
Years Old
Old Master's Ardmore 1980
Bladnoch Aged 10 Years (Flora
and Fauna)
Bowmore Voyage
Old Malt Cask Bruichladdich Aged 13
Years dist Mar 90

Caol Ila Aged 21 Rare Malts Selection

Duncan Taylor Caperdonich 1970
Aged 33 Years cask 4380

Signatory Cardhu Millenium
Edition 1974

Blackadder Raw Cask Clynelish 1976

Dalwhinnie 15 Years Old

Dun Bheagan Convalmore 1985
Aged 18 Years

Glenfiddich 1937

Adelphi Glen Grant 31 Years Old
cask 1706

Old Masters Glen Grant 1969

Glenmorangie 10 Years Old

Glen Moray Mountain Oak

The Glenrothes 1967

The Glenrothes 1974 bott 03

Scotch Malt Whisky Society Cask
93.10 Aged 11 Years *(Glen Scotia)*

Highland Park Aged 25 Years *(50.7%)*

Chieftain's Ledaig 31 Years Old

Mission Range Highland Park 1979

Knockdhu 23 Years Old

Laphroaig Aged 30 Years

Laphroaig Aged 40 Years

The Macallan 1989

Macallan 1985 bott 03

The Macallan Fine Oak 25 Years Old

Scott's Selection Macallan 1985
bott 03

Old Malt Cask Millburn Aged 34 Years

Adelphi Port Ellen 24 Years Old

Rosebank Aged 20 Years Rare
Malts Selection

Aberdeen Distillers Rosebank 12
Years Old

Royal Lochnagar Aged 23 Years Rare
Malts Selection

Old Malt Cask Scapa Aged 25 Years
(dist Nov 74)

Berry's Own Selection Springbank
1968 35 Years Old

Dun Bheagan Springbank 1969
Aged 35 Years

Dun Bheagan Teaninich 1984
Aged 18 Years

Connoisseurs Choice Tullibardine 1994

Unspecified Single Malt Scotch

Finlaggan Old Reserve Islay
Single Malt

The Ileach Peaty Islay Single Malt

Vatted Scotch Malt

Century of Malts

Safeway Islay Pure Malt 10 Years Old

The Six Isles Pure Island Malt

Blended Scotch

Chivas Brothers Oldest and Finest

William Grant's Family Reserve

Irish Single Malt

Knappogue Castle 1992

Blended Irish

Jameson 1780 Matured 12 Years

Jameson Gold

American Single Malt

McCarthy's Oregon Single Malt
Aged 3 Years

Bourbon

Blanton's Silver Edition barrel no 53

Buffalo Trace

Eagle Rare 17 Years Old

Scotch Malt Whisky Society Heaven
Hill Aged 12 Years 1992

Jefferson's Reserve 15 Year Old

Old Forrester Birthday Bourbon
Vintage 1989

Vintage Bourbon 1976

Wild Turkey Rare Breed *(batch
W-T-02-91)*

Single Malt Rye

Old Potrero *(Essay 8 RW ARM 8 A)*

Japanese Single Malt

Karuizawa 1979 Aged 24 Years

Karuizawa 1986 Aged 17 Years

Suntory Pure Malt Hakushu
Aged 20 Years

Shirakawa 32 Years Old Single Malt

Yoichi 15 Years Old

Scotch Malt Whisky Society Cask
116.1 Aged 16 Years *(Yoichi)*

Japanese Blended

Special Reserve 10 Years Old

Canadian

Seagram's VO

Austrian Oat Whisky

Waldviestler Hafer Whisky 2000

93

Scotch Single Malt

Aberlour Aged 15 Years Cuvee
Marie d'Ecosse

Ardbeg 10 Years Old

Ardbeg 1976 Single Cask 2395

Connoisseurs Choice Ardbeg 1974
(bottled 95)

Old Malt Cask Ardbeg Aged 29 Years

Provenance Autumn Distillation
Ardbeg Over 9 Years

Old Malt Cask Auchentoshan
Aged 25 Years

The Balvenie Aged 15 Years Single

Barrel

The Maltmill Speyside (Balvenie)
Single Malt 11 Years

Peerless Benriach 1968 (cask 2590)

Bladnoch 15 Years Old

Bowmore 17 Years Old

Brora Aged 24 Years Rare Malts
Selection

Platinum Brora 1972

Old Malt Cask Bunnahabhain
Aged 16 Years

Spirit of the Isles Bunnahabhain 1982

Murray McDavid Mission III
Craigellachie 1970

Scotch Malt Whisky Society Cask
122.1 (Croftengea) Aged 11 Years

Adelphi Dailuaine 22 Years Old

The Dalmore 1973 Gonzalez Byass
Sherry Cask Finish

Glenfarclas Vintage 1987 Refill
Oloroso Cask

Glenfiddich Aged 15 Years
Solera Reserve

Glenfiddich 1982 Private Collection
for The Craigellachie Hotel

Usquebaugh Society Glen Garioch
Aged 16 Years

Cadenhead's Glenglassaugh
25 Years Old

Glengoyne 1985 Cask 103

Peerless Glen Grant 1974

Scotch Malt Whisky Society 18th
Anniversary Cask No. 9.30
(Glen Grant)

The Glenlivet Cellar Collection 30
Years Old American Oak Finish

The Glenlivet Vintage 1970

Berry's Own Selection Glenlivet 1975

Glenmorangie Distillery Manager's
Choice 2001

Glenmorangie Golden Rum
Cask Finish

Glenmorangie Madeira Matured

Chieftain's Glenrothes 1993 Aged 10
Years Rum Finish

Blackadder Glenturret 17 Years Old

Highland Park Bicentenary Vintage
1977 Reserve

Old Malt Cask Highland Park
Aged 25 Years

Isle of Jura 1973 Vintage

Lagavulin 12 Years Old

Laphroaig 10 Years Old Original
Cask Strength

Laphroaig 17 Years Old Islay Festival

of Malt and Music 2004

Old Malt Cask Laphroaig
Aged 15 Years

Private Cellar Longmorn-
Glenlivet 1970

The Macallan 1946 Select Reserve

The Macallan 1951 (51 Years Old)
cask no.644

The Macallan 1967 (35 Years Old)
cask no.1195

The Macallan 1972 29 Years Old

The Macallan 1973 (30 Years Old)
cask no.6098

Oban Bicentenary Manager's Dram
16 Years Old

The Whisky Shop Port Ellen 1978

Coopers Choice Rosebank 1993

Provenance Rosebank Over 12 Years

Scotch malt Whisky Society Cask
25.30 Aged 13 Years (Rosebank)

"Green" Brackla 1975 27 Years Old

Springbank Wood Expression 12 Year
Old Rum Wood

Juul's Private Bottling Springbank
Vintage 1966 Aged 34 Years

Murray McDavid Springbank 1965
Cask Strathisla 1974

Talisker 20 Years Old bott 03

Vatted Scotch Malt

Compass Box Eleuthera All Malt

Kelt Tour du Mond Very Rare Extra
Old Pure Malt

Blended Scotch

The Bailie Nicol Jarvie

Blue Hanger 25 Years Old bott 03

Buchanan's Special Reserve

Classic Cask 35 Years Old batch 202

Compass Box Asyla
(2003 bottling)

Compass Box Asyla bottle
identification L4097

Dewar's 18 Years Old

Dewar's Signature

Islay Mist Premium Aged 17 Years

Isle of Skye 8 Years Old

Royal Salute 21 Years Old

Royal Silk Reserve

Whyte & Mackay 30 Years Old

William Grant's Classic Reserve
21 Year Old

Irish Pure Pot Still

Knappogue Castle 1951

Irish Single Malt

Bushmills 16 Years Old Triple Wood

Blended Irish
Golden Irish
Midleton Very Rare 1990
Bourbon
Ancient Ancient Age 10 Years Old
Blanton's Gold Edition
Blanton's Single Barrel barrel no 240
Booker's 7 Yrs 3 Months
Cougar
Maker's Mark (Black Wax Seal)
Old Heaven Hill Very Rare
    Aged 10 Years 100 Proof
Old Rip 12 Years Old
Rip Van Winkle 15
Old Heaven Hill Very Rare
    Aged 10 Years 100 Proof
Rip Van Winkle 15 Years Old
Thedford Colonial Style Batch no 001
Single Malt Rye
Old Potrero (*Essay 5 RW ARM 2 A*)
Old Potrero Single Malt Straight Rye
    Essay 10-SRW-ARM-A
Straight Rye
Fleischmann's Straight Rye
Jim Beam Rye
American Single Malt
McCarthy's Oregon Single Malt
    Aged 3 Years bottling No. 4

Edgefield Distillery Hogshead db
    bott 4 Sep 03
Japanese Single Malt
Scotch Malt Whisky Society Cask
    120.1 Aged 21 Years (*Hakushu*)
Karuizawa 1987 Aged 16 Years
"Hokuto" Suntory Pure Malt
    Aged 12 Years
Nikka Single CaskMalt Whisky 10
    Years Old (*Yoichi*)
Yoichi 10 Years Old
Japanese Single Grain
Nikka Single Cask Coffey Grain
    Whisky 1991
Japanese Vatted Malt
Southern Alps Pure Malt
Japanese Blended
Golden Horse Busyuu Deluxe
Hibiki 21 Years Old
The Nikka Whisky Aged 34 Years
Super Nikka
Tsuru
Canadian
Crown Royal
Gibson's Finest Rare
    Lot No 40
Schenley OFC Aged 8 Years
Wiser's De Luxe 10 Years Old

Scottish Malts

For those of you deciding to take the plunge and head off into the labyrinthine world of Scotch malt whisky, a piece of advice. And that is, be careful who you take your advice from. Because, too often, I hear that you should leave the Islays until you have tackled the featherlight Speysiders and the bolder, weightier Highlanders. This is just complete, patronising nonsense. The only time that rings true is if you are tasting a number of whiskies in one day. Then leave the smoky ones to last, so the lighter chaps get a fair hearing.

I know many people who didn't like whisky until they got a Talisker from Skye inside them, or a Lagavulin to swamp their tastebuds with oily iodine. The fact is, you can take your map of malt whisky, start at any point and head in any direction you feel. There are no hard and fast rules. Certainly with well over 1,000 tasting notes here you should have some help in picking where this journey of a lifetime begins.

DISTILLERY LOCATOR

1	Highland Park	21	Tullibardine
	Scapa	22	Glengoyne
2	Pulteney	23	Loch Lomond
3	Clynelish		Littlemill
4	Balblair		Auchentoshan
5	Glenmorangie		Interleven
6	Dalmore	24	Rosebank
	Teaninich	25	St. Magdalene
7	Glen Ord	26	Glenkinchie
8	Talisker	27	Isle of Arran
9	Ben Nevis	28	Sprinbank
10	Dalwhinnie		Glen Scotia
11	Royal Lochnagar	29	Tobermory
12	Glen Garioch	**A**	Bunnahabhain
13	Oban	**B**	Caol Ila
14	Edradour	**C**	Jura
15	Fettercairn	**D**	Bruichladdich
16	Blair Athol	**E**	Bowmore
17	Glencadam	**F**	Ardbeg
18	Aberfeldy		Lagavulin
19	Glenturret		Laphroaig
20	Deanston	**G**	Port Ellen

H	Glasgow
I	Edingburgh
J	Perth
K	Dundee
L	Aberdeen
M	Inverness
N	Ben Nevis

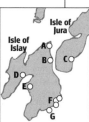

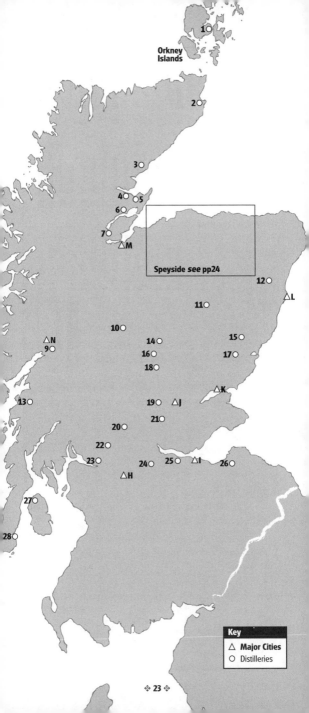

Orkney Islands

Speyside *see* pp24

Key

△ Major Cities
○ Distilleries

Speyside

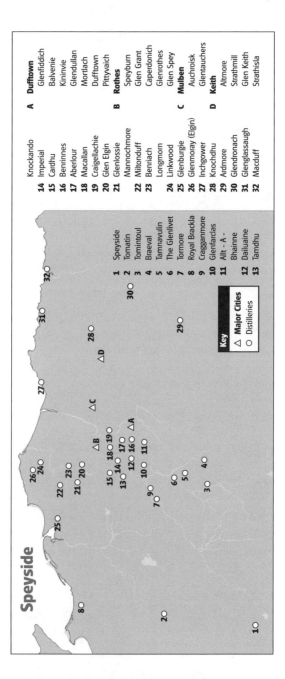

A Dufftown
- Glenfiddich
- Balvenie
- Kininvie
- Glendullan
- Mortlach
- Dufftown
- Pittyvaich

B Rothes
- Speyburn
- Glen Grant
- Caperdonich
- Glenrothes
- Glen Spey

C Mulben
- Auchroisk
- Glentauchers

D Keith
- Altmore
- Strathmill
- Glen Keith
- Strathisla

14 Knockando
15 Imperial
16 Cardhu
17 Benrinnes
18 Aberlour
19 Macallan
20 Craigellachie
21 Glen Elgin
22 Glenlossie
23 Mannochmore
24 Miltonduff
25 Benriach
26 Longmorn
27 Linkwood
28 Glenburgie
29 Glenmoray (Elgin)
30 Inchgower
31 Knochdhu
32 Macduff

1 Speyside
2 Tomatin
3 Tomintoul
4 Braeval
5 Tamnavulin
6 The Glenlivet
7 Tormore
8 Royal Brackla
9 Cragganmore
10 Glenfarclas
11 Allt - A - Bhainne
12 Dailuaine
13 Tamdhu

Key
△ Major Cities
○ Distilleries

Single Malts
ABERFELDY

Highlands (Perthshire), 1898. John Dewar & Sons. Working.

Aberfeldy Aged 12 Years db **(89) n**_22_ softly honied, rich and clean; **t**_23_ lighter in body than the nose suggests, a prick of first smoke, then spice, but the honey develops; **f**_22_ pretty long with developing vanilla and soft oils and very late honey again; **b**_22_ I have long loved this malt and it shows to good effect here although I'm not sure if the strength does it any favours. **40%**

Aberfeldy Aged 25 Years db **(85) n**_24_ this might fool a few Highland Park devotees: heather and honey in abundance, and beautifully weighted with very soft peat, too; **t**_21_ the oak has played havoc with the balance here and the honey is patchy and sparse; **f**_19_ dry, chalky, tired; **b**_21_ just doesn't live up to the nose. When Tommy Dewar wrote, "We have a great regard for old age when it is bottled," as quoted on the label, I'm not sure he had as many as 25 years in mind. **40%**

Aberfeldy 1980 Cask Strength bott 97 db **(92) n**_23_ **t**_24_ **f**_22_ **b**_23_. This is brilliant malt that displays the distillery's beauty to its fullest extent. **62%**

Connoisseurs Choice Aberfeldy 1975 (81) n_20_ **t**_22_ **f**_19_ **b**_20_. Slightly smoky and sweet. **40%**. _Gordon & MacPhail._

Connoisseurs Choice Aberfeldy 1977 (83) n_20_ **t**_21_ **f**_22_ **b**_20_. A soft, mildly honied dram with a surprising appearance of shy peat. **40%**. _Gordon & MacPhail._

Connoisseurs Choice Aberfeldy 1978 (84) n_22_ **t**_22_ **f**_20_ **b**_20_. Floral and lots of barley sugar. **40%**. _Gordon & MacPhail._

⠴ **Coopers Choice Aberfeldy 1974 Aged 29 Years** bott 03 **(88) n**_22_ new cut American bread and tinned peaches; **t**_22_ satin-textured with an early prod of oak jabbing into the lush barley; **f**_22_ beautifully layered oak; **b**_22_ a bitter-sweet delight that does the reputation of this excellent distillery no harm. **46%**. _The Vintage Malt Whisky Co._

Old Malt Cask Aberfeldy Aged 23 Years dist Oct 78 **(86) n**_22_ a salty aroma with an old wooden garden shed feel to it. Perhaps a little too much oak; **t**_20_ big and not a little coastal for a distillery in the heart of Perthshire! Briny, but the honey thread unravels and intensifies towards the oaky middle; **f**_24_ lashings of rich honey, a little burnt toast around the edges, remaining spicy and salty, but seriously yummy; **b**_20_ there is an oaky stand-off at first, but the finish is the stuff of dreams. **50%**. _Douglas Laing._

Scotch Malt Whisky Society Cask 60.25 Aged 27 Years (89) n_22_ big stuff: curiously coastal for a Perthshire malt with a briny, citrus freshness blending perfectly with seasoned oak; **t**_22_ no less shy on the palate with the same combination restructuring in a different formation on the palate. A touch of smoke is added for effect; **f**_23_ such a tease: softens down towards a more coffee-demerara finale with the oak threat receding; **b**_22_ absolutely stunning stuff playing the oak brinkmanship card to perfection. **55.2%. nc ncf sc.**

⠴ **Scott's Selection Aberfeldy 1975** bott 03 **(81) n**_19_ **t**_23_ **f**_20_ b21. Dried dates and spicy fruit. Brilliant mouth arrival but just a shade too oaky for its own good. **56%**

ABERLOUR

Speyside, 1826. Chivas Bros. Working.

Aberlour 10 Years Old db **(86) n**_20_ mint and freshly sliced cucumber; **t**_22_ big fruit presence but teasing, spicy malts battle through; **f**_23_ very long and weighty for a Speysider of this age with formulating fruit; **b**_21_ there is evidence of a decent percentage of clean sherry butts at work here: the spiciness stars for the malt. **43%**

Aberlour a'bunadh db **(88) n**_23_ liquorice and hickory, coal dust, oloroso and even a gentle waft of peat. Any heavier and the aroma wouldn't leave the glass; **t**_22_ big spice and oak hit the tastebuds running, the malt is an afterthought; **f**_21_ remains spicy and heavy with a return of liquorice (red candy style, this time); **b**22 phew! This is heavy-duty malt that blasts holes through your palate, unique in style for any Speyside malt. If anything, it's too big at **59.8%**! This is a single malt that varies in style slightly from bottling to bottling. Sadly the bottling marks are often too small to make head or tail of, or I would include different tasting notes as I have done with Yoichi. However below, to give some idea of the variance in style, are the notes and evaluation from one of the earliest bottlings in 1998.

Aberlour a'bunadh db **(91) n**23 firm malt and sherry but punctuated by overripe mango and rich honey tones; **t**23 immediate spice and then an eruption of honey and barley with some liquorice diving in. A soft dispersal of peat around the palate adds an extra surprise; **f**22 the intensity remains at first but quietens as vanilla makes its mark and some cocoa trickles in; **b**23 brilliantly balanced and displaying a fruity-malty and mildly peaty complexity which is jaw-dropping. **59.6%**

Aberlour a'bunadh 12 Years Old Sterling Silver Label db **(94) n**24 stupendous stuff: heavier and oakier than the age suggests but with a big, waxy sherry note offering a cleaner, richer dimension; **t**22 quite massive with a big sherry and ripe date surge that breaks against a malt middle and delicious spices; **f**23 long, magnificently oaky and proud. Pure cocoa and clean sherry fight for the finish but intertwine for a dead heat; **b**23 don't try and convince me all the malts in here are 12 – the average age seems a whole lot greater. Just startling and just about deserving a 24-carat gold label. **58.7%**. *Limited edition.*

Aberlour 12 Years Old Double Cask Matured db **(79) n**19 **t**21 **f**19 **b**20. Fresh mint on the nose and finish but the taste, though rich, lacks structure. **43%**

Aberlour 12 Years Old Sherry Cask Matured db **(85) n**20 bizarrely toothpastey; what is it about mint and Aberlour? **t**22 stunningly textured, rich fruit, with succulent grape edging out the malt; **f**22 long, with fingers of oak on the malt; **b**21 this is a big, clean dram where the malt is just about strong enough to hold onto the sherry. **40%**

Aberlour Aged 15 Years Cuvee Marie d'Ecosse db **(93) n**23 sublime fresh sherry with kumquats and lime for extra zest; **t**24 beautifully ethereal with the malt drifting in all directions while the fruit, though rich, has virtually no weight at all, magical malt; **f**22 some light vanilla apologetically drifts in to replace what appeared to be a hint of smoke; **b**24 this, and the a'bunadh Sterling Silver, lift Aberlour into the super league of malt whiskies. It is sold primarily in France, and one can assume only that this is God's way of making amends for that pretentious, over-rated, caramel-ridden rubbish called Cognac they've had to endure for the last couple of centuries. Hope there'll be enough to go around the rest of the world one day. **43%**

Aberlour Aged 15 Years Sherry Wood Finish db **(84) n**19 **t**21 **f**23 **b**21. The sherry slowly builds to a chewy, spicy crescendo. **40%**

Aberlour Aged 21 Years db **(77) n**21 **t**21 **f**17 **b**18. Hard as nails with the finish really closing in with little compassion. **43%**

Aberlour Aged 30 Years db **(89) n**23 a clean, deep sherry aroma with a lemon and mint residue: compelling stuff; **t**22 deep, moderately dry throughout with a slow build-up of spices and smoke. Malty, grapey succulence together with some cocoa bitterness adds extra complexity; **f**22 long and brilliantly weighted, the fruitiness helps sweeten the malt gracefully; **b**22 a classy Aberlour with great complexity. **43%**. *1,000 bottles.*

Aberlour 1976 db **(85) n**22 suety, sultanas, lots of vanilla; **t**20 a sweet malt blast is immediately swamped by wave upon wave of encroaching oak; **f**22 more vanilla but malt stretches complicate the length; **b**21 pleasant and wellmeasured; lacking complexity until the finish. **43%**

Aberlour 1980 db **(89) n**21 sawdust and sultanas; **t**22 exceptionally clean malt and fruit with a subtle prickly backdrop; **f**24 immensely complex with warming hints of everything from spice to sherry with malt and smoke in between:

a legendary phase for any whisky; **b**22 a quality dram offering enormous subtlety and charisma. **43%**

Aberlour 1988 Distillers Selection db **(69)** n17 t19 f16 b17. Sulphur tainted, I'm afraid. **40%**

Aberlour 100 Proof db **(91)** n23 beneath this sherried, volcanic start there is something rather sweet and honied. One of the most two-toned noses you'll find in a long while; **t**23 sweet to begin and honied, too. The maltiness keeps its shape for some time. Between the middle and end an ebulliient spiciness takes hold; **f**22 massively long and fruity; **b**23 stunning, sensational whisky, the most extraordinary Speysider of them all ...which it was when I wrote those official notes for the bottling back in '97, I think. Other malts have superseded it now, but on re-tasting I stand by those original notes, though I disassociate myself entirely with the rubbish: "In order to savour Aberlour 100 at its best add 1/3 to 1/2 pure water". **57.1%**

Aberlour Warehouse No. 1 Aged 12 Years cask no. 11552 filled into cask 12/12/90, first-fill bourbon cask db **(86)** n22 nutty, biscuity; **t**22 sweet with ripe cherries and rich malt; **f**21 long and slightly toasty, good sweet malt follow-up; **b**21 great to see a bourbon-cask Aberlour for once. Strength not stated – around **60%. sc.**

Aberlour Warehouse No. 1 Aged 13 Years sherry cask matured 6524 filled into cask 26/5/89 db **(90)** n22 raw oloroso but not even a hint of an off-note: almost overpowering; **t**23 just about the cleanest oloroso you could wish for: thankfully the malt has body enough to pick a spicy route through the fruity onslaught; **f**22 the fruit slowly subsides leaving a slightly roasty, burnt oaky note at the death: even a pinch of salt and smoke, maybe; **b**23 for those who love their sherried whisky. Come and get it! No strength stated – about **59%.**

Blackadder Raw Cask Aberlour 1990 sherry hogshead 3318, dist 7 May 90, bott Apr 02 **(70)** n17 t19 f17 b17. Rich, but a poor cask. **59.9%. nc ncf sc.**

Blackadder Raw Cask Aberlour 1990 bourbon hogshead 3319, dist 7 May 90, bott Mar 03 **(87)** n21 fresh, immature for its age, but quite mouthwatering and appealing; **t**23 classic, sharp, grassy notes, enormous gristy malt; **f**22 clean, malty, chewy; **b**21 lack of complexity thanks to almost zero oak input but a delicious Speysider. **60%. nc ncf sc.**

Cadenhead's Aberlour-Glenlivet 13 Years Old dist 89, bott 03/03 **(86)** n21 fresh, grassy; **t**22 mouthwatering, fresh, uninterrupted malt; **f**22 medium length, remains grassy and clean; **b**21 if you ever wanted to know what a blender looks for in 12-ish-year-old Speyside from a cask that is on its second or third filling, this is just about the perfect example. **46%**

⋅⋇⋅ **Celtic Legends Aberlour 1990** bott 02 hogshead no 11521 **(81)** n19 t21 f21 b20. A trifle sappy with some soft bourbon. **46%. Liquid Gold/John MacDougall.**

Old Malt Cask Aberlour Aged 12 Years (83) n21 t21 f20 b21. Demure and subtle, a textbook quality Speysider. **50%. Douglas Laing.**

⋅⋇⋅ **Old Malt Cask Aberlour Aged 14 Years** dist Nov 89, bott Feb 04 **(80)** n20 t21 f20 b19. Malty and mouthwatering, but a little on the hot side. **50%. nc ncf sc. Douglas Laing.**

⋅⋇⋅ **Old Master's Aberlour 1989** bott 04 cask no. 12198 **(73)** n18 t19 f19 b17. Unyielding and fiery it never quite settles into a comfort zone. **56.8%. James MacArthur.**

The Single Barrel Collection Aberlour 1987 dist Mar 87, bott Dec 01, cask no. 1806 **(77)** n19 t18 f21 b19. Pleasant but rather one-dimensional. **55.43%. nc nf.**

Whisky Galore Aberlour 1989 14 Years Old (84) n19 t23 f21 b21. Really clean and delicious (especially on the mouth arrival), the malt running riot unimpeded by oak. But perhaps too young for its age. Even so, just so massively drinkable! **46%. Duncan Taylor & Co.**

ALLT-A-BHAINNE
Speyside, 1975. Chivas Bros. Silent.

Old Malt Cask Allt A Bhainne Aged 16 Years dist Apr 85, bott May 01 **(66)** n*15* t*18* f*16* b*17*. Allt-a-sorts. **50%. nc ncf.** Douglas Laing. 114 bottles.

·:·:· **Connoisseurs Choice Allt A Bhainne 1991 (83)** n*20* t*22* f*20* b*21*. Clean, sexy and simpering, the honeyed thread makes up for bulimic body. **43%.** Gordon & MacPhail

ANCNOC (see Knockdhu)

ARDBEG
Islay, 1815. Glenmorangie Plc. Working.

Ardbeg 10 Years Old db **(93)** n*23* oily, slapped-on-all-over-with-a-trowel-peat that leaves nothing uncoated. A lovely salty tang gives an extra tweak; t*23* sweet, equally oily arrival with a massive malt surge. When that has passed the serious work of picking out the intense seaweedy, oaky complexity begins; f*24* stupendous spices add an extra dimension to the already complex story unfolding on the palate; b*23* close your eyes and enjoy. **46%**

Ardbeg 17 Years Old (earlier bottlings) db **(92)** n*23* a gentle, seductive, sweet peat leads the way to a complex arrival of malt and vanilla; t*22* soft and languid at first, brilliant, sweet chewy malt with just a shade of cocoa adding depth and balance; f*23* a delightful level of residual peat which ensures a long, sophisticated finish and just shows the extent of Ardbeg's complexity even without peat screaming at you; b*24* OK, I admit I had a big hand in this, creating it with the help of Glenmorangie Plc's John Smith. It was designed to take the weight off the better vintages of Ardbeg whilst ensuring a constant if limited supply around the world. Certainly one of the more subtle expressions you are likely to find, though criticised by some for not being peaty enough. As the whisky's creator, all I can say is they are missing the point. **40%**

Ardbeg 17 Years Old (present bottlings) db **(90)** n*22* enormously fruity and flighty. The peat though present is just a mere echo of what it once was, with lashings of sweet marmalade where peat used to be, but still lightly salted and malty; t*23* moist Madeira cake with cherries; softly malted and sweet with a lovely encrustation of salt that slowly grows; f*22* the sweet fruit continues on its classy course; the shape in the mouth is sublime, the smoke almost a mirage; b*23* the peat has all but vanished and cannot really be compared to the original 17-year-old: maybe it's time to give this beauty a new name. It's a bit like tasting a Macallan without the sherry: fascinating to see the naked body underneath, and certainly more of a turn on. Peat or no peat, great whisky by any standards. **40%**

Ardbeg 21 Years Old db **(95)** n*24* the kind of aroma that has made a legend of a distillery: marmalade on slightly burnt toast while in the background a peat fire smoulders and salt melts on porridge; t*24* arrives on the palate like a snowflake, deft, weightless for all its enormity of character, lush citrus fruits for all the rich peat; f*22* for its age, sweet and tender: the oak is taking a day off and offers no more than a token bitterness to counter the malt, beautifully spiced; b*25* we all have bad days, weeks, months in our life when we wonder why we were put on this earth then you open a bottle like this and discover the reason. This is a dram of dreams, an inspiration and reminder that something does not have to be perfect to achieve greatness. The distillery manager Stuart Thomson oft told me of his affection for this bottling. It was one of the few Ardbegs that had slipped through my net over the last 25 years. So I tasted it for the first time to mark the 1500th whisky in this book. Stuart's confidence was well-founded: the remaining few hundred bottlings have a tough act to follow. **56.3%.** Limited edition from 12 casks.

Ardbeg Guaranteed 30 Years Old db **(91)** n24 slightly burnt toast, raisins on the highest point of a freshly baked bun; sensuous malt and peat-reek on a vanilla bed; t23 silky and increasingly sweet, none of the enormity one might expect and the oak plays lip-service; f21 perhaps too gentle for an Ardbeg with limited shoreline complexity; b23 an unsual beast, one of the last ever bottled by Allied. The charm and complexity early on is enormous, but the fade rate is surprising. That said, still a dram of considerable magnificence. **40%**

Ardbeg 1975 Single Cask No. 4701 db **(87)** n22 dry and oaky, the peat arrives in salty waves; t22 rich and estery with a distinct maltiness that is set apart from the smoke; f21 more salty esters and vanilla; b22 unusual mouthfeel for an Ardbeg: hard and relatively unyielding for this distillery. **46.4%**

Ardbeg 1975 Single Cask No. 4703 db **(91)** n22 hard, flinty malt, peat hovers around, complex salts; t23 brilliantly fills the mouth with an ever-increasing smoke presence, begins dry and then sweetens out: a profound malt; f23 softens but the complexity levels refuse to fall, quite salty by the end with rich fruit adding depth; b23 a lovely Ardbeg that is quite lethargic despite its obvious riches. The bitter-sweet balance nears perfection. **47.7%**

Ardbeg 1975 Single Cask No. 4716 db **(86)** n21 dank stables, smoke and salt; t22 sweet malt with some vanilla and peat giving something to chew on; f22 light vanilla, cocoa, oranges and smoke; b21 doesn't quite take off and develop like the average Ardbeg of this era. Still a little gem, though. **45%**

Ardbeg 1975 Single Cask No, 4718 db **(83)** n20 t22 f20 b21. The least inspiring of the individual casks, revealing that Ardbeg is mortal after all. Still amasses a complexity other whiskies dream about but the finish, like the nose, is bitter and less than perfect. **46.7%**

Ardbeg 1976 Single Cask No. 2390 sherry butt filled 24 Nov 76, hand bott at dist 27 Apr 02 db **(96)** n24 biting brine despite the sherry. The cask seems to have been held under water for 25 years, not in a warehouse: remarkable and quite brilliant; t25 a stupendous marriage of ripe grape, perfectly weighted peat-reek and juicy malt. It simply doesn't get better than this. Come to think of it, few things in life actually do; f23 relatively medium but again it is the brine that stars, bringing out the intensity of the barley yet keeping the oak at bay, some deep liquorice underlines the age; b24 when you die, have a bottle of this put beside you in the coffin to take to the afterworld: this is just one of those drams of a lifetime. Distillery manager Stuart Thomson has proved to be an inspired choice: not only can he make a fine malt, he can pick a bloody incredible dram. Respect. **53.1%**. *494 bottles; sold only at distillery.*

Ardbeg 1976 Single Cask No. 2395 db **(93)** n24 salty and a lot peatier than the sherry usually allows. Let it lay, unwatered, in the glass for 10 minutes for the most extraordinary results. Then it becomes farmyardy, organic and just so alive; t23 very sweet malt arrival then an explosion of peat, big with some juicy fruit; f22 decent oak arrival and teasing spices and chocolate; b24 really supremely weighted malt with a bit more oak than it needs but enough charisma to see it off. **54.4%**

Ardbeg 1976 Single Cask No. 2396 db **(91)** n24 mildly hot and nippy, even so, just wonderful peat complexity. No joking: take 5–10 minutes over this one before drinking. Incredible; t23 labyrinthine peat and malt delve deep into the oak, liquorice and aniseed form a fascinating sub committee; f21 mildly tame compared to the complexity of earlier, sweetens with vanilla and gristy malt starring. The final burst is pretty hard and brittle; b23 at first this was marked in the mid-80s. Then I tasted again ... and again ... and again.... Superb. **53.5%**

⋅⋅⋅ **Ardbeg 1976 Single Cask No. 2398** db **(89)** n23 nose-twitching stuff: the oak and peat are sharp-edged and bold; sandalwood, marshmallow and damp leather football boots add to the bitter-sweet enigma; t22 equally punchy on the palate with a fizzing oak dryness perfectly countered by a peaty-Demerara sweetness; **f**22 much drier now but the malt digs deep for some weighty barley; **b**22 old and noble; **52.3%**

Ardbeg 1976 Single Cask No. 3275 db **(85) n**22 thin, quite hard, orangey and bourbony; **t**21 biting. malty, soft peat; **f**21 lots of vanilla and custard; **b**21 a quite different, light dram highlighting the scope of the peating levels in those own-made malt days. Those who thought the lightly peated 17-year-old vatting a recent un-Ardbegian invention and vociferously decried it are in for a reality check and a large slice of humble pie. **44.6%**

Ardbeg 1977 db **(96) n**25 an aroma your nose sinks into and you have to prise it away from the glass: thick, weighty, gently oiled peat offers so much more. The barley is still intact, there is coke smoke and a million things you might find from the sea. Never sweet, never dry; **t**24 probably the sweetest Ardbeg arrival on the palate of all time: an absorbing mixture of one part sugar cane juice to 20 parts concentrated malt, and heavily peated malt at that; **f**23 lighter here than I might have expected when I first tasted the casks in '97, the oak has fizzed through like I anticipated, so there is a lightness towards the end slightly unusual for an Ardbeg. Even so, the mouthfeel remains nothing short of perfect; **b**24 when working through the Ardbeg stocks, I earmarked '77 a special vintage, the sweetest of them all. So it has proved. Only the '74 absorbed that extra oak that gave greater all-round complexity. Either way, sweet, or slightly dryer, the quality of the distillate is beyond measure: simply one of the greatest experiences – whisky or otherwise – of your life. **46%**

Ardbeg 1978 db **(91) n**23 dry, the oak has already made telling inroads, but kept in check by brilliant salty, coastal notes; **t**24 wave upon wave of peated malt crashes on the tastebuds, the sweetness level rising with each landing, quite salty and chewy; **f**22 the oak remains confident but allows the mildly sweet malt a very free hand, slightly bitter towards the end; **b**22 an Ardbeg on the edge of losing it because of encroaching oak, hence the decision made by John Smith and I to bottle this vintage early alongside the 17-year-old. Five years on, still looks a pretty decent dram, though slightly under strength! **43%**

⋰ **Ardbeg Single Cask 2740** db **(83) n**21 **t**21 **f**20 **b**21. A bit hot with lots of oak to chew on. **52.3%**. *Belgium only.*

⋰ **Ardbeg Single Cask 2782** db **(87) n**22 salty, sharp, gristy peat; exceptionally dry; **t**22 magnificent sweet malt delivery with just enough oil to soften the dry oaky punches; **f**21 thins out towards vanilla; **b**22 positively schizophrenic. **52.3%**. *Italy only.*

Ardbeg Committee Reserve bott 02, db **(96) n**24 punchy, salty and oily, there is a mildly Taliskeresque, peppery bite to this one ... perfect for starting the tasting day at 7am!!! My God, am I awake now, or what??? **t**24 brilliant spray of all things sweet and salty and so much more besides. The peat seems to operate on several different levels, each one displaying slightly different coastal tones or pure vegetable: outstanding; **f**23 surprising toffee-fudge finish but before then the quality of the chocolate would shame the Belgians; **b**25 absolutely faultless balance: Ardbeg personified. You take the first mouthful and wonder: is this the best Ardbeg of them all? Had I been drinking this at the distillery and not in my tasting lab, I would probably have said yes. But this lab is a great leveller, devoid of all romantic contact with the exception, perhaps, of sultry, dark brown Brazilian eyes flashing at you at the other side of my desk ... but I digress. What a way to start the day ... does this rate alongside the OMC '75 or the Provenance '74, or even the Ardbeg '77? It is a hard choice. More mouthfuls are required at full cask strength: it's a tough life. But then that toffee note detected is further concentrated upon: this is not something normally in the Ardbeg armoury and is for me, I decide, a chink. A mark is lost. The ACR is not the greatest Ardbeg of all time. It's not yet 8 in the morning. Nearly an hour has passed in near silence trying to unravel this conundrum. Time for breakfast after Ardbeg. Do I have any caviar left ...? **55.3%**. *3,000 bottles.*

Ardbeg Lord of the Isles db **(87)** n*23* as if two peat types are working in tandem: one soft, toffeed and lilting, the other firmer, drier; t*23* big peat kick at first then a more sombre maltiness; f*20* slightly flat and disappointing; b*21* a dram that starts well enough but complexity becomes scarcer as a cream-toffee effect mingles with the peat. **46%**

Ardbeg Provenance 1974 bott 99, db **(96)** n*24* the peat courses through the aroma in perfect balance and harmony with the soft, gently spiced and salted oak, touches of something citrus here and there, too; t*25* the malt is soft and sweet at first but then the peatiness gathers momentum and intensity until it absolutely glows; f*23* the oak bourbon-malt-peat-cocoa characters all ebb and flow but are joined by a more bitter note that counters the earlier sweet maltiness, some toffee-character in there as well: all-in-all, pretty enormous; b*24* this is an exercise in subtlety and charisma, the beauty and the beast drawn into one. Until I came across the 25-year-old OMC verson during a thunderstorm in Denmark, this was arguably the finest whisky I had ever tasted: I opened this and drank from it to see in the year 2000. When I went through the Ardbeg warehouse stocks in 1997 I earmarked the '74 and '77 vintages as something special. This bottling has done me proud. **55.6%**

◌ **Ardbeg Uigeadail** db **(89)** n*25* awesome package of intense peat reek amid complex fruitcake and leather notes. Everything about this nose is broadside-big yet the massive oak never once oversteps its mark. A whiff of engine oil compliments the kippers. Perfection; t*22* begins with a mind-blowing array of bitter-sweet oaky notes and then a strangely fruity peat entry; real scattergun whisky; f*20* very odd finish with an off-key fruit element that flattens the usual Ardbeg grand finale; b*22* a curious Ardbeg with a nose to die for. Some tinkering regarding the finish may lift this to being a true classic **54.1%**

◌ **Ardbeg Very Young** db **(91)** n*22* cured bacon on rye bread; a seasoning saltiness compliments the firmer peat while a second, lighter, level floats around. Complex stuff; t*24* the initial strike is sweet malt followed by a bombardment of spicy peat; the middle sees some cocoa turn up; f*22* slightly oily and at length carries sweat, smoky malt all the way; b*23* much more complex in its structure than content, this bottling helps demonstrate the true genius of Ardbeg's versatility. **58.9%**

Connoisseurs Choice Ardbeg 1974 (bottled 95 – old-fashioned cream label) **(93)** n*24* massive depth that cocks a snook at the 40% strength. Complexity goes off the scale here as orangey-fig notes dovetail with brooding, mildly sinister smokiness, ye olde Ardbeg at its most nose-tweaking; t*23* beautiful marmalade notes melt into the peaty inferno, lots going on here, but in a very gentlemanly way; f*23* fruit and malt sit comfortably with the bitter cocoa and lingering peat, the fade is a slow one; b*23* a dram that is etched in the hearts of many Ardbeg lovers discovering the distillery for the first time. Understandably and rightly so. **40%**. *Gordon & MacPhail.*

Connoisseurs Choice Ardbeg 1974 (bottled 97 – newer, purple label) **(89)** n*22* pines among the peat; t*22* very sweet malt, the peat level has dropped on the previous bottling though the complexity continues along a fruity path; f*23* long, light and flighty, the malt is fabulously textured and offers a late, salty burst; b*22* a slightly different animal to the previous bottling, lacking a kind of all-round brilliance in a way that is so subtle you struggle to put your finger on exactly why, no matter how many times you taste it and re-taste it ... (hic!) On such is the finest line between genius and mere excellence drawn. **40%**. *Gordon & MacPhail.*

◌ **Connoiseurs Choice Ardbeg 1975 (91)** n*24* more honeyed than most, the vanilla forms a useful backdrop to the layered peat. Wonderfully underplayed; t*22* sweet, biscuity start then gentle prod of the tastebuds by peat; f*23* the honey returns as the peat takes a more enveloping role; the vanilla dries and spices prickle; b*22* a seemingly demure dram that sends all kinds of hidden, delicious messages. **43%**. *Gordon & MacPhail.*

Connoisseurs Choice Ardbeg 1990 (88) n*23* like much of 1990-distilled Ardbeg drawn at this time, the peat is pastel-shaded rather than punchy, fragile rather than forceful; t*22* sweet and almost a little green, the style that was preferred in the 50s: chewy, though; f*22* the smoke drifts effortlessly to the end where it meets a slight bitterness, moderate complexity: b*21*. **40%**. *Gordon & MacPhail.*

Connoisseurs Choice Ardbeg 1991 (88) n*22* young in character and light, the peat drifts effortlessly about but hasn't cranked up the phenols; t*23* oily and genuinely mouthfilling. The new Ardbeg texture begins here, with the malt being slightly like grist dissolving on the tongue with an extra sprinkling of sugar for good measure: this is one of the sweeter renditions; f*22* soft with just the merest detail of oak, otherwise it's peated malt grist all the way; b*21* sweet, oily and so easy to drink. **40%**. *Gordon & MacPhail.*

Glen Denny Ardbeg 1990 Aged 11 Years (91) n*21* a dry marzipan nose almost outweighs the sweeter peat-reek. Light and refined by Ardbeg standards, there is marmalade to enrich it slightly; t*23* so soft it dissolves on the palate, leaving a sweet, smoky residue. Waves of vanilla and peat vie for control, but neither take it; f*24* long, enormously complex, a touch salty with the peat now taking a warming, spiced form. Ardbeg at its most teasing and luxurious; b*23* cracking stuff that, despite the lazy nose, dominates, confuses, confounds and tantalises the tastebuds. Wonderful. **43%**. *Hunter Hamilton Co. 419 hand-filled bottles.*

Kieler Whisky Club Ardbeg Germania dist 26/12/75, bott 26/03/02, cask no. 4716 **(88)** n*22* dry, oak chippings; sappy peat; t*23* dry, then a roast coffee middle builds into a fuller peaty effect; f*21* very laid-back with sweet malt; b*22* a gentle, softly bodied, complex dram that thankfully doesn't deliver the oak threatened on the nose. **44.8%**. *35 samples issued for the Kiel Whisky Club, Germany.*

⬩⬩⬩ **La Reserve Ardbeg 9 Years Old (83)** n*20* t*22* f*20* b*21*. Exceptionally clean, big peat but the complexity has not fully developed. **60.9%**

Murray McDavid Ardbeg 1991 bourbon cask MM2999, dist Feb 91, bott Feb 00 **(86)** n*20* green, young, lots of nibbling, flapping, nowhere near fully fledged peat; t*22* massively lively, as might be expected, the youth of the dram finding a mouthwatering barley note through the thickish peat; f*22* very light vanilla picks a course around the smoke, some light oils maintain a sweetness while the barley continues to offer fresh complexity; b*22* an intriguing and genuinely fun Ardbeg that helps complete a learning curve. **46%. nc ncf sc.**

Old Malt Cask Aged 11 Years dist May 90 **(84)** n*20* t*22* f*21* b*21*. Curiously over-sweet and, for all the moutainous peat, the usual Ardbeg complexity fails to fully materialise. **50%. nc ncf.** *342 bottles.*

⬩⬩⬩ **Old Malt Cask Ardbeg 1992 Aged 10 Years** dist Mar 92, bott Feb 03 **(85)** n*23* very hard peat, spirity, biting, salty; t*21* slightly oily, thin middle with the peat struggling to form a shape; f*20* one of the shortest Ardbegs in a long time with the usual waves becoming ripples; b*21* lovely, lively nose, good early delivery and yet..and yet... **50%. sc nc ncf.** *Douglas Laing. 360 bottles.*

⬩⬩⬩ **Old Malt Cask Ardbeg 1993 Aged 10 Years** dist Mar 93, bott Jan 04 **(85)** n*22* peaty grist and youth gang together; t*21* above average spice grips the palate while the peat ducks and weaves amid firm malt; f*21* a touch of vanilla; b*21* was on its way to becoming a top grade cask. **50%. nc ncf.** *Douglas Laing.*

⬩⬩⬩ **Old Malt Cask Ardbeg 1993 Aged 10 Years** dist Mar 93, bottApr 04 **(80)** n*19* t*20* f*21* b*20*. Recovers from below par nose for an attractive, flinty-peat finish. **50%. nc ncf.** *Douglas Laing. 634 bottles.*

Old Malt Cask Ardbeg 1975 Aged 24 Years dist Oct 75, bott May 00 **(94)** n*23* salty and slightly sweaty, the seaweed and peat form enticing layers; t*24* fabulous bite, then soft peat arrival allowing a multi-layered, lingering attack on the tastebuds in which cocoa plays no little part; f*23* elegantly brawny, muscles everywhere but the complexity is superb: just so amazingly bitter-sweet; b*24* this is a dram that will be preferred over the 25-year-old version (75/00) by those looking for raw aggression over finesse. I won't argue either way – it's a personal thing. **50%. nc ncf.** *Douglas Laing. 713 bottles.*

Old Malt Cask Ardbeg 1975 Aged 25 Years dist Oct 75, bott Oct 00 **(97) n**25 the peat is big, but like all great Ardbegs, its intensity is diffracted through several layers of malt. Some salt adds piquancy and as the malt warms in your hand some orangey fruit arrives, but under the heavy guard of the firm peat. Both dry and sweet, heavy and light, salty and peppered, flowery yet a little fruity, this has it all. There is even that lovely, oiled smell of a warm-running model train. As close to perfection to make no difference; **t**24 mouthfilling and chewy, the peat shows the soft and delicate side to its nature at first before becoming pretty firm. Almost Taliskeresque peppers pummel the tastebuds, but these, too, are fleeting. There is a quick outburst of something honied and fruity and then wave upon wave of gristy malt and toffee; **f**23 eventually, much drier with 25 years of oak having a calming influence. Even so, the peat returns with soft ripples of smoke and vanilla acts as a mute recipient; **b**25 is this the best independent bottling of whisky of all time? I would say yes. And it would be a hard job to find a better single cask throughout Ardbeg's warehouses. I have tasted more individual casks of Ardbeg than any other whisky critic living, but never have I found one that so captures the brilliance of the world's greatest distillery – even my mark of 97 is me just nit-picking and being mean! Just one single glass at bottle strength – don't you dare add a single drop of water to this one – a quiet room, and you will be lost in the labyrinth of this great whisky for hours if not days. Will you ever get to the bottom of it? I very much doubt it. **50%.** *Douglas Laing. 702 bottles.*

Old Malt Cask Ardbeg 25 Years Old dist Oct 75, bott May 01 **(96) n**23 curiously less prominently peated than other OMC '75 bottlings with a much heavier oak influence, remains coastal and cunning, though, with a tidal, salty impact to add to the abrasiveness; **t**25 a dry initial impact that slowly and gloriously increases in sweet-malty intensity as it spreads around the palate. This is the stuff of genius; **f**24 salty, cocoa-crusted, a devaluing of the sweet peat that has gently gathered on the palate. The perfect climb-down to the perfect build-up; **b**24 just a little imbalance on the nose and slight bitterness to the finish dock a few points – but who cares? If you don't have this in your Ardbeg collection, consider it incomplete. But don't let it sit there gathering dust: experience ...! **50%. nc ncf.** *Douglas Laing. 243 bottles.*

Old Malt Cask Ardbeg Aged 27 Years dist Mar 75 **(92) n**22 amazingly delicate peat that meanders around the equally soft sherry, fabulously clean and complex, everything is gentle and understated. Everything is hinted at, but nothing stated, except the obvious magnificence of this aroma; **t**24 nothing short of outstanding: the arrival on the palate is a fanfare of sweet malt followed by soft murmurings of peat then no less delicate lush sherry. The oak arrives last, almost apologetically, alongside some gentle spice; **f**22 a gathering of warming, peppery spices – not unlike a Talisker – but the sherry remains clean and the peat simply flickers around the palate; **b**24 proof positive that to be a great Ardbeg it does not have to be swimming in peat. We are talking sheer unadulterated elegance and complexity from the world's greatest distillery when it was in its prime. What more can one say? **50%. ncf.**

Old Malt Cask Ardbeg Aged 28 Years dist Nov 72, bott 01 **(87) n**20 hot and biting; toasty and dry, the peat is heavy but quite dull, almost sinister, in character; **t**22 hard malt meets even harder oak. An early oak bitterness is softened by some battling sugars; **f**23 very light, showing signs of a little wear and tear but still enormous and chewy, brilliant late rallying complexity with spices and more waves of malt; **b**22 vaguely battered and bruised, but some genuine class shines through.

Old Malt Cask Ardbeg Aged 29 Years dist Mar 72 **(93) n**24 much of the distillate of '72 possessed a deep, earthy resonance to the peat, as if they were using fuel cut from the deepest parts of the bed. This enormous character is in full play here; **t**24 enormous sweet and lush, though not in the oily style of today. Chewy, big malt and some liquorice-toffee oak add extra depth. Lovely marmalade fruitiness clings to the mouth, too; **f**22 surprisingly light, as if spent. The oak hangs around to add a bitterish edge though doesn't intrude too much on the dying embers of peat; **b**23 a malt on the cusp of brilliance, but just a summer or two over its time. Good to see a '72 vintage showing its own peculiar qualities, though. **50%. nc ncf.** *Douglas Laing. 432 bottles.*

⁖ **Platinum Old and Rare Ardbeg Aged 29 Years** dist 73, bott 02 **(94)** **n**25 crofter's lumbs reeking; flakey peat that is both deep yet ethereal. Salty, seaweedy, distinctly coastal in every way. And yet never not even mildly over the top. Simply perfection; **t**24 pounding peat and then a zillion levels of sweetness; **f**22 flattens surprisingly quickly with a shade of natural caramel. Some spices carry out a minor uprising; **b**23 absolutely brilliant whisky made at a time when Ardbeg was making probably the finest spirit in its long history. One for every true Ardbeg officianado...therefore with just 137 bottles a fight to the death. **51.4%. sc nc.** *Douglas Laing. 137 bottles.*

⁖ **Platinum Old and Rare Cask Ardbeg Aged 29 Years** dist 75, bott 04 **(94)** **n**24 some marmalade and nuts freshens the delicate peat reek: classic old Ardbeg that embraces the oak; **t**24 immediately the mouth is cluttered by peat of varying enormity; just the odd flake of toasted honeycomb can be found; **f**23 beautiful mocha just so compliments the vanilla and smoke; some soft toffee leaves a gentle trail and controls the mounting oak; **b**23 a beautiful Ardbeg that just holds back from going full frontal. **58.3%.** *Douglas Laing.*

⁖ **Platinum Old and Rare Ardbeg Aged 30 Years** dist 73, bott 02 **(89)** **n**24 a shade oily but the complexity of the peat remains spellbinding and beyond words; **t**22 sweet and fruity at first with a mouthwatering barley rush. The peat gathers momentum, as does the salt; **f**21 unusually sweet and sugary in part; surprising lack of oak; **b**22 quality malt, but by no means Ardbeg at its most bemusing. **48.9%.** *Douglas Laing. 197 bottles.*

Premier Malts Ardbeg 11 Years Old dist 28/3/91, bott Nov 02 **(88)** **n**22 the peat is thick, punchy and intense; **t**23 this is a rich dram, an Ardbeg of the full, fat variety where oak is still to play a key role; **f**22 remains oily so the peat barely subsides; **b**21 a big, uncomplicated Ardbeg of the new oily school. **60.6%.** *Malcolm Pride.*

Provenance Ardbeg Autumn Distillation Over 9 Years dist Autumn 90, bott Summer 00 **(93)** **n**23 young, vibrant, lively and drenched in peat. Fresh it may be, but the complexity of that peatiness takes some unravelling. All the usual suspects with iodine, seaweed, salt and so on, but this time with the sweet malt is dried peppers – not a usual Ardbeg feature in bottled form; **t**23 a pounding mixture of concentrated grist and hot peppers. An oily sweetness creeps across the palate to offer a cocoa-peat middle. Very chewy and uncompromising, but the complexity is in saga form; **f**23 so enormously long that, after the third mouthful, you can just sit back and enjoy the long-haul flight. It all ends in vanilla but the peat refuses to go away; **b**24 this one takes me back, about the closest bottling to the first Ardbeg I tasted 20 years ago I have found. The Lagavulin may be a little more intense than this, but you will be hard pushed to find any other whisky offering such complexity. Though unusually spicy and dry, this is a classic for Ardbegophiles. **43%.** *Douglas McGibbon & Co.*

Provenance Ardbeg Autumn Distillation Over 10 Years dist Autumn 90, bott Winter 00 **(83)** **n**19 **t**23 **f**20 **b**21. Brilliant middle, a tad off the mark elsewhere. Not to be confused with Ardbeg Provenance! **43%.** *Douglas McGibbon & Co.*

⁖ **Silver Seal Ardbeg 26 Years Old** **(79)** **n**20 **t**21 **f**19 **b**19. Spiced, sweet but flattened by caramel base line. **46%**

Spirit of Scotland Ardbeg 1974 (86) n22 big fruit; an unusual, almost (and I so hate to say it) ancient Cognacy feel to the friction-free oakiness; the peat is powerful but sweet and controlled; **t**22 as silky as the nose suggests with a massive wave of improbably sweet barley while the oak outguns the peat; **f**20 pretty bitter once the barley vanishes; **b**21 oddball by Ardbeg standards with everything in black and white and with complexity at a minimum. **40%**

Spirit of Scotland Ardbeg 1993 db cask no. 1091 bott Jul 03 **(88) n**23 salty, farmyardy and bracing; **t**22 slow start then a steady development of vanilla and peat; pretty salty and puckering throughout; **f**21 dry toast while the peat rolls in; **b**21 one to be taken in large mouthfuls for full eye-watering effect. **52.3%. Potstill, Vienna. 295 bottles.**

Symposium International Ardbeg 1991 (89) n22 thick and oily, lots of vegetation among the liquid barley, dense and uncompromising; **t**23 a very sweet, malty arrival that then takes off as the peat leaves, clean and attractive; **f**22 yields seriously to reveal the barley; **b**22 unambiguous Ardbeg.

ARDMORE
Speyide, 1899. Allied. Working.

Ardmore 100th Anniversary 12 Years Old db dist 86, bott 99 **(94) n**24 beautifully clean, sweet peat with none of the salty freshness that one associates with island malts. A crisp, firm almost hard and angular nose that displays heaps of character; **t**23 intense and complex from the start with a wonderful shape-changing style. One moment it is hard and biting into the roof of the mouth, the next it is soft and sweet and caressing the tastebuds, peaty and smoky throughout and fabulously malty and intense; **f**23 sweet, flour-gristy softness at first, smoky and then it sharpens and becomes steely hard, delicate vanilla oak and for the first time a touch of honeycomb; **b**24 this was to be one of the great whiskies of 1999. As this didn't get Allied switched on to what a truly great malt this is, nothing will. Quite fantastic.

Ardmore 100th Anniversary 21 Years Old db **(91) n**24 lovely weight of smoke to counter the confident fruit and oak; **t**22 silky, gently peated malt and lush fruit make for the most gentle combination; **f**22 very light vanillas and an echo of smoke and spice; **b**23 a malt which simply caresses the tastebuds. The fruit influence is important but the malt and smoke are intriguingly subtle. It just gets better each time you taste it. **43%** *Very rare. One or two only available exclusively at Glendronach distillery shop and the odd one has slipped into specialist outlets. Bottled exclusively for guests of the distillery's centenary bash.*

Cask Ardmore 1990 (94) n24 the peat arrives in a gristy, powdered form; the barley remains fresh and young with hints of orange; **t**23 mouthfilling, gently oiled, the peat fills around the palate at leisure while the oak offers the dryer chalky backdrop; **f**23 the mouthwatering, fresh properties continue, and the peat gently caresses whatever its contacts. Sweet and beguiling; **b**24 one of the peatiest, most sublime Ardmores ever to hit the market, yet its genius is in its improbable dexterity and balance: just look beyond the peat and discover a living dram!! For late-coming Islayphiles, this loquacious, Lothario of a malt is closest you will ever get to seeing Port Ellen at its long-lost peak. **55.8%.** *Gordon & MacPhail.*

Gordon & MacPhail Ardmore (91) n23 perfectly peated, soft and lumbering, allowing some wonderful malty tones egality. Just sniff and enjoy! **t**24 the arrival on the palate is a tapestry of all things magical. The peats are subtle, complex and a little spicy, there is early chocolate as the oak grabs hold and then there is an oaty, honeycomb thread. Just staggering; **f**21 flattens a little, but the honeycomb and spice continue; **b**23 arguably the best Gordon and MacPhail standard bottling of the last decade. **40%**

Gordon & MacPhail Ardmore 1985 (90) n23 classic Ardmore charm: delightfully smoky yet offering a hint of lavender and bitter-sweetness among the complex malts. Exhilarating; **t**22 there is a controlled surge of smoke that immediately rises and then levels off as a superbly textured almost biting maltiness comes through; **f**22 very similar to a Very Old Barton bourbon with the mouth popping with oaky-malty notes that keep the lips smacking; **b**23 considering the main theme is peat-oak-malt, the complexity is truly astonishing. One of G&M's most assured malts and worth hunting down. **40%**

Gordon & MacPhail Ardmore 1987 (85) n21 honied and surprisingly peatless; **t**22 silky sweet, ultra intense malt with a whiff of smoke; **f**21 a procession of vanillas; **b**21 a silky, sweet expression with little more than a hint of smoke. **40%**

Old Malt Cask Ardmore 21 Years Old dist Nov 79, bott Mar 01 **(90)** n23 charming display of untarnished softly peated barley: just so subtle! **t**23 follows on from the nose without missing a beat: glorious malt with a touch of smoke and oil; **f**21 light and vanilla-rich; **b**23 probably from a second or even third-fill bourbon cask, the malt has almost unrestrained dominance. Just sniff the glass after it has gone! **50%**. *Douglas Laing. 648 bottles.*

Old Master's Ardmore 1980 (94) n23 a supreme dovetailing of soft yet confident peats and mouthwatering, grassy malt. Clean and much younger than you might expect from the age, despite some background oak; **t**24 classic Ardmore with the sweet peat with a controlled explosion on lift off but then a fabulous follow-through of crisp, brittle barley. The complexity and clarity is glorious; **f**23 the most subtle oak is around but it's mainly cocoa on the finale, all slowly drying. Still the peat remains a nagging whisper and the backbone malt remain erect and sturdy and, miraculously, salivating to the very end; **b**24 what can you say? Yet another example of why Ardmore is probably the world's greatest undiscovered malt. This is surely one of the most mouthwatering drams for an 18-year-old year-old-malt you'll ever find, and the luscious subtlety of the peat is more than a bonus. With such fabulous balance and complexity, if you want to discover what a subtlety in whisky is all about, have a gander at this. For this is a Masterpiece Malt. **51.4%** *James MacArthur.*

⋅∷⋅ **Scott's Selection Ardmore 1977 Sherry Wood** bott 03 **(86)** n22 a gentle, playful argument between clean, soft grape, shy peat reek and vanilla; **t**22 the oak helps make for a puckering start and the salty sherry also adds to the sharpness of flavours; **f**21 some smoke comes out of hiding for the softest of finales; **b**21 another summer or two in cask and the balance would have been lost. **58.1%**

⋅∷⋅ **The Un-chillfiltered Collection Ardmore 1990 Aged 12 Years** cask 2695 dist 31 May 90, bott 6 Jun 03 **(89)** n23 almost an echo of peat reverberating around the glass; **t**22 softly oiled with sweet peat offering smokey riches; **f**22 long, sweet malt and gathering vanilla; **b**22 a more lughtly peated version but the suspense is awesome. **46%**. *Signatory.*

Ultimate Selection Ardmore 1992 dist 25/2/92, bott 28/11/02 **(86)** n21 oily smoke diffuses with clean barley; **t**22 sweet and oily with intense, chewy maltiness; **f**21 simmering peat just gets above the gathering oak; **b**22 a bold and classy version. **43%**. *Van Wees. NL.*

ARRAN (*see* Isle of Arran)

AUCHENTOSHAN
Lowlands, 1800. Morrison Bowmore. Working.

Auchentoshan 10 Years Old db **(79)** n17 **t**21 **f**21 **b**20. A lively, malty chap that coats the mouth with a soft oil and cocoa. **40%**

Auchentoshan 18 Years Old dist 78 db **(87)** n22 gooseberries and riesling with fresh barley; **t**21 rich, busy malt with complex oak infusion; **f**22 soft brown sugars mixing with the rich malt. Long and lingering; **b**22 a really delightful Lowlander full of complexity. **58.8%**

Auchentoshan 21 Years Old db **(84)** n*20* t*20* f*23* b*21*. Recovers from a surprisingly hot start to generate some really gorgeous spicy and ultra malty complexity for the outstanding finale. **43%**

Auchentoshan 29 Years Old dist 73, cask 793 db **(89)** n*24* exceptional sherry butt: a touch of coffee fringes the fruit, slightly salty and dry. Oloroso is near peak performance; **t***24* my, oh, my: a supreme combination of seasoned, clean oloroso and bourbon. The malt kicks in to add further sweetness. Simply sublime; **f***19* oak begins to make its mark with a touch of bitterness, but the complexity remains; **b***22* maybe one or two summers too long – the oak has crept in to unravel the finish, but until then the experience is one of sheer joy. **55.8%**

Auchentoshan 1978 (*see* Auchentoshan 18 Years Old)

Auchentoshan Select db **(72)** n*18* t*19* f*17* b*18*. Malty but thin and a little hot. **40%**

Auchentoshan Three Wood db **(74)** n*19* t*17* f*20* b*18*. An attractive finish. The mouthfeel still isn't right, but this is so much better than the dreadful first-ever bottling. **43%**

⁙ **Aberdeen Distillers Auchentoshan 1992** cask 6196 dist Oct 92, bott Nov 03 **(82)** n*20* t*21* f*21* b*20*. They don't come much more youthful or sweeter than this. **43%**. *Blackadder.*

Cadenhead's Auchentoshan 10 Years Old dist 92, bott 03/03 **(85)** n*20* Clean, attractive though a bit thin and lifeless; **t***23* superb maltfest arrival on the palate, aided by some weak spices; **f***21* slightly oily, sweet malt; **b***21* the fun is all upfront: brilliant malt sparkle. **46%**

MacLeod's Lowland Single Malt Aged 8 Years **(74)** n*17* t*20* f*18* b*19*. Thin, malty and cream-toffee sweet. **40%**. *Ian MacLeod (Auchentoshan, though not stated).*

⁙ **Murray McDavid Auchentoshan 1992** **(89)** n*22* Bushmills in disguise; **t***23* delicate malt, a touch of apple and then gathering honey; **f***22* some powerful vanilla and a dash of coffee reveals the spread of oak; **b***22* a really classy expression of a distillery that too often shows itself to faltering effect. As a 10-year-old this has to be the serious whisky lover's benchmark. **46%. nc ncf.**

⁙ **Old Malt Cask Auchentoshan Aged 25 Years** dist Oct 78, bott Oct 03 **(93)** n*24* magnificently different: plain omelette sizzling in groundnut oil; freshly baked egg custard tart; a drizzle of citrus; toasted rye bread – simply an awesome aroma of brain-busting complexity; **t***23* uncanny sweetness for a triple-distilled malt this age; the barley offers a comforting background as oak-induced spices indulge; vanilla forms the middle with slightly overdone toast; **f***22* very, very long – improbably so – with a charming if not almost unique development of mouthwatering barley towards the finale. Traces of mango chutney kick in for good and almost surreal measure; **b***24* not what I expected … in fact, an entirely unique fingerprint to any Lowlander (indeed perhaps any malt) I have tasted before, and that is saying something. For any Lowland fans, you miss this at your peril. For others, find a good half hour to simply sit back, drink, close eyes, and be truly entertained and amazed. **50%. nc ncf sc.** *Douglas Laing.*

Old Malt Cask Auchentoshan Aged 33 Years dist Nov 67, bott Feb 01 **(77)** n*21* t*21* f*17* b*18*. Inside of garage showroom: new car smell. Hot and biting. **45.3%. nc ncf.** *Douglas Laing.* 162 bottles.

Old Masters Auchentoshan 1992 bott 02 **(79)** n*18* t*22* f*19* b*20*. Rougher than an oil-less engine. But the malty punch on the palate is memorable. **64.2%.** *James MacArthur.*

Scott's Selection Auchentoshan 1978 bott 96 **(72)** n*20* t*18* f*16* b*18*. Has some sweet, bourbony moments. **51.2%.** *Robert Scott & Co.*

⁙ **Whisky Galore Auchentoshan 1990 Aged 12 Years** **(78)** n*19* t*20* f*19* b*20*. Young, thin, sharp and tangy. **46%**

Whisky Galore Auchentoshan 1992 Aged 10 Years (88) n*21* deliciously young and undermatured, so fresh and malty; t*23* mouthwatering grassy, clean malt… amazingly a slight hint of peat! f*22* more of the same, sweetens out and spices arrive; b*22* just so rare to find Auchentoshan of this age that is so brilliantly distilled. A treat. **46%**

AUCHROISK
Speyside, 1974. Diageo. Working.

Auchroisk Aged 10 Years db **(75)** n*19* t*20* f*17* b*19*. The really disappointing, toffee-laden and bitter finish undermines the sweet, grassy, malty intensity on the arrival on the palate. One of Speyside's lighter, most delicate drams, this has to be treated with very tender care and sensitivity which appears not to have happened here. **43%**. *Flora and Fauna.*

∵ **Auchroisk Rare Malt 28 Years Old** dist 74, db **(83)** n*21* t*21* f*22* b*21*. Just enough charisma to recover from the mildly butiric nose, and the bourbony, spicy sub-plot is exceedingly good fun. **56.8%**

∵ **Blackadder Raw Cask Auchroisk 1989** cask no 30264 dist Jun 89, bott Nov 03 **(84)** n*22* t*21* f*21* b*20*. The distillers were surprised how light their malt was then the distillery began operation – hence the use of sherry finishing in The Singleton. Here we have confirmation: a Speysider that tastes like a very good young bourbon, or an old grain whisky. Delicious it may be, but I've marked it down slightly as I like my Speysiders to taste of malt. **61.9%. nc ncf sc.**

Old Malt Cask Auchroisk Aged 27 Years dist Dec 74, bott, Dec 01 **(83)** n*21* t*22* f*19* b*21*. A light, malty, grassy Speysider, even after all these years in the cask. Thoroughly enjoyable. **43.8%. nc ncf.** *Douglas Laing. 246 bottles.*

The Single Barrel Collection Auchroisk 1989 12 Years Old dist June 89, bott Dec 2001 cask no. 30257 **(69)** n*17* t*18* f*17* b*17*. Too oaky and aged, despite little colour. **65.92%. nc nf.**

AULTMORE
Speyside, 1896. John Dewar & Son. Working.

∵ **Aultmore 12 Years Old** db **(86)** n*22* freshly diced apple; clean and salivating despite encroaching oak; a slight citrus mask there, too; t*22* the mouth arrival is every bit as crisp and mouthwatering as the nose suggests, only a little extra intensity towards the middle; f*20* vanilla, bitter toffee and some very late spice amid the platforms of oak; b*22* do any of you remember the old DCL distillery bottling of this from, what, 25 years ago? Well, this is nothing like it. **40%** *John Dewar & Sons.*

Aultmore 1983 Cask Strength bott 97 db **(79)** n*20* t*19* f*20* b*20*. Some pleasant malt-barley sugar notes, but it's some battle to get there. **58.8%**

Adelphi Aultmore 14 Years old cask 2900 dist 85, bott 99 **(69)** n*17* t*19* f*17* b*16*. A less than impressive cask – sulphur tainted. **60.1%. sc.**

∵ **Connoisseurs Choice Aultmore 1989 (87)** n*21* freshly sandpapered floors plus some honey and under-ripe fig. A distant hint of peat-smoke; t*22* excellent clarity to the clean barley; intelligent sparring between barley and vanilla-oak; f*22* a delightful smoke-fade returns ensuring excellent bitter-sweet character; b*22* clean, impressive whisky that perfectly captures the distillery fingerprint: about time, too, for this usually an ill-served Speyside. **43%**

Hart Brothers Aultmore Aged 10 Years dist 1990 **(86)** n*21* crispish barley; t*22* clean, refreshing malt, a blender's delight; f*21* firm oak and malt with waves of spice; b*22* nothing flash or spectacular, just extremely good quality and very well-made Speyside malt. **43%**

Inverarity 10 Years Old Speyside (81) n*19* t*22* f*20* b*20*. A light, flitting malt, but with the toffee on the finish, not quite light enough. Exceptional, faintly smoked, ultra-malty middle. **40%.** *From Aultmore, though not stated.*

Old Malt Cask Aultmore Aged 16 Years dist Apr 84, bott Jul 01 **(77) n**18 **t**22 **f**18 **b**19. A light Speysider slightly out of breath at this age on nose and finish but glories in a sensational cream toffee-rich arrival on the palate. **50%**

⠿ **Old Master's Aultmore 1989** cask 2454 bott 03 **(86) n**21 solid fruit, unripe gooseberry; a shade of soft oak; **t**22 seriously big malt despite all the chewy fruit; **f**22 long, excellent texture and bitter-sweet charm; **b**21 this Speysider was much more like this 25 years ago: a welcome return to an old and effective style. **60.5%**

⠿ **Scott's Selection Aultmore 1987** bott 02 **(80) n**19 **t**21 **f**20 **b**20. Good juicy barley throughout. **56.6%**

⠿ **Whisky Galore Aultmore 1987 Aged 15 Years (85) n**22 fat, clean, rich barley; **t**21 mouthwatering and simplistic barley with a gentle spice buzz; **f**21 vanilla and barley; **b**21 the clean, uncluttered stuff blenders crave for. **46%**

⠿ **Whisky Galore Aultmore 1989 Aged 14 Years (78) n**20 **t**20 **f**19 **b**19. A pleasantish dram, but the sherry is indistinct. **46%**

BALBLAIR
Highlands (Northern), 1872. Inver House. Working.

Balblair 10 Years Old db **(75) n**24 **t**18 **f**16 **b**17. The mild, peated nose is just amazing: just like being by the sea, with salt and seaweed etc. But to taste: bland, bland, bland!!. Too much caramel. **40%**

Balblair 16 years Old db **(78) n**21 **t**21 **f**18 **b**18. Sweet and enticing at first but lacking depth and complexity on the finish. Not a patch on previous bottlings. **43%**

⠿ **Balblair Aged 24 Years Limited Edition** db dist 1979, bott Oct 03 **(90) n**23 a riot of mixed fruit ranging from apple and pear to nectarine, all dusted with vanilla and custard; the oak offers some intriguing spice, too; **t**22 more early spice then an avalanche of fresh, mouthwatering malt. The oak remains refined and controlled; **f**22 medium length and subtle thanks to an oak input that is tune with the sweet barley; **b**23 absolutely spot-on whisky from a truly great distillery. The absence of colouring on this underlines my assertion that this is a distillery that is far too good to be tampered with at any age. **46%**. *3150 bottles.*

Balblair 27 Years Old Limited Edition Sherry Cask db **(91) n**23 coffee and intense sherry: a dense aroma for wine lovers especially; **t**23 the sherry influence is profound, though not overwhelming. Sparks fly as the peppery spices arrive; **f**22 thick oak softened by and sweetened by raisins. Heavy roast Java returns for the finale; **b**23 an outrageously big sherry cask of the old school that has much to say and is worth listening to. Fabulous. **46%**

⠿ **Balblair Aged 31 Years Limited Edition** db dist 1969 **(86) n**23 honeycomb and bourbon star with the vanilla adding a softening dustiness, clean and subtle; t22 a pretty lively dram for its age and strength with the honey taking the lead but being pegged back by a bitter-sweet oakiness; **f**20 slightly limp by comparison with the malt dying off and a hard, thin edge forming; **b**21 starts brilliantly, especially with the nose and early honey spurt. The finish though is surprisingly mean. **45%**

Balblair Aged 33 Years db bott 2002 **(89) n**22 sweet, ripened peaches despite the marauding oak. Excellent charm and balance. The complexity is understated; **t**23 Quite a sugary offering: the sweetness runs from start to middle. Not unlike German coffee biscuits with the barley flour crisp then chewy. The oak is telling and fabulously controlled with a lovely mocha layer; **f**21 long, even and sweet with gentle spices drifting around. The oak is deft and balances supremely with some very late orangey notes; **b**23 sexy stuff designed for late nights, a silent, gently lit room and an elegant, blonde and beautiful woman, the same age as the whisky, called Andrea by your side.... Everything is softly done and the complexity is almost alarming. **45.4%**

∴ **Balblair 1989 Limited Edition** db **(82) n**_21_ **t**_21_ **f**_20_ **b**_20_. Good honey in places. **46% ncf**

Balblair Elements db **(87) n**_22_ heather-honey and clean malt; **t**_22_ very sweet start, lush with developing malt and spice; **f**_21_ slightly bitter fruit, with compensating smoke; **b**_22_ This is such an improvement on the first, elementary, Elements that it is barely comparable. Much sweeter and confident. **40%**

Adelphi Balblair 37 Years Old cask 893 dist 65, bott 02 **(82) n**_21_ **t**_19_ **f**_22_ **b**_20_. A shade too much sap to make this a great whisky, but the honey and kiwi fruit on the finish is sublime. **54.3%**

Gordon & MacPhail Balblair 10 Years Old (85) n_21_ honey, spice and chalky oak; **t**_22_ brilliant malt flourish that runs through from dry and chewy to sweet; **f**_21_ tails off towards oak, but always remains intact; **b**_21_ a chewy, clean dram. **40%**

Old Malt Cask Balblair Aged 35 Years dist May 66, bott Aug 01 **(85) n**_22_ **t**_21_ **f**_22_ **b**_20_. Just a few years beyond brilliance, but still packs a punch. **40.4%. nc ncf.** Douglas Laing. 151 bottles.

∴ **Scotch Single Malt Circle Balblair 1975** cask 7275 dist 26 Nov 75 bott Jan 98 **(91) n**_22_ heavy duty, oily malt **t**_24_ apples of enormous density and then a wave of brilliantly fresh barley **f**_22_ gentle spices and vanilla with many layers of barley **b**_23_ a classic Balblair for club members to get their teeth into **57.9%** Germany

BALMENACH
Speyside, 1824. Inver House. Working.

Balmenach 27 Year Old db **(86) n**_21_ unusual mixture of peat and coal smoke and some sharpish oaky notes; **t**_22_ a thread of peat weaves its way around the toasted honeycomb: silky and sexy; **f**_21_ long, silky, smoky, spiced; **b**_22_ confirmation of this distillery's ability to dazzle at great age. **46%**

Balmenach Aged 25 Years Golden Jubilee db **(89) n**_21_ towering vanilla, slightly chalky and dry where the oak is beginning to gain hold. Decent if unsophisticated spices kick but interweave attractively with the stewed apples. Threatens to be slightly too oaky but just enough sweet honeycomb keeps it under control; **t**_23_ spicy, robust and bourbony. Now complexity is the key word as the peppers buzz around the palate and the charging oak clashes head on with the roasty, malty notes. Some burnt honeycomb in there, too. Delicious cocoa peaks very early on; **f**_22_ perhaps slightly on the tired at first side but enough demerara sweetness carries it through to a fabulously long and beautifully weighted conclusion. Lots and lots of toffee hangs around seemingly forever; **b**_23_ What a glorious old charmer this is! An essay in balance despite the bludgeoning nature of the beast early on. Takes a little time to get to know and appreciate: persevere with this belter because it is classic stuff for its age. Bottled in special still-shaped decanter to mark the occasion of the Queen's Golden Jubilee. **58%.** Around 800 decanters.

Adelphi Balmenach 13 Years Old cask 3560, dist 90, bott 03 **(88) n**_21_ firm and malty; **t**_23_ massive malt, absolutely mountainous stuff; **f**_22_ a saner, more complex phase, lightened by a subtle citrus note; **b**_22_ I have never come across a malt from this distillery with such a massive malt character. Incredible. And so delicious! **60.1%**

Connoisseurs Choice Balmenach 1973 (72) n_17_ **t**_19_ **f**_18_ **b**_18_. Not quite the cleanest of drams. **40%**

Connoisseurs Choice Balmenach 1974 (86) n_22_ hints of honey and smoke; **t**_22_ fine malt-honey oak-cocoa balance, lovely texture; **f**_20_ dries gently and reintroduces the smoke; **b**_22_ a Speyside, laid-back version of a Highland Park! **40%.** Gordon & MacPhail.

Deerstalker Balmenach Aged 12 Years (85) n_21_ really excellent malt-oak balance: complex; **t**_22_ sheds of honey and rich oak suggest something older than 12; **f**21 delicate malt and butterscotch, more hints of age; **b**21 an elegant, beautifully structured Speysider. **40%**. *Aberfoyle & Knight.*

Deerstalker Balmenach Aged 18 Years (81) n20 **t**21 **f**19 **b**21. A delicate, butterscotch malt with charm, character and a touch of age. **40%**. *Aberfoyle & Knight.*

Hart Brothers Balmenach 18 Years Old dist 1979 **(81) n**21 **t**21 **f**19 **b**20. Silky, sweet and gently oaked. **43%**

Hart Brothers Balmenach Aged 30 Years dist Jan 72, bott 02 **(85) n**20 a few signs of oak bruising, but the fruit patches it up; **t**22 massive sherry, spice and chocolate, powering and majestic; **f**22 long with continued and absolutely delicious sweetened cocoa notes; **b**21 this is big, impressive whisky that should keep sherry lovers amused for a while. **50.1%**

Inverarity Ancestral 14 Years Old (74) n18 **t**19 **f**19 **b**18. Fusty and fruity with toffee on the finish. 40% Although not stated on label, this is Balmenach. **40%**

Scott`s Selection Balmenach 1979 bott 96 **(83) n**21 **t**21 **f**20 **b**21. A highly drinkable expression from a distillery that rarely stands up so contentedly at this kind of age. **62.4%**. *Robert Scott & Co.*

The Single Barrel Collection Balmenach 1988 13-y-o cask 2774, dist Oct 88, bott Dec 01 **(85) n**19 **t**23 **f**21. Calmed by lashings of vanilla and barley. Slightly brooding; **b**22 An absolute treat: the arrival on the palate is near flawless. **59.79%. nc nf.**

THE BALVENIE

Speyside, 1892. William Grant & Sons. Working.

The Balvenie Aged 10 Years Founders Reserve db **(90) n**23 astonishing complexity: the fruit is relaxed, crushed sultanas and malty suet. A sliver of smoke and no more: everything is hinted and nudged at rather than stated. Superb; **t**24 here we go again: threads of malt binding together barely detectable nuances. Thin liquorice here, grape there, smoke and vanilla somewhere else; **f**20 Light muscovado-toffee flattens out the earlier complexity. The bitter-sweet balance remains brilliant to the end; **b**23 just one of those all-time-great standard 10-year-olds from a great distillery. **40%**

The Balvenie Aged 12 Years Double Wood db **(79) n**22 **t**21 **f**17 **b**19. Sledgehammer sherry offers the fruitiest of welcomes while good spice doubles up on the malt-sherry front. The caramel has a too leading role on the finish, though. Usually better than this. **40%**

The Balvenie Aged 15 Years Single Barrel db **(93) n**23 cracking vanilla-malt split. Complex, intriguing, something to really get your nose into. Quite maltings-floorish; **t**24 massive malt surge is invigorating and mouthwatering. Glorious; **f**22 keeps clean and relatively oak-free; **b**24 just one of those drams that should be within touching distance at strategic points around the house. **50.4%** *Being single barrel the bottlings do change quite regularly: fortunately the magnificence of the quality rarely does.*

The Balvenie Aged 21 Years Port Wood db **(87) n**23 clean, mouthwatering evidence of fresh port pipes; **t**22 the wine swamps the malt for a while, but being Balvenie the complexity returns, a softly smoked, sweet maltiness leading the way; **f**21 vanilla and toffee; **b**21 using port pipes like this can backfire on a malt as complex as Balvenie, but this one comes through with flying Scottish and Portuguese colours. **40%**

The Balvenie 25 Years Old Single Barrel cask no. 14439 **(88) n**23 sturdy yet fresh malt surrounded by soft mint. The oak is wheezing a bit, but beautifully couched; **t**22 lively and minty with intense malt of varying sharpness; **f**21 some late oiliness, then vanilla and a sprinkling of spice and cocoa; **b**22 tremendous stuff: complex and charming.

The Balvenie Aged 50 Years db cask 191 **(87)** n23 coffee and biscuits alongside the ultra-ripe, thick sherry, not unlike moist cherry fruitcake. Smoke remains after the sherry is burnt out; t23 some suppressed oak does its best to escape, but has a major battle to fight its way through the layers of big grape. Lovely spices point in the direction of some peat; f19 pretty shattered oak offers a bitter finale, but the fruit does all it can to soften things and lengthen out matters; b22 a noble dram battered by oak but comes through with a degree of nobility. Natural strength.

The Balvenie 1967 Vintage Cask db **(89)** n24 beautifully delicate and floral with a layer of peat. Bourbon-style vanilla adds age, approaching perfection in Balvenie terms; t22 oily rush of malt. Now Canadian-style vanilla infuses with spices and dry cocoa; f21 dries to become vanilla-rich, remains cocoa dominant; b22 dry and complex.

The Balvenie 1968 Vintage Cask db **(86)** n23 firm and flinty, deep oak with a hint of the berry fruit about it, and buttered crumpets for good measure; t22 creamy malt then a surge of unspecified fruitiness; f20 hardens into brittle toffee with the Balvenie-esque light muscovado sweetness lingering from the middle until it fades as the oak grabs hold; b21 the delicate sweetness accentuates the dry finale. Pretty delicious. **50.8%**

The Balvenie 1972 Vintage Cask db **(88)** n22 melon and ginger: beautifully oaked, bourbon style; t23 immediate spices, more ginger plus peppers and a touch of apple then bright malty notes; f21 some smoke appears with the cocoa and a late touch of honey; b22 a superb, lightly smoked Balvenie that shows some age but wears it well. Natural strength.

⠂⠿⠂ **The Balvenie 1973 Vintage Cask** db **(92)** n22 distinctly bourbony with sweet leathery tones sitting beside vanilla and a trickle of honey. Just a distant waft of peat brings us back to Scotland; t24 this is the acceptable face of oak: delicate bourbony notes gush at you, then a honey spice middle with vanilla ice cream; f22 natural caramel slows it all down but still waves of bourbony sweetness both rattle and caress the tastebuds; b24 some purists will find too many stars and stripes to the character if this malt. Even I thought I was in a Wild Turkey warehouse for a moment or two. But sheer quality cannot be denied. **49.7%**

The Balvenie 1989 Port Wood db n20 t22 f21 b20. The nose is remarkably undemonstrative, all the fruity action arriving up front early on the tastebuds. Good follow-through. **40%**

The Maltmill Speyside Single Malt 11 Years cask 3008, dist 1990, bott 2001 **(93)** n24 t24 f22 b23. Exquisite stuff: Balvenie unplugged in some ways. It would be great to see the distillery carry on where the Germans left off. 55% Is it Balvenie? "The distillery founded in 1892 in Dufftown is named after the castle nearby. It is still owned by an independent company and uses its own floor malting...." Sadly, I understand The Maltmill in Hamburg who bottled this are no longer in business. William Grant keeps a close eye on each and every Balvenie cask so it doesn't find its way as a single malt onto the open market. So a real collector's item ... in every sense. **55%. sc.** *Germany.*

BANFF
Speyside, 1863–1983. Demolished.

Chieftain's Choice Banff Aged 18 Years dist 80 **(80)** n19 t22 f19 b20. Excellent coppery texture; big and chewy. **43%.** *Ian MacLeod.*

Connoisseurs Choice Banff 1974 (74) n17 t20 f18 b19. Slightly feinty when warmed, so big and oily, too. Sweet and malty. **40%.** *Gordon & MacPhail.*

Connoisseurs Choice Banff 1976 (76) n19 t20 f19 b18. Soft with chalky oak. **40%.** *Gordon & MacPhail.*

Coopers Choice Banff 1978 Aged 22 Years bott 01 **(82)** n22 t21 f19 b20. Struggles at the end, but the nose and mouth arrival in particular are excellent for a Banff. **56%.** *Vintage Malt Company.*

Old Malt Cask Banff Aged 24 Years dist Dec 77 **(88)** n*19* grinding oak appears to knock the wind out of the lighter, slightly honied orangey tones, just a fraction sappy; **t***24* outstanding mouthfeel and arrival on palate. The sweet malt is also fantastically spiced and for a moment all-consuming. A hint of peat wafts across the mouth but the rich honeycomb is a meal in itself. The intensity and complexity has to be tasted to be believed! **f***22* long, tapering, clean with a build-up of some piney, oaky notes. Lots of natural caramel with chewy cream toffee and again some attractive soft orange. Perhaps a fraction overcooked in the oak department at the absolute finale ... though not by much; **b***23* only the nose prevents this from hitting the 90s. This is heady and unquestionably beautiful stuff: the sweetness is almost liquor-like at times and women will adore this one. **50%.** *Douglas Laing.*

Old Malt Cask Banff Aged 31 Years dist Nov, 66 bott Aug 98 **(88)** n*23* t*22* f*21* b*22.* Hangs together well with the oak having the final say. Good whisky for its age. **50%. nc ncf.** *Douglas Laing. 181 bottles.*

Old Malt Cask Banff Aged 35 Years (Sherry) dist Feb 66, bott Mar 01 **(76)** n*19* t*19* f*19* b*19.* A tired old soul, but one with a dry, spicy tale to tell. **46.4% nc ncf.** *Douglas Laing. 192 bottles.*

Old Masters Banff 1976 bott 01 **(86)** n*20* foraging oak; **t***22* brittle barley and excellent mouthfeel; **f***22* loads of oak-barley character with late cocoa and smoke; **b***22* fit for its age. **57.1%** *James MacArthur.*

BEN NEVIS
Highland (Western), 1825. Nikka. Working.

Ben Nevis Ten Years Old db **(85)** n*19* oily, nutty but a little off-key **t***22* such a massive introduction to the palate: soft oils, citrus notes and very big oak on the malt but sweet enough to chew for ever; **f***23* the integration of the oak really makes for some finish: long, hints of bitter roast coffee against the sweet oils; **b***21* the nose makes you say oh-oh, but you need a knife, fork, spoon and napkin for the taste. **46%**

Ben Nevis Ten Years Old db **(88)** n*21* typically weighty, nutty and oily, though there are some powering, over-ripe orange tones. Mountainous stuff; **t***24* no less massive on the palate: the intensity of the malt is awesome. Much cleaner than the nose, and the degree of sweetness is surprising. Fat, chewy and entirely delicious with no shortage of fruity notes countering a vague hint of smoke; **f***20* much, much harder as the sweetness dissolves. Firm vanilla and brittle malt and a faint echo of cocoa; **b***23* bottled exclusively for the Japanese market, this expression shows Ben Nevis at its most colourful, characterful and complex: no shrinking violet, this. The mouth arrival is spellbinding. The definitive 10-year-old Ben Nevis for whisky clubs to chase. **43%.** *bott 03 Japan only*

Ben Nevis 21 Years Old db dist 74, bott 95 **(91)** n*23* t*23* f*22* b*23.* Although bottled in 1995 and from a single cask spotted for its brilliance by the manager, apparently some bottles are still doing the rounds at great prices as this is regarded as near enough the ultimate Ben Nevis. I, for one, will not disagree too loudly. This bottling underlines the enormity of this great distillery. **60.5%.** *192 bottles.*

Ben Nevis 1973 Age 26 Years cask no. 747, bott 99 db **(91)** n*22* t*23* f*23* b*23.* Ben Nevis has its detractors, though I have never been entirely sure why. This bottling was one of my favourites in the world through 1999 and firmly put the distillery among the greats of Scotland. This is lush and magnificent: cask 747 produced a jumbo of a malt that has no problem taking off. When it'll land, your guess is as good as mine! **52.7%. sc.** *252 bottles.*

Ben Nevis 26 Years Old cask 952, dist 75, bott 01 db **(91)** n*23* t*23* f*21* b*24.* Another cask from the Ben Nevis of Improbable Complexity. A connoisseur's dram and a half. **53.9%**

Ben Nevis 30 Years Old cask 2519 db **(86)** n*22* ripe dates concentrate, soft bourbon and lemon: this is a big nose with oak and age stamped all over it; t*22* sweet malt, amazingly, to the fore then a surge of big cocoa-led oak; f*20* bitter with heavy roast Costa Rican coffee joining the cocoa, but finally the oak takes complete control; b*22* a malt living on the edge: just about over the top oak but there is enough sweetness around not only too see it through but to make for a fascinating dram. **56.9%**

🞙 **Ben Nevis 1990 Port Wood Finish** bott 04 db **(92)** n*21* nutty and fruity, there is some freshly ground coffee – and smoke – lurking, too. Marked down only by a slight sulphur-ish blemish; t*24* bloody hell!! Few whiskies have quite so many flavour profiles landing simultaneously on the palate. There is a distinct metallic note that seems to explode in harmony with rich honey and about the most intense barley you will ever find. Oily, and coats the mouth with a fruity, suety layer. The fruitiness just disappears off the scale; f*23* a very slight peat smoke drifts out towards the sweet barley while the oak offers a drier level; b*24* pouring into the glass is a startling experience: it is like a Beaujolais. To quote: "first filled into refills hogsheads on 9th November 1990. It was then transferred into a port bodega butt number 03/01/01 on 12th February 2003 and allowed to mature for a further 12 months." I replicate this from the label because in 30 years of nosing my way around whisky warehouses and labs, never have I come across something as entirely unique as this. You will either love it or hate it. Either way, distillery manager Colin Ross deserves a medal struck for producing something so extraordinary. Collectors around the world will eventually trade their spouse for bottles of this. **61.6%**

Blackadder Raw Cask Ben Nevis 1984 sherry cask 258, dist 21 Nov 84, bott May 02 **(83)** n*21* t*21* f*21* b*20*. Good, clean sherry butt, blackberries on the middle, a little hot. **61.2%. nc ncf sc.**

Blackadder Raw Cask Ben Nevis 1992 bourbon hogshead 687, dist 24 Feb 92, bott Apr 03 **(77)** n*18* t*20* f*19* b*20*. Light and mouthwatering, but not entirely on song. **59.6%. ncf nc sc.**

Cadenhead's Ben Nevis 17 Years Old dist 86, bott 03/03 **(86)** n*22* fit-to-burst gooseberries, newly mown hay and a touch of honey: entrancing; t*22* rich malt that becomes slightly oilier as it develops with spice arrival; f*21* more low-key simple malt; b*21* one of the lightest examples of Ben Nevis bottled in recent years. **46%**

Hart Brothers Ben Nevis Aged 35 Years sherry wood dist 67 **(84)** n*21* t*22* f*21* b*20*. Enormous ginger through the middle and finish. A hard-punching middleweight. **50.1%**

Old Malt Cask Ben Nevis Aged 34 Years dist Apr 66, bott Jan 01 **(78)** n*18* t*22* f*19* b*19*. Flavoursome but hot and slightly off key. **50%. nc ncf.** *Douglas Laing. 168 bottles.*

Old Malt Cask Ben Nevis Aged 36 Years dist Dec 64, bott Mar 01 **(87)** n*23* t*22* f*21* b*21*. This bourbon-style is not unusual in a well-aged Ben Nevis. Excellent. **50%. nc ncf.** *Douglas Laing. 156 bottles.*

🞙 **Platinum Ben Nevis 1963** cask 03/08/07 **(75)** n*21* t*19* f*17* b*18*. Crushing, eye-watering oak saved only by a sweet, bourbony element. **45.8%.** *Douglas Laing.*

BENRIACH
Speyside, 1898. The Benriach Distillery Co. Working.

Benriach 10 Years Old db **(77)** n*18* t*22* f*18* b*19*. Disappointing, non-existent nose but a really excellent malty mouth arrival. Lost in toffee on the finish. **43%**

🞙 **Benriach Over 12 Years** (db) **(83)** n*20* t*21* f*21* b*21*. A barley sugar fest: one of Speyside's most intensely, naturally sweet malts that's a blender's dream and a Godsend for lovers of honeyed malt. **Natural Cask Strength**

🞙 **Benriach Over 16 Years** (db) **(85)** n*20* deft oak; t*22* lush and playful with strands of acacia honey; f*21* dries out elegantly with vanilla; b*22* a beautifully gentle dram that plays up to its full sweet character.

⬥ **Benriach Over 20 Years** (db) **(94)** n24 superb, understated buttery peat: like sticking your nose in the grist mill; t23 an avalanche of honeyed peat, highly unusual and distinctive; hard and flinty on the palate; f23 spices drift over the palate as the peat enters into cocoa mode; b24 unique: never come across such a bone-hard onslaught of peat and honey in one glass.

⬥ **Benriach Over 25 Years** (db) **(74)** n18 t19 f19 b18. Candy store stuff.

⬥ **Benriach Over 30 Years** (db) **(84)** n19 t22 f22 b21. A delicious amalgam of honey and spice; a distant rumble of peat towards the finish.

⬥ **Benriach Over 34 Years** (db) **(90)** n23 improbably clean sherry with thick barley deeply embedded into it; t22 just so sweet: but the sherry acts as a buffer to offer some controlled bitter-dryness; f22 finishes like an old Demerara rum, full bodied, still with sweetness coating the oak; b23 a quite different form of sherry style: as in your face as Terry Hurlock in a Millwall or Rangers shirt.

Cask Benriach 1982 casks 5211–3, dist 4/5/82, bott Sep 93 **(89)** n22 t23 f22 b22. This was for a long time the finest Benriach ever bottled. Although bottled 10 years ago, if you still see the odd bottle around, treat yourself. **60.6%.** *Gordon & MacPhail.*

Connoisseurs Choice Benriach 1980 (71) n20 t19 f16 b16. Charisma bypass. **40%.** *Gordon & MacPhail.*

Connoisseurs Choice Benriach 1981 (78) n20 t21 f18 b19. Beautiful grassy nose and mouth arrival, but otherwise typically thin. **40%.** *Gordon & MacPhail.*

Connoisseurs Choice Benriach 1982 (83) n21 t21 f20 b21. Excellent example of a fresh, light Speysider offering a clean, unpretentious blending malt. **40%.** *Gordon & MacPhail.*

⬥ **Duncan Taylor Benriach 1968 Aged 34 Years (91)** n23 faultless sherry, slight spice; many layers of fruit; t23 fabulously mouthwatering despite all the sherry: the fruit is in total harmony with the barley; f22 dries with a touch of salt; b23 a vague, bitter smokiness drifts around the ripe fruit. **50%**

⬥ **Hart Brothers Benriach Aged 34 Years** dist Nov 68, bott May 03 **(76)** n19 t20 f18 b19. The mildly soapy, sappy nose suggests it has gone through the wood and there is little to suggest otherwise on the palate despite a brief, malty moment. **49.8%.**

Peerless Benriach 1968 cask 2590, dist Nov 68 **(93)** n23 deft oak, hints of chocolate lime; t24 brilliantly mouthwatering, fruity with sharp malt; f23 lots of natural caramel softens the oak, sweet malt continues; b23 this bottling puts Benriach into another dimension. Superb. **50.4%.** *Duncan Taylor & Co.*

Peerless Benriach 1968 cask 2593, dist Nov 68 **(76)** n22 t20 f17 b17. Delightfully fruity, bit over-oaked **51.4%.** *Duncan Taylor & Co.*

BENRINNES

Speyside, 1826. Diageo. Working.

Centenary Reserve Benrinnes 1978 bott 95 **(78)** n20 t22 f17 b19. A so-so dram with a hint of peat to mark the centenary of G&M, not the distillery. **40%.** *Gordon & MacPhail.*

Connoisseurs Choice Benrinnes 1972 (79) n18 t22 f19 b20. Not convinced about the nose, but nothing wrong with the big sultana middle. **40%.** *Gordon & MacPhail.*

Connoisseurs Choice Benrinness 1973 (79) n20 t21 f18 b20. Clean, oily and malty. Very sweet. **40%.** *Gordon & MacPhail.*

Dun Bheagan Benrinnes Aged 20 Years dist 79, bott 00 **(74)** n19 t20 f17 b18. Trademark coal-gas nose and pleasant spice, but rather caramel-jaded and ordinary. **43%.** *William Maxwell.*

Milroy's Benrinnes Over 11 Years Old dist 89, bott 00 **(79)** n21 t20 f19 b19. A pretty biggish version of this unusual, triple-distilled dram. **43%**

Old Malt Cask Benrinnes Aged 19 Years Sherry dist Jul 81, bott Jan 01 **(79) n**18 t22 f20 b19. Big and chewy, but if anything slightly too sweet and cloying. **50%. nc ncf.** *Douglas Laing.*

⋰ **Scotch Malt Whisky Society Cask 36.25 Aged 32 Years 1971 (78) n**19 t19 f21 b19. Takes no prisoners: burnt raisins and Fishermen's Friends cough sweets. **53.5%. nc ncf sc.**

BENROMACH
Sepyside, 1898. Gordon & MacPhail. Working.

Benromach Aged 18 Years db **(78) n**18 t21 f20 b19. Rich textured. **40%.** *Gordon & MacPhail.*

Benromach 19 Years Old Port Wood Finish db **(91) n**22 incredibly fresh, winey, juicy fruit gums and clean; **t**23 mouthwateringly clean and juicy with a sensational mixture of ultra-clean barley and quite amazing sweet grape; **f**22 some lazy spices and bristling oak marry superbly with that elegant barley thread; **b**24 these must be absolutely brand new, first-fill sherry pipes to get this intensity of flavour. A classic among port finishes, reminding others how it should be done. **45%.** *Gordon & MacPhail.*

Benromach 25 Years Old db **(85) n**21 a waft of oak interrupts a blanket of barley concentrate; **t**22 staggeringly intense malt: sweet, lip-smacking stuff; **f**21 remains unbelievably sweet and relatively oak-free until the very dying moments; **b**21 very sweet, highly enjoyable but lacking the all-round complexity or even age one might expect of a 25-year-old. *Gordon & MacPhail.*

Benromach 1973 Vintage db **(80) n**22 t20 f19 b19. Bitter oak finish compliments the light, sweet barley. **40%.** *Gordon and MacPhail.*

Benromach 1974 db **(79) n**21 t21 f18 b19. A delicate flower lacking any sort of "ooomph". **40%.** *Gordon & MacPhail.*

Benromach Centenary 17 Years Old db **(80) n**20 t21 f19 b20. Light and elegant, a delicate malt selected to mark the re-opening of this excellent Speyside distillery. Some undertstated sherry and soft malt make for a typically understated dram **40%.** *Gordon & MacPhail.*

⋰ **Benromach Traditional** db **(85) n**22. Sexy, teasing peat is light enough to sweeten and embolden the youthful malt; **t**23 God! I so love this. It takes a second or third mouthful before you really get the true picture here: the peating level is just high enough to really give weight and depth, yet low enough to allow the barley to come at you with the freshness of rain-soaked grass. Unusual and a bit special; **f**20 more simplistic with a cocoa-smoky dryness; **b**20 a very young, softly smoked Speysider that would be recognisable to those working at the distillery between the two wars. Beautifully made and quite unique. **40%**

⋰ **Cask Benromach 1980** db **(86) n**19 a little closed; **t**22 a rich, intense, bossy dram with mouthwatering properties despite the spice; **f**23 the powering barley has extraordinary stamina and even builds in sweetness; **b**22 one hell of a delicious mouthful. **58.1%**

Cask Benromach 1982 db casks 1335, 1341, dist 15/10/82, bott Jun 96 **(92) n**23 t24 f23 b22. It was probably bottlings like this that convinced G&M of the need to buy this distillery. Masterful. **63%.** *Gordon & MacPhail.*

Cask Benromach 1982 db casks 112, 114, dist 2/2/82 bott 24/10/01 db **(84) n**20 t22 f22 b20. Incredibly sweet and almost syrupy. One of the most intensely malted drams on the market, but perhaps lacks balance – even with some late spices. **59.7%.** *Gordon & MacPhail.*

Connoisseurs Choice Benromach 1969 (82) n21 t22 f19 b20. One of those annoying G&Ms from that period that starts off brightly and then just dies on you! Probably caramel is to blame. **40%.** *Gordon & MacPhail.*

Connoisseurs Choice Benromach 1971 (90) n22 heavy sherry nose, soft spices; **t**23 clean sherry, really juicy grape with a sweet malt counter thrust;

f23 a hint of smoke digs in as the sherry continues its mouthwatering cruise around the palate; **b**22 one of the most memorable CCs from that period, hoisting the sherry flag with some aplomb. **40%.** *Gordon & MacPhail.*

BEN WYVIS
Highland (Northern) 1965–1977. Demolished.

Ben Wyvis Aged 27 Years cask 1061, dist 72 db **(78) n**21 vanilla, soft oak with a sweet structure and the malt is intact – amazing for a light whisky for this age – with some softening caramel; **t**20 big malt, toffee presence then becoming gradually hotter, not peppery, simply from the way it has been distilled; **f**18 very thin, surprisingly little oak, meagre malt and more bite: the finale is sweet and coated with late oil; **b**19 this is by no means great whisky, but it is certainly among the most rare you will ever locate. There are hints here of why the distillery closed: certainly even after all these years the oak cannot paper over the cracks. That said, you are drinking history and romance and it should be enjoyed with due reverence. **43.1%.** *146 bottles.*

BLADNOCH
Lowland, 1817. Working.

Bladnoch Aged 10 Years db **(94) n**23 lemon and lime, marmalade on fresh-sliced flour-topped crusty bread; **t**24 immensely fruity and chewy, lush and mouthwatering and then the most beguiling build-up of spices: the mouthfeel is full and faultless; **f**23 long, remains mildly peppery and then a dryer advance of oak. The line between bitter and sweet is not once crossed; **b**24 this is probably the ultimate Bladnoch, certainly the best I have tasted in over 25 years. This Flora and Fauna bottling by then owners United Distillers should be regarded as the must-get-at-all-costs Bladnoch. If the new owner can create something even to hang on to this one's coat-tails then he has excelled himself. For those few of us lucky enough to experience this, this dram is nothing short of a piece of Lowland legend and folklore. **43%** *For those of you with a nervous disposition, the author would like to point out that not a single drop of this whisky was spat out during the creation of these tasting notes.*

⨳ **Bladnoch 13 Years Old** db dist July 91 **(84) n**20 t20 f22 b22. A refined dram that celebrates the gentleness of the malt with a pleasing bitter-sweet melody. A hint of citrus and honey on the excellent finish but the oak plays slightly too enthusiastic a part early on. **40%. nc.**

⨳ **Bladnoch 15 Years Old** db dist Sep 88 **(86) n**22 astonishing fruit: like an old cider-brandy; **t**22 more massive apple early on; the sweetness is coy and hangs on top the coat-tail of the ever-deepening barley; **f**21 the cider-brandy effect fades to leave ears of barley sticking out from the vanilla; **b**21 deeply unusual and delicious. **46%. nc ncf.**

⨳ **Bladnoch 15 Years Old** db dist Sep 88 **(93) n**22 not dissimilar to a 6-7 years old Moneymusk rum, mildly estery with a lingering, oily sweetness; **t**24 mouth-filling and sweet, an early rum character dissolves into unfettered, ultra-rich, unambiguous barley that fills out further towards the middle with light roasted Santos. Fabulous; **f**23 dries to offer more coffee and cocoa but there is something of the cream cake about this, too; a distant fruitiness lurks from first to last for good measure; **b**24 I can't remember the last time I was so marvellously entertained by a Bladnoch of this relative antiquity. One for any collection. **55%. nc ncf.**

Cask Bladnoch 1985 cask nos 318, 352, 870–1, dist Jan/Feb 85, bott Jun 96 **(88) n**22 t22 f22 b22. A charming, slightly unusual Bladnoch: fruity, as is its wont, but in a quite unusual direction. Lovely stuff. **56.8%.** *Gordon & MacPhail.*

⨳ **Cask Strength Bladnoch 1991 (82) n**19 t22 f21 b20. A thuggish, bullying nose compensated by a mouth arrival of the most intense, unambiguous malt imaginable. **54.8%.** *Gordon & MacPhail*

Connoisseurs Choice Bladnoch 1980 (77) n*19* t*20* f*19* b*19*. Easy-going and malty. **40%.** *Gordon & MacPhail.*

Gordon & MacPhail Bladnoch 1988 Cask Strength (81) n*20* t*21* f*20* b*20*. Well-structured and beautifully chewable. **58.8%**

James MacArthur Bladnoch 10 Year Old (78) n*22* t*19* f*18* b*19*. Immensely chalky and dry despite some rich early malt. **43%**

Old Masters Bladnoch 1992 bott 02 **(88)** n*22* big malt and oak sitting comfortably; t*22* fabulous, mouthwatering bitter-sweet chap and so, so malty; f*22* a zesty fruitiness, marmalade and malt with some chunky oak arriving; b*22* classically clean, fresh Lowland whisky. I would use this in any blend. **58.5%.** *James MacArthur.*

⠿ **Provenance Bladnoch Over 12 Years** dist Autumn 91, bott Winter 03 **(87)** n*21* attractively flinty and firm, there is almost a snap to the barley; distant lemon zest adds to the freshness; t*23* cracking palate arrival with crisp barley forming a mouthwatering fanfare; the middle is emboldened by a surprising oiliness; f*21* long with the oak having a drying effect; some natural toffee towards the finale also helps with the lingering chewability; b*22* confirmation that this distillery has no problem making an absorbing dram. **50%. nc ncf sc.** *Douglas McGibon.*

Private Cellar Bladnoch 1987 bott Feb 03 **(77)** n*20* t*20* f*18* b*19*. A bit lively and nippy with thin malt. Characterful and hot to handle despite a begrudging sweetness. **43%.** *Forbes Ross Co. Ltd.*

Royal Mile Whiskies Bladnoch 16 Years Old dist Jun 80, bott Jan 97 **(87)** n*22* t*22* f*21* b*22*. Absolutely top drawer Bladnoch. *From RMW shop, Edinburgh.*

⠿ **Scott's Selection Bladnoch 1984** bott 03 **(83)** n*20* t*22* f*20* b*21*. Candy store aroma and a beautiful mouthwatering grassy attack on the palate. **58%**

The Ultimate Selection Bladnoch 1991 bourbon barrel 4011, dist 17/7/91, bott 11/9/02 **(77)** n*17* t*20* f*20* b*20*. Not quite firing on all cylinders but there is good cocoa at the finish. *Van Wees NL.*

BLAIR ATHOL
Highlands (Perthshire), 1798. Diageo. Working.

Blair Athol Aged 12 Years db **(77)** n*18* t*19* f*21* b*19*. Thick, fruity, syrupy and a little sulphury and heavy. The finish has some attractive complexity among the chunkyness. **43%.** *Flora and Fauna range.*

⠿ **Blair Athol Aged 27 Years Rare Malts Collection** dist 75, db **(81)** n*20* t*22* f*19* b*20*. Buttery, spicy with a sliver of honey. A shade too much fade, though. **54.7%**

⠿ **Old Malt Cask Blair Athol Aged 13 Years** dist May 90, bott Oct 03 **(85)** n*21* clean, uncluttered with some fruit and salt; t*22* excellent mouth buzz that offers an enjoyable skirmish amid the complex oak layers; lots of fresh barley abounding; f*20* holds out pleasantly at first but some off-key bitterness at the very death; b*22* not often you find a younger Blair Athol charming you, but this is one. **50%. nc ncf sc.** *Douglas Laing. 300 bottles.*

Old Malt Cask Blair Athol Aged 25 Years dist March 75 **(80)** n*21* t*20* f*19* b*20*. Don't look for complexity, but still one of the better – and these days few – Blair Athols on the market. **50%.** *Douglas Laing.*

⠿ **Old Malt Cask Blair Athol Aged 27 Years** dist May 76, bott Mar 04 **(87)** n*23* a sherry pie in your face; t*22* a fascinating argument between the full on sherry and the distillery's natural inclination at that time to make bad whisky: the sherry wins; f*21* some spice overcomes the natural caramel; b*21* seriously heavyweight malt in sherry you could stand a spoon in; enjoyable and from a very good sherry butt. **50%. nc ncf sc.** *Douglas Laing.*

⠿ **Platinum Old and Rare Blair Athol 37 Years Old** dist Jan 66 **(85)** n*22* very breakfasty: marmalade on toast with porridge oats topped with melted brown sugar in the background: big, big stuff; **t21** thick mouthfeel with ultra-intense malt; viscous and full-bodied; **f21** lingers impressively with the oak well contained by the sheer, immovable mass of barley; **b21** unusual and unyielding, few malts come quite so thick-set as this. **41.8%.** *Douglas Laing.*

BOWMORE
Islay, 1779. Suntory. Working.

Bowmore 12 Years Old db **(85) n21** delicate, buttery peat; **t22** sweet intense malt with a peaty shadow; **f21** light, clean, hint of vanilla; **b21** a real sweetie in every sense. **40%**

Bowmore 17 Years Old db **(93) n23** the peat could be made from helium, so light is it. Even so, it remains the dominant feature in a complex aroma; **t23** sweat peat at first, then juicy malt; **f23** long, fragile with the peat lingering but refusing to undermine the complexity; **b24** a masterpiece. Back to its old self: an exercise in understatement and refinement. Always my favourite aged Bowmore of them all – with only Voyage offering something more extraordinary and beautiful – and this bottling shows exactly why. Sublime.

Bowmore 25 Years Old db **(90) n21** nutty, toasty; **t23** silky fruit, glazed cherries and tantalising spices; **f22** a final tilt of clean sherry then creamy malt and vanilla; **b24** bit of a tastebud Lothario, seducing the palate with a cool, oozing charm. Beware. **43%**

Bowmore 1957 db **(91) n23** tangerines and marzipan: Lubec's finest. The peat is so laid back it could be chewing straw. So, so delicate and attractive; unobtrusive oak; **t23** firm malt with a chewy, oily coating. The peat offers itself as a volley of prickly spice, followed by the softest, most gentle malt follow-through; **f22** long, more malt oil and a reintroduction of something vaguely fruity and juicy; **b23** nothing from 1957 has the right to be this well preserved and sophisticated. It appears I have a challenger... **40.1%**

The Vintage House Bowmore 20 Years Old (91) n22 a curious lacing of bourbon and distant peat with something heathery thrown in. Delicate and complex; **t23** big and explosive from mouth entry with dry oak booming through but softened by rich malt and touch of honey; **f23** long, sweetening despite the growling, deep oak and spicy peat. Enormously big finale with liquorice and toast and cocoa powder; **b23** another brinkman's malt with the oak going as far as is safe. Enormous depth and complex peat that, beyond the spice, has to be sought. **52.7%. ncf.** *From The Vintage House, London only.*

Bowmore 1964 Vintage Bourbon Cask db **(86) n23** the oak, perhaps in conjunction with the apparently vanished peat, has given an attractive rye character; **t21** fruity and mouthwatering start but the malt gives way to budding oak; **f21** dry finale as the oak makes its stand; **b21** just about holds together for a very enjoyable dram. The peat has been absorbed to create an unusual rye effect – and for those new to this game, this has nothing to do with the fact that this has been matured in a bourbon cask: that spirit has had no influence whatsoever. **43.2%**

Bowmore 1964 Vintage Fino Cask db **(90) n21** biting and hot, but the malt is impressive as is the sultry, fleeting fruit; **t23** gentle fruit now but still there is bite and truculence; **f23** long, lots of sultanas and still that lovely malt/spice mix; **b23** sheer quality. Curiously, much more Bushmills in style than Bowmore. Exquisite stuff. **49.6%**

Bowmore Cask Strength db **(80) n19 t21 f21 b20.** A buttery, malt-rich very lightly smoked dram which lingers on the oil. **56%**

Bowmore Claret Bordeaux Wine Cask db **(62) n16 t16 f17 b13.** When this first came out the then distillery boss Jim Mcewan and I fell out (temporarily, of course!): he loved it, I loathed it. For the sake of this book (and it needed a good reason) I re-visited this whisky. And I still loathe it. The whisky has been swamped by the wine, is raw and the character of a distillery I love has been obliterated with all balance sacrificed. Oh dear, oh dear. **56%**

Bowmore Darkest db **(69)** n18 t18 f17. b16 Raw and slightly wild. I adore youth on a whisky but this is just not my scene at all. **43%**

Bowmore Dawn db **(89)** n21 busy, complex, firm peat; t23 mouthwatering, malty and full bodied; f22 lovely fruit follow-through then long, long toasty, vaguely honied malt; b23 there appears to be some youngish malt in this, but it has been superbly honed to create a malt of blistering complexity. Superb. **51.5%**

Bowmore Dusk db **(80)** n18 t19 f23 b20. Another youngster, almost a mirror image to the Oddbins exclusive bottling of Bowmore or Islay (can't remember) of about 12 or 13 years ago. Memorable for the astonishing finish after a so-so start. Love it!! **50%**

Bowmore Legend db **(80)** n19 t21 f20 b20. A very even, almost docile Bowmore but possessing great shape around the palate. The peat is raw but well-mannered. **40%**

Bowmore Mariner db **(89)** n20 young and ungainly; t23 packs a stupendous punch. Young this malt may be, but it's as clean as a whistle and the peat is unfettered and rich; f23 long, smoky with brilliant malt complexity; b23 a big, peaty number, lumbering but genuinely charismatic and delicious This is sheer, unpretentious fun – a session dram for when you are wanting to rough it like an old tar... and I speak as a former member of the Swedish Merchant Navy (well, I had to escape from Lagos somehow), I'll have you know. Talk about ship shape. **43%**

Bowmore Surf db **(75)** n19 t20 f18 b18. More of a ripple. **40%**

Bowmore Voyage db **(94)** n24 salt spray and peat-reek on a cottage lumb: intoxicating, but not from the alcohol; t24 an intriguing display of young and old malts clashing together then harmonising with a massive sweet malt heave-ho; f23 longer than a sailing to Sydney. The peat simply moulds into every crevice in the mouth; b23 a more apposite name I can't think of. Despite some apparent youth, this whisky has done the rounds and has the salty scars to prove it. Brilliant, me 'arties. Ah, ha, an' don't ye all knock it back at once. **56%** *(the Moody Blues obviously had a premonition of this whisky's arrival when in the 70s they wrote: "My ship's sailed stormy seas/battled oceans filled with tears/At last my port's in view/now that I've discovered you...")*

Blackadder Bowmore 25 Years Old cask 3174, dist Apr 73, bott Apr 98 **(89)** n22 t23 f20 b24. A supremely balanced whisky.

Blackadder Raw Cask Bowmore 1989 cask 22533, dist 21 Sep 89, bott Apr 02 **(79)** n20 t19 f20 b20. Clean, lightly peated dram with mouth-filling sweet properties but a bit hot, alcohol apart. **63.3%. nc ncf sc.**

Blackadder Raw Cask Bowmore 1989 bourbon barrel no. 22535 dist 21 Sep 89, bott Mar 03 **(79)** n20 t19 f20 b20. As cask 22533 above. **62.9%. nc ncf sc.**

⠐ **Blackadder Raw Cask Bowmore 1989** cask 22536 dist Sep 89, bott Nov 03 **(85)** n23 coastal, with fresh multi-layered salty peat; t20 despite all the sweet peat, there is a hottishness too; f21 lots of milk chocolate on the finale; b21 despite being a hot-head there is enough complexity to search for. **60.2%**

⠐ **Blackadder Raw Cask Bowmore 1991** cask no. 10597 dist Sep 91, bott Nov 03 **(81)** n22 t19 f20 b20. Great nose but just a fraction unwieldy on the palate. **60.3%**

Blackadder Raw Cask Bowmore 1991 cask no. 15093, dist Sep 91, bott Apr 02 **(89)** n22 gristy, lively and fresh; t23 exploding peat then malty-peaty shockwaves;f22 amazingly long with sublime cocoa and hints of Columbian coffee; b22 Just a really superb malt, full of character and life. Brilliant for its age. **61.2%. nc ncf sc.**

Blackadder Raw Cask Bowmore 1991 refill sherry cask 22535, dist Sep 91, bott Mar 03 **(89)** n22 t23 f22 b22. A complete re-run of cask 15093. I suspect the cask number for this bottling is a mistake. **60.7%**

Coopers Choice Bowmore 1990 bott 03 (12 Years Old) **(88)** n*21* still slightly green, but the peat is gentle and sensuous; t*22* early sweet malt start, then a fascinating bitter oak surge before the sweetness returns; f*23* quite long with this toing-and-froing between oak and barley continuing for some time; **b***22* as impressive an example of Bowmore of this age as you could hope for. **43%.** *The Vintage Malt Whisky Co.*

Dun Bheagan Bowmore Aged 21 Years dist 80, bott 01 **(79)** n*19* t*21* f*19* **b***20*. Very unusual Bowmore, much more peppery and fragmented than the norm for this age. Lively but not quite in tune. **43%.** *William Maxwell.*

⇌ **Duncan Taylor 1968 Aged 35 Years** cask 1424 **(88)** n*22* playful, sweat peat amid toasty vanilla; t*22* clean barley with some leathery, waxy honey neo-bourbony notes; f*22* the peat returns – just – to add a modicum of weight to the clean, fruity finish; **b***22* classy, but one of the most lightweight 35 y-o of all time: and probably the lightest from a medium to heavyweight Islay. There must have been a peat shortage that year... **42.05%**

Hart Brothers Bowmore 11 Years Old dist 90 **(84)** n*22* t*22* f*21* **b***19*. The serious lack of colour suggests, correctly, that this is taken from a pretty well-used cask. The result is a new-make, youngish single malt, one of not inconsiderable charm and clarity of nose and taste. Love it! **46%**

⇌ **Hart Brothers Bowmore Aged 12 Years** dist 91 **(87)** n*21* citrus amid firm peat; t*23* mouthwateringly fresh and gristy, clean and stunningly malty; f*22* very little oak from this many times used cask, leaving a clean, simplistic and malty finale; **b***21* a thirst-quenching Islay of few frills. **46%**

Hart Brothers Bowmore Aged 34 Years dist Feb 68, bott Oct 02 **(85)** n*21* gooseberry jam and a hint of smoke; t*22* silky fruit and incredibly sweet malt; f*21* a puff of smoke and some buzzing spices remind you it's an Islay dram; **b***21* amazingly delicate and beautifully preserved. **40.2%**

⇌ **Jim McEwan's Celtic Heartlands Bowmore 1968 (86)** n*22* minor esters; banana and custard, negligible smoke; t*21* custard again, this time with stewed apples and developing vanilla and spice; f*22* long, melt-in-the-mouth barley with just the occasional wave of something smoky; dry vanilla at death; soft bourbon notes zigzag their way from first to last; **b***21* an unusual Bowmore (though not for a '68) where the peat has almost drifted out of the equation to be replaced by soft stewed fruit and bourbon. **40.6%**

⇌ **Old Malt Cask Bowmore Aged 12 Years** dist Apr 91, bott Feb 04 **(84)** n*23* t*20* f*21* **b***20*. The brilliant, ultra delicate nose isn't quite fully backed up on the palate. **50%.** *Douglas Laing.*

⇌ **Old Malt Cask Bowmore Aged 14 Years** dist Feb 89, bott Aug 03 **(80)** n*19* t*21* f*20* **b***20*. One of the more lightly peated bottlings of recent times displaying lots of natural caramel. **50%.** *Douglas Laing.*

⇌ **Old Malt Cask Bowmore Aged 15 Years** dist Apr 88, bott Mar 04 **(84)** n*22* t*21* f*21* **b***20*. More hot whisky from a time when those stills were obviously getting a bit of stick; there is a sweet malty complexity, too. But it battles hard to make itself heard. **50%.** *Douglas Laing.*

Old Malt Cask Bowmore Aged 18 Years dist Mar 83, bott Feb 02 **(91)** n*24* peat and raspberries (seriously folks, it really is!!): what a fabulous and nearly unique combo! t*23* mouthwateringly fruity with the peat leaking about palate amid firm malt; f*22* loads of light muscovado amid the dying malt; **b***22* question: what kind of whisky do you buy a person (like me) whose favourite fruit is raspberry and who is a bit partial to some peat? Answer: this. Absolutely unique. Take my word for it. **50%. nc ncf.** *Douglas Laing. 270 bottles.*

Old Malt Cask Bowmore Aged 34 Years dist May 66, bot Mar 01 **(79)** n*22* t*20* f*18* **b***19*. Bowmore by name, certainly not by nature. The fruit pastel fruitiness is lovely, but something essential is missing. **45.15%. nc ncf sc.** *Douglas Laing. 96 bottles.*

Old Malt Cask Bowmore Aged 35 Years dist May 66, bott May 01 **(86)** n*22* t*22* f*21* b*21*. They must have run out of peat on the island. Very unusual, amazingly fruity. **44% nc ncf sc.** *Douglas Laing. 192 bottles.*

⠿ **Old Masters Bowmore 1989** bott 03 **(83)** n*21* t*20* f*22* b*20*. A fruity, attractive expression that is as sweet and oily as this distillery ever gets. **57.3%.** *James MacArthur.*

Old Masters Bowmore 1990 bott 02 **(77)** n*17* t*21* f*20* b*19*. Liqueur-sweet, but a tad out of kilter. **56.7%.** *James MacArthur.*

Peerless Bowmore 1966 cask 3311, dist May 66 36-y-o **(84)** n*22* t*19* f*22* b*21*. Astonishing array of orange-related fruits, kumquats the fore; the arrival is oaky-tired but the finish is full of soft, spicy life. Virtully peatless. **42%.** *Duncan Taylor & Co.*

Peerless Bowmore 1968 cask 3819, dist Oct 68 34-y-o **(83)** n*21* t*22* f*20* b*20*. Another curiously peatless offering, though the depth of the sweet malt is very impressive. **40.3%.** *Duncan Taylor & Co.*

Peerless Bowmore 1969 cask 6085, dist Nov 69 33-y-o **(77)** n*21* t*20* f*18* b*18*. Thin and a bit oaky. **42.5%.** *Duncan Taylor & Co.*

⠿ **Provenance Bowmore Over 12 Years** dist Spring 91, bott Winter 04 **(90)** n*22* soft, hints of lemon and mildly gristy; the smoke is there but surprisingly distant; t*23* light, tenderly melts on the tongue but the gathering malt sweetness is met by powdery smoke and exploding spice f*22* vanilla intermingles playfully with the smoke while the pepper notes guarantee a steamy finish; b*23* there's a really sexy, elegant shape to this one; younger than its years and caresses the senses expertly. **46%.** *Douglas McGibbon for Premium Spirits, Belgium.*

⠿ **Provenance Bowmore Over 15 Years** dist Autumn 91, bott Winter 03 **(87)** n*23* some serious coffee-crusted peat on the nose: pungent yet subtle and a little oily; the thrust of the smoke is quite striking; t*23* immensely mouth-filling at first then sweetness with some banana notes and then ripe, juicy dates; f*20* slightly too sugary towards the finale; b*21* a dram that makes its presence felt, especially for those with a sweet tooth. **46%.** *Douglas McGibbon.*

Murray McDavid Bowmore 1989 bourbon cask MM5133 bott 00 **(86)** n*22* t*22* f*21* b*21*. A full-on Bowmore that lingers around. **46%. nc ncf sc.**

Murray McDavid Bowmore 1989 bourbon cask MM20975, dist Jun 89, bott May 02 **(87)** n*22* softly peated, sweet, almost winey; t*22* sweet, moderately spiced malt. The oak says no more than hullo; f*21* vanilla and deft smoke; b*22* this is about as gentle a peaty dram as you could ask for. **46%**

Scotch Malt Whisky Society Cask 3.77 Aged 13 Years (83) n*20* t*22* f*21* b*20*. For all the natural colour, a pretty youthful aroma and mouthfeel; the peat pretty chilled and allowing barley-character to help provide something fruity and eventually chalky. **55.9%. nc ncf.**

Signatory Bowmore Rare Reserve 33 Years Old dist 28/2/68, bott 23/7/01 cask 1431 **(91)** n*23* t*23* f*22* b*23*. Seriously remarkable malt that needs a bit of time in the glass to get going. A classic Bowmore of its genre without doubt and proof to some that you don't need cart-loads of peat to be a great Islay. **46.2%.** *218 bottles.*

Signatory Bowmore 11 Years Old Unchill filtered Collection hogshead 2220, dist 6/5/92, bott 26/3/03, **(88)** n*22* peat kilns or Scottish coastal villages on a cold day; t*22* soft, intensely sweet at first with the malt; f*22* some black coffee with the peat, but sugared; b*22* a cask just about every blender in the country will recognise: Bowmore at 10–11 years of age that is clean with a delicate peaty punch. Spot on. **46%.** *378 bottles.*

Ultimate Selection Bowmore 1992 cask 2216 dist 6/5/92, bott 11/9/02 **(85)** n*20* young, fresh barley, scarcely peated; t*22* refreshing grassy malt with an echo of smoke; f*22* long, incredibly clean and beautifully sweet; b*21* a near colourless dram untroubled either by oak or, by Bowmore standards, even peat. That said, it is so faultless in construction that it makes the perfect summer quaffing dram. **43%**. *Van Wees NL.*

⁘ **Usquebaugh Society Bowmore Aged 13 Years** cask 6130, dist Jun 89, bott Mar 03 **(91)** n*23* excellent citrus notes accentuating the smoke; t*23* big and chewy with the peat buzzing and soft fruits in harmony with the salivating barley; f*22* soft oils help fatten the smoke effect; the late complexity is superb as vanilla tucks in; b*23* way above regulation Bowmore and at a fractionally higher peating level. **52.1%. sc ucf.** *NL 200 bottles.*

Whisky Galore Bowmore 1989 (70) n*16* t*18* f*18* b*18*. Hugely disappointing from the off-note nose to the lifeless finale. **46%.** *Duncan Taylor & Co.*

⁘ **Wilson & Morgan Barrel Selection Bowmore 1993** bott 04 **(86)** n*21* clean, medium, youthful peat; t*22* buttery, slightly salty yet sweet throughout; f*22* lush finale with soft spices; b*21* a standard, clean, sweet and attractive expression. **50%**

BRAES OF GLENLIVET
Speyside, 1974. Chivas. Silent.

Connoisseurs Choice Braes of Glenlivet 1975 (89) n*23* sexy and alluring, gristy and fresh despite so many years in wood, even a touch of peat; t*23* just astonishingly fresh and grassy despite the massive age, mouthwatering, clean, sweet, deftly smoked and glorious; f*22* light, the softest of oak presence; b*21* there will be those that argue that such an old whisky should offer more. Obviously the cask has done the rounds, but one must judge on quality. And in this context we are talking really first-class Speyside malt that is sensuously lip-smacking. I could start the day on this anytime. **40%**. *Gordon & MacPhail.*

BREAVAL (*see* Braes of Glenlivet)

BRECHIN (*see* North Port)

BRORA
Highland (northern), 1819–1983. Diageo. Closed.

⁘ **Brora Rare Malt 20 Years Old** dist 82, db **(89)** n*21* honeyed pine nuts encrusted in barley. The most distant smoke signals are barely perceptible; t*23* starts lazily, but soon builds into a profoundly rich crescendo with barley at the fore and fruit and honey nougat at the edges; f*22* long with pleasing cocoa effects. A vague spiced smokiness sits comfortably with the natural sheen; the honey lasts longer than expected; b*23* good whisky. A characterful little soul with an improbable honey theme. Though lacking the smoke that the average Brora lover demands, it offers other sweet glories. **58.1%**

Brora Aged 22 Years Rare Malts Selection dist 72 db **(87)** n*21* smoking bonfires and a few chunks of peat tossed in; pretty dry; t*22* firm entrenched oak at first then a sweet malty rush; f*22* dries again with the oak returning nipping and biting; bitter chocolate on the late finish; b*22* a thought-provoking dram: much more there than a cursory tasting will reveal. Big, big stuff. **56.7%**

⁘ **Brora Aged 24 Years Rare Malts Selection** db distilled 77, bott Oct 01 **(93)** n*23* just so delicate and just such clean peat; memories of Brora a dozen years back when it was at its peak; slight Marmite (Vegemite) edge with citrus, intact and without a single blemish; t*22* lively, rich, intensely malty with a beautiful underlying moulten brown sugar sweetness, the peat forms several thin layers which cannot be avoided – nor would you want to; f*24* amazingly long with a wonderful cocoa depth that perfectly compliments the smoke; b*24* we are getting down to the last bottles of Brora before it disappears forever. This is one you will always remember with affection. **56.1%**

·:·· **Brora 30 Years Old** db **(92)** n23 supremely balanced and intact after all these years. The full-on smoke offers a sweet counter to the well-behaved oak. An apologetic hint of pine reveals some of the age. Majestic, nonetheless; t22 the full strength plays into the hands of the beguiling oak-peat character. Despite the wood chippings, the sweetness of the barley keeps the tastebuds panting: this is sexy stuff; f23 good breeding here as the oak backs off to offer nibbling vanilla and marmalade and just the right percentages of smoke-fuelled spice; b24 oh, it does the heart such good to find aged malts like this. Near sublime. **55.7%**

Celtic Cross Brora 1980 (92) n23 one of the best Brora noses of recent years: lively peat, a dash of salt yet somehow not coastal in style. With some delicate oak around, this is beautifully weighted and complex; t23 intricate patterns of malt and spice, a touch of sugar here, dryer oaks there, totally harmonious and symmetrical; f22 dries but slowly and in sychronisation with everything else around it: almost like a green olive by the finish; b24 a gem of a bottling. There have been some run-of-the-mill Broras of late as age has taken its toll, but this is absolutely top of the tree. **46%.** *Scotch Malt Sales Ltd According to bottle code, bottled in 02.*

Connoisseurs Choice Brora 1972 (74) n18 t19 f19 b18. One of those malts that doesn't quite gel, the peat in particular being off beam. **40%.** *Gordon & MacPhail.*

Connoisseurs Choice Brora 1982 (74) n19 t20 f17 b18. Very lightly peated with sweet vanilla. **40%.** *Gordon & MacPhail.*

·:·· **Dun Bheagan Brora 1980 Aged 23 Years** bott 29 Jan 04 **(84)** n21 t22 f21 b20. Quite freaky Brora with a blast of peat early on, but lurches around the palate as if drunk. Some odd (as in strange) fruit notes, but enjoyable in an eccentric kind of way. **50%.** *William Maxwell.*

Old Malt Cask Brora Aged 19 Years Sherry dist Sep 81, bott Dec 00 **(86)** n21 t22 f22 b21. Genuine charm. **50%. nc ncf.** *Douglas Laing. 564 bottles.*

Old Malt Cask Brora Aged 19 Years dist Nov 82 **(75)** n18 t20 f19 b18. Warms the tastebuds and lacks the normal peaty glow. **50%.** *Douglas Laing. 744 bottles.*

Old Malt Cask Brora Aged 20 Years dist Jun 81, bott Jul 01 **(86)** n21 t22 f22 b21. This is a really big, smoky, salty, mother-of-all peated mainlanders. **50%. nc ncf.** *Douglas Laing. 560 bottles.*

·:·· **Old Malt Cask Brora Aged 21 Years** dist Jun 82, bott Apr 04 **(75)** n19 t19 f18 b19. Cowsheds: tail-swishing livestock. And that's just the nose ... **50%.** *Douglas Laing. 708 bottles.*

Old Malt Cask Brora Aged 26 Years dist Nov 74, bott Apr 01 **(82)** n19 t23 f20 b20. The nose, though smoky, is delicate, so what follows next is big honey-peat surprise. **50%. nc ncf.** *Douglas Laing. 258 bottles.*

Scotch Malt Whisky Society Cask 61.15 Aged 26 Years (83) n18 t22 f21 b22. Quite a hot, nippy chap this. The smoke has burnt itself out slightly leaving an attractive, naturally sugared malt-oak bitter-sweet finish. A dram with attitude. **54.8%. nc ncf sc.**

·:·· **Scotch Malt Whisky Society Cask 61.20 Aged 25 Years (87)** n19 antiseptic; unsophisticated; t22 a gratifying bitter-sweet dust-up from the off with the sweetness gaining the upper hand by the second; about as mouthwatering as Brora ever gets; f23 intense malt by the finish with some burnt fudge entering the fray; b23 no prizes for the nose but just gets better and better as it goes along. **57%. nc ncf sc.**

Signatory Brora 20 Years Old Cask Strength cask 273, dist 25/2/82, bott 11/11/02 **(82)** n18 t22 f21 b21. A seeringly hot dram with little or no peat to soften the blow. The intensity of the sweet, sugared malt is attractive, though. **58.6%.** *292 bottles.*

Platinum Brora 1972 (93) n22 sharp, brittle grassy/malty notes get the mouth salivating. A hint of something peaty can be found amid something fruity and, to be honest, something a little farmyardy, too! t24 big and even more salivating! Sweet, mildly sugary start with some soft peats arriving at the middle: massive yet fabulously subtle; f23 loads of silky, gristy malt that revels in its clean, peaty smokiness. This is big stuff that just gets better the longer it stays on the palate; b24 you taste a whisky this magnificent, and you can't help but wonder as to the thinking behind closing down such a brilliant distillery. There must be good reasons, but they are entirely lost in the stunning beauty and enormity of this classic bottling. **59.5%.** *Douglas Laing.*

Platinum Brora Aged 30 Years dist Mar 72, bott Jan 03 **(91)** n24 the closest aroma to a peat-reeked distillery kiln I have ever come to: an old-fashioned maltings in a bottle; t23 a big fruit influence – tinned peaches and sultana – helps play down the sweet peat and threatening oak; f22 the oaky tones fade, kept in their place by roasty, gristy, smoky malt that lingers to the nth degree; b22 a real one-off whisky that tells its very own story. **49.7%.** *Douglas Laing.*

Provenance Autumn Distillation Brora Over 25 Years dist Autumn 75, bott Winter 01 **(87)** n22 t22 f21 b22. Decidedly non-Islay in style and quite magnificent in every respect. However, you can only wonder at the enormity of this had it been delivered at full cask strength. **43%. nc ncf.** *Douglas McGibbon & Co.*

BRUICHLADDICH
Islay, 1881. Bruichladdich Ltd, Working.

Bruichladdich Aged 10 Years db **(88)** n21 beautifully clean and zesty, the malt is young and almost juvenile; t23 a sweet, fruity then malty charge along the tastebuds that gets the mouth salivating; f22 soft vanilla and custard tart; b22 this is really great stuff: a whole lot lighter and less oily than a generation ago with the casks appearing to have limited influence. Few island whiskies come more refreshing than this. **46%**

⋰�∴ **Bruichladdich 12 Years Old** db **(87)** n21 salivatingly sharp Seville oranges with some sub strata of grape juice and unusually firm malt; t22 a big, almost riotous arrival of fruit and grain: about as mouthwatering an Islay as you'll find; f22 a bevvy of delicate spices and vanilla; b22 a busy Laddie full of juicy fun. **46%**

Bruichladdich Aged 15 Years db **(89)** n22 quite salty with just a faint honey note; sea-breezy and fresh; t22 lots more saltiness alongside the firm oak and gentle malt; f22 long and malty with developing spice brushed with cocoa; b23 a very coastal, laid-back dram where the complexity has to be spotted by the tastebuds in the same way that eyes become accustomed to the dark. One of Scotland's more subtle malts worthy of time and exploration. **46%**

⋰�∴ **Bruichladdich Full Strength 1989** db **(89)** n21 freshly crushed cocoa bean, oily, clean; t21 concentrated barley sugar; f24 brilliant finale as the intensity of the barley dissipates into a bedrock of vanilla; from the late middle to the end the bitter-sweet balance is nigh faultless; b23 the kind of dram built for a shitty day: first it thumps you back to life with its high alcohol barley and then spends the next two minutes making love to your tastebuds. Aaaaahhhhh... **57.1%**

Bruichladdich XVII db **(87)** n22 pears and clean malt; t21 an oily signature heralds some enormous malt; f22 quite long with a steady build-up of vanilla and salt, offset by some sweeter malty tones; b22 another sensuous and well-balanced dram. **46%**

Bruichladdich Aged 20 Years db **(87)** n19 malty but a little soapy; t21 warming, massive, sweet malt; f24 roast chestnuts and brilliant bitter-sweet malt: fabulous complexity unravels; b23 not a confident start, but well worth a long hard study. Brilliant complexity. **46%**

∵ **Bruichladdich Legacy 1965** db **(90)** n22 amazingly floral and muscular: a bit like a men's changing room after the talc has been thrown about; t23 improbably slick on the palate with a degree of bourbony sweet liquorish and natural caramel but the malt remains intact; f22 dries attractively with some spices as an extra; b23 well, I don't now how it did it, but a malt as gentle as Bruichladdich has survived nearly 40 years in the cask with barely a wrinkle. Not a single off note! **41.8%.** *1,500 bottles.*

Bruichladdich Legacy 1966 db **(92)** n23 a yielding aroma not short on fruit and a vague smokiness: dreamy stuff; t23 stupendous softness, so the malt moulds itself to the mouth while the fruit offers something mouthwatering ... at this age! There really is a hint of something smoky in there, which fits beautifully with mercurial oaky notes; f23 the oak is so in tune with the malt: no sappiness or bitterness here, just grace, charm, melting malt, cocoa ... oh, and that hint of smoke again! b23 that's my laddie! **40.6%**

∵ **Bruichladdich "Links" Royal Troon 14 Years Old** db **(89)** n23 although from a refill sherry, there is clean, uncluttered grape enough here to offer a spiced weightiness against the briney malt; t23 big and well spiced arrival with a big, confrontational fruitiness so unusual with a 'Laddie, the middle sings with powering coffee-cocoa to accompany the pulsating dry fruit; f21 almost a grainy feel to the finale with a steely hardness; b22 a very different sort of 'Laddie that eschews its usual malty softness for a hard-edged charisma. **46%. nc ncf.** *12,000 bottles.*

∵ **Bruichladdich Links 14 Years Old** db **(82)** n22 t22 f19 b19. Oily, beautifully spiced but not as multi-layered as the usual Laddie. **46%**

Bruichladdich Vintage 1970 db **(87)** n23 all the weight on this is oak but it harmonises impeccably with a barley-sugar, honey sweetness; t23 again the skeleton is oak, the meat is a chewy, oily maltiness; f20 dries to leave a salty, slightly sappy shadow; b21 before the oak kicks in it is utter bliss. **44.2%**

∵ **Bruichladdich Vintage 1973** db **(88)** n22 blackened bananas and sultanas. The oak, with an early touch of sap, is at first suggesting that the cask is just holding out but closer inspection reveals a complex sub-plot of even more fruit with freshly boiled gooseberries among them; t22 good oily structure for the now busy barley to get hooked on; astonishingly soft middle where the oak offers a dryish, toasty counterplay to the overall sweetness; f21 pretty long with some attractive bourbony notes towards the end; b23 first sight suggests that the oak is too intrusive; give it time and instead you get a genuinely delicious bourbony strata to a fabulously complex whisky. **40.2% nc ncf.** *4,200 bottles.*

Bruichladdich Vintage 1984 db **(86)** n22 new-mown grass and honey. How un-Islay can you get?!? t22 wonderful oily character that coats the roof of the mouth with soft malt-vanilla f21 very dry with a marked degree of saltiness; b21 surprising amount of age present considering the richness of the malt. **46%**

Blackadder Raw Cask Bruichladdich 1970 hogshead 4840, dist 16 Nov 70, bott Apr 02 **(89)** n23 teasingly sweet, honey, heather and very fresh malt; t23 brilliantly lush as spices add an extra dimension to what is otherwise repeated from the nose; f21 dry oaky tones with a touch of salt; b22 first-class aged Islay. **53.8%. nc ncf sc.**

Blackadder Raw Cask Bruichladdich 1991 hogshead 3264, dist 22 Nov 81, bott Apr 02 **(83)** n19 t22 f21 b21. Typically oily and extremely malty and clean. **56.1%. nc ncf sc.**

Berry's Own Bruichladdich 1993 bott 03 **(89)** n22 exceptionally clean, light and young. It's almost as if you can still get the CO_2 off the washbacks; t24 a wonderful arrival of mouthwatering barley: fresh, lively and mouth-puckeringly sharp; f21 soft oak and slowly dawning layers of increasingly oily malt; pretty dry and spent at the death; b22 an absolute charmer, full of fizz and vitality. The most Speysidey Islay you're ever likely to find. **57%.** *Berry Bros*

Cadenhead's Bruichladdich 16 Years Old dist 86, bott 03/03 **(88)** n20 very flakey oak lightens what appears to be delicate peat-reek; t23 massive malt arrival, enormously rich, sweet ... and smoked? f22 long with some trace elements of peat: just so beautifully weighted malt; b23 if I didn't know better, I'd say there was some peat influence in there somewhere. In fact, I will say there is some ... what a collector's item! **59.9%. nc ncf sc.**

∵ **Coopers Choice Bruichladdich 1991 Port Wood Finish 12 Years Old** bott 03 **(85)** n22 a rock-hard aroma of diced fresh carrots and spices; t23 superb early arrival of lush fruit and then an oily, spicy attack as the barley surges forward; f19 ungainly and dry; b21 loses it towards the finish, but the mouth arrival would turn on any tastebud. **46%.** *Vintage Malt Whisky Co.*

James MacArthur Bruichladdich 10 Years Old (89) n21 over-ripe bananas and sweet malt; t23 flawlessly intact malt and soft oak, brilliantly made whisky with not a single off-note or blemish; f23 more bananas and malt; b22 pastel-shaded flavours that are fruity and invigorating. A little gem. **43%**

Gordon & MacPhail Bruichladdich 1969 Cask (77) n19 t20 f19 b19. Very sweet and intense, but the oak just takes too large a slice of the action. **52.5%**

Gordon & MacPhail Bruichladdich 1969 Cask (82) n21 t22 f19 b20. Lightly oiled, not unlike Canadian with the cream toffee oak effect. **54.2%**

Gordon & MacPhail Bruichladdich 1988 Cask (86) n22 the vaguest touch of smoke on the deeply malty nose; t22 enveloping oils help the sweetish, malty vanilla cling to the palate; f21 lazy wafts of smoke re-surface as some drier, oaky, cocoa notes drift in; b21 a collector's item: peat on a Bruichladdich. It is barely detectable, but it is there. A very more-ish dram. **54.2%**

Lochindaal 10 Years Old Bruichladdich (78) n18 t20 f20 b20. A pleasant malty dram once you get past the mildly off-key nose. **43%.** *Associated Distillers Ltd.*

Murray McDavid Bruichladdich 1986 cask MM514, bott 03 db **(80)** n21 t20 f20 b19. Good oak and gooseberries on the nose and malty-salt on the body. **46%**

∵ **Murray McDavid Bruichladdich 1989 (89)** n23 eggy batter, vanilla and sultana; t23 clean, uncluttered barley; attractively oily with a drier, sawdusty middle and excellent spice counterblast; f21 medium length, soft vanilla and fading barley; b22 little wonder MM can pick a spot-on Laddie! **46%**

∵ **Old Malt Cask Bruichladdich Aged 13 Years** dist Mar 90, bott Oct 03 **(94)** n24 old banana skins and freshly squeezed pear juice; one of the cleanest, most subtle noses around, you feel like dabbing it behind your lover's ears; t24 faultlessly clean with mouthwatering barley juice sluicing through the jagged spices; stunningly beautiful; f22 much oakier with a rapid drying effect that leads to late coffee-cocoa notes. Also, amazingly, some Brazil nuts in there, too; b24 one of those rare occasions where you would love to hug the cask this matured in. This is near faultless whisky that simply beguiles you with each understated, tastebud-teasing mouthful. By far the best single cask from this great distillery I've come across. **50%. nc ncf sc.** *Douglas Laing. 330 bottles.*

Old Malt Cask Bruichladdich Aged 13 Years dist Oct 88 **(79)** n19 t21 f20 b19. Rather charming – Speyside in style. **50%.** *Douglas Laing.*

∵ **Old Malt Cask Bruichladdich Aged 17 Years** dist Nov 86, bott Dec 03 **(87)** n20 big, but signs of fatigue; t23 in-your-face oil and spice with a chewy barley intense sweetness; f22 excellent oak battles bravely against the barley; some lime juice helps the complexity; b22 a punchy, heavyweight that eschews subtlety for effect. **50%. nc ncf sc.** *Douglas Laing.*

∵ **Old Master's Bruichladdich 1991** bott 04 cask 2295 **(90)** n20 rhubarb and distant orange peel, but a touch sappy; t24 a firm, clean arrival that has the trademark oily maltiness burrows deep into the roof of the mouth: intense, slick and almost faultless; f23 pans out for the vanilla to shine plus some residual mouthwatering malt; the late cocoa is really impressive; **b**23 after an average nose the arrival on the palate is a celebration of exceptionally well made, complex malt. **58.7%.** *James MacArthur.*

Peerless Bruichladdich 1969 cask 2329, dist May 69 33-y-o **(88) n**22 very softly honied with honeysuckle, too, and the very faintest trace of peat; **t**23 brilliant mouth arrival with a rich, coppery texture then a riot of clean, gently sugared malt; **f**21 dries as the vanilla arrives; **b**22 certainly one of the richest and most distinguished unmalted Islays bottled in the last decade. **48.7%.** *Duncan Taylor & Co.*

⋅∷⋅ **Provenance Bruichladdich Over 13 Years** dist Spring 90, bott Autumn 03 **(88) n**21 light, ethereal, ultra-clean, delicate malt with very little oak interference apart from a touch of custard; **t**22 fabulously fresh and clean with the accent on sweet barley; **f**22 now the complexity arrives as a spicy element; combines with cocoa powder and burnt raisins for a surprisingly weighty finale; **b**23 a really excellent cask – probably second fill bourbon – give a perfect insight into the depth of this distillery. Tremendous stuff. **46%** *Douglas McGibbon.*

Royal Mile Whiskies Bruichladdich 12 Year Old dist Jul 85, bott Apr 98 **(88) n**21 **t**23 **f**22 **b**22. This is one of the few Bruichladdichs still to be found that holds the exact character that for many years made this the island's favoured dram. Available from only Royal Mile Whiskies, Edinburgh.

Scott´s Selection Bruichladdich 1986 bott 01 **(71) n**19 **t**18 **f**17 **b**17. Slightly too unevenly developed for its age. **55%.** *Robert Scott & Co.*

⋅∷⋅ **Scott's Selection Bruichladdich 1986** bott 03 **(88) n**21 rounded, bananary feel to the oak; the barley is confident; **t**22 lush, even barley, clean with distinctive malt-sweetness; **f**23 lengthy, unhurried with the oak adding a toasty dimension; **b**22 one of those high-quality whiskies that offers a bit of everything ... except peat. **60%**

⋅∷⋅ **Spirit of the Isles Bruichladdich 1991 Rum Cask Finish** bott 03 **(85) n**22 crushed pine nuts, diced bacon rind and salted barley; **t**23 a mountainous arrival of busy malt and intense fruit; heaps of Demerara sugars and juicy dates; **f**19 a hint of spice, but loses its bearings as the uneven rum interferes; **b**21 was doing well until the rum arrived: worth trying just for the mouth arrival alone. **46%.** *Liquid Gold/John MacDougall.*

⋅∷⋅ **Whisky Galore Bruichladdich 1991 Aged 12 Years** **(87) n**22 clean, gentle barley; mouthwatering and missing the usual background salt; **t**22 salivating barley; **f**21 maybe a hint of distant vanilla but the barley still remains complete; **b**22 unusual to find Laddie in a second (ot third) fill cask: the distillery's output in its most natural, naked state. **46%**

⋅∷⋅ **Wilson & Morgan Barrel Selection Bruichladdich 1993** bott 04 **(90) n**21 salty, punchy, nipping, malty, charismatic; **t**23 beautifully rich malt with lots of bounce and shape to the intense barley; **f**23 even hints of honey to this one, then milk chocolate; long and intense to the deliciously juicy dregs; **b**23 exemplary bitter-sweet balance. A minor classic. Beware: Jim McEwen will be chasing you for every last bottle. **50%**

BUNNAHABHAIN
Islay, 1881. Burn Stewart. Working.

Bunnahabhain Aged 12 Years db **(87) n**21 soft hint of sultana and sea-breeze, even a vague waft of smoke – something new; **t**22 mouth-filling and mouthwatering fruit had takes a lead role then a gradual build-up of intense malt, flanked by salt; **f**22 remains salty and dries as vanilla approaches and sweetens for a short burst of malt. Dries for a second, final time as the oak and salt move back in; **b**22 a greatly improved dram in recent years thanks to better quality casks and a slight toning down of the sherry. But still not a patch on 20 years ago when it was Scotland's most bracing, provocative dram. Hopefully the new owners will be able to restore it to its former superstar (though little-known) glory. **40%**

Bunnahabhain 1968 Family Silver Vintage Reserve db **(85)** n21 gentle sherry pepped up by a salty breeze; t22 fat and malt-lush with the sherry and oak fighting for second spot; f21 dries towards oak and cocoa; b21 just about hanging on in there, but the sherry is a delight. **40%**

Berrys' Own Selection Bunnahabhain 1980 bott 02 **(88)** n22 stupendous fresh salt breeze: pure Bunna! t23 silky, honied start, more brine and barley; f21 doesn't quite pan out in terms of complexity as one might have hoped, but the oak behaves well and offers limited vanilla; b22 a big honied, high-quality version that is just so Bunna. **55.6%.** Berry Bros & Rudd.

⁖ **Blackadder Bunnahabhain 1985** cask 1472 dist 16th Dec 85, bott Aug 01 **(82)** n20 t22 f20 b20. Salty and earthy with decent late malt. **51.8%**

Dun Bheagan Bunnahabhain 22 Year Old cask 5899 **(87)** n21 lots of honey and salted butter; t23 chewy and spicy with a massive malt surge; f21 signs of liquorice and mocha amid the salt and spice; b22 genuine quality and a cask emptied just at the right time. **58%**

⁖ **Duncan Taylor Bannahabhain 1966 Aged 36 Years** cask 4874 **(77)** n23 t19 f17 b18. The nose is outstandingly complex but age catches up with it. **40.7%**

⁖ **Duncan Taylor Bunnahabhain 1967 Aged 35 Years** cask 3325 **(86)** n22 diluted tangerines and gentle salt; t23 fresh barley and fruit at first then a gathering of oak f20 a bit musty and dusty; b21 starts brilliantly but fades.. **40.2%**

Hart Brothers Bunnahabhain Aged 35 Years dist Mar 67, bott Sep 02 **(87)** n23 dank fruitcake: just beautiful; t22 mouthwatering and surprisingly malty and fresh, lovely toasty notes and grape juice; f21 the oak is a bit on the tired side but still sits well with the barley and fruit; b21 a dram to be savoured. **40.5%**

The MacPhail's Collection Bunnahabhain 1988 (78) n19 t21 f19 b19. Exceptionally light even for a Bunna, with moderate salty intervention **40%.** Gordon & MacPhail.

The MacPhail's Collection Bunnahabhain 1989 (83) n20 t22 f20 b21. Salty and biting, a fierce dram for its strength. **40%.** Gordon & MacPhail.

Murray McDavid Bunnahabhain 1979 Bourbon cask MM 2080, dist Mar 79, bott Apr 99 **(53)** n5 t17 f16 b15. A curry-nosed entirely flawed disaster. **46%. nc ncf sc.**

Murray McDavid Bunnahabhain 1979 Sherry caskMM 2081, dist Mar 79, bott Apr 99 **(79)** n21 t20 f19 b19. The rich sherry papers over some cracks; great spice with the fresh, plummy fruit dominating. **46%. nc ncf sc.**

⁖ **Old Malt Cask Bunnahabhain Aged 14 Years** dist Mar 89, bott Nov 03 **(76)** n19 t20 f17 b18. A rather mouthwatering yet strangely off-balance Bunna with a bitter finish. **50%. nc ncf sc.** Douglas Laing. 282 bottles.

Old Malt Cask Bunnahabhain Aged 16 Years dist Mar 85, bott Mar 01 **(94)** n23 t24 f23 b24. Simply, unambiguously, the best Bunna I have ever found in bottled form ... though over the years I have spotted similar peaches in their warehouses. It has lashings of everything that makes the distillery tick: new owners Burn Stewart could do worse than grab a bottle of this and use it as a template for their future range. **50%. nc ncf.** Douglas Laing. 366 bottles.

Old Masters Bunnahabhain 1979 bott 99 **(82)** n19 t23 f20 b20. Excellent fruit on arrival; finishes like watered bitters. **57%.** James MacArthur.

Peerless Bunnahabhain 1966 cask 4872, dist Jun 66 **(89)** n22 salty, refreshing, mildly honied barley; t23 really intense heather-honey spruced up by salt and a hint of bourbon; f21 mildly spicy with soft oak drifting about; b23 this is a stupendous Bunna, the best at this age I have ever found. And bottled in the nick of time if the strength is anything to go by ... **40.1%.** Duncan Taylor & Co.

⁖ **Peerless Bunnahabhain 1966** (see Duncan Taylor Bunna 66)

⁖ **Peerless Bunnahabhain 1967** (see Duncan Taylor Bunna 67)

Peerless Bunnahabhain 1969 cask 6717, dist Jun 69 33-y-o **(82) n**20 **t**21 **f**21 **b**20. Zesty on the nose and bitter marmalade on the palate. **42.8%.** *Duncan Taylor & Co.*

Private Cellar Bunnahabhain 1988 bott Feb 03 **(84) n**20 **t**22 **f**20 **b**22. Bracing, fresh and gently honied. **43%**

⋯ **Provenance Bunnahabhain Over 14 Years** dist Spring 89, bott Winter 03 **(78) n**18 **t**21 **f**19 **b**20. Mouthwatering, mildly salty middle with decent oak support. **46%.** *Douglas McGibbon.*

Rare Old Bunnahabhain 1965 (82) n22 **t**21 **f**19 **b**20. The sherry starts brightly enough and then flattens with curious haste. **40%**

⋯ **Scotch Malt Whisky Society Cask 10.56 Aged 6 Years (80) n**20 **t**19 **f**21 **b**20. More of a chick than a fledgling, there are no professional faults to this delicious but understandably unfulfilled Islay. **59.4%. nc ncf sc.**

Single Barrel Collection Bunnahabhain 1988 dist June 88, bott Dec 01 **(79) n**20 **t**18 **f**21 **b**20. Brusque, islandy but quite unlike the distiller's own version. **55.93%. nc ncf.**

⋯ **Spirit of the Isles Bunnahabhain 1982** bott 03 **(93) n**24 crashing waves against limpet-encrusted rocks, salt on porridge, sea spray on a warm face: monumentally beautiful and sheer Bunna; **t**22 an early barley-grist followed by spiced oak and fresh coffee; **f**23 back to the salt and malt; long and embracing with enough juicy barley and citrus to make this outstanding; **b**24 the guy who chose this cask and I have known each other the best part of 20 years: I have never known him to use his life-long insight into whisky with more telling effect. Bunna in aspic. **46%.** *Liquid Gold/John MacDougall.*

CAOL ILA
Islay, 1846. Diageo. Working.

Caol Ila Aged 12 Years db **(86) n**21 oily, pungent peat coats the nosebuds; **t**22 big sweet peat swamps the palate with some gristy, mildly green notes balancing out some rich vanilla; **f**21 very soft, peaty, peppery spices form alongside some toffee tones; **b**22 toffee on the finish apart, this is a quite beautiful dram whose power-packing peatiness does not hinder the sensual ride. **43%**

Caol Ila Aged 18 Years db **(77) n**20 **t**20 **f**18 **b**19. Meanders, sometimes big and spicy, sometimes dead on the palate. Very odd and overall pretty frustrating and disappointing. **43%**

Caol Ila Aged 21 Years Rare Malts Selection dist 75 db **(94) n**24 biting, searing peat on an oily bed; **t**22 enormous peat of the highest order battles it out with some vanilla notes; **f**24 spellbinding complexity: the sweet-dry ratio is entirely in sync; some enormously arousing fresh malty notes survive despite the enormous age: amazing; **b**24 perhaps this bottling represents the first time the owners took this distillery entirely seriously and produced arguably the definitive dram. It's off the Richter scale. **61.3%**

Caol Ila Aged 23 Years Rare Malts Selection dist 78, bott May 02 db **(91) n**22 lively coastal attack: salty, iodine-peat; dry and decent oak presence; **t**23 sweet malt, then the most linear build-up of peat imaginable with little explosions all around the palate for good measure; **f**23 some liquorice and coffee join the peat for a really deep, chewy and very long finish; **b**23 less a malt and more of a saga, the flavours always going that extra chapter further. Superb. **61.7%.** *6,000 bottles.*

Caol Ila Cask Strength db **(91) n**22 pungent lead weight; atypical for this distillery; **t**23 massive peat attack; **f**23 softens, sweetens and charms; **b**23 this is a bruiser, enormously sweet and the phenol level is surely way over the usual 35ppms. Mysteriously, the back label instructs the drinker to drink one part Caol Ila for two parts water to "enjoy a single malt cask at its best". Bizarre: you might just as well buy it at 43%. Take it from me: for best results add one part Caol Ila to one part Caol Ila and, if in doubt, add another part Caol Ila. Then warm in the hand. If you need water, add it to some lemon squash before going to bed. **55%. ncf.**

⋰∴ **Aberdeen Distillers Caol Ila 1993** dist May 93, bott Oct 03 **(83)** n21 t20 f22 b20. Light but chewy peat within a vanilla frame. **43%**

⋰∴ **Adelphi Caol Ila 1988 Aged 15 Years** cask 4247 **(84)** n20 t21 f22 b21. Tart, citrus-dominated, sweet barley but at times violently assertive. **59.3%**

⋰∴ **Adelphi Caol Ila 1990 Aged 13 Years** cask 4842 **(79)** n22 t19 f20 b18. Estery, mildly rummy, hot and sweet in part. **59.6%**

⋰∴ **Adelphi Caol Ila 1991 Aged 12 Years** cask 13374 **(92)** n24 stunning bluebells (honestly!) and other wild, natural aromas – cider brandy (honest again!!) – an almost perfect balance against the salty, multi-layered peatiness. One of the best Caol Ila noses on the market; t23 subtle oils plus a gristy sweetness offer a resounding opus; f22 falls away slightly as the smoky vanilla dominates; b23 exceptional Caol Ilas are getting harder to find: this is one. **57.5%**

Berrys' Own Selection Caol Ila 1983 bott 02 **(85)** n23 pretty crispish for a Caol Ila, with some oilier notes wandering leisurely through: big time peat; t21 fills the mouth with gently oiled peat and the barley does spread out to form something brittle. Pleasant fruit-tones; f20 dries with oak making some toasty notes; b21 a very decent dram with attractive complexity. **46%**

⋰∴ **Blackadder Raw Cask Caol Ila 1990** cask 4161 dist Apr 90, bott Nov 03 **(76)** n20 t19 f18 b19. Hot and just doesn't sit comfortably. **57.7%**

Blackadder Raw Cask Caol Ila 1992 cask 10637, dist 19 June 92, bott Apr 02 **(86)** n22 clean, young, full-bodied and slightly oily peat; t22 vibrant malt arrival on palate, dark chocolate drops in on the chewy peat; f21 cocoa and vanilla plus waves of smoke; b21 sweet and confident. A typical Caol Ila of this age. **58.6%. nc ncf sc.**

Cadenhead's Caol Ila 10 Years Old dist 93, bott 03/03 **(92)** n23 classic, unmistakable: oily, fat and phenolic; t24 superb spices hit the tastebuds in waves. The malt is sweet and peaty and beautifully clean; f22 oily but light with lots of vanilla and banana replacing the spice; b23 with minimum oak interference from a wrung-out cask Caol Ila, as a 10-year-old, is rarely found any better than this. **60.8%**

Cask Caol Ila 1980 casks 10540–3, bott 94 **(84)** n20 t22 f21 b21. Both explosive and gentle in equal measures, but just a little raw through the middle. **62.6%.** *Gordon & MacPhail.*

Cask Caol Ila 1981 casks 2081–6, bott Nov 96 **(83)** n21 t21 f20 b21. Attractively buttery and biscuity amid the very soft peat. Enormously sweet. **63.4%.** *Gordon & MacPhail.*

Cask Caol Ila 1988 casks 1084–7 (refill hogsheads), dist 4/5/88, bott 17/1/02 **(87)** n23 unambiguously Caol Ila offering a hint of grist; t22 big at first then settles down to a zingy, zesty citrus freshness among the peat; f21 soft vanilla kicks in; b21 quality Caol Ila. **57.6%.** *Gordon & MacPhail.*

⋰∴ **Chieftain's Caol Ila 1993 Aged 11 Years Rum Finish** bott 26 Mar 04 **(84)** n23 t22 f19 b20. The nose is at its industrial best but despite a bright, animated start on the palate the balance is lost towards the bitter end. **46%.** *Ian Macleod.*

Connoisseurs Choice Caol Ila 1980 (88) n24 a monster of a nose, peaty and beechy. Just about spot-on balance between malt and oak. It doesn't come much better than this; t22 the flavour doesn't follow through with the peat at first, more emphasis on fruit, but the smoke gathers momentum; f20 lots of vanilla and salt; b22 the closest in style to the old CC that used to accompany me around the island in the early 80s. Delicious. **40%.** *Gordon & MacPhail.*

Connoisseurs Choice Caol Ila 1981 (73) n19 t19 f17 b18. A bizarrely passionless Caol Ila. **40%**

Connoisseurs Choice Caol Ila 1988 (83) n20 t20 f23 b20. Sweet and relaxed peat encounters little resistance. The complexity arrives all on the long, quite wonderful finish. **40%. Gordon & MacPhail.**

Coopers Choice Caol Ila 1991 bott 03 (11 Years old) **(83)** n20 t21 f20 b22. So, now you have it – the UNPEATED! Caol Ila. From a cask that could sit undetected a mile or two along the coast at Bunnahabhain, this bottling ranks alongside the latter Ardbeg 17-y-o and the bourbon cask Macallans. Not the first time I have tasted Caol Ila in this form, but the first time I can ever remember seeing it bottled. A really fascinating dram in which a softly salty character thrives but suffers slightly for some so-so fruit influence which probably masks the higher complexity. Anyway, well done for bringing this one to us: a must for every Islay-phile. **43%. The Vintage Malt Whisky Co.**

⸭ **Distillery No. 2 Caol Ila 1989** cask no 4655 **(78)** n20 t19 f20 b19. Bitumen, newly tarred road on the nose, slightly off course on the palate. **56.2%. Denmark.**

⸭ **Dun Bheagan Caol Ila 1993 Aged 10 Years** bott 15 Mar 04 **(87)** n22 a big-peated, oily Caol Ila template; t22 silky with some definite malt getting above the smoke; f21 toffee and vanilla amid the gentle smoke; b22 slightly plodding but above average Caol Ila these days. **43%. William Maxwell.**

Dun Bheagan Caol Ila Aged 10 Years dist 90, bott 00 **(91)** n24 t23 f21 b23. Ladies and gentleman, we have a genuine classic on our hands. It really amazes me when the actual distillery bottling described Caol Ila as less pungent than some other Islays. This is pungent enough. **43%. William Maxwell.**

⸭ **Gordon & MacPhail Reserve Caol Ila 1995 Aged 8 Years (81)** n20 t21 f20 b20. Punchy, biting big Charlie peat but needs a dose of complexity. **55.5%. Scoma Germany.**

⸭ **Hart Brothers Caol Ila Aged 10 Years** dist May 93 bott Nov 03 **(87)** n22 delicate, mildly complex and wonderfully gristy; t21 medium, very sweet peat envelops the mouth; f22 fabulous tail to this with the gristiness returning with a fine balance against the oak; b22 for once a Caol Ila not swamped in exaggerated oil. **57.3%**

Hart Brothers Caol Ila Aged 23 Years dist 75, bott 98 **(79)** n19 t20 f21 b19. A noble, attractive, complex if rather tired version of one of the first-ever makes of the new-style Caol Ila after its rebuilding in 1974. **43%**

Milroy's Caol Ila Over 10 Years Old (89) n23 absolutely typical Caol Ila: a flat-ish oily aroma lifted by sweet peat and more jolting salty, coastal notes. Unmistakably from this distillery: could be used as a blueprint for any 10-y-o Caol Ila! t22 real sweetie, in every sense. The oaky vanilla holds out for only a matter of seconds before being swept away by a majestic wave of chunky peat. Softens back to its oily norm for the chewy middle; f21 lingering peat and dark chocolate echo around the palate for an impressively long period. Dries delightfully at the very end, as a delicate spiciness emerges; b23 what a cracker! Caol Ila at probably its best age and from a well-used cask which allows the massive peat free rein to do its, sweet, oily best. This is Caol Ila at its most bruising and confident. **43%. UK.**

Murray McDavid Caol Ila 1989 bourbon cask 2107, dist Dec 89, bott Dec 01 **(85)** n22 oily, gristy; t21 big spice kick from start; f21 gentle oak follow-through and a hint of something citrussy; b21 complex sweet-dry character: oily and big. **46%. nc ncf sc.**

⸭ **Old Malt Cask Caol Ila Aged 12 Years** dist Nov 90, bott Aug 03 **(87)** n20 quite flinty and brittle for this distillery, the peat offers minimum yield and decent punch; t23 fun, crunching mouth arrival with an extra shovel or two of peat that forms starburst around the palate; f22 some citrus is blasted away by the continuing peat; exceptionally long with decent oak dryness, too; b22 much better than the tight nose suggests: in fact it's a joy. **50%. nc ncf sc. Douglas Laing.**

Old Malt Cask Caol Ila Aged 12 Years Sherry Finish dist Sep 91, bott Feb 04 **(78)** n23 t19 f18 b18. The nose is classic but, hard as nails, this loses balance somewhat on the palate. Only after I re-read the label did I see a possible reason why. **50%. nc ncf sc**. *Douglas Laing. 360 bottles.*

Old Malt Cask Caol Ila Aged 14 Years dist Jan 90, bott Feb 04 **(92)** **n**24 you can almost smell the reek from the mash tuns; fresh and fruity despite the age and peat; **t**23 dissolves effortlessly as soon as hitting the tastebuds, leaving a trail of walnut oil and sweet figs to battle it out with the intense barley and lingering smoke; **f**22 long, elegant and still billowing smoke; the oak acts as no more than a frame to a stunning picture; **b**23 a Caol Ila that every Islay-phile will recognise every time. A sexy little charmer. **50%. nc ncf sc**. *Douglas Laing.*

Old Malt Cask Caol Ila Aged 17 Years dist Nov 84 **(88)** n22 vanilla and peat; t24 peat and peat; f22 peat ... errr ... and vanilla; b20 the peat level is way above the norm for a Caol Ila, but the complexity has been lost. A sweet, oily, rambling, rumbling dram that is sheer bliss for those who love to chew turf. **50%. nc ncf**. *Douglas Laing. 408 bottles.*

Old Malt Cask Caol Ila Aged 19 Years (Sherry) dist Feb 81, bott Jun 00 **(85)** n21 t22 f21 b21. Lots of sultanas to go with the subdued peat. **50%. nc ncf**. *Douglas Laing. 793 bottles.*

Old Malt Cask Caol Ila 26 Years Old dist Dec 74, bott Apr 01 **(88)** n23 t22 f21 b22. Really tastebud-rattling stuff with a kick far greater than the alcohol strength suggests. Beautiful. **50%. nc ncf**. *Douglas Laing. 294 bottles.*

Private Collection Caol Ila 1965 (79) n21 t18 f20 b20. Lovely nose, but then a big oaky dive on the palate. Recovers beautifully, though. **45.6%.** *Gordon & MacPhail.*

Private Collection Caol Ila Calvados Finish 1988 (85) n22 sharp burst of flighty peat and etheric apple-based fruits; t20 refreshing; f22 spicy and fruity with the peat unable to decide whether to stay or go; b21 a malt I have warmed to over the years in a big way. Certainly shows more complexity and charm than I first thought and a revitalising dram when drunk chilled. **40%.** *Gordon & MacPhail.*

Private Collection Caol Ila Claret 1988 (83) n18 t22 f22 b21. That most unique of beasts: a light, fruity, mouthwatering thirst-slaking Caol Ila. Yes, such a thing exists and allows a hefty degree of peat to filter through for good measure. The nose is a bit of a challenge for old-fashioned Islay-philes like me, but worth a place in any collection or simply for a unique experience. Didn't originally think much of it: has grown on me. **40%.** *Gordon & MacPhail.*

Private Collection Caol Ila Cognac Finish 1988 (83) n22 t20 f21 b20. Very odd: hard as nails, flinty and green. Great nose. **40%.** *Gordon & MacPhail.*

Private Collection Caol Ila Cognac Finish 1990 (74) n16 t20 f19 b19. Almost the complete opposite of the '88: nose apart, too soft and shapeless. **40%.** *Gordon & MacPhail.*

Private Collection Caol Ila Port Wood Finish 1990 (77) n20 t20 f19 b18. Some juicy, fruity moments, but doesn't quite cling together. **40%.** *Gordon & MacPhail.*

Private Collection Caol Ila Sherry 1988 (76) n20 t19 f18 b19. Sherry and peat out of step. **40%.** *Gordon & MacPhail.*

Provenance Caol Ila 13 Years Old dist Autumn 91, bott Spring 04 **(82)** n21 t21 f20 b20. A medium peated, easy going Islay. **46%**

Scotch Malt Whisky Society Cask 53.80 Aged 11 Years 1993 (83) n20 t21 f22 b20. Sweet, massively peated and in many ways devoid of structural fault, but the oiliness limits the complexity severely. **53.80%. nc ncf sc**.

Shieldaig Caol Ila Aged 17 Years dist 83 **(78)** n20 t21 f18 b19. A steady, dram: lightly peated by CI standards. **43%.** *William Maxwell France.*

Signatory Caol Ila 11 Years Old Cask Strength sherry butt 5360, dist 1/12/89, bott 24/11/01 **(83)** n23 t21 f19 b20. Superb nose, but the soft sherry is tying one hand behind the malt's back and you feel it could do so much more **58.1%**. *586 bottles.*

Ultimate Selection Caol Ila 1994 cask 10836, dist 6/9/94, bott 19/9/02 **(88)** n*22* clean unrestricted peat balancing out grassy barley; t*23* refreshing, crisp dram, mouthwatering with a beautiful build-up of oily peat; f*22* a minor incursion of vanilla as the salty peat drifts off; **b***21* there is not a blender in Scotland who won't recognise this young-ish Caol Ila for its gristy-peaty-grassy yet slightly oily quality from a cask on its second or, more likely, third time around the block. Fabulous to get the chance to buy in bottled form. **43%**. *Van Wees NL.*

Usquebaugh Society Caol Ila 1989 dist 2/5/98, bott Sep 99 **(85)** n*23* t*22* f*20* b*20*. A curiously oak-advanced Caol Ila for its age. **45%**. *NL.*

Whisky Galore Caol Ila 1989 (88) n*22* peaty and oily; t*22* sweet peat; more oil; f*22* soft vanilla on the peat. Gentle and simplistic; **b***22* Caol Ila at 12 years in a nutshell: all delicious effect, little complexity. **46%**. *Duncan Taylor & Co*

⠿ **Whisky Galore Caol Ila 1990 Aged 12 Years (83)** n*20* t*22* f*21* **b***20*. Another clean and delicious Caol Ila that is just missing out on the complexity. **46%**. *Duncan Taylor.*

⠿ **Wilson & Morgan Barrel Selection Caol Ila 12 Years Old** dist 90 cask no 13943 **(86)** n*21* punchy, oily, in your face peat; t*22* assertive arrival of blistering peat; f*21* some natural caramels soften the explosion; **b***22* for those who love their peat on a trowel. **58.6%**

⠿ **Wilson & Morgan Barrel Selection Caol Ila 1992** bott 04 **(87)** n*22* gristy, clean peat; t*22* sweet, oily and slick; f*21* vanilla with a touch of zest amid the smoke; **b***22* one of the most delicate Caol Ila expressions for a while. **46%**

CAPERDONICH
Speyside, 1898. Chivas. Silent.

Caledonian Selection Caperdonich 1970 cask 3337 bott (in decanter) 01 **(78)** n*20* t*20* f*20* b*18*. Oaky, pleasant but perhaps lacking guile. **46%**. *nc ncf. Liquid Gold Enterprises. From hogshead.*

Connoisseurs Choice Caperdonich 1968 (77) n*21* t*20* f*17* b*19*. Clean malt, but a little thin and hot. **40%**. *Gordon & MacPhail.*

Connoisseurs Choice Caperdonich 1980 bott 2000 **(73)** n*20* t*19* f*17* b*17*. Ordinary fare. **40%**. *Gordon & MacPhail.*

⠿ **Connoisseurs Choice Caperdonich 1980 (74)** n*19* t*19* f*18* b*18*. Typical of the distillery: thin and hot, though there is a decent early malt surge. **46%**. *Gordon & MacPhail.*

⠿ **Duncan Taylor Caperdonich 1968 Aged 34 Years** cask 3568 **(85)** n*22* just love this under-ripe banana with fresh grist; t*22* brilliant vanilla-barley delivery: excellent sweetness; f*20* dries with a fraction too much enthusiasm; **b***21* Caper being its usual confusing self. **41.8%**

⠿ **Duncan Taylor Caperdonich 1970 Aged 33 Years** cask 4380 **(94)** n*23* unusually coastal and saline with white-wine sharpness by no means in keeping with its age; a hint of smoke? t*24* angels sing as the most salivating barley imaginable forms a juicy alliance with understated grape; some peat makes a half-hearted attempt to reach the middle; f*23* long, a touch of smoke and cocoa, but still the barley fizzes; **b***24* another masterpiece from the slowest-maturing whisky distillery on earth. **50.7%**

⠿ **Hart Brothers Caperdonich Aged 30 Years** dist Nov, 72 bott May 03 **(89)** n*22* some weary oak is blasted away by beeswax and crushed sultanas; t*22* beautifully weighted with chewy honey-dipped malt to the fore, the bourbony tones are intense and spellbinding; f*22* heavy; returns to its oaky thread with gathering liquorice – quite extraordinary length, just so amazingly bourbony; **b***22* yet another top-notch example from a distillery that rarely performs in its younger days but commands respect in old age: a very passable imitation of a 12/14-year-old Wild Turkey cask. **50.1%**

Hart Brothers Caperdonich Aged 32 Years dist 1968 **(85)** n*21* apples and bananas; t*22* very tasty, mouthwatering malt, at times sweet; f*21* quite long with the barley keeping the oak at arm's length and even some peat drifts in at the death; b*21* a quite juicy Caper, thankfully displaying little of its great age. **44.5%**

Lombard Caperdonich 1968 (59) n*12* t*17* f*15* b*15*. A fleeting moment of rich malt fruit on the palate, but otherwise soapy. **46%**

᠅᠅ **Murray MacDavid Mission 2 Caperdonich 1968** (82) n*21* t*21* f*20* b*20*. Some oily butter follows on from the oaked barley; lots of nip. **46%. nc ncf.**

The Old Malt Cask Caperdonich Aged 27 Years dist Oct 74 **(88)** n*23* exquisitely delicate, floral, rose petals with hints of cinnamon and cucumber. Honestly, folks! Some good old-fashioned spice and honey also on standby. The oak is weaving one of the most complicated patterns of 2002's releases; t*22* beautifully sweet and gently honied, the barley has a minor role but it is the complexity of the oak that astonishes: really pleasing build-up of rumbling spices; f*21* classic soft cocoa notes as you might expect from an oak-dominated malt, and a lick of liquorice gives some extra length; b*22* Old Masters don't come more delicate than this. The brilliant nose is no way let down by what follows. Fabulous and one of the great Caperdonichs of all time. **50%**. *Douglas Laing.*

Old Malt Cask Caperdonich Aged 30 Years dist May 70, bott Jun 00 **(74)** n*20* t*19* f*17* b*18*. Displays the usual Caperdonich butteriness, but also its fragility. A touch too oaky, especially at the finish. **50%**. *Dougls Laing. nc ncf. 180 bottles.*

᠅᠅ **Peerless Caperdonich 1968** (*see* Duncan Taylor Caperdonich 1968)

᠅᠅ **Peerless Caperdonich 1970** (*see* Duncan Taylor Caperdonich 1970)

᠅᠅ **Platinum Old and Rare Caperdonich Aged 36 Years** dist Nov 67 **(96)** n*24* bourbon and butter; even slight wisps of juniper and pear. No off notes, clean and singing fruity vaguely Kentuckian lullabies. I dare you to find a fault with this; t*24* now the bourbon is kicking in, but there is a genuinely astonishing alcohol tidal wave and surfing in on it are those gloriously gentle juniper notes tucked inside marmalade and peanut butter oil (without the peanut taste, if you see what I mean). Like an uncharted tunnel, full of stalactites and stalagmites but without dead ends. The vanilla is evident but never confident, the barley retains a certain brittleness and not once does a single off note find a voice; f*24* like the most beautiful of orgasms, hard to find where things start and end. This is one continuous experience with a gathering of gentle spices which is prompted by the most benign oak imaginable. The level sweetness hardly deviates until the very death when oak does give off a vanilla dryness. But even three or four minutes after you think the final embers have guttered, there is the tang of marmalade and lime. Awesome; b*24* so there we have it. A distillery that can't live day to day because its general spirit is so average can, in the right conditions, offer one of the greatest whisky experiences on Earth. Such is the beauty – and tragedy – of whisky. **57.9%**. *Douglas Laing.*

Scotch Malt Whisky Society Cask 38.11 Aged 32 Years (91) n*24* unquestionably the most complex Caperdonich I have nosed. Shy and retiring, you seriously have to hunt the aromas: not unlike your eyes acclimatising to the night sky to realise just how many stars are visible. The most subtle of floral and citrus notes combine with a faintly bourbony oak: spiced yet sweet, dry yet fruity, Caperdonich but fantastic; t*23* now we are in the realms of Kentucky: slightly more bourbon signs here than Scotch, but with a lightweight 32-y-o what do you expect? Lovely oils coat the mouth, slapping on the last malt traces; f*21* slightly creosote-ish (yes, I have drunk creosote...) with the oak now in total control, still sweet against the odds; b*23* this Scotch has turned bourbon in pursuit of brilliance, and who cares? Great whisky is great whisky. And this is great whisky. Believe me: for a Caperdonich, it's better than great! **53.6%. nc ncf sc.**

CARDHU
Speyside, 1824. Diageo. Working.

Cardhu 12 Years Old db **(90) n**23 just about the cleanest, most uncluttered, pure, sweet malt you will ever find, a touch of apple, perhaps, giving an extra dimension; **t**24 again the malt is pure and rich, just a thread of oak adding some dryness and depth; **f**21 vanilla and malt; **b**22 I remember at a tasting in America once being asked to define "malt whisky". I answered with one word: Cardhu. Because no whisky, even the exceptional Glen Moray, is quite as intensely malty as this and, although it may lack overall complexity, the sheer beauty of this malt has been one I have savoured for over 20 years and never once seen a drop in quality or been disappointed by it. I don't think there's a blender in the land, including this author, who would not give his left little pinky for unlimited supplies of this astonishing malt. Johnnie Walker use the distillery as their home base: hardly any surprise there. The bad news is that for the foreseeable future this is the last bottling of Cardhu as a single malt in a bid to preserve stock. The distillery has been given back its original name of Cardow and there are no plans to bottle under this title. Future Cardhu will be in vatted form. **40%**

(*see* also Cardhu Pure Malt)

⋰ **Signatory Cardhu Millenium Edition 1974** dist 24, Apr 74, bott 2 Aug 99 **(94) n**24 busy, peppered fruitcake beside mango and blood orange, simply launches into a fruit cocktail as it warms, clean, not a hint of an off note from this sherry butt; **t**24 again, an explosion of clean fruit with intense barley blasting its way into the grapefest; layers of soft and vicious spices – even a hint of very distant smoke; **f**22 soft oils gather as do the cocoa notes; **b**24 sensational! An astonishing interplay between gutsy barley and laid back sherry; it's all about intensity marrying with subtlety. The rarest Cardhu of them all: a real must find at all costs. Somehow I tracked one down to Fawsley Hall Hotel in deepest Northamptonshire where it is little coicidence that the byword is elegance. Make your way there before it is too late. **56%.** *498 bottles.*

CLYNELISH
Highlands (Northern), 1968. Diageo. Working.

Clynelish 14 Years Old (old Flora and Fauna label) db **(86) n**22 weighty, toasty malt with some rich fruity notes and a three-quarters-strangled smokiness; **t**20 light yet very sweet malts, then an assertive spiciness; **f**22 enormous emphasis on the malt still, with the sweetness becoming heavier as oak intervenes; **b**22 a lovely dram with a sweet malt dependency rather than the usual Clynelish complexity. **43%**

Clynelish 14 Years Old (new "Coastal Highland" label) db **(88) n**22 weighty, toasty malt with some rich fruity notes and a half-strangled smokiness; **t**21 sweet, absorbing, mildly gristy malt, coated lightly with muscovado sugar; **f**22 slightly more fruity, yet bitter. Some delicate (perhaps peaty?) spices see out the late brittle barley notes; **b**23 a high-quality dram that is firmer than most Clynelish on the market and is not afraid to throw its weight round. **46%**

Clynelish 24 Years Old Rare Malts Slection db dist 72 **(84) n**21 t22 f20 **b**21. Lots of toasted barley but a tad to much oak. Has some lovely honey moments, though. **61.3%**

Adelphi Clynelish 11 Years Old cask 1698, dist 88, bott 99 **(79) n**21 t21 f18 **b**19. Bananas and malt but thin and hot on the finish. **59.8%**

Adelphi Clynelish 12 Years Old cask 3280, dist 89, bott 01 **(64) n**17 t16 f15 **b**16. Something not right about this one at all. **57.2%**

⋰⋱ **Adelphi Clynelish 13 Years Old** cask 3281 dist 89, bott 02 **(77)** n19 t20 f19 b19. Estery with evidence of honey and spice, but splutters along not seeming to fire on all cylinders. **56.7%**

Adelphi Clynelish 16 Years Old cask 3077, bott 00 **(83)** n20 t22 f20 b21. Impressively malty, delicate for its age. **54%**

Adelphi Clynelish 27 Years Old cask 2565, dist 74, bott 01 **(89)** n23 t22 f22 b22. **56.3%**. A collector's item to some as the label spells the distillery as "Clynelsh".

Adelphi Clynelish 28 Years Old cask 14264, dist 72, bott 00 **(92)** n24 t24 f22 b22. I'm a sucker for this kind of grassy yet peaty conundrum. Brilliant. **57.3%**

Berrys' Own Selection Clynelish 1972 bott 02 **(92)** n23 subtle, suety and salty; t23 a soft smoke drifts through a procession of passing tones of malt. A gradual build-up of soft, sugary notes makes it more edible still; f23 still hints of smoke as a little oak gains a toe-hold; b23 a dream: a malt that just floats round the tastebuds like a hostess in a ballgown. **43%**. *Berry Bros & Rudd.*

Blackadder Raw Cask Clynelish 1976 sherry cask 6501, dist 5/8/76, bott Apr 02 **(94)** n23 tangy, zesty orange amid layers of oak, malt and peat, bunches of succulent white grapes, too. t24 sensational. Absolutely astonishing depth which you can chew until your jaws ache. Aided by some sweet peat, the fruit and malt melt into one. There is even some wonderful nip and bite to keep you on your toes; f23 long, with some fruit chocolate and smoke; b24 here you have it, folks: arguably the best single cask bottled in 2002, certainly one to rival Macallan's ESC IV. A true masterpiece and one which reveals Clynelish to the unitiated as one of the great Scottish distilleries. **59%. nc ncf sc.**

Blackadder Raw Cask Clynelish 1989 bourbon barrel 6088, dist 26 Sep 89, bott Mar 03 **(89)** n22 bracing sea air, a salty bite to sweet malt; t23 beautiful and fresh with buzzing spices against the wall of salty malt; f22 long, vanilla and malt; b22 really excellent malt thrust, complexity and bitter-sweet balance. **60.6%. nc ncf sc.**

⋰⋱ **Blackadder Raw Cask Clynelish 1990** cask no 3593 one year sherry finish dist 11 May 90, bott Nov 03 **(78)** n20 t20 f20 b18 a decent mouthfiller but the sherry and malt aren't on speaking terms **59.3%** *258 bottles*

⋰⋱ **Chieftain's Clynelish 1989 Aged 18 Years** in South Africa Sherry Cask bott 10 Feb 04 **(84)** n19 t21 f22 b22. Starts poorly on the nose and then blossoms on the palate with a sweet, fruit-invigorated barley surge. **46%**. *William Maxwell.*

Connoisseurs Choice Clynelish 1984 **(79)** n19 t21 f19 b20. Chewy and rich, big hickory-oak finale **40%**

Connoisseurs Choice Clynelish 1990 **(80)** n22 t20 f19 b19. Great nose and early riches. **40%**. *Gordon & MacPhail.*

Coopers Choice Clynelish 1990 bott 02 (12 Years Old) **(84)** n23 t20 f20 b21. Amazingly light and malty. A beautifully soft dram. **43%**. *The Vintage Malt Whisky Co.*

Coopers Choice Clynelish 1990 Port Finish bott 02 (12 Years old) **(91)** n23 lovely peppers and spices on top of a malt-fruit marriage; t22 an immediate array of invigorating fruit, pretty sweet but with some comforting vanilla, pounds around the palate; f23 spices return for a subtle fade-out: majestically complex; b23 my hat is off for a job well done: one of the best wine finishes to have come on the market in the last few years. A sensational achievement – congrats to all concerned. **46%**. *The Vintage Malt Whisky Co.*

Coopers Choice Clynelish Aged 16 Years dist 83, bott 00 **(85)** n22 t22 f21 b20. A grassy, succulent dram that grows on you. **43%. sc.**

⋰⋱ **Distillery No 5 Clynelish 1990** **(86)** n21 sugared barley, grassy; sharp, bitter lemon fresh and clean; t21 massive barley, mouthfilling, sugary, a tad sappy but with mesmerising malt intensity; f22 a vanilla-custard follow-through with the barley still sparking; b22 what a pleasure to find Clynelish in its most naked, blendable state. **46%**

Gordon & MacPhail Clynelish 1989 Cask Strength (77) n*19* t*19* f*20* **b***19*. Not quite the cleanest sherry you could ask for. **57.9%**

Hart Brothers Clynelish Aged 14 Years dist Mar 88, bott Sep 02 **(79)** n*21* t*21* f*18* **b***19*. Some very decent honey. **53.3%**

James MacArthur Clynelish 10 Year Old (88) n*21* lively and complex: pure Clynelish for its age; t*23* so sensuous: the mouthfeel is lush and has clinging to it stupendous toasted honey malt and soft oak; f*22* the spicy oak intensifies the age, but the dryness counters the early sweet tones; **b***22* a real monster for a 10-y-o: the tastebuds are swamped with goodies. **43%**

Mission Range Clynelish 1972 (92) n*22* elegantly aged with just the right amount of oak dryness; t*24* absolutely stunning: the malt-barley fit is just about perfect and spices evolve early on; f*23* thins out slightly with the oak now in the ascendency but still shows class and compensating silky sweetness; **b***23* a real gem. The mouthfeel is textbook. **46%. nc ncf.** *Murray McDavid.*

⠿ **Murray McDavid Mission III Clynelish 1983 (79)** n*20* t*21* f*19* **b***19*. Tired and unemotional. **46%**

⠿ **Old Malt Cask Clynelish Aged 14 Years** dist Jan 90, bott Feb 04 **(84)** n*23* t*22* f*19* **b***20*. As mouthwatering as the barley may be it is the fabulous covertly smoked aroma that impresses most. **50%. nc ncf sc.** *Douglas Laing.*

⠿ **Old Malt Cask Clynelish Aged 14 Years** Rum Finish cask no 3850 dist June 89, bott Sep 03 **(85)** n*22* fabulously busy and floral; the spices add pungency to the lurking fruit. Exciting stuff; t*23* enormous mouth arrival again with spices crashing into rich plums and sultanas and a waft of peat smoke; the vanilla and barley are firm but quiet; f*19* disintegrates towards the mildly off-key, bitter end; **b***21* despite the untidy unravelling at the finish, there are many mouth-puckering moments here. Great fun. **50%. nc ncf sc.** *Douglas Laing. 312 bottles.*

Old Malt Cask Clynelish Aged 30 Years dist Sep 70, bott Apr 01 **(90)** n*23* t*23* f*22* **b***22*. This is how you dream a 30-y-o should be, but so rarely is. **42%. nc ncf.** *Douglas Laing.*

Old Malt Cask Clynelish Aged 31 Years Sherry Finish dist Sep 70, bott Sep 01 **(89)** n*23* t*23* f*21* **b***22*. Quality malt with a few hidden extras that need searching for. **48.4% nc ncf sc.** *Douglas Laing. 186 bottles.*

Old Masters Clynelish Aged 10 Years (89) n*22* gentle smoke and citrus tones: very refreshing; t*23* massive malt, beautifully shiny and honied on palate; f*22* gentle smoke and vanilla; **b***22* near faultless for its age. **59.8%**

Old Masters Clynelish 1989 (88) n*22* chocolate lime and smoke: superb; t*22* trademark Clynelish silkiness and ultra-intense malt; f*22* hints of smoke; **b***22* a superb all-round single malt. **59.1%.** *James MacArthur.*

Provenance Summer Distillation Clynelish Over 11 Years dist Summer 89, bott Autumn 00 **(89)** n*22* t*23* f*21* **b***23*. No colouring, not chill filtered: you can see why blenders love this stuff. It doesn't half make a bad single malt, either! This bottling shows just what complexity it can muster from apparently nowhere. **43%. nc ncf.** *Douglas McGibbon & Co.*

⠿ **Scotch Single Malt Circle Clynelish 1972** dist 14 Oct 72 bott Oct 02 cask 14287 **(91)** n*23* this one could have been sitting in a puffin's nest for the last 30 years; you couldn't get much more coastal t*22* an immediate impact of soft honey running alongside thick barley f*23* fabulously long with some oaky saltiness leaking into the barleyfest **b***23* any Clynelish that doesn't offer a degree of honey is missing a trick: this one won't let you down. **56.3%** *Germany*

⠿ **Scotch Single Malt Circle Clynelish 1990** dist May 90, bott Oct 04 cask 3963 **(86)** n*21* a salty edge to the sharp barley: you could slice your nose on it despite the softer water melon counter; t*22* mouthwatering barley then a tobacco character not unknown for this period at the distillery; f*21* lingering barley; **b***21* a bitter-sweet dram that leans more closely to bitter. **57.4%.** *Germany.*

∴ **Signatory Clynelish Vintage 1983** cask 2695, dist 11May 83, bott 3 Oct 03 **(84)** n*22* t*22* f*20* b*20*. Brilliant nose offering just a touch of honey, but fades after the promisingly malty start. **43% nc.** *343 bottles.*

Signatory Clynelish 12 Years South African Sherry Butt cask 3239, dist 17/05/89, bott 05/11/01 **(81)** n*19* t*21* f*20* b*21*. Interesting, unquestionably fruity and sweet with a spicy background. **43%.** *868 bottles.*

Ultimate Selection Clynelish 1992 (73) dist 5/11/92, bott 15/8/02 n*16* t*19* f*20* b*18*. Fails to gel early on but the middle and early finish are fine. **43%.** *Van Wees NL.*

∴ **The Un-chillfiltered Collection Clynelish Vintage 1992** cask 6302, dist 12 May 92, bott 24 Feb 02 **(89)** n*23* find a more subtle honey aroma and you'll do well; t*23* has no hesitation to ofer both bite and soothing malt at the kick off; thins out towards middle; f*21* fades a little too easily with little more than toffeed vanilla keeping fort; some spice does offer relief; b*22* early on this Clynelish at its most alluringly stylish. **46%.** *Signatory 398 bottles.*

∴ **Whisky Galore Clynelish 1990 Aged 13 Years (78)** n*20* t*19* f*20* b*19*. Some tobacco notes amid the barley. **46%**

∴ **Whisky Galore Clynelish 1992 Aged 11 Years (84)** n*22* t*22* f*20* b*20*. Gristy, beautifully clean malt with a slight peat accent but lacks development. **46%**

∴ **Wilson & Morgan Barrel Selection Clynelish 1989** Marsala Finish bott 03 **(91)** n*21* dusty but several stratum of clean malt underneath t*22* soft spices attack the tongue; elsewhere the barley links grapefully the remainder of the palate f*24* goes into complexity overdrive: some serious juicy white grape intermingles with spice and light roast Costa Rican coffee sweetened by raw Demerara b*24* dusty nose but a real spicefest on the juicy palate. A sensual sensation. **46%**

COLEBURN
Speyside, 1897–1985. Diageo. Closed.

Connoisseurs Choice Coleburn 1972 (72) n*17* t*20* f*18* b*17*. A strange, off-balanced, rather sweet malt. One for collectors rather than purists. **40%.** *Gordon & MacPhail.*

Old Malt Cask Coleburn Aged 20 Years (Sherry) dist Sep 80, dist Jan 01 **(71)** n*16* t*21* f*17* b*17*. Big mouth arrival, but little else works. **50%.** *648 bottles.*

CONVALMORE
Speyside, 1894–1985. Closed.

∴ **Convalmore Rare Malt 24 Years Old** dist 78, db **(88)** n*23* Peaches and cream ... and pretty juicy peach at that. One of the fruitiest noses on the market; t*23* not even a straffing of searing spices can reduce the peachy onslaught. About as juicy and salivating as it gets for a malt so old; f*20* an abrupt entry of cocoa-dusted oak plus some lingering barley; b*22* another stunning version of a much-missed distillery, begging the question as to why it was ever closed. **59.4%**

Connoisseurs Choice Convalmore 1969 (86) n*21* suet pudding with diced fruit, a slight hint of smoke; t*22* beautifully silky, sweet malt-rich but succulent fruit; f*22* attractive vanilla, a touch of spice and trailing peat; b*21* a wonderful old Convalmore from a bottling from the 90s still doing the rounds in Europe. **40%.** *Gordon & MacPhail.*

Dun Bheagan Convalmore Aged 16 Years dist 84, bott 00 **(78)** n*20* t*19* f*20* b*19*. Spicy and oaky, no shortage of character. **43%.** *William Maxwell.*

∴ **Dun Bheagan Convalmore 1985 Aged 18 Years** bott 22 May 03 **(94)** n*23* banana split; dessert sweetness countering the drier oak elements and wonderfully covert and silently influential peat; t*24* fabulous mouth arrival; near perfection in fact. Few malts are quite this silky on the palate or possess a weight to the barley which is so even; there is even a hint of peat to balance out perfectly against the mouthwatering quality of the barley; **f**22 some cocoa butter and cocoa-bitter oak notes plus a hint of spice but despite the obvious age this is a glorious warm down; **b**25 just one of those whiskies that work. The nose needs extra time to fathom; the experience on the palate is the stuff of legend. Something that experienced whisky watchers will savour. **43%.** *William Maxwell.*

Rare Old Convalmore 1960 (86) n22 violets and muted cloves with light honey and a touch of bourbon; **t**22 soft malt and honeycomb with restrained oak. More bourbon towards the end of the middle as the oak digs in; **f**21 long, oily with some liquorice and chicory for extra effect; **b**21 takes some studying to get to the bottom of this one: take your time. **40%.** *Gordon & MacPhail.*

Old Malt Cask Convalmore Aged 22 Years dist Jan 78, bott Jun 00 **(80)** n19 t20 f21 b20. Threatened on the nose by oak, but boasts sufficient barley intensity to make an impressively chewy-tofffee dram of it. **50%. nc ncf.** *Douglas Laing.* 336 bottles.

Signatory Convalmore 1981 dist 18/3/81, bott 8/1/02 **(86)** n21 gristy, fresh and clean; **t**21 direct translation onto the tastebuds: rich textured and signs of good copper involvement; **f**22 highly complex with some subtle spices playing against the intense barley; **b**22 a well-used cask has thankfully preserved this malt so it retains a grassy, mildly honey shape. **43%.** *462 bottles.*

CRAGGANMORE
Speyside, 1870. Diageo. Working.

Cragganmore 12 Years Old db **(85)** n21 a layer of crushed sultana overlooked by coke smoke; **t**22 soft, extremely sweet and fruit-influenced; **f**21 long, the smoke returns with a degree of buzzing spice; **b**21 I admit it has been a couple of years since I last tasted Cragganmore, and this is not what I expected to find: those, like me, who remember the dry, crusty malty-oaky complex dram are in for a sherried surprise. **40%**

⋅⋰⋅ **Cragganmore 29 Years Old** dist 73, db **(69)** n17 t19 f16 b16. Less than pleasant malt handicapped by poor cask selection. **52.5%**

Cragganmore Distillers Edition Double Matured 1988 bott 2002, port-wine cask wood finish, db **(88)** n23 genuinely different to anything else around: the heaviness of the fruit does not contain the usual spice from port but rather a strange diffused mixture of unripened gooseberry juice and elderberry, genuinely odd, but very attractive; **t**22 the spice arrives now, but softly so with some bitterness creeping in to counter an instant malt-sweetness; **f**20 throat grabbingly dry with bitter almonds popping up; **b**23 this is one very weird whisky, the like of which cannot be found outside this bottling. Sit back and marvel. **40%**

Blackadder Raw Cask Cragganmore 1989 cask 1966, dist 13 Sep 89, bott Jun 00 **(89)** n22 t23 f22 b22. Absolutely cracking chewy, coffeed Cragganmore. **59.6%. nc ncf sc.**

Cask Cragganmore 1978 cask 4959, dist 13/9/78, bott Nov 96 **(92)** n23 t24 f22 b23. One of those little pieces of genius that G&M has a tendency to unleash on us every now and again. **60.1%.** *Gordon & MacPhail.*

Connoisseurs Choice Cragganmore 1976 (81) n20 t21 f19 b21. Chocolate fruit and nut. Sweet and chewy. **40%.** *Gordon & MacPhail.*

Connoisseurs Choice Cragganmore 1978 (70) n19 t18 f16 b17. Pretty boring stuff: never gets even close to getting off the ground. **40%.** *Gordon & MacPhail.*

Murray McDavid Cragganmore 1990 bourbon cask MM9833, dist Apr 90, bott Oct 01 **(87)** n22 t23 f21 b21. Simply a good Speyside cask: blender's fodder. **46%. nc ncf sc.**

Murray McDavid Cragganmore 1990 bourbon cask MM1410, dist April 90, bott Nov 01 **(88)** n*22* t*23* f*22* b*21*. A re-run of cask MM9833 except the finish has more spice and malt on the finale. **46% nc ncf sc.**

⠿ **Murray McDavid Cragganmore 1990 (85)** n*21* very young malt; t*22* pre-teen malt; f*21* malty; b*21* pure blending fodder. **46%**

Signatory Cragganmore 13 Years Old dist 89, bott 02 **(89)** n*22* clean, fresh, mouthwatering malt; t*23* brilliant sharp barley arrival with young grass, fabulously juicy; f*22* some spice and soft vanilla; b*22* frankly, this is how the official Classic Malt Cragganmore should be: screaming undisguised Speyside at you.

Ultimate Selection Cragganmore 1989 cask 96, dist 18/4/89, bott 14/1/03 **(79)** n*21* t*21* f*18* b*19*. Big malt start, but becomes furry and chalky. Just 1000 casks before the Blackadder Cragganmore, but they are poles apart. **sc.** *Van Wees NL.*

CRAIGELLACHIE

Speyside, 1891. Dewar's. Working.

⠿ **Craigellachie 14 Years Old** db **(82)** n*21* t*22* f*19* b*21*. Complex nose and battles deliciously and maltily before the indifferent finish; quite a bit of bite. **40%.** *John Dewar & Sons.*

Connoisseurs Choice Craigellachie 1982 (76) n*20* t*20* f*17* b*19*. You get the feeling that disruptive caramel has crept in from somewhere. **40%.** *Gordon & MacPhail.*

Connoisseurs Choice Craigellachie 1987 (87) n*21* floral, violets; hint of smoke, confident oak; t*22* succulent, juicy, oily malt with no mean dash of low-profile peat to weight things down and spice things up; f*22* pretty long and sweet with decent oak fade; b*22* a really punchy Speysider that's no shrinking violet. **40%**

⠿ **The Craigellachie Hotel Craigellachie Single Cask Bottling 2003** cask 1416, dist 3 Mar 82, bott 28 Oct 03 **(77)** n*19* t*20* f*18* b*19*. A disappointing bottling that despite an early malt surge on the palate falls victim to a less than glorious cask. **??%**

⠿ **Murray McDavid Mission III Craigellachie 1970** refill sherry **(93)** n*23* oaky spice off-set by damson plums in custard; t*24* stunning!!! The arrival simply glimmers with fabulous barley in that sweet custardy setting; an usual form of sweetness, this, fruity and refined, though not in a sugary way; f*22* some natural caramel blunts the richer tones but there is soft sherry back-up; b*24* when I tell people that Craigellachie can be a God, I am looked upon with incredulity. Well, get your lips around this minor masterpiece; also rare to find this distillery in any form of sherry. **46%**

Old Malt Cask Craigellachie Aged 12 Years dist Oct 88 **(79)** n*20* t*21* f*18* b*20*. Beautifully fresh with a very lively personality. **50%. nc ncf.** *Douglas Laing.*

⠿ **Scotch Single Malt Circle Craigellachie 1977** dist 13 Dec 77, bott Oct 01 cask 95/64/13 **(82)** n*19* t*22* f*20* b*21*. Delicious, attractively oily but otherwise lightweight barley and a little hot. A pretty old and worn cask in use here. **59.4%** *Germany.*

Scott's Selection Craigellachie 1982 bott 99 **(81)** n*19* t*23* f*19* b*20*. Craigellachie can sometimes be the bruiser of Speyside and here it takes no prisoners with its sweetness. **62.3%.** *Robert Scott & Co.*

CROFTENGEA (*see* Loch Lomond)

DAILUAINE

Speyside, 1854. Diageo. Working.

Dailuaine Aged 16 Years db **(83)** n*19* t*22* f*21* b*21*. Checking through my old tasting notes, I see I have scored this higher than any previous Flora and Fauna bottling from this distillery. Mildly lighter, yet more smoked than some, it offers a charming, mouthwatering freshness. Solid and delicious. **43%**

Adelphi Dailuaine 22 Years Old cask 4151, dist 80, bott 02 **(93) n**24 one of the all-time-great Dailuaine noses: honied with just about bang on malt-oak balance and very, very faintest hint of peat; **t**24 sensational! Fabulous sweet malt is wrapped in a softly oiled body and then more manuka honey and soft spice; **f**22 slightly bitter by comparison as oak makes a stand, but the malt remains superb; **b**23 I have waited many years for a really premier Dailuaine to turn up and here it is. A superb blend of weighty Highland style and grassy Speyside. **55.2%**

Berry's Own Dailuaine 1975 bott 03 **(91) n**22 appears at first to have oaky bags under its eyes, but a distant hint of spiced smoke plus some intense barley offers life and intrigue enough; **t**23 enlivened further by an intensely malty, chewy middle. The sweet, succulent barley is wonderfully clean and invigorating for its great age; **f**23 again trails off towards oak at the finale, but the middle and finale sparkle with no little complexity. Quite estery at the death: very rum-like; **b**23 a seriously impressive and enjoyable old malt that takes a little time to fathom. Really outstanding stuff and unquestionably one of the great bottled Dailuaines of our time. **46%.** *Berry Bros*

∴ **Blackadder Raw Cask Dailuaine 30 Years Old** cask 15956 dist 14 Dec 73, bott Mar 04 **(84) n**20 **t**22 **f**22 **b**20. A bit over-tired but enough riches to make for a chewy middle. **59.9%**

∴ **Blackadder Raw Cask Dailuaine 30 Years Old** cask 15957 dist 14 Dec 73, bott Mar 04 **(79) n**21 **t**19 **f**20 **b**19. Impressive nose but the whisky is becoming oak saturated. **57.7%**

Connoisseurs Choice Dailuaine 1974 (84) n21 **t**22 **f**20 **b**21. Sweet, sensuously silky and malty. A lovely dram. **40%.** *Gordon & MacPhail.*

Connoisseurs Choice Dailuaine 1975 (81) n20 **t**22 **f**19 **b**20. Rhubarb on the nose and a lot to say for itself on the extremely malt-rich middle palate. **40%.** *Gordon & MacPhail.*

Old Malt Cask Dailuaine Aged 20 Years dist Feb 80, bott Feb 00 **(83) n**21 **t**21 **f**20 **b**21. A linear, clean, peachy malt that is a blender's dream. **50%. nc ncf.** *Douglas Laing. 368 bottles.*

Old Malt Cask Dailuaine Aged 23 Years Sherry Finish dist Sep 78, bott Sep 01 **(83) n**19 **t**22 **f**21 **b**21. Dull nose, but plenty to compensate in a lively mouth-explosion. **50%. nc ncf.** *Douglas Laing. 276 bottles.*

∴ **Old Master's Dailuaine 1976** bott 04 cask 5967 **(84) n**21 **t**22 **f**21 **b**20. A strapping malt abounding in spices and fruit; a sweetie with no shortage of oak and punch. **57.1%.** *James MacArthur.*

DALLAS DHU
Speyside, 1899–1983. Closed. Now a museum.

Dallas Dhu 21 Years Old Rare Malts Selection (83) n21 **t**21 **f**20 **b**21. An uncompromising barley-rich effort as one might expect, but otherwise a bit thin and lacking that usual extra depth. **61.9%.** *United Distillers/Diageo.*

Cadenhead's Dallas Dhu 23 Years Old dist 79, bott 03/03 **(89) n**20 pleasant, but a bit lazy; **t**23 trademark rich honey that was always so apparent from 10–12 years old has been preserved and improved upon; **f**23 enormously long with deft fingers of smoke stimulating the honey; **b**23 a true gem from one of the most-missed distilleries in the world. **60.8%**

Connoisseurs Choice Dallas Dhu 1971 (87) n23 smoky and honied, quite weighty; **t**22 soft, chewy malt and a hint of peat; **f**21 vanilla, cocoa, soft and silky; **b**21 a really clean, rich Dallas Dhu with quite beautiful smoke. **40%**

Gordon & MacPhail Dallas Dhu 1980 (85) n23 hot cross buns, doughy, icing sugar: genuinely beautiful; **t**21 early oak surrounds the barley, but is just in balance; **f**20 sugared almonds and oak; **b**21 the oak has done some damage, but the charisma of a great malt still shimmers through. **40%**

Mission Range Dallas Dhu 1979 (90) n*23* beautiful raisiny, resiny oak: rich: t*22* wave upon wave of barley with a little more oak as each one lands; f*23* the most tender, sweet oak imaginable, a wisp of peat at the death; b*22* this is such a classy, classic whisky. Age cannot dim its shafts of gold. **46%**. *Murray McDavid.*

∴ **Murray McDavid Mission III Dallas Dhu 1974 (91)** n*22* sliced cucumber beside a glass of sweet sherry; t*24* does sherry come any cleaner or cleverly covert than this? Boiled fruit sweets and Fishermen's Friends make a warming, mouthwatering combination; f*22* a hint of Jenever and natural caramel rounds it off beautifully; b*23* are they sure they can't re-open this distillery...? **46%**

Old Malt Cask Dallas Dhu Aged 20 Year dist Nov 79, bott Apr 00 **(76)** n*19* t*21* f*18* b*18*. Pretty rich middle, but a little hot and splutters about a bit. **50%. nc ncf.** *Douglas Laing. 324 bottles.*

Old Malt Cask Dallas Dhu Aged 21 Years dist Mar 80, bott May 01 **(79)** n*20* t*20* f*19* b*20*. Soft and malty. **50%. nc ncf.** *Douglas Laing. 348 bottles.*

Old Malt Cask Dallas Dhu Aged 24 Years dist Oct 76, bott Jan 01 **(76)** n*20* t*20* f*19* b*17*. Attractively powerful early arrival but otherwise uninspiring. **50%. nc ncf.** *Douglas Laing. 630 bottles.*

Old Malt Cask Dallas Dhu 31 Years Old dist Dec 68, bott May 00 **(88)** n*21* t*23* f*22* b*22*. Chocolate honeycomb bliss. **50%.** *Douglas Laing. 253 bottles.*

∴ **Provenance Dallas Dhu Over 19 Years** dist Summer 81, bott Winter 03 **(72)** n*15* t*20* f*18* b*19*. Sadly sulphurous. **46%.** *Douglas McGibbon.*

Signatory Rare Reserve Dallas Dhu 30 Years Old refill sherry butt 673, dist 6/3/70, bott 25/7/00 **(84)** n*20* t*23* f*20* b*21*. The oak does little damage at first, offering lavender to the nose and a jagged spicy counter to the lush sweet malt in the fabulous middle. But it catches up in the end. **56.5%.** *378 bottles.*

DALMORE
Highand (northern), 1839. Whyte and Mackay. Working.

Dalmore 12 Years Old db **(91)** n*22* big, fruity, firm, a threat of smoke, weighty; t*24* well-muscled malt surge followed by clean fruity tones, immaculate mouth-presence and bitter-sweet balance; f*22* long, tapering fruit-malt residue, some brown sugar coating and uncomplicated oak; b*23* simply one of the great Highland malt whiskies at just about the perfect age: what I would do to see this unplugged at 46% minimum and no bottling hall interference. **40%**

The Dalmore 21 Years Old db **(87)** n*22* just how many citrus notes can we find here? Answers on a postcard ... on second thoughts, don't. Just beautifully light and effervescent for its age: a genuine delight; t*23* again, wonderfully fruity though this time the malt pushes through confidently to create its own chewy island: fabulous texture; f*20* simplifies towards toffee slightly too much in the interests of great balance. But a lovely coffee flourish late on; b*22* bottled elegance. **43%**

The Dalmore 30 Years Old Stillman's Dram (89) n*23* nuts and oranges in a rich fruitcake, lime marmalade adds to the fruit cocktail: seductive; t*22* enormous fruit explosion, silky malt then an injection of bitter oak; f*22* medium length, but the emphasis is on the malt as the oakiness burns off. The complexity levels rise as the fruit recedes and some spices arrive late; b*22* in some ways the ultimate bitter-sweet dram, with the burnt-toast oak fighting against the sweet fruit and malt. It's a battle royale. **45%**

The Dalmore 50 Years Old db **(88)** n*21* buxom and bourbony, the oak makes no secret of the antiquity; t*19* again the oak arrives first and without apology, some salty malt creaking in later. Ripe cherries offer a mouthwatering backdrop; f*25* comes into its own as harmony is achieved as the oak quietens to allow a beautiful malt-cherry interplay. Spices arrive for good measure in an absolutely has-it-all, faultless finish: really as much a privilege to taste as a delight; b*23* takes a little while to warm up, but when it does becomes a genuinely classy and memorable dram befitting one of the world's great and undervalued distilleries. **52%**

The Dalmore 62 Years Old db **(95) n**23 PM or REV marked demerara pot-still rum, surely? Massive coffee presence, clean and enormous, stunning, top-drawer peat just to round things off; **t**25 this is brilliant: pure silk wrapping fabulous moist fruitcake soaked in finest oloroso sherry and then weighed with peat which somehow has defied nature and survived in cask all these years. I really cannot fault this: I sit here stunned in and in awe; **f**24 perfect spices with flecks of ginger and lemon rind; **b**24 if I am just half as beautiful, elegant and fascinating as this by the time I reach 62, I'll be a happy man. Somehow I doubt it. A once-in-a-lifetime whisky – something that comes around every 62 years, in fact. Forget Dalmore Cigar Malt – even I might be tempted to start smoking just to get a full bottle of this. **40.5%**

The Dalmore 1966 db **(86) n**23 marzipan-orange, apple and malt; **t**22 clean, lush mouth arrival with superb, sparky spice; **f**20 flattens considerably as the vanilla kicks in; **b**21 a remakable dram for the years that it has kept its fruity integrity despite the big age. **44.6%**

The Dalmore 1973 Gonzalez Byass Sherry Cask Finish db **(93) n**24 outstanding fruit-spice: one of the cleaner sherry butts you are likely to find. This is dry and as delicate as an eighteenth-century Wedgewood figurine. Grapes, a touch of banana and very distant coal smoke. Don't sniff too hard: you might break it; **t**23 clean, almost Speyside light by Dalmore standards then a slow rolling in of crisp, dry sherry. The body is lightly oiled; **f**22 takes on an entirely new phase as oak arrives and the malt begins to vanish. Hints of cocoa and distant peat. Everything unravels in slow motion; **b**24 What happens when you get one of Scotland's greatest – if entirely undervalued – drams and fill it into what what was obviously a special, hand-picked, clean and flawless sherry butt? You get this. **52.3%**

The Dalmore Black Isle db **(77) n**19 **t**20 **f**19 **b**19. Very little of the complexity I automatically associate with Dalmore; slightly furry and a little drab. **40%**

The Dalmore Cigar Malt db **(71) n**17 **t**20 **f**16 **b**18. For me, flat and un-Dalmore-like. But there again I have never smoked as much as a cigarette in all my life – so what do I know? **43%**

Adelphi Dalmore 11 Years Old cask 998, dist 89, bott 00 **(69) n**16 **t**19 **f**17 **b**17. Sulphur to the fore, pure demerara sugar to the middle and sour, bitter notes aft. Some people will love this: for me this is not in the usual sure-footed mould of either the distillery or the bottlers. **57.2%. sc.**

⋰ **Old Malt Cask Dalmore Aged 10 Years** dist Oct 93, bott Feb 04 **(82) n**22 **t**23 **f**18 **b**19. Cracklingly beautiful nose and early mouth development; the finish is bitter and dry. **50%. nc ncf sc.** *Douglas Laing. 395 bottles.*

Provenance Dalmore Over 11 Years Winter Distillation dist Winter 88, bott Autumn 00 **(89) n**22 **t**24 **f**22 **b**21. Oh, if only more malt were bottled with this zest and youthfulness! Some may say it's undercooked: rather raw than burnt to a crisp, I say. **43%. nc ncf.** *Douglas McGibbon & Co.*

⋰ **Provenance Dalmore Over 14 Years** dist Spring 89, bott Autumn 03 **(86) n**21 lazy and lush, hints of fruit and dough; **t**22 the clarity of the nose continues with the mouthwatering, ultra-malty, spicy mouth arrival; **f**21 the soft vanillas on the middle pan out attractively; **b**22 a charming, faultless, unspectacular yet rewarding bottling. **46%.** *Douglas McGibbon.*

DALWHINNIE
Highlands (central), 1898. Diageo. Working.

Dalwhinnie 15 Years Old db **(94) n**23 sublime stuff: a curious mixture of coke smoke and peat-reek wafts teasingly over the gently honied malt. A hint of melon offers some fruit but the caressing malt stars; **t**24 that rarest of combinations: at once silky and malt intense, yet at the same time peppery and tin-hat time for the tastebuds, but the silk wins out and a sheen of barley sugar coats everything, soft peat included; **f**23 some cocoa and coffee notes, yet the pervading slightly honied sweetness means that there is no bitterness that cannot be controlled; **b**24 a malt it is hard to decide whether to drink or bath in: I suggest you do both. One of the most complete mainland malts of them all. Know anyone who reckons they don't like whisky? Give them a glass of this – that's them cured. Oh, if only the average masterpiece could be this good. **43%**

Dalwhinnie Distillers Edition 1986 Double Matured oloroso finish, bott 02 db **(87)** n23 exceptionally clean sherry freshens up the nose without too much cost to the honey; **t**23 beautiful mouth arrival and then radiating out of fruit, the malt regroups but is outnumbered; **f**20 quite dry and oak rich; **b**21 good sherry butt, but if anything goes to prove how sherry influence can reduce the all-round complexity of a great malt. **43%**

⋰ **Dalwhinnie 29 Years Old** dist 73, db **(85)** n21 very curious graininess not unlike a blend; lots of bite amid the soft oak and light sap; **t**20 fighting whisky; an old bruiser for its age that early on shows little of its fine breeding but plenty of tongue-pulverising oomph; **f**23 at last settles with the trademark honey showing shyly with layers of barley and then a massive oak surge that for a moment threatens to overwhelm and then recedes; **b**21 one for those hunting the atypical. **57.8%**

Dalwhinnie 36 Years Old db **(92)** n23 well-peated and weird for a Highlander: there is something distinctly coastal for a whisky matured up a mountain, though the heather is quite fitting; **t**24 brilliant oak and salt seep into the tastebuds leaving a honey stain wherever they go. Soft peats are also very evident; **f**22 much drier, with a soft, oaky-peaty buzz; **b**23 rarely does a Dalwhinnie of this antiquity make it to market. Even rarer is it for a Perthshire-style whisky to retain its smoky-heather-honey shape to this degree. Brilliant. **47.2%**

DEANSTON
Highlands (Perthshire), 1966. Burn Stewart. Working.

⋰ **Deanston 6 Years Old** db **(83)** n20 t21 f22 b20. Great news for those of us who remember how good Deanston was a decade or two ago: it's on its way back. A delightfully clean dram with its trademark honey character restored. A little beauty slightly undermined by caramel. **40%**

Deanston 12 Year Old db **(66)** n15 t18 f16 b17. Butyric and thin. **40%**

Deanston 17 Year Old db **(68)** n17 t17 f17 b17. A 17-year-old anorexic with agoraphobia: painfully thin and goes nowhere. **40%**

⋰ **Deanston 1967** db filled Friday 31st Mar 67 cask nos 1051-2 **(90)** n23 the very faintest hint of peat rubs shoulders with high fluting honey and polished pine floors; **t**23 the loud oak influence is perfectly tempered by rich barley concentrate. Sweet towards the middle with hints of honey and peat; **f**21 spiced and softening towards vanilla; **b**23 the oak is full on but there is so much class around that cannot gain control. A Perthshire beauty. **50.7%. nc.**

⋰ **Lombard Deanston 1977 (89)** n23 honey and salted butter on toast; a hint of vague sap but the sweetness is balanced; **t**22 excellent translation onto the palate: an immediate sweetness arrives with some of the most intense barley you can imagine; **f**22 the dry, oaky tones are controlled and offer hickory and spice; **b**22 a Perthshire thoroughbred just champing at the bit with honey. **49.6%. ncf nc.** *Lombard International.*

⋰ **Scotch Single Malt Circle Deanston 1992** dist 17 Jun 92, bott 14 Oct 02 **(87)** n22 the usual Deanston honey; **t**22 weightier than many official bottlings have been of late with the honey bristling with malt and spice; no shortage of bite and attitude; **f**21 vanilla sweetened with a few grains of raw brown sugar; **b**22 an agreeable rough diamond. **59.8%.** *Germany.*

DUFFTOWN
Speyside, 1898. Diageo. Silent.

Dufftown Aged 15 Years db **(69)** n16 t19 f17 b17. Rubbery, syrupy and sickly sweet: Dufftown in a nutshell. **43%.** *Flora and Fauna range.*

Dufftown Rare Malts Aged 21 Years db dist 1975 **(59)** n14 t17 f14 b14. Not rare enough. **54.8%**

Berry's Own Dufftown 1979 (78) n21 t20 f18 b19. Promising at first, especially with the deep and rich malt intensity on mouth arrival. But there is that trademark, odd – dirty almost – kick and residue to be countered. **46%.** *Berry Bros*

Berrys' Own Selection Dufftown 1984 bott 02 **(86)** n22 very attractive spice amid ... well, something (being Dufftown, you are never quite sure what); t22 I don't believe it: the landing on the palate is superb, concentrated malt with a dash of molassed sugar tipped in for good measure; f21 a slight rubberyness dissolves into the gristy-sugary malt, but decent oak helps to counter; b21 well, it had to happen one day: a Dufftown under 20 years old I can actually offer to people without the use of a brown paper bag. Hats off to that other prince of St James's Dougie McIvor at Berrys', owner of the best nose of Scotch never to find its way into a blending lab. Never did I ever expect to heap such lavish praise on a Charlton supporter... or this particular distillery. **56.8%** *Berry Bros & Rudd.*

Coopers Choice Dufftown 1982 bott 01 sherry cask (19 Years Old) **(72)** n19 t18 f16 b19. Whenever I see a sherry cask Dufftown pour into a glass I shudder ... Pavlov, dogs, that kind of thing. However that strange tinned-tomatoes-meets-demerara-rum nose wasn't too bad and this is pretty drinkable. **46%**

⁙ **Old Malt Cask Dufftown Aged 12 Years** dist Dec 91, bott Feb 04 **(83)** n21 t22 f20 b20. Easily one of the most pleasant bottlings from this distillery; unusually clean, untroubled by complexity. **50%. nc ncf sc.** *Douglas Laing.*

⁙ **Old Malt Cask Dufftown Aged 14 Years** dist Sep 88, bott Aug 03 **(73)** n20 t19 f16 b18. Typically unbalanced, it lurches all over the palate with a mildly cloying mouthfeel. Enjoy the ride! **50%. nc ncf sc.** *Douglas Laing.*

Old Malt Cask Dufftown Aged 20 Years Sherry dist Feb 80, bott Jun 00 **(82)** n19 t22 f21 b20. A collector's item: a very drinkable post-'60s Dufftown. Big-chested and brazen, this is one for big boys. Hefty and edible. **50%. nc ncf.** *Douglas Laing.*

Old Malt Cask Dufftown Aged 20 Years dist Oct 81 **(69)** n15 t18 f19 b17. Trademark dirty nose, but has some big moments afterwards. **50%. nc ncf.** *Douglas Laing.*

Old Malt Cask Dufftown Aged 35 Years Sherry dist Oct 62, bott Apr 01 **(88)** n23 t22 f21 b22. Forget sherry: what we are talking here is fine quality bourbon! **49.6%. nc ncf sc.** *Douglas Laing. 228 bottles.*

Provenance Spring Distillation Dufftown Over 11 Years dist Spring 90, bott Autumn 01 **(50)** n10 t15 f13 b12. Proof in a bottle as to why this distillery closed. **43%. nc ncf.** *Douglas McGibbon & Co.*

Royal Mile Whiskies Dufftown 17 Years Old dist Dec 79, bott Nov 97 **(69)** n15 t18 f19 b17. Run-a-mile whisky from the normally dependable Royal Mile. Bottled in the days before they knew better. **sc.** *Edinburgh UK.*

Ultimate Collection Dufftown 17 Years Old sherry butt 6030, dist 27/11/85 **(69)** n17 t18 f18 b16. Tinned tomatoes meets golden syrup. **sc.** *Van Wees NL.*

Whisky Galore Dufftown 1987 15-y-o (85) n20 sparkling, light malt despite the usual slightly dirty off-notes; t22 mouthwatering, fresh and, for a Dufftown, remarkably clean; f21 the rich malt continues; b22 not the most complex of whiskies, but perhaps the use of a round-the-block cask or two has helped settle this whisky down. Truly outstanding for a Dufftown. **46%.** *Duncan Taylor & Co.*

⁙ **Wilson & Morgan Barrel Selection Dufftown 15 Years Old** dist 85 **(73)** n18 t19 f18 b18. Oaky spice attack loses battle against the cloying, dirty-ish intensity. Big and brawny. **56.8%**

❖ **Wilson & Morgan Barrel Selection Dufftown 1989** Marsala Finish bott 03 **(85) n**19 peppery agave with vanilla and grape; **t**21 slightly oversweet at first, but fattens out on the palate; **f**23 develops impressively around juicy fruit and intense barley; **b**22 a distinctly better-class dram from a consistently poor distillery. The fruity-spice is genuinely delicious. **46%**

DUNGLASS (*see* Littlemill)

EDRADOUR
Highland (Perthshire), 1837. Signatory. Working.

Edradour 10 Years Old db **(86) n**21 charmingly heathery with soft citrus and a glimmer of honey; **t**22 unusual sweet malt and saccharine with very soft oak; **f**22 nodules of honey on the encroaching oak and oil; **b**21 too rarely do you get bottlings from this distillery particularly close and this one is very different, though the honey is a constant. Some of you may have tasted a feinty disaster of a bottling from 2002 – I experienced it while giving a tasting in Stockholm: hopefully that was a one-off and you can return to this brand with a degree of confidence. **40%**

Signatory Edradour 10 Years Old Un-chillfiltered dist 92, bott 02 db **(81) n**20 **t**21 **f**20 **b**20. Some pleasant honey flits around. **46%**

Signatory Edradour 1989 Glass Decanter Collection cask 354, dist 26/09/89, bott 22/01/03 db **(74) n**17 **t**20 **f**18 **b**19. A very disappointing, below-average cask. **57.2%**. *608 bottles*.

Old Masters Edradour 1976 bott 02 **(81) n**21 **f**22 **f**18 **b**20. As one might expect, a very distinctive and different dram: heavy with unusual spices but some honey to see off some slightly bitter notes on the finish. **49%**. *James MacArthur*.

❖ **Edradour Signatory Aged 10 Years** cask 361, dist Oct 93, bott 24 Feb 04, db **(89) n**22 firm sherry; ample rich fruitcake; **t**23 lots of youthful, rich barley and then wave upon wave of faultlessly clean grape; **f**21 remains young in character; **b**23 a very unusual but entertaining marriage between young barley and big sherry. **46%**

Signatory Edradour 24 Years Old dist 76, bott 01 **(63) n**15 **t**17 **f**15 **b**16. Soapy. Flawed. **50.8%**. *432 bottles*.

FETTERCAIRN
Highland (Eastern), 1824. Whyte and Mackay. Working.

Fettercairn 1824 db **(69) n**17 **t**19 **f**16 **b**17 By Fettercairn standards, not a bad offering. Relatively free from its inherent sulphury and rubbery qualities, this displays a sweet nutty character not altogther unattractive – though I think caramel plays a calming role here. Still need my arm twisting for a second glass, though. **40%**

❖ **Connoisseurs Choice Fettercairn 1992 (61) n**13 **t**17 **f**16 **b**15. Sulphury, burning car tyres on the nose and cloying sweetness on the palate with a dirty finish. Business as usual at Fettercairn, then. **46%**. *Gordon & MacPhail*.

Old Fettercairn Stillman's Dram 26 Years Old db **(88) n**22 beauty and the beast ... there are some strange off-notes but they are rendered completely irrelevant by the most gorgeous fruity fanfare you could wish for. Anyone who has ever plucked over-ripe figs off the tree will know where I am coming from here, **t**23 charismatic and playful, the malt offers an astonishingly rich theme for even more fruit to develop; **f**22 a hint of spice and a few thickening oaky tones amid the rebuilding rubber. But it's a joy; **b**21 OK folks time to lie down: I am about to say it. It's Fettercairn. And I love it. A flawed gem maybe, but a gem nonetheless. **45%** *(Note to readers: I have just counted and discovered this is the 888th distillery-recognised Scotch single malt I have tasted for this book. And it gets a mark of 88 ... what's the chances of that happening, eh?)*

Old Fettercairn Stillman's Dram 30 Years Old db **(84) n**21 **t**22 **f**20 **b**21. To celebrate my 1,000th named distillery Scotch single malt tasted specially for this book I turned to my old nemesis, Fettercairn. And I celebrated in style: a chunky, clean dram with plenty of orangey notes on the nose and deep malt on the palate. **45%**

James MacArthur Fettercairn 1992 bott 02 **(63) n**16 t16 f15 b16. Ah! Pure Fettercairn! **60.5%**

GLEN ALBYN
Highland (Northern) 1846–1983. Demolished.

Glen Albyn Aged 26 Years Rare Malts Collection dist 75 db **(88) n**22 fruity and floral there is still some surprising gristy freshness; **t**23 big kick, but not from the alcohol. The spices seem to have a sugary coating to which the malt is attached. A very unusual mouthfeel but wholly delicious; **f**21 yet more spice with oak massaging and nibbling the tastebuds **b**22 quite a sensual whisky, full of clout but the sweetness disguises the collosal nature of the beast. **54.8%**. *6,000 bottles.*

Connoisseurs Choice Glen Albyn 1972 (85) n23 very softly peated, dreamy; **t**21 malty and sweet with some drying oak; **f**20 sugar-coated soft peat; **b**21 a complex, delicate dram. **40%**. *Gordon & MacPail.*

Connoisseurs Choice Glen Albyn 1974 (83) n19 t23 f20 b21. Skip the nose and finish and concentrate directly on the sugar-barley palate. **40%**

Old Malt Cask Glen Albyn 26 Years Old dist Apr 74, bott Jun 00 **(69) n**18 t19 f15 b17. Thin, overly or sickly sweet, one-dimensional. The finish is a bit grim. **50%**. *Douglas Laing. 264 bottles.*

Old Malt Cask Glen Albyn Aged 34 Years dist Dec 66, bott May 01 **(79) n**21 t20 f19 b19. Toasty, burny honeycomb. Just slightly too aged. But single casks don't come any rarer than this! **42%. nc ncf.** *Douglas Laing. 66 bottles.*

GLENALLACHIE
Speyside, 1968. Chivas. Working.

❖ **Dun Bheagan Glenallachie 1991 Aged 12 Years** bourbon barrel bott 11 Sept 03 **(86) n**21 crisp, spotlessly clean barley; **t**22 easily the most friendly delivery of malt from a bottle of Glenallachie in living memory; **f**21 not overly long but just a shaft of honey to help soften the more bitter oak; **b**22 it appears the raging fire that normally accompanies Glenallachie has been doused. **43%**. *William Maxwell.*

❖ **Scotch Single Malt Circle Glenallachie 1981** cask 600 dist 18 May 81, bott 4 Nov 03 **(79) n**21 t20 f19 b19. A malty, fudgy sweetness negates the burning undercurrent. By no means the worst Glenallachie I've tasted. **55.9%** *Germany.*

Usquebaugh Society Glenallachie 1991 dist 5/3/91, bott 16/3/01 **(76) n**19 t21 f18 b18. Rock-hard and barley-sharp; pleasant, refreshing blending fodder. **46%. ncf.** *NL.*

GLENBURGIE
Speyside, 1810. Allied. Working.

Cask Glenburgie 1984 (87) n22 clean malt: grassy, rich, oak-toffee; **t**23 mouthwatering, clean, exemplary Speyside; **f**20 shortish with some vanilla driving home; **b**22 Glenburgie at its most illustrious. **62.3%**. *Gordon & MacPail.*

❖ **Douglas Taylor Glenburgie 1969 Aged 34 Years** cask 6753 **(78) n**21 t20 f18 b19. Begins maltily, but later a fraction too resinous. **45.7%**

❖ **Gordon and MacPhail Glenburgie 1964 (91) n**22 blood oranges and putty; quite attractive, really; **t**22 dense barley-oak body but the sweetness from the malt really is excellent; **f**24 serious amounts of very dark chocolate dissipate as an oily maltfest returns with some late citrus and spice; almost too well orchestrated and beautifully behaved to be true; **b**23 this is one of those really old numbers that defy age and belief. Just so, so beautiful. **40%**

Gordon & MacPhail Glenburgie Aged 10 Years (77) n19 t20 f19 b19. Chewy, with curious coal-smoke weight. **40%**

Hart Brothers Glenburgie aged 35 Years (84) n21 t22 f20 b21. Like a prim Edwardian village maid, it exudes old fashioned grace, subtle scents and a dry, dusty charm.

⠶ **Old Malt Cask Glenburgie Aged 13 Years** dist Nov 90, bott Nov 03 **(91)** n23 a seductive peppering of faultless floral tones sweetly strengthened by biscuits and barley. So delicious! t23 complimentary complexity that mirrors the nose; a quite brilliant saltiness adds piquancy; f22 much more oak apparent here with some cocoa tones continuing the drying trend; b23 this is a sophisticated malt offering a fabulous coastal tang. The complexity goes through the roof: a golden nugget of a malt. **50%. nc ncf sc.** Douglas Laing. 240 bottles.

GLENCADAM
Highland (Eastern), 1825. Angus Dundee. Working.

Cadenhead's Glencadam 13 Years Old dist 89, bott 03/03 **(80)** n19 t22 f20 b19. Syrupy stuff: sweet, sugar-coated malt that's more candy than whisky. **59.4%**

Connoisseurs Choice Glencadam 1974 (75) n20 t19 f18 b18. Pleasant, middle-of-the-road. **40%.** Gordon & MacPhail.

Connoisseurs Choice Glencadam 1987 (80) n21 t22 f18 b19. An abrupt finish to something that promised much on nose and early malt start. **40%.** Gordon & MacPhail.

⠶ **Mackillop's Choice Glencadam 1974** cask no 10 dist 23 Dec 74, bott Oct 01 **(88)** n22 winey; toffee apples; t23 massive arrival on the palate full of oily, mildly molassed barley; f21 long and warming with just an injection of natural caramel; b22 a way above average expression from this distillery, absolutely full of mouthwatering complexity. The best Glencadam around. **59.9%. nc ncf.** Iain Mackillop & Co.

Old Malt Cask Glencadam 28 Year Old dist Dec 71. bott July 00 **(72)** n16 t21 f19 b16. Massively sweet and intense middle, otherwise all over the place. Not, I suspect, from the world's greatest cask. **50%.** Douglas Laing. 268 bottles.

⠶ **Whisky Galore Glencadam 1991 Aged 12 Years (83)** n20 t22 f21 b20. What we are talking here is clean, simple, uncomplicated and pretty delicious malt – with the emphasis on malt. **46%.** Douglas Taylor & Co.

GLENCRAIG
Speyside, 1958. Allied. Two Lomond stills operating within the Glenburgie plant. Now silent.

Connoisseurs Choice Glencraig 1970 (90) n22 oily, malty notes of considerable weight and brilliant bitter-sweet balance. The fruit is ripe and salivating; t22 big malt, with deft oiliness that gives weight to the body. Silky and sits perfectly on the palate. A touch of smoke is an added bonus; f22 vanilla and sweet malt; b24 this is absolutely brilliant malt: why it was discontinued I'll never know. Few Speysiders achieve such harmony in weight and balance. If you ever see a bottle, grab it if it's the last thing you do. And heartfelt congrats to G&M for preserving posterity: and priceless posterity at that. A company way ahead of its time. **40%.** Gordon & MacPhail.

Connoisseurs Choice Glencraig 1975 (85) n21 crushed bananas in milk sprinkled with brown sugar. Oily malts filter through for company; t22 the oak is doing its best to dry out the enormous malt kick and to an extent succeeds; f21 slightly bitter thanks to the oak, but that sugared malt refuses to give up the fight, sticking grimly to the roof of the mouth, offering a brief flicker of peat into the bargain; b21 a once great whisky that has seen better days and trying for all its worth to maintain dignity. It suceeds this time, but for how much longer only later bottlings will reveal. **40%.** Gordon & MacPhail.

GLENDRONACH
Speyside, 1826. Allied. Working.

⋄⋄ **Glendronach 12 Years Old Double Matured** db **(83)** n*20* t*20* f*22* b*21*. Coal gas and minor smoke amid the sweet barley and fruit, including bitter blood orange. I still say the best Glendronach 12 was abandoned about a decade ago which was, I think, all from ex-bourbon. I wonder if that short-lived classic will ever return. **40%**. *Allied Distillers.*

Glendronach 15 Years Old db **(83)** n*20* t*22* f*20* b*21*. Chocolate fudge and grape juice to start then tails off towards a slightly bitter, dry finish. **40%**

⋄⋄ **The Glendronach 1968** db **(92)** n*23* nuts, clean sherry of the highest order; t*22* exceptionally together with the most vibrant oloroso: not a single off note; f*23* astonishing depth, with more than a touch of pot still Demerara (PM mark to be precise); b*24* an almost extinct style of sherry that is faultless in its firmness and clarity. This was bottled in 1993 – I remember it well. Astonishingly, some bottles have just turned up in Whisky of the World Duty Free in UK and this is how it tastes now. Grab while you can. **43%**

Berry's Own Glendronach 1990 bott 03 **(81)** n*18* t*22* f*20* b*21*. A very curious Glendronach, having absorbed very little colour but enough on the nose to suggest this is not from the greatest of casks. A hint of peat and some beautifully intense malt make for a magic few moments on entering the mouth, but the finish is closed and hard. **46%**. *Berry Bros*

⋄⋄ **Blackadder Raw Cask Glendronach 28 Years Old** cask 3407 dist Dec 74, bott Nov 03 **(85)** n*19* closed, except for a little sap, and unpromising; t*22* a miraculous recovery of rich barley amid some eager oak; f*22* surprisingly sugary as the barley fights back against the liquorice; b*22* limps its way to an attractive conclusion. **48.6%**

Old Malt Cask Glendronach Aged 22 Years (87) n*21* malty, clean but thin; t*23* complex: sweet yet spicy ,fruity yet malty; f*22* the spice continues and gathers sweetness; b*21* a confused and confusing dram that can't make its mind up where it wants to go: superb nonetheless. **50%. nc ncf.** *Douglas Laing. 252 bottles.*

Old Malt Cask Glendronach Aged 24 Years dist Nov 76, bott Sept 01 **(91)** n*22* t*24* f*22* b*23*. Better than anything bottled so far by the distillery. Possibly the ultimate Glendronach. **50%. nc ncf.** *Douglas Laing. 228 bottles.*

Old Malt Cask Aged 26 Years dist Dec 74, bott Aug 01 **(86)** n*23* t*22* f*20* b*21*. A malt on the edge. **47.5%. nc ncf.** *Douglas Laing. 198 bottles.*

⋄⋄ **Whisky Galore Glendronach 1990 Aged 13 Years (86)** n*21* that not unfamiliar coal-gassy very distantly peated aroma on a bed of firm barley; t*22* sweet fresh barley with a mildly bitter, tangy twist; subtle smoke; f*21* a simple denouemont of vanilla and barley; b*22* Glendronach being outwardly simple, but a little more classy and complex than it first appears.

⋄⋄ **Wilson & Morgan Barrel Selection Glendronach 1990** Port Finish bott 04 **(86)** n*18* a faint wisp of something irritatingly sulphury blunts the spicey charge; t*23* so light and delicate it's the souffle of single malts, except there is more of the trifle about this with the fruit and custard notes that abound; f*23* continues on its spotlessly clean course with a development of that spice stifled on the nose and some massive grassy barley and bitter cocoa for good measure; b*22* this must have come from a fresh port pipe after years in a second fill bourbon. The result looks like distilled flamingo, but a lot more mouthwatering. **46%**

GLENDULLAN (*see also below*)
Speyside, 1898–1985. Closed.

Platinum Old and Rare Glendullan Aged 34 Years dist Mar 72, bott Jan 03 **(78)** n*20* t*22* f*18* b*18*. Big malty mouth arrival but the balance suffers later. **46.8%. nc ncf.**

Platinum Old and Rare Glendullan 36 Years Old (89) n*20* the oak is in the vanguard followed by a train of marginally sweeter elements. Malt and vanilla intertwine plus spice and sultanas. A dash of peat is in there for extra weight; t*23* outstanding arrival of beautifully textured and sweetened malt – almost gristy in the way it dissolves in the mouth. The oak is much less pronounced than on the nose except for the very initialimpact. Wonderfully spiced; f*23* long, very subtly smoked with a bombardment of peppers giving way to cocoa; b*23* a whisky of brilliance from the original old stills of this little-known but reliable Speysider. **55.1%. nc ncf.** *Douglas Laing.*

GLENDULLAN (*see* also above)
Speyside, 1972. Diageo. Working.

Glendullan Aged 8 Years db **(89)** n*20* fresh, gingery, zesty; t*22* distinctly mealy and malty. f*24* brilliant – really stunning grassy malt powers through. Speyside in a glass – and a nutshell; b*23* this is just how I like my Speysiders: young fresh and uplifting. A charming malt.

Glendullan Aged 12 Years (old stock circa 99, bottling mark – on reverse of label – LLJB0461179, light green print) db **(90)** n*22* t*23* f*22* b*23*. This is a great Speyside dram: big, strong yet never muscular. Superb. **43%.** *Flora and Fauna range.*

Glendullan Aged 12 Years (new stock circa 03, bottling mark – on reverse of label – L19R01457997, dark green print) db **(77)** n*19* t*20* f*19* b*19*. Oily, flat and bitter towards the finish. Really disappointing. **43%.** *Flora and Fauna range.*

GLEN ELGIN
Speyside, 1900. Diageo. Working.

Glen Elgin Aged 12 Years db **(89)** n*23* blistering, mouthwatering fruit of unspecified origin. The intensity of the malt is breathtaking; t*24* stunning fresh malt arrival, salivating barley that is both crisp and lush: then a big round of spice amid some squashed, over-ripe plums. Faultless mouthfeel; f*20* the spice continues as does the intense malt but is devalued dramatically by a bitter-toffee effect; b*22* absolutely murders Cragganmore as Diageo's top dog bottled Speysider. The marks would be several points further north if one – rightly or wrongly – didn't get the feeling that some caramel was weaving a derogatory spell. Brilliant stuff nonetheless. States Pot Still on label – not to be confused with Irish Pot Still. This is 100% malt... and it shows! **43%**

⠴ **Glen Elgin Aged 32 Years** db **(68)** n*15* t*19* f*17* b*17.* Unacceptably soapy and sappy, even for its age. Really disappointing. **42.3%**

Adelphi Glen Elgin 26 Years Old cask 3, dist 74, bott 00 **(82)** n*21* t*20* f*20* b*21.* Plenty of quality about this dram, but I would love to have tasted it as a 10-year-old! **57.3%**

Connoisseurs Choice Glen Elgin 1968 (77) n*20* t*19* f*19* b*19.* Big chewy, sweet malt, but totters very slightly under some unwieldy oak. **40%**

⠴ **Scotch Single Malt Circle Glen Elgin 1991** cask 4062 bott Mar 04, Oct 02 **(69)** n*17* t*18* f*17* b*17.* Sulphur tainted and hot. **61.9%.** *Germany.*

⠴ **Whisky Galore Glen Elgin 1991 Aged 12 Years (71)** n*17* t*19* f*17* b*18.* No shortage of bitter orange; at time teeth-tingling sweet but the odd off note too many. **46%.** *Duncan Taylor.*

GLENESK
Highland (Eastern), 1897–1985. Closed.

Hillside 25 Years Old Rare Malts Selection db **(83)** n*20* t*23* f*20* b*20.* Hot as Hades, but for a Glenesk this gets off to a cracking start and is let down only by the paucity of the finale. Plenty to enjoy, though, with some really top-rate malt-honey notes. **62%**

Connoisseurs Choice Glenesk 1982 (68) n*17* t*18* f*16* b*17*. Poorly made whisky. Not at all pleasant. **40%**. *Gordon & MacPhail.*

Connoisseurs Choice Glenesk 1984 (77) n*19* t*20* f*19* b*19*. Sticky and syrupy. **40%**. *Gordon & MacPhail.*

Connoisseurs Choice Glenesk 1985 bott 00 **(67)** n*19* t*17* f*15* b*16*. Attractive nose, goes downhill rapidly. **40%**. *Gordon & MacPhail.*

GLENFARCLAS
Speyside, 1836. J&G Grant. Working.

Glenfarclas 8 Years Old db **(76)** n*18* t*20* f*19* b*19*. Fresh, tangy, fruity and chewy. **40%**. *J&G Grant.*

Glenfarclas 10 Years Old db **(77)** n*15* t*21* f*21* b*20*. Great honey notes. **40%**. *J&G Grant.*

Glenfarclas 12 Years Old db **(90)** n*22* honeycomb and barley concentrate; t*23* just about perfect mouthfeel: a touch oily but gloriously sweet barley, a dash of fruit and drying vanilla; f*23* much less demonstrative, but the oak is sublime, the length eternal; b*22* it is unlikely Speyside offers a much better 12-year-old. **43%**. *J&G Grant.*

Glenfarclas 15 Years Old db **(74)** n*17* t*20* f*19* b*18*. Never quite gets going. **46%**. *J&G Grant.*

Glenfarclas 21 Years Old db **(89)** n*24* a touch of peat adds weight to a stunning, nigh-on faultless aroma; t*22* honey and oak form parallel layers, with something smoky in between; f*21* vanilla and honey plus some grape-juice sweetness. The smoke also hangs on; b*22* what genuinely top quality malt this is. **43%**. *J&G Grant.*

Glenfarclas 25 Years Old db **(91)** n*22* beautifully developed oak, yet remains light and malty; t*23* the complexity on the mouth-arrival is glorious: fruit and malt abound, honey confirms the age; f*23* some wonderful spices percolate, firm oak finale. b*23* this is just great whisky. Absolutely top class. **43%**. *J&G Grant.*

Glenfarclas 30 Years Old db **(82)** n*22* t*20* f*21* b*19*. Delicious, but a few wrinkles. **43%**. *J&G Grant.*

Glenfarclas 40 Years Old Millennium Edition db **(92)** n*23* beautifully defined oak which has taken on a handsomely sweet bourbon character. This is almost chestnut sweet, very softly peated and enticingly gentle. Steps up a gear when warmed in the hand with tantalising spices keeping in harmony with waxy malt and ultra-clean sherry. The way the old oak behaves itself and toes the line is nothing short of wonderful; t*23* the oak is again first to show but remains soft and laid back and teasingly spicy. The initial burst of oak does suggest a worn dryness, but this is soon counterbalanced by a demerara sweetness. This blends effortlessly with some heavy, intense malt and a lingering but quite unmistakable hint of liquorice which emerges from the refined sherry-trifle middle; f*23* long, chewy, smoky and initially sweet with the liquorice continuing, but dries very slowly to deliver an oaky encore. Stays just the right side of being vanilla rich to ensure continuing charm and quality; b*23* an almost immaculate portrayal of an old-fashioned, high-quality malt with unblemished sherry freshness and depth. The hallmark of quality is the sherry's refusal to dominate the spicy, softly peated malt. The oak offers a bourbony sweetness but ensures a rich depth throughout. Quite outstanding for its age. **nc ncf**. *J&G Grant.*

Glenfarclas 105 Cask Strength db **(75)** n*18* t*19* f*20* b*18*. Sweet and raw. **60%** *J&G Grant.*

Glenfarclas 1968 db **(82)** n*20* t*22* f*19* b*21*. Initially hot and spicy, but some wonderful natural toffee and honey in there. Another effortless beauty from a great distillery. **54.1%. nc ncf**. *J&G Grant.*

Glenfarclas 1968 Cask 684 db bott 00 **(90)** n*24* t*21* f*23* b*22*. If you ever wonder why I mark down so many latter-day sherry casks, just try this for size.

An almost lost style of sherry: one of flawless intensity. Only a touch of deliciously OTT oak prevents this from being a masterpiece. **54.2%. nc ncf.** *J&G Grant.*

◌ **Glenfarclas Vintage 1968** db **(92)** n23 Glenfarclas at its most slick with the grape possessing a sheen which balances so well with the orange-vanilla; hard to detect which, if either is leading or the base note – which means textbook complexity; t23 no shortage of burnt raisins and bourbon; f23 burnt fudge and some grapey remnants amid the burgeoning barley; b23 just one of those sherry casks that was destined for greatness in Scotland. **43%.** *USA.*

Glenfarclas 1968 Vintage (88) n24 an exhibition of subtlety. slightly nutty with no more than a hint of oak and a coating of sherry: refined and sophisticated; t21 sweet barley and soft vanillins; f21 a succession of soft oak tones, with vanilla dominant; b22 never quite lives up to the mercurial nose, but sheer quality nonetheless. **43%.** *J & G Grant.*

Glenfarclas 1970 db **(83)** n20 t20 f22 b21. Rich and spicy. **50.1%. nc ncf.** *J&G Grant.*

Glenfarclas 1973 Sherry 1st Fill db **(88)** n21 a massive nose with even some gentle smoke escaping through the sherry and oak; t23 intense, sweet, gloriously fruity; f22 soft oak that dries at a very slow pace; b22 a mountain of a whisky to start with significant oak presence, but quietens into a delicate thing by the finish. Great stuff. **51.4%. nc ncf.** *J&G Grant.*

◌ **Glenfarclas Vintage 1973** db **(89)** n24 wood, but as perfect in aromatic form as the sound of a crack through the covers for four (that will baffle our American friends...) The sherry is profound but sculpted like the wood; hints of old Demerara rum complete the picture of a beauty in velvet robes; t21 thin mouth arrival at first and then grape dominates; some vanilla forces much-needed depth; f22 stupendously nutty, softly oiled and clean, there is a lingering bitter-sweet swan song; b22 a deceptively delicate malt where some complexity is over-ridden by oil. **46%.** *Germany.*

Glenfarclas 1974 Vintage db **(89)** n22 light, fino-style sherry influence with the malt its usual subtle self; t22 dry oak arrival vanished quickly to allow the sweetest malt: great spice; f22 lashings of rich malt and very late cocoa; b23 for all the sweetness, this is just so delicate. **43%. nc ncf.** *J&G Grant.*

Glenfarclas 1978 db **(83)** n22 t21 f20 b20. Sweet chestnuts and malt to nose; hot, sweet and malty to taste. **53.3%.nc ncf.** *J&G Grant.*

Glenfarclas 1979 db **(89)** n22 big, sweet, chocolate pudding and fruit; t23 spicy from the off and a lovely fanning out of chewy malt and burnt fudge; f22 very long with some toasted honeycomb in there; b22 a big, bruising, full-flavoured malt that takes no prisoners. **51.8%. nc ncf.** *J&G Grant.*

Glenfarclas 1980 db **(69)** n16 t19 f17 b17 . Rich but sulphur-stained. **55%.** *J&G Grant.*

Glenfarclas 1983 db dist 9/3/83, bott 16/12/02 **(78)** n18 t21 f20 b19. Punchy fruit and some bite. **43%.** *J&G Grant.*

◌ **Glenfarclas Vintage 1987 Refill Oloroso Cask** db **(93)** n23 spiced toffee apple, ripe greengages and even the most distant hint of something smoky; t23 puckeringly dry at first, the sherry effect is pure fresh oloroso. Sweetens out as the malt battles through; f23 seriously long and complex: thankfully lots of very natural toffee fails to take the edge off the malt sharpness while the spices gather momentum; b24 sherry bottlings of this integrity and class are appallingly thin on the ground. I have come all the way to Europe to track it down: and worth every mile travelled, too. **46%.** *Imported by Mahler-Besse, Bordeaux.*

Glenfarclas 1988 Vintage 12 Years Old Oloroso sherry bott 2000 db **(84)** n21 t22 f20 b21. Subtle, with lovely natural toffee and above-average oak for its age. **43%.** *J&G Grant.*

Glenfarclas 1986 Fino Sherry Cask db **(90)** n22 appears thin by Glenfarclas standards but genuinely complex with dry oak and sweeter toffeed malt; **t**22 an explosion of very sweet malt followed rapidly by something much drier; **f**23 very dry and mildly salty with some bitter cocoa; **b**23 an eye-closing, think-about-it dram. A laid-back classic. **43%.** *J&G Grant.*

Glenfarclas 1989 Oloroso Sherry Cask 1st Fill db **(90) n**24 cream toffee, mocha, brown sugar – and not an off-note in sight; **t**23 mouthwatering sweet malt despite the forming dry notes. The oak is quite chunky for its age, but the malt and sherry are wonderfully sure-footed. Not dissimilar to a demerara pot-still rum in mouthfeel; **f**21 the oak gathers pace to offer liquorice and soft oils; **b**22 it says "1st fill Sherry" on the label. A waste of ink. Just one sniff will tell you! **43%. nc ncf.** *J&G Grant.*

⁘ **Glenfarclas Vintage 1990** db **(88) n**23 flawless sherry with thick barley refusing to be outdone. Impressive; **t**22 dry sherry leads the way before a grapey sweeting and spicy richness intervenes; **f**21 a bit sluggish towards the finale with a sherry-toffee simplicity; **b**22 just refuses to go that extra mile for complexity. **46%.** *Germany.*

Glenfarclas 1990 Family Malt Collection db **(79) n**18 **t**20 **f**22 **b**19. Rich, chewy, salty with big finish. **43%.** *J&G Grant.*

⁘ **Glenfarclas 105 Cask Strength 10 Years Old** db **(84) n**20 **t**21 **f**22 **b**21. Much better than the old 8-year-old version with nothing like the helter-skelter ride and surprising late oil **60%**

⁘ **Adelphi The Whisky That Cannot Be Named 1953** cask 1668 dist 53 **(89) n**23 defies the years with a cushioned impact of natural caramel, vanilla and grape; lovely bourbony sub-plot; **t**23 confident nuggets of oak but the intense, slightly honeyed, barley-grape counter delights; **f**20 runs slightly out of steam towards the softly oaked finale, but after 50 years, who wouldn't; **b**22 they won't say which distillery this comes from but, to me, Glenfarclas is written all over this: few can display such sherried countenance after so many years. The perfect birthday dram for all those born in that year. **54.3%**

⁘ **Blackadder Blairfindy Aged 23 Years** cask 2003/BF/01 dist Jun 80, bott Nov 03 **(77) n**19 **t**20 **f**19 **b**19. Heavily oaked. **57.5%**

Blackadder Raw Cask Blairfindy Aged 40 Years first-fill sherry cask 5, dist 9 Jan 1963, bott Mar 03 **(89) n**23 salty, pulsating sherry and heavy roast Brazilian coffee; **t**24 ridiculously clean and beautifully defined fruit, lush and sensuously spiced with a hint of something a tad smoky; **f**20 rather hard and bitter as the oak kicks in without remorse. Just enough fruit to hold shape; **b**22 even the severe finish cannot take away from the joy of the nose and mouth arrival. **52.3%.** The label doesn't mention Glenfarclas. Blackadder won't confirm or deny, but didn't the Grant family have a farm called by some similar name? Anyway, sheer Glenfarclas in character: it is hard to think of many other distilleries quite capable of producing something this good.

Blackadder Raw Cask Blairfindy 1990 cask 5983, dist 6 Jun 80, bott May 02 **(91) n**22 thick sherry: wild blackcurrants and peppery spices about; **t**24 a dry oaky edge to a pulsing, peppery start then sweetness with malt and fruit: massive; **f**22 quite long with a good malt flow-through that softens the big oak impact. Rich sherry holds its ground; **b**23 enormous whisky of unquestionable quality. **57.6%**

Cadenhead's Glenfarclas 31 Years Old dist 70, bott 06/02 **(88) n**21 big, weighty fruit – diced apple, banana, plums and grape. And some malt squeezes in while a bourbony character develops to show the oak; **t**23 clean as a whistle. The fruit and malt combine with soft caresses for a wonderfully rich, chewy middle. Still a little bourbony in style; **f**22 long, natural toffee joining the lingering fruit and malt; **b**22 an elegant and refined non-distillery version of a fine, rich malt. **54.4%**

Craigellachie Hotel of Speyside Glenfarclas 1972 Single Cask Bottling 2001 cask 3540, dist 30/05/72, bott 7/12/01 **(87) n**22 **t**22 **f**21 **b**22. A bracing dram for chilly midwinters beside a roaring fire and for those who like oak in the glass as well as the panelling around them. **51.2%.** *UK. 602 bottles.*

⊹ **Distillery No 3 Glenfarclas 1990** cask no 1106 **(88) n**18 very slightly tainted; fruit-barley background; **t**23 outstanding weight and mouthfeel; the very softest of honey deliveries armed with a sweet fruit salad; **f**24 the honey drives on, this time into a darker, deeper honeycomb: your tastebuds can only marvel at the deliciousness of the onslaught; **b**23 the honey that surges through this malt, unusual for this distillery in bottled form, is stuff of dreams. Highly unusual Glenfarclas in bottled form and, nose apart, quite outstanding. **46%. ncf.** *Denmark.*

MacLeod's Speyside Aged 8 Years (86) n21 slightly nutty, crisp barley with some distinctive tangerine notes. Some digestive biscuit saltiness combines with soft oak trace: delicate and complex; **t**22 fresh, sharp, mildly green arrival on palate with some silky barley playing off against subtle citrus. Lovely sheen offering an oily coating to the roof of the mouth from which some oaky weight hangs; **f**21 amazingly clean and uncluttered with some coffee hanging on to the barley, quite chewy but always fresh; **b**22 a real delight of a dram: busy and fresh on the tastebuds. Just love the soft coffee tones as the first oak notes kick in. **40%.** *Ian MacLeod (Glenfarclas malt used, though not stated).*

Peerless Glenfarclas 1967 cask 5811, dist Oct 67 **(69) n**21 **t**17 **f**16 **b**15. Several summers too old. **42.9%.** *Duncan Taylor & Co. Ltd.*

⊹ **Scotch Malt Whisky Society Cask 1.107 Aged 38 Years (80) n**21 light with gentle marzipan; **t**20 deft malt offers a wonderful sweetness; the oak closes fast; **f**19 unobstructed oaky tones; **b**20 the Society has made 107 trips to this, its first, distillery: perhaps this was not its most successful. **48%. nc ncf sc.**

GLENFIDDICH
Speyside, 1887. William Grant & Sons. Working.

Glenfiddich Special Reserve (no age statement) db **(88) n**21 fresh, grassy, clean, salivating; **t**23 perhaps the crispest, freshest most mouthwatering malts known to mankind: young yet energetic clean beyond measure and a waft of gentle peat for a hint of weight; **f**22 such wonderful, unequalled grassy malt with a touch of vanilla; **b**22 no longer produced and now a malt for collectors: one that brings a tear to the eye of us 40-somethings. This is malt that kept us going when none others were obtainable. Never has the term "familiarity breeds contempt" ever been more apposite to any whisky as this. It's become de rigueur in recent years for connoisseurs to rubbish this whisky (though, it has to be said, never by me) as a poor man's malt. A brilliant, effervescent whisky missed more sorely than words can describe. I never thought I would find myself writing those words, but there you have it. I believe in honesty: I have built my reputation on it. And in all honesty, the whisky world is poorer without this unpretentious, landmark malt. The official "Bring Back The No-Age Statement Glenfiddich Special Reserve" campaign starts here. **40%**

Glenfiddich Aged 12 Years Caoran Reserve db **(84) n**19 **t**23 **f**21 **b**21. Juicy, lively, deliciously spiced, crisp malt, mildly smoky. **40%**

Glenfiddich Aged 12 Years Special Reserve db **(80) n**20 **t**22 **f**19 **b**19. Delicious malt but perhaps a touch too much caramel subtracts from the otherwise juicy maltfest. Just not the same as the old (younger) version. Much flatter and less fun than its predecessor. **40%**

Glenfiddich Aged 15 Years Cask Strength db **(80) n**21 **t**21 **f**19 **b**19 Very toffeed: is it the oak or possibly caramel? Big dram, all the same. **51%**

Glenfiddich Aged 15 Years Solera Reserve db **(93) n**24 a marriage of citrus notes (especially oranges) subtle spices and oak; **t**23 honey leads the way with balancing spices and oak. The malt remains fresh and refreshing; **f**23 medium to long with soft sherry and gently building cocoa; **b**23 this is one of my regular drams, and the one I immediately display to people who rubbish Glenfiddich. Over the years I have noticed a shift in quality in both directions, the best being two marks higher, the worst cropping six points, mainly due to traces of sulphur on the sherry. However, this sample is pretty representative of a quite brilliant Speyside malt of awesome complexity. Just wish they'd up the strength and make it nonchillfiltered and noncoloured. **40%**

Glenfiddich Aged 18 Years Ancient Reserve db **(92) n**24 blood oranges, apples, the most gentle of smoke and oaky saltiness: delicate, complex and enormously sexy; **t**23 those oranges are there again as the malt melts in the mouth. Quite salty still but sherry and sultanas to fatten things up, brown sugar sweetens things a little; **f**22 a dry finale of medium length with unsweetened mocha: clean, chewy and well-defined; **b**23 another nail in the coffin of those who sniffily insist that Glenfiddich can't make good whisky. Taste this – and Solera Reserve – then find me two distillery-bottled malts of this age anywhere on Speyside that offers this enormity of complexity and sheer élan.

Glenfiddich Aged 21 Years Havana Reserve db **(75) n**19 **t**20 **f**18 **b**18. I know a lot of people are jumping up and down about this one in excitement. But, sorry, I just don't get the picture. Cuban rums tend to be light in character, so in theory it should marry with the distillery's elegant character. However, we seem to have everything cancelling each other out leaving a pleasant experience with a decent cream coffee-toffee middle/finish, but little else besides to really get the pulses racing. **40%**

Glenfiddich Aged 21 Years Millennium Reserve db **(86) n**22 spritely barley; vaguely doughy and suet-like, a wisp of smoke; **t**22 refreshing barley juice with lovely build-up in sweetness; **f**21 a move towads a bourbon/Canadian style but intervention by toffee; **b**21 a very shy, delicate dram best at full strength and not quite fully warmed. **43%**

·:::· **Glenfiddich 1974 Aged 29 Years** cask 2336 db **(88) n**23 softly, softly sherry punctuated by delicate and complex bourbon notes and the most distant hint of peat: just so sophisticated **t**23 that bourbon theme arrives immediately, with fabulous "small grain" depth; a heavier fruit layer holds the roof of the mouth **f**19 thins out rather with grapey vanilla holding court **b**23 not all Glenfiddich casks show such class at this age but this realy is a minor gem of almost hypnotic complexity **48.9%** *Exclusive to The Whisky Exchange*

Glenfiddich 30 Years Old db **(85) n**22 the sweetness is so similar to when you open up a tin of "Quality Street" chocolates: cocoa and nuts, marzipan, coconut, plastic wrappers ... well, maybe not the wrappers; **t**22 delicate malt notes, a swift wave of peaty spice and then a slight menthol oakiness; **f**20 very light, clean and gently toffeed. Dry oak gathers momentum for the finale; **b**21 comes through just about unscathed by time, or at least the scars don't show too badly. **40%**

Glenfiddich Rare Collection 40 Years Old db **(92) n**23 curiously and attractively smoked, lots of sweet vanilla and stunning spices: remarkable and beautiful; **t**24 brimming with oaky, toasty vanilla, malt punching through for silky, rich and mildly honied middle. Signs of oaky wear and tear, but do not detract from the overall beauty; **f**22 remains silky with a return of peat, mixed with cocoa; **b**23 quite brilliant for a Glenfiddich of this antiquity: rarely does it survive to this age. In fact, brilliant for any distillery. **43.6%**. *600 bottles.*

Glenfiddich 1937 db **(94) n**24 smoky, almost agricultural farmyardy, with kippers spitting on the range, salted butter melting into them. Quite beautiful, the peat almost hitting perfection. Truly unique; **t**23 sweet malt that just dissolves around the mouth but leaving traces of the most elegant oak, almost too soft to be true. Again the smoke is just stunning in its elegance; **f**23 long, silky, soft oak and – amazingly – clean barley; **b**24 when this was distilled my football team, Millwall, reached the FA Cup semi final. My late dad went to the game in my old mate Michael Jackson's country, 'uddersfield. We lost 2–1. They haven't reached the FA Cup semi finals since. I'll taste this again the next time we do ... it could be a long wait. From a sheer whisky perspective, proof – alongside some older Macallans – that Speyside once made a much peatier dram, one which perhaps only Ardmore can today match. How this whisky has remained this truly fabulous for so long has been entirely in the lap of the Gods. To whoever, whatever, is responsible: thank you!! NOTE TO 2005 EDITION: On April 4th, 2004, Millwall did, miraculously, reach another FA Cup semi-final. And beat the team they lost to in 1937. So my wait to taste it was shorter than I could even dream … **40%. 61 bottles only** (going for in the region of £10,000 each).

Glenfiddich 1961 Vintage Reserve db **(75) n**20 lots of toffee-fudge and barley; **t**19 honied and soft with a wave of gentle peat that is not evident on the nose and various oaky notes; **f**18 a bit flat and oaky-dimensional; **b**18 hasn't withstood the test of time quite as well as might be hoped. **43.2%. sc.**

Glenfiddich 1967 Vintage Reserve db **(87) n**23 sensuous, softly spiced and boasting a maple sweetness to counter the mouthwatering barley sharpness, beautifully fruity and balanced; **t**22 early oak then a surge of sweet, deliciously textured malt, soft, peppery and a hint of fudge; **f**21 dry and slightly oaky but with barley-richness, late hints of milk chocolate and liquorice; **b**21 an unusually refreshing dram for such age. **43.6%. sc.**

⠿ **Glenfiddich Vintage Cask 1972** db **(82) n**20 **t**19 **f**22 **b**21. On the sappy side throughout but good honey depth. **48.9%**

Glenfiddich 1973 Vintage Reserve db **(88) n**23 fresh, fruity, tangy, enormously live and a hint of peat; **t**23 heaps of oak arrive first, but the malt is intense and crisp and spices chase anything that moves: an enormous mouthful; **f**21 dies slightly as some vanilla and toffee-fudge arrive; **b**21 great to find a Glenfiddich at natural srength. **49.8% sc**

⠿ **Glenfiddich Reserve 1984** db **(90) n**21 tart, unripened gooseberries; something of a young Austrian Danube-side wine. Mouthwatering and full of promise; **t**24 expectations are fulfilled by a shimmering arrival of juicy, grassy barley. The sweetness is surprising and all embracing but there is still enough oak and sharp barley to keep it in check; **f**22 pretty long with the oak gathering weight until it hits a semi-bitter tone; **b**23 Glenfiddich at its most exuberant defying its age with a nonchalant charisma. A must for serious Speyside lovers. **40%**

⠿ **Glenfiddich 1982 Private Collection for The Craigellachie Hotel** cask 3672, bott 03 db **(93) n**23 gloriously mouthwatering with an almost coastal saltiness underlining the big malt dais, the oak is wonderfully balanced; **t**24 wave upon wave of complex barley crashes home, that saltiness is still evident but it is the crispness of the mouthwatering, grassy sweetness that really stuns; **f**22 very long with mounting bitter oak; some soft natural toffee and nut dusted with cocoa; **b**24 the kind of star-studded bottling that makes you wonder why Glenfiddich don't do this kind of thing at this kind of age – or younger – more often. *288 bottles available at The Craigellachie Hotel, Speyside.*

GLENFLAGLER
Lowland, 1965–1982. Demolished.

Glenflagler 29 Years Old db **(88) n**22 pretty ripe tangerines on vanilla ice cream. The oak makes for just about perfect bitter-sweet balance; **t**23 massive fresh fruity to start – citrus again – then an astounding intense and clean malty follow-through; **f**21 a quiet finale with the malt remaining confident, the oak adding a slight bitterness, but all under control; **b**22 I've tasted some Glenflagler over the years, but nothing quite as accomplished as this. Lowlander it might be, but this has seen off the years with the grace and élan of the noblest Highlander. Forget about collector's item: eminently drinkable in its own right. **46%.** *A unique malt, as it was run through a Kentucky-type beer still before entering a pot still: a Lowlander made the American way.*

Killyloch 35 Years Old db **(80) n**20 thin, malty nose, but strong enough to see off the oak; **t**20 again a thin, wispy start wth the malt offering sweetness but always in the shadow of something oaky; **f**20 holds together reasonably well: the oak does play the major role but behaves itself while again the malt makes a valiant stand.; **b**20 only the fourth Killyloch I have ever tasted – even including lab sample form – and, I admit, a lot better than I thought it might be. It doesn't have either the muscle or complexity to guarantee a great malt, but very few faults, either. Rather, it hangs on in there proudly – like a frail old lady successfully crossing a busy road – so you can relax and enjoy it for the pretty decent dram it is. **40%**

GLEN GARIOCH
Highland (Eastern), 1798. Suntory. Working.

Glen Garioch 10 Years Old db **(80)** **n**19 **t**22 **f**19 **b**20. Chunky and charming, this is a malt that once would have ripped your tonsils out. Much more sedate and even a touch of honey to the rich body. Toffeed at the finish. **40%**

Glen Garioch 15 Years Old db **(79)** **n**20 **t**21 **f**19 **b**19, The proud owner of a distinctive Glen Garioch character, a hint of rubber on nose and taste (once common here) but compensated by some brown sugar sweetness. A really characterful dram. **40%**

Glen Garioch 16 Years Old db **(88)** **n**20 fruity and spiced: a real heavyweight with a hint of peat thrown in; **t**23 clean, fresh oloroso character massively chewy with a fine malt thread; **f**22 lengthy, sweetening malt, a hint of peat and spice returns; **b**23 lovely whisky, setting off a bit like a Dufftown but heading into a galaxy that poor old Speysider can only dream of. Really high grade malt with bags of character and attitude. **55.4%**

Glen Garioch 21 Years Old db **(83)** **n**18 **t**21 **f**23 **b**21. For a start, the nose is truly weird. I mean, cuckooland nuts. An entirely one-off. By no means unpleasant, but so hard to know exactly what it is trying to say, or just who or what, rather, is saying it. It could be some strange hybrid between peat and sherry. The slightly peaty mouthfeel is silky and the all-round experience is quite lovely. The elegance of the finish in particular is impressive: one that grows on you. Whisky Club alert: worth buying just to fathom the nose. **43%**

Glen Garioch Highland Tradition db **(80)** **n**19 **t**21 **f**20 **b**20. Light and fresh, there is an effervescent complexity that is always enjoyable. **40%**

Glen Garioch 12 Years The National Trust for Scotland db **(77)** **n**18 **t**21 d19 **b**19. Mouthwatering, and would be even more so but for a toffeed intrusion. **43%**

Cadenhead's Glengarioch 11 Years Old dist 90, bott 07/01 **(72)** **n**15 **t**20 **f**19 **b**18. The feinty nose is compensated – to a point – by the big, rich body, as one might expect. **56.6%**

⠿ **Old Malt Cask Glen Garioch Aged 15 Years** dist Sep 88, bott Oct 03 **(82)** **n**18 **t**22 **f**21 **b**21. A bourbony edge to the lively malt-rich middle. Good spice, cocoa and overall body feel. **50%. nc ncf sc.** *Douglas Laing. 336 bottles.*

⠿ **Platinum Old and Rare Cask Glen Garioch Aged 35 Years** dist 68 **(75)** **n**18 **t**20 **f**18 **b**19. Like watching an ancient rock band having one come back too many. **56%.** *Douglas Laing.*

⠿ **Platinum Old and Rare Cask Glen Garioch Aged 36 Years** dist Mar 67 **(82)** **n**19 **t**22 **f**21 **b**20. I was expecting something a lot peatier than this; no more than a hint of smoke: not enough to paper over the cracks though the torrid battle between oak and malt is entertaining. **55.5%.** *Douglas Laing.*

⠿ **Usquebaugh Society Glen Garioch Aged 16 Years** cask 1550, dist 18 Apr 88, bott 22 Apr 04 **(93)** **n**23 bliss ... so rare these days to come across a Glen Garioch still offering peat: the smoke here is delicate amid the sharper barley and citrus; just so much fruit lurking about here and astonishing honey drifts in if the glass is left for a while; **t**23 old fashioned "Geary" with a stupendous buzz of alcohol and malt combined tightly and a few layers of smoky bacon; **f**23 the sweet malt holds ground while cocoa gathers, lashings of chocolate raisins also aids the intensity; **b**24 when this was distilled it would have been a fireball of a spirit.

Sixteen years on it has been tamed slightly by the oak but there is still no shortage of attitude. A throwback and one of the most entertaining bottlings from this distillery in quite a while. If you are looking for a reason to join a Dutch Whisky Society, this is it... **54.4% sc ucf.** Holland 280 bottles.

⋯⊱ **Whisky Galore Glen Garioch 1988 Aged 15 Years (75) n**17 t20 f19 b19. Poor nose; to taste – sweetness on full throttle. **46%**

GLENGLASSAUGH
Speyside, 1875. Edrington. Silent since 1986.

Glenglassaugh 1973 Family Silver (95) n23 fruity and exceptionally complex: quite coastal with something vaguely citrussy, orange in particular; t24 melt-in-the-mouth malt that intensifies by the second. Never becomes either too sweet or vaguely woody. There is a soft hint of peat around the spices; f24 virtually without a blemish as the malt continues on its rich and merry way. Some sublime marmalade follows through on the spice; b24 from first to last this whisky caresses and teases. It is old but shows no over-ageing. It offers what appears to be malt veneer but is complexity itself. Brilliant. And now, sadly, almost impossible to find. Except, possibly, at the Mansefield Hotel, Elgin. **40%**

Cadenhead's Glenglassaugh 25 Years Old dist 78, bott 03/03 **(93) n**23 fresh oloroso, salt, light oak, yet sweet and deep as well. t24 soft, melting fruit that leads into lilting malt. Almost too clean and perfectly sweet to be true; f22 relatively short, but perfectly formed. Loads of natural toffee-apple richness and the most friendly oak of all time; b24 this is just one of those bottlings never to be forgotten. I have tasted perhaps more individual casks from this distillery than anyone outside the old Highland Distillers company. And oloroso versions of this style from there are rarer than 20-something, know-nothing whisky ambassadors not on an ego trip. Trust those magnificent lifetime-of-whisky-in-their-blood stalwarts at Cadenhead to come up with a gem like this. A bottling that will rightly become a legend, mark my words. **45.2%**

Connoisseurs Choice Glenglassaugh 1983 (81) n20 t22 f20 b19. Quite rich, rounded, buttery and sweet. Thin towards the finish. **40%.** Gordon & MacPhail.

GLENGOYNE
Highlands (Southwest), 1833. Peter Russell. Working.

Glengoyne 10 Years Old db **(88) n**21 beautifully clean despite coal-gas bite. The barley is almost in concentrate form with a marmalade sweetness adding richness; t22 crisp, firm arrival with massive barley surge, seriously chewy and textbook bitter-sweet balance; f22 incredibly long and refined for such a light malt. The oak, which made soft noises in the middle now intensifies, but harmonises with the intense barley; b23 proof that to create balance you do not have to have peat at work. The secret is the intensity of barley intermingling with oak. Not a single negative note from first to last. A little beauty. **43%**

⋯⊱ **Glengoyne 12 Years old Cask Strength** db bott Oct 03 **(85) n**19 sherry out-manoeuvres the barley but a dodgy butt has crept in somewhere; t21 slightly off key sherry arrival at first and then wave upon wave of grape and barley take turns to compensate; f23 such a quality finish with a rich fruit pastel sharpness; b22 shame about the slight sulphur blemish to the nose but this has such inbuilt charisma and elan that the middle and finish are worth the uncomfortable early segments. **57.2%**

⋯⊱ **Glengoyne 16 Years old** db bott Oct 03 **(85) n**24 sticky toffee pudding, rich fruit and nut Christmas cake, molasses and sherry: I think you are getting the pungent picture; t23 the sherry is just about too over the top with the malt failing to really get a toe hold; it has to be said, though, that the grape shape is; f18 distinctly out of harmony at the death as is so often the case with these types of big sherry jobs; b20 one of those real monsters that crop up from time to time: the nose and immediate impact is nothing short of astonishing. But for every action, there's an equal and opposite reaction. **55.5%**. *For Clan Des Grands Malts, Paris*

Glengoyne 17 Years Old db (**76**) n*19* t*22* f*17* d*18*. Elegant and charming at first, but the malt is too light to hold the oak. **43%**

Glengoyne 21 Years Old db (**79**) n*17* t*22* f*20* b*20*. The middle is honied, waxy and fabulous, but caramel flattens the fun. **43%**

⋄⋅⋄ **Glengoyne 22 Years** old db bott 8 Apr 04 (**88**) n*23* celery and bread with a jar of honey open somewhere; t*22* the malt is embracing and stands up manfully against the oak; best though is the background sweetness offering malt at a second level; f*21* surprisingly quick despite the hint of tannin; b*22* excellent whisky showing little age damage. **43%**. *For Whisky Festival, Limburg.*

⋄⋅⋄ **Glengoyne Single Cask 1** db dist 72, bott 98 cask no 1428 (**87**) n*21* the first sign of a bourbony embrace rather smothers the usual high barley aroma. Well-balanced though with the oak also offering drier tones to the bourbony sweetness; t*22* a genuinely powering arrival of ultra firm tannins heads off the gathering sweetness and a modest hint of smoke (despite the label stating it being an unpeated malt!); f*21* some spirit nip and bite with lashings of vanilla; b*23* an exceptionally well-balanced dram that holds up well for a distillery that rarely feels comfortable at this kind of age. A malt bourbon drinkers are likely to appreciate. **55%**. *180 bottles. Thought long extinct, a few cases of this have recently surfaced in Australia.*

Glengoyne 2000 AD 30 Years Old db (**91**) n*23* big age, no shortage of ripe, grapey fruit and, dare I say it, a hint of smoke...! t*23* fat, full and fruity, mouthwateringly ripe, superb spices and drifting peat; f*22* sweet, long, very attactive vanilla, toffee and raisins; b*23* top-of-the-range, chewy malt that sets the pulse racing. **51.3%**

Glengoyne 1985 Cask 103 dist Feb 85, bott 97 db (**93**) n*23* t*23* f*23* b*24*. Just so complex and rewarding. Masterful malt. Why did Highland stop producing such one-off drams? The new owners have a near flawless template: let the hunt begin for 12-y-o of such magnitude and magnificence. **57.8%**

Glengoyne 1985 Cask 104 dist Feb 85, bott 97 db (**91**) n*24* t*23* f*22* b*22*. A very unusual malt offering a shape on the palate that is highly distinctive and far from the norm. **59.1%**

GLEN GRANT
Speyside, 1840. Chivas. Working.

Glen Grant db (**89**) n*22* young, clean malt doesn't come much cleaner, maltier – or even younger than this: drooling stuff; t*23* crisp, brittle grain nibbling at the tastebuds, lovely and mouthwatering; f*22* more of the same: the intensity of the malt is stunning, yet it remains delicate throughout; b*22* little oak, so not much complexity, but the balance and quality is nothing short of superb. **40%. nc.** *France.*

Glen Grant 5 Years Old db (**84**) n*21* t*21* f*21* b*21*. Enormous malt, much more oily than the non-age-statement version with an unusual lack of crispness for a Glen Grant. Still mouthwateringly delicious, though! **40%. nc.** *Italy.*

Glen Grant 10 Years Old db (**87**) n*21* fine, flinty grain, quite hard and with limited oak interference; t*23* really mouthwatering, clean and fresh: not an off-note in sight; f*21* gentle, almost half sleeping, just malt and a faint buzz of oak; b*22* a relaxed, confident malt from a distillery that makes great whisky with effortless charm and each mouthful seems to show that it knows it. **43%. nc.**

Adelphi Glen Grant 27 Years Old cask 7638, dist 74, bott 01 (**92**) n*22* t*23* f*23* b*24*. Stunning whisky, its beauty underlined by the crispness of outline. Fine old whisky of unblemished quality. **56.9%**

Adelphi Glen Grant 31 Years Old cask 1706, bott 99 (**94**) n*23* t*24* f*23* b*24*. If the man behind Adelphi, Jamie Walker ever has an off day, he can take this bottle in hand and say: "Well, at least I gave the world this ... !" By the way, boys and girls: consume at full strength for maximum effect. A sweet masterpiece. **57.7%. sc.**

Adelphi Glen Grant 31 Years Old cask 1772, bott 99 **(87) n**22 t23 f21 b21. Dour sherry, dry and weighty like an American news anchorman who takes himself very seriously indeed. **53.9%. sc.**

Berrys' Own Selection Glen Grant 1970 bott 01 **(86) n**20 t23 f22 b21. I would love to have seen the sherry butt this came from: an interesting history, I'd say. A few blemishes on this one, like foxing on a rare first edition. But readable all the same. **55%.** Berry Bros & Rudd.

Berry's Own Glen Grant 1972 bott 03 **(87) n**23 absolutely top class sherry, whistle-clean, dry, weighty yet subtle enough to allow the development of vanilla and various floral-oaky notes; **t**23 lush, soft arrival of sherry on the palate: a mouthwateringly juicy affair at first; followed by a wave of barley; and then firmer oak, chocolate eclairs and faint peat; **f**20 pretty dry, flint embedded in chalk; **b**21 rock hard Glen Grant with a grey beard, but the sherry really has that touch of class. **46%.** Berry Bros

Berry's Own Glen Grant 1973 bott 03 **(86) n**23 sultanas and warming spices; clean, clear and crisp; **t**23 brilliant delivery of intense fruit coupled with enormous spices that nip, bite and chatter around the palate. The oak takes its time before arriving, allowing the barley-sherry combo full and unrestricted reign; **f**19 rock-hard and almost impenetrable in the most classic of Glen Grant styles. The oak is bolder now and showing a little sap along with some very late cocoa. Still the spice persists; **b**21 an old malt that at first displays Glen Grant in a near classic pose, but ultimately just a fraction too sappy around the gills. **52%.** Berry Bros

Berrys' Own Selection Glen Grant 30 Years Old bott 02 **(82) n**21 t20 f21 b20. A pervasive bitterness creeps in and undermines the sherried bliss. **43%.** Berry Bros & Rudd.

Berrys' Own Selection Glen Grant 31 Year Old cask 1041, bott 01 **(88) n**22 t22 f23 b21. Massive whisky that shoots prisoners on sight. **55.6%.** Berry Bros & Rudd.

⁖ **Coopers Choice Glen Grant 1988 Port Wood Finish 15 Years Old** bott 03 **(79) n**22 t20 f18 b19. A natural caramel effect has blasted the fruit out of the glass. **46%.** Vintage Malt Whisky Co.

⁖ **Distillery No. 4 Glen Grant 1989** cask 23057 **(83) n**20 t21 f22 b20. A faultlessly simplistic expression: what it loses on complexity it makes up for with uncomplicated, deliciously honest malt. **46%**

⁖ **Duncan Taylor Glen Grant 1970 Aged 24 Years** cask 831 **(85) n**22 peppery sherry and other muscular oak notes; **t**22 massive clean sherry at first then a slow development of semi-sap; **f**20 pretty exhausted towards the finish with a shade too much bitter pine and liquorice; **b**21 very drinkable, very big and very over-aged. **54.2%**

Gordon & MacPhail Glen Grant 21 Year Old (76) n22 t19 f17 b18. The weakest of the Glen Grants bottled by G&M. Caramel-flattened and lifeless. **40%.** Gordon & MacPhail.

Gordon & MacPhail Glen Grant 1948 (90) n23 big oranges, oak and smoke; **t**24 massive malt intensity, with the oak being nothing like as threatening as the nose suggests. Some peat drifts around, filling in some age-cracks, but the malt is quite overwhelming; **f**21 lots of toffee-vanilla; **b**22 a real cracker of a malt displaying controlled power and aggression. Stunning. **40%**

Gordon & MacPhail Glen Grant 1950 (90) n23 remarkable: the oak, presumably, takes the form of newly opened horsechestnuts while soft grapey notes waft around: highly unusual and very enticing; **t**23 massively sweet: both malt and sultana concentrate congregate for a whisky version of the noble rot; **f**22 some smoke and cocoa take a bow; **b**22 no spitting out of this one: this has to be one of the world's most extraordinary bottlings. Not only is it of enormous age, but it remains entirely intact and revelling in its sweet glory. Defiant and utterly delightful. **40%**

Gordon & MacPhail Glen Grant 1952 (85) n*24* Arbroath smokies, sweet and malty: stunning; **t***21* some early oak creates a chalky field in which the fruit and grassy malt works; **f***19* tiring rapidly, the oak is really giving the malt a hard time. Some very late smoke helps cushion the attack; **b***21* in 1992 I bought a bottle of this to mark my wife's 40th birthday. Seven months later we were no longer an item: obviously she didn't like the whisky, so I kept it ... **40%**

Hart Brothers Glen Grant Aged 29 Years dist Oct 72 **(96) n***24* slightly smoky, seeing off the heavy grape. The malt is compacted and forms banks on either side of the fruit. Just so sensuous; **t***24* unbelievably nubile sherry: deft grapes happily give way to the most fabulous malt arrival imaginable: enormous; **f***24* longer than War and Peace. And a lot easier going, too. Fruity and fresh, it defies age and challenges your tastebuds. Massively thick malt is meeting the demarara-sugared fruit head on; **b***24* if only my sex life was this good. Possibly one of the top twenty whiskies I have ever tasted: certainly one of the greatest moments in my (not inconsiderable) whisky life. It has everything. If you can find it, life will take on a slightly different dimension. October 72: I had just set a personal record for 1,500 metres: 4 mins 46 seconds. Meanwhile, someone in Speyside was filling a cask ... **53.6%.** *Matured in sherry wood.*

Hart Brothers Glen Grant Aged 33 Years dist Oct 69, bott Jan 03 **(83) n***21* **t***22* **f***20* **b***20*. A sweet, uncomplicated malty dram with a buttery sheen. **51.5%**

Murray McDavid Glen Grant 1989 bourbon cask MM2105, dist Oct 89, bott Dec 01 **(79) n***20* **t***20* **f***19* **b***20*. A thinnish, buttery dram, a bit on the warm side.

·:·:· **Murray McDavid Mission Glen Grant 1969 (80) n***20* **t***19* **f***20* **b***21*. Tangy, sharp orange coated in chocolate. **46%. nc ncf.**

·:·:· **Old Malt Cask Glen Grant Aged 12 Years** dist Apr 91, bott Jan 04 **(84) n***19* **t***23* **f***21* **b***21*. A bitty, busy malt full of enjoyably stereotypical Speyside characteristics. The malt is well defined and very clean, the oak well behaved and adding a salty twist. Only the surprisingly tired nose loses points. **50%. nc ncf sc.** *Douglas Laing. 324 bottles.*

Old Malt Cask Glen Grant Aged 27 Years dist Sep 72, bott Jul 02 **(76) n***17* **t***23* **f***17* **b***19*. I'm speechless: just not what you expect from an OMC. The nose is off-key and confirmation that all is not right in the world comes with the bitter finish. But the arrival on the palate is awesome.

Old Masters Glen Grant 1969 bott 01 **(94) n***23* **t***25* **f***23* **b***23*. If only the finish could have kept pace with the unbelievable start, we would have had something to battle the monumental Hart Brothers 29-y-o. As it is, the initial flavour and thrust goes down in the book as perfection. **57.1%.** *James Macarthur.*

Peerless Glen Grant 1970 cask 811, dist Feb 70 32-y-o **(89) n***22* a forest of oak but such is the quality of oloroso the splinters are absorbed by the fruit and soft spices: hints of bourbon, cocoa and smoke complete the romp in the woods; **t***23* a thick marriage of sherry, oaky and orange with some malt still being heard; **f***22* slightly bitter oak but the malt now does have a say: gentle spices still play around; **b***22* this is big, macho stuff that retains a fabulous sense of theatre. **46.6%.** *Duncan Taylor & Co.*

Peerless Glen Grant 1972 cask 1640, dist Feb 72 30-y-o **(89) n***21* spiced, a hint of stem ginger; **t***23* big, oily, honied and unbelievably intense: a real mouthful; **f***22* vanilla and honey combine while the malt intensifies without the oil: the oak offers cocoa; **b***23* a wonderfully controlled dram where the oak stays in the background. The sweetness is of almost perfect intensity. Excellent.

Peerless Glen Grant 1972 cask 1643, dist Feb 72 **(85) n***20* some worrying partly hidden signs of tired oak, but there is enough apple and cream to offer hope; **t***22* an intensely malty start that sweetens impressively. A lovely oiliness also develops and all is surprisingly well-balanced. There is even a touch of honey to improve and enrich things further. Truly massive and complex; **f**22 long and vanilla-rich but the oak, though hinting slightly of burnt toast, behaves itself. The oily, honied malt lasts the distance; **b**21 a turn up for the book, this. The nose, though quite sweet and full, shows tell-tale signs of tiredness which is not confirmed on the very characterful palate. A really enjoyable old dram offering much class. **60.6%.** *Duncan Taylor & Co.*

Peerless Glen Grant 1974 cask 16587, dist Nov 74 28-y-o **(93)** **n**23 Speyside it may be, but salty it is; **t**23 massive salt-malt arrival encompasses the firm, chewy oak: amazingly complex; **f**24 very softly smoked with an amazingly long barley fade-out. Brilliant; **b**23 man, this is whisky! **55.1%.** *Duncan Taylor & Co.*

⸬ **Platinum Old and Rare Cask Glen Grant 1967** bott 04 **(92)** **n**22 freshly roasted coffee offers a more Demerara rum characteristic than Speyside. Hints of tired oak but the rich intensity just about conquers all; **t**23 only a lifetime in a fresh oloroso butt can offer this type of bitter-sweet, softly spiced gentle giant; **f**24 continues on its brilliantly chewy way with liquorice adding to the coffee and sherry. Elephantine stuff; **b**23 half whisky half Demerara rum yet entirely astonishing. The enormity of the dram never quit subtracts from the underlying delicacy of this beast. From the Golden Age of sherry butts, this is now a dying breed. **49.6%.** *Douglas Laing.*

Private Collection Glen Grant 1953 (95) **n**24 mountainous oloroso. Pretty crisp and shapely for the great age, though some salt has crept in; **t**24 salty and spicy, the oloroso develops a life of its own. Loads of coffee notes and excellent bitter-sweet ratio; **f**23 a silky coating of salty sherry encrusts the tastebuds guaranteeing an amazingly long and deep finale; **b**24 What can be said? Except that this malt has no right whatsoever to be anything close to this good. G&M have their detractors, and sometimes they do make life hard for themselves. But when it comes to delivering golden treasures from the past they are the Lord Caernarvon of the whisky world. A dry masterpiece. **45%.** *Gordon & MacPhail.*

Scotch Malt Whisky Society 18th Anniversary Special Bottling Cask No. 9.30 dist Oct 72, bott Sep 01 **(93)** **n**24 beautifully sculpted: slightly nutty but any sherry-oaky dryness is countered by extraordinary fruits, including (honestly!) strawberries! **t**23 incredibe arrival of natural toffee, glutinous in character, carrying with it oak, liquorice and salt; **f**23 the curtain is brought down gently with a little more salt, toffee and spice. The vanilla treads softly; **b**23 a massive whisky with a strangely coastal resonance for a Speysider and always triumphalist about coming from such a wonderfully clean sherry cask. Tasted blind I would have sworn this to be top-notch Springbank! **56.6%**

Scotch Malt Whisky Society Cask 9.32 Aged 30 Years (85) **n**23 weighty sweet oak and cream coffee, burnt raisins on top, roasty and rich, almost demerara rum in style; **t**22 dry, massive spice attack with a pinch of salt, fruity, plum jam on burnt toast; **f**19 long, the sweetness increasing at first but a lot of tannin in there still and becoming bitter to the point of off-key; **b**21 big, chewy and challenging. The oak contributes much but becomes rather over-excited on the finish. **56.2%. nc ncf sc.**

Scott's Selection Glen Grant 1977 bott Jun 03 **(89)** **n**21 slightly mean, with the oak offering the lion's share; **t**23 opens up towards enormous bitter-sweet, almost crunchy malt with a surging wave of honied spice and then darker oak tones; **f**22 pretty long, a distant hint of smoke but the oak slowly begins to take command from the rigid oak; **b**23 really impressive malt from a great distillery and holds off the oak brilliantly. **55.4%.** *Robert Scott & Co.*

GLEN KEITH
Speyside, 1957. Chivas. Silent.

Glen Keith 10 Years Old db **(80)** **n**22 **t**21 **f**18 **b**19. A malty if thin dram that finishes with a whimper after an impressively refreshing, grassy start. **43%**

Glen Keith Distilled Before 1983 db **(79)** n21 t21 f18 b19. Lemon-drop nose of concentrated malt in palate; pleasant but fades just too much towards oaky bitterness. **43%**

Cadenhead's Glen Keith 16 Years Old dist 85, bott 07/01 **(72)** n17 t19 f18 b18. Hot as hell and mildly off-key. **59.2%**

Connoiseurs Choice Glen Keith 1967 (86) n23 the best nose to any Glen Keith I have found in over 20 years. Total complexity as rival factions of sweet/dry malty/oaky fruity/spicy battle it out with feathers; t20 starts almost too softly to register, then builds up sweetly, then some telling spice; f22 long vanilla and malty notes take an age to fade; b21 an unusually fine example of a pretty rare malt these days. **40%**. Gordon & MacPhail.

⋯ **Old Malt Cask Glen Keith Aged 14 Years** dist Mar 89, bott Sep 03 **(80)** n19 t21 f20 b20. Thin nose but compensated by sweet and spicy barley attack on the palate; bitter almond finish. **50%. nc ncf sc.** Douglas Laing. 378 bottles.

⋯ **Old Master's Glen Keith 1974 (78)** n21 t20 f19 b18. Attractive, rich bourbon notes, but never quite gets into gear. **52.7%.** James MacArthur.

Scotch Malt Whisky Society Cask 81.3 Aged 33 Years (83) n21 t22 f20 b20. Low-ester Jamaica rum for the nose and a superb honey-malt middle. This is really attractive whisky. Sweet and warming. **58.3%. nc ncf sc.**

GLENKINCHIE
Lowland, 1837. Diageo. Working.

Glenkinchie 10 Years Old db **(80)** n20 t21 f19 b20. This has been more jazzed up in recent years; certainly much more robust on nose and palate with fruit and toffee replacing malt as the main theme. **43%**

Glenkinchie Distillers Edition Glenkinchie 1989 Double Matured amontillado cask finish, bott 02 db **(83)** n21 t22 f20 b20. A strange thing happened: I opened this bottle absent-mindedly without realising what it was. Suddenly I thought I had opened up a bottle of sherry by mistake, such was the power of the wine on popping the cork. Now that may be good news to some, but I come from that strange old school of wanting to drink light Lowland whisky when I have it in my hand ... having said that, the nose is lovely, but the amontillado wipes the floor with the usual subtleties of a Glenkinchie aroma. Clean, enjoyable, near faultless stuff in many ways: from a technical point of view one of the best Double Matured I have tasted from there and the casks must have been quite superb. **43%**

⋯ **Scotch Malt Whisky Society Cask 22.9 Aged 16 Years (92)** n23 an off-note-free zone. The barley is complex and intact throughout; the oak offer almost perfect weight; t23 mouthwatering, playful malt jinks around the tastebuds; the intensity seems to double every three or four seconds; f24 one of the longest finishes of a Lowlander you will encounter with natural toffee being so light as to not interfere with the lush barley; b22 not the most complex but a delightful surprise to those of us who have not been overly entertained by 'Kinchie in recent years. As a blender you would treat this as Speyside top dressing. This is supremely made and beautifully matured whisky: easily the best expression of this distillery I can remember. **58.9%. nc ncf sc.**

THE GLENLIVET
Speyside 1824. Chivas. Working.

The Glenlivet Aged 12 Years db **(83)** n20 t22 f20 b21. A surfeit of apples on both nose and body. The malt is quite rich at first but thins out for the vanilla at the death. **40%**

The Glenlivet Aged 12 Years American Oak Finish db **(86)** n21 light malt and delicate oak; t22 lush, mildly oily body, the malt coming through in small waves with soft pear-like fruit just behind with a lovely spice sub-stratum;

f22 long and chewy; the fruit remains clean and harmonised with the budding vanilla and spice; **b**21 stylish and under-stated in every department. **40%**

The Glenlivet Aged 12 Years French Oak Finished db **(83) n**21 t22 f20 **b**20. The oak is extraordinary and offers an unusual style of spiciness, though the finish is flatter than might be expected. Good bitter-sweet sync. **40%**. *Finished in French Limousin oak.*

The Glenlivet Aged 15 Years db **(84) n**22 t21 f20 **b**21. Good spice and complexity. Very well-weighted throughout. **43%**

∴ **The Glenlivet Aged 15 Years French Oak** bott 04 db **(86) n**21 deep vanilla and echoes of grape; t22 silky, malty mouth arrival, then a salivating sweetness; f21 as the fruit returns the bitterness escalates; **b**22 a by no means straightforward Glenlivet with an accentuated bitter-sweet theme. **43%**

The Glenlivet Aged 18 Years db **(87) n**22 fresh for its age and mildly smoked; t23 attractive fruity complexity adds to the busy malt; f21 quietens and dries rapidly, lots of vanilla; **b**21 another Glenlivet that starts beautifully but lacks stamina. **43%**

The Glenlivet Archive Aged 21 Years db **(77) n**21 t20 f18 **b**18. The more I have got to know this whisky, the more I despair of it. After a lovely fruity start, way too much toffee-caramel, I'm afraid. **43%**

The Glenlivet Cellar Collection 1959 bott 02 db **(90) n**22 diced apples and raisins, a hint of allspice; t23 enormously silky and spicy then a wave of concentrated malt and hints of cocoa; f22 light smatterings of vanilla and liquorice, beautifully bitter-sweet with more than a bit of the old bourbon about it; **b**23 no malt has any right to be this good at this kind of age. Oak has done very little damage, apart from giving a mildly bourbony feel amid some indulgent liquorice, and that can hardly be construed as damage at all. It is the élan of the fruitiness jousting with the rich malt that impresses most. If anyone was born in 1959, this is the bottle you must buy: a 2cl nip every birthday should be enough to see you through to the end in style. **42.28%**

∴ **The Glenlivet Cellar Collection 1964** bott 04 db **(82) n**23 t20 f19 **b**20. Curious, delightful nose with memories of school at that time: polished floors and plasticine with oranges at break. However, it is just too oaky on the palate. **45.05% ncf**

The Glenlivet Cellar Collection 1967 bott 00 db **(88) n**23 t23 f20 **b**22. Marks would be higher if I didn't detect caramel on the finish. But distillery manager Jim Cryle did a great job selecting these casks. **46%**

The Glenlivet Cellar Collection 1983 Finished in French Oak bott 03 db **(88) n**22 busy and bubbly: lots of vanillins pepper the big malt, quite unusual; t23 the mouth is gripped by a mini malty-oak battle with lots of spicy sub plots. Lovely fruity richness, too; f21 more spice lingering with the oak, slightly Jamaica rum-like in its fade; **b**22 sophistication and attitude rolled into one. **46%**

The Glenlivet Cellar Collection 30 Years Old American Oak Finish bott 01 db **(93) n**23 t24 f23 **b**23. Love quiet old whiskies? You know, the sort that nose of leather chairs and taste of toasty, oaky malt and then die quietly on the finish? If so, don't get this, for this is the dram that flew over the cuckoo's nest, needing several straitjackets to keep it in control. There is more than a touch of bourbon about this one; hardly surprising seeing the kind of oak it ended up in. But what has surprised – nay, shocked, readers – is the bucking bronco violence of the malt in retaliation at being treated this way. Anyone who seriously adores whisky has to stump up for this one. See if you can ride it. **48%**

The Glenlivet Vintage 1967 db **(85) n**21 hints of old leather and smoke; t22 oily wave of sweet sherry-malt; f21 chocolate and a hard-metallic tang; **b**21 excellent complexity and no over-ageing.

The Glenlivet Vintage 1968 db **(82) n**20 t22 f20 **b**20. Firm oak, interesting bite.

The Glenlivet Vintage 1969 db **(89)** n22 fabulouly clean and precise sherry, deftly smoked; t24 Dry oak to begin then salt and fruitcake; f21 soft oak and bitter-sweet chewy finale; b22 brilliant whisky with great but controlled age.

The Glenlivet Vintage 1970 db **(93)** n24 honey replaces sherry: tangerine, salty oak and coconut milk; t23 oiled and intense honey richness, perfectly balanced with roast oak and malt; f22 brilliant, bitter-sweet, oaky dry with some lingering honey; b24 outstanding. The finest and probably most delicate distillery-bottled Glenlivet I have tasted.

The Glenlivet Vintage 1972 db **(84)** n21 t22 f20 b21. Very dry sherry ensures complexity and maximum spice.

⋰ **Adelphi Glenlivet 26 Years Old** cask 13120 dist 77, bott 03 **(84)** n21 t22 f21 b20. Firm to the point of brittle; the rich malt dominates especially in the early rounds. **57%**

⋰ **Adelphi Glenlivet 23 Years Old** cask 13743 dist 80 bott 03 **(86)** n21 the barley nips and bites for all the years; t21 amazingly mouthwatering despite the oak; the barley concentrates towards the middle and some syrupy notes arrive; f22 the intensity of the vanilla in conjunction with the barley goes into overdrive as the slightly burnt toasty oak arrives; b22 Speyside for this age at its most entertaining and resourceful: the complexity is superb. **50.6%**

Adelphi Glenlivet 27 Years Old dist 75 bott 02 **(87)** n21 a hint of peat and marzipan amid powering malt; t22 fat and oily with a touch of smoke; f22 long vanilla and malty strands offer some late honey and then drier oak; b22 effortlessly elegant. **55.4%**

Berry's Own Glenlivet 1971 bott 03 **(82)** n23 t22 f18 b19. A heavyweight, yet nimble, bout between massed ranks of oak and tar-brushed sherry. Sherry, it must be said, that is dry and of the very finest order; to taste, though, an enormous spice attack, heaps of prickle and pepper and early wave of thick oak. A subtle, sweet backdrop softens the thudding blows but even traces of cocoa fail to entirely shield us from the OTT oak. Not without charm, character and quality but, alas, several summers too old. **55%.** *Berry Bros*

Berrys' Own Selection Glenlivet 1975 bott 02 **(93)** n24 this is a baby: soft honey and the cleanest of rich malt. Aaaaah! t24 the silk honey dissolves around the tastebuds leaving oaky strands and flighty malt; f22 slighly bitter as the oak kicks in, but plenty of silk still to go around; b23 you know Lawson's 12-y-o, the blend? Well, this seems to be the honey section of it in single malt form. A real treat that seduces without any shame whatsoever. **43%.** *Berry Bros & Rudd.*

Blackadder Raw Cask Glenlivet 1966 sherry cask 3898, dist 30 Nov 66, bott Apr 02 **(77)** n19 t20 f19 b19. Faded despite some serious malt incursions in the late middle of the palate. **64.2%. nc ncf.**

Cask Glenlivet 1973 refill American hogshead 8847, 8850, dist 16/11/73, bott 7/6/02 **(92)** n21 crisp malt, almost brick-hard and impenetrable; t25 for those of you who love intense, silky concentrated malt just take a mouthful of this: multi-orgasmic; f23 more of the same but with a gentle letting-in of some guest oak; b23 made in the days when The Glenlivet distillery produced the finest malt in Speyside. I still remember them – just. **55.9%.** *Gordon & MacPhail.*

Cask Glenlivet 1978 casks 16419–16423, dist 13/10/78, bott Nov 96 **(91)** n22 t24 f22 b23. This, clearly, is what Gordon & MacPhail do best. **60.2%**

⋰ **Coopers Choice Glenlivet 1972 Sherry Cask Aged 30 Years** bott 03 **(88)** n22 the dry sherry dominates with the expansiveness of an oloroso in peculiar tandem with the sharpness of fino: very unusual; t21 a surprisingly thin, grapey start then a pounding arrival of altogether fatter fruit and barley; f23 more harmonious, especially with the oak providing a drier floor for the sugary grape to lie; b22 an oddly behaved sherry butt, but after 30 years strange things do sometimes happen. **46%.** *Vintage Malt Whisky Company.*

Craigellachie Hotel of Speyside Glenlivet 1980 Single Cask Bottling 2002 cask 1520, dist 22/01/80, bott 17/12/02 **(89)** n*23* beautifully clean and spicy fruit, egg custard pie and rich malt: impressive; **t***23* a real mouthful of a dram: amazingly clean fruit combining with sweet, mouthwatering malt, beautifully textured. Just so Speyside; .f*21* a buzz of spice and some oak working its way into the fruity fray; **b***22* for all its age there is still a wonderful freshness to this dram. The crescendo of spice is a classy touch. **59.1%. 222 bottles.**

⠿ **Duncan Taylor Glenlivet 1968 Aged 35 Years** cask 2840 **(86)** n*21* briny barley; **t***22* exceptionally clean for its age with the barley still in total command; **f***21* slightly sugary and hints of sap but the barley remains robust; **b***22* salty and delicate for its age: a bit like a Springbank but with only two thirds the complexity. **43.6%**

George & J.G Smith's 15 Year Old Glenlivet 40% (81) n*20* t*21* f*20* b*20*. A veritable maltfest, but perhaps lacking complexity. *Gordon & MacPhail.*

George & J G Smith's 15 Year Old Glenlivet 46% (84) n*19* t*22* f*22* b*21*. Dustier nose, but the extra intensity makes for happier malt. *Gordon & MacPhail.*

⠿ **Glenscoma Glenlivet 1986 17 Years Old (88)** n*21* nutty, a hint of smoke and a nip of warming sherry; **t***22* mouthwatering, lush malt and then a wall of bristling spice; **f***23* a few estery hints of rye-fruited bourbon; **b***22* quite a dashing fellow with a petulant streak. **57.8%.** *Scoma, Germany.*

⠿ **Hart Brothers Glenrothes Aged 10 Years** dist Nov 92, bott Sep 03 **(86)** n*18* over oaked for its age, sappy; **t***22* big, juicy malt; sweet and refined; f*23* brown sugar on egg custard; **b***22* the nose is a horror show; the finish is fabulously memorable. **46%**

Hart Brothers Glenlivet Aged 34 Years dist Oct 68, bott Jan 03 **(81)** n*20* t*22* f*19* b*20*. A few grey hairs, as one might expect from an old smoothie. **50.6%**

Mission Range Glenlivet 1974 (89) n*22* honey and golden syrup with a sprinkling of malt; **t***23* even more honey this time with vanilla in tandem; **f***22* deft malt, a touch of salt and some cocoa; **b***22* stupendous mouthfeel. A wonderful non-peated nightcap. **46%. nc ncf.** *Murray McDavid.*

Old Malt Cask Glenlivet Aged 20 Years dist Dec 81, bott Feb 02 **(87)** n*22* honey, malt and spice; r*22* typical high-octane malt with a sweet edge; **f***22* very easy-going and relaxed malt-oak marriage; **b***21* don't bother with complexity here: it just tastes good. **46.7%. nc ncf sc.** *Douglas Laing. 108 bottles.*

Old Malt Cask Glenlivet Aged 26 Years dist May 74, bott Jan 01 **(84)** n*20* t*22* f*22* b*20*. Molten toffee, delicious, though. **50%. nc ncf.** *Douglas Laing. 306 bottles*

Old Malt Cask Glenlivet Aged 29 Years dist Aug 71, bott Jan 01 **(82)** n*22* t*21* f*19* b*20*. For all the coffee and toffee apples, can't really make my mind up here. Sometimes I mark very high when tasting this, but on the weight of evidence I'd say bottled on its way down, probably five or six years after being brilliant. You missed this one, boys!! First time for everything, I suppose... **50%. nc ncf.** *Douglas Laing. 558 bottles.*

Old Masters Glenlivet 1976 (69) n*15* t*21* f*17* b*16*. I am sure there are those who will swoon at this. But it is one of those with which I have problems with the sherry cask. It does have some gloriously rich moments in the middle. But... **59.9%. nc ncf.** *James MacArthur.*

Peerless Glenlivet 1968 cask 5254, dist Sep 68 34-y-o **(75)** n*19* t*19* f*18* b*19*. Sharp, malty, spicy middle but it never escapes the big oak. **50%.** *Duncan Taylor & Co.*

Private Collection Smith's Glenlivet 1943 (87) n*21* an astonishing mixture of understated oaky notes intertwined with clean, distinctive malt and the most distant aroma of peat: a gentleman of an aroma; **t***20* maintains a malty integrity despite the accompaniment of oak; **f***23* for its age, quite astounding: no over-the-top oak or dryness, just soothing waves of malty-oak which are neither bitter nor sweet; **b**23 remarkable. How a whisky remains this enjoyable after so many years is what makes spending a lifetime investigating the world's greatest drink such a great profession! No off-notes and, whilst it is not the greatest dram you will ever find, it is certainly the finest wartime relic you can find to keep you company whilst watching Whisky Galore. **40%**. Gordon & MacPhail.

Scotch Malt Whisky Society Cask 2.46 Aged 13 Years (83) n21 t22 **f**19 **b**21. Natural toffee sweetens it, but quite chalky from the oak. Plenty to chew on. **60.3%. nc ncf sc.**

⋄⋄⋄ **Scotch Malt Whisky Society Cask 2.53 Aged 32 Years (89)** n24 an exceptional nose so complex you can fancy you can almost spot the molecules: no big aromas here, just myriad tiny ones making an astonishing, perfectly-balanced whole; **t**20 those tiny flavours don't quite gel on mouth arrival leaving the oak too much room to dominate; **f**23 the malt finally finds its voice and the mind-blowing complexity is resumed; **b**22 genuinely fine whisky. **46.3%. nc ncf sc.**

Scott's Selection Glenlivet Sherry Wood 1976 bott 01 **(88)** n23 t22 f21 **b**22. Oh that all Glenlivets were like this! Fifteen years ago I came across samples like this quite regularly. Not now. How often will we see it like again? **56.9%**. Robert Scott & Co.

Smith's Glenlivet 1948 (85) n21 marmalade and toast; t22 really intense malt with lovely fruity edge; **f**21 slighly biting oak, dry with some peat softening things a little; **b**21 good whisky which is impressive on its own merits, let alone the great age.

Smith's Glenlivet 1951 (82) n19 a touch on the oaky side; t21 sweet malts dominate. and a hint of smoke registers in the background; **f**21 light, delicate oak and malt; **b**21 silky and sweet with delicious milky, malty depth. Not half as oaky as the nose threatens. **40%**. Gordon & MacPhail.

Smith's Glenlivet 1955 (87) n23 big ripe fruit, sensuously clean within a frame of oak and malt; **t**20 oak immediately asserts itself, then a follow-through of fruit and soft peat, fruitcake rich; **f**22 much more sensible and structured with some mouthwatering malt adding complexity; **b**22 absolutely hypnotic whisky. **40%**. Gordon & MacPhail.

Smith's Glenlivet 21 Years Old (88) n21 teasing malts ranging from grassy to very mildly smoked; **t**23 silky, malt-rich with exceptional balance; f22 long, lightly spiced rich vanilla dulled by caramel; **b**22 what a cracking dram this is. There is a caramel effect which could be natural that prevents this from hitting the 90s. Superb nonetheless. Gordon & MacPhail.

⋄⋄⋄ **The Un-chillfiltered Collection Glenrothes Vintage 1990** cask 10985, dist 11 May 90, bott 23 Jan 04 **(69)** n18 t18 f16 **b**17. Sulphur spoiled. **46%**. Signatory 709 bottles.

⋄⋄⋄ **Wilson & Morgan Barrel Selection Glenlivet TwentyEight Years Old** dist 75, bott 03 Hogshead No 5727 **(92)** n22 salty, grapey, a hint of paprika and honeysuckle: pretty complex stuff!! **t**23 the salty tale continues with a mixture of ripe and dried dates with burnt raisins for company and an assortment of warming spices for balance; **f**24 one or two light roast coffee notes engage with the stunningly structured fruit: the salt lingers but only to rejuvenate the soft oak; **b**23 this whisky has spent 28 years in the kind of characterful cask that us long-in-the-tooth whisky specialists shed a tear or two over. Masterful for its antiquity. **46%**

GLENLOCHY
Highland (Western), 1898–1983. Closed.

Connoisseurs Choice Glenlochy 1977 (77) n20 t21 f18 **b**18. Decent malt and texture, a shade too much caramel. **40%**. Gordon & MacPhail.

Gordon & MacPhail Glenlochy 1965 (87) n22 a hint of smoke; t22 beautifully fruity, really lovely honey and complexity; **f**21 lip-smacking honey and oak; **b**22 brilliant stuff. **40%**

Old Malt Cask Glenlochy Aged 26 Years dist Mar 75, bott Jun 01 **(91)** n24 t23 f21 b23. Yet another bottle that begs the question: why the hell was this distillery closed? **50%. nc ncf.** Douglas Laing. 258 bottles.

⁖ **Platinum Old and Rare Glenlochy 38 Years Old** dist May 65 **(78)** n21 t19 f19 b19. Fruity and juicy but you are still left picking out the splinters. **42.5%.** Douglas Laing.

⁖ **Platinum Old and Rare Glenlochy 38 Years Old** dist 65 bott 03 **(84)** n22 t21 f20 b21. Softly smoked and sweet. Big oak but remains in bounds. **42.3%.** Douglas Laing. 171 bottles.

GLENLOSSIE
Speyside, 1876. Diageo. Working.

Glenlossie Aged 10 Years db **(91)** n23 brilliant: big, big malt with a distant glazed stem ginger echo; t23 so rich-textured and beatifully lush, the malt is mega intense with soft spice, a touch of salt and oak; f22 sweet malt with mounting vanilla and a rumble of distant smoke; b23 first-class Speyside malt with excellent weight and good distance on the palate. Easily one of the best Flora and Fauna bottlings of them all. **43%**

Adelphi Glenlossie 17 Years Old cask 1679, dist 81, bott 98 **(89)** n23 t23 f21 b22. Glenlossie peaks a lot younger than this: rare to find one from this distillery in such good sherry form and of such unspoiled antiquity.

⁖ **Chieftain's Glenlossie 1992 Aged 10 Years** bott 6 Mar 03 **(88)** n21 clean, grassy, fresh, simplistic barley; t22 an essay in mouthwatering barley; f23 really comes into its own now as the little oak there is firms out and even fattens the clean malt; b22 another excellent, technically faultless, example of what the latter day Speyside malt is all about. **43%.** Ian Macleod.

Connoisseurs Choice Glenlossie 1974 (78) 20 t22 f17 b19. The finish is bitter and twisted, the build-up beautiful. 40% Gordon & McPhail.

Connoisseurs Choice Glenlossie 1975 (79) n19 t21 f19 b20. Molassed and well-oaked. **40%.** Gordon & MacPhail.

Coopers Choice Glenlossie 1978 bott 01 (22 Years Old) **(69)** n17 t18 f17 b17. Sorry, just not the kind of sherry butt I get along with. **43%.** The Vintage Malt Co.

⁖ **Duncan Taylor Glenlossie 1978 Aged 25 Years** cask no 4802 **(88)** n20 sappy, bacon fat; t22 mouthwatering, rich malt; the oak has a mildly bourbony resonance; f23 takes off into honey heaven as the oak and barley embrace with passion: more liquorice-honey bourbon notes towards the end; b23 enough malts survives to take on the bourbon. A genuinely beautiful whisky. **54%**

Gordon & MacPhail Glenlossie 1961 bott 02 **(87)** n22 toasted brown bread, soft vanilla and honey. A dab of smoke hangs in there; t22 fabulous mouth-arrival, at first sweet malt then the toastiness arrives with, again, a subtle hint of honey; f21 cocoa, burnt fudge and a late waft of peat; b22 a really lovely old dram that has seen off the years with some style. **40%**

⁖ **Murray McDavid Mission 2 Glenlossie 1975 (77)** n19 t21 f18 b19 good, sturdy, mouthwatering arrival on the palate, but runs out of puff. **46% nc ncf**

⁖ **Murray McDavid Glenlossie 1993 (86)** n22 young barley and ripe fig; t22 magnificent, mouthwatering barley with a spoonful of unrefined sugar; f21 medium length with barley leading the way as gentle vanilla reaches for footing; b21 absolutely prime example of Glenlossie at its most malt intense: great example as to why it's such a great blender. This is the Speyside Way. **46%**

⁖ **Peerless Glenlossie 1978** (see Duncan Taylor Glenlossie 1978)

Provenance Autumn distillation Glenlossie Over 10 Years dist Autumn 89, bott Spring 00 **(79)** n20 t21 b18 f20. A light, refreshing grassy malt that charms rather than seduces. **43%.** Douglas McGibbon & Co.

⁖ **Provenance Glenlossie Over 14 Years** dist Autumn 89, bott Autumn 03 **(85)** n21 laid back barley on a bed of uncooked rhubarb; t22 fresh, mouthwatering arrival in classic Glenlossie style; clean, crispish malt is unhindered by oak though a swift peppery blast adds a necessary contrast; **f21** just a slow cooling of the malt; **b21** much younger and fresher than its 14 years suggests: delicious stuff, about as good as you will get from a cask this well used. **46%. Douglas McGibbon.**

GLEN MHOR
Highland (Northern), 1892–1983. Demolished.

Cask Glen Mhor 1979 cask 2376, dist 25/5/79, bott May 94 **(85)** **n**19 **t**23 **f**21 **b**22. Worth checking a few labels for: won't see it at this relative youth again. **66.7%.** *Gordon & MacPhail.*

Cask Glen Mhor 1979 cask 2379, dist 25/5/79, bott Sep 99 **(80)** **n**18 **t**22 **f**20 **b**20. Big, biscuity malt, beautifully structured though mildly flawed. **66.3%.** *Gordon & MacPhail.*

Coopers Choice Glen Mhor 1980 bott 01 (20 Years Old) **(90)** **n**23 **t**23 **f**21 **b**23. Just wonderful whisky from a lost source: unlikely we shall see quality like this too often from Glen Mhor. A must buy.

Gordon & MacPhail Glen Mhor 1965 (74) **n**19 **t**20 **f**18 **b**17. Somewhat bitty and unbalanced. **40%**

Gordon & MacPhail Glen Mhor 1979 (74) **n**17 **t**19 **f**19 **b**19. A long way from their best-ever bottling from this distillery. **40%**

Hart Brothers Glen Mhor Aged 21 Years dist 76 **(81)** **n**19 **t**21 **f**20 **b**21. Glossy and attractively weighted with heavy malt. Lovely bitter-sweet balance **43%**

Old Malt Cask Glen Mhor Aged 24 Years dist Jul 75, bott Apr 00 **(92)** **n**22 **t**23 **f**23 **b**24. Honey enriched fireworks: the stuff of legend. **50%. nc ncf.** *Douglas Laing. 263 bottles.*

Old Malt Cask Glen Mhor Aged 25 Years dist Dec 75, bott Apr 01 **(88)** **n**22 a bit of nip and bite amid the lavender; **t**23 hot but sweet; **f**21 healthy oak and honey: lovely spice; **b**22 a busy, fascinating and delicious dram. **50%. nc ncf.** *Douglas Laing. 270 bottles.*

Old Malt Cask Glen Mhor Aged 34 Years dist Feb 66, bott Jul 00 **(89)** **n**24 **t**23 **f**21 **b**21. Fantastic sherry – to blow your mind, vat a tiny amount with some OMC Glen Mhor 24-y-o.... **50%. nc ncf.** *Douglas Laing. 396 bottles.*

GLENMORANGIE
Highland (Northern), 1843. Glenmorangie plc. Working.

Glenmorangie 10 Years Old db **(94)** **n**24 perhaps the most enigmatic aroma of them all: delicate yet assertive, sweet yet dry, young yet oaky: a malty tone poem; **t**22 flaky oakiness throughout but there is an impossibly complex toastiness to the barley which seems to suggest the lightest hint of smoke; **f**24 amazingly long for such a light dram, drying from the initial sweetness but with flaked almonds amid the oakier, rich cocoa notes; **b**24 remains one of the great single malts: a whisky of uncompromising aesthetic beauty from the first enigmatic whiff to the last teasing and tantalising gulp. Complexity at its most complex. **40%**

Glenmorangie 15 Years Old db **(89)** **n**23 fruitier with dense grapey tones, malty yet not as complex as the 10; **t**23 the most silky mouthfeel then delicious, controlled explosion of malty, peppery notes around the palate. Clean fruit, including the juiciest of plums, balances nicely; **f**21 remains warm and lingering with more emphasis on simple vanilla and malt; **b**22 rich by Glenmorangie standards and very warming. **43%**

···· **Glenmorangie 15 Years Old Sauternes Wood Finish** db **(68)** **n**14 **t**17 **f**19 **b**18. Only the intense fruit and finish saves this sulphury one ... to a degree. Not a patch on the standard Sauternes. **46%.** *Duty Free.*

Glenmorangie 18 Years Old (87) **n**23 big citrus presence: fresh and sparkling; **t**22 big, yet somehow subdued, as though on best behaviour. The sweet fruit dominates through a silky sheen, though the malt recovers; f21 the oak battles grimly for control, but the malt holds fast, supported by the fruit. The finale is pure custard tart. Lovely! b21 a real sweet, smoothie. 43%

Glenmorangie 25 Years Old db (84) n21 t22 f20 b21. Soft as a baby's bum, but for all its clean tones needs an injection of complexity. 43%

Glenmorangie 25 Year Old Malaga Wood db (89) n23 delicious infusion of sweet, highly perfumed notes of the candy shop: toasted mallows, lemon drops, perhaps, and fruity boiled sweets, all dusted with a sprinkling of oak; t22 that sweetness is evident early on, but soon diminishes as a fruity lustre gives way to a significant build-up of spices; f22 extremely long, peppery at first then fine malt interacts with oak and just a little smoke; b22 of all the many finishes Glenmorangie have provided over the last five years this is perhaps the most arresting: complex and downright deliciously unusual. 43%

Glenmorangie 1977 db (84) n22 t22 f20 b20. Complex and tasty, but feels an oaky pinch at the finish. 43%

Glenmorangie Burgundy Wood Finish db (78) n17 t21 f20 b20. The nose is a curious and less than wonderful mix of pepper and sweaty armpits and the spice really does go for it on mouth arrival. A wave of fresh fruit and barley sugar cushions the blows and though the finish is shortish it has an attractive chewability. 43%

⠿ **Glenmorangie Burgundy Finish** db (69) n16 t19 f17 b17. Sulphur traces and very ordinary. 43%

⠿ **Glenmorangie Cellar 13 Ten Years Old** db (90) n22 the very first threads of bourbon notes are filtering through; the butterscotch and honey notes mentioned on the label are spot on; t22 more glorious honey makes for an unusually intense maltiness; f23 that wonderful honey swarms all over the finale. The vanilla picks up in weight, as do some spices; b23 oddly enough, as much as this is the most honey-rich Glenmorangie of them all and a tastebud pleaser from first to last, the use of 100% first-fill bourbon has slightly detracted from the all round brilliance and complexity of the standard 10-y-o. 43%

Glenmorangie Cognac Matured db (83) n21 t21 f20 b21. Complex, but the famous Glenmorangie top notes have been flattened slightly. About as soft a Glenmorangie you are likely to find. 43%

Glenmorangie Cote de Beaune db (63) n10 t18 f19 b16. Hard to get past the disastrous nose. Improves towards the end, but too little, too late. 46%

Glenmorangie Cote de Nuits db (77) n19 t20 f19 b19. One of those whiskies where things never quite fall into place, though a second mouthful is no chore whatsoever. Fruity and dry. 43%

Glenmorangie Fino Sherry Wood Finish (85) n22 crisp, dry with some hiding smoke. It's all very delicate and striking; t21 remains clean and dry and understated; f21 It's all about delicacy and sweet-dry balance; b21 rather lovely and unusual stuff. They don't come more delicate and reserved than this. 43%

⠿ **Glenmorangie Golden Rum Cask Finish** db (94) n23 much of the usual 'Morangie complexity except there is also a syrupy sweetness to this one; t23 after a hesitant first second or two, the flavours sing in diverse harmonisation like a morning chorus: any more delicate it would snap; f24 some honeyed strands are coated in soft rum notes while the vanilla purrs along contently; b24 as limited a fan of finishes as I may be, a standing ovation here is richly deserved. The complexity fair boggles the mind. 40%. *Glenmorangie for Sainsbury's.*

Glenmorangie Distillery Manager's Choice 1983 db bott 00 (91) n22 t24 f22 b23. A malty exhibition of intense complexity. 53.2%

Glenmorangie Distillery Manager's Choice 2001 db (93) n23 fresh fruit, almost cut-glass clarity; t24 Oh, you little beauty! The arrival in the mouth is just so charismatic: spicy, fruity, malty, oaky, all at different levels but at some stage touching; f22 relaxed, end-of-season kick-about with emphasis on technical ability rather than thrills, but each goal scored is a stunner; **b**24 What can you say? Don't have the label to hand, but the effect is similar to extremely fresh port pipes. Astonishing whisky: every whisky club should try and get a bottle of this to share. **57.2%**

Glenmorangie Madeira Matured db **(93) n**21 big, wilful, spiced fruit and, despite carrying a slight blemish, big, bruising and belligerent; **t**24 the enormity of the flavour takes some serious map-making. A moderately-spiced grape leads the way, but beneath this the pulse of the barley beats strongly; sweetens fabulously and unexpectedly around the middle. The most mouthwatering 'Morangie of all time? **f**24 long, with less flaws now but the marrying and then slow fade of the fruit, barley and oak is a treat; **b**24 this is like a scarred, bare-knuckled, fist-fighter knocking 50 types of crap out of a classically trained world champion boxer: not one for the purists, but you cannot but admire and gasp in awe … **56%**

Glenmorangie Madeira Wood Finish db **(82) n**17 **t**22 **f**22 **b**21. Like all the Glenmorangie wood finishes the quality can vary dramatically. It's all part of the fun. Here a poor nose is rescued by a wonderful fruit-pastel, candy, mouthwatering arrival. Succulent and sweet. **43%**

Genmorangie Millennium Malt Aged 12 Years db **(83) n**21 **t**22 **f**20 **b**20. This is from entirely 100% first fill bourbon barrels and because of this – and the extra two years – the enchanting spell that makes Glenmorangie the most complex malt on mainland Scotland has been broken. Delicious, make no mistake, but simply too much of a good thing. **40%**

Glenmorangie Missouri Oak db **(88) n**21 well I'll be darned tootin': this is Scotch, ain't it? Had me goin' for a minute it were one of them thar bourbons; **t**23 a tornado of tannins and sweet sap. The barley recovers, but it's some shoot-out; **f**23 fabulous spices sit brilliantly with the simmering oak. The barley is a just a side-kick; **b**21 Yes-siree. This is one hell of a bourbon for a Scotch … technically; appears slightly too butyric ever to be a classic. But this ain't no one-horse whisky. Howdy stranger! Welcome into town. **56.2%**

Glenmorangie Port Wood Finish db **(84) n**22 **t**23 **f**19 **b**20. Perhaps because of the nature of the beast – finishing the whisky for a while in port pipes – this can be a variable dram. Not at its best here, it still shows an early complexity that defies belief, then superb spices. Just too sweet and toffee-rich on the finish in this bottling. **43%**

Glenmorangie Sauternes Wood Finish db **(89) n**21 spices and dark chocolate; **t**22 at first falls apart, but quickly regains composure for the intense grapeyness to hold the malt in place for good weight; **f**24 just so long and deft: the fruit-malt-oak ratio is brilliant – liquid Manor House cake. **b**22 one of the success stories of the wood-finishing programme: superb.

Glenmorangie Sherry Wood Finish db **(80) n**21 **t**23 **f**17 **b**19. The finish here is more cream toffee than sherry: somewhat disappointing, knowing how good it can be. The initial mouth arrival is superb, though. **43%**

Glenmorangie Tain L'Hermitage db **(88) n**22 a busy aroma, full of darting coal gas (at times an improbable hint of very weak peat reek), wild berries crushed in the hand and vanilla-tangerine; **t**21 flat at first, then a rush of ultra-ripe fruity notes: the middle merges effortlessly into the finish; **f**23 much more together here, with pleasing, mouthwatering fruit outlines against a deepening chocolate kick and those bizarre peat tones again; **b**22 a see-saw of a dram full of rich, mouth-bulging entertainment. **46%.**

Glenmorangie 3 Cask Matured db **(77) n**20 **t**20 **f**18 **f**19. Chalky and dry with fleeting fruit. **40%**

Glenmorangie Warehouse Three Reserve db **(92) n**22 dry, yet effervescent malt offers a fruity barley thrust; **t**23 slightly oily perhaps, it's all about thrusting barley and a mouth-puckering sharpness; **f**23 excellent arrival of light oak adding a touch of extra class and charisma to the finale. Lovely cocoa notes radiate warmly; **b**24 another genuinely outstanding expression, a cathartic catalogue of complexity, from a distillery that shows its greatness when allowed. **40%**. *Glenmorangie for Asda.*

GLEN MORAY
Speyside, 1897. Glenmorangie plc. Working.

Glen Moray (no age statement) db **(82)** n*19* t*22* f*21* b*20*. Young, vibrant, fresh malt, beautifully made. Has the feeling of a young blend – without the grain! **40%**

·:·· **Glen Moray 8 Years Old** db **(83)** n*21* t*20* f*22* b*20*. Clean but unusually fat for a Glen Moray. **40%**

·:·· **Glen Moray 12 Years Old** db **(85)** n*22* despite a surprising hint of sap, the oak holds the deep barley aloft; **t***21* threatens mouthwatering mode, but checked by gathering vanilla; **f***21* the finish is pure Glen Moray: layer after layer of barley that is clean and increasingly chewy. Still weightier than it was at this age 20 years ago; **b***21* never heads into great complexity but it does what it does well. **40%**

Glen Moray 12 Years Old db **(91)** n*23* a comfortable straddle between very light, teasing malt and soft vanilla; **t***22* lazy flavour entry: the malt saunters round the palate as if it owns the place, perfect harmony between sweet malt and drier oak; **f***23* here's where we get to business with the delicate complexity between malt and oak which is simply sublime. Some minor bourbony notes make a subdued approach; **b***23* one of my favourite Speyside malts for the last 17 years simply because it is so unfailingly consistent and the delicate nature of the whisky has to be experienced to be believed. **40%**

Glen Moray 12 Years Old Chenin Blanc db **(87)** n*22* big, over-ripe sultanas and some unusual oaky tones; **t***23* oily and lush. The malt and grape go hand in glove; **f***21* lots of vanilla, dries, becomes a little flakey; **b***21* a malt that feels good about itself in this slightly exotic form. **40%**

Glen Moray 16 Years Old db **(79)** n*21* t*21* f*18* b*19*. A heavier, fruitier expression but one that could come from any Speyside distillery and lacks the unambiguous characteristics of Glen Moray. **43%**

·:·· **Glen Moray 16 Years Old** db **(88)** n*23* pears and passion fruit amid the pounding malt; **t***21* a very soft and even mouth arrival with a barley-sugar middle; **f***22* more complexity here as lazy oak arrives to add a drying depth; **b***22* seriously easy drinking with not a single note out of tune. **40%**

Glen Moray 16 Years Old Chenin Blanc db **(85)** n*20* apples and sultanas sit well with the intense malt and a hint of smoke; **t***22* the oak makes for fuller mouthfeel on the oil and lush malt and fruit; **f***22* complex and medium dry with hints of coffee breaking through the chalky oak and softer fruit; **b***21* a dram just brimming with complexity. **40%**

·:·· **Glen Moray Mountain Oak** db **(94)** n*24* it must be the Appalachians, because there is a distinct bourbony aroma here: the malt rings clear but some oranges and something like beech smoke filter through; **t***22* the malty meltdown is not all because of the strength: a mixture of fresh, lip-smacking barley crashes head-first into something brimming with liquid spice and a smoky, biscuity depth; **f***24* astonishing length and weight but the real star is the near perfect bitter-sweet balance. The cut-glass barley sparkles to the very end; **b***24* Unquestionably the best Glen Moray I have ever tasted: a masterpiece Speysider that, if this quality can be maintained, is set to become a legend through its sheer complexity and depth. **60.5%**

Glen Moray 1959 Rare Vintage db **(91)** n*25* various orangey-tangerine notes amid a waft of smoke and a touch of bourbon keeps the nose intrigued. Probably the best nose of a malt this age you'll ever find; **t***23* beautiful mouthfeel then a wave of clear, clean oak and then sweeter, surprisingly gristy malt; **f***21* fades, as might be expected but there is no bitterness as one might expect from this age, just lots of sweet toffee; **b**22 they must have been keeping their eyes on this one for a long time: a stunning malt that just about defies nature. The nose reaches absolute perfection. **50.9%**

Glen Moray 1971 db bott 99 **(83)** n22 t21 f20 b20. Fruity yet a little dry and chalky. **43%**. *(bott 99)*

Glen Moray 1974 Distillery Manager's Choice bott 02 db **(88)** n23 this is all about just how subtle oak can be: the malt has a walk-on part but tannin-induced spices abound; **t**23 fabulous natural cream toffee. You can just chew and chew: the malt has come to life but still it's about controlled oak; **f**21 dries and loses some of its earlier pliability. The spice – and dab of smoke that one suspects on the nose – offers a third dimension; **b**21 this is brinkmanship of the highest level: this shows just how far a malt can be stretched by oak without snapping. **53.4%. ncf.**

Glen Moray 1981 Distillery Manager's Choice db **(92)** n25 classic sherry nose: tomatoes, figs, crushed raisins, bitter chocolate, coffee etc. Entirely faultless – a freak; **t**23 exceptionally well-balanced in terms of mouthfeel and bitter-sweet ratio, but the oak gets just a little too assertive too early; **f**22 lots of spices and dancing oak; **b**22 always said my old mate Ed at Glen Moray was a bit of a whisky genius. He should be struck a medal for finding this stunner.

Glen Moray Vallée du Rhône **(75)** n17 t20 f19 b19. C'est comme ci comme ça. **46%**

MacLeod's Highland Aged 8 Years **(89)** n22 stunning honey, so beautifully clean that the mouth salivates! Crisp barley concentrate that is firm and full and hardly troubled by oak, quite sensuous and very, very delicately smoked; **t**21 really malty with a highly accentuated barley thrust that offers brilliant sweet/dry ratio. Hardly complex by way of invading flavours, but the shape of the whisky is so delicious! **f**23 lots of bitter cocoa that perfectly counters the hinted sweetness of the barley. Some smoke simmers through; **b**23 Wow! This may be a Highlander by name on the label, though the source of the whisky is Speyside. But it is Highland by nature with some enormous earthy, resonance. Absolutely top-class stuff that bites and teases deliciously. Love to have seen this at 46% nonchillfiltered: might have had a minor classic on our hands. Glen Moray, though not stated on label. **40%**

Signatory Glen Moray Aged 9 Years sherry butt 4670, dist 29/06/89, bott 5/10/98, **(81)** n21 t21 f19 b20. The fruit influence appears to nullify the malt; the stand-off results in a peppery dram with more grape and oak than barley. **59.2%**

GLEN ORD
Highland (Northern) 1838. Diageo. Working.

Glen Ord Aged 12 Years db **(88)** n23 busy spices fail to interrupt the fruity malt flow; **t**22 more spice, then wave upon wave of quite brittle malt before a hint of smoke and vanilla appears; **f**21 a tad lazy as the malts luxuriate in a soft, sweet glow; **b**22 enormously improved on the boring old bottling with the trademark spices re-introduced and the malt spanning several layers of complexity. Much closer to how I remember it 20 years ago: the sherry style has been dropped and the malts reign. A very well-made malt ... welcome back! **43%**

Glen Ord Aged 23 Years db dist 1974, bott Oct 98 Rare Malts Selection **(84)** n21 t21 f21 b21. Big, chewy, fat, oaky, some honey and smoke. **60.8%**

⠿ **Glen Ord 28 Years Old** db **(90)** n22 malt and mint bound together by soft liquorice and dark fudge; **t**23 delightful barley-sugar theme that forms a stupendously rigid middle with the most delicate hints of smoke and coffee. The body weight is perfect; **f**22 amazingly long finale with lashings of cocoa to go with the mollassed sugar and powering barley; **b**23 this is mega whisky showing slight traces of sap, especially on the nose, but otherwise a concentrate of many of the qualities I remember from this distillery before it was bottled in a much ruined form. Blisteringly beautiful. **58.3%**.

Cadenhead's Ord 19 Years Old dist 83, bott 03/03 **(85)** n*22* a hint of coal smoke against brittle malt; t*21* biting, irrascible, nippy but the malt is crisp and constant; f*22* superb softening of malt alongside some natural cream toffee-fudge; b*20* a mouthwatering dram that was born to blend. **57%**

Signatory Glen Ord 18 Years Old refill sherry butt 377, dist 02/02/83, bott 24/08/01 **(84)** n*19* t*22* f*21* b*22*. Cream toffee, raisin. **58.3%**. *226 bottles.*

GLENROTHES
Speyside, 1878. Edrington. Working.

The Glenrothes 1966 cask 1437, bott 02 db **(87)** n*24* rich, heady toffee apple and demerara pot-still rum, beautifully clean with fruity red liquorice candy; t*21* massive oak and grape hand in hand, but the oak has the harder, more bitter grip; f*21* more liquorice and molassed sugar and the malt snaps and snarls at the marginally sappy, salty oak; b*21* really lovely stuff, but the oak punishes just a little too hard for this to be a true classic. **52.8%. nc.** *216 bottles.*

The Glenrothes 1967 cask 6998, bott 02 db **(94)** n*24* amiable malt blunders into vanilla: this relaxed, seriously laid-back yet ultra-complex malt keeps you sniffing until your nose bleeds; t*24* glorious. Just a celebration of all things malty yet softly spiced, fruity yet grained, sweet yet at times slightly dry; f*23* a slight hint of something smoky as the peppers tone down to something softer amid the sweet vanilla; b*23* Glenrothes at its most seductive and complex. Now this is a classic: not just as a Speysider but among all Scotland malts. Almost Sprinbankesque in sheer, unfettered élan. **46.3%. nc.** *180 bottles.*

The Glenrothes 1971 db bott 99 **(89)** n*23* t*22* f*21* b*23*. Big age on this, but kept in shape by firm malt and rich fruit. **43%**

The Glenrothes 1973 db bott 00 **(91)** n*22* t*24* f*23* b*22*. Great malt from a Speysider that dares to offer something big and bruising yet somehow complex and sophisticated. **43%**

⠴ **The Glenrothes 1974** bott 03 db **(94)** n*24* old leather handbags, honeycomb, slight peat; t*24* stupendous honey-malt arrival with burned fudge and then malted barley at its most pure; some liquorice and peat are also in there somewhere; f*23* oak offers a vanilla reprise from the marauding honey, malt and soft peat; b*23* I know people who are Glenrothes aficionados: their lives revolve around this distillery. Without this truly classic dram, those lives will be incomplete. **43%**

The Glenrothes 1979 db bott 02 **(92)** n*22* a complex, grainy nose with bite: not unlike a very good blend; t*24* just love this: fresh, crisp, clean then honied; f*23* back to that grainy crispness and a soft, floating smokiness; b*23* a very unusual Glenrothes of alluring and memorable complexity. A must for us blend lovers! **43%**

The Glenrothes 1987 db bott 99 **(84)** n*21* t*22* f*20*. b*21* Soft cream-toffee-caramel checks the development of an otherwise lovely-weighted and fruity malt. **43%**

The Glenrothes 1989 db bott 01 **(75)** n*19* t*20* f*18* b*18*. Disappointingly dull and caramel rich. **43%**

The Glenrothes 1989 db bott 00 **(76)** n*19* t*21* f*18* b*18*. Cloakroomy, musty rainjackets, dusty churches. Makes for an interesting nose, shame it's nothing like as curious to taste. I think '89, with the odd exception here and there, must have been a sub-standard vintage for this usually impeccable distillery. **43%**

⠴ **The Glenrothes 1992** bott 04 db **(76)** n*17* t*20* f*19* b*20*. Just a hint of red liquorice on the finale heads it away from the malt. The nose is poor, though. **43%**

Adelphi Glenrothes 10 Years Old cask 10965, dist 92, bott 02 **(79)** n*20* t*19* f*20* b*20*. Toasty and dry for the most part; hot and malty in others. **57.1%**

⫶ **Adelphi Glenrothes 13 Years Old** cask 15355 dist 90 bott 03 **(79)** n*19* t*19* f*21* b*20*. Despite that impressive toffee-apple sherry effect on the middle and finish just the odd flaw marks this one down slightly. **59.6%**

Adelphi Glenrothes 24 Years Old cask 2711, dist 76 bott 00 **(78)** n*19* t*21* f*19* b*19*. Mildly feinty and enormously oily. **52.7%. sc.**

Cadenhead's Glenrothes 12 Years Old dist 90, bott 10/02 **(69)** n*17* t*19* f*17* b*16*. Sulphur-tainted throughout. **46%**

⫶ **Chieftain's Glenrothes 1992 Aged 10 Years Port Finish** bott 27 Mar 04 **(90)** n*21* the malt hasn't quite merged with the port; t*23* no such problems here: the arrival on the palate is one of harmony with the softness of the wine laying a fruity foundation for the increasingly intense barley; f*23* some oak arrives to add a touch of welcome bitterness to the gathering sweet barley; b*23* from such an unpromising nose has sprung a port finish that keeps the tastebuds guessing until the last. Brilliant!! **43%. Ian Macleod.**

⫶ **Chieftain's Glenrothes 1993 Aged 10 Years Rum Finish** bott 25 Mar 04 **(93)** n*22* as rum-soaked as a sea wind; t*24* from the very start the mouth goes into overtime to come to terms with the sheer enormity of the flavour profile: the sweetness is intense but the barley richness matches the rum richness. Just so wonderfully complex; f*23* some extra oak for its age which really does work well with the natural caramel notes which linger with the peppery spices and barley; b*24* one that you can chew until your jaw drops off. **43%. Ian Macleod.**

Coopers Choice Glenrothes 1985 dist 01 (15 Years Old) **(89)** n*22* stem ginger and molasses; t*22* big, chewy, malty; f*22* tufts of liquorice amid dry oak and sweet sugars; b*23* an absolute little cracker. **56%. The Vintage Malt Whisky Co.**

Coopers Choice Glenrothes 1975 dist 02 (26 Years old) **(87)** n*22* fresh fruit and spices with just a hint of something smoky; t*21* big mouthfeel, wave upon wave of buttery sherry; f*22* soft, sultanas and raisins and some spices; b*22* a fine sherry cask without an off-note. In some ways too perfect! **51%. The Vintage Malt Whisky Co.**

Gordon & MacPhail Glenrothes 1961 (82) n*20* t*21* f*21* b*20*. Gooseberries on the nose and malty-silk on the palate. No off-notes or oak deterioration whatsoever. **40%**

Hart Brothers Glenrothes Aged 33 Years dist Oct 69, bott Jan 03 **(80)** n*21* t*21* f*19* b*19*. Chalky but cheerful. **46.8%**

James MacArthur Glenrothes 12 Year Old (85) n*21* firm, wth a mixture of tangerine and nicotine; t*22* fresh and fruity at first then a wave of grassy malt and spice. f*21* busy oak; b*21* very big and weighty. **43%**

The MacPhail's Collection Glenrothes 8 Years Old (80) n*19* t*22* f*20* b*19*. Really complex middle stars. **40%**

⫶ **MacPhail's Collection Glenrothes 30 Years Old (82)** n*20* t*21* f*21* b*20*. Good honey spice, enthusiastic oak. **43%. Gordon & MacPhail.**

⫶ **Old Malt Cask Glenrothes Aged 17 Years** dist Dec 85, bott Sep 03 **(72)** n*17* t*19* f*18* b*18*. Sultanas, raisins and high roast Java coffee offer riches, but the lurking sulphur from the sherry has the most telling say. **50%. nc ncf sc. Douglas Laing. 581 bottles.**

Old Malt Cask Glenrothes Aged 31 Years dist Jun 69, bott Feb 01 **(72)** n*18* t*19* f*17* b*18*. Off the pace. **50%. nc ncf. Douglas Laing. 174 bottles.**

Old Masters Glenrothes 1989 bott 01 **(86)** n*21* buttery, cream toffee; t*22* uncomplicated malt: clean, intense and naturally toffeed; f*22* long with some soft oaks intruding on the malt; b*21* a real mouthful. Blenders die for this stuff. **64.7%. James MacArthur.**

Peerless Glenrothes 1967 cask 8389, dist May 67 **(74)** n*20* t*18* f*18* b*18*. Some honied moments, but pretty tired. **40.9%. Duncan Taylor & Co.**

Peerless Glenrothes 1968 cask 13481, dist Nov 68 34-y-o **(80)** n*19* t*21* f*20* b*20*. An oaky, substantial beast. **57%. Duncan Taylor & Co.**

Peerless Glenrothes 1969 cask 382, dist Jan 69 **(86) n**20 light and just a little shy for its great age, the oak strikes an impressively delicate balance with the malt but insists on a degree of superiority. Some spice does bite hard but the toffee softens it all down; **t**23 Wow! Piledriving spices hammer home but are consumed by the most extraordinary sweetness. This takes an oily form that coats the mouth with an unusual mixture of coffee-cocoa and honey. Excellent; **f**21 long and fat with many variations on a drying oaky theme. Perhaps just a little too bitter at the death, but that can be forgiven; **b**22 an impressive bottling. **50.7%.** *Duncan Taylor & Co Ltd.*

⠿ **Provenance Glenrothes Over 13 Years** dist Winter 90, bott Winter 03 **(89) n**22 toffee and burnt raisin: massive sherry influence for once not ruined by sulphur!! **t**23 breathtaking intensity and spice to start; the sweetness appears only when it thinks it is safe and brings with it vanilla and treacle; **f**22 ripe plums and burnt sugar; the oak labours in its dryness and finally offers a sawdusty finale; **b**22 oh, the bliss of finding a true sherry butt in good shape. **46%.** *Douglas McGibbon.*

Scott's Selection Glenrothes 1973 bott May 03 **(92) n**23 this is glorious: the malt and oak have combined for golden shafts of honey to fall on some delicate smoky tones: light and heavy, sweet and dry; **t**24 carries on from the nose with a shimmering, concentrated honied maltiness; **f**22 heaps of spice, with that softly spoken peat on the nose making another murmur; **b**23 I know those who regard Glenrothes as the finest of all Speyside distilleries: on the evidence of this it is hard to offer too much of an argument. **50.2%.** *Robert Scott & Co.*

Ultimate Selection Glenrothes 1994 sherry butt 6882, dist 10/6/94, bott 4/3/02 **(89) n**21 fresh, young, youthful malt with just enough oak; **t**24 absolutely beautiful malt: grassy, crystal clear in flavour and wonderfully bitter-sweet; **f**23 slightly short but the malt persists and some late dark chocolate suggests some oak involvement; **b**21 if this were any cleaner you could wash yourself with it. Delicious: the sherry butt has obviously done the rounds as it plays no part in the malt's development. Everybody should have a bottle of this. **43%.** *Van Wees NL.*

⠿ **Wilson & Morgan Barrel Selection Glenrothes 1989 Rum Finish** bott 03 **(75) n**20 **t**19 **f**18 **b**18. Mildly cloying and off the pace. **46%.**

GLEN SCOTIA
Campbeltown, 1832. Glen Catrine. Working.

Glen Scotia 14 Years Old db **(90) n**23 complex, with darting malty notes nipping around, almost like the small grains in a bourbon: really top-quality stuff; **t**22 busy, light maltiness with flickering intensity. The malty sweetness is never more than a passing illumination amid the gathering cocoa oakiness; **f**22 gristy malt and soft oak intertwine; **b**23 if Glen Scotia had been this good in the past it wouldn't have suffered such a chequered career. Absolutely engrossing malt with fabulous complexity. **40%**

⠿ **Cask Glen Scotia 1992 (81) n**18 **t**22 **f**21 **b**20. Not exactly text-book whisky (troubled times at t'distillery) but the excellence of the unexpected peat makes for a delicious dram. **62.1%.** *Gordon & MacPhail.*

⠿ **Chieftain's Glen Scotia Aged 30 Years Rum Barrel** bott 31 Mar 04 **(83) n**22 **t**21 **f**19 **b**21. Enormously sweet, salty, oaky with a toffee creaminess. **41.2%.** *Ian Macleod.*

The MacPhail's Collection Glen Scotia 1990 (86) n21 peat and honey; **t**22 peat and honey **f**22 guess what? ... peat and honey ... and oak; **b**21 for those in search of a softly peated and honied dram. A real collector's item for Glen Scotia – the peatiest I have ever come across bottled by some margin. Simple, but delicious. **40%.** *Gordon & MacPhail.*

Milroy's Glen Scotia Aged Over 10 Years (75) n19 **t**17 **f**20 **b**19. Big whisky with power and bite, but hard as nails and a little spirity. **43%**

⠿ **Murray McDavid Mission III Glen Scotia 1975 (73)** n18 t19 f18 **b**18. There are those who will lie down and die for this; however, to me this is more like an OTT flavoured aquavit. **46%**

Scotch Malt Whisky Society Cask 93.10 Aged 11 Years (94) n23 for something so rich and honied there is no shortage of weight: such an enticing mildly peaty dram; t24 a raucous arrival of sweet malt and thumping oak, a punch-up in which much honey is spilt; f23 some smoke lingers with the spices and lush, rich malty notes; **b**24 like a top-rate Talisker ... with honey! If you have a friend who is a member of the society, let him have your wife for the weekend in exchange for a miniature of this distillery's finest in bottled form. For the entire bottle, it might be worth allowing him to keep her. (For the PC – only joking (yeah, right!)) **63.8%. nc ncf sc.**

GLEN SPEY
Speyside, 1885. Diageo. Working.

Glen Spey Aged 12 Years db **(85)** n21 a soothing, softly malted aroma, hints of toffee maybe but definite oak; t22 refreshing and grassy malt battles through some toffee-heaviness most uncharacteristic of Glen Spey. Vague hints of something molassed and oaky; f21 quite long with some bitter cocoa and distant peppers; **b**21 for those of us brought up on Glen Spey being light, crystalline and grassy, this is a strange bottling to get to grips with. The heaviest Glen Spey I've come across in 20 years which, though not quite representative of the distillery's character, offers an acceptably intriguing and complex dram. **43%**

⠿ **The Master of Malt Glen Spey 12 Year Old** dist 85 **(82)** n20 t22 f20 **b**20. Clean, a tad fruity and very mouthwateringly malty. Overall, though, sweet, simple and unchallenging. Although bottled in the late 1990s, I have found a few cases of this rarest of Speysiders still floating around Denmark. **43%.** *The Master of Malt.*

GLENTAUCHERS
Speyside, 1898. Allied. Working.

Gordon & MacPhail Glentauchers 1990 (86) n21 a tantalising mixture of soft malts and oaks with just a sprinkling of peat for good measure; t22 stupendous mouthfeel with again subtle nuances found of the three major contributors; f21 moves towards oaky vanilla with a hint of spice; **b**22 this is an unspectacular malt that somehow contrives to be quite charming. Everything is delicate and understated, but the journey is wonderful. **40%**

The Master of Malt Glentauchers 11 Years Old (84) n21 t22 f21 **b**21. Really impressive chewing malt with a healthy streak of peat and a little nip. **43%**

⠿ **Old Master's Glentauchers 1990** bott 04 cask 14422 **(91)** n22 firm, clean, almost rye-hard nose offering perfect poise; t23 brittle, mouthwatering barley explodes on impact. The fallout includes gentle vanilla; f22 a sophisticated sweetness lingers with ginger and coffee as the barley-oak balance stays in sync; **b**24 stylish and subtle, this is textbook Glentauchers. **59.2%.** *James MacArthur.*

⠿ **Whisky Galore Glentauchers 1990 Aged 12 Years (88)** n21 textbook 'Tauchers with flint-hard malt you could fire bullets with; t23 absolutely no give on the palate: the barley thuds meteorite-like into the tastebuds; f22 some mouthwatering malt falls out from the blast and some vanilla, too; **b**22 I love this distillery. Clean, delicious and entirely uncompromising. **46%**

⠿ **Wilson & Morgan Barrel Selection Glentauchers 1990 Rum Finish** bott 04 **(75)** n20 t19 f18 **b**18. Rarely has the old adage of "if it ain't broke, don't fix it" been more apposite. The rum character is discernible, but only at the cost of the more complex, delicate malt trying to be heard. **46%**

GLENTURRET
Highlands (Perthshire), 1775. Edrington. Working.

Glenturret 10 Years Old db **(86) n**21 firm honey thread, exceptionally clean malt with the most teasing hint of ginger; **t**22 rich Glenturret mouthfeel, as if lots of copper has been used in the process. Again the malts are clean and slick; **f**21 mild hints of something spicy enlivens the malt-honey processsion; **b**22 those of you into Lochnagar will recognise this style of rich, intense whisky. Amazing coppery mouthfeel, softened by the trademark honey: very well-made whisky, indeed. **40%**

The Glenturret Aged 15 Years db **(87) n**21 honey and cherry tomato: rich yet clean; **t**22 highly intense malt that sweetens, mildly oily with a hint of oak; **f**21 honey returns, vaguely waxy with a mild spice finale; **b**22 a beautifully clean, small-still style dram that would have benefitted from being bottled at a fuller strength. A discontinued bottling now: if you see it, it is worth the small investment. **40%**

The Glenturret Aged 18 Years db **(86) n**21 floral and herbal: a gardener's dram; **t**22 good grip in the palate with acacia honey booming in; **f**21 cream toffee and marmalade. Just a faint hint of honey battles through; **b**22 very delicate and holds its age well. Discontinued. If you see it, it's the last of the line. **40%**

The Glenturret Aged 21 Years db **(85) n**20 fruity, honied but a tad soapy; **t**22 beautifully oiled with the honey going into orbit and even a hint of peat; **f**21 lots of cream toffee with cocoa, then the soapiness returns; **b**21 a soft, honied dram that is way understrength for its age and style. **40%**

Glenturret 1972 bott Dec 02 db **(87) n**22 I don't think I've come across so much vanilla on a nose, especially one that is already overflowing with honey; **t**21 slightly soapy, but acceptably so, then a wave of intense malt and honey; **f**22 back to the massive vanilla wall: those long strands of honey just keep on going; **b**22 a really unusual dram, a bit on the soapy side, but such is the enormity of honey/vanilla mix, wholly acceptable. **47%**. *Four hogsheads producing just 522 bottles.*

Blackadder Glenturret 17 Years Old cask 4906, dist 7 April 80, bott May 97 **(93) n**23 **t**23 **f**23 **b**24. This is a Glenturret classic, damp millet and budgie seed! A perfect dram for budgies, as my son's one, Borat, will testify. He loves to nose it ... and with very good reason! **53.7%. sc.**

Cadenhead's Glenturret 15 Years Old dist 86, bott 10/02 **(89) n**21 lively and a tad soapy, but slowly some very piercing malt notes appear; **t**22 sublime texture of yielding yet biting malt – excellent complexity; **f**24 now the honey arives for Glenturret overdrive. Few other distilleries have this kind of flourish to their signature: cocoa mixes brilliantly with the soft honey; **b**22 for all its playful bite and nip, a dram you can sink into. **54%**

⸭ **Chieftain's Glenturret Aged 13 Years Port Finish** bott 25 Mar 04 **(86) n**23 the malt has been over-run slightly by the port, but my word: this is port and malt at its most noble; **t**21 stirring oak from the off with the wine sweetening the proceedings; **f**21 mildly bitter finale – not dissimilar to grape pips – but the vanilla and fruit until then are enjoyable; **b**21 never quite lives up to the nose ... but what a nose!! **43%**. *Ian Macleod.*

Hart Brothers Glenturret Aged 11 Years dist Jun 91, bott Sep 02 **(83) n**19 **t**22 **f**21 **b**21. Slightly dusty, but the palate arrival is pure Perthshire! **55.5%**

MacPhail's Collection Glenturret 1990 Vintage (84) n21 **t**22 **f**20 **b**21. Beautiful honey, dry on finish. **40%**. *Gordon & MacPhail.*

Old Malt Cask Glenturret Aged 15 Years dist 86, bott 02 **(84) n**21 **t**22 **f**19 **b**22. A whisky of beguiling enormity that reeks of rich Perthshire honey. There are one or two minor flaws here, almost certainly cask-related, but so lush and sweet is this whisky that a blind eye can be turned. **50%. nc ncf.** *Douglas Laing.*

⸭ **Old Malt Cask Glenturret Aged 17 Years** dist Dec 85, bott Sep 03 **(72) n**17 **t**19 **f**18 **b**18. Oh dear. **50%. nc ncf sc.** *Douglas Laing.*

Old Masters Glenturret 1986 bott 02 **(88)** n*21* standard mildly oily Glenturret aroma; t*23* rich oils fill the mouth: sweet yet sharp malt rules the roost; f*22* a hint of honey as the vanilla arrives; b*22* this is a very good cask selection. **51.3%.** *James MacArthur.*

Ultimate Selection Glenturret 1985 cask 119, dist 12/7/85, bott 4/3/02 **(90)** n*23* honey and diced raw carrots; t*23* perfect mouthfeel and wonderful marriage of sweet malt and toffee bonbons; f*22* soft, chalky oak; b*22* ask to be shown a first-class cask of 16-y-o Glenturret, and you'll get this. **43%. sc.** *Van Wees NL.*

GLENUGIE
Highland (Eastern). 1834–1983. Closed.

Connoisseurs Choice Glenugie 1967 (89) n*23* tangerines, grist and vanilla: a wonderful combination; t*23* softly oiled and massive, sweet malt. The barley just revels. A touch of peat, too; f*21* soft vanilla and lingering malt; b*22* the first Glenugie I ever tasted: has never been bettered in bottle. **40%.** *Gordon & MacPhail.*

Gordon & MacPhail Glenugie 1968 (86) n*22* oaky and a little starchy, big, big malt; t*22* oak first again, but levels out to let in very sweet, biscuity barley; f*21* lovely balance here as the oak recedes to allow in figs and vanilla; b*21* incredibly sweet and malty. Really lovely stuff, with fine oak. **40%**

Old Malt Cask Glenugie Aged 26 Years dist March 76 **(76)** n*22* t*20* f*16* b*18*. Brilliant fruit and custard nose, but the palate – after the initial malty burst – shows inevitable signs of wear and tear. **50%.** *Douglas Laing.*

GLENURY ROYAL
Highland (Eastern), 1868–1985. Demolished.

⋮⋮ **Glenury Royal 50 Years Old** dist 53, db **(91)** n*23* marvellous freshness to the sherry butt; this had obviously been a high quality cask in its day and the intensity of the fruit sweetened slightly by the most delicate marzipan and old leather oozes class; a little mint reveals some worry lines; t*24* the early arrival is sweet and nimble with the barley, against the odds, still having the major say after all these years. The oak is waiting in the wings and with a burst of soft liquorice and velvety, understated spice beginning to make an impression; the sweetness is very similar to a traditional British child's candy of "tobacco" made from strands of coconut and sugar; f*22* masses of oak yet, somehow, refuses to go over the top and that slightly molassed sweetness sits very comfortably with the mildly oily body; b*22* I am always touched when sampling a whisky like this from a now departed distillery. My first whisky of a new tasting day: no need for the spittoon with this one and things can go only downhill from here...(well, not quite: joy of joys, I have just received a phone call to confirm I have tickets for my beloved Millwall's FA Cup Final appearance with Manchester United. An event even rarer than a 50-y-o Glenury...!) **42.8%**

Connoisseurs Choice Glenury Royal 1976 (83) n*21* t*22* f*20*. b*20*. Malt and clean with lovely citrus freshness. **40%**

Gordon & MacPhail Glenury Royal 1972 (70) n*18* t*19* f*16* b*17*. Decent early show, then dies. **40%**

Old Malt Cask Glenury Aged 21 Years (sherry) dist March 80, bott May 01 **(83)** n*21* t*22* f*20* b*20*. Big, chewy, oaky. Lots of natural toffee. **50%. nc ncf.** *Douglas Laing. 504 bottles.*

Old Malt Cask Glenury Aged 32 Years dist Nov 68, bott Feb 01 **(89)** n*22* t*23* f*22* b*22*. A strappingly big laddie. **49.4%. nc ncf.** *Douglas Laing. 258 bottles.*

Platinum Glenury 34 Years Old dist Nov 68, bott Jan 03 **(72)** n*18* T19 f*17* b*18*. Honey but too aged. **43.4%.** *Douglas Laing.*

HIGHLAND PARK
Highland (Island–Orkney), 1795. Edrington. Working.

Highland Park 8 Years Old db **(87) n**22 firm young, honied malt with food coke/peat smoke; **t**22 silky honey and excellent complexity for a malt so young; **f**22 complex layers of vanilla and soft peat at first than caramel grabs hold: shame; **b**21 a journey back in time for some of us: this is the orginal distillery bottling of the 70s and 80s, bottles of which are still doing the rounds in obscure Japanese bars and specialist outlets such as the Whisky Exchange. **40%**

Highland Park Aged 12 Years db **(92) n**24 sublime: the peat is almost sprinkled on by hand in exact measures, the honey and vague molasses guaranteeing contolled sweetness, salt, old leather and apples in there, too; **t**22 moderately weighty mouth arrival, sweet yet enough oak to offer some bitter complexity. This fabulour bitter-sweet balance pans out in favour of the honey though there is enough peat around to add extra weight; **f**22 long, spicy, some earthy heather and more oak than usual. Excellent cocoa hangs about with the peat; **b**24 it defies belief that an international brand can maintain this quality, more or less, year in year out. Few drams are as silkily enveloped as this gem. **40%**

Highland Park Aged 15 Years db **(83) n**20 **t**22 **f**21 **b**20. The new kid on the block has yet to show the voluptuous expansiveness of its brothers. The nose is surprisingly closed and the flavours never fully open on the palate, either. Good smoke and spice, though. **40%. For Sainsbury UK.**

Highland Park Aged 18 Years db **(95) n**24 an empty honey jar which once held peaty embers. An enormous nose of excellent consistency, with salty butter and burnt honeycomb is always present; **t**23 beautifully sweet, in some ways sweeter than even the 12-y-o thanks to some manuka honey, which is accentuated against the drier oaky tones and rumbling peat towards the back of the palate: beautifully chewy, a touch oily and wholly substantial; **f**24 some citrus, heathery notes, controlled oak and outstanding cocoa and peat: long and rewarding; **b**24 a consistent dram of enormous weight and complexity, bottle after bottle, and never short of breathtakingly brilliant: the ace in the Highland Park pack. **43%**

Highland Park Aged 25 Years db **(94) n**23 enormous sherry, but enough spice and peat battles through to guarantee balance. A zesty, honied maltiness can also be found; the oak is also loud and clear; **t**24 seriously rich and weighty; oily textured, fruity but a really gripping spiciness buzzes around the palate. The crescendo is silk-textured and honey sweet with some grape and cocoa; **f**23 long, with the cocoa taking its time to clear. Late heather but the oak is restrained by comparison with the nose and the esters remain fat and sparkling; **b**24 since the launch of the 18 and 25, for me there has always been a wide gap in quality with the 18 always on top. This latest bottling suggests the gap is closing fast. Brilliant use of some sherry, it seems, has calmed the former excesses of the oak and we are left with an aged whisky that is an essay in balance and sophistication. **50.7%**

Highland Park Aged 25 Years db **(89) n**23 emphasis on the heather-honey though significant fruit – apple especially – abounds. Some pulsating oak, but the theme is sweetish and gently spiced. No more than a hint of smoke; **t**23 firm bodied with soft, smoky spices forming a guard around the burnt honey and barley; much more rigid and crisp than normal HP but this doesn't detract from the radiating complexity; **f**21 layers of vanilla and rich honey. Pretty short, though; **b**22 a very different animal to the 50.7% version with less expansion, depth and expression. Not a bad dram, though... **51.5%**

꙳ **Highland Park 1967** cask 10252, db **(87) n**22 a heady mix of oak, honey, smoke and raisin; **t**22 a raunchy, massively oaked beast that survives the chunky onslaught through sweetening honey and a rich smoke layer; **f**21 calmer and better-behaved with the balance at last restored with honey maintaining its line and a raisiny smokiness providng the depth, the oak is just a little too noisy at the finale; **b**22 the sum is better than the parts but this is massive whisky caught at the moment it falls over the oaky edge. **49.7%.** *Exclusive to the Whisky Exchange.*

Highland Park Bicentenary Vintage 1977 Reserve db **(93)** n*24* herbal and salty. The heather is in full bloom; t*25* the early peat dissolves in the mouth allowing the honey and vanilla the stage. Lovely greengages and salt add to the complexity: truly fantastic, to the point of faultless; f*21* cocoa and Jamaican coffee compensate for an otherwise lazy though lightly spiced finale; b*23* should have been bottled at 46–50% for full effect: they were making great whisky at this time at HP and this is a pretty peaty version. **40%**

⠸⠿ **Highland Park Capella Special Edition** db **(87)** n*23* that unique buzz of smoke that so comfortably sits with distinctive heather/gorse and honey. Genuinely awesome how this distillery does it; t*23* smoke and some grapey, fruity notes, then thick fudge; f*20* spice but dampened and embittered by toffee; b*21* the caramel (natural or otherwise) that has arrived towards the middle and end flattens an until then intensely glorious bottling. **40%**

Adelphi Highland Park 20 Years Old cask 1286, dist 82, bott 02 **(90)** n*21* quite sharp malt, honied of course; t*23* so rich … enormous malt-honey start but some peat sneaks in slowly; f*23* touches of cocoa make for a brilliant counter-dryness and some salt in there, too; b*23* the cocoa at the end adds an extra supreme dimension to an already fabulous whisky. Brilliant. **56.4%**

Adelphi Highland Park 21 Years Old cask 4146, dist 79, bott 00 **(84)** n*21* t*23* f*20* b*20*. A strangely listless malt from Adelphi. The fore and middle are big and long, offering lots of sweetness. But the smoke and complexity just isn't there all round and is replaced by toffee. **51.7%. sc.**

Blackadder Highland Park 10 Years Old refill sherry cask 20569, dist 11 Nov 92, bott Mar 03 **(80)** n*19* t*22* f*20* b*19*. Very sweet and refreshing. **45%**

Blackadder Old Man of Hoy (89) n*22* winey and rich, softly oaked with an oily peatiness. Flower-scented sweetness and heather: the kind of malt that would send bees into a frenzy; t*23* fat and oily; a wave of intensely sweet malt upon successive waves of gentle peat. Thick, intense and chewy; f*22* a long strand of peat compliments the heather and oak; b*22* the label doesn't say which Orkney distillery this hails from, but two seconds alone with a glass of it leaves no doubt whatsoever. **58%**

⠸⠿ **Blackadder Raw Cask Highland Park 14 Years Old** cask 10039 dist Mar 89, bott Nov 03 **(91)** n*22* bales of straw; a little sappy but some impressive covering peat-reek and honey; t*23* heads directly into the heather-honey zone without passing go; f*23* soft peat returns and battles it out with rich, oily spices; b*24* massive amounts of complexity, and all in the fingerprints of HP despite above average peat: most excellent. **57.1%**

Blackadder Raw Cask Highland Park 1989 sherry hogshead cask 10042, dist 1 March 89, bott April 02 **(88)** n*21* lively, spicy, heathery; t*23* usual honey tang and delicious sweetness with some vanilla balancing the middle out a bit; f*22* very long with vanilla and busy spices; b*22* a relatively light HP with limited smoke inclusion but the soft honey complexity is quite lovely.

Cadenhead's Highland Park 22 Years Old dist 79, bott 10/02 **(79)** n*19* t*22* f*18* b*20*. Honied, but a little hidden soapiness just takes it down a peg or two. **50.4%**

Cask Highland Park 1989 (79) n*20* t*22* f*18* b*19*. The usual honey and stuff and some berry chewy moments, but otherwise not firing on all cylinders. **58.4%.** *Gordon & MacPhail.*

⠸⠿ **Duncan Taylor Highland Park 1966 Aged 36 Years** cask 6410 **(79)** n*19* t*20* f*20* b*20*. A malt straffed by rampaging oak but there is enough honey in there for running repairs. **40.1%**

⠸⠿ **Duncan Taylor Highland Park 1966 Aged 37 Years** cask 4637 **(85)** n*19* piney, tired oak; t*21* brilliant mouth arrival with the oak trying to gain fatal control but waves of waxy honey and soft peat hold sway; **f**23 real, thick old honey offers countless waves of toasted sweetness; **b**22 sees off the worst of the oak with waxy honey to spare. **40.9%**

Gordon & MacPhail Highland Park 1970 (78) n22 t20 f18 b18. Honied nose (surprise, surprise) but the body is just a fraction too thin and oaky. **40%**

Hart Brothers Highland Park Aged 10 Years dist 89, bott 00 **(82)** **n**20 **t**22 **f**20 **b**20. Lots of soft vanilla douses the usual honey. The spices are excellent, though. **43%**

꜒꜒꜒ **Hart Brothers Highland Park Aged 10 Years** dist July 93 bott Sep 03 **(82)** n21 t22 f19 b20. One of the most intense citrus noses I've come across with slight pine and peat giving it a character the like of which I guarantee you've never seen before from this or probably any other distillery! **46%**

Hart Brothers Highland Park 20 Years Old dist 77 **(83)** n20 t22 f21 **b**20. The malt has thinned and soft vanilla holds sway. Delightfully delicate all the same. **43%**

Hart Brothers Highland Park 25 Years Old dist 75 **(89)** n23 ripping honey and oak balance with glorious peaty side-dish. The oak threatens towards big age, but so what! **t**22 heather-honey and leather Winchesters and soft oak: it's like drinking a library; f22 dries with a honied sheen; **b**22 this is just one hell of a Highland Park. Thinks about going over the woody edge, but stays the right side of the warning line. **43%**

꜒꜒꜒ **Jim Wiebers Whisky World Old Train Line Highland Park 30 Years** Cask No. 8396 dist Jun 73, bott Aug 03 **(91)** n22 the barley remains mercifully intact, a slight bourbon element sweetens things and a second layer of weighty oak adds depth; **t**24 yesssss!!! Just wonderful, perfectly balanced arrival with softly oiled barley battling it out with the rampaging heather-honey. Just too good to be true; f22 gloriously long with lots of cocoa and a playful hint of peat; **b**23 rarely does one cask nutshell Highland Park so comprehensively as this. A must have. **58.7%** *.Germany. 168 bottles.*

꜒꜒꜒ **Jim McEwan's Celtic Heartlands Highland Park 1967 (87)** n22 a salted heatherfest; **t**22 enormously fat with a buttery-vanilla-barley theme and a hint of honey towards the middle; f21 soft and curiously oak free: the butteriness remains; **b**22 I have drunk some '67 HP over the years, but nothing quite as oily, as this curious – and delicious – chap. **40.1%**. *Bruichladdich.com.*

Lombard Highland Park 1989 (86) n20 coal smoke and a hint of lime; **t**24 the gradual arrival of honey amid the intense malt is a sheer delight. Couched in equally increasing smoke, this is so soft it is almost unreal. A great whisky moment! f20 what follows is a relative let-down as the malt-honey growth stops and drier, more toffeed tones appear; **b**22 one of the better bottlings by some distance from Lombard. **50%**

The MacPhail's Collection Highland Park 8 Years Old (86) n 21 honey and smoke; **t**22 velvety malt and the heather honey makes its guest appearance; f22 long with hints of delicious cocoa; **b**21 straight as a die: smoke and honey all the way with no hesitation or deviation. **40%**

꜒꜒꜒ **The MacPhail's Collection Highland Park 30 Years Old (89)** n22 quite some honeyfest; **t**21 decidedly off-balance at first, but regains its poise towards the middle as some smoke arrives; f24 now goes into overdrive as all the old suspects, honey, heather and smoke combine like old pros to steer the dram home to a near perfect conclusion; **b**22 starts unpromisingly but finishes a thoroughbred. **43%**. *Gordon & MacPhail.*

Mission Range Highland Park 1979 (94) n22 coke and seaweed, quite salty plus soft oak; **t**24 just an amazing infusion of varying honey tones with the most delicate peat; f24 complexity goes into overdrive here as the heathery, earthy tones gain a healthy foothold and rock with the smoke and oak: sweet massive and long. Great spices kick in, too; **b**24 just wicked whisky: simple as that. Another extraordinary dram that helps put the Mission Range among the most impossibly brilliant in world bottlings. **46%**. *Murray McDavid.*

Murray McDavid Highland Park 1979 cask 7749 dist May 79, bott Jun 97 **(89)** n22 t24 f21 b22. Peat and honey of the very highest order. One of the better independent bottlings at non-cask strength. **46%. nc ncf sc.**

⸬ **Old Malt Cask Highland Park Aged 16 Years** cask 984 dist Apr 87, bott Sep 03 **(82)** n20 t22 f20 b20. A delicious honeyball at times, but the oak has fraction too loud a shout. **50%, nc ncf sc.** *Douglas Laing. 306 bottles.*

⸬ **Old Malt Cask Highland Park Aged 16 Years** dist Dec 87, bott Mar 04 **(91)** n21 warming and honeyed if a little thin; t23 brilliant combination of spicy punches softens you up for the gushing honey; f24 just a hint of vanilla is all that shows of the oak; the honey and very soft smoke have the field to themselves: maximum effect with minimum effort – outstanding! b23 HP at its most abstract and alluring: the secret is the minimum oak interference. **50%. nc ncf sc.** *Douglas Laing. 186 bottles.*

Old Malt Cask Highland Park Aged 17 Years sherry dist May 84, bott May 01 **(72)** n17 t20 f18 b17. Cloyingly sweet, poor balanced, less than impressive cask. Apart from that ... **50%. nc ncf.** *Douglas Laing. 786 bottles.*

⸬ **Old Malt Cask Highland Park Aged 19 Years** dist May 84, bott Jun 03 **(78)** n19 t21 f19 b19. Attractively sweet at times, but otherwise fuzzy and ill-defined. **50%. nc ncf sc.** *Douglas Laing. 636 bottles.*

Old Malt Cask Highland Park Aged 23 Years dist Feb 78, bott Apr 01 **(77)** n19 t20 f19 b19. Decent, quite rich but not classic. **50%. nc ncf.** *Douglas Laing. 606 bottles.*

Old Malt Cask Highland Park Aged 25 Years dist Nov 75, bott May 01 **(93)** n23 t24 f23 b23. The nose may be less than promising, but all else afterwards is sheer bliss. Truly mind-blowing and tastebud-raping. **50%.** *Douglas Laing. 288 bottles.*

⸬ **Old Master's Highland Park 1989** bott 04 cask 10535 **(83)** n21 t21 f20 b21. Blood orange vies with the pounding oak for the honeyed hand. **53.5%.** *James MacArthur.*

Old Malt Cask Highland Park Aged 30 Years dist Nov 70, bott Apr 01 **(83)** n20 t20 f23 b20. Too much oak and sherry early on, perhaps, but the finish is Highland Park heaven. **50%. nc ncf.** *Douglas Laing. 570 bottles.*

⸬ **Peerless Highland Park 1966 Aged 36 Years** (*see* Duncan Taylor Highland Park)

⸬ **Peerless Highland Park 1966 Aged 37 Years** (*see* Duncan Taylor Highland Park)

Peerless Highland Park 1966 cask 4627, dist May 66 36-y-o **(89)** n21 certainly some oak around, but the honey sings; t23 silky with soft peaty spices and burgeoning honey; f22 excellent follow-through of complex heather-honey and oak; b23 this really is a charming malt: it has held its head high over the years. **43.4%.** *Duncan Taylor & Co.*

Private Cellar Highland Park 1985 bott Feb 03 **(88)** n21 beautiful citrus-honey tones; t23 rich, honied malt with just a soft fade of peat. More fruit gathers towards the middle; f22 curvaceous to the very end with the malt still sparkling and offering gentle honey/brown sugar sweetness; b22 I have always said that 18 years is the optimum age for this distillery, and while there are more complex versions around this is a little stunner. **43%**

⸬ **Provenance Highland Park Aged 10 Years** dist Summer 93, bott Winter 03 **(87)** n21 anthracite-smoke and a touch of peat amid the barley; t22 lively arrival but soon settles into a soothing honey routine; f22 gentle with intense barley background and developing spice; b22 subtle, mildly simmering and full of guile. **46%.** *Douglas McGibbon.*

Provenance Winter Distillation Highland Park Over 10 Years cask DI Ref 726*, dist Spring 92, bott Winter 02 **(82)** n*19* t*22* f*21* b*20*. Slightly raw and un-refined but, as usual, the honey notes are a delight. **46%. nc ncf sc.** *Douglas McGibbon & Co.*

Rare Old Highland Park 1964 (92) n*24* peaty, but in a diffused, fruity way. Cocoa and chocolate mingles with the malt: so very complex; t*24* heather-honey, HP trademark, then a rush of peat and spices with more softening cocoa; f*21* the Achilles heel: is it natural or unnatural toffee that flattens out the high points of this great malt? Loads of fruit, either way; b*23* one of the great Gordon & MacPhail bottlings of all time still found on Japanese shelves at mortgage requiring prices **40%.** *Gordon & MacPhail.*

Scotch Malt Whisky Society Cask 4.73 (91) n*24* toffee apple and cocoa, clean oloroso at its most luxuriant; t*23* natural toffee bedding down with intense malt. Some bitter chocolate battles it out with the sweet fruit puree; f*22* myriad oak notes, most of them sweet and lingering malt; b*22* a handsome whisky by any standards, the only problem being that the sherry butt is so good the character of the distillery is lost somewhat. Still, not a bad price to pay if it is effect you are after.

Scott's Selection Highland Park 1975 bott 00 **(87)** n*24* t*22* f*20* b*21*. If the middle and finish were as good as the nose and entry on the palate, we would be in for something amazing. As it is, this is big, sweet, lively and pretty delicious. **52%.** *Robert Scott & Co.*

Scott's Selection Highland Park 1977 bott 98 **(89)** n*21* t*24* f*22* b*22*. The complexity is sheer Highland Park, the arrival in the palate is sheer theatre. Keep this one in the mouth for longer than normal before swallowing. **52.9%.** *Robert Scott & Co.*

☼ **Scott's Selection Highland Park 1977** bott 02 **(92)** n*21* thin, peaty brushstrokes on a canvas of vanilla and honey; t*23* sweet honeycomb, heather and all the usual suspects. Except the proportions here are near perfect, as is the top layer of spice; f*24* the slow acceleration of peat is spellbindingly beautiful; b*24* the nose is ordinary by HP standards by the denouement on the palate is sheer, naked beauty. **55.6%**

Single Barrel Collection Highland Park 1988 cask 10001, dist Mar 88, bott Dec 01 **(83)** n*18* t*22* f*22* b*21*. A confrontational HP with the honey upfront to the point of rudeness. Oddly, more like a Jamaican pot-still rum long in the bottle than a typical Highland Park. Quite a shock on first meeting, this is a dram that grows and grows on you big time. **59.39%. sc nc ncf.** *Germany.*

☼ **The Un-chillfiltered collection Highland Park Vintage 1990** cask 3925, dist 23 Apr 90, bott 23 Jan 04 (87) n*22* delicate smoke on honey; t*22* charming malt and honey, lush without being too oily; f21 plenty of warming, biting spices buzz around the sweeter notes; b*22* sweet and spicy throughout. **46%.** *Signatory 422 bottles.*

Usquebaugh Society Highland Park 1992 dist 11/11/92, bott 12/3/02 **(86)** n*21* gristy, slightly smoked malt; t*23* clean, fresh, vaguely honied; f*21* delicate oak and fine cocoa; b*21* an understated and refined dram. **46%.** *NL.*

Whisky Galore Highland Park 1989 (58) n*18* t*15* f*12* b*13*. If the whisky was attached to a cardiograph, there would be a straight line. **40%.** *Duncan Taylor & Co Ltd.*

☼ **Whisky Galore Highland Park 1990 Aged 13 Years (87)** n*21* heather-honey and not a stitch else; t*23* refreshing light and tender with those stunning honey notes blazing through the softly peated, malty heaven; f*22* apologetic vanilla with soft barley; b*21* with this pale, second (or even third) fill bourbon expression, proof were it ever needed that the heather-honey effect does not come from maturation. **46%.** *Duncan Taylor.*

HILLSIDE (*see* Glenesk)

IMPERIAL
Speyside, 1897. Allied. Silent.

⋰ **Imperial 17 Years Old** db **(82)** n19 t21 f21 b21. Seems lethargic at first, but it's so complex in the middle it's difficult to say where the middle ends and the end starts ... a real mouth-pleaser. **40%.** *Korea only.*

Cadenhead's Imperial-Glenlivet 24 Years Old dist 77, bott 10/02 **(87)** n22 very beautifully shaped oak but it is the integrity of the enormous malt that really impresses; t22 a re-run of the nose. The enormity of the malt on landing is immense, with a few orangey notes too; f21 soft malt and vanilla; b22 you could almost shed a tear when realising the likely fate of this distillery **57.6%**

Gordon & MacPhail Imperial 1979 (87) n22 grassy and smoky; t22 mouthwatering, clean, refreshing: fresh, soft malt all the way; f22 very light vanilla but still the sweet malt dominates; b21 a very simple, light and enjoyable Speysider. **40%.** *Gordon & MacPhail.*

Gordon & MacPhail Imperial 1990 (82) n20 t22 f19 b21. Very good example of clean, light, mouthwatering Speyside blending malt. Delicious. **40%**

Private Collection Imperial Calvados Finish 1990 (56) n14 t15 f14 b13. Just doesn't work. A disaster that should have been tipped (with care) into a blend. **40%.** *Gordon & MacPhail.*

Private Collection Imperial Claret Finish 1990 (83) n22 t21 f20 b20. Superb stuff with a glorious, concentrated Turkish-delight nose and start. Trails slightly at end.

Private Collection Imperial Cognac Finish 1990 (88) n21 malty, fruity, elegant, simple and one-dimensional – but delightfully so; t23 beautifully complex from start with delighful interplay between malt and oak, quite malty and mealy; f22 charmingly bitter-sweet with soft vanilla and spice; b22 great stuff. **40%.** *Gordon & MacPhail.*

Private Collection Imperial Cognac Finish 1991 (79) n18 t21 f19 b21. Enjoyable, but missing much of the élan of the '90. **40%.** *Gordon & MacPhail.*

Private Collection Imperial Port Wood Finish 1991 (83) n20 t22 f20 f21. Very sweet and maybe short on complexity but deliciously chewy with good spice. **40%.** *Gordon & McPhail.*

Private Collection Imperial Sherry Wood Finish 1990 (72) n19 t19 f18 b16. Not very exciting and slightly off-key, towards the finish especially. **40%.** *Gordon & MacPhail.*

Provenance Imperial Winter Distillation Over 11 Years dist Winter 89, bott Winter 00 **(68)** n15 t19 f17 b17. Half-hearted. Doesn't sit right at all. **43%. nc ncf.** *Douglas McGibbon & Co.*

INCHGOWER
Speyside, 1872. Diageo. Working.

Inchgower Aged 14 Years db **(77)** n19 t20 f19 b19. A vague hint of peat and a sprinkling of spice lifts the dram above something treacly and over-sweet. **43%.** *Flora and Fauna.*

Berry's Own Inchgower 1975 bott 03 **(87)** n23 weighty and very well balanced; barley sugar and the faintest hint of smoke merges effortlessly with some crushed green leaf and oaky notes; t22 a very sweet, fat chap with massive chewing power. The malt rules the roost but in the background earthier, smokier notes are lightened, highlighted even, by hints of citrus; f20 dry with subtle vanilla on one plain, deft, sweeter smoke on another; b22 an impressively balanced dram that shows really good weight. **46%.** *Berry Bros*

Hart Brothers Inchgower Aged 26 Years dist Aug 76, bott Sep 02 **(89)** n21 slightly sharp, but the malt is crisp; t23 liquid honey, lightly oiled and with some spices to pep it up; **f***23* long malt fade, soft vanilla; **b***22* this is exactly how I remember tasting Inchgower at the distillery 20-odd years ago. A magnificent malt for any collector. **49.9%**

Old Malt Cask Inchgower Aged 25 Years dist Nov 74, bott Jun 00 **(88)** **n***20* **t***22* **f***24* **b***22*. Glorious full-bodied whisky from an under-stated distillery. **50%.** *Douglas Laing. 234 bottles.*

⋆⋆⋆ **Whisky Galore Inchgower 1989 Aged 13 Years (76)** **n***18* **t***20* **f***19* **b***19*. The nose display all the tell-tale signs of a still worked into the ground. The sweetness is uneven and strained. **46%.** *Duncan Taylor & Co.*

INCHMURRIN (*see* Loch Lomond)

INVERLEVEN
Lowland, 1938–1991. Closed.
⋆⋆⋆ **Duncan Taylor Inverleven 1977 Aged 26 Years (78)** **n***20* **t***18* **f***20* **b***20*. They rarely come much more warming than this, though when the flames are doused the sweet malt is attractive. **57%**

Gordon & MacPhail Inverleven 1986 (89) **n***22* scrumptious apples and pears, feather light, malty and enticing; **t***23* mouth-filling malt, excellent body and more soft fruit; **f***22* gentle coating of vanilla, sprinkled with barley sugar; **b***22* this is just the most simplistic, but sexy dram you could wish for. Easily the best expression by G&M of this distillery to date. **40%**

⋆⋆⋆ **Gordon and MacPhail Inverleven 1989 (79)** **n***19* **t***20* **f***20* **b***20*. Though thin and shy, it is also clean, barley-rich and refreshing. **40%**

⋆⋆⋆ **Peerless Inverleven 1977** (*see* Duncan Taylor Inverleven 1977)

ISLE OF ARRAN
Highland (Island–Arran), 1995. Isle of Arran Distillers. Working.
Arran db **(87)** **n***21* fat and massively malty, not as fruity as some bottlings; **t***22* unbelievably oily with a subtle malt sweetness that also offers the faintest trace of oak. The voluptuous viscosity is unique; **f***22* long and sensuous with the thickest coating of malt you will ever find; **b***22* there is not enough oak interference here to get the complexity going, but putting on my blending hat for a minute I must say that it occurs to me that a little Arran goes a long, long way. This is great malt that is one of a kind. **40%**

⋆⋆⋆ **Arran First** db dist 95, bott Apr 04 **(87)** **n***21* melt-in-the-nose gently sweetened malt; **t***22* a double layer of malt – one hard, juicy and purposeful, the other soft, sweet and undisciplined; **f***22* some almost chalky vanilla puts the brake on the malty celebrations; **b***22* quite beautifully made malt. **46%.** *2,784 bottles.*

The Arran Malt Non Chill Filtered db **(84)** **n***18* **t***23* **f***22* **b***21*. A young, raw nose is an ingeniously false lead to the magnificent story that unfolds on the palate. Mouthwatering and intense, a subtle oiliness holds gathering spices to the roof of the mouth. What a cracking wee dram. **46%. ncf.**

The Arran Malt db **(87)** **n***22* buttery, fresh, soft, a pinch of coke-smoke, very complex, with some apples thrown in; **t***22* sweet, silky, natural cream-toffee and vanilla: the malt intensity is phenomenal, the weight on the palate confident and rewarding; **f***21* remains gentle with further vanilla which is chewy and long. Some really tantalising spices make a late extra addition; **b***22* an immensely soft and soothing dram showing rich creamy style. I have tasted the last two bottlings, the last of which was in March 2003. And I have to say it is getting better and better. For all its relatively tender years, this is unambiguously great whisky – and one must now ask: a classic in the making? **43%**

The Arran Malt Limited Edition 1996 db dist 12/8/96, bott 14/4/03 **(88)** **n***22* intense malt with a hint of spearmint and heavy oak for its age; **t***23* big and softly spiced, with the trademark oiliness clinging to the roof of the mouth along with some charming citrus; **f**21 subtle stuff: the malt remains massive and chewy. The contrast between bitter and sweet is minimal and the oak input is telling with some chewy toffee rounding things off; **b**22 when Arran whisky was little more than an embryo, I predicted rapid maturation. Even I didn't expect something quite like this from a six-year-old. Astonishing and massively drinkable. **57%.** *175 bottles.*

The Arran Malt Limited Edition 1997 db dist 18/7/97, bott 15/10/02 from hogshead **(82) n**21 **t**21 **f**20 **b**20. Decent single cask but falling between fruit or oak influence. **58.3%.** *341 bottles.*

∴ **The Arran Malt Single Cask Finished in Calvados** db **(83) n**19 **t**22 **f**21 **b**21. A strange, indecisive whisky that never quite settles on the character it wishes to be. Undermined by a slight soapiness on the nose it still has one or two astonishing moments of wanton wild, fruity passion, especially on the early mouth arrival. One that may terrify you at first but will grow on you. **62.1%**

∴ **Arran Port Finish** bott 14 Jun 04 db **(87) n**19 raw, fruity yet imbalanced; **t**22 an astonishing transformation on the palate, the malt is still amazingly young but the port effect is like boiled candy, especially as the intense, sweet malt congregates; **f**23 very long, immensely fruity and then a delicious chocolate-cherry finale; **b**23 a highly unusual Scotch that is like weak cranberry juice on the eye and a malty fruitfest on the palate thanks most to most probably a first-fill port pipe. Just ignore the nose. **57.5%**

Robert Burns World Federation Arran Single Island Malt db **(84) n**19 **t**22 **f**22 **b**21. Fat, creamy, full-bodied. The malt sweetens by the second to become something like a good old-fashioned American malt milkshake: amazing but there is enough oak for a drying balance. One of the most intense young malts on the market, only the naivety of the nose preventing it from hitting the heights. A delightful, tastebud-massaging malt experience. **40%.** *Isle of Arran.*

Blackadder Raw Cask Lochranza 1996 dist 24/1/96, bott Apr 02 **(90) n**22 charismatic and rich, the malt is thick, with no hint of sweetness; **t**23 absolutely beautifully shaped with the most lovely cream-toffee imaginable. The spices arrive hand-in-hand with the sweeter malt tones; **f**23 spicy oak, long, lovely and oily; **b**22 there is no other six-year-old single malt that compares to this: in giving my speech at the opening ceremony of the distillery I stuck my neck out and predicted this would become a fast-maturing malt. Isn't it just!!!! **56.8%. nc ncf.**

∴ **Provenance Arran Over 8 Years** dist Winter 95, bott Winter 03 **(73) n**16 **t**21 **f**18 **b**18. Oh, how disappointing! Tragic, even. One of the very first independent bottlings of Arran and a trace of sulphur on the sherry butt has blighted it. That said, the extraordinary quality of the malt managed to see off the worst excesses early on, and although balance has been compromised by the lurking bitterness – especially at the death – it has some fine moments against the odds. **50%. nc ncf sc.** *Douglas McGibbon & Co.*

∴ **Scotch Malt Whisky Society Cask 121.1 Aged 7 Years (82) n**19 **t**19 **f**23 **b**21. The first-ever bottling from this distillery. A fast maturer but evidence, perhaps, that this is not from the world's greatest cask. But there is plenty to admire towards the slightly spicy, intense finish. **59.4%. nc ncf sc.**

ISLE OF JURA
Highland (Island–Jura), 1810. Whyte and Mackay. Working.

∴ **Isle of Jura 5 Years Old 1999** db **(83) n**19 **t**23 **f**21 **b**20. Absolutely enormously peated, but has reached that awkward time in its life when it is massively sweet and as well balanced as a two-hour-old foal. **46%** *Exclusive to The Whisky Exchange*

Isle of Jura 10 Years Old db **(77) n**18 **t**19 **f**21 **b**19. A tangy malt that seems younger than its 10 years. The finish is long and offers the faintest hint of smoke on the rich malt. **40%**

Isle of Jura 16 Years Old db **(80)** 18 t22 f20 b20. Some lovely, mildly salty honey thorugh the middle. But an indefinable something is missing. A variable dram at the best of times, this expression is pleasant but ... variable. **40%**

Isle of Jura Aged 21 Years db **(78)** n20 t21 f19 b18. Pleasant enough, but surprisingly short of charisma. **40%**

Isle of Jura 21 Years Old Cask Strength db **(92)** n22 something hard and grainy against the ultra-clean fruit; t24 fabulous mouth arrival, just such a brilliant fruit-spice combo held together in a malty soup; f23 long and intensely malty; b23 every mouthful exudes class and quality. A must-have for Scottish Island collector ... or those who know how to appreciate a damn fine malt **58.1%**

Isle of Jura Aged 36 Years (dist 1965) db **(96)** n25 bloody hell's bells! I didn't expect to be thumped by peat quite like that: light and tangy phenols, offering something quite different in character to anything offered across the other side of the Port Askaig ferry; t25 honey at its honiest meets peat at its peatiest. It's like a bee trapped in a smoke chamber; a Perthshire distillery dumped on Islay. Unique in style in all my experience and something to tell the grandchildren about or, preferably, give them some to be weaned on. f23 becomes so soft you feel your teeth dissolve into it ... I'm now down to the gums. The smoke is now more subdued and a few tannins break sweat for an oaky intervention; b23 I remember 20-odd years ago being taken into a corner of Jura's warehouse and tasting a cask of something big and smoky. It was different to all the other Juras around, but had none of this honey. Is this the same cask, a generation on? Most probably. I then returned to the hotel opposite for a dram (and a bottle) of their own Jura and wondered what would become of that peaty one-off. Now I know. **44%**

Isle of Jura 1973 Vintage db bott 23/2/03 **(93)** n25 Aaaaahhhhh!!! A sherry butt from heaven sent: clean, full of big, ripe cherries and fruitcake and, of its type, faultless; t23 the oak shows signs of deterioration, but the complete brilliance of sherry plugs the holes: chewy, spicy, burnt raisins and, of course, big oak; f21 long, with the remaining malt hard and flinty. Stays fruity and offers majestic bitter-sweet balance to the very end; b24 if you want to know what a truly great sherry nose is like, start here. The balance isn't bad, either. Brilliant! **55.6%**

Isle of Jura 1984 db **(69)** n15 t18 f18 b18. Big brother ... with sulphur. All whiskies are equal, but some are more equal than others. Oops, wrong book. **42%**. *Bottled to commemorate George Orwell who wrote the book 1984 while on the island.*

⸭ **Jura Festival of Malt and Music Distilled 1989** db dist Mar 89, bott 04 (87) n19 the two year influence of the young "Anada" sherry butt has left a slight blemish though an agave pepperiness is interesting; t23 very unusual delivery of barley, almost glass textured at first and mildly cooling before those massive peppers return to torch the outside of the tongue; f23 opens up later on to reveal a saltier tang to the storming spice and a distant waft of smoke; b22 not entirely flawless but one of the most unusual, fascinating and, it must be said, at times delicious drams of the year. **57.9%**. *850 bottles.*

Isle of Jura 1989 db bott 23/2/03 **(66)** n16 t17 f17 b16. Wrong kind of sherry influence: off-key. Not my cup of tea at all. **57.2%**

Isle of Jura Legacy db **(82)** n19 t22 f20 b21. Some very chewy honeycomb on the middle. Pretty big stuff. **40%**

Isle of Jura Stillman's Dram Limited Edition Aged 27 Years db **(90)** n24 a single thread of peat holds together a toasty-honeycomb malt and oak combination: outstanding; t23 the zesty middle follows a honied start, some buttery notes, too; f21 medium length with roast malt and budding oak, very discreet peat at the death; b22 one of the most complex Juras yet bottled. **45%**

Isle of Jura Superstition db **(86)** n21 busy, peat and spice-led. Seems young despite some distingushed oak: very unusual; t22 a beguiling array of soft barley and oak tones pinned to the tastebuds by green peat; **f**20 much thinner and more relaxed than the intense mouth arrival; **b**23 a rare case of where the whole is better than the parts. A malt that wins through because of a superb balance between peat and sweeter barley. Distinctive to the point of being almost unique. **45%**

Adelphi Isle of Jura 6 Years Old cask 1917, dist 96, bott 02 **(82) n**21 **t**22 **f**19 **b**20. A lush and magnificent malt-honey nose and mouthfeel is undone slightly by a build-up of toffee on the finish. **60.5%**

Blackadder Raw Cask Jura 1988 cask 1639, dist Oct 88, bott Apr 02, **(75) n**18 **t**20 **f**19 **b**18. A bit on the thin side despite a quick maltburst on arrival. **59.4%. nc ncf.** *Hogshead.*

Connoisseurs Choice Jura 1989 (72) n19 **t**19 **f**17 **b**17. Little impact. **40%.** *Gordon & MacPhail.*

⁙ **Connoisseurs Choice Jura 1991 (74) n**18 **t**21 **f**17 **b**18. Pleasing barley kick, but otherwise not happy with itself. **43%.** *Gordon & MacPhail.*

Dun Bheagan Isle of Jura Aged 14 Years dist 86, bott 01 **(67) n**16 **t**18 **f**17 **b**16. Sulphur-tainted sherry butt. **43%.** *William Maxwell.*

⁙ **Murray McDavid Isle of Jura 1989 13 Years Old** bourbon cask **(77) n**18 **t**20 **f**19 **b**20. Decidedly unscintillating fare. **46%**

Old Malt Cask Isle of Jura Aged 35 Years dist Apr 66, bott May 01 **(75) n**19 **t**20 **f**18 **b**18. Some tangy, sweet fruit, but the oak is a little too loud. **47.8%. nc ncf.** *Douglas Laing.* 204 bottles.

Scotch Malt Whisky Society Cask 31.10 Aged 18 Years (84) n22 **t**22 **f**20 **b**20. Salty nose and mouth arrival with brimming spices. Quick toffee-fudge fade. **59.9%. nc ncf sc.**

⁙ **Signatory Isle of Jura 1988** cask 2679, dist 21 Dec 88, bott 23 Jan 04 **(82) n**19 **t**22 **f**21 **b**20. **46%.** *Signatory* 268 bottles.

⁙ **Spirit of the Isles Isle of Jura 1988 Rum Cask Finish** bott 03 **(75) n**18 **t**20 **f**18 **b**19. Teasingly smoked, oily malted but ultimately lazy dram. **40%.** Liquid Gold/John MacDougall.

Ultimate Selection Isle of Jura 1988 dist 12/10/88, bott 19/9/02 **(73) n**17 **t**18 **f** 20 **b**18. Chewy finish, but an early struggle. **43%.** *Van Wees NL.*

KNOCKANDO

Speyside, 1898. Diageo. Working.

Knockando 1990 bott 23 db **(83) n**21 **t**22 **f**20 **b**20. The most fruity Knockando I've come across with some attractive salty notes. Dry, but a little extra malty sweetness these days. **40%**

KNOCKDHU

Speyside, 1894. Inver House. Working.

AnCnoc 12 Year Old db **(90) n**22 massive aroma with a grassy maltiness enriching a grapey-juicy fruitiness, lovely coal smoke for good measure; **t**23 absolutely fabulous, near-perfect, malt arrival, perhaps the most clean, yet intense of any in Scotland. The complexity is staggering with not only multi-layers of malt but a distant peat and oak infusion; **f**22 deliciously spicy; **b**23 if there is a more complete 12-year-old Speyside malt on the market, I have yet to find it. A malt that should adorn a shelf in every whisky-drinking home.

AnCnoc 13 Year Old Highland Selection db **(85) n**21 usual coal smoke with ripe pears and oak for company; **t**23 rich, juicy, spicy and then so, so malty! **f**20 flattens rather unexpectedly; **b**21 a big Knockdhu, but something is dulling the complexity. **46%**

⁙ **AnCnoc 1990** bott Mar 04 db **(90) n**21 dry-ish and sawdusty; the barley puts up firmer than usual resistance; **t**23 pure Knockdhu with its sturdy barley lines offering a mouthwatering embrace; **f**23 a faint hint of bourbon as the oak adds a cocoa-tinged edge to the oily and enormously long finish; **b**23 strikingly attractive and textbook clean; the extra oak has detracted slightly from the usual honeyed complexity but has provided instead an interesting weight. Speyside at its most alluring. **46%. ncf.**

AnCnoc 26 Years Old Highland Selection db **(89) n**23 profound. Everything is big, but perfectly proportioned: massive grapey fruit and malt concentrate; **t**22 pure Knockdhu: intense malt carrying some beautiful spices and an obscure but refreshing fruit; **f**23 the lull after a minor storm: rich vanilla and echoes of malt; **b**21 there is a little flat moment between the middle and finish for which I have chipped off a point or two. That apart, superb. **48.2%**

Knockdhu 23 Years Old db **(94) n**23 coal gas and fruit (getting the pattern?): telling oak, but wonderfully crafted with the malt untarnished and rich beyond your wildest dreams; **t**24 the spiced malt makes violent love to your tastebuds. It's no-holds-barred, bodice-ripping stuff. Toasty honey tries to play a more gentle role, but gets caught up in the taste orgy: really hot stuff; **f**23 spent passion and a bewildering afterglow of malt, honey and fading spice; **b**24 pass the smelling salts. This is whisky to knock you out. A malt that confirms Knockdhu as simply one of the great Speysiders, but unquestionably among the world's elite. **57.4%**. *Limited edition.*

LADYBURN
Lowland, 1966–1974. Closed.

Ladyburn 1973 db **(60) n**15 varying shades of light oak have not entirely dimmed the malt, just a tad spirity but pleasant with minimum complexity; **t**15 oak, oak and more (spicy) oak; **f**17 oak; **b**13 this has lost all trace of shape and form. Pretty one-dimensional yet easily drinkable thanks to a singular malty sweetness, especially towards the very end. Don't bother opening.

Old Rare Malt Ayrshire Distillery 1970 (71) n16 t17 f21 b17. A mildly soapy nose, uncomfortably hot on the palate but redeemed by a superb, clean malt surge at the end that is deliciously out of character. **40%.** *Gordon & MacPhail.*

LAGAVULIN
Islay, 1816. Diageo. Working.

❖ **Lagavulin 12 Years Old** db **(93) n**24 disarmingly gentle peat, much of its younger oils have miraculously vanished, lots of fresh fruit – including mandarin – available and mildly nutty, too. Pretty faultless material; **t**23 the smokescreen of the nose is laid bare on the palate: oil enough for heart attacks, peat laid on thickly and the oak offering an extra surge of spice that is man-marked by gristy, sweet barley; **f**23 long and at times almost too soft to be heard. Impressive vanilla to thin out the smoke, but the peat with the cocoa still lingers for a good five or ten minutes; **b**23 really, all you can ask from a Lagavulin at this age: weighty yet delicate enough for impressive complexity. Just try not having a second of this … **57.8%**

Lagavulin 12 Years Old db **(92) n**24 clean sea-brine and peat: first class; **t**23 explosive peat and soft barley make delicious bedfellows; **f**22 cocoa and smoke. The barley hangs sweetly around; **b**23 really charming Islay with a frisky peatiness that is sweet and lingering. One to savour and reminisce for those of us who were hooked on the Lagavulin in pre-Classic Malt era. **58%**

Lagavulin 15 Years Old db (in ceramic decanter from late 80s) **(89) n**22 t23 f22 b22. This reminds me of how I discovered Lagavulin nearly a quarter of a century ago: proof indeed that styles within distilleries change. A real belter, nonetheless. **45%**

Lagavulin Aged 16 Years db **(88) n**23 the peat, though full, is also unusually linear and lacking its trademark complexity: much more gristy than normal; **t**22 exceedingly soft with a quick surge of vanilla followed by some fruity notes. The sweet peat, of course, is everywhere; **f**_21_ slightly oilier than usual and bitter, too; **b**_22_ a bit unfair to pass judgement on this bottling: looking at my notes since year 2000, the average mark runs out at a fraction under 92 ... !!

Lagavulin 25 Years Old db bott 2002 **(78)** n_21_ t 21 f_19_ **b**_19_. Apart from the early mouth arrival, blunt and disappointing. Lagavulin, says Jim, but not as we know it. **57.2%.** _9,000 bottles._

Lagavulin 1986 Distillers Edition Double Matured bott 02 Pedro-Ximenez finish db **(86)** n_22_ big peat and crushed ripe cherries, sweet pipe tobacco smoke; **t**_22_ fresh wine gives a bitter-sweet but glass-like countenance that seems to keep the peat at bay, though it does sneak up impressively whilst you're not watching; **f**_21_ juicy, boiled-sweet fruitiness and virtually peatless; **b**_21_ I really can't believe what I'm reading on the back label: "This is the definitive Islay Malt – untameable with the strongest peat flavour of any of the malt whiskies from this wild island shore." Well, sorry. But someone's had a bottle too many there. Big peat on the nose, sure, but then after that a whimper. It doesn't even begin to compare with the 12 and 16-y-o. Still, a good 'un for the juicy ones amongst us. **43%**

Aom 11 Years Old Single Islay Cask (89) n_22_ oily and spicy, really very rich – very atypical of the distillery in bottled form; **t**_23_ exceptionally sweet peat syrup, incredibly oily – very Caol Ila-ish in style, but the phenolic intensity must be around the 50ppm – hence Lagavulin; **f**_21_ fades surpisingly to allow in some vanilla. But the peat stays the course, as does that amazing sweetness; **b**_23_ this is one hell of a Lagavulin and it is from that famed distillery that my dear friend Tatsuya Minagawa personally selected it for the now defunct M's bar in Edinburgh. The bottles have now re-surfaced in Japan. **46%**

Mission Range Lagavulin 1979 in oak casks for 23 years **(90)** n_22_ sturdy and stimulating, the peat is aggressive and very oily for this distillery. Shows no wear or tear for such great age; **t**_23_ sweet and glossy with the peat forming varying layers of intensity; **f**_22_ brilliant oak arrival which is flakey and surprisingly light; **b**_23_ it's hardly possible that a malt of this age can maintain an almost youthful lightness and dexterity at the same time as offering thumping peat! Fabulous. **46%.** _Murray McDavid. 600 bottles._

MacLeod's Islay 8 Years Old (90) n_24_ an astonishing array of citrus (lime and orange) battles with some success against the crashing waves of clean peat that is iodine-rich and enticingly green. Something that no true whisky lover should fail to experience; **t**_22_ fresh-faced and tender, there is an enveloping sweetness that is like liquid grist. The peat almost pings around the mouth, so crisp is it. Only on the middle does the lack of age seem to offer an unfilled hole; **f**_21_ lengthy and luscious, it is still spritely and fun and boasts massive liquoricey chewability, but so very green and immature – fabulous all the same! **b**_23_ the nose is Islay, pure Islay. At half the age of what you would normally taste Lagavulin this effervescent malt helps you learn so much more about this great distillery. No Islay malt on the market comes cleaner than this: only the old Bowmore 5-y-o used to show such childish abandon. This dram should be in every serious collector's or Islay-phile's home. I'm 100% certain this is Lagavulin. **40%**

Signatory Vintage Islay Malt (Lagavulin 5 Years Old) **(85)** n_20_ raw yet quite beautiful, powering peat; **t**_23_ fruity, oranges in particular, with rich, velvety peat juice; **f**_21_ quietens a little and the youth returns; **b**_21_ an advanced Lagavulin for its tender years but still hasn't quite reached puberty. A stupendous blending malt in this state and a fascinating singleton. **58.4%**

LAPHROAIG
Islay, 1820. Allied. Working.

Laphroaig 10 Years Old db **(90)** n_24_ impossible not to nose this and think of Islay: no other aroma so perfectly encapsulates the island – clean despite the rampaging peat-reek and soft oak, raggy coast-scapes and screeching gulls – all in a glass; **t**23 one of the crispiest, peaty malts of them all, the barley standing out alone, brittle and unbowed, before the peat comes rushing in like the tide: iodine and soft salty tones; **f**21 the peat now takes control for a sweet, distinguished finish; **b**22 quite light compared to of old with the peat taking a more subdued, harmonious stance. But it is every bit as good if not better simply because there is now clearer definition and shape. This, undisputably, is classic whisky. The favourite of Prince Charles, apparently: he will make a wise king ... **40%**

Laphroaig 10 Years Old Original Cask Strength db **(93)** **n**23 explosive peat, sweet malts as well and no shortage of dry vanilla; **t**24 a mouthful of this is one of life's little treasures: a stunning unravelling of peat at various levels of intensity, sometimes accompanied by brine, other times by subtle oils or vanilla; **f**23 gristy and sweet, with long, pounding waves of soft smoke and iodine. Salty to the end ... and that end is a long time in coming; **b**23 a home without one of these around is barely worth visiting. This is Laphroaig nutshelled: wild and windswept yet calm and controlled. Marvellous malt. **57.3%**

Laphroaig Aged 15 Years db **(79)** **n**20 **t**20 **f**19 **b**20. A hugely disappointing, lacklustre dram that is oily and woefully short on complexity. Not what one comes to expect from either this distillery or age. **43%**

⠸⠾ **Laphroaig 17 Years Old Islay Festival of Malt and Music 2004** db **(93)** **n**23 just a whimper of smoke by Laphroaig standards – and smoked cod at that – but the malt itself if thick and gristy, the soft intensity of the oak offers a bitter-sweet narrative, **t**24 lush and loaded with malt, there is almost a sugar-cane element to this one with the smoke gathering in intensity as the mouth is coated; **f**22 the demerara sugar-peat combination lingers with some soft vanilla acting as the perfect foil; **b**24 reminds me very much of the original Ardbeg 17-year-old I created with the peat hiding at first and then slowly trying to take command ... but failing. Most probably will be panned by those looking for in your face peat, but this is a sophisticated and highly unusual single cask Laphroaig that needs time to get to know. Congratulations to blender Robert Hick on spotting a real one off. **55.2%**. *250 bottles.*

Laphroaig Aged 30 Years db **(94)** **n**24 subtle, sweet peat-reek from distant lumbs, coupled with pungent sea spray: outstanding; **t**23 ultra-delicate peat tiptoes over the tastebuds. The malt and oak combine effortlessly to create a sweet vanilla-toffee package; **f**23 long, vanilla-peat echoes; **b**24 the best Laphroaig of all time? Nope, because the 40-y-o is perhaps better still... just. However, Laphroaig of this subtlety and charm gives even the very finest Ardbeg a run for its money. A sheer treat that should be bottled at greater strength. **43%**

Laphroaig Aged 40 Years db **(94)** **n**23 smoky oranges, salty kippers: can this really be such a gigantic age? **t**24 clean, precise peated malt at first, almost soft and welcoming, then a slow procession of oak halting as it reaches bitter cocoa mixed with the smoke; **f**23 more fruit and some developing oils that guarantees a sweet and fabulously long finish; **b**24 mind-blowing. This is a malt that defies all logic and theory to be in this kind of shape at such enormous age. The Jane Fonda of Islay whisky. **43%**

⠸⠾ **Distillery No 1 Laphroaig 1988** cask no 3881 **(89)** **n**22 clean, uncluttered Laphroaig that's a little young for its age but enjoys excellent depth; **t**23 again, brilliant distillate with no off notes and after the initial peaty exclamation, some sweeter barley-liquorice notes arrive; **f**22 shows its age now with plenty of oak to soften the peaty, seaweedy blows; **b**22 a touch of natural (?) caramel at the death but until then a warts-and-all, macho bottling. **62.9%**

Limited Editions Laphroaig 1979 dist July 79, bott Sep 97 **(92)** **n**23 **t**24 **f**23 **b**22. Grab yourself a standard 14–15 year old cask of Laphroaig that has been faultlessly made and contains all its briny, smoky hallmarks... and you get this. Except this is a couple of years older and still unblemished. I have spotted the odd bottle of this still around. Give it a go!!!. **54.5%. nc ncf sc.** *Blackadder.*

Murray McDavid Laphroaig 1988 bourbon cask 2108, dist July 88, bott Dec 01 **(90) n**23 **t**23 **f**22 **b**22. Laphroaig in its purest form: if ever you want to know what happens to a Laphroaig when put into a tired cask offering limited year-on-year development, here's your chance to find out. Lacks the obvious complexity gained from oak but at the same time the youthful edges have been rounded for the most brilliant natural hybrid. I'd have this over porridge for breakfast any day. **46%**

Murray McDavid Leapfrog 1987 bourbon cask MM2868, dist Mar 87, bott Apr 99 **(91) n**23 **t**23 **f**22 **b**23. Due to legal action by Allied the bottlers were not allowed to state the distillery of origin. So they simply called it "Leapfrog". A folklore collector's item for what is in and outside of the bottle. **46%**

⁘ **Old Malt Cask Laphroaig Aged 11 Years** dist Apr 92, bott Nov 03 **(89) n**23 exemplary (probably) second fill bourbon, allowing the buttery peat to flutter sweetly around unhindered with hints of dry marzipan for company; **t**23 a near faultless template for all Laphroaigs of this age with a gristy, mealy edge to the smoke and the oily body providing the desired sheen; **f**21 long and dries attractively allowing cocoa and vanilla to blend with the flaky peat; **b**22 delightful, supremely made whisky. **50%. nc ncf sc.** *Douglas Laing. 540 bottles.*

⁘ **Old Malt Cask Laphroaig Aged 14 Years** dist Mar 89, bott Sep 03 **(79) n**19 **t**21 **f**19 **b**20. Astonishing, delicate Laphroaig with about the lowest phenol level I have seen in a bottle. Sugary in part with the smoke drifting around the palate. The bitter finale doesn't help. **50%. nc ncf sc.** *Douglas Laing. 300 bottles.*

⁘ **Old Malt Cask Laphroaig Aged 15 Years** dist Apr 88, bott Jan 04 **(93) n**23 liniment; a leaking bottle of bromine; a hint of salt; **t**23 the peat dissolves on the palate with ripples of clean malt carrying with it a spicy flotsam; **f**23 the sweetness continues for a minute or two more before some drier wafer-notes start dissolving again; the spices are persistent but harmonious; **b**24 a memorable Laphroaig in top form. **50%. nc ncf sc.** *Douglas Laing. 162 bottles.*

⁘ **Old Malt Cask Laphroaig Aged 15 Years** dist Apr 88, bott Mar 04 **(83) n**22 **t**21 **f**20 **b**20. An oily, machine-room nose but the palate, though sweet, never quite gets out of third gear. **50%. nc ncf sc.** *Douglas Laing. 112 bottles.*

⁘ **Old Malt Cask Laphroaig Aged 15 Years** dist Mar 89, bott Apr 04 **(90) n**23 farmyards and haystacks plus plenty of cottage peat-reek **t**22 sweet oils even catch a honeyed strand amid the ultra-clean peat; **f**23 one of the softest finishes to a Laphroaig for quite a few years: the malt and peat are inextricably intertwined, it is all very soft yet the oak advances no more than a distant hint of vanilla while the peat becomes supremely assertive; **b**22 Laphroaig at its cleanest and best behaved while still displaying its unique charms. **50%. nc ncf sc.** *Douglas Laing. 289 bottles.*

⁘ **Old Malt Cask Laphroaig Aged 15 Years** dist Feb 87, bott Jan 04 **(90) n**18 tainted and sweet, not exactly the perfect nose; **t**24 time to sit down: the intensity of the sweet sherry backed to the hilt by writhing peat makes this one hell of an experience; **f**24 the big sprinkling of spices still cannot dampen the enormous, mind-blowing sherry-peat theme; **b**24 if you went by the nose alone, you'd probably not go any further. But do. Your reward will be a one-off, an oral orgy, for all bottlings in the last year. Brilliant ... very few whiskies have been awarded a 90 after such a poor start on the nose. Hey, but that's whisky ...! **50%. nc ncf sc.** *Douglas Laing. 309 bottles.*

The Old Malt Cask Laphroaig Aged 15 Years dist Feb 87, bott Apr 02 **(86) n**21 yieldingly pungent and very young in style for age with crisp iodine, very delicate despite the obvious peat; **t**21 lively and lovely with big spice arrival to complement the peaty surround. The malt is especially sweet and clean; **f**21 long with ever-increasing soft-oaked vanilla blending with the malt. But it is the clarity of the spiky malt that wins through: enormously spicy towards the end; **b**22 an immense whisky that is among the sweetest Laphroaigs to have been bottled in recent years. The spicy fizz adds fun. A genuine joy. **50%. nc ncf.** Douglas Laing. 336 bottles.

⋅⋅⋅ **Old Malt Cask Laphroaig Aged 16 Years** dist Feb 87, bott Sep 03 **(83) n**22 **t**20 **f**20 **b**21. A strangely synthetic nose while the malt is dazzlingly sweet. **50%. nc ncf sc.** Douglas Laing. 270 bottles.

Old Malt Cask Laphroaig Aged 17 Years dist Feb 85, bott Apr 02 **(75) n**19 **t**20 **f**18 **b**18. One bloody weird whisky. The aroma took me back over 30 years to the peculiar, carbolic aroma of the Morris Minor driven by Miss Nora Bavin, the spinster school secretary of the Grammar I attended. I never thought of that aroma in many decades: why should I? But there it is, in bottled form, in the guise of a Laphroaig. Life – whisky – never ceases to amaze... **50%. nc ncf.** Douglas Laing. 306 bottles.

Premier Malts Laphroaig 12 Years Old dist 30/10/90, bott Nov 02 **(80) n**20 **t**21 **f**19 **b**20. Begins with bite and nip but settles as a silky dram. **56.2%.** Malcolm Pride.

Signatory Laphroaig 15 Years Old Un-chillfiltered Collection refill sherry butt 3600, dist 16/3/88, bott 22/3/03 **(79) n**21 **t**20 **f**19 **b**19, Has its pretty chewy moments. But you are left feeling disappointed at the lack of overall development and complexity: a bit like lusting after the village beauty for a couple of years and, when the passionless deed is done, thinking: "Was that it... ?" **46%.** 625 bottles.

Ultimate Selection Laphroaig 1988 refill sherry butt 3598, dist 16/3/88, bott 25/3/03 **(88) n**23 clean, utterly faultless. The peat is sweet, salty and coastal; **t**23 crisp malt pretty young in style, grassy for all the peat; **f**21 soft vanilla lightens the peat; **b**21 a cask refilled more than once on the evidence of this. Very young for its age and about the cleanest Laphroaig you'll ever find. A minor treat: a brilliant bottling for those trying to find every character in the Laphroaig personality. **43%.** Van Wees NL.

⋅⋅⋅ **The Un-chillfiltered Collection Laphroaig Vintage 1992** cask 3613, dist 16 Mar 88, bott 23 Jan 04 **(91) n**22 young in character but the peat really is of the most well-proportion type imaginable, lovely; **t**23 text-book mouth arrival with the peat at first arriving in a dense cloud, vanishing momentarily to allow in the barley and then returning slowly again; **f**23 long, delicate, late sawdusty, flasky smoke; **b**23 the epitome of a gentle giant. **46%.** Signatory 819 bottles.

LEDAIG (see Tobermory)

LINKWOOD
Speyside, 1820. Diageo. Working.

Linkwood 12 Years Old db **(90) n**22 custard pie and crispy malt; **t**23 sensuous: a blistering arrival of among the cleanest malt you will find, slightly sweet and enormously chewy – any cleaner and you could wash yourself in it; **f**22 hints of smoke keep the vanilla in check. Still the malt carries on and on and on...; **b**23 this is one hell of a Speysider. Being part of the Flora and Fauna range, the bottle depicts a swan on the label. Nothing could have been more apt. **43%**

Linkwood Aged 26 Years Rare Malts Selection dist 75 bott, May 02 db **(89) n**21 hints of bourbon plus lavender and tangerine, but all so very subtle; **t**22 an even, if bourbony, start at first with sweet malt overcoming an oily wave...; **f**24 ... then wow, does this baby take off! Not in a big way, but in the must delicate manner with orange on vanilla, all spread around the palate by this amazing oiliness. Cocoa and further bourbon notes go that extra yard on a seemingly never-ending finale. One of the longest finishes in the whisky world! **b**22 a great dram that, by Speyside standards especially, takes an eternity to complete each memorable mouthful. **56.1%**

❖ **Adelphi Linkwood 13 Years Old** dist 90, bott 03 **(76)** n18 t20 f19 b19. Aggressive, hot and off-key but not entirely without merit. **56%**

Adelphi Linkwood 17 Years Old cask 4592, dist 82, bott 99 **(91)** n22 t23 f23 b23. Rarely do you find light, grassy-style Speysiders this good at this age: the total lack of oak interference is the key. A must if you can still find it. **64.2%**

Blackadder Raw Cask Linkwood 1989 sherry butt 5624, dist Oct 89, bott Apr 02 **(83)** n20 t22 f20 b21. Solid malt, clean sherry and spicy. Blackadder with bite. **59.2%. nc ncf sc.**

Blackadder Raw Cask Linkwood 1989 first-fill sherry butt 5624, dist Oct 89, bott Mar 03 **(84)** n20 t22 f21 b21. Just a little extra salt and depth on the finish by comparison with the earlier bottling from this cask. **59.3%. nc ncf sc.**

Cask Linkwood 1989 dist 3/10/89, bott 29/3/01 **(76)** n19 t20 f18 b19. A bit thin and salty for all the strength. **61%**. Gordon & MacPhail.

Celtic Legends Single Cask Linkwood 1989 hogshead 3193, bott 01 **(75)** n15 t21 f20 b19. A complex and delicious dram that does its best to make up for the poor nose. **46%. ncf.** Liquid Gold.

Coopers Choice Linkwood 1990 bott 03 (12 Years Old) **(79)** n18 t21 f20 b20. Slightly syrupy, but decent spices. **43%**. The Vintage Malt Whisky Co.

❖ **Dun Bheagan Linkwood 1991 Aged 12 Years Port Finish** bott 15 Mar 04 **(79)** n21 t20 f19 b19. Many years back I discovered the now famous "green" whisky, the port-cask Springbanks. Now, ladies and gentlemen, I unveil the first-ever truly pink whisky, followed by the later bottled Glendronach – also from port). Here the listless Linkwood is outgunned by the mildly unbalanced port. Tasty, though. **43%**. William Maxwell.

Gordon & MacPhail Linkwood 1954 (69) n18 vanilla and cream-coffee; t16 a slight malty thrust can be felt amid the oak; f17 very salty and oaky; b18 one for birthdays and anniversaries only. **40%**

Gordon & MacPhail Linkwood 1969 (69) n17 t18 f16 b18. Old, tired and awaiting the grim reaper. **40%**. Gordon & MacPhail.

Gordon & MacPhail Linkwood 1972 (72) n20 t18 f17 b17. Decent vanilla, but just a shade too heavily oaked. **40%**. Gordon & MacPhail.

Hart Brothers Linkwood Aged 12 Years Sherry Cask dist May 90, bott Jan 03 **(68)** n17 t17 f17 b17. Some blenders at the distiller's parent company don't like working with their sherry casks. You can see why. Just not my type at all. **46%**

Murray McDavid Linkwood 1989 fresh sherry cask MM5117, bott 01 **(83)** n20 t22 f20 b21. Very fruity but slightly cramped for complexity. **46%. nc ncf sc.**

❖ **Murray McDavid Linkwood 1990 (69)** n17 t18 f17 b17. Screwed by mild sulphur. **46%.**

❖ **Murray McDavid Mission 2 Linkwood 1973 (84)** n21 t20 f22 b21. Delightful hints of citrus and honey plus background smoke amid the pounding vanilla. **46%. nc ncf.**

Old Malt Cask Linkwood Aged 20 Years Sherry dist Jul 79, bott Apr 00 **(76)** n17 t21 f19 b19. Some sulphur has crept in to spoil a very malty party. **50%. nc ncf.** Douglas Laing.

Old Masters Linkwood 1990 bott 01 **(72)** n16 t20 f18 b18. Some off-notes ruin what would have been a rich dram. **59.2%.** James MacArthur.

❖ **Provenance Linkwood Over 11 Years** dist Winter 93, bott Winter 04 **(82)** n20 t22 f20 b20. youthful, fresh, mouthwatering barley and zesty. **46%**. Douglas McGibbon.

❖ **Scotch Malt Whisky Circle Linkwood 1978** cask 7 dist Apr 78, bott Jul 00 **(82)** n20 t22 f19 b21. A good example of a good, simplistic Speysider keeping its head below the parapet. **58%**. Germany.

Signatory Decanter Collection Linkwood 1987 dist 12/11/87, bott 21/11/02 cask 4132 **(84)** n19 t22 f21 b22. A better malt than it noses being rich-textured, young and mouthwatering for its age. **43%**. 928 bottles.

Usquebaugh Society Linkwood 1988 dist 31/5/88, bott Nov 97 **(85) n**_21_ **t**_22_ **f**_21_ **b**_21_. Everything one might expect from a decent cask of Linkwood at this age. **43%.** NL

⋄⋄ **The Wee Dram Linkwood Aged 12 Years (85) n**_21_ dense grape-barley character softened by lychee and vanilla ice cream; **t**_22_ the sweetness comes as a bit of a shock but the intensity of the barley sees off some half-hearted grape noises; **f**_21_ lashings of barley with a light sherry fade; **b**_21_ twelve years ago I was discussing with United Distillers the strange effect their rather unnatural sherry wood policy will have further down the road. They said no-one would spot the difference; I said they would. The result has been a clutch of Sellafield-style sulphured monsters (especially from Mortlach), and a few disarmingly eccentric chaps like this. One for every collector. **43%.** The Wee Dram, Bakewell, UK.

Whisky Galore Linkwood 1987 15-y-o (81) n_20_ **t**_22_ **f**_19_ **b**_20_. A decent Speysider, biscuity and malty. **46%.** Duncan Taylor & Co.

⋄⋄ **Whiskymessen V.I.P. Club Linkwood 1987** Hogshead No. 452 bott 02 **(83) n**_20_ **t**_21_ **f**_21_ **b**_21_. Some subtle honey amid the grassy barley. **46%.** Denmark.

LINLITHGOW (see St Magdalene)

LITTLEMILL
Lowland, 1772. Glen Catrine Now closed awaiting demolition.

Littlemill 8 Years Old db **(81) n**_20_ **t**_20_ **f**_21_ **b**_20_. This malt has moved on a lot since its days as the byword for paintstripper. The malt in here is not eight but at least 13 or so and the oak absorbed into the system has had a calming and sweetening effect. Now a fruity, mouthwatering Lowlander of no little charm and finesse. A real shock to the system. **40%**

Littlemill 1964 db **(82) n**_21_ **t**_20_ **f**_21_ **b**_20_. A soft-natured, bourbony chap that shows little of the manic tendencies that made this one of Scotland's most-feared malts. Talk about mellowing with age ... **40%**

Connoisseurs Choice Littlemill 1985 (86) n_22_ gristy, young intense malt; **t**_22_ beautifully sweet with ultra-clean barley dissolving on the tongue; **f**_20_ thin but clean; **b**_22_ I'd like this distillery to be remembered for this charming and, to be frank, unrepresentative bottling. Clean as a whistle, there is a wonderful barley grist air about the nose and palate arrival. Limited complexity and troubled even less by oak, this is a delightful little version which everybody should try and get hold of. Had its whisky always been this good the distillery would never have closed. **40%.** Gordon & MacPhail.

⋄⋄ **Dun Bheagan Littlemill 1984 Aged 19 Years** bott 14 Jul 03 **(81) n**_20_ **t**_19_ **f**_21_ **b**_21_. The years have been kind to this dram: a stylish fresh-barley intensity that was never evident in its youth, despite recognisable early blemish. **43%.** William Maxwell.

Dunglas (17) n_6_ classic butyric (baby sick) qualities and something else besides: soapy beyond belief; **t**_7_ malty, but the off-key oils suggest a still out of control **f**_0_ oak fails to save an impossible situation: it might even be adding to it. The soapiness will be with you for days. I had to stop tasting for the day after this one; **b**_4_ the stills at Littlemill often caused problems at the best of times. When they experimented with the rectifier to produce Dunglas it was as if they were trying to perfect the art of making bad whisky. This is one of the rarest whisky bottlings in the world and worth being in any collection. Buy it for the experience and to learn. But don't expect to enjoy that experience. Interestingly, and in fairness to Littlemill, I have discovered these same faults with some casks in Scotland and beyond. An educated guess is that the stillman had major problems keeping the still under control and used large chunks of soap to calm down the frothing wash. There was probably a soap shortage in the area for some months after. **46%.** Bravely bottled by The Whisky Exchange, London. (www.thewhiskyexchange.com). 102 bottles. For serious whisky devotees or people with a serious grudge against their tastebuds.

Old Malt Cask Littlemill Aged 35 Years dist Oct 65, bott Jan 01 **(81)** n18 t22 f20 b21. A hot and fruity old chap that radiates lush, sweet malt in its really good moments. **47.4%. nc ncf.** Douglas Laing.

⋯❖⋯ **Whisky Galore Littlemill 1992 Aged 10 Years (77)** n18 t21 f19 b19. An attractive malty early mouth arrval outshines the indifferent nose and finish. **46%.** Duncan Taylor.

LOCH LOMOND
Highland (Southwestern), 1966. Glen Catrine. Working.
Inchmurrin 10 Years Old db **(81)** n21 t21 f19 b20. A sturdy, sweet and indulgently complex malt that struggles very slightly on the mildly bitter finale. **40%**

Loch Lomond db **(80)** n20 t22 f19 b19. Bold, fruity start. Big, silky body clipped in its prime presumably by caramel. **40%.** No age mentioned but varies between five and eight years.

⋯❖⋯ **Old Rhosdhu 1967** db bott Dec 96 **(78)** n19 t20 f19 b20. Some early barley sugar but lacks charisma. A few bottles still doing the rounds, amazingly. **40%**

Cadenhead's Inchmurrin 29 Years Old dist 74, bott 03/03 **(84)** n20 t23 f21 b20. Lots of vanilla and tangerines amid the malt and muscovado sugar. Really delicious. **54.4%**

Gordon & MacPhail Inchmurrin 1973 (78) n20 t19 f20 b19. Curiously very similar to some oily old corn whiskies I used to find in the States 20 years ago. **40%**

⋯❖⋯ **Murray McDavid Mission III Old Rhosdhu 1979 (81)** n20 t21 f20 f20. Typically well built and chewy with a handsome milk-toffee richness to the barley. **46%**

⋯❖⋯ **Scotch Malt Whisky Society Cask 122.1 Aged 11 Years (93)** n23 clean, clearly defined peat on a weighty malt background, frighteningly Islay-ish in style; t24 the fatness helps the sweetness blossom around the tastebuds; there is decent bite and kick that is not spice related but the intensity and development of the peat is stunning; f23 long with some medium roast Blue Mountain coffee keeping the peat company; b23 unlikely you will come across a more top grade "Islay" from the Scottish mainland. The SMWS have given this a new number (122) because it is Croftengea rather than just a standard Loch Lomond. A much more heavily peated version than the very decent Limburg Whisky Fair bottling and, frankly, a class above. One every collector should get their hands on: if you aren't a member of the SMWS, you'd better join.... **58.6%. nc ncf sc.**

⋯❖⋯ **The Whisky Fair Croftengea 1993** dist 23 Aug 93, bott 15 Jan 04 **(86)** n18 heavy, oily, a touch feinty with awkward peat t22 at first it takes the tastebuds to acclimatise: amid the oily fog are those feinty notes again and then a slow, incredibly intense build-up of peat: dense and murky stuff f23 honeyed smoke and a continuation of the sweet barey concentrate that has gathered throughout b23 this is the first time I have tasted Croftengea in bottled form, though it has changed little since I first tasted it at the distillery about eight years ago. All the main components are still there – as are the flaws. An enormous, curious dram that challenges and entertains and hangs around the palate for hours on end... **54.8%.** Germany. 208 bottles for the Limburg Whisky Fair.

LOCHSIDE
Highland (Eastern), 1957–1992. Closed.
Connoisseurs Choice Lochside 1981 (77) n18 t21 f19 b19. Light, chalky and fruity. **40%.** Gordon & MacPhail.

∴ **Connoisseurs Choice Lochside 1991 (85)** n*20* slight bite but the citrus attracts; t*22* the development of the barley is laboured but linear; a slow crescendo is achieved with spice amid the buttery malt; f*21* excellent follow through with the distant mollased sweetness drying into liquorice; b*22* deceptively complex and rewarding. **43%**. *Gordon & MacPhail.*

Berrys' Own Selection Lochside 1981 bott 02 **(76)** n*19* t*20* f*18* b*19*. Chewy sweet malt but lacking staying power and depth. **43%**. *Berry Bros & Rudd.*

Gordon & MacPhail Lochside 1981 bott 00 **(61)** n*15* t*17* f*14* b*15*. Poor whisky. **40%**

∴ **Jack Wiebers The Lochside 37 Years** Cask No. 7543 dist Dec 66, bott Mar 04 **(87)** n*21* pretty tired but just enough lemon zestiness to lighten the bourbony oak; t*22* kumquat peel and mouthwatering barley; surprisingly clean and soft; f*22* seems to be standing still, but your tongue continuously licking the roof of your mouth confirms that some covert cocoa-coated complexity is keeping you entertained; b*22* a cask picked just in the nick of time shows delicious insight into this lost distillery. **58.7%. nc ncf sc.** *Germany. 168 bottles.*

Lombard Lochside 1981 (85) n*21* beautiful marmalade; t*23* fresh fruit, mouthwatering in style, clean malt, exemplary Lochside style; f*20* bit too much toffee on the finish; b*21* a lovely dram marred perhaps by too much either natural or unnatural caramel. **50%**

Murray-McDavid Lochside 1981 cask MM 2106, dist May 81, bottled Dec 01 **(82)** n*23* t*20* f*19* b*20*. The nose stars and nothing quite lives up to it. Pretty classy number, nonetheless.

∴ **Old Malt Cask Lochside 14 Years Old** dist Jul 89, bott Mar 04 **(78)** n*19* t*21* f*19* b*19*. Just too intensely sweet ever to be a great whisky, but a jolly exhibitionist all the same. **50%. nc ncf sc.** *Douglas Laing.*

Old Malt Cask Lochside Aged 21 Years dist May 79, bott June 00 **(87)** n*22* t*22* f*22* b*21*. Quality malt. **50%. nc ncf.** *Douglas Laing. 306 bottles.*

Old Malt Cask Lochside Aged 35 Years dist Dec 66, bott Jan 02 **(74)** n*19* t*19* f*18* b*18*. Hot whisky. **50%. nc ncf**. *Douglas Laing. 216 bottles.*

∴ **Scotch Malt Whisky Society Cask 92.10 Aged 20 Years (83)** n*21* t*20* f*22* b*20*. Clean, mouthwatering with lots of citrus and bite. **61%. nc ncf sc.**

Scotch Malt Whisky Society Cask 92.9 Aged 30 Years dist May 81, bott Jun 01 **(85)** n*21* bourbony with no shortage of citrus fruit and ripe banana; t*22* more bourbon oakiness to the fore, sweet malts abound; f*21* long and very well-spiced. The oak softens out; b*21* still mothwaterng after all these years. **61.2%**

LONGMORN
Speyside, 1895. Chivas. Working.

Longmorn 15 Years Old db **(93)** n*23* curiously salty and coastal for a Speysider, really beautifully structured oak but the malt offers both African violets and barley sugar; t*24* your mouth aches from the enormity of the complexity, while your tongue wipes grooves into the roof of your mouth. Just about flawless bitter-sweet balance, the intensity of the malt is enormous, yet – even after 15 years – it maintains a cut-grass Speyside character; f*22* long, acceptably sappy and salty with chewy malt and oak. Just refuses to end; b*24* this latest bottling is the best yet: previous ones had shown just a little too much oak but this has hit a perfect compromise. An all-time Speyside great. **45%**

Blackadder Raw Cask 1973 sherry cask 3974, dist 8 May 73, bott May 02 **(91)** n*23* intense, thick oloroso covers some hefty oak: a 16-ton weight in a glass; t*24* sweet, over-ripe figs and plums sprinkled with brown sugar, nutmeg and pepper, stunningly lush and chewy; f*22* something has to crack and the oak comes out on top; b*22* a dram that takes no prisoners: wimpy tastebuds should stand well clear. Glorious! **56.9%. nc ncf sc.**

Cask Longmorn 1969 (92) n24 supreme sherry: ripe cherries and zesty; t24 magnificent: an explosion of spices, scattering with it intense malt and soft oak. Loads of natural toffee; f22 surprisingly light; b22 this is one of those give-away classics that can still be bought relatively cheaply. Find it! **61.2%.** *Gordon & MacPhail.*

Cask Longmorn 1973 cask 3235, dist 13/4/73, bott Jul 00 **(94)** n23 t24 f23 b24. Good old Gordon & MacPhail. Longmorn has long been one of their mainstays and here they have done each other proud. Probably the pick of the entire G&M range. **55.7%.** *Gordon & MacPhail.*

⠿ **The Coopers Choice Longmorn 1988 Aged 14 Years** bott 03 **(86)** n22 fruit and nut; t21 mouthwatering delivery of soft barley; f22 a bedazzling array of muted dark sugars amid the rich malt; b21 hefty and weighted to the very end: a more than passable example of Longmorn at this age. **43%.** *Vintage Malt Whisky Co.*

⠿ **Old Malt Cask Longmorn Aged 15 Years** dist Nov 88, bott Feb 04 **(91)** n23 first-class interplay between busy coal-gas/peaty smoky notes, soft honey, unripened oranges and unmalted barley flour; t22 really delicate malt with wafer-thin strands of oak underpinning it at first and then attempting to take control; bitter oranges and honey form a complex diversion. Mouthwatering throughout; f22 the odd waft of peat reek sweetens the lightly charred toast; b24 this is something to spend time over: a bitter-sweet tale if ever there was one. **50%. nc ncf sc.** *Douglas Laing.*

Gordon & MacPhail Longmorn-Glenlivet Age 12 Years (75) n18 t20 f19 b18. Been drinking (as opposed to tasting!) this chap regularly for some 20 years: it's normally a lot better than this. Too much age and fruit – just doesn't hang right. **40%**

Gordon & MacPhail Longmorn 25 Years Old (81) n20 t22 f19 b20. Fruit biscuit, with dry finish. **40%**

⠿ **Gordon & MacPhail Longmorn 1971 (91)** n22 whistle-clean sherry has soaked up rich oak comforatably; t23 again the grape is towering but such is the clarity the malt makes delicious inroads; f23 laced with cocoa and prunes, the bitter-sweet finish is a joy; b23 one of those exceptional Seagram sherry butts of the early '70s. Unmistakable and unmissable. **40%.** *Gordon & MacPhail*

Gordon & MacPhail Longmorn 1970 (85) n22 salt and honey and harmony, especially with that wisp of smoke; t22 more honey with a lovely malt and cucumber middle (really!); f20 the oak kicks in with a chalky dryness; b21 just enough all-round weight and complexity to make into a very decent dram. **40%**

⠿ **Duncan Taylor Longmorn 1978 Aged 25 Years** cask 5556 **(96)** n23 dream-like complexity with near perfect salt seasoning the vanilla-dried, barley-sweetened theme t24 wow...!!! No easy task to get to grips with what is happening here: that saltiness peppers the mouth but the honey edge to the barley quietens the liquorice/coffee oak f24 some fruit edges into the equation but still we have a briny quarter to the barley; the oak is dry and has weight and purpose and some late honeycomb arrives to even it up a little b25 ladies and gentleman, I introduce to you complexity... **58.1%**

Old Malt Cask Longmorn Aged 20 Years Sherry dist Nov 81, bott Nov 01 **(87)** n21 t22 f22 b22. I shall start blending some malt with pot-still Jamaican to see if I can recreate this one. **50%. nc ncf.** *Douglas Laing. 570 bottles.*

Old Malt Cask Longmorn Aged 31 Years dist May 69, bott Feb 01 **(91)** n23 t24 f22 b22. An ambiguous quality. **45.6%. nc ncf.** *Douglas Laing. 210 bottles.*

Old Masters Longmorn 1967 bott 2002 **(90)** n21 exceptionally firm malt and oak softened only by grapey fruit and a vague hint of smoke; t23 multi-layered oak, all of the the softest, most yielding character. The sweet malt can be chewed, the soft fruits offering mouthwatering complexity; f23 chocolate fruit and nut bar in liquid form; **b**23 this is wonderful whisky: warm it in the hand and see it come alive. **57.1%**. James MacArthur.

Peerless Longmorn 1969 cask 2948, dist May 69 **(90) n**23 rich honey and a barely perceptible stratum of menthyl. Fruity physalis stars amid the barley concentrate: beautiful; **t**22 silky and soft, the honey and fruit dovetail brilliantly. A wonderful breeze of smoke wafts elegantly through the palate, barely distracting from the busy, popping malt notes in the middle; **f**21 smoky with plenty of oaky, toasty notes to balance the sweeter malt: terrific style and balance; **b**24 a supreme old whisky from a truly great distillery. Few Speysiders show such poise, grace and complexity at this age. A must. **44.1%**. Duncan Taylor & Co Ltd.

⠿ **Platinum Old and Rare Longmorn 35 Years Old** dist May 68 **(88) n**23 a strange mix of model kit glue and oranges left in the sun a day too long. Pungent, bourbony, lively and, against the odds, highly attractive; **t**22 hotly spiced cherry tomatoes and some towering bourbony tones; the middle fills up with massed ranks of cocoa-ey oak and lashings of old acacia honey; **f**21 calms down surprisingly quickly leaving a trace of barley amid the vanilla; **b**22 if you a glue-sniffing, vindaloo-eating, apiary-keeping chocoholic, there is finally a whisky just for you...**57.8%**. Douglas Laing. 94 bottles.

Private Cellar Longmorn-Glenlivet 1970 bott 03 **(93) n**23 oranges and ripe physalis combine with juicy pears and malt. Some oak offers weight; **t**24 an astonishing mixture of fresh fruit and weighty, oaky depth, unusual and delicious; **f**22 spicy but wave upon wave of succulent, fruity malt; **b**24 some say there is no such thing as vintages: let's just say that in the late 60s and early 70s God smiled benevolently on Longmorn. **43%**. Forbes Ross Co.

Scotch Malt Whisky Society Cask 7.21 Aged 33 Years (82) n19 **t**22 **f**21 **b**20. Malty and spiced but heading south. **60.3%. nc ncf sc.**

Scott's Selection Longmorn-Glenlivet 1971 bott 99 **(95) n**24 **t**24 **f**23 **b**24. My indifference to over-sherried whiskies is well-documented. But if they were all like this absolute gem then you wouldn't hear a word of complaint from me. This is nothing short of stupendous. It is how every distiller dreams his whisky will taste 28 years after filling the cask ... but believes it to be impossible. A classic among classics. **57.8%**. Robert Scott & Co.

⠿ **Scott's Selection Longmorn-Glenlivet 1983** Sherry Wood bott 03 **(89) n**23 boiled, unsugared gooseberries or what!! Some bread-pudding for good measure; lively, spiced, pulsating stuff; **t**25 outwardly, dry sherry with a sub-plot sweet enough to set your teeth of edge; the counter-blast of ruffian spices is perfect; **f**22 much more civilised with vanilla calming down the manic start and some cocoa adding late balance; **b**22 no prisoners taken here in this unusual chewathon. **54.5%**

Whisky Galore Longmorn 1990 12-y-o (86) n21 coal-smoky; **t**23 bright, clean and a little nutty: the intensity of the malt is startling; **f**20 malty but becomes just a little bitter; **b**22 a really big Speysider. **46%**. Duncan Taylor & Co.

LONGROW (see Springbank)

MACALLAN
Speyside, 1824. Edrington. Working.
The Macallan 7 Years Old db **(87) n**22 beautifully clean sherry, lively, salty, gentle peppers; **t**21 mouth-filling and slightly oily. Some coffee tones intertwine with deep barley and fruit; **f**22 unravels to reveal very soft oak and lingering fruity spice; **b**22 an outstanding dram that underlines just how good young malts can be. Fun and fabulous. **40%**

The Macallan 10 Years Old db **(81) n**20 **t**21 **f**21 **b**19. Delicious, but perhaps a little too slick to allow for full complexity **40%**

The Macallan 10 Years Old Cask Strength db **(87)** n*20* aggressive but beautifully clean and sweet oloroso; t*23* outstanding sherry-barley balance with a biscuity chewiness; f*22* long, clean sherry, molassed and silky; b*22* everything the standard 10-y-o wants to be. Stunning, controlled aggression. **58.8%.** *Duty free.*

The Macallan 12 Years Old db **(77)** n*17* t*20* f*21* b*19*. A slightly bitter, off-key bottling with some lingering, mouthwatering, sherry-rich moments – but usually much better than this. **40%**

The Macallan 18 Years Old 1982 db **(83)** n*21* t*20* f*21* b*21*. An intense malt with excellent barley core. **43%**

The Macallan 18 Years Old 1983 db **(85)** n*21* a thick, punchy sherried aroma of enormous weight; t*22* fat, mouth-filling starting softly then building a caramel-biscuit middle; f*21* lightens in body but spices evolve pleasantly; b*21* sparkling sherry-barley on the palate. Good oils. **43%**

The Macallan 18 Years Old 1984 db **(88)** n*21* controlled oak showing a hint of smoke amid the plums and apples; t*22* beautifully sweet and intense barley and very clean fruit; f*21* excellent sherry-barley balance; b*24* exceptionally well-balanced, revealing some lingering youth on the barley and fruit with older, oaky notes. Impressive. **43%**

The Macallan 25 Years Old db **(80)** n*20* t*22* f*19* b*19*. Decent, but a much thinner, oak-dominant expression than usual. The quality of this Macallan can vary dramatically. **43%**

The Macallan 30 Years Old db **(92)** n*24* orange pith and oak, really charming and incredibly sexy and complex; t*23* mouth-filling with a mixture of full fruits and beguiling spices, brilliant layer of honied barley; f*22* slightly medium to short after the brilliance of the palate, but lovely vanilla and lingering, silky sweet malt; b*23* a greatly improved dram than a few years back. An astounding mixture of age and beauty. **43%**

The Macallan 1841 Replica db **(83)** n*21* t*21* f*20* b*21*. Cultured, classy, well-balanced malt, fresh with a lovely whiff of smoke. **41.7%**

The Macallan 1861 Replica db **(82)** n*19* t*21* f*22* b*20*. The nose is a miss, the rest is bliss. A pageant of honey and spice. **42.7%**

⁖ **The Macallan 1876 Replica** db **(83)** n*21* t*21* f*21* b*20*. Lovely oak-malt nose while the palate is silky and relaxed. **40.6%**

⁖ **The Macallan 1937** bott 69 db **(92)** n*23* an outline of barley can eventually be made in the oaky mist; becomes better defined as a honeyed sweetness cuts in. Fingers of smoke tease. When nosing in the glass hours later the fresh, smoky gristiness is to die for ... and takes you back to the mill room 67 years ago; t*22* pleasantly sweet start as the barley piles in – even a touch of melon in there; this time the oak takes second place and acts as a perfect counter; f*24* excellent weight with soft peat softening the oak; b*23* a subtle if not overly complex whisky where there are few characters but each play its part exceptionally well. One to get out with a DVD of Will Hay's sublime *Oh Mr Porter* which was being made in Britain at the same time as this whisky and as Laurel and Hardy were singing about a Lonesome Pine on the other side of the pond; or any Pathe film of Millwall's FA Cup semi-final with Sunderland. **43%**

⁖ **The Macallan 1937** bott 74 db **(83)** t*19* a little oak-tired but invigorated by marmalade and threatening spice; t*24* beautiful delivery of silky, almost concentrated, barley with the spice arriving followed by deep waves of oak; f*20* the oak gets a little too embedded as the finish takes a bitter turn; b*20* it's all about the superb initial mouth impact. **43%.**

⁖ **The Macallan 1938** bott 73 db **(90)** n*21* hint of apple blossoms on oak; t*23* stupendous balance and poise as the barley rolls, wave after wave over the palate bringing with it a sweet sugar-almond biscuity quality; f*23* fabulous finish of great length. Spices dovetail with an almost perfect barley-oak charm; b*23* no hint of tiredness here at all: a malt that has all the freshness and charisma yet old-world charm and mystery of Hitchcock's *The Lady Vanishes*, which was made at the same time as this whisky. **43%**

·:· **The Macallan 1938 (31 Years Old)** dist 38, first bott 69, re-bottled 02 db **(83) n**20 rigid barley slaps into uncompromising oak; a touch of sugared cold tea, too. The sherry does soften the blow; **t**22 massive brown sugar implosion with the barley offering a mouthwatering edge; slightly rummy; **f**20 some coffee amid the ultra stern oak; **b**21 some wonderful trills of barley early on but the oak dominates. **43%.**

·:· **The Macallan 1939** bott 79 db **(90) n**23 pleasing peaty edges to the thick malt; a touch of hickory for extra weight and Highland Park-esque heather-honey; **t**22 spot on barley gives an unmolested mouthwatering performance; the oak tags on reluctantly drying towards cocoa at the middle; **f**22 the integrity is kept as the oak backs off and little wisps of smoke re-surface; some brown sugar keeps the bitter-sweet pot boiling; **b**23 enormous complexity confidence to a whisky distilled at a time of uncertainty; one to accompany the original *Goodbye Mr Chips*, though the whisky seems nothing like so faded. **43%**

·:· **The Macallan 1940** bott 75 db **(83) n**20 the oldest Macallan to display sherried traits, though they are a little clumsy, perhaps because of a vague peatiness, but improve slightly with warming; **t**22 fresh sherry is punctuated by mouthwatering malt; **f**21 big oak charge sees the balance being tortured somewhat but just stays within acceptable levels; **b**20 easily the most modern style discernible from this distillery; a Macallan recogisable as an ancestor of today's famous dram, even with one or two warts apparent. **43%**

·:· **The Macallan 1940 (37 Years Old)** dist 40, first bott 77, re-bottled 02 db **(91) n**22 not dissimilar to an old sherried Irish of this era with the barley having a firm, crisp, almost abrasive quality. Rather lovely especially with the most subtle wisps of peat imaginable; **t**23 bracing, full-on barley where the flintiness from the nose is transferred perfectly to the palate; a touch of spice and hint of smoke towards the middle; **f**23 clean, long finale where the barley pulsates its rock hard message; **b**23 blind-tasting I would have declared this Irish, though slightly mystified by the distant hints of peat. Hard to believe that something so sublime could have been made by a nation under siege. Obviously nothing can distract a Scotsman from making great whisky ... **43%**

·:· **The Macallan 1945 (56 Years Old)** cask no.262 bott 02 db **(89) n**22 extraordinary to the point of improbability: the sherry is fresh and keeping at bay logjams of chunky oak, though the fruitiness burns off the longer it remains in the glass; the smoke hovers and soars like pin-prick eagles on the wing; **t**23 battling oak fizzes against the sweeter, mouthwatering barley; the fruit is subtle though there is a pineapple sharpness amid the still lush grape; **f**22 really impressive, slow development of peat that offers no spice but a smoky overlay to the oak; **b**22 how can a whisky retain so much freshness and character after so long in the cask? This game never ceases to amaze me. **51.5%**

The Macallan 1946 Select Reserve db **(93) n**25 does peat arrive any more delicately than this? The sherry, barley and oak offer perfect harmony: perfect and faultless; **t**23 teasingly mouthwatering and fruity. Crushed sultanas cruise with the peat; **f**22 the oak makes inroads at the expense of the barley. Remains chewy and tantalisingly smoky, though; **b**23 I have never found a finer nose to any whisky. Once-in-a-lifetime whisky. **40%**

·:· **The Macallan 1946 (56 Years Old)** cask no.46/3M bott 02 db **(84) n**21hints of ginger and toast **t**21 citrussy and refreshing with the oak outrunning the barley **f**20 some tender strands of barley see off the toasty, oaky follow through **b**22 the most peat-free '46 I've come across yet **44.3%**

·:· **The Macallan 1948 (53 Years Old)** cask no.609 bott 02 db **(77) n**18 a bit sappy and tired; **t**21 initial burst of rich malt and fruit then hollows out; **f**19 faint traces of peat aren't enough to galvanise the oak; **b**19 drinkable, but showing some cracks. **45.3%**

The Macallan 1948 Select Reserve db **(75)** n22 t19 f17 **b**17. What a fabulous nose! Sadly the package trails behind the '46. **40%**

⌇ **The Macallan 1949 (53 Years Old)** cask no.136 bott 02 db **(95)** n23 wonderfully lively fruit interwoven with waxy, polished wooden floors and acacia honey; a touch of salt sharpens it further; **t**24 nothing extinct about this old Scottish volcano as oak-led spices assert their grip on the tastebuds while soft, sultry sherry tries to act as placator; **f**24 oaky-cocoa/liquorice and intense barley; remains mouthwatering yet spicy for seemingly hours; **b**24 hold on to your trilbies: this punchy malt knows exactly where it is going. What a year: Carol Reed makes the incomparable *The Third Man* and Macallan can come up with something like this. Oh, to swap Orson Welles for H. G. Wells and his time machine. Sheer, unrepeatable class. **49.8%**

⌇ **The Macallan 1949 (52 Years Old)** cask no.935 bott 02 db **(82)** n23 by far the most intense of this range with oloroso dripping from the nose even after all this time, further fortified by molten black chocolate and an adroit peachy sweetness: amazingly clean for its age; **t**21 the fruit dominates and is much lighter than the nose. Because of this the oak makes its mark a bit quicker; **f**19 thin and mildly tart; **b**19 faded and slightly tired, it has problems living up to the heaven-made nose. **41.1%**

⌇ **The Macallan 1950 (52 Years Old)** cask no.598 bott 02 db **(83)** n22 a frisson of peat slips between the standard malt/peat horn-locking; **t**22 mouthwatering at first and then a burst of spice; the oak quickly closes most else down; **f**18 some peat returns to quieten the oaky onslaught; **b**21 probably about two or three summers past being a truly excellent whisky. **46.7%**

⌇ **The Macallan 1950 (52 Years Old)** cask no.600 bott 02 db **(91)** n20 the early fruit quickly evaporates to leave a clear path for the oak; **t**24 stunning sherry: the grape absolutely sparkles yet is soft enough to allow through a tidal wave of malt, on which peat is sensuously surfing; **f**23 spices from the middle carry through as does the chewy peat. Some fabulous undercurrents of burnt raisin and healthy malt continue; **b**24 only two casks apart, but this is almost a mirror image of the first, in the sense that everything is the other way round... **51.7%**

⌇ **The Macallan 1951 (51 Years Old)** cask no.644 bott 02 db **(93)** n23 a minor fruitfest with withering grapes and raisins the main attraction but over-ripe greengages and raspberries bulk up the sub-plot: needs this to see off the firm oak. A gentle, barely discernible peatiness drifts over it all with absolutely no signs of over-aging; **t**24 fascinating detail to the barley: it is fresh and still mildly gristy at first but the sherry builds a dark path towards it. All the time the sherry remains clean and in harmony; some confident peat weaves a delicious path through the complexity; **f**23 unrefined brown sugar digs in with the barley to see off the encroaching oak; the most delicate wafts of peat imaginable caress the senses; **b**23 a malt instantly recognisable to Macallan lovers of the last two decades. Simply outstanding. **52.3%**

⌇ **The Macallan 1952 (50 Years Old)** cask no.627 bott 02 db **(80)** n20 firm and slightly honeyed **t**20 bubbling with spices the sherry is aloof and soft **f**21 lots of vanilla and butterscotch **b**19 good, clean sherry but it all seems a little detached **50.8%**

⌇ **The Macallan 1952 (49 Years Old)** cask no. 1250 bott 02 db **(74)** n19 seriously odd: a fruit salad of lychee and passion fruit with boiled blackcurrants for good measure; grassy compost; **t**19 full-blown sherry but there is a strange background noise that fits with the curious nose; **f**18 slightly vegetable; **b**18 ye olde weirde Macallane. **48%**

⌇ **The Macallan 1953 (49 Years Old)** cask no. 516 bott 02 db **(92)** n22 a shade meaty with the oak offering a big counter to the thumping sherry and delicate smoke; **t**24 full sherry alert as the fruitcake richness goes into overdrive, as do the spices; **f**23 some medium roast Santos lightens the oak while enrichening the barley; **b**23 deliciously big and unflinching in its Christmas pudding intensity. **51%**

✑ **The Macallan 1954 (47 Years Old)** cask no. 1902 bott 02 db **(77) n**19 enormous oak held together by sherry; something of an old bourbon about this; **t**18 too much oak makes for a puckering start: you almost feel as if you can pick out the splinters; **f**21 enormous milk coffee character helps sweeten the eye-watering oak; **b**19 the line between success and failure is thin: outwardly the '53 and 54 are similar but the 53 controls the oak much tighter. I love the astonishing coffee finale on this, though. **50.2%**

✑ **The Macallan 1955 (46 Years Old)** cask no. 1851 49 bott 02 db **(88) n**21 more burnt raisins and apples; **t**22 the tastebuds get a good spicy peppering as the barley rootles about the palate; the sherry is clear and intact; **f**23 amazingly long with the oak falling short of its desired palate domination; **b**22 close call: one more Speyside August and this dram would have been matchwood. **45.9%**

✑ **The Macallan 1958 (43 Years Old)** cask no. 2682 bott 02 db **(86) n**17 sappy; **t**22 a shocking and delicious meeting of sweet and spicy; **f**24 honey on several different levels; **b**23 one fears the worst from the nose but the taste is sheer Highland Park in its honey depth. **52.9%**

✑ **The Macallan 1959 (43 Years Old)** cask no. 360 bott 02 db **(79) n**19 tired and unemotional; **t**21 burnt toffee fudge; **f**19 lots of oaky stress on the muscavado sweetness; **b**20 the oak is giving the whisky a good hiding but it just hangs on to a delicious plot. **46.7%**

✑ **The Macallan 1964 (37 Years Old)** cask no. 3312 bott 02 db **(86) n**24 beautiful butterscotch tart laced with honey and a light dry sherry; outstandingly clean and complex; **t**22 disarming arrival of honeyed barley and peat but the oak bounds in early; **f**20 spice, alcohol bite and militant honey makes this one chewy finale; **b**20 promised to be so much better, but a real chewing whisky if ever there was one. **58.2%**

✑ **The Macallan 1965 (36 Years Old)** cask no. 4402 bott 02 db **(91) n**22 pretty well oaked but wonderful balance from blood oranges; **t**23 again lovely mouthfeel as the fabulously balanced and lush barley hits the palate; fruit and oak are dished out in even measures with the spice: this is top notch whisky; **f**22 after the big bust comes the ample arse: heaps of chewy barley fortified by sultanas and raisins; **b**24 if this was a woman it would be Marilyn Monroe. **56.3%**

✑ **The Macallan 1966 (35 Years Old)** cask no. 7878 bott 02 db **(83) n**21 spicy sherry with a mildly tart sub stratum; **t**22 booming malt kick with the sherry being light and distant; **f**20 slightly flat and toffees; **b**20 a malt which never quite works out where it is going but gives a comfortable ride all the same. **55.5%**

✑ **The Macallan 1967 (35 Years Old)** cask no. 1195 bott 02 db **(93) n**23 top notch uncompromised sherry with some lovely nutty touches; **t**24 the sherry deftly flicks each individual tastebud while the burnt fudge offers a bitter-sweet distraction; **f**23 coffee ice cream but a whole lot warmer as the spices pop about the mouth. Vanilla and raisins gather around the spicy centrepiece; some lovely salt towards the finale; **b**23 this is what happens when you get a great sherry cask free of sulphur and marauding oak: whisky the way God intended. Unquestionably classic Macallan. **55.9%**

✑ **The Macallan 1968 (34 Years Old)** cask no. 2875 bott 02 db **(92) n**23 lemon curd tart and barley; **t**23 full frontal barley with a grape chaperone; **f**22 continues to mouthwater now with late cocoa adding depth and finesse; **b**24 possibly the most sophisticated and delicate malt in the pack despite the strength. **51%**

✑ **The Macallan 1968 (33 Years Old)** cask no. 5913 bott 02 db **(84) n**17 sappy and a little soapy; **t**23 the malt seems unphased by the poor nose and intensity of the barley and praline is sublime; f22 very long and before it fades back to sap there is a continuation of that cocoa theme; **b**22 flawed genius: how can a whisky with such a poor nose produce the goods like this? **46.6%**

⠂⠅ **The Macallan 1969** cask no. 9369 db **(75) n**19 tinned tomatoes and salt; **t**18 the palate disappears in sludgy sherry-oak; f20 sweetens slightly to offer some barley; **b**18 one of those ungainly sherry butts that swamps everything in sight. **52.7%**

⠂⠅ **The Macallan 1969 (32 Years Old)** cask no. 10412 bott 02 db **(76) n**18 splinters, anybody? **t**20 the early oak forest partitially obliterates a lovely peaty layer flanked by soft fruit; **f**18 pretty exhausted in its battle against the oak; **b**20 one small sip for man, one ordinary vintage for Macallan. **59%**

⠂⠅ **The Macallan 1970 (32 Years Old)** cask no. 241 bott 02 db **(95) n**23 another heavyweight but this time with some honey and ripe fig to offer complexity; passable impersonation of ancient bourbon blended with old Demerara rum; **t**24 quite massive with strands of brown sugar bringing out the best of the grape; **f**23 very long and so subtle: the barley and vanilla stretch a long distance with some natural toffee rounding things off; **b**25 Brazil win the World Cup with the finest team and performance of all time, my girlfriend born there soon after and Macallan receive a butt from Heaven via Jerez. 1970 was some year ... **54.9%**

⠂⠅ **The Macallan 1970 (31 Years Old)** cask no. 9033 bott 02 db **(81) n**20 dry with coffee and oak; **t**20 unconvincing arrival of OTT oak puts sherry and barley off balance; **f**22 vanilla dives in to help steady the ship with the burnt raisin effect seeing off some late resins; **b**19 a butt bottled on its way down. **52.4%**

⠂⠅ **The Macallan 1971 (30 Years Old)** cask no. 4280 bott 02 db **(86) n**21 coffee-flavoured party ring biscuits; **t**22 viscous grape is set about by vicious spice; **f**22 some hallmark Macallan lushness; medium length; **b**21 imagine the trusty 10 years old from about 1980 with a grey beard ... **56.4%**

⠂⠅ **The Macallan 1971 (30 Years Old)** cask no. 7556 bott 02 db **(91) n**22 delicate salt helps develop the barley; **t**22 vivid barley with rather soft sherry and then spice; **f**24 lengthy, subtle end with waves of rich sherry carrying a Demerara sweetness and coffee; **b**23 a complex dram that is comfortable with its age. **55.9%**

⠂⠅ **The Macallan 1972 (29 Years Old)** cask no. 4041 bott 02 db **(92) n**23 hell's teeth!!! This is probably what an explosion in a bodega would smell like. The most awesomely powerful sherry I can probably ever remember on a whisky, much more one dimensional than cask 4043, though; **t**24 that trademark coffeeness is there (in this case something of a heavy roast Costa Rican) then some tomato and burnt raisin; **f**22 bitter and slightly nutty as the oak begins to gain some control; **b**23 once, I would have hated this type of malt. But I have come across so many sulphur-tainted casks over recent years that I have learned to have fun with monsters like this. Snatched from an awesome clutch of butts. **49.2%**

The Macallan 1972 29 Years Old cask 4043, bott 02 db **(93) n**25 well, it has to be said: a quite faultless nose. The spices are entirely in true with the perfect sherry-oak balance. This is big stuff, but perfectly proportioned: seems almost a shame to drink it ...; **t**24 stupendous spice-plum-giant-boiled-Italian-tomato: enormous with a waft of smoke through the middle; **f**21 slightly bitter as the oak nibbles but still lots of complexity; **b**23 the sherry butt used for this was a classic: the intensity of the whisky memorable. If, as Macallan claim, the sherry accounts for only 5% of the flavour, I'd like to know what happened to the other 95.... **58.4%**

⠂⠅ **The Macallan 1973 (30 Years Old)** cask no.6098 bott 03 db **(93) n**23 the grape is brittle and nestles behind barley and honey; some ripe pears add to the freshness; **t**24 the honey is at the vanguard of a brilliant display of intense, sugar-coated barley; **f**23 the sweetness vanishes to leave the more mouthwatering, grassy malt elements; **b**23 a superbly chosen cask for those with a sweet tooth in particular. If you know any women who claim not to like whisky, seduce them with this. **60.9%**

⋙ **The Macallan 1989** cask no 552 db **(94)** n*23* stunningly clean sherry with wonderful nuttiness amid spice and oak; moist Melton Hunt cake at its most subtle; t*23* explosive entrance with spices and a superbly full-on oakiness that bathes in the luxuriant, simply flawless, leathery sherry; the sweetness is not entirely unlike Demerara rum; f*24* calms down for wave upon wave of chocolate fruit and nut ... only without the excessive sweetness; b*24* there are countless people out there who cut their whisky teeth 20 years ago on Macallan. Battle to get a bottle of this and the grey hairs will return to black, the eyesight will improve and your clothes will fit more easily. This is timewarp Macallan it its most dangerously seductive. **59.2%**

The Macallan Distillers Choice db **(80)** n*21* t*22* f*18* b*19*. Seems like young stuff, lively, mouthwatering and good, clean sherry influence. Something wild, raw and different amongst Macallans. Great fun.

The Macallan Cask Strength (78) n*18* t*21* f*20* b*19*. A straight-up-and-down malt with few surprises. **58.6%**. *USA*.

The Macallan Gran Reserva 1981 db **(90)** n*23* fully ripe wild cherries, a thin stratum of smoke, luxuriant grape plus barley, spice and oak. Pretty damn good! t*22* succulent, mouthwatering grape and barley with a lovely rumble of deeper oak and smoke; f*22* long, oaky, toast and marmalade; b*23* Macallan in a nutshell. Brilliant. But could do with being at 46% for full effect. **40%**

The Macallan Gran Reserva 1982 db **(82)** n*21* t*22* f*20* b*19*. Big, clean, sweet sherry influence from first to last but doesn't open up and sing like the '81 vintage. **40%**

The Macallan Elegancia 1990 db **(70)** n*16* t*19* f*17* b*18*. Struggles to get past the sulphur. Ironic, considering this is the only Macallan bottled by the distillery that contains bourbon as well as sherry casks. **40%**

⋙ **The Macallan Elegancia 1991** db **(79)** n*19* t*21* f*19* b*20*. Distinctly citrusy with fresh-squeezed blood orange intermingling with vanilla and fresh malt; sadly, a distant murmer of sulphur on both nose and finish docks a point or three. **40%**

⋙ **The Macallan Elegancia 1992** db **(85)** n*19* a busy, if imperfect, aroma showing more oak and age than the years suggest t*21* very firm malt followed by soft fruit f*23* a true whisky-lover's finish which is seemingly endless with countless twists and turns. There even appears to be a high copper-input into the lush and cocoa-sprinkled finale b*22* a marvellous improvement on the '90 edition **43%**

The Macallan ESC IV 1990 cask 24690 db **(95)** n*24* the cleanest sherry cask you can find: spices intermingle with crisp barley and cut-glass grape: extraordinary; t*24* the tastebuds are completely over-run by an intense infusion of salivating barley and succulent fruit with some spice and a hint of peat to round off the show; f*23* hints of cocoa as the curtain comes down on an almost unbelievable choreography of bitter-sweet dexterity. The oak, though present, plays the perfect background role; b*24*. What can you say? These notes are just a sketch of something that words cannot adequately describe. ESC stands for Extra Special Cask. They are not kidding. For this, unquestionably, is the greatest Macallan of them all. Not an off-note. No domination by any character in the drama. Not too sweet. Not too dry. Not too smooth. Savour at full strength. Do not add water. Do not add ice. Just drink something that approaches an absolutely perfect whisky. **57.2%**

⋙ **The Macallan Fine Oak 8 Years Old** db **(89)** n*21* entirely different to any other Macallan around: the brash freshness of the sherry appears to be magnified by the young barley, playful, kindergarten stuff; t*23* the youthful exuberance on the nose is matched by the live-wire arrival on the palate. The shape it takes in the mouth is fascinating with the initially mouthwatering grape effect at first breathlessly rushing in and then calming to dissolve in every corner of the palate, gentle spices trickle down as does the very faintest of honey notes; f22 a lot of cocoa butter as the oak shows a surprising depth, burnt raisins also guarantee a bitter edge to the sweet malt; b23 a distinctly different, young and proud Macallan that settles into a satisfying middle and finish where the soft grapey tones break through for a mottled effect with the intense malt. Seriously tasty stuff and great fun. **43%**

⠿ **The Macallan Fine Oak 10 Years Old** db **(83)** n20 t21 f21 b21. The faintest blemish on the grass and citrus nose disappears after the bottle's been open a day or two; elsewhere soft malt dissolves leaving a more bitter biscuity oatiness in its wake. The malt-fruit combination is mouth-cleansing as it gathers in intensity. A pleasingly delicate Macallan. **40%**

⠿ **The Macallan Fine Oak 12 Years Old** db **(89)** n22 clean, dry sherry is bolstered by competent fresh barley and even a hint of ginger when warmed; t23 seriously mouthwatering with the barley coating the palate with its ultra-clean bitter-sweet charms; vanilla arrives earlier than usual – especially for a Macallan; f21 quite a dry, chalky finish but only after the barley is given an almost free run. If you have chewed malt, then you will recognise this beautiful character; late natural toffee muscles in on the vanilla fade; b23 a dram to be taken at body temp for best results: when sampled cold the balance edges towards subtle fruit and crispness; when warmed the barley makes the most stunning impact. A suave dram of near flawless character. **40%**

⠿ **The Macallan Fine Oak 15 Years Old** db **(95)** n24 over-ripe bananas on toast with freshly-picked spring grass as a side dish and plenty of floral notes to round it off: a sublime and probably unique official Macallan aroma! t23 the malt, complete with distant peat, simply dissolves in the mouth; beautifully weighted with the distinctive Macallan brown-sugar sweetness hitting the red zone for a while before it is pulled back by drier vanilla; f24 just so, so long!! Excellent playful peaty spice development late on helps punctuate the continuation of the rich barley theme that expands out into low key butterscotch/toffee; dovetailing is a distant grapey sub-plot; b24 true story: I have for years played about in my lab with bourbon and sherry cask Macallan and come to the conclusion that a truly great whisky was waiting to happen. This could be it. You have to travel a long way to find a whisky with quite the same refreshing all round harmony as this. The balance is the stuff of legend ... and genius. **43%**

⠿ **The Macallan Fine Oak 18 Years Old** db **(91)** n23 inside the dry sherried shell is sweeter malt and vanilla; a touch of salt gives a slightly coastal air, even with some far-off peat-reek on the breeze; t22 myriad malt characteristics on varying levels of sweetness; there is mesmerising spice and grape varying between pungent and juicy; f23 remains young at heart with the barley dominating; mouthwatering to the end, distant smoke returns flanked by spineless grape juice and toffee plus oak that lays bitterness on sweet; even a touch of bourbon-style ageing at the death; b23 a dram much truer to the old Macallan style but with enough overt barley to make a difference. **43%**

⠿ **The Macallan Fine Oak 21 Years Old** db **(89)** n22 an attractive honeyed thread weaves through the oak and grape; some beautiful marmalade off-cuts toys with a ghostly peatiness; t22 oily and sultry with some stiff oak softened by the barley which is yielding and mouthwatering; f23 remains butter-creamy, that vague, ethereal peatiness plays peak-a-boo but the vanilla continues as does the marmalade on toast; b22 by far the richest textured Macallan of all time with a fascinating distant peatiness. **43%**

⠿ **The Macallan Fine Oak 25 Years Old** db **(94)** n24 probably the first Macallan since '46 to show such little shyness with peat, though here it is more fleeting; the second wave is proud, clean sherry. The third is vanilla ice-cream with pears and peaches; the fourth is pure bourbon. Speyside bliss; **t**23 the oak offers a framework in which the sherry thrives while the barley punches its weight; an assortment of fruit also make an entrance as does an almost underground spiciness; **f**23 back to vanilla for the undetectable touchdown; I can think of no whisky this age which has such a velvety feel right to the very end. Guys, if it were a woman you wouldn't know whether to make love or snuggle up in a silky embrace and go to sleep: I suggest both; **b**24 the blenders have obviously worked overtime on this: what a star! **43%**

⌐∴⌐ **The Macallan Fine Oak 30 Years Old** db **(90) n**23 lots of nose-nipping oaky weight softened by crushed gooseberries and grape; a mild and deeply attractive bourbony character develops **t**23 delicate spices arrives from nowhere, there is a quick flash of half-hearted peat and then we are left in a custard-sweet and enormous world of malty-oaky-grapiness; a certain fatness to the whisky develops **f**22 where's the oak? An improbable finale that is all about barley arm-in-arm with sherry and nut oil. At last the oakiness appears but immediately tapers out **b**22 the oak threatened on the nose never quite materialises. Few whiskies of this maturity are quite so polite regarding the age **43%**

The Macallan Millennium 50 Years Old (1949) decanter db **(90) n**23 toffee and sherry hand in hand, alongside ripe apples and grape: sweet and sexy; **t**22 mouth-filling and malt, sandwiched by some fine and extremely clean sherry notes and intense oak; **f**22 lingering oloroso and liquorice, good age but light enough for the malt, spice and smoke to appear; **b**23 magnificent finesse and charm despite some big oak makes this a Macallan to die for. **40%**

The Macallan Travel 1920s db **(67) n**17 **t**18 **f**15 **b**17. Does absolutely nothing for me at all. Totally off-key, no finish. Nothing roaring about this one. **40%**

The Macallan Travel 1930s db **(91) n**22 beautiful peat and sherry combo; **t**23 the cleanest, most mouthwatering sherry you could pray for; **f**23 soft vanilla and lingering, lazy smoke; **b**23 an essay in complexity and balance. Clean sherry at its finest. You little darling! **40%**

The Macallan Travel 1940s db **(81) n**21 **t**22 **f**17 **b**21. Lovely smoke and complexity, but let down by the sherry and a faltering finish. **40%**

The Macallan Travel 1950s db **(92) n**24 intense, immaculate sherry and blood orange with playful spices adding nose prickle; **t**22 massive but voluptuous sherry, then a wave of malt concentrate; **f**23 more barley, a touch of smoke and then juicy sultanas and lingering spice; **b**23 sit back, take a deep, mouth-filling draught, close your eyes and listen to Hogie Carmichael's "Stardust", for this is just what this whisky is. **40%**

Adelphi Macallan 12 Years Old (83) n20 **t**22 **f**21 **b**20. An unusually honied and sweet Macallan, almost malt syrup, with no sherry influence whatsoever considering it is from bourbon cask. But plenty of spices to go round. **57.4%.** *For Michael Skurnik Wines New York.*

Adelphi Macallan 12 Years Old dist 88, bott 00 **(66) n**15 **t**19 **f**16 **b**16. Ooops. Sul-phar, sul-bad. Least said the better. **57.5%**

"As We Get It" Macallan-Glenlivet dist 90, bott 02 **(80) n**18 **t**22 **f**20 **b**20. Unusually sweet Macallan: tastes and finishes a lot better than it noses. **55.6%.** *Kirsch-Import Skye.*

Blackadder Raw Cask Macallan 1990 bourbon hogshead 1051 dist 23, Jan 90 bott Apr 03 **(79) n**20 **t**21 **f**19 **b**19. Sweet and malty. **55%**

Cadenhead's Macallan-Glenlivet 12 Years Old dist 89, bott 10/01 **(73) n**17 **t**20 **f**18 **b**18. Blemished by sulphur, though from the colour doesn't look like a sherry cask bottling. Strange! Decent malt middle. **46%**

Coopers Choice Macallan 1988 bott 01 (12 Years Old) **(86) n**20 **t**22 **f**22 **b**22. A big, lumbering malt, sometimes a little off-balance yet somehow completes the job it set out to do: entertain. **55.5%.** *The Vintage Malt Whisky Co.*

❖ **Distillery No 7 Macallan 1990** **(81)** n*19* t*20* f*21* b*21* attractively malty and mouthwatering with some chewey cocoa notes **46%**

❖ **Duncan Taylor Macallan 1968 Aged 35 Years** cask 5593 **(90)** n*20* a hint of citrus t*24* massive injection of barley leaves the tastebuds gasping f*23* amazingly long with an irresistable combination of cocoa and very late smoke b*23* all understated and gentle, this oozes class **53.1%**

❖ **Earl of Zetland Malt Tasting Club Macallan 1975** bott 00 cask 17112 **(95)** n*24* absolutely exemplary. Faultless, almost certainly first fill sherry, that offers a very rarely found clarity and intensity. Lots of nuts and even a smattering of honey amid the caressing sherry. A template for how sherried whisky should be; t*24* quite astonishing riches, offering at varying degrees tones of moist dates, cocoa, juicy sultana, burnt raisin, heavy roast Java coffee and Demerara sugar. But just so the tastebuds don't vanish under this bitter-sweet massage there is a distinct volley of spices to add a third dimension. Unforgettable and quite astounding; f*23* some malt and vanilla at last make themselves heard as the sherry begins to tail off. The oak remains well behaved and refuses to offer more than a frame for the fruity, spiced picture; b*24* just one of those malts you encounter and never, ever forget. Sadly only 36 bottles. But if you find one then be prepared to kill for it. Only rarely does a sherry butt of such faultless charm and charisma come along like this and stay so fresh and alluring after so many years. An all-time classic. **54%.** *Malt Whisky Wholesalers Australia. 36 bottles.*

❖ **Hart Brothers Macallan Aged 12 Years Sherry Cask** dist Jun 90, bott Feb 03 **(69)** n*16* t*18* f*17* b*18*. Sulphur stained. **46%**

Hart Brothers Macallan Aged 12 Years Sherry Cask dist Jun 90, bott Feb 03 **(75)** n*18* t*20* f*18* b*19*. Brilliant mouth entry but a hint of something sulphury undermines the dram. **46%**

❖ **Hart Brothers Macllan Aged 15 Years** dist Oct 88, bott Nov 03 **(92)** n*21* fresh barley but enough citrus for zestiness; t*23* spot-on oak-malt ratio and then wave upon wave of salivating, honeyed, grassy, mouthwatering barley; f*24* the finish meanders around the palate for ever: a soft oiliness develops but the barley remains intense and chewy. Superb; b*24* for a Macallanophiles out there: this is bourbon-Macallan at its finest for its vintage. **46%**

❖ **Jim McEwan's Celtic Heartlands Macallan 1968 (84)** n*19* t*23* f*21* b*21*. Although from bourbon cask, this is a very curious re-run of Macallan '54, only without quite so much honey; the early freshness of the barley is excellent. **40.2%**

Murray McDavid Macallan-Glenlivet 1974 cask MM 6024, fresh sherry wood, dist Dec 74, bott Nov 96 **(92)** n*24* t*23* f*22* b*23*. A minor classic among independently bottled Macallans, bottles of which can still be found, I hear. **46%**

Murray McDavid Macallan 1990 cask MM 10242, fresh sherry, dist Dec 90, bott March 01 **(85)** n*19* the Achilles heel: decent toffee but green and a slight, heavily-disguised off-note; t*23* now it comes alive with magnificent intensity on the palate: just about perfect mouthfeel incorporates stunning barley brilliance with an oily, sherry, mildly smoky background; f*21* lots of vanilla and decent depth; b*22* if it wasn't for the nose, this would be right up there. **46%. ncf nc.**

❖ **Murray McDavid Macallan 1990 Aged 13 Years (70)** n*18* t*18* f*17* b*17*. Sulphur blighted and off-key. **46%**

❖ **Old Malt Cask Macallan Aged 13 Years** dist Jun 90, bott Feb 04 **(88)** n*22* flakes of honey enrich the lazy barley and soft oak: relaxed and enticing; t*23* sumptuous mouthfeel with that honey really making its mark from early on; soft additions of vanilla and peach work well with the faintest of smoke tones; f*21* not quite so complex as the early arrival and dries as the oak broadens, but a lingering sweetness does the trick; b*22* really lovely Macallan shorn of sherry and bringing about the exhibitionist in its nudity. **50%. nc ncf sc.** *Douglas Laing. 307 bottles.*

⁑ **Old Malt Cask Macallan Aged 25 Years** dist Oct 78, bott Dec 03 **(89)** n21 diced fruit and fresh leather, a real softie; t23 now the malt comes alive with a bracing, refreshing arrival on the palate. Spices abound but early on it is the buttery interaction between intense malt and top rate oak that spellbinds. Some abstract honey notes add to the riches; f22 the silkiness is blunted by some toffee-oak tones; b23 Macallan unplugged: confirmation that it has weight enough to hold its own in a non-sherried environment. **50%. nc ncf sc.** *Douglas Laing. 138 bottles.*

⁑ **Old Malt Cask Macallan Aged 26 Years** cask no DL988 dist May 77, bott Oct 03 **(76)** n18 t20 f19 b19. Overly honey sweet, off-balance, ordinary fare with a bit of a kick. **50%. nc ncf sc.** *Douglas Laing. 240 bottles.*

⁑ **Old Malt Cask Macallan Aged 26 Years** dist Jun 90, bott Feb 04 **(85)** n19 oops! A bit sappy, gassy and oak-exhausted. Just enough clean barley does save the day; t23 makes up for nose with a glittering mouth arrival. The oak is never far from home but there is enough barley concentrate garlanded by honeycomb; f22 pretty lengthy and with a touch of liquorice. A softly oiled mouthfeel lasts the pace; b21 Creaking and patched up, there is just enough class and lingering sweetness to make this a very decent dram. **50%. nc ncf sc.** *Douglas Laing. 240 bottles.*

⁑ **Old Malt Cask Macallan 1976 Aged 26 Years** dist May 76 bott Oct 02 **(81)** n22 t22 f18 b19. A tight little whisky with a clean sherry touch that promises much but doesn't entirely deliver. **49.7%.** *252 bottles*

Old Masters Macallan 1979 Cask Strength Selection bott 2001 **(82)** n21 t22 f20 b19. Without a sherry shield, the oak is slightly dominant. But some lovely, honey-sweet charm. **55.5%.** *James MacArthur.*

Peerless Macallan 1967 cask 7678, dist Sep 67 35-y-o **(89)** n22 quite dry for all the spice, malt and honey; t23 massively intense and rich with a sublime chocolate-lime and rich copper-estery middle; f22 pretty long with the malt expanding in every direction; b22 a brilliant non-sherried Macallan of a very rare richness. **45.1%.** *Duncan Taylor & Co.*

Peerless Macallan 1969 cask 5390, dist May 69 33-y-o **(75)** n20 t19 f18 b18. Malty and soufflé light. **40.3%.** *Duncan Taylor & Co.*

Private Cellar Macallan 1971 bott Feb 03 **(79)** n20 t21 f19 b19. A very odd whisky; almost green with being under-ripe. There is a stunning malt surge early on in the palate but while generally pleasant something doesn't shape up right. **43%.** *Forbes Ross Co.*

⁑ **Provenance Macallan Over 10 Years** dist Autumn 93, bott Spring 04 **(88)** n21 fresh, grassy, new make-ish; t22 despite the overall lightness, there is a weightiness to the malt; f23 stupendous clarity and goes into mouthwatering overdrive; b22 an outstanding example of Macallan without make up: no sherry, little oak to speak of due to old bourbon cask. Top notch distillate and so delicious! **46%.** *Douglas McGibbon.*

⁑ **Provenance Macallan Over 12 Years** dist Summer 92, bott Winter 04 **(77)** n18 t21 f20 b18. A distant hint of sulphur, sadly. Sweet, robust arival on the palate works well with peppery finish, though. **46%.** *Douglas McGibbon.*

⁑ **Provenance Macallan Over 14 Years** two cask bottling dist Summer 90, bott Summer 04 **(77)** n17 t21 f19 b20. Sulphur-spoiled, but recovers some ground thanks probably to the malt-honey richness of a top quality cask included. **46%.** *Douglas McGibbon.*

Provenance Summer Distillation Macallan Over 10 Years dist Summer 1990, bott Winter 2001 **(75)** n17 t19 f20 b19. Very slightly flawed nose; brilliant recovering finish. **43%.** *Douglas McGibbon.*

Royal Mile Whiskies Macallan 25 Years Old (88) n22 gristy and clean and very lightly peated, no sign of a quarter of century's work in barrel; t23 slight oily texture to the massive, gristy maltiness; f21 some citrus amid the barley and then the; b22 Macallan in aspic: this must have come from a second fill bourbon. **40%**

Scotch Malt Whisky Society Cask 24.76 Aged 14 Years (88) n22 the peatiest, oiliest Macallan from bottle in many years; t23 bounds around the palate like a Caol Ila, especially with the accompanying oils, but the lively barley makes some impact; f21 soft vanilla and cocoa; b22 if you are a Macallan-loving Islayphile then your prayers have been answered. **61.2%**.

Scott's Selection Macallan 1973 bott 99 **(85)** n23 t23 f19 b20. Forget the finish: just enjoy the unfettered brilliance of its arrival on the palate. One of the most honied Macallans around, enjoying its freedom from sherry. **50.9%**. *Robert Scott & Co.*

Scott's Selection Macallan 1985 bott 03 **(94)** n23 exceptionally fine sherry butt, not a single blemish and offering spice and leather in near perfect parcels; t23 the spice on the nose hits the mark from the first second. Excellent sweet background of intense barley tinged with unrefined brown sugar and burnt honey: quite bourbonesque; f24 the fruit from the sherry waves a white flag under the spicy, barley intense onslaught; the degree of sweetness perfectly matches the drier, oaky undertones; b24 Macallan at its cleanest, most bullish and recognisable. A rare bottling that takes me back 30 years to its finest days. Brilliant. **51.2%**

Single Barrel Collection Macallan 1989 cask 18072, dist Oct 89, bott 01 **(74)** n18 t19 f18 b19. A Macallan shorn of its sherried skin that is much lighter than the norm from ex-bourbon cask and one never ascending great heights. **58.14%. nc ncf sc.** *Germany.*

Speymalt from Macallan 1966 (92) n24 pantheon of oak, but still displays lovely, soft peat and cracking barley: dreamy; t23 silky oak and then a build-up of burnt honeycomb and smoke; f22 softer vanillas and lingering barley; b23 an absolutely outstanding bottling from the Speyside specialists. **40%.** *Gordon & MacPhail.*

Speymalt from Macallan 1978 (79) n22 t20 f19 b18. Lovely butterscotch nose, but a shade too dry and oaked. **40%.** *Gordon & MacPhail.*

Speymalt from Macallan 1990 (76) n17 t20 f20 b19. A big Speysider, but some sulphur notes spoil it. **40%.** *Gordon & MacPhail.*

Speymalt from Macallan 1994 (88) n24 too beautifully honied to be true; t22 clean-cut sweet barley and simple vanillas; f21 long, deftly oaked and big, clean barley; b21 little sherry evidence. Worth getting for the nose alone. **40%.** *Gordon & MacPhail.*

Whisky Galore Macallan 1989 (58) n17 t15 f13 b13. One of the most boring Macallans I have happened across in over 25 years. I hope someone didn´t just add caramel to make up for the lack of sherry. **40%.** *Duncan Taylor & Co.*

Whisky Galore Macallan 1989 (71) n17 t18 f18 b18. Big improvement on the earlier, coloured version. But still unimpressive. **46%.** *Duncan Taylor & Co.*

Wilson & Morgan Barrel Selection Macallan 12 Years Old dist 90 **(87)** n22 toffee apple and nougat topped with a sherry dressing; t23 first class arrival on palate with no shortage of heather and spices; f20 just a little bitter as the oak arrives; b22 a thoughtful, busy dram that demands time for exploration. **57.7%**

Wilson & Morgan Barrel Selection Macallan 1990 Rum Finish bott 04 **(84)** n20 t21 f22 b21. A diamond of a Macallan: not that it particularly dazzles, just that it is the hardest on the palate I've ever come across. Has its attractively fruity, mouthwatering moments, though: even with a hint of peat thrown in. **46%**

MACDUFF
Speyside, 1963. Dewar's. Working

Glen Deveron Aged 10 Years dist 1992 db **(72)** n19 t18 f17 b18. A peculiar, oily, softly smoked nose of a hot-running model train engine, but like the remainder of the malt off-key and altogether odd. **40%**

Glen Deveron Aged 12 Years dist 1984 db **(86)** n21 rich, biscuity malt, well-balanced; t21 really big barley which sweetens; f22 softest wisps of honey on vanilla; b22 a clean absolutely delicious malt that is honied but never overly sweet. **40%**

Coinnoisseurs Choice Macduff 1980 (83) n20 t23 f21 b19. A pot of light honey: quintessential Macduff – make a bee-line for it. **40%**. *Gordon & MacPhail.*

Connoisseurs Choice Macduff 1988 **(79)** n19 t21 f19 b20. Honied and charming, but a little thin for a usual MacDuff. **40%**

Peerless Macduff 1969 cask 3672, dist Apr 69 33-y-o **(78)** n19 t21 f19 b19. Sweet, a touch oily but rich. **40.3%.** *Duncan Taylor & Co.*

Platinum Old and Rare Macduff 36 Years old db **(84)** n23 t22 f18 b21. Forget the exhausted finale. With a whisky of such improbable age, that is forgivable. The nose and arrival on the palate are moments to genuinely savour. **49.2%.** *From Douglas Laing and Co.*

MANNOCHMORE
Speyside, 1971. Diageo. Working.

Mannochmore Aged 12 Years db **(84)** n22 t21 f20 b21. As usual the mouth arrival fails to live up to the great nose. Quite a greasy dram with sweet malt and bitter oak. **43%.** *Flora and Fauna.*

Mannochmore 22 Years Old Rare Malts Selection db dist 74 **(87)** n22 hazelnut and malt; t22 silky oils offer a superb richness to the malt; f21 vanilla kicks in, sweetens and becomes quite chewy with late cocoa; b22 lively, warming dram with a big malt character. **60.1%**

Connoisseurs Choice Mannochmore 1984 (79) n22 t20 f18 b19. What a tragedy the flat palate no way matches the fruity exuberance of the nose. **40%.** *Gordon & MacPhail.*

⠿ **Old Malt Cask Mannochmore Aged 14 Years Sherry Finish** dist Feb 90, bott Oct 03 **(88)** n19 there is a nip and bite to this which is unusual for the distillery; the sherry transference is noticeable, but hasn't quite gelled; t22 fabulous richness from the very start; the body is muscular and flexes both sharp barley and a strangely flinty sherry note in equal proportions; f24 the complexity of the palate arrival now goes into overdrive as soft saline notes ingratiate themselves into the developing fruit and honey. Great stuff; b23 a less demanding person than I would be slightly more forgiving with the nose. **50%. nc ncf sc.** *Douglas Laing. 354 bottles.*

Old Masters Mannochmore 1990 bott 01 **(86)** n22 t22 f21 b21. Honeycomb malt with attitude. Delicious. **59.8%.** *James MacArthur.*

⠿ **Provenance Mannochmore Over 12 Years** dist Spring 91, bott Winter 04 **(87)** n23 fluting barley notes that never hit a bum note; textbook clarity and bitter-sweet charm; t22 green and young in part, the mouthwatering elements contrast sharply with the abrupt arrival of chunky oak; f21 more bitter than sweet, the barley-sheen remains profound although the oak has a surprisingly big say; b21 most probably a first-fill bourbon cask to the fore here: it's older than its age should suggest but the all-round complexity is quite wonderful. **46%.** *Douglas McGibbon.*

⠿ **Signatory Vintage Mannochmore 1991 South African Sherry Butt** cask 16587, dist 7 Nov 91, bott 19 Jun 03 **(87)** n23 a big spicy nose, a green leafy tinge to counter the building oak; t23 massive, jolting spice that is all the more impressive due to the massive mouthwatering malt surge, fabulous stuff; f20 disappointing natural toffee flattens it out; b21 fascinating start. **60.2%.** *596 bottles*

MILLBURN
Highland (Northern), 1807–1985. Closed.

⚙ **Blackadder Raw Cask Millburn 1974** cask 4615 dist Nov 74, bott Nov 03 **(90)** n*24* it is tempting not to drink when the nose is so complex and sexy: ripe red grapes with steamed breadfruit and tired lavender; t*23* a much more aggressive attack than the nose suggests but the involvement of watered down Demerara sugar on the towering barley softens the blow; f*21* remains biting; limp fruit, but the oak offers drier comfort; b*23* a top-notch dram that has experienced a summer or two: in Nov 74 I was a £5-a-week cub reporter still working on the Lord Lucan case and took my first driving lesson; in Nov 03 I celebrated my 46th birthday with my 32-year-old Brazilian girlfriend and launched the 2004 *Whisky Bible*: tough call on whether the Millburn or I have aged the better in the passing 28 years ... **56.8%**

Connoisseurs Choice Millburn 1972 (80) n*20* t*22* f*18* b*20* A hint of something sulphury on the nose is adequately countered by peat. It's a gentle, malty chew, though. **40%**

Connoisseurs Choice Millburn 1976 (75) n*21* t*20* f*18* b*16*. Pleasant, but lacks direction or depth. **40%**. *Gordon & MacPhail.*

Gordon & MacPhail Millburn 1978 cask 3166, cask dist 9/8/78, bott June 97 **(83)** n*20* t*22* f*21* b*20*. Silky, ultra-sweet and malty. **65.6%**

The Old Malt Cask Millburn Aged 34 Years dist Nov 67, bott Dec 01 **(94)** n*23* t*23* f*24* b*24*. What a way for this long-lost distillery to be remembered! One of the finest sherry-cask bottlings you will ever find, this casts a shadow over the quality of present sherry butts. Though Millburn's character has been lost somewhat amid the splendour of the wood, it still had to have sufficient depth to add to the complexity and balance, both of which are near faultless. One of the whiskies of a lifetime, just buy and savour it if you ever see it around. **50%**. *Douglas Laing. 552 bottles.*

⚙ **Scott's Selection Milburn 1983** bott 03 **(77)** n*19* t*21* f*19* b*18*. The watercress spice is fine, but thin overall and just not enough complexity to see it through. **58%**

Signatory Silent Stills Millburn 20 Years Old sherry butt 3632A, dist 11/12/80, bott 7/3/01 **(77)** n*17* t*22* f*19* b*19*. Disappointing, sulphur-tainted sherry but it does hit a delicious, though short-lived high on the palate. **58.7%**. *240 bottles.*

The Whisky Shop Millburn 1976 (89) n*23* heather-honey with a hint of spice ... is it HP in disguise? Reassuring oak for the age; t*23* dense malt that is wonderfully rich and chewy accompanied by some pretty busy spices; f*21* the oak is more confident and towards the end becomes a little loud. But the malt retains its shape to add to the cream-toffee effect; b*22* lost distilleries like these don't die: they just fade on the palate. **58.9%**. *The Whisky Shop, Scotland. 276 bottles.*

MILTONDUFF
Speyside, 1824. Allied. Working.

Gordon & MacPhail Miltonduff 10 Years Old (73) n*19* t*21* f*16* b*17*. A steady, rich middleweight but a slack finish. **40%**

Gordon & MacPhail Miltonduff 1968 (79) n*20* t*21* f*19* b*19*. A bit sappy and dry for all the fruit. **40%**

Hart Brothers Miltonduff 10 Years Old (73) n*16* t*21* f*17* b*19*. Good spice and a hint of honey but slightly cask tainted. **40%**

Peerless Miltonduff 1966 cask 1014, dist Feb 66 36-y-o **(83)** n*21* t*20* f*21* b*21*. The Speyside character remains intact on the nose, amazingly for its age. Dies on entry but resurfaces later with some splendid malt-oak complexity and spice. **42.7%**. *Duncan Taylor & Co.*

⚙ **Scott's Selection Miltonduff 1987** bott 02 **(82)** n*21* t*20* f*20* b*21*. An honest Speysider with a bit of toffee among the barley. **56.4%**

Single Barrel Collection Miltonduff 1989 bott 01 **(74)** n*17* t*20* f*18* b*19*. Not a dram for the faint- – or feint – hearted. Big, bustling stuff that for all its obvious flaws offers massive compensation when sampled at full strength. **65.28%. nc ncf sc.** Germany.

Ultimate Selection Miltonduff 1989 bourbon barrel 67180, dist 3/9/89, bott 28/11/02 **(76)** n*19* t*21* f*17* b*19*. The fresh, malty intensity is up front. **43%.** Van Wees NL.

MORTLACH
Speyside, 1824. Diageo. Working.

Mortlach Aged 16 Years db **(87)** n*20* big, big sherry, but not exactly without a blemish or two; t*23* sumptuous fruit and then a really outstanding malt and melon mouthwatering rush; f*22* returns to heavier duty with a touch of spice, too; b*22* once it gets past the bold if very mildly sulphured nose, the rest of the journey is superb. Earlier Mortlachs in this range had a slightly unclean feel to them and the nose here doesn't inspire confidence. But from arrival on the palate onwards, it's sure-footed, fruity and even refreshing ... and always delicious. **43%.** Flora and Fauna range.

Mortlach 1980 Limited Bottling bott 97 db **(66)** n*16* t*18* f*16* b*16*. A sulphur-ridden disaster. A bit like the hilarious tasting notes on the bottle. **63.1%**

Adelphi Mortlach 13 Years Old (83) n*19* t*23* f*20* b*21*. A big whisky with ripe cherries with the massive malt middle. Toffeed finish.

Adelphi Mortlach 19 Years Old cask 2166, dist 1980, bott 99 **(74)** n*20* t*20* f*17* b*17*. Should come complete with fire extinguisher.... **59.3%. sc.**

Adelphi Mortlach 1990 (86) n*23* supreme sherry, clean and faultless enough, but maybe needs more input from the malt; t*22* hot and spicy with enormous sherry bite, sweet, fruity middle; f*21* some toffee and oak with some late malt; b*20* delicious but could be integrated better.

Berry's Own Mortlach 1989 bott 03 **(92)** n*22* a hint of new make, but it has seen just enough oak to pick up balance with the intense and tart young malt. Fresh and mouth-watering: those who remember the old Glenfiddich will recognise this guy; t*24* bracing and clean, there is wave upon wave of succulent malt, interspersed with vague sugar-biscuit notes. Wonderful liveliness and youth; f*23* remains clean and mouth-watering to the very death, with some vanilla weight to balance the barley onslaught; b*23* once I wrote an article saying how Mortlach made one of Speyside's great whiskies, based on tasting samples of the stuff since the 1970s. Recent bottlings have been disappointing to almost heartbreak proportions. This, though, is a stupendous example of first-class distillate in aspic. The cask was probably on its third lap around the warehouses, which has given the tastebuds free access to what makes this distillery tick. Light and lacking its complexity of old, this is still the best Mortlach bottled in the last five or six years. Refreshingly brilliant: the perfect pre-prandial dram. **46%.** Berry Bros

Blackadder Raw Cask Mortlach 1989 sherry butt 5149, dist Oct 89, bott Apr 02 **(73)** n*16* t*18* f*21* b*18*. Big, juicy-sweet and fruity, but tainted by sulphur. **59.4%. nc ncf sc.**

Blackadder Raw Cask Mortlach 1989 first-fill sherry butt 5149, dist Oct 89, bott Mar 03 **(74)** n*17* t*18* f*20* b*19*. Still slightly sulphured but a little more comfortable. **59.9%. nc ncf sc.**

Chieftain's Choice Mortlach Aged 10 Years dist 1988 **(79)** n*21* t*21* f*18* b*19*. Starts well but falters. **43%**

Coopers Choice Mortlach 1989 first-fill sherry, bott 00 **(77)** n*20* t*21* f*18* b*18*. Never quite gets out of bed, for all the sherry. **43%. nc sc.**

Coopers Choice Mortlach 1989 sherry ask bott 02 (aged 12 Years) **(79)** n*20* t*21* f*19* b*19*. A sweeter version of a previous Coopers Choice Mortlach, with plenty of attractive tones, including a touch of peat, but none that quicken the pulse. **43%.** The Vintage Malt Whisky Co.

·⊙· **Fortnum & Mason Old Malt Cask Mortlach Aged 13 Years** dist jun 90 bott Nov 03 **(71)** n*17* t*20* f*16* b*18*. Not a great vintage at Mortlach for sherry butts. **50% nc ncf sc.** *Douglas Laing. 241 bottles.*

Gordon & MacPhail Mortlach 1954 (78) n*20* very soft, gentle toffee apple; t*20* the oak chokes the barley slightly but enough juice makes its way through; f*18* big oak, but just enough sweetness to see out the balance, good late spice; b*20* survived the oak attack well – enough character to enjoy on a cold night

Gordon & MacPhail Mortlach 1959 (82) n*22* deep, sweet oak to the point of bourbon: lovely, though; t*20* trademark, mildly honied bourbon style with some malt arriving in the vanilla middle; f*21* surprisingly graceful and soft; b*19* what it lacks in complexity it makes up for in effortless charm. **40%**

Gordon & MacPhail Mortlach 1980 Cask Strength (90) n*23* glorious mix of raisins and spice, penetrating oak, but beautifully balanced; t*23* a massive outbreak of mouthwatering fruit with undertones of the softest peat, liquorice and honey; f*22* medium to long with some cocoa amid lingering, silky malt; b*22* sit back, close your eyes and bask in sheer beauty. **63.8%**

Gordon & MacPhail Mortlach 15 Years Old (79) n*21* t 23 f*16* b*19*. The stupendously sweet and complex taste is failed by the blandest of finishes. **40%**

Hart Brothers Mortlach Aged 12 Years dist May 90, bott Jan 03 **(69)** n*15* t*18* f*18* b*18*. United Distiller's sherry wood policy of the early 90s leaves a little to be desired. **46%**

James MacArthur's Mortlach 1989 (87) n*22* oily, fat malt, clean and intense with a sweet development; t*22* chewy, intense malt; f*22* a welcome arrival of some spicy notes as the malt clings to the roof of the mouth; b*21* forget about complexity: this is like alcoholic malt extract. **43%**

Lombard Mortlach 1990 (83) n*20* t*23* f*20* b*20*. Astonishing degree of malt throughout with a very sweet edge. Not much complexity, but a superb ride. **50%**

Milroys Mortlach Over 12 Years Old dist 88, bott 00 **(71)** n*15* t*18* f*19* b*19*, A whisky that improves the further it travels from the sulphured nose and early mouth arrival. **43%**. *UK.*

Murray McDavid Mortlach 1989 dist Aug 89, bott 01 **(73)** n*13* t*19* f*23* b*18*. A moody and magnificent finale works heroically to make up for earlier failings. Just try and ignore the sulphur-ruined nose: it is worth tasting just for the fabulous finish alone. **46%. nc ncf sc.**

·⊙· **Murray McDavid Mortlach 1990 (70)** n*17* t*18* f*17* b*18*. Whatever passed for sherry butts in those days at UDG should be taken out and unceremoniously torched. **46%**

The Old Malt Cask Mortlach Aged 10 Years dist Nov 90 **(74)** n*17* t*21* f*18* b*18*. Green and barley-rich. **50%**

·⊙· **Old Malt Cask Mortlach Aged 13 Years Sherry Cask** dist Jun 90, bott Jan 04 **(78)** n*17* t*23* f*19* b*19*. A brilliantly bullish mouth arrival offers all kinds of natural dark sugars and rich barley. But the bitter, off-key fade is in tune with the poor nose. **50%. nc ncf sc.** *Douglas Laing. 384 bottles.*

·⊙· **Old Malt Cask Fortnum and Mason Mortlach Aged 13 Years** (*see* Fortnum & Mason OMC Motlach)

·⊙· **Old Malt Cask Mortlach Aged 20 Years** dist May 83, bott Aug 03 **(90)** n*23* molten brown sugar with fresh green barley, a hint of bourbon and grape juice. Cluttered, though clean and gloriously balanced; t*23* a sweet arrival sets up the coffee and spice middle; slightly oily body adds intensity; f*22* no shortage of vanilla here and a natural toffee apple development; b*22* this is big stuff, a type of Mortlach I have not found in the best part of a decade and I was wondering if lost to us. One to take your time over. **50%. nc ncf sc.** *Douglas Laing. 384 bottles.*

Old Masters Mortlach 14 Year Old (85) n*22* sheer joy! A delicate array of oak and barley; t*22* barley-rich, green for its age and mouthwatering, lovely spices and a hint of honey; **f**_20_ soft oak that dries slowly; **b**_21_ an attractive expression of Mortlach at this age. **43%.** *James MacArthur.*

Old Masters Mortlach 1990 (87) n_21_ lovely signs of sherry influence: deep, clean and spiced; **t**_23_ incredible arrival of intense young barley and succulent grape. The tastebuds are almost overwhelmed; **f**_21_ dissipates quickly to leave a warming, fruity, oaky finale; **b**_22_ excellent.

⠿ **The Peebles Malt Mortlach 12 Years Old (75)** n_18_ t_20_ f_18_ b_19_. A pleasant honeyed thread does its best to mend the sulphured tear. **43%.** *Villeneuve Wines.*

⠿ **Provenance Mortlach Over 12 Years** dist Spring 92, bott Winter 04 **(85)** n_22_ coal gas and apples; **t**_22_ mouthwatering, young, and at times gristy-sweet; **f**_20_ a dull fruitiness undermines the early promise; **b**_21_ one of the better Mortlach expressions of recent years. **46%.** *Douglas McGibbon.*

⠿ **Provenance Mortlach Over 13 Years** dist Summer 90, bott Autumn 03 **(61)** n_12_ t_17_ f_16_ b_16_. A touch of attractive honey through the middle, but never survives the sulphurous wounds. **46%.** *Douglas McGibbon.*

Usquebaugh Society Mortlach 1988 dist 26/5/88, bott 6/98 **(75)** n_18_ t_20_ f_19_ b_18_. Rich middle. **43%.** *NL.*

The Wee Dram Mortlach Aged 12 Years (77) matured in a sherry butt n_17_ t_21_ f_20_ b_19_. Fresh, grassy middle for all the sherry. Lovely spice and sweetness. **43%.** *Exclusive to The Wee Dram, Bakewell, UK.*

Whisky Galore Mortlach 1990 40% (60) n_18_ t_18_ f_13_ b_11_. Grinds to a halt with caramel digging deep. Dull as ditchwater **40%.** *Duncan Taylor & Co Ltd.*

Whisky Galore Mortlach 1990 46% (84) n_21_ t_21_ f_21_ b_21_. Good grief! Same brand name, same distillery and year ... yet. If this is not proof enough of what damage caramel does to a whisky, nothing is. This is fresh, light, mouthwatering – the unfettered essence of Speyside. Even some smoke on the finish. A little treat. **46%.** *Duncan Taylor & Co.*

⠿ **Whisky Galore Mortlach 1993 Aged 10 Years (87)** n_22_ the second fill bourbon cask has left a clear path for the sparkling, apple-juicy, grassy barley; **t**_23_ mouthwatering and refreshing barley-sugar; **f**_21_ a touch of spice to the barley; **b**_21_ at last! For almost the first time in a decade a Mortlach not screwed by being filled into a cask of the very crappiest order. Wonderful to show what this distillery can really do without someone doing their best to ruin it. **46%.** *Duncan Taylor.*

⠿ **Wilson & Morgan Barrel Selection Mortlach 10 Years Old** dist 89 **(73)** n_18_ t_19_ f_18_ b_18_. Spot the difference between this and a typically inept Dufftown: blowed if I can. **57.2%**

MOSSTOWIE

Speyside, 1964–1981. Two Lomond stills located within Miltonduff Distillery. Now dismantled.

Connoisseurs Choice Mosstowie 1975 (85) n_22_ fat and fruity, surprisingly clean and malty in style despite the body; **t**_21_ spicy from the off then a flowering of varied malty tones; **f**_20_ very light for Mosstowie wth the malt dominating; **b**_22_ a busy dram with massive malt influence. **40%**

Connoisseurs Choice Mosstowie 1979 (86) n_20_ oily enough to fry chips in, malty and sweet, too, with surprisingly little oak restraint; **t**_23_ still unbelievably fat and malt-rich after all these years: few whiskies boast such a shimmering, intense maltiness as this. What a joy! **f**_22_ buttery yet remains sweet and clean; **b**_21_ not the most complex of drams, but the weight of the malt is amazing: not entirely unlike an old-fashioned Scottish heavy ale but in sweeter form.

NORTH PORT

Highland (Eastern), 1820–1983. Demolished.

Adelphi Brechin 24 Years Old cask 3897, dist 76, bott 00 **(83)** n_22_ t_21_

f20 **b**20. The nose doesn't warn you about the firewater about to come, but experience should have. This takes me back to when it was a young make incinerating my youthful tastebuds. Still has some malty, sweet moments. **60.4%**

Connoisseurs Choice North Port-Brechin 1974 (84) n19 **t**21 **f**23 **b**21. A seriously good dram, about as clean as you are likely to find from this distillery. Just gets better as it stays on the palate, thanks to some fruit pudding and peaty ingredients. One to find. **40%**

Connoisseurs Choice North Port-Brechin 1981 (74) n18 **t**19 **f**19 **b**18. Gristy, oaty. **40%**. *Gordon & MacPhail.*

Old Malt Cask North Port Aged 35 Years dist Mar 66, bott Jul 01 **(84) n**21 **t**20 **f**22 **b**21. Lots of marmalade and oak. Deliciously chewy, with some smoke thrown in for extra ballast. **50%. nc ncf sc.** *Douglas Laing.* 186 bottles.

Old Malt Cask North Port Aged 36 Years (75) n19 **t**21 **f**19 **b**16. Big sherry number with powerful palate presence but never quite gets into balance. **50%.** *Douglas Laing.*

⁖ **Scott's Selection North Port 1982** bott 03 **(86) n**21 crushed cereals, lively mash tun, nippy and playful but always clean; **t**22 blistering spice/alcohol attack singes the palate but some honeycomb does withstand the inferno to soothe the tastebuds; **f**22 the honey has less hassle now, but there is still sufficient bite to keep you on your guard; **b**21 hot as Hades. But, d'ya know, for all the fire this is serious fun and worth enduring the tastebud blitz. A rare North Port worth finding. **52.5%**

OBAN

Highland (Western), 1794. Diageo. Working.

Oban 14 db **(84) n**20 **t**22 **f**21 **b**21. Slick and fruity, you can close your eyes and think of Jerez. Oban seems a long way away. A very decent dram, I grant you. But I want my old, bracing, mildly smoky, fruitless Oban back!! Those who prefer malts with a sheen, sweet and with enormous fruit depth won't be disappointed. **43%**

Oban The Distillers Edition Double Matured 1987 bott 02, montillo mino finish, db **(80) n**22 **t**20 **f**18 **b**20. Dry despite the apricot and tinned tangerine edge on the nose; the body seems frustratingly flat, especially on the finish. Pleasant in parts but disappointing overall. **43%**

Oban Bicentenary Manager's Dram 16 Years Old 1794–1994 db **(93) n**24 oloroso at its finest: fruit and a slight hint of peat but the malt remains enormous; **t**23 an explosion of spices: the grapey fruit leads the way but the malt remains steadfast and crunchy; **f**23 smoky, sherried and late, late malt; **b**23 when you get a distillery manager, such as Ian Williams, so in touch with the distillery in which he worked, there is little surprise that he comes up with something quite as enormous and enriching as this. Massive and magnificent: a true collector's dram not to sit on a shelf but to be savoured in the glass. **64%**

OLD RHOSDHU (*see* Loch Lomond)

PITTYVAICH

Speyside 1975–1993. Closed.

Pittyvaich Aged 12 Years (new stock circa 99 – no bottling mark, light brown print) db **(70) n**17 **t**20 **f**16 **b**17. The nose is scuffed in classic neighbouring Dufftown distillery style, but the simmering malts are kept in check by the same brute forces. Grim going. **43%**. *Flora and Fauna range.*

Pittyvaich Aged 12 Years (new stock circa 03 – bottling number L19R01941144, dark brown print) db **(84) n**22 **t**21 **f**20 **b**21. For a dram that will tear your throat out as soon as look at you, this has been tempered dramatically by the use of some exceptionally clean sherry casks which show to their best on the nose. Pittyvaich in a form I thought I'd never see it in my lifetime ... drinkable! And deliciously so. **43%**. *Flora and Fauna range.*

PORT ELLEN
Islay, 1825–1983. Closed.

Port Ellen Aged 20 Years Rare Malts Collection dist 78 db **(89)** n*22* a crisp, lively nose with gentle spice to the peat-reek, salty and nutty, chunky iodine, ripe pears; t*23* explosive stuff with heavy, chewy peat, nothing like as complex as the nose but the vanilla does offer a calming diversion; f*22* good age with intense vanilla lingering on a higher layer than the deeper yet sweeter peat; **b***22* a big whisky that has successfully withstood the test of time. Top rate and memorable. **60.9%**

Port Ellen Aged 24 Years Distilled 1978 second year release db **(86)** n*21* light, floral, smoked kippers; t*23* explosive, sweet peat and chewable until your tongue drops off; f*22* delicate, subtle and suave; **b***20* a really fine malt, though not if you have a sweet tooth. **59.3%**

⁘ **Port Ellen 24 Years Old** dist 79, bott 03 db **(90)** n*23* unusually oily and weighty for a Port Ellen with the peat hammering with chisels; stonking stuff worthy of sticking your nose in for a few minutes; t*24* confirmed as an oily, prisoner-slaughtering beast, with an immediate sweet, estery impact starts drying as oak is announced and then sweetening again as a distinctive maltiness arrives and then rich mocca; f*21* falls away rapidly and a little off-key but enough peat rumbles through to complete the show; **b***22* pow!! Port Ellen at something over its usual 35ppm phenols here, acting like a 50ppm monster. On a blind tasting I'd swear it was Lagavulin!

Adelphi Port Ellen 24 Years Old cask 1765, dist 75, bott 99 **(94)** n*23* t*24* f*23* **b***24*. A must-buy malt. Despite the age of the whisky, it acts very much like a Port Ellen of half those years. One of the all-time Adelphi – and Port Ellen – greats. **56%**

Cask Port Ellen 1980 casks 5090, 5101–4, dist 19/11/80, bott Jun 96 **(95)** n*24* t*24* f*23* **b***24*. A Port Ellen that is more like a 12-y-o than the 16 you must ransack every wine and spirit merchants to find. A piece of Port Ellen folklore. For me the greatest Port Ellen bottling of all time, eclipsing even the Adelphi offering. A Gordon and MacPhail legend. **63.9%**. *Gordon & MacPhail.*

Connoisseurs Choice Port Ellen 1980 (88) n*24* just so gristy, you could eat it. Allow to warm in glass, unwatered, for maximum effect; t*22* sweet and uncomplicated: soft malted peat; f*21*some vanilla gets a toe-hold but the peat remains at two levels: calm yet increasingly spicy; **b***21* a gentle giant, bottled in the 90s when still relatively youthful. **40%**. *Gordon & MacPhail.*

Connoisseurs Choice Port Ellen 1982 (90) n*23* totally classic, clean, smoky grist, uniquely Port Ellen; t*23* melt-in-the-mouth peat that allows in just enough oak for balance; f*22* sweet with lingering gristy barley; **b***22* if anyone asked me to describe Port Ellen, I would hold up this bottle and say: "It tastes exactly like this." Truly classic and representative of how it was at its peak as a 12-year-old. Time has stood still. Spooky. **40%**. *Gordon & MacPhail.*

Islay Whisky Shop Port Ellen 18 Years Old dist 1982 **(91)** n*23* a really raw medium betwixt massive peat and rich sherry: big and boisterous; t*24* a fantastic arrival of peat dovetails with the cleanest sherry available. This is the stuff of dreams; f*22* hard and uncompromising malt with equally big peat; **b***22* if you are ever on the Isle of Islay, you have only yourself to blame for not grabbing a bottle of something very different and absolutely superb. **50%**. *Islay UK.*

Old Malt Cask Port Ellen Aged 18 Years (sherry) dist Sep 82, bott Aug 01 **(82)** n*22* t*22* f*18* **b***20*. Very salty with the sherry outweighing the peat. **50%**. nc ncf. *Douglas Laing. 777 bottles.*

Old Malt Cask Port Ellen Aged 18 Years cask 2740, dist Nov 82, **(85) n**22 clean sherry, coffee but little peat; **t**22 silky grape notes, big malt middle; **f**21 more ripe plums; **b**20 delicious Port Ellen but curious because the peat has all but vanished under the weight of the sherry. **50%. nc ncf.** Douglas Laing.

Old Malt Cask Port Ellen Aged 19 Years (sherry) dist Feb 82, bott Sep 01 **(77) n**20 **t**20 **f**18 **b**19. 50% The nose has a curious, though not entirely unattractive, coal-dust effect. The remainder is central heating. **50%. nc ncf.** Douglas Laing. 720 bottles.

⁖ **Old Malt Cask Port Ellen Aged 20 Years** dist Feb 83, bott Dec 03 **(87) n**23 sparkling peat for all the age on a distinctive butterscotch and pear field; **t**20 a sharpness to the arrival reveals that the peat and oak are not entirely in harmony; **f**23 that sweet, gristy fingerprint of the distillery arrives against the odds for a long and beautifully cured finale; **b**21 limps about in old age a bit but still has style. **50%. nc ncf sc.** Douglas Laing.

Old Malt Cask Port Ellen Aged 21 Years (sherry) dist Sep 79, bott Feb 01 **(87) n**22 sherry and peat that works together. Hurrah! **t**22 pounding, gutsy peat floating in a sea of ripe grapes; **f**21 the oak says hullo after the massive peat-malt-sherry orgy; **b**22 big whisky: pure fun. **50%.** Douglas Laing. 546 bottles.

Old Malt Cask Port Ellen Aged 21 Years dist Jan 79, bott Jul 00 **(79) n**23 **t**21 **f**17 **b**18. Very peculiar: very bitty-flavoured with a winey finish. Do not drink cold. The gristy nose, though, is extraordinary. **50%. nc ncf.** Douglas Laing. 336 bottles.

Old Malt Cask Port Ellen Aged 22 Years dist Mar 78, bott Feb 01 **(82) n**21 **t**21 **f**20 **b**20. Fruity malt and subdued peat. **50%. nc ncf.** Douglas Laing. 352 bottles.

Old Malt Cask Port Ellen Aged 23 Years Sherry Finished dist Jan 78, bott Sep 01 Years **(68) n**16 **t**19 **f**17 **b**16. Massive peat but spoiled by sulphur from six months in sherry cask. A shame. **50%. nc ncf.** Douglas Laing. 764 bottles.

Old Malt Cask Port Ellen Aged 25 Years bott Mar 76, bott Apr 01 **(82) n**22 **t**22 **f**18 **b**20. Salty and peaty and delicious, but a little unsympathetic oak. **50%. nc ncf.** Douglas Laing. 522 bottles.

⁖ **Old Malt Cask Port Ellen Aged 25 Years** dist Sept 78, bott Feb 04 **(95) n**24 this is prime Port Ellen: absolutely perfectly balanced peat, offering a mild sweetness that just sings with the oak-induced vanilla and sprig of lavender; **t**23 very few 25-years-olds can be so delicate on the palate; the peat, like the underlying barley is fragile yet the building medium roast Java coffee cannot dislodge it; **f**23 lengthy, with a delicate sprinkling of Muscovado sugar helping to counter the formulating liquorice and strengthening coffee; **b**25 one of those great whiskies you search for and rarely find. It has captured the gentle magnificence of Port Ellen that very few bottlings, not least because of a later downgrade in cask quality, are ever ever likely to again. **50%. nc ncf sc.** Douglas Laing. 604 bottles.

Provenance Winter Distillation Port Ellen Over 18 Years dist Winter 81, bott Spring 00 **(81) n**20 **t**21 **f**20 **b**20. This is Port Ellen, reader, but not as we know it. Not the very best sherry butt ever to be delivered to the island, but one with enough about it to ensure complexity and not a little intrigue. **43%. nc ncf.** Douglas McGibbon & Co.

⁖ **Provenance Port Ellen Over 21 Years** dist Winter 82, bott Autumn 03 **(76) n**19 **t**19 **f**19 **b**19. As spicy as a Cumberland sausage but a bit murky and lacks guile. **46%.** Douglas McGibbon.

Scott's Selection Port Ellen 1981 bott 00 **(80) n**19 **t**21 **f**20 **b**20. This must have started as an only fairly peated Port Ellen and age has softened it further still. Even so, chewy and attractive stuff, though maybe a little world-weary at times. **56.3%.** Robert Scott & Co.

Scott's Selection Port Ellen 1982 bott May 03 **(90) n**22 massive peat with soft fruits to calm it down slightly; one of the bigger Port Ellen noses in recent years; t23 the enormity of the peat-reek translates directly onto the massively spiced palate: quite dry and chewy for its type; f23 some gristy malt offers a soothing sweetness before deep, sensual oak intervenes; b22 go for it folks: this will be among the last bottlings of Port Ellen in this kind of mega and irresistible form. **56.5%.** *Robert Scott & Co.*

Signatory Port Ellen 23 Years Old Cask Strength sherry butt 464, dist 5/9/78, bott 18/2/02 **(85)** n23 a ravishing nose: the cleanest sherry mixed with some punchy peat; t21 starts brilliantly with a thick wave of spicy peat then starts to go all toffee-fied: odd; f20 more vaguely faint peat with lots of toffee; b21 comes out the blocks like a champ but limps lamely to the finish. **60.9%.** *464 bottles.*

Signatory Port Ellen 1979 dist 28 Aug 79, bott 5 Mar 02 **(76)** n21 t19 f18 b18. The peat is striking on the nose but wear and tear takes its toll as the experience continues. **43%**

Signatory Silent Stills Port Ellen 1979 sherry refill butt 6792, dist 16/11/79, bott 9/11/02 **(87)** n20 pretty crisp peat even now, quite kippery; t22 a bit of the rough stuff early on then settles towards melt-in-the-mouth gristy malt; f23 here it comes into its own as the sweet peat heads towards liquorice and vanilla: highly complex; b22 a very decent Port Ellen that shows some of its youth in old age. **50.3%.** *Switzerland. 518 bottles.*

The Whisky Shop Port Ellen 1978 (93) n25 very young and fresh for its age, the famous Port Ellen grist is back, outrageously beautiful: for Port Ellen, perfection; t23 sweet peated malt, very light in style with lovely early vanilla balance; f23 typically simplistic, clean.and peaty; b22 this doesn't blow your mind like an Ardbeg and complexity is at a premium. It's as naturally beautiful, though, as a proud, naked woman in the prime of her life. And equally as enjoyable. **57.9%.** *The Whisky Shop Scotland 10th anniversary bottling. 602 bottles.*

PULTENEY
Highland (Northern), 1826. Inver House. Working.

Old Pulteney 12 Years Old db **(83)** n21 t22 f20 b20. The nose is floral; malty; polished floorboards; to taste razor-sharp malt, firm and brittle; stays hard despite softening oak; wonderfully energetic malt. **40%**

⋅⋅⋅ **Old Pulteney Aged 15 Years Old Single Cask Selection** cask 2340, dist 23 Jun 89, bott 23 Jun 04 db **(88)** n22 sharp, clean and lively; citrus abounds, with salty, bourbony notes adding further riches; t23 every bit as busy and biting as the nose suggests, only with more oil and much earlier oak than you might expect, only a hint of smoke seems to be in there, a little hot, maybe, but forgivably so; f21 long, with lashings of dark chocolate; b22 a mouthful of a dram that is delightful reward for making the long trip north. **63.2%.** *Available exclusively from distillery where drawn directly from cask.*

Old Pulteney 18 Years Old Cask 546 db **(83)** n22 t21 f20 b20. Fresh and zesty despite the age. Chalky finale. **40%**

⋅⋅⋅ **Old Pulteney Cask Strength Sherry Wood 18 Years Old** cask 1500 db **(91)** n22 sharp sherry; spiced fruitcake; t22 early fresh sherry, ultra-clean green grape and lumps of brown sugar; f24 mildly bitter at first and then a clarion call of spices reverberating around the palate; b23 a malt that cleverly builds up into something a little special. **58.8%**

⋅⋅⋅ **Old Pulteney Aged 20 Years Distilled in 1982 Bourbon Cask Limited Edition** db **(79)** n20 t20 f19 b20. Pleasant but never quite takes off. **46%.** *275 bottles.*

Old Pulteney Aged 26 Years Limited Bourbon Cask Edition (82) n23 t17 f22 b20. A lovely northern Highland malt to be enjoyed by those who love straight Glenmorangie. Suffers a little early in palate development from a lack of character and direction, but this is redeemed by the busy and entertaining finale. The tangerine-led nose, though, is to die for. **46%.** *1,600 bottles.*

Old Pulteney 1983 Cask No. 6181 db **(91)** n22 tangerines and malt in massive quantities and of unimpeachable quality; t24 faultlessly clean, intense barley with the usual citric suspects hanging around with a touch of peat to complete the picture; f23 long, with lovely malty tones now hand in glove with delicate oak; b22 a whisky for late night, when you've had a tough day and you need something to take your mind off everything except what is occupying your tastebuds. Gloriously indulgent. **57.5%**

⋅∷⋅ **Old Pulteney Cask Strength Sherry Wood 1983** db cask 929 **(85)** n23 dripping with Oloroso, there is also freshly sliced, sugared orange: a genuine fruitfest with a background of floral perfume; t21 lots of natural toffee-caramel and a hint of bourbon to further beef up the sherry; f20 dry with a dried date background sweetness; b21 after the pungent sherry nose it is a touch too predictable on the palate. **58.4%**

Adelphi Pulteney 19 Years Old cask 2610, dist 84 bott 03 **(84)** n23 t22 f19 b20. Nose to die for and taste absolutely mercurial, but let down by the short, thin finish. **51.9%**

Blackadder Raw Cask Pulteney 1990 bourbon barrel 3952, dist 13 Aug 90, bott Mar 03 **(87)** n21 quite hard, fruity and yet not unlike a young bourbon; t23 usual Pulteney lift-off on the palate, massive malty sweetness, almost "Malteser"-like, with a chocolate hint; f21 vanilla and more very sweet malt; b22 a cracking example of a fine malt at an age that suits it. Ripe for drinking. **62.7%**

Cadenhead's Pulteney 12 Years Old dist 90, bott 10/02 **(90)** n22 a firm malt aroma softened by something vaguely orangey; t23 stupendous mouth arrival: silky, mildly gristy malt and accompanying spices flushed with a very vague fruitiness; f22 that wonderful oily body remains, this time with some cold-coffee notes clinging to it; b23 you can't ask much more of any 12-y-o than this. **59%**

⋅∷⋅ **Duncan Taylor Pulteney 1977 Aged 26 Years** cask 3078 **(86)** n20 sandalwood; sawdusty, leathery malt; t22 mildly oily malt with an unusual and sweet development of bready, toasty, corn; f22 vanilla and spice; b22 slick and sweet. **58.3%**

Gordon & MacPhail Old Pulteney Aged 8 Years (85) n22 kumquats and malt; t22 more orangey fruit with teeming barley, f20 quietens rapidly with caramel; b21 a fine dram. **40%**

Gordon & MacPhail Old Pulteney 1966 (87) n23 switched-on oak; massive orangey, pithy presence; t21 malt then tangerines and soft oak; f22 a hint of smoke adds weight to the fruit; b21 remarkable whisky for its age, perfect for vitamin C lovers. **40%**

Gordon & MacPhail Old Pulteney 1990 Cask first-fill sherry butt cask 5471, dist 5/10/90, bott 31/12/02 **(85)** n21 almost immaculate butt: irritating sulphur distant echo apart, sherry clean to the point of squeaking and spices pinging all over the nose; t22 consumes the mouth and tastebuds with neat sherry, dry and chewy; f21 some malt has the temerity to show its face; b21 the most apologetic trace of sulphur prevents this from being a minor classic. Impressive all the same. **59.4%**

Hart Brothers Pulteney 10 Years Old (87) n20 hint of young bourbon; t22 malty, oily; f23 big, impressive finish with honey and smoke; b22 seriously good quality malt. **55.6%**

⋅∷⋅ **Private Collection Old Pulteney 1973 (72)** n19 t19 f16 b18. An entirely odd fish, this, with some attractive sweet coffee notes at times but a mysterious, bitter off-note that gives it an irony, Fisherman's Friend character. **45%** *Gordon & MacPhail.*

Ultimate Selection Old Pulteney 1990 bourbon barrel 25005, dist 26/4/90, bott 6/11/02 **(89)** n22 soft peat frames some wonderfully crisp malt; t22 mouthwatering, refreshing. The malt plays lead role with some vanilla ganging up in the middle; **f**23 very complex with tangerines mingling with soft smoke and relaxed, sweet malt; **b**22 this is, quite simply, first-class malt whisky. **43%.** *Van Wees NL.*

ROSEBANK
Lowland 1840–1993. Closed. (But if there is a God will surely one day re-open.)

Rosebank Aged 12 Years db **(87) n**21 sawdusty and dry; **t**23 supreme complex maltiness, rich tea biscuit and spice; **f**22 a soft diffusion of those busy malty tones, surprising sweetness; **b**21 a few years past its best, but still offers a malt of awesome natural beauty. The soft, malty sweetness is remarkable; **43%.** *Flora and Fauna range.*

Rosebank Aged 19 Years Rare Malts Selection dist 79 db **(85) n**22 peppery, bristling malt; **t**22 excellent mouthfeel but the early intense barley loses shape slightly; **f**20 bitter vanilla saved by good malt follow-through; **b**21 pleasant enough but bottled 10 years too late. **60.2%**

Rosebank Aged 20 Years Rare Malts Selection dist 81, bott May 02 db **(94) n**23 a volley of peppery spices are fired across the nosebuds: oak is present but takes shelter from the fire. Does some of that smoke contain peat? **t**24 f*** my old boots. This is a Rosebank? At 20 Years? Incredible. This is tin-hat whisky, explosive and just so brilliantly balanced with sweet and sour running hand in hand. There are some vague fruits, but it's the malt that stars until a coffee-laden oakiness begins to assert itself; **f**23 long, long, long with the oak trying to take control but complex malt notes fighting a rearguard action. Even a tad of peat adds to the mayhem; **b**24 well I had always said that the best Rosebank should be tasted at eight years old. Time to rip up my notebook: this one has re-written the rules. For Christ's sake re-open this distillery! How many can make a malt that sends us to heaven and back from eight to 20 years? **62.3%.** *6,000 bottles.*

⋰ **Aberdeen Distillers Rosebank 12 Years Old** cask 236 dist Feb 91 ,bott Oct 03 **(94) n**23 sweet and honeyed; **t**24 just slides into the palate and fits a treat: the barley/honey balance is to die for; **f**23 remains intense with malt leaping all over the tastebuds. A hind of spice towards the end; **b**24 if you can find better Lowland whisky at this age, then show me it. **43%.** *Blackadder International.*

Adelphi Rosebank 9 Years Old cask no. 1447 **(92) n**23 amazing dry marzipan and delicate malts. So complex! **t**24 celery and sweet malt combine with a touch of salt and an outline of oak; **f**22 vanilla and natural toffee represents the oak, myriad hits on the tastebuds, and even a tiny degree of smoke is there for the malts; **b**23 a Lowlander? A closed distillery? Shurely shome mishtake ... this is nothing short of sensational. **61%**

Blackadder Raw Cask Rosebank 1992 hogshead cask no. 1452 distilled 25/3/92, bott Apr 02 **(87) n**22 beautiful malt, dry and touched by oak.; **t**22 full-bodied malt, fleetingly sweet and intense but reverts to a more languid dry and spicy posture; **f**21 soft oaks and straggling malt; **b**22 solidly good whisky with loads to keep the tastebuds amused. **61%. nc ncf sc.**

Cadenhead's Rosebank 12 Years Old dist 89, bott 07/01 **(88) n**22 **t**23 **f**21 **b**22. 12 years is a bit old for this distillery but the complexity is still superb. **56.4%**

Connoisseurs Choice Rosebank 1984 (90) n22 diced almonds and cherry cake; **t**23 supreme mouth texture: medium sweetness with rich malt and such sexy oaky interventions. A touch of smoke lends weight; **f**22 dries to bitter chocolate; **b**23 quite excellent **40%.** *Gordon & MacPhail.*

Connoisseurs Choice Rosebank 1988 (82) n24 **t**21 **f**18 **b**19. A stunning whisky until it all goes flat at the finish. The smoke and marzipan nose is stupendous, though. **40%.** *Gordon & MacPhail.*

Connoisseurs Choice Rosebank 1989 (89) n23 dovetailing of sandalwood and marzipan; **t**23 really beautiful context that seems to accentuate the clever malt-oak complexity. Lovely spices abound; **f**21 quiet and sweet with vanilla; **b**22 sophisticated stuff. *Gordon & MacPhail.*

Coopers Choice Rosebank 1992 bott 00 **(93)** n*24* t*24* f*22* b*23*. Flawless example of the most luscious and complex Lowlander of them all, bottled at exactly the right time. Pity it wasn't at a purer strength. **40%**

⋯ **Hart Brothers Rosebank Aged 13 Years** Cask Strength dist Nov 90, bott Nov 03 **(89)** n*21* clean, faint fruit and vanilla; t*23* steps into overdrive as the a tidal wave of barley crashes into the tastebuds leaving a honeyed foam; f*22* impressive soft vanilla plus spice and butterscotch; b*23* at once energetic yet delicate whisky of very high quality. **58.3%**

Lombard Rosebank 1989 (85) n*21* green 'n' grassy; t*22* lovely weight on the palate: malt zings around, no more of a hint of vanilla amid some spices; f*21* very malty; b*21* an old cask fails to provide depth, but the fresh richness of the malt is reward enough. **50%**

Milroy's Rosebank Over 13 Years Old dist 89, bott 02 **(89)** n*22* intriguing and mouthwatering, the freshness of the aroma matches the extraordinary paleness of the whisky and is remarkable for a whisky of such age. The barley is fresh and flitting: coal-gas notes tweak the nose as does a very soft peat and barely a hint of oak is detectable. Absolutely charming; t*22* exactly how it noses and looks! A beautiful, subtle sweetness becomes ultra-malty and grassy. Clean, refreshing, youthful with an arrival of cocoa powder reminding us that it has, after all, spent a long time in a cask; f*22* surprisingly long and teasing with an incredible barley fade that lasts forever. Even a hint of peat can be found: for something so light, the chewiness is superb! b*23* a one-off classic. From perhaps a third- or even fourth-filled cask, the whisky is all but colourless. But the charisma and charm of a whisky from one of the great distilleries unfolds tantalisingly and deliciously on the palate. For those, like me, who love a great blend this has absolutely everything you will ever need and more.

Murray McDavid Rosebank 1990 bourbon cask MM 517, dist Feb 90, bott May 98 **(76)** n*15* t*22* f*20* b*19*. The label quotes from one of my books, referring to Rosebank: "If you ever find one aged 8, re-mortgage the house for it." What I had in mind was the distillery bottling or one like Coopers Choice 1992, launched a few years after I typed those words. What I didn't have in mind was this: the cask must have been around the warehouses a few times; having said that, this dram does have a fresh, irresistible middle. I do actually like it: but not as a Rosebank 8-year-old! **46%**

Murray McDavid Rosebank 1990 cask MM 2113, dist Mar 90, bott Dec 01 **(72)** n*17* t*17* f*20* b*18*. Another slightly odd Rosebank from MM: some years back they produced a young-un that never quite got off the ground. That mysterious, lurking juniper is an attractive tease, though. **46%. nc ncf sc.**

⋯ **Murray McDavid Rosebank 1990 (79)** n*22* t*20* f*18* b*19*. A degree too much natural caramel blunts the early malt promise. **46%**

Murray McDavid Rosebank 1992 cask MM 1413, dist Mar 92, bott May 02 **(88)** n*21* clean with big barley; t*23* the arrival on the palate is like so many butterflies landing on the tastebuds. Spices accentuate its delicate nature; f*22* long, remains fresh, sparkling and fizzy; b*22* a real little cracker. **46%**

Old Malt Cask Rosebank Aged 12 Years dist Feb 89 **(86)** n*21* primroses lead the way in a very floral aroma, lovely sweet sub-stratum of honey, the oak is softly seasoned: about as delicate as it gets; t*23* light, flitting malt becomes increasingly more intense, hints of coffee towards the middle, but with plenty of lumps of brown sugar. The complexity and balance is exemplary; f*21* very long and sweet for what appears at first as a lightweight. Excellent oak retention that offers superb balance; b*21* a gilded malt that could crack under the oak if the intensity and complexity of spirit was not so powerful. Magnificent stuff. **50%. nc ncf sc.** *Douglas Laing.*

⋯ **Old Malt Cask Rosebank Aged 12 Years** dist Jan 91, bott Nov 03 **(71)** n*15* t*20* f*18* b*18*. Unusually robust for Rosebank but off notes have crept in from somewhere. **50% nc ncf sc.** *Douglas Laing. 354 bottles.*

❧ **Old Malt Cask Rosebank Aged 13 Years** dist Feb 89, bott Oct 02 **(87)** n*19* dusty and non-committal; t*23* molten brown sugar over barley concentrate: chew on this; f*22* some oak makes a whimpering intervention; the finale is chalky and dry; b*23* liquid breakfast cereal and toast. **50%. nc ncf sc.** *Douglas Laing. 248 bottles.*

Old Malt Cask Rosebank Aged 20 Years dist Feb 81, bott May 01 **(82)** n*20* t*21* f*21* b*20*. A lively, clean dram with a wisp of late smoke. But age has eroded slightly the unique Rosebank style. **50%.** *Douglas Laing. 828 bottles.*

Old Malt Cask Rosebank Aged 22 Years dist Sept 78, bott May 01 **(80)** n*19* t*21* f*20* b*20*. Bright and refreshing with some lovely cocoa. **50%. nc ncf.** *Douglas Laing. 444 bottles.*

❧ **Provenance Rosebank Over 12 Years** dist Summer 91, bott Summer 03 **(93)** n*22* soft bourbon notes; like a 7-y-o Heaven Hill with dollops of honey for good measure; t*24* charismatic and heart-pounding arrival of clean barley enriched by golden honey and fudge candy; quite superb spices; more bourbony sub-notes are fed by some mildly herbal tone; f*23* long, vanilla-led with gentle sugars to soften the landing: the spices persist delightfully; b*24* I was tut-tutted by some a decade ago when I wrote that Rosebank at its best can match anything most other Scotch distilleries can offer. Well, try this. The early bourbon theme is rendered a side-show: the balance between honey and spice is equal to Highland Park at its most sophisticated and eloquent. Absolutely tastebud-smackingly brilliant. **46%.** *Douglas McGibbon.*

❧ **Provenance Rosebank Over 13 Years** dist Winter 91 bott Spring 04 **(83)** n*20* t*21* f*22* b*20* the coal dust nose is followed by prisoner-shooting barley: a hard and bitter little cuss **46%** *Douglas McGibbon*

Provenance Spring Distillation Rosebank Over 11 Years dist Spring 89, bott Autumn 00 **(82)** n*22* t*21* f*19* b*20*. Fabulous whisky from a fabulous distillery. Can't help wondering what this would have been like if bottled three years earlier – even more complex and beautiful I suspect. **43%. nc ncf.** *Douglas McGibbon & Co.*

Scotch Malt Whisky Society Cask 25.30 Aged 13 Years (93) n*22* old lavender and spiced oak; t*24* a tidal wave of peppered honey and rich malt. salty and spiced: enormous; f*23* fades to a degree, but slowly and not without upping the complexity, the length is almost immeasurable; b*24* Rosebank in younger years offers something remarkable: this is the best sample yet of something much older and confirming just what a top-of-the-line malt this is. The oak is bold, but the depth of the malt – plus the stunning sweet-sour balance – is up to the challenge. A distillery milestone. **59.7%. nc ncf sc.**

❧ **Signatory Vintage Rosebank Vintage 1989** cask 727, dist 5 Apr 89, bott 20 Sept 02 **(83)** n*21* t*22* f*20* b*20*. By no means the most complex, but really a velvety ride. **43%.** *427 bottles*

Ultimate Dram Rosebank 1991 dist 18/2/91, bott 6/11/02 **(85)** n*22* soft vanilla, almost like soft ice cream cone; t*22* refreshing malt, clean and lip-smacking delicious early entry; f*20* a touch of salt gives it a life; b*21* clean and chewy. *Van Wees NL*

❧ **Whisky Galore Rosebank 1990 Aged 13 Years (83)** n*19* t*23* f*20* b*21*. Weighted beyond a Lowlander with thick, mildly honeyed, malt, but just a fraction too much age for a Rosebank to fully blossom. **46%.** *Duncan Taylor.*

ROYAL BRACKLA
Speyside, 1812. Dewar's. Working.

Royal Brackla db **(80)** n*21* t*20* f*19* b*20*. A very soft, young and steady dram. **40%**

❧ **Royal Brackla 10 Years Old** db **(82)** n*21* t*22* f*18* b*21*. A rich dram with lots of depth but perhaps a shade too much toffee amid the spice. **40%.** *John Dewar & Son.*

Royal Brackla Aged 10 Years db **(72)** n*18* t*19* f*17* b*18*. Malty, but unusally hot and nippy. **43%**. *Flora and Fauna range.*

Royal Brackla Rare Malts Selection Aged 20 Years dist 78 db **(78)** n*19* t*22* f*18* b*19*. Apart from a rousing early chorus of malt on the tastebuds, pretty tired stuff. **59.8%**

Royal Brackla Aged 25 Years dist 78, bott Mar 03 db **(88)** n*23* old walnuts, tangerines and slightly green melon; t*22* firm-bodied, curiously grainy at first then the slow evolution of creamy pulped fruit and chewy malt; f*21* much drier despite a hint of toasted raisin; b*22* a very complex malt that for a light Speysider has survived the passing summers much better than can be expected and is bold enough to display its own richness of style. Some excellent cask selection has gone into this one. **43%**

Connoisseurs Choice Royal Brackla 1974 (76) n*19* t*20* f*18* b*19*. Somewhat thin despite some distant peat. **40%**

⋰⋱ **Connoisseurs Choice Royal Brackla 1976 (84)** n*19* t*21* f*22* b*22*. Bit thick on the oak early and very late on but all in between is a riot of weighty barley sugar ripping off in a warming, bourbony direction. **46%**

Coopers Choice Royal Brackla 1975 bott 01 (25 Years Old) **(79)** n*20* t*22* f*18* b*19*. You know, it crossed my mind to do two sets of scores for this one. On the one hand I like it a lot, on the other I'm just not sure about it at all. The scores fall between two stools, although the strange flavour on the finish tends to confirm the suspicions aroused by the weirdly peated nose. Yet, on the other hand ... **43%**. *The Vintage Malt Whisky Co.*

Coopers Choice Royal Brackla 1984 (13 Years Old) bott 98 **(85)** n*22* orange and marmalade notes; t*22* complex malt and tangy fruit; f*21*a spicy flourish; b*20* a decent dram better served slightly cold. **43%. sc.**

"Green" Brackla 1975 27 Years Old cask 5471, bott 28 Oct 02 **(93)** n*24* intense floral and citrus combined with some sweet demerara notes – rum not sugar: beautifully weighted; t*24* imperious malt-sugar notes then a big arrival of intact oak, Mouth-coating and gloriously crisp and precise; f*22* fabulously long with outstanding barley-sugar characteristics and spice; b*23* the cask type says "unknown" on the label, but this is almost certainly ex-rum, most probably a demerara wooden column still. The type of whisky where one glass can last you an hour: complexity of extraordinary rarity. Moments like this make my job very rewarding. **www.thewhiskyexchange.com** 204 bottles.

Mission Range Royal Brackla 1975 (92) n*22* unripened kumquats and seven-year-old bourbon. t*24* Sssssh! Don't make a sound: listen to the extraordinary subtlety and deftness as the fruit and malt dovetails. The weight and mouthfeel is near enough perfect; f*22* hints of smoke, but the oak-malt interplay intrigues; b*24* this is a whisky that is essentially all about complexity and secret messages. Find a silent room, save for a ticking clock or the crackle of the fire, lights dimmed to twilight, and just concentrate on something rather special. **46%**

Provenance Winter Distillation Brackla Over 6 Years dist Winter 94, bott Winter 00 **(84)** n*20* b*22* t*21* f*21*. What a treat to find a delicate Speysider bottled at an age that suits the whisky rather than a marketing department. Also reveals why young blended Scotch can be so satisfying. One of the most refreshing, thirst-quenching drams you'll find. **43%. nc ncf.** *Douglas McGibbon & Co.*

Scott's Selection Royal Brackla 1976 bott May 03 **(83)** n*20* t*23* f*19* b*21*. Wonderful, clean, sweet malt through the middle. **57.2%**. *Robert Scott & Co.*

ROYAL LOCHNAGAR
Highland (Eastern), 1826. Diageo. Working.

Royal Lochnagar Aged 12 Years db **(79)** n*20* t*21* 19 f*19*. Disappointing: a bit on the hot side with toffee where the malt should be. **40%**

Royal Lochnagar Aged 23 Years Rare Malts Selection db **(94)** n23 toasted honeycomb and nougat, slightly nutty; t24 magnificent richness, with some early tired oakiness repaired by the sheer enormity of the malt: a dram for grown-ups; f23 now the oak gets in with liquorice but some demerara sugar keeps the balance; b24 This is great whisky: seems at times over the edge, but some invisible force of greatness is holding it back. About as good a Lochnagar you will ever find. **59.7%**

Royal Lochnagar Selected Reserve db **(89)** n23 superb oloroso, clean and spicy with apples and pears; t23 stupendous spice lift-off which really starts showing the malts to great effect; f21 the malts fade as the toffee progresses; b22 quite brilliant sherry influence. The spices are a treat. **43%**

Old Malt Cask Lochnagar Aged 28 Years dist May 73, bott 01 **(76)** n20 t20 f17 b19. Beginning to fall apart. **50%. nc ncf.** Douglas Laing. 252 bottles.

⁖ **Platinum Old and Rare Lochnagar 32 Years Old** dist 72, bott 04 **(85)** n23 quite beautiful: strands of honey thread through soft vanilla and even the most delicate hint of peat; the oak is showing but the lavender and toast are wonderfully understated; t19 a dry oaky wall hits the palate but then there is a second shock wave this time of slicker, sweeter, gently oiled barley and warming spices; f22 much more at ease with the oak now fully under control and the cocoa offering a very long and tasty finale; b21 a malt that hangs in there by the skin of its teeth but most extraordinary is the strength for the age. **60.5%.** Douglas Laing.

Platinum Old And Rare Lochnagar 30 Years Old (72) n22 t17 f16 b17. Stunning sherry nose, but a little aged. **57.6%.** Douglas Laing.

Scotch Malt Whisky Society Cask 103.8 Aged 34 Years (79) n19 t21 f20 b19. An old, big-oaked malt, not unlike some old Irish pot still that turns up now and again. The ageing process has left scars across the malt. But a hint of molassed sugar fills some of the holes though not all. A dram for those who like their malt sweet but with warts and all. **66.1%. nc ncf sc.**

ST MAGDALENE
Lowland, 1798–1983. Closed.

St Magdalene Aged 19 Years Rare Malts Selection db dist 79, bott Oct 98 **(87)** n19 t23 f23 b22. Quite outstanding Lowland malt. As good as this distillery gets. **63.8%**

Blackadder Raw Cask Linlithgow 1975 hogshead 30012, dist 2/6/75, bott Apr 02 **(86)** n22 exceptionally clean and intense malt with layers of oaky complexity; t21 the malt arrives softly at first, then there is a massive second wave, gentle smoke is also there: pleasingly oiled; f21 drier oak; b22 an exceptional quality Linlithgow, displaying massive malt. **59.3%. nc ncf sc.**

Connoisseurs Choice St Magdalene 1966 (83) n20 t22 f21 b20. Chewy toffee and sweet. Fabulous mouthfeel but perhaps too much caramel chips at the complexity? **40%.** Gordon & MacPhail.

⁖ **Duncan Taylor Linlithgow 1982 Aged 21 Years** cask 2211 **(80)** n19 t20 f21 b20. Thin and hot, but the clarity of the malt is without question. **63%**

Gordon & MacPhail St Magdalene 1982 (90) n21 greengages and cream with just a dab of oak; t23 perfect sweetness: the barley is all guns blazing and cleaner than a freshly scrubbed nun; f23 lovely spice drifts with the vanilla oak, longer than a Sunday sermon. b23 a minor miracle from G&M: a classic, sweet-velvet dram from a malt that in its youth would have burnt your throat out. **40%**

⁖ **Hart Brothers St. Magdalene Aged 21 Years Cask Strength** dist Sep 82, bott Nov 03 **(86)** n20 mustard and carrot cake; t22 thinks about ripping into the tastebuds but backs off when the Heavens open and shafts of Demerara-sugared barley arrives and sweetens things up beautifully as angels pluck at their harps; f22 impressive oily weight and longevity, but it's barley all the way; **b**22 there are two types of St Magdalene. Vicious or serene. Here you taste with angels. **56.6%**

Old Malt Cask Linlithgow Aged 26 Years dist Jun 75, bott Dec 01 **(79)** **n**21 **t**20 **f**19 **b**19. Very malty sweet, but overall thin and warming. **50%. nc ncf sc.** *Douglas Laing. 288 bottles*

Scott's Selection Linlithgow 1975 bott 99 **(77)** **n**18 **t**20 **f**19 **b**20. Has withstood the test of time to present an attractive Lowland, sweet and rich in charm. **56.3%.** *Robert Scott & Co.*

SCAPA
Highland (Island–Orkney), 1885. Allied. Full-time production from late 2004.

Scapa 12 Years Old db **(88)** **n**23 honeydew melon, soft salt and myriad styles of barley: really complex with a sprinkling of coal dust on the fruit; **t**22 truly brilliant mouth arrival: the most complex display of malt and cocoa, the fruit is ripe figs with a thread of honey; **f**21 a slight bitterness with some developing toffee, but the malt stays the distance; **b**22 always a joy. **40%**

⬥ **Scapa 14 Years Old** db **(88)** **n**20 hints of honey and kumquats, but a tad sappy; **t**22 relays of mouthwatering barley sprinting between the shards of honey; **f**23 toasty, a subtle bitterness blends well with the lingering barley-honey; **b**23 the tongue works overtime trying to work out the multi-layered structure of a superb malt from a distillery at last being recognised for its excellence. **40%**

⬥ **Chieftain's Scapa 1979 Aged 23 Years** sherry wood bott 6 Mar 03 **(87)** **n**21 cumbersome, very vaguely sulphured, but punchy with fruit; **t**23 some early imbalances are overcome by a lush, oily wave of sherry: hardly subtle but effective; the middle is steadied by some natural soft caramel; **f**21 dries out rigorously but the barley remains; **b**22 bit of a scud missile this: hit and miss but impressive when it hits its target. **55.6%.** *Ian Macleod.*

Gordon & MacPhail Scapa 1984 **(79)** **n**23 **t**20 **f**17 **b**19. Great – no, brilliant! – nose, then the Viking ship depicted on the label just sinks without trace. **40%.** *Gordon & MacPhail.*

Gordon & MacPhail Scapa 1985 (83) n 22 **t**22 **f**19 **b**20. Fresh, lemon-zesty nose and alluring maltiness on the palate but the toffee-fudge gets greedy. **40%**

Gordon & MacPhail Scapa 1987 (75) **n**22 **t**18 **f**18 **b**17. Rather simplistic and lacking its usual cocoa depth. **40%**

Gordon & MacPhail Scapa 1988 (76) **n**21 **t**20 **f**17 **b**18. Fine malt, but some numbing caramel bites deep from somewhere. **40%**

Gordon & MacPhail Scapa 1990 (89) **n**22 coal dust, timber and exceptionally clean malt: quite lovely; **t**22 mouthwatering entry with the malt just zooming off in all directions; **f**23 brilliant fall-out with a touch of smoke clinging to the cocoa and malt; **b**22 immeasurably better than recent bottlings, the subtle character of the distillery sketched beautifully in an awesome dram.

⬥ **Old Malt Cask Scapa Aged 14 Years** dist Oct 89, bott Mar 04 **(83)** **n**20 **t**21 **f**21 **b**21. A neat and tidy dram with a rich cocoa finale but perhaps just a shade too fierce in places. **50%. nc ncf sc.** *Douglas Laing. 269 bottles.*

⬥ **Old Malt Cask Scapa Aged 15 Years** dist Oct 88, bott Mar 03 **(88)** **n**19 thin and unpromising; **t**23 mouthwatering malt that is clean and refined. The barley is almost in concentrate with the oak offering a textured vanilla; **f**24 can't really ask for more: fresh barley interacts almost perfectly with the dry cocoa. Long with late, lingering spices. Textbook; **b**22 after the disappointing nose all that follows is simply glorious. Sheer Scapa! **50%. nc ncf sc.** *Douglas Laing.*

Old Malt Cask Scapa Aged 25 Years dist Nov 74, bott May 00 **(94)** **n**22 **t**23 **f**25 **b**24. There are times you have to hold your hands up and say: words alone cannot do this justice. Except to say that every member of Allied should taste this so they can get the distillery back into full-time operation. And, a year after writing these notes, what do you know? They have!! **50%. nc ncf.** *Douglas Laing. 524 bottles.*

Old Malt Cask Scapa Aged 25 Years dist Aug 75, bott Feb 01 **(92)** n23 t24 f23 b22. Spicy and lively, this is a whisky that defines complexity. **50%. nc ncf.** Douglas Laing. 438 bottles.

Old Malt Cask Scapa Aged 25 Years Sherry dist Aug 75, bott Jun 01 **(91)** n22 t23 f23 b23. This is obviously a relation to OMC's previous bottling, but do twins come more beautiful than this? **50%. nc ncf.** Douglas Laing.

⌁ **Provenance Scapa Over 14 Years** dist Autumn 88, bott Winter 04 **(86)** n19 lively and a touch spirity, the main theme is the subtlety of the oak; t22 outstanding malt arrival helped by a gentle oiliness that seems to thicken the soft honey notes and apple fruitiness; f23 now extremely complex with the tell-tale cocoa notes embracing the intense malt. Long and rewarding; b22 devilishly complex with some fruit and honey mixing well with the oaky cocoa. **46%. nc ncf.** Douglas McGibbon.

SPEYBURN
Speyside, 1897. Inver House. Working.

Speyburn 10 Years Old db **(81)** n19 t21 f21 b20. Soft, slightly smoked, sweet, syrupy, simple: Speyburn so stylish. **40%**

Speyburn 21 Years Old Single Malt db cask 2711 **(84)** n20 t22 f21 b21. Sherried, sultana-sweet, smoky, spiced. **40%**

Speyburn 21 Year Old Single Cask cask 1811, dist 77, bott 99 db **(83)** n23 t20 f20 b20. A very rare specimen of an old-fashioned Speyside type. The original lightness of the make means that the malt struggles to be heard amid the fruit and oak. But despite a degree of tiredness and some ragged edges towards the finish, it holds together impressively. **61.9%**

Speyburn 25 Years Old db cask 1810 **(88)** n19 pulped and slightly burnt raisins, about as heavy as sherry gets (with a slight crack) so the malt barely troubles the aroma, if at all; t22 total sherry saturation but there are plenty of soft spices to kick life into the fruity onslaught; f24 fat gooseberries lighten it a little while heavy roast, dry cocoa heads towards the finale. Becomes salty as the oak really kicks in and then – would you believe? – some malt has the temerity to make itself heard; b23 I know there are those who will mark this a lot higher. But I can't say I'm a great lover of the nose and the mouth arrival is just too one-dimensional. It is only on the very long, absolutely outstanding and extraordinary finish that the tangled web is unwoven and much-needed lightening of body complexity arrives. Love it or otherwise, not a dram you forget in a hurry. **61.6%**

Connoisseurs Choice Speyburn 1971 (87) n22 fruit and smoke in same, moderate proportions; t22 refreshing, grassy, Speysidey malt with tinned fruit but bolstering spices f21 quite long, smoky, zesty with lingering malt; b22 really a complex, lingering dram of some serious quality. A minor classic in terms of the distillery. One I used to drink a lot of many years back and worth hunting today. **40%.** Gordon & MacPhail.

Connoisseurs Choice Speyburn 1974 (72) n17 t19 f18 b18. Sweet, malty and silky. But not quite hanging together. **40%.** Gordon & MacPhail.

SPEYSIDE
Speyside, 1990. Working.

Drumguish db **(78)** n18 t21 f19 b20. A very fruity and malty young Speysider (three years old, to be precise) that is hard and intense. This bottling is pretty sweet, though hot. Some, though, are on the feinty side. **40%**

⌁ **Hart Brothers Speyside Aged 10 Years** Sherry Cask dist Oct 93, bott Nov 03 **(73)** n17 t18 f20 b18. A slight feintiness to the nose and early mouth arrival but the grapiness magnifies and prospers the longer it remains on the palate. **46%**

Speyside 10 Years Old db **(81)** n*19* t*21* f*20* b*21*. Plenty of sharp oranges around; the malt is towering and the bite is deep. A weighty Speysider with no shortage of mouth prickle. **40%**

Cu Dhub **(66)** n*15* b*18* t*16* b*17*. A whisky bottled exclusively by Danish whisky importers Mac Y for their home market after requests to find a "Black Whisky". This is, basically, young malt from the Speyside distillery with lashings of caramel colouring. It does have one all too brief golden moment a few seconds after hitting the palate. But don't expect anything too much beyond the novelty. One for ice and coke. **40%**

SPRINGBANK
Campbeltown, 1828. J&A Mitchell & Co. Working.

Longrow 10 Years Old 1993 db **(89)** n*22* deft peat flies sweetly around. There is something young and alluring about this; t*23* mouthfilling, sweet malt offers limited complexity but the peat makes it a dram to savour; f*22* clean, sweet, gristy, b*22* not unlike a Port Ellen at about the same age. Certainly the closest we'll ever get to it again. **46%**

Longrow 10 Years Old Bourbon Cask db bott 00 **(88)** n*22* t*23* f*22* b*21*. A very simple malt, beautifully made, though the peating level is lower than previous distillations. That said, it's just glorious. **46%**

Longrow 10 Years Old Sherry Cask db bott 00 **(82)** n*20* t*22* f*20* b*20*. Technically, beautifully made, clean and flawless. Talking from the heart, the peat and sherry seem to rub each other out leaving an attractive dram but one short of those special Longrow moments **46%**

Longrow 13 Years Old Sherry Cask db bott 02 **(91)** n*23* clever peat-fruit interplay, traces of oak as a third dimension; t*23* fat and full mouthfeel, brilliant sweet peat-dry sherry balance with a spicy side-dish; f*22* sweetens towards the malt as the sherry thins out; b*23* glorious whisky which just goes to show how malt from this distillery takes a few years to get cracking **53.2%**

Springbank 10 Year Old db **(90)** n*22* fresh, unusual complexity with remarkable barley-oak jousting; t*23* massive: an Etna of an arrival with the main explosion being pure malt then a descending pyroclastic of salty vanilla notes and amazing spice; f*22* medium length but the malt remains indescribably lucid; b*23* I am in my third decade as a Springbank devotee. Never, though, has their 10-year-old been even close to being quite this good. Masterful. **46%. nc ncf.**

⊹ **Springbank Aged 10 Years 100 Proof** db **(90)** n*22* enormously bright with strands of honey and ginger thrown in delicious effect; t*23* massive malt arrival with some vanilla trying to dig its way in but with only limited success; f*23* stunning brown sugar and melt-in-the-mouth malt at the very death: what is going on? b*22* this really is a quite diferent Springbank, due to its comparative youth lacking its usual briney compexity, but the tale told is sweet and engrossing. Easily one of the best 10-y-o from this distillery I've ever tasted. **57%**

Springbank 12 Years Old 175th Anniversary db **(86)** n*20* gentle; t*24* malt, malt, malt and malt. Oh, and some malt; f*21* long, oily and very velvety, displaying – guess what? – with the oak...; b*21* an unusually soft Springbank with less complexity than usual but displaying amazing intensity. **46%.** *12,000 bottles worldwide from Apr 03. The age may not be stated.*

Springbank 15 Year Old db **(85)** n*22* punchy, lively malt which remains fresh despite some salty age with a surprising degree of oak; t*22* very intense malt concentrate that starts sweet then dries spectacularly; f*20* pretty dry oak, cocoa and marmalade; b*21* a decent but not great Springbank. **46%. nc ncf.**

Springbank Aged 25 Years **(91)** n*24* sherry oak was made for this: the cleanest, fruitiest, crushed grape aroma imaginable dovetailing with rich, salty, malty waves; t*22* really deep malt, like layers of an onion: the inherent malty sweetness is always lurking despite the oak; **f**22 long, chewy and deep: late hints of citrus burst from nowhere; **b**23 I think complex is the word. **46%**

Springbank FFF 25 Year Old db **(90) n**23 salty with the usual complex oaky-malty battles raging; **t**22 lovely oils bring out the richness of the oak, malt bounces around the tastebuds with hints of some citrus; **f**22 long finale with the accent on oaky-malty things: a real jaw-acher in its chewiness; **b**23 the words Springbank and complexity seem conjoined: they are again here. **46%**

Springbank Aged 35 Years limited edition, bott 99 db **(95) n**24 t24 f23 **b**24. No whisky of this age should be quite this faultless or good. One of the great sherry casks of recent times. **46%. nc ncf.**

Springbank Wood Expression 12 Year Old Rum Wood (93) db **n**22 quiet yet complex; **t**25 Bloody hell! One is given the impression that one's tastebuds have just exploded. It's a bit of a mess: there is no rhyme nor reason to what is happening, it just happens ...; **f**23 heavy shades of cocoa and high roast Java; **b**23 uncontrolled, unstable, explosive Springbank at its most deadly ... and for a while too delicious to be true. **54.6%. Seven years in bourbon cask. Five years in demerara barrel. 25 years minimum in the memory bank.**

Springbank 1966 cask 500, dist Feb 66, bott Aug 98 db **(92) n**23 t23 f23 **b**23. This is sublime, complex whisky. It is entirely typical of the distillery style of the mid-60s from bourbon. **54.2%**

Springbank Wood Expression 1989 Port Wood 13 Years Old db **(90) n**20 very clean and fresh port wood influence – but at the cost of some complexity, though spice is not in short supply; **t**23 astonishing, succulent fruit with the most wonderful peppery attack, the most mouthwatering Springbank bottled in the last 25 years; **f**23 absolutely top-class chocolate and malt finale; **b**24 yet another piece of freaky genius from Springbank. **54.2%. 10 years refill bourbon, three years port pipes. Mainland Europe only.**

⋰⋰ **Adelphi Springbank 1970** cask 1622 **(92) n**23 a warming, peppery nose has a Demerara rum and sugar edge and a touch of sweetened tequila; look carefully and malt seeps out, too; **t**22 a big, threatening oakiness is checked by a sherry-malt resistance and overcome by gentle brown sugar; **f**24 mouthwatering, chewy with layers of plummy fruit and liquorice; **b**23 brilliant, complex whisky that two years earlier may have been quite exceptional. **54.4%**

⋰⋰ **Berry's Own Selection Springbank 1968 35 Years Old** bott 03 **(94) n**23 orange peel doused in salt and pepper; also an intriguing bond of molassed sugar and vanilla-rich oak; **t**22 big, chewy with increasing weight; teasing spices blend with barley sugar; **f**25 long, almost rum-like in its liquorice-coffee Demerara weight with an estery follow-through. The salty, sea-shore tang continues and intensifies; more fruit at the very death, but you have to wait a long time for the finish to finally arrive; **b**24 a whisky this age almost has no right to offer this degree of complexity on the entirely faultless finish. The bitter-sweet ratio is the stuff of dreams; the integrity of the barley remains unsullied despite the trickery of the oak. A Springbank classic for the collector. **46%. nc ncf.** Berry Bros & Rudd.

Blackadder Raw Cask Springbank 1991 hogshead 04, dist Jun 91, bott Apr 02 db **n**22 light, complex but mainly coal-gas; **t**25 trademark malt explosion carried along with some rich oils, and spice: pretty hot but unmistakably brilliant. The malt starts sweet then settles: truly faultless; **f**23 digestive biscuit, complete with salt but with lashings of malt on top; **b**23 there is a certain burn to this whisky that has nothing to do with the alcohol content. The specific flavour of the malt is about as good as it ever gets in whisky. Had I owned this cask it would never have seen the light of day. It would have been mine, I tell you ... all mine!!! If you ever spot a bottle, knock yourself out. **57.4%. nc ncf sc.**

⋰⋰ **Blackadder Raw Cask Springbank 1993** cask no. 340 dist Jun 93, bott Jun 93 **(85) n**22 oloroso at its most dense with lots of peripheral spicy moments; t20 big juicy raisin kick; f22 the barley regroups to offer some sweetness to counter the sherry; b21 too young for this ever to be a great Springbank, but the quality of the butt is awesome. As it happens, I was at Springbank in June '93 and saw some butts being filled: I wonder... **46%**

⫶⫶ **Chieftains Springbank 1969 Aged 34 Years** rum barrel bott 27 Nov 03 **(92)** n24 get your hooter around this: one of the most delicate and complex fruitfests of all time. Quite stunning; t23 the malt dissolves in the mouth leaving traces of soft fruits and spices; the vanilla is quite perfectly weighted and the age heads towards a bourbon-style sweetness; f22 has little more to say except on the bourbony-vanilla theme which is flawless; b23 a bigger finish would have made this one of the all-time greats. As it is, just enjoy the astonishing early harmony. **43.2%**

Chieftain's Springbank 1972 (30 years old) **(88)** n20 initially showing some signs of tiredness, a fraction too much oak leading to a slight bourbony character, but the fruit here is massive for all that: orange concentrate with big, big toffee; t23 silky with the most intense natural caramel you can imagine: again the bitter-sweetness is absolutely spot on, buttery and chewy with the most intense barley richness imaginable; f23 deep, the slightest hint of liquorice and some sweet malts until a much drier oakiness kicks in. Some spice in there, too; b22 a whisky you have to get to know – you will be rewarded. **57.8%**

Chieftain's Springbank 1974 (27 years old) **(84)** n21 t21 f21 b21. Fat, oily and resounding. This is big, big whisky – again not of a character that one immediately associates with Springbank. But the raw quality will not be denied. **56.6%**

Chieftain's Springbank 1974 (28 years old) **(81)** n21 t22 f18 b20. Light and amazingly delicate for a Springbank, but missing the usual saline intensity. **46%**

Da Mhile Organic Springbank 1992 Aged 7 Years dist June 92, bott Sept 99 **(74)** n17 t20 f19 b18. Really big, oily and chewy. Also a bit feinty, but a real one-off. The only organic whisky around. **46%**. *Made for organic farmer John Savage-Onstwedder.*

⫶⫶ **Dun Bheagan Springbank 1969 Aged 35 Years** bott 15 Mar 04 **(94)** n24 classic Springbank, the salty/oaky complexity of aroma is quite different from the Chieftains rum version but the stuff on which some of us discovered the genius of Campbeltown single malt nearly 30 years ago; t23 fills the mouth with an oaky frame in which the battle between barley and grape, brown sugar and dry tanin is staged; f23 almost too long to register; there is an oaky bitterness that includes some medium roast coffee but the saltiness and perfect oil density makes this one to just sit back and melt into; b24 when a Springbank can stand the test of time, little can live with it for sheer élan and complexity. **50%**

⫶⫶ **Duncan Taylor Springbank 1967 Aged 37 Years** cask 1943 **(82)** n21 t21 f20 b20. Some barley-rich moments but just a shade sappy. **41%**

Juul's Private Bottling Springbank Vintage 1966 Aged 34 Years **(93)** n23 a rich fruitcake nose not without some bourbony-style oakiness; t24 a mind-blowing array of salty, oaky notes neatly wrapped in lush fruit: outstanding mouthfeel; f22 the salty theme continues, with some pepper for company plus hickory, liquorice and Blue Mountain coffee; b24 a stupendous cask which marked Copenhagen's landmark whisky shop's 75th anniversary in 2001 in awesome style. **47.1%**. *190 bottles.*

Lombard Jewels of Scotland Springbank Distilled 1991 bott 2001 **(72)** n17 t21 f17 b17. Disappointing due to a pervading natural caramel effect. Unfortunate. Flat nose and finish but delicious mouth arrival. **50%**

⫶⫶ **Murray McDavid Springbank 1993/1965 (83)** n20 t22 f21 b20. Curious, fruity mix of youth and prime wrinkliness works, but only just; youth sprints into the lead with fresh malt but the oldies gather for an oaky sherry party; no shortage of spice, either. **46%**

Murray McDavid Springbank 1965 bott 99 **(93) n**24 t24 f22 b23. With its tidal wave of spicy, oaky tones, a truly brilliant whisky, once tasted never forgotten. Classic, classy stuff. **46%. nc ncf sc.**

⋯ **Old Malt Cask Springbank Aged 10 Years** dist Jun 92, bott Feb 03 **(74) n**19 t20 f17 b18. Would make Queen Elizabeth I look like Dolly Parton: ultimately about the flattest Springbank I've happened across in 25 years. Shame, the malt start is bright and lively. **50%. nc ncf sc.** *Douglas Laing for Alambique Classique, Germany. 311 bottles.*

⋯ **Old Malt Cask Springbank Aged 10 Years** dist Jun 93, bott Jan 04 **(81) n**19 t22 f20 b20. Disappointingly sappy nose translates to the finale. Some bright, typically weighty, salty and complex moments on the early arrival and middle, though. **50%. nc ncf sc.** *Douglas Laing. 628 bottles.*

Old Malt Cask Springbank Aged 33 Years dist May 67, bott Feb 01 **(78) n**23 t20 f17 b18. The nose suggested we were in for a classic. It was not to be. **41.4%. nc ncf sc.** *Douglas Laing. 204 bottles.*

Open Championship 2000 Bottling Campbeltown Single Malt cask 600R, dist 93 **(88) n**22 meaty oloroso. The malt chimes in but the oak stays quiet: very clean with some wonderful coffee notes; **t**23 massive. The sherry is dripping off the tastebuds with a malt-extracty sweetness adding to the weight. The spices are almost alarming; **f**21 charming and slightly reserved, with neither the youthful malt nor sherry quite having the confidence to take the lead; **b**22 sheer class. I'd be tempted to buy a bottle, shove the contents into a tiny oak barrel and let it reach brilliance. **59.2%.** *Available from only Luvians Bottleshop of Cupar, Scotland. States 300 bottles – there were only 258 produced. This is Springbank, though not stated on bottle.*

Peerless Springbank 1967 cask 1940, dist May 67 36-y-o **(86) n**22 lemon drops, very sharp malt and some heavier oak; **t**19 some over-weighty oak at first but complex malts gather; **f**23 enormously long, the complexity levels going off the scales: bitter-sweet balance just about perfect despite the persistent oak; **b**22 takes time to settle but well worth the wait. **41.1%.** *Duncan Taylor & Co.*

Scotch Malt Whisky Society Millennium Malt Nine Years Old First Release Distillery 114 (Longrow) **(87) n**21 delicately peaty and curiously gristy; **t**22 now the peat arives big time, fruity and malty-sweet; **f**23 chewy, vanilla-rich, kippery, buttery, still gristy and young but very long; **b**21 a cask culled in its youth. A joyous dram, but one that still has a long way to go before maturity. **58.1%**

Scotch Malt Whisky Society "27.49" 12 Years Old dist Dec 89, bott Aug 02 **(86) n**23 salty, sea-swept and malty: archetypal Springbank; **t**22 youthful, exuberant, zesty, malty; **f**20 slightly green and tart, but no shortage of complexity; **b**21 it may not say Springbank on the label, but there's just no mistaking it. **54.7%**

Signatory Springbank 9 Years Old sherry cask, dist 90, bott 00 **(85) n**21 t22 f21 b21. A really enjoyable dram with plenty going on, though you feel that, given time, there could have been so much more. **46%.** *215 bottles.*

⋯ **Whisky Galore Springbank Aged 10 Years** (79) **n**19 t21 f20 b19 No screaming off-notes except perhaps a strange tobacco character. A brief flash of peaty smoke, but pretty half-baked by Springbank standards. **46%**

STRATHISLA
Speyside, 1786. Chivas. Working.

Strathisla 12 Years Old db **(87) n**21 a dab of distant peat adds even more weight to something that is malt-heavy already; **t**22 pleasant, sultana-fruity with a very rich malt follow-through; **f**22 some almost apologetic oak breaks into the rich maltiness. Some hints of cocoa and more smoke elongate the finale; **b**22 an infinitely better dram than a few years back that was a bit oily and shapeless. Today the heavily-weighted, full-bodied malt engages the tastebuds from first to last with a complexity and richness of genuine class. **43%**

⸭ **Aberdeen Distillers Strathisla 13 Years Old** dist Nov 89, bott Nov 03 **(87)** n*21* basic barley, maybe a tad youthful and new-makish, but clears the head; t*22* the palate is wiped clean by the most uncomplicated barley attack imaginable; f*23* some weak vanilla does show here and though complexity remains at a premium, the refreshing, thirst-quenching properties cling to the very death; b*21* some people will keep shy of such an anaemic-looking malt. But after a day of tasting one sherry butt after another, the beauty – and relief – of indulging in the clarity offered by a second or, most likely, third fill bourbon cask is almost beyond description. This is Strathisla unmasked. **43%**

Blackadder Raw Cask 1989 sherry cask 9411, dist 6 Nov 89, bott Apr 02 **(87)** n*22* big grassy malts, a waft of smoke; t*23* massive malt gangs up and thumps the tastebuds mercilessly, hints of oak and smoke; f*21* medium length, vanilla and bitter chocolate; b*21* sherry cask, but the influence is non-existent. **61.3%**

Cask Strathisla 1974 casks 2206–7, dist 25/3/74, bott Jul 92 **(93)** n*24* t*24* f*22* b*23*. One of G&M's masterpieces still (amazingly) available in places like Vintage House, London. Close your eyes and go for the ride. **57.8%**. *Gordon & MacPhail.*

⸭ **Coopers Choice Strathisla 1976 Aged 27 Years** bott 03 **(87)** n*22* crushed sultanas in a fruit bun; lovely barley-rich background t*22* such a gentle assortment of delicate fruity-barley notes; f*21* soft, oaky vanilla but slightly shorter than expected; b*22* what us Surreyites would call a "little darling", were that not now considered sexist. **46%**. *Vintage Malt Whisky Co.*

Gordon & MacPhail Strathisla 25 Year Old **(89)** n*24* Oh my word! A sprinkling of everything, except OTT oak. It seems almost a shame to drink it; t*23* sweet, sugary malt. The subtle smoke on the nose doesn't filter down, though; f*20* just a little flat and vanilla-bound; b*22* a quite remarkable malt, never quite living up to the nose in terms of complexity – but that would have been asking a bit too much. **40%**

Gordon & MacPhail Strathisla 1953 **(90)** n*22* heavy duty and dense, very big vanilla oak but enough fruit for balance; t*22* Well done! The oak is kept at bay as massively intense malt and rich sultanas take centre stage. Some spices hover as does a welcome hint of smoke; f*23* more grapes just melt in the mouth as does the malt; b*23* whisky of this antiquity has no right to be this good or clean. An undisputed classic of its type. **40%**

Gordon & MacPhail Strathisla 1963 **(90)** n*23* ripened wild cherries and mushy greengages. Some nose! t*23* a malt extravaganza, at once both mouthwatering and dry – always chewy; f*22* some bitterness creeps in as the oak arrives, but the malt continues to the end; b*22* good old Gordon & MacPhail to unearth a little cracker. **40%**

Gordon & MacPhail Strathisla 1982 **(83)** n*22* t*21* f*20* b*20*. Solid, juicy, well-made malt that runs out of steam slightly at the finish. **40%**

Gordon & MacPhail Strathisla 1987 **(76)** n*19* t*20* f*18* b*19*. Regulation Speyside. **40%**

⸭ **Murray McDavid Mission Strathisla 1976** **(83)** n*20* t*23* f*20* b*20*. The barley-rich fullness of the body has helped overcome some upfront oak: a real tastebud pleaser. **46%**

⸭ **Old Malt Cask Strathisla Aged 28 Years** dist Nov 75, bott Dec 03 **(79)** n*18* t*23* f*19* b*19*. A summer or two too many for this one. Still sparkles with the fabulous mock bourbon on the fruity mouth arrival and offers a glorious mouthful. But the nose and tail show some cracks. **50%. nc ncf sc.** *Douglas Laing.*

Peerless Strathisla 1967 cask 1533, dist Feb 67 35-y-o **(92)** n*22* a fraction smoky; honied and rich; t*24* spellbinding series of crystal-clear, powering flavours starting with sweet butterscotch through avocado to honied malt; f*22* liquoricy and muscovado sugar: the peat-smoke returns slightly at the death; **b**24 this is dreamy stuff with balance and complexity by the bucketful. **51.1%.** *Duncan Taylor & Co.*

⠿ **Private Collection Strathisla 1955 (84) n**23 coffee iced biscuit; thick, sweetish sherry and biting spice: classic ye-olde sherry butt and one, in its day, of the very highest order; **t**23 hold on to your seat: the spice latches on to your throat and tastebuds and refuse to let go; the sherry really is heavyweight stuff that is brilliantly balanced between sweet toffee and bitter pear-drops; **f**18 pretty shattered: an oak-exhausted bitterness softened by liquorice; **b**20 full tasting notes because this old timer deserves it. **59.2%.** *Gordon & MacPhail.*

⠿ **Provenance Strathisla Over 10 Years** dist Winter 92 bott Autumn 03 **(86) n**21 light and distinctively floral; intriguing mix of rice paper and tangerine; **t**20 surprising early oak arrival. Pretty warming too; **f**23 comes into its own with a fabulous malty texture offering extra dimension to the massive cocoa: not unlike a malt chocolate night drink; **b**22 brilliant mouthfeel combines well with a delicious finish. **46%. nc ncf.**

Scotch Malt Whisky Society "58.5" 32 Years Old dist Nov 69, bott Aug 02 **(85) n**23 enormous clean oloroso (one suspects through the oaky haze), sprinkled with spice and generously topped with top-rate old bourbon; **t**24 an exhibition of clean fruit and punchy spice with chewy burnt toffee for good measure; **f**18 threatens to fall off the tracks age-wise and does so, spectacularly: slightly sappy and bitter; **b**20 fun at the beginning while it lasted. **56.4%**

Signatory Rare Reserve Strathisla 33 Years Old cask 2372, dist 11/04/68, bott 23/07/01 **(88) n**23 **t**22 **f**21 **b**22. A pretty tired dram, but one with enough character and complexity to ensure a long and enjoyable mouthful. **50.2%.** 148 bottles.

Ultimate Selection Strathisla 1989 dist 7/6/89, bott 14/1/03 **(79) n**19 **t**21 **f**19 **b**20. Pleasant, sweet and malty. **43%.** *Van Wees NL.*

STRATHMILL
Speyside, 1891. Diageo. Working.

Strathmill Aged 12 Years db **(79) n**21 **t**21 **f**18 **b**19. A big malt for a normally light, delicate Speysider. Brilliant spice and rich mouthfeel but fatally let down by caramel-toffee. Strathmill, but not as God intended. **43%.** *Flora and Fauna range.*

Connoisseurs Choice Strathmill 1991 (71) n17 **t**20 **f**17 **b**17. Strangely bitter and off-key. **40%.** *Gordon & MacPhail.*

⠿ **Duncan Taylor Strathmill 1975 Aged 28 Years** cask 1891 **(79) n**18 **t**21 **f**20 **b**20. Some lovely nougat-honey moments, but also hot and ungainly: the make is too delicate to take the weight. **48.7%**

The Old Malt Cask Bottling Strathmill Aged 11 Years dist Oct 88, bott Jun 00 **(85) n**20 **t**21 **f**22 **b**22. A real odd-ball of a Strathmill, not entirely in keeping with malt of this age from there. But its propensity for leading the tastebuds up blind alleys and into otherwise uncharted territory makes for intriguing drinking. Love it! No added colouring. **50%. nc ncf sc.** *Douglas Laing. 420 bottles.*

The Old Malt Cask Strathmill Aged 39 Years sherry, dist Apr 62, bott May 01 **(82) n**20 **t**19 **f**23 **b**20. Powerful oak and sherry dominate. Just enough sweetness and malty follow-through on the finish to make this a good 'un. **45.2%. nc ncf sc.** *Douglas Laing. 270 bottles.*

⠿ **Old Malt Cask Strathmill Aged 40 Years** dist Apr 63, bott Aug 03 **(89) n**22 the nose drips antiquity buoyed by an almost decadent barley-rich charisma; distinct weighty oaky tones softened with dried dates and sweet barley; **t**23 no shortage of oomph amid the sweet, caramelised biscuit note; **f**22 sweet vanilla abounds but the barley does battle through for a lengthy finish that eschews complexity for effect; **b**22 on the edge of going over the top, we have almost nerveless brinkmanship here. Quite superb malt and rare to see such a light and delicate dram last the pace. **50%. nc ncf sc.** *Douglas Laing.*

Old Masters Strathmill 1992 bott 03 **(81) n**19 **t**22 **f**20 **b**20. Real high-propane, heavy-duty Speysider at its very maltiest. **64.2%. nc ncf.** *James MacArthur.*

TALISKER
Highland (Island–Skye), 1832. Diageo. Working.

Talisker Ten Years Old db **(86) n**22 Cumberland sausage and kippers side by side; **t**21 worrying shades of toffee arrive early on; **f**22 the big peat explosion but muffled, dulled by caramel; **b**21 the natural brilliance of this whisky gets it into the high 80s, but someone has gone nuts with the caramel machine here and done their best to flatten those uniquely massive notes that set this distillery apart. As a rule, I give 25 for the finish as a matter of course as normally it is the greatest in the world. **45.8%**

Talisker Aged 20 Years db **(95) n**24 an exceptional sherry butt that brilliantly allows full scope for the spicy excesses of the distillery to spill over: sensational; **t**24 almost unreal marriage of ultra rich and clean sherry with explosive peat. The usual Talisker viciousness with the sherry somehow hanging on for the ride; **f**23 quietens to something approaching mere fireworks with the spices now being slightly subdued by the fruit ... though not quite; **b**24 I have been tasting Talisker for 28 years. This is the best bottling ever. Miss this and your life will be incomplete. **62%**

⋰⋱ **Talisker 20 Years Old** db bott 03 **(93) n**21 slightly fruity, smoky, but just a shade limp; **t**24 simply magnificent: subtle oils help control the explosion of peaty spice. There is a development of some single distillation Demerara rum characterist as well as natural caramel and coffee; in the background is a delicate fruitiness (sultana maybe) and a hint of nut; **f**24 continues for ever. Just more of the same, but in a less conspicuous manner; **b**24 this is major whisky for most the demanding of palates. Absolutely no signs of weakness for its age. **58.8%**

Talisker Aged 25 Years db **(83) n**20 **t**23 **f**20 **b**20. The 20-y-o is simply too hard an act to follow: the nose is surprisingly flat, weighted down by oak. The palate is superb with those spices gathering intensity to a brilliant crescendo. But then it all dies rapidly. By no means a bad whisky, but once you have experienced the 20-y-o... **59.9%**

Talisker 1989 Distillers Edition Double Matured Jerez Amoroso finish, bott 02 **(87) n**22 fruity, Turkish delight and soft smoke; **t**22 spicy and lively with good malt-fruit interplay; **f**21 winey notes replace the usual kaboom you get at this point: succulent redberries and vanilla... and toffee...; **b**22 an enjoyable dram that you wouldn't recognise as a Talisker unless you read the label. But doubtless quality, nonetheless. **45.8%**

Talisker Limited Edition For Sale Only at Distillery db **(88) n**23 kumquats, spices, red liquorice candy and biting peat; **t**22 searing peat and sweet malt: vanilla gangs up impressively **f**21 long, incredibly malty and sweet, almost gristy in style; **b**22 this is one heck of a dram: fresh yet explosive, sweet yet deep and chewy. The last time I tasted this I nearly died the very same day and was ill and unable to work for the next nine months. If you are reading this book, then it was only a coincidence ... **60%**

⋰⋱ **Black Cuillin 8 Years Old** db **(78) n**19 **t**21 **f**18 **b**20. Pleasant initial peatless sweet malt but lacking telling depth or cutting edge. **40%.** *The Highlands and Islands Scotch Whisky Co.*

Old Malt Cask Tactical Aged 20 Years **(62) n**12 **t**18 **f**16 **b**16. Sulphured sherry butt sadly ruins it. **50%.** *Douglas Laing & Co.*

Old Malt Cask Tactical Aged 22 Years **(90) n**23 rich, spicy honey and well-aged, this aroma offers brilliant balance and magnificent character. The smoke has softened towards something like dry Darjeeling while the sweetness also carries hints of raisins: really quite lovely. Dissolve-in-the-mouth malt carries softly honied riches; **t**23 the peat forms a base layer of its own that now and again raises to intermingle with the higher malty-honey notes; **f**22 back to Darjeeling with a hint of some medium roast Costa Rica coffee; **b**22 pretty long and satisfying. Is this where Talisker meets Highland Park? Quite amazing stuff with heaps of honied character but with a disarming peatiness that has lost its younger fizz. **50%. nc ncf.**

Old Malt Cask Tactical Aged 31 Years (73) n19 **t**18 **f**18 **b**18. Finished in sherry cask for six months. Like watching a great old boxer, slugging it out for the very last time when clearly past it. Even so, shows a little of the old magic early on. Doesn't name distillery on label. **50%.** *Douglas Laing.*

⠿ **Scotch Malt Whisky Society Cask 14.8 Aged 15 Years 1989 (91) n**21 a striking, surprisingly oily peat kick with background fruit; **t**24 soft, gristy malt at first and then a mind-blowing explosion of peat that appears to be out of control until a bizarre citrus-fruity-oaky note appears; **f**23 the oil returns, the peat backs off and a Santos coffee dryness appears; **b**23 a Talisker displaying all its temperamental hallmarks but though showing signs of brilliance just falls short of greatness. **58.6%. nc ncf sc.**

TAMDHU
Speyside, 1897. Edrington. Working.

Tamdhu db (87) n23 grassy, fresh, juicy, youthful, boiled fruit candy, coke smoke: pure Speyside in a sniff; **t**22 very light malt, extremely clean, newly cut grass, deliciously chewy; **f**21 perhaps a hint of toffee but the malty show rumbles on with good weight and late burst of non-peated smoke; **b**21 nothing like as oily as of old, but charmingly refreshing, non-threatening and enormously enjoyable. **40%**

Adelphi Tamdhu 1967 34 Years Old cask 7 **(85) n**23 seductive honey, some vanilla bite; **t**21 intense malt and spice; **f**20 the oak is surprisingly shy for a Tamdhu of this age; **b**21 a warming dram with an even spread of oak. **49.9%. sc.**

Adelphi Tamdhu 12 Years Old cask 4593, dist 90, bott 02 **(89) n**23 I think we have found Tamdhu's nose at optimum age: so honied, clean and rich! **t**22 silky malt, a hint of smoke and honey and a little bite; **f**22 rich biscuity malt and very mildly molassed sugar; **b**22 a different Tamdhu: big but less oil and more sweet malt. **53.6%**

Adelphi Tamdhu 15 Years Old cask 9032, dist 85, bott 00 **(84) n**19 **t**22 **f**22 **b**21. Fabulous malty thrust at the middle, a bit ragged around the edges. **55.3%**

⠿ **Duncan Taylor Tamdhu 1969 Aged 34 Years** cask 7314 **(83) n**21 **t**21 **f**20 **b**21. Oily, malt younger than its years and sweet vanilla; attractive whisky displaying little sign of great age. **42.6%**

Gordon & MacPhail Tamdhu 1960 (85) n21 big, big oak: we are talking sap amid the sweet malt. But it works; **t**22 beautifully complex: sweet malt battles with very deep oak, neither quite getting the upper hand; **f**21 remains oaky, but a good traditional Tamdhu oiliness keeps the malt on course; **b**21 talk about brinkmanship. The oak is way over the top, but in this case the intensity of the oily malt is such that it leads to a really fascinating dual. Not for the purists, perhaps. But grizzly, macho entertainment. **40%**

Gordon & MacPhail Tamdhu 1961 (83) n20 **t**22 **f**21 **b**20. The oak influence is such, we are talking very decent bourbon! **40%**

⠿ **Hart Brothers Tamdhu Aged 33 Years** dist Nov 69, bott May 03 **(77) n**20 **t**20 **f**18 **b**19. The old tangerines on the nose is intriguing, but the immediate sweet and chewy bourbon theme suggests big age. **40.5%**

The MacPhail's Collection Tamdhu 8 Years Old (80) n19 **t**22 **f**19 **b**20. Grassy, bright and mouthwatering. **40%.** *Gordon & MacPhail.*

⠿ **MacPhail's Collection Tamdhu 30 Years Old (90) n**21 old bananas and leather; **t**23 just dreamy honeycomb that melts into every tastebud while the oak adds backbone; **f**23 nearer old bourbon than malt, we now have some sumptuous red liquorice sweetening the drier, toasty oak; **b**23 not getting away from this being pretty exhausted, but it still conjures some bitter-sweet magic. Excellent. **43%**. Gordon & MacPhail.

Old Malt Cask Tamdhu Aged 23 Years dist Feb 77, bott Jun 00 **(89)** **n**22 **t**22 **f**23 **b**22. Steady, top-quality spicy malt. **50%. nc ncf**. Douglas Laing. 301 bottles.

Old Malt Cask Tamdhu Aged 34 Years dist Oct 66, bott Oct 00 **(77)** **n**20 **t**20 **f**18 **b**19. Marmalade spread thinly over slightly burnt toast; some fine, delicate peat creeps in. **50%. nc ncf**. Douglas Laing. 198 bottles.

Old Malt Cask Tamdhu Aged 34 Years dist Jan 67, bott Sep 01 **(87)** **n**23 10-y-o top dog bourbon from the middle of the warehouse; **t**22 sweet, bourbony, toffee-rich and chewy, excellent oak control; **f**21 drier oak; **b**21 the perfect malt for bourbon lovers. **50%**. Douglas Laing. 186 bottles.

Peerless Tamdhu 1968 cask 4104, dist Jun 68 34-y-o **(88)** **n**22 very gently smoked and clean; **t**22 dissolving malt, sharp and fresh; **f**22 lovely malty finale with a soft wisper of peat once again; **b**22 a straight-down-the-line, high-quality whisky. **40.1%**. Duncan Taylor & Co.

TAMNAVULIN
Speyside. 1966. Whyte and Mackay.

Tamnavulin 12 Years Old db **(79)** **n**19 **t**20 **f**21 **b**19. Quite weighty for a Speysider with a deliciously massive malty kick. But missing out on complexity somewhat. **40%**

Tamnavulin Stillman's Dram 30 Years Old db **(87)** **n**22 subtle hints of bourbon amid a rigid malt frame; **t**23 again the malt is big and sweetens by the second. The soft oiliness helps the bourbony sweetness cling to the palate: really lovely; **f**21 short but clean; **b**21 a great example of when bourbon meets malt. Not enormously complex, just enjoyable. **45%**

Gordon & MacPhail Tamnavulin 1988 Cask casks 4706–9, dist 6/12/88, bott May 97 **(83)** **n**20 **t**22 **f**20 **b**21. Buttery, soft and oily, the gentle malt spreads evenly over the palate. **58.9%**

⋅⋅⋅ **Old Malt Cask Tamnavulin Aged 13 Years** dist Nov 90, bott Feb 04 **(88)** **n**21 some stewed apples go well with the intense barley **t**23 really beautifully weighted malt with just slightly gristy sub-plot allows the barley full play; the oiliness is almost Caol Ila-ish in effect **f**22 slightly fresh bready with gathering vanilla and spice **b**22 thoroughly enjoyable and tastebud provoking. **50% nc ncf sc** Douglas Laing.

⋅⋅⋅ **Provenance Tamnavulin Over 10 Years** dist Autumn 93 bott Winter 04 **(81)** **n**20 **t**21 **f**20 **b**20 if you wanted to know exactly what Tamna offers at this age from decent bourbon cask, you have a spot-on example here. Weighty, a touch oily, malt intense with oak involvement from the nose onwards. No off notes, but minimal complexity, either. Enjoyable blending fodder. **46% nc ncf** Douglas McGibbon & Co.

TEANINICH
Highland (Northern), 1817. Diageo. Working.

Teaninich Aged 10 Years db **(84)** **n**21 **t**21 **f**21 **b**21. A very even, ultra-malty, outwardly light dram with some pleasantly lurking spice. Flora and Fauna bottlings I have tasted over the years have ranged from 82–84 in marks, being similar in clean, malty style but varying in degree of oiliness. **43%**. The notes above are from the latest bottling, L15N00298941.

Teaninich Aged 23 Years Rare Malts Selection dist 73 db **(74)** **n**19 **t**20 **f**17 **b**18. Lightly smoked and sweet, but disappointingly lacking in direction. **57.1%**

Adelphi Teaninich 31 Years Old cask 3576, dist 71, bott 02 **(82) n**20 **t**22 **f**20 **b**20. Bold and oaky with firm, fruity body. **57.8%**

Berrys' Own Selection Teaninich 1973 bott 02 **(85) n**19 subtly smoked, though a tad off balance; **t**22 a real flavour free-for-all. No discipline at all as fudgy, oaky, raisiny, smoky notes go on a walkabout. Some spice enters the fray; **f**22 remains busy and disorganised; **b**22 a roller-coaster malt that doesn't quite settle or decide what it wants to be. Softly smoked but the complexity seems to lead to cul-de-sacs. Even so, a real roof-of-mouth-licking dram. **43%**

Chieftain's Choice Teaninich Port Barrel aged 16 years (Double Wood Maturation) **(85) n**20 delicate fruit; incredibly light with unripe bananas; **t**23 indescribably complex with a teasing light barley being flanked by astonishing fruit and spice. A real silky mouthful that refuses to settle – as busy as any whisky gets; **f**21 much closer to a Jamaican pot-still rum than a single malt. Incredible riches! **b**21 an absolute one-off – so, so different. The port barrel has moved this malt into a weird and wonderful dimension where the port is hardly noticeable, but rum is!! This job doesn't get easier. **43%**. *Ian MacLeod.*

Chieftain's Choice Teaninich Aged 19 Years dist 1980 **(87) n**23 honied, rich and astonishingly sweet with a pinch of peat; **t**22 big oak arrival, more honey and beautifully silky; **f**21 big vanilla and drying oak, some late, lingering peat; **b**21 worth finding for the nose alone. **43%**. *Ian Macleod.*

Chieftain's Choice Teaninich Aged 21 Years dist 1979 **(73) n**18 **t**19 **f**18 **b**18. Good spice but a little dull. **43%**. *Ian Macleod.*

Connoisseurs Choice Teaninich 1975 (72) n22 **t**17 **f**16 **b**17. Great nose, some ginger on the finish but otherwise dead in the bottle. **40%**. *Gordon & MacPhail.*

Connoisseurs Choice Teaninich 1982 (90) n23 ginger, a hint of smoke, salty; **t**23 lively, salty, big malt kick and sweet; **f**22 levels out but the vanilla and malt keep going strong; **b**22 wonderfully complex and dangerously moreish. **40%**. *Gordon & MacPhail.*

⋰ **Connoisseurs Choice Teaninich 1983 (85) n**22 pears and apricots form a fresh, fruity facade **t**22 delightful delivery of malt backed by soft spice **f**20 sweet barley grist and bitter burned toast **b**21 refreshing and never dull **46%** *Gordon and MacPhail*

⋰ **Dun Bheagan Teaninich 1984 Aged 18 Years** sherry wood bott 11 Sep 03 **(94) n**24 what a brilliant array of contrary tones: an aroma that spans absolutely pristine sherry to diced fresh apple with a ripple of honey and the most distant smoke imaginable. Just a touch of bourbon for good measure. Stick your head in a trough of this and you won't re-surface for some weeks; **t**24 raspberry and cream Swiss roll, but only after there has been a fanfare of rampant barley; **f**23 elegant oak and soft fruits; **b**23 always had a soft spot for this distillery. But when it appears like this, one can only swoon. **59%**. *William Maxwell.*

Hart Brothers Teaninich Aged 13 Years dist 83 **(84) n**19 **t**22 **f**21 **b**22. A mildly butyric nose is the only blemish on an otherwise resounding malt, one that has a sensuous copper-rich mouthfeel and the usual hint of honey. **43%**

Hedges & Butler Teaninich Aged 21 Years cask 13668, dist 79, bott 00 **(88) n**22 **t**22 **f**21 **b**23. Bottled just in time before the oak took hold. **43%**. *Ian Macleod.*

⋰ **Scotch Malt Whisky Society Cask 59.25 Aged 20 Years 1983 (83) n**19 **t**22 **f**21 **b**21. Unusually simplistic for this distillery but the barley content is clean and faultless. **59.25%. nc ncf sc.**

TOBERMORY

Highland (Island–Mull), 1795. Burn Stewart. Working.

⋰ **Ledaig Peated 7 Years Old** db **(80) n**19 **t**21 **f**19 **b**21. Young and a little raw in parts, but the sweet chewability of the smoke is delicious. Drops points though for a dumbing down caramel effect. **43%.**

Ledaig Aged 15 Years db **(90)** n*23* honeyed, waxed floors, silky barley and even the peat has sheen: unique; **t***23* melts in the mouth and just crumbles on the tastebuds. The peat lands like snowflakes; **f***22* more gentle honey and slow development of vanilla; **b***22* beautiful whisky from one of the most temperamental distilleries – and ages. **43%**

Ledaig Aged 20 Years db **(86)** n*22* thoroughly well-oaked with a trace of waxy honey, deep and softly smoked; **t***22* intensely sweet with a swelling of soft peat. The sheer intensity creeps up on you; **f***20* medium length with intense barley, layers of smoke and clean oak; **b***22* a lazy, laid-back, subtle malt that is much more heavily peated than it originally seems. **43%**

⠿ **Ledaig 1974 Vintage** db **(77)** n*20* t*20* f*18* b*19*. Good looking, sweet but overly polite peat and a bit of a stuffed shirt. Bottled some time ago; some bottles still doing the rounds. **43%**

Ledaig 1979 Vintage db **(74)** n*17* t*22* f*18* b*17*. By no means a classic Ledaig and one quite lacking in telling peatiness. Only the big arrival on the palate saves it from being really disappointing by Ledaig standards. **43%**

Ledaig Light db **(84)** n*21* t*22* f*21* b*20*. A fabulously youthful dram, obviously with a lot of growing up to do – especially on the nose which introduces an amusing tequila note. That said, the magnitude of the peat, the oiliness and sweetness of the body and the clarity of the malt makes this one to go to Korea just to find. High-quality malt especially, us bachelors please note, for women – and great fun to boot! An idiosyncratic bottle I'd pour for anybody, anytime. **42%**. *Korea.*

Ledaig Sherry Malt db **(73)** n*18* t*19* f*18* b*18*. There are some powerful forces here refusing to gel. A bit of a mish-mash. **42%**. *Japan/Asia Pacific.*

Cadenhead's Ledaig 10 Years Old dist 92, bott 03/03 **(84)** n*19* t*23* f*21* **b***21*. Not quite on top form: the nose has an off-beat and there hasn't been enough oak in the cask to effect sufficient complexity. That said, pretty fresh, green, chewy and more-ish stuff. **59.9%**

⠿ **Chieftain's Ledaig 31 Years Old** sherry hogshead **(94)** n*24* strikingly beautiful with a faint smokiness linking arms with the faultless and intense grape **t***23* like jewels glittering in a golden crown juicy grape fills the mouth as intense, crisp barley and sweeter smoke add wonderfully to the clutter, the start of something spicy; **f***23* a little toffee intervenes as the grape wins back control for a long, gently peated finale that can be counted over a great many waves; **b***24* an essay in depth and balance; by far the best Ledaig I've come across since the late 1980s. **54.8%.**

Connoisseurs Choice Ledaig 1990 **(77)** n*18* t*20* f*20* b*19*. Honied and waxy, but fails to develop. **40%**. *Gordon & MacPhail.*

⠿ **Gent Malt Whisky Festival Ledaig 1993** bott Mar 04 **(89)** n*21* young, a playful hint of smoke, clean maltiness with minimum oak intervention; **t***23* the smoky start vanishes, then a mouthwatering, lip-smacking delivery of fresh, grassy barley that has outwardly retained its youth but reacted with the oak just enough to allow a cocoa dusting to the developing honey; **f***22* a hint of vanilla and butter with that cocoa but the barley retains its freshness; **b***23* a superb little bottling extracted directly from cask at the first Belgium International Whisky Festival showing how a decent old cask can spring a surprise. **56%.** *Maison du Whisky, Belgium.*

Gordon & MacPhail Ledaig 1975 **(87)** n*23* absolutely glorious: trademark honey and soft peat abound while the vanilla cushions all impact; **t***23* honey-heather, waxy with a big surge of malt and oak; **f***20* thins rapidly but some gentle spices arrive; **b***21* a honied and waxy little charmer wth just the faintest hint of peat. A delight. **40%**

⠿ **Iona Atoll** **(69)** n*16* t*18* f*18* b*17.* Young and for all the heavy peating the lack of structure, plus the fact this is not a particularly well-made batch of whisky, cannot be disguised. **40%**

⫶⫶⫶ **Old Masters Ledaig 10 Years Old (82) n**_20_ **t**_21_ **f**_21_ **b**_20_. The superbly rich, malty-dark fudge, roasty middle and curtain call makes up for some overly youthful smudges. **56.7%.** *James MacArthur.*

Tobermory Aged 10 Years db **(75) n**_17_ **t**_19_ **f**_20_ **b**_19_. Delightful custardy finish. **40%**

TOMATIN
Speyside, 1897. Working.

Tomatin Aged 12 Years db **(73) n**_20_ **t**_18_ **f**_17_ **b**_18_. Some seriously weird sherry influence has done no favours to this bottling. I can't believe it: Tomatin makes one of Speyside's most consistently brilliant drams, full of malty, grassy promise especially when matured in bourbon and then ... this!!! Drinkable, but for us Tomatin lovers just so hugely disappointing. **40%**

Connoisseurs Choice Tomatin 1968 (69) n_16_ **t**_20_ **f**_16_ **b**_17_. Disappointingly flat. **40%.** *Gordon & MacPhail.*

⫶⫶⫶ **Hart Brothers Tomatin Aged 37 Years** dist Nov 65, bott May 03 **(84) n**_19_ **t**_23_ **f**_22_ **b**_20_. Plenty of grey hairs but bourbony-malty middle is a treat. **47.2%**

Old Malt Cask Tomatin Aged 23 Years dist Nov 76, bott Feb 00 **(80) n**_20_ **t**_21_ **f**_19_ **b**_20_. Big, sweet and spicy. **50%. nc ncf.** *Douglas Laing. 293 bottles.*

James Macarthur's Tomatin 12 Year Old (84) n_21_ **t**_22_ **f**_20_ **b**_21_. Silky, malty ultra-sweet and very typical version of a very sound Speysider. **43%**

Old Malt Cask Tomatin Aged 33 Years Sherry dist Jan 67, bott Jun 00 **(72) n**_18_ **t**_19_ **f**_18_ **b**_17_. Either too dry or syrupy: not my type of sherry. **50%. nc ncf.** *Douglas Laing. 594 bottles.*

Old Malt Cask Tomatin Aged 36 Years dist Jan 65, bott Feb 01 **(88) n**_22_ **t**_22_ **f**_21_ **b**_23_. Beautifully complex, balanced and in improbably good condition for its great age. **49.7%. nc ncf.** *Douglas Laing. 216 bottles.*

Old Malt Cask Tomatin Aged 38 Years dist Sep 62, bott Jan 01 **(81) n**_20_ **t**_22_ **f**_19_ **b**_20_. A frail malt that has maintained its posture and elegance despite the passing years. **41%. nc ncf.** *Douglas Laing. 186 bottles.*

Peerless Tomatin 1965 cask 1867 dist Jan 65 **(72) n**_20_ **t**_18_ **f**_16_ **b**_18_. Big, oily and oaked, but the nose sparkles. **49.7%.** *Duncan Taylor & Co Ltd.*

Peerless Tomatin 1965 cask 1909 dist Jan 65 37-y-o **(81) n**_20_ **t**_21_ **f**_20_ **b**_20_. Heaps of natural toffee and vanilla: well-aged and well-behaved. Bourbony and honied. **48%.** *Duncan Taylor & Co.*

Single Barrel Collection Tomatin 1988 cask 1967, dist Jun 88, bott 01 **(90) n**_23_ **t**_23_ **f**_21_ **b**_23_. This is about as good a Tomatin as you are likely to find. If you are looking for a study of balance and grace, this is it. **56.2%. sc nc ncf.** *Germany.*

TOMINTOUL
Speyside, 1965. Angus Dundee. Working.

Tomintoul Aged 10 Years db **(79) n**_20_ **t**_21_ **f**_19_ **b**_19_. A fresh, clean, malty dram but leading to toffee fudge simplicity. **40%**

Tomintoul Aged 16 Years db **(88) n**_21_ Weetabix in full fat milk with crushed raisins; **t**_23_ magnificent mouth arrival: as soft as you could pray for. Toffee-apple and malt melt in the mouth while some crisper, more mouthwatering barley notes filter through; **f**_22_ a long finale that remains chewy and soft; **b**_22_ "The gentle dram" claims the label, and so it is. In fact, few Scotch malts can match this whisky's uncanny ability to dissolve on contact with the tastebuds. Excellent bitter-sweet balance, though it tends towards sweetness with the oak kept at a safe distance until the very end. For all the toffee-effect, a real treat. A deadly more-ish dram with all the deftness of a Zola lob. **40%**

⫶⫶⫶ **Tomintoul Aged 27 Years** db **(86) n**_21_ plum jam on toast with unsalted butter and barley; **t**_23_ stunning mouth arrival, genuinely silky and yielding with a light arrival of very fresh and clean honey, apparent for only a few seconds before some oaky vanilla turns up; the most gentle of spices further the complexity; **t**20 one or two bitter, burnt currant notes which work in context with the sweeter build-up; a degree of caramel sadly blunts the finale; **b**22 an accomplished malt that shows few cracks despite the obvious great age for a Speysider. Further evidence that this is a very impressive distillery with more under the bonnet than many once thought. Would be a cracker at a fuller strength and perhaps colour-free ... **40%**

Adelphi Tomintoul 23 Years Old cask 7320, dist 76, bott 99 **(84) n**21 **t**22 **f**21 **b**20. Enormously sweet and delicious with added coal smoke. **54.3%. sc.**

Adelphi Tomintoul 34 Years Old cask 532, dist 66, bott 00 **(89) n**23 **t**23 **f**21 **b**22. Perhaps a couple of years too old for being a true classic: pretty fabulous anyway. **52.1%**

⁙ **Adelphi Tomintoul 1967** cask 4479 **(78) n**19 **t**20 **f**19 **b**20. Feels its age. **47%**

⁙ **Adelphi Tomintoul 1967** cask 4481 **(85) n**22 soft, clean hints of bourbon; highly attractive; **t**21 a bit sharp and fiery but the malt really does sweetly blossom; **f**21 soft vanilla mingles with spice; **b**21 a malt hanging on for dear life, but succeeds rather attractively where a cask two down the line fails. **47.3%**

Gordon & MacPhail Tomintoul 1967 (84) n23 **t**21 **f**20 **b**20. The clean sherry nose is classically majestic, even offering stewed tomato! But after the early initial sweet and rich flavour arrival becomes rather too bitter. Shame, but a real honey for the nose alone. **40%**

Old Malt Cask Tomintoul 34 Years Old dist Feb 66, bott June 00 **(78) n**19 **t**21 **f**18 **b**20. A curious one, especially on the tangy nose and finish

TORMORE
Speyside, 1960. Allied. Working.

Tormore 12 Years Old db **(75) n**19 **t**20 **f**18 **b**18. Greatly improved on the old days: much more yielding and accessible now, even boasting a touch of honey. **40%**

Blackadder Tormore 1990 Raw Cask cask 1964, dist 2/2/90, bott Apr 02 **(79) n**19 **t**21 **f**19 **b**20. Marzipan and sugar. And something to chew. **65.9%. nc ncf.**

Provenance Spring Distillation Tormore Over 10 Years dist Spring 90, bott Autumn 00 **(78) n**17 **t**22 **f**20 **b**19. The tasting notes on the bottle state marzipan, and they are right. Not the rubbishy British variety, but the almost unsugared stuff from Lübeck. Slightly toasty and some toffee apparent. A little ragged and bitter at the finale but otherwise very good. **43%**. *Douglas McGibbon & Co.*

Ultimate Selection Tormore 1989 sherry butt 920259, dist 11/5/89, bott 13/11/00 **(72) n**17 **t**19 **f**18 **b**18. Sugary sweet and not quite hitting the heights. *Van Wees NL.*

TULLIBARDINE
Highland (Perthshire), 1949. Tullibardine Ltd. Working.

Tullibardine 10 Years Old db **(86) n**21 really lovely hint of Seville oranges refreshes an otherwise big malty theme; **t**22 voluptuous mouthfeel, clean malt and gentle spices; **f**21 good oak adding to the spice and upping the weight with a light dusting of cocoa; **b**22 a simple, superbly weighted and charming dram with a lovely mouth presence. **40%**

Tullibardine Stillman's Dram Aged 30 Years db **(88) n**22 full, fat, fabulously fruity, with a tun-room aroma; **t**23 lush and oily; oak-induced spice topped by demerara sweetness; **f**21 long, intense barley lingering on with a tinge of oak and molassed raisins; **b**22 a complex, hearty and stylish dram. **45%**

⋄ **Tullibardine Vintage 1993** db bott 03 **(79)** n21 t22 f18 b18. Lots of early spicy fruit and vanilla but, sadly, the caramel dumbs it down and embitters it. Just brilliant to see this fabulous malt back on the market. But one this rich and rewarding should always come as natural and pure as the water on which the distillery sits ... **40%**

Adelphi Tullibardine 35 Years Old cask 2122, dist 66, bott 01 **(78)** n17 t23 f19 b19. Big, massively sherried and salty. Some will flip and call this the best thing they have ever tasted. I have a slightly more reserved feel for it: for all its many highlights, the nose is poor and the balance seems to have drifted. **54.6%**

Blackadder Raw Cask Tullibardine 1966 sherry cask 2118, dist 23 April 66, bott May 02 **(73)** n19 t19 f18 b17. The pine from over-ageing makes this more like Swedish aquavit than Scotch. **52.1%. nc ncf sc.**

⋄ **Connoisseurs Choice Tullibardine 1994 (94)** n24 stupendous aroma of juicy white grape and near-exploding gooseberries, almost too fresh and mouthwatering to be true; t24 what a treat! The intensity of the barley mixed with the juicy fruit misses only some soft smoke for harmony ... until it arrives; f22 gentle oils roll over the hint of smoke and drying, vanilla-rich oak; b24 when they closed this distillery soon after the barrel was filled, I was left scratching my head in perplexity. On this mouthwatering evidence, my belief in this distillery was by no means misplaced...**46%** *Gordon and MacPhail*

⋄ **Old Malt Cask Tullibardine Aged 14 Years** dist Jun 89, bott Jan 04 **(90)** n23 steaming suet pudding with freshly mashed barley malt; clean and sharp; t24 astonishingly clean and refined barley of the very top order; the mouth waters as the malt then sensual spices play havoc with the tastebuds; f21 slightly on the bitter side, a cross between European bitters and pungent marmalade; b22 a refreshing and at times explosive concoction. A minor gem like this just makes you wonder at the folly of this distillery being closed for so long. **50%. nc ncf sc.** *Douglas Laing. 360 bottles.*

UNSPECIFIED SINGLE MALTS (Campbeltown)
Open Championship 2000 Bottling Campbeltown Single Malt from Luvians (*see* Springbank)

UNSPECIFIED SINGLE MALTS (Highland)
Asda Single Malt (see Douglas MacNiven)

⋄ **"As We Get It" Aged 8 Years (85)** n18 not the best sherry butt but characteristic enough to offer a roughhouse of bitter-sweet oaky Demerara notes. Finesse-free; t23 the arrival is robust with a chunky toffee-apple core and massive, oily barley. Beware: this one has knuckles; f22 at last some sanity as the barley notes dip and vanilla forms an alliance with some improbable and very late honey. Spices, naturally; b22 Ker-pow, zap, ka-boom...Batman stuff for a good punch up on the tastebuds. Despite the distant threat of sulphur, appeals to the Millwall supporter within me ... **58.5%.** *Ian MacLeod.*

Douglas MacNiven Highland Single Malt 12 Years Old (80) n20 t21 f19 b20. Pretty compact maltiness with some developing fruit and demerara sugar. Guess what I think about the caramel ...? **40%.** *Asda UK.*

⋄ **Dun Bheagan Highland Single Malt 8 Years old (89)** n22 fruity, a shade oaky with unbelievably intense yet clean barley: quite dazzling, in its own simplistic way; t22 lush, barley-rich and just so amazingly salivating; all that and still it has an extra oaky-fruity weightiness, too; f22 a touch of lingering cocoa-oakiness; b23 further evidence, were it needed, that fabulous, nigh-on faultless single malt whisky doesn't have to come with a two-figure age statement. **43%**

Dun Bheagan Highland Aged 15 Years (82) n19 t22 f21 b20. Enormously sweet and malty with long toffee finish. **46%. ncf.** *William Maxwell.*

Glen Andrew Highland Single Malt 10 Years Old (87) n*22* apple pie and custard; t*22* wonderfully mouthfilling and chewy: great character. f*22* the malty sweetness filters through and works well with developing spice; b*21* what a pleasant, fun, unpretentious malt. More, please! **40%.** *Highland & Islands Whisky Co.*

Glenbeg Single Highland Malt (82) n*21* t*21* f*20* b*20*. Young, tasty stuff that might be tastier still without the evident toffee. **40%**

Glenfoyle Highland Single Malt Aged 12 Years (82) n*20* t*22* f*20* b*20*. Barley sugar on the nose; to taste clean malt, rich in texture and sweetens by the second. The finish is a bit fudgy. **40%.** *Longman Distillers for Tesco UK.*

Glenfoyle Highland Single Malt Aged 17 Years dist 85 **(72)** n*17* t*19* f*18* b*18*. Sweet, ungainly and bitter towards the finish. I know those who love this style of malt – but not my cup of tea, so to speak. **40%.** *Longman Distillers for Tesco.*

Glen Gordon 1957 Single Highland Malt (88) n*23* beautiful spices dart out from the rich sherry; t*22* intense from the start, the spice bringing with it dry oak and a hint of liquorice; f*21* pretty dry and tired around the edges, but still impressive; b*22* that supreme Glen Grant/Glenfarclas sherry style that displays sheer class despite the age. **40%**

⠿ **Ian MacLeod's "As We Get It"** (*see* As We Get It)

Inverey Single Highland Malt Aged 12 Years (78) n*20* t*20* f*18* b*20*. Subtle and satisfying. **40%.** *Marks & Spencer UK.*

Majestic Wine Warehouse Mature Highland Malt Aged 8 Years (77) n*20* t*20* f*19* b*18*. Decent malt struggles to penetrate the caramel. **40%.** *Majestic UK.*

McClelland's Highland Single Malt Sherry Cask (78) n*19* t*21* f*19* b*19*. Silky and succulent but limited complexity **40%.** *Morrison Bowmore.*

McClelland's Highland Single Malt Aged 10 Years (76) n*17* t*21* f*20* b*18*. A malty, spicy recovery after an indifferent start on the nose. Too sweet in places, though, and the balance suffers. **40%.** *Somerfield Stores UK.*

McClelland's Highland Single Malt 16 Years Old (79) n*20* t*21* f*19* b*19*. A rich dram with lots of chewability. **40%.** *Morrison Bowmore.*

MacLeod's Highland Aged 8 Years (*see* Glen Moray)

Safeway Highland Single Malt 12 Years Old (89) n*22* lemon, lime and kumquat softened by fresh-crushed barley; t*23* massive citrus character that is clean and mouthwatering. The malt almost crackles on the palate; f*22* genuinely lip-smacking and moreish with a late hint of smoke; b*22* a very impressive own-label brand that has a lot to say for itself. A gem of its genre – absolutely adore it! **40%.** *UK.*

Sainsbury's Single Highland Malt Aged 12 Years (84) n*21* t*23* f*19* b*21*. An impressively tempered dram allowing full vent to a complex range of malty-vanilla tones. Cut the finish-deadening caramel and it would be right up there. **40%.** *UK.*

Stronachie Single Highland Malt Aged 12 Years (82) n*18* t*21* f*22* b*21*. An enjoyably busy dram with impressive soft spice follow-through. The nose is so-so, but some decent esters make for a chewy mouthful. Very slightly smoked, but seeing how this is meant to be the spirit of a malt distillery closed in 1928 a little more peat wouldn't go amiss for authenticity's sake. **43%.** *A Dewar Rattray.*

Tantallan 10 Years Old Highland Single Malt (89) n*22* fresh figs and moist barley, a hint of clove; t*23* the nose tells you what's coming and there is no disappointment: massive malt surge, mouthwatering and refreshing; f*21* beautifully textured finish as the barley unites with the light oak; b*23* the sheer brilliance of this whisky is its simplicity. Limited colouring interference and a severe lack of sherry means that the barley can do as it pleases. And pleases, it does. **40%.** *The Vintage Malt Whisky Co.*

Waitrose 12 Years Old Highland Single Malt (72) n*18* t*20* f*17* b*17*. Some malty thrust, but the caramel is all-conquering. *Waitrose Stores. UK.*

Walker & Scott 12 Years Old Single Highland Malt (77) n*19* t*19* f*20* b*19*. Citrussy, but quite hot and furry. Decent late spice and mild honey thread. **40%**

Wm Morrison Highland Single Malt Aged 10 Years (80) n*21* t*21* f*18* b*20*. Really superb nose and mouth arrival but dulls as the oak and caramel combine. Overall, though, pretty good chewing whisky. *Morrison Supermarkets UK.*

UNSPECIFIED SINGLE MALTS (Island)

Majestic Wine Warehouses Island Single Malt 8 Years Old (88) n*24* a nigh-faultless, clean, crisp peat aroma dovetails some youngish oaky notes: really fabulous; t*22* complex interplay between fresh but mature sweet peat and first-class oak; f*20* dies slightly and becomes a little bitter as complexity is lost; b*22* although delivered to my tasting lab in May 2003, the bottler's date suggests early November 1999. Surely a malt as deliciously good as this hasn't been hanging around on the shelves that long? **40%**. *Majestic Wine Warehouses UK.*

Waitrose 10 Year Old Island from the Orkney Isles (87) n*22* surprisingly well-peated, really delicate; t*23* again the peat has a big input with some barley-sugar malt that is hard and flinty in contrast; f*20* soft oak, smoke, burnt honey and caramel; b*22* a seriously odd dram. Not even Highland Park is usually this peaty. Either we have a delightful, magnificent freak, or someone didn't change the filters after bottling the Islay – not! Either way, a real treat of a dram!! **40%**. *Waitrose Stores UK.*

UNSPECIFIED SINGLE MALTS (Islay)

Ardnave Single Islay Malt Aged 12 Years (88) n*22* clean, oily, intense malt with a mildly salty edge to the sweetness; t*23* glorious gathering of barley, sprinkled with light muscovado sugar, followed by delicate oak; f*21* mildly bitter by comparison, a hint of toffee but still the buttery malt battles through; b*22* there will be those who buy this as an Islay single malt disappointed that it is not bursting from the cork-top with peat. However true Islay-philes will recognise this as a really outstanding example of the unpeated variety: if this isn't Bruichladdich, then my name's Ricardo Patermismo. Having gone non-chill filtered, just wish they had the confidence to go non-coloured (I suspect). **41.2%. ncf.** *Grey Rodgers for Tesco UK.*

⋅∺⋅ **Dun Bheagan Islay Single Malt 8 Years old (91)** n*23* so this is what happens if you get your head stuck in a grist mill ... t*23* does any Islay come more silky than this? The young age allows for a wonderful horn-locking between frisky peat and fresh fruit. The result is salivating; f*22* a slight bitterness as some oak at last makes an appearance; the peat level lightens but never thinks of vanishing; b*23* when you get faultlessly clean and supremely made distillate, the matter of age seems to matter not. This is outstanding stuff. **43%**

⋅∺⋅ **Finlaggan Islay Single Malt 10 Years Old Lightly Peated (76)** n*20* t*19* f*19* b*18*. Promises something quite delicate and complex but is strangled by caramel. **40%**. *Vintage Malt Whisky Co.*

Finlaggen Islay Single Malt 17 Years Old (72) n*20* t*20* f*15* b*17*. Sweet and chewy, but lots of toffee drowning out the complexity. Can't say I'm that impressed. **46%**. *The Vintage Malt Whisky Co.*

Finlaggen Islay Single Malt 21 Years Old (75) n*20* t*19* f*18* b*18*. Some chewy moments, but overall strangely off-beam. **46%**. *The Vintage Malt Whisky Co.*

Finlaggen Old Reserve Islay Single Malt (94) n*23* big breakfast fruitiness (Old Preserve, more like), plus nuts and chocolate. What a start! t*23* fat mouth arrival, more chocolate and ... oh, peat, lashings of it; f*24* back to fruit again, then a chocolate mousse; all interlocked by peat. Brilliant; b*24* this is simply awesome. Someone has had access to one or two of the best casks the east coast of Islay has to offer. If you don't get a bottle of this, you'll regret it for the rest of your life. **40%**. *The Vintage Malt whisky Co.*

❖ **Glenscoma Single Cask Single Islay Malt 5 Years Old (85)** n*22* massive, high octane clean peat; t*22* crisp, semi-sweet peat with some grassy barley offering mouthwatering freshness; f*21* slightly dim but clean; b*20* one dimensional peat, but great fun. **46%**. *Scoma, Germany.*

The Ileach Peaty Islay Single Malt (94) n*24* a thick chunk of peat has been dissolved in my glass; t*24* the oil-peat-barley balance is spot on, as is the bitter-sweet tone: just stunning; f*23* the peat dissipates slowly to leave a slightly bitterish, oaky influence. But the spices compensate; b*23* couldn't be an Islay single malt, perchance? Fabulous stuff, a bottle of which should sit in every household cabinet. A wonder dram. **40%**. *The Highlands & Islands Scotch Whisky Co.*

The Islay Whisky Shop Islay Single Malt Aged 9 Years (85) n*21* clean, malty, soft vanilla; t*22* silky texture and intense malt: dissolves in the mouth and never becomes too sweet; f*21* vanilla and toffee; b*21* try and convince me this isn't a Bruichladdich.... **43%**. *Islay only.*

McClelland's Islay Single Malt (87) n*23* crisp, sea-breeze and kippery malt; t*21* sweet malt and banana, softly oiled and enormous barley character. The peat drifts serenely along; f*21* very light vanilla and fading peat; b*22* what a really elegant and gentle whisky this is, quite unlike what the nose at first suggests. A reflective dram. **40%**. *Morrison Bowmore.*

MacLeod's Islay 8-y-o (*see* Lagavulin)

Majestic Wine Warehouses Islay Malt 8 Years Old ("this whisky has been aged in oak casks at the distillery") **(89)** n*22* soft, creamy, clean peat; t*22* rich, oily, smoked malt, lazy vanilla tones; f*23* spice arrives as the textures changes from creamy to layered. With it comes a lovely bitter-sweet battle; b*22* so refreshing to find an Islay malt at this relatively young age. The marks would be higher still but for the caramel: 46% non-coloured, non-chill filtered? The mind boggles. This is sumptuous, top-drawer whisky by any standards: truly Majestic. **40%**. *UK.*

Marks & Spencer Islay Single Malt Aged 10 Years (86) n*23* the most delicate of peaty Islays: softly salted, almost crisp peat and malt, no more than a hint of oak. Just like being there; t*21* soft and very silky malt, then an oily-oaky dryness; f*21* remains dry at first, then sweet peat re-emerges; b*21* doesn't quite live up to the nose, but a lovely dram all the same and a decent example of its genre. **40%**. *For Marks & Spencer UK.*

Old Masters Islay 1992 cask 3200 (89) n*23* fabulous, clean, gristy and punchy peat; t*24* young yet old enough to reveal enormous complexity amid the sparkling peat, sweet, but one or two oaky notches; f*20* flattens slightly, toffee amid the dying embers; b*22* no prisoners taken early on, but relents toward the end. **59.9%**. *James MacArthur.*

The Pibroch 12 Years Old Islay Single Malt (87) n*22* oily and softly peated; t*21* oily and sweet malt carries with it a clinging, silky smokiness; f*22* softens to allow decent oak to arrive; b*22* this was the name I wanted to launch my own Islay single malt brand with, some 20-odd years ago. But I have been beaten to it: damn! This is classical Caol Ila-style: oily with the peat subdued but still pretty rich. A very evocative dram in many ways. **43%**. *The Highlands & Islands Scotch Whisky Co.*

Waitrose 10 Year Old Islay (79) n*20* t*21* f*18* b*20*. Velvet smooth and malt-sweet. But just about peatless. **40%**. *Waitrose Stores UK.*

❖ **W&M Born on Islay House Malt** dist Jan 95, bott Jan 04 casks no. 655-672 **(71)** n*20* t*18* f*16* b*17*. Unusually dull and disappointing from what is normally an excellent independent bottler. Rightly or wrongly, one detects the evil, nullifying hand of caramel at work here. **43%**. *Wilson & Morgan Barrel Selection.*

UNSPECIFIED SINGLE MALTS (Lowland)

Dun Bheagan Lowland Single Malt 8 Years old (87) n*19* thin, apologetic barley; t*23* whoa!! Steady on, there!! From an insipid nose to a massive, sparklingly clean barley injection that almost knocks you off your seat. In seconds ... Don't look for complexity, just effect; f*23* now there's complexity as a series of pulsing barley notes interlock with something slightly more citrussy; deft vanilla binds the whole; b*23* just shows you: don't read a book by its cover ... I think it has to be said that the present Dun Bheagan regional range is about the best I have ever encountered outside Classic Malts. **43%**

McClelland's Lowland Single Malt (85) n*21* lively fruits, citrus in particular; t*22* stunningly clean mouthfeel, then a tidal wave of grassy and fresh malt. The attractive sweetness is checked by a little spice; f*21* remains a tad spicy with some vanilla offering ballast; b*21* never spectacular, this is always just very good whisky with a steady development of complexity: in others words, a lovely dram. **40%.** *Morrison Bowmore.*

MacLeod's Lowland Single Malt Aged 8 Years (see Auchentoshan)

UNSPECIFIED SINGLE MALTS (Speyside)

Asda Speyside Single Malt 12 Years Old (83) n*19* t*22* f*21* b*21*. A long, chewy malty dram that really spreads its wings for a refreshing middle. **40%.** *Douglas MacNiven. Asda UK.*

Ben Bracken 12 Years Old (88) n*20* lazy malt and oak, clean but void of any great complexity; t*23* fabulously mouthwatering and clean: the malt reaches out to caress every tastebud; some honeyed strands are beautifully in tune with the intense barley; f*23* long, deftly sweet, a hint of oil to the body with still that big barley/honey theme, some vanilla arrives; b*22* the blurb claims peat – in fact none is here – but what you do have is uncluttered and intense beauty in abundance. **40%.** *Clydesdale Scotch Whisky Co. Glasgow*

Celtique Connexion (see Unspecified Single Malts (General))

Glen Darbach Single Speyside Malt Aged 12 Years (71) n*18* t*19* f*17* b*17*. Heather and honey say the label notes: oak says the nose. Just doesn't turn me on. **40%.** *Marks & Spencer UK.*

Glen Marnoch Single Speyside Malt Aged 12 Years (77) n*19* t*21* f*18* b*19*. Malty middle with impressive bite. **40%.** *Alistair Graham Aldi Stores.*

Glen Parker (see GlenParker)

Glen Parker Speyside Single Malt (77) n*19* t*20* f*19* b*19*. Younger on nose and palate than the colour might suggest: good, sprightly chewing malt. Toffee on finish. **40%.** *Angus Dundee.*

Glinne Parras Single Speyside Malt Aged 12 Years (86) n*22* fresh sliced cucumber and dry oak; t*22* really big malt theme, richly textured; f*21* long, sweet, confident with a mildly spicy counterattack; b*21* solid, chewy, well-made whisky. **40%.** *Eaux de Vie.*

Hart Brothers Ballindalloch Aged 35 Years dist May 67, bott Sep 02 **(88)** n*23* unreal: how can something spend this amount of time in wood and come out so fresh and malt-intense? The minty oak adds the faintest marmalade tang to the elegant complexity; t*20* and it's that tart, citrussy note that shows first on the palate. The oak is weighty but not a blight, the malt firm and chewy; f*23* big oak now with liquorice and cocoa taking the lead with some dashing spices in pursuit. The toasty flavours still include the stubborn malt which cling on to the oily body that forms by the second. This is now very big whisky; b*22* this takes oak just about as far as I like to see it go. There is little sign of it on the nose, but it makes itself felt on arrival. But really it's the complexity of the oaky tones that gives such an enormous finish. Memorable stuff. **48.5%** *There is no such distillery as Ballindalloch. One can safely deduce that it is from the distillery in the area that takes a dim legal view of its name being used on a label* *it does not own: Glenfarclas. It's also a safe bet that a whisky of this enormous complexity at such an age is more likely to come from that Speyside distillery than any other.*

Lochruan Speyside Single Malt Scotch Aged 12 Years (86) n21 citrus-fresh, beautifully light with some curvaceous malty notes; t22 mouthwatering malt with more citrus sneaking in, fresh and only mildly oaked; f21 a pinch of peat wafts in from somewhere, the malt dominates, but a Brownie point lost for the toffee; b22 a charming malt with good weight despite the citrus sub-stratum. I guess from the finish this has been coloured: would have been a belter in natural form. **40%.** *Leith Distillers for Tesco UK.*

McClelland's Speyside Single Malt (74) n17 t19 f20 b18. Heavy and oily. A good chew but somehow lacking a typical Speyside charm. **40%.** *Morrison Bowmore.*

McClelland's Speyside Single Malt Aged 10 Years (73) n19 t19 f17 b18. Surprisingly heavy for the region; oily and rumbustious but ultimately lacking the aplomb the region desires. **40%.** *Exclusive to Somerfield Stores UK.*

MacLeod's Speyside Aged 8 Years (*see* Glenfarclas)

Safeway Speyside Single Malt 12 Years Old (77) n19 t19 f20 b19. Clean, malty, rich but a little bland in character. **40%.** *UK.*

Sainsbury's Single Speyside Malt Aged 12 Years (78) n18 t21 f19 b20. Above-average fruitiness and sweetness. **40%.** *UK.*

⋄ **Sainsbury's Speyside Single Malt Matured for 15 Years Cognac Finish (88)** n22 undeniably complex; light, busy, floral tones with sound vanilla; t21 quite a biting, nippy arrival that seems a little ill-at-ease; f23 now finds its path with a luxuriant, never-ending bathing of cocoa over myriad fruity-floral notes; b22 for a moment it appears the Cognac barrels have thrown this out of sync, but its recovery is stunning. **40%**

Sainsbury's Speyside Single Malt Matured for 15 Years Claret Finish (87) n23 a crisp fruitiness succeeds in accentuating some very clean malt: charming and stylish; t23 heavy-textured with the wine and grain labouring to hit a rhythm. The early mouthfeel, though, is lovely. The malts somersault around the tastebuds with abandon. The degree of sweetness is spot on; f20 surprisingly fresh for its age, remains confrontational but guarantees complexity; b21 an intriguing and on the whole pretty enjoyable dram. To be churlish and technical, could do with a little tightening up: that said, no way I'd say, "No." if offered a second one. Fun and fruity! **40%.** *UK.*

Waitrose 12 Year Old Speyside (72) n18 t20 f16 b18. Some lovely, sharp moments but dulled by caramel. **40%.** *Waitrose Stores UK.*

Waitrose Single Speyside Malt Whisky Matured in Port Wood for 21 Years dist 81 **(89)** n24 the malt and port just seem to fit like hand in glove, teasing spicy notes amid succulent, juice-dripping fruit notes: rare and ravishing; t22 impressively clean winey feel and a texture not unlike wine-gum candy, playful spices throughout and for a brief second a surge of something vaguely smoky; f21 at last the malt emerges from the fruit and intertwines with the vanilla; b22 it could be argued the port has taken too firm a grip, but to be honest I don't care … and I actually don't think so. Very rare to find port pipes of this quality and whisky matured in it for this long – usually finishing the done thing. An almost unique whisky for which Waitrose deserve enormous credit in adding to their own-label portfolio. A real dram for real whisky lovers to learn a little more about the world's greatest spirit. I can see droves of European malt whisky lovers taking special flights just to get hold of this one … **40%.** *William Maxwell for Waitrose UK.*

Wm Morrison Speyside Single Malt Aged 10 Years (86) n21 classic green, grassy maltiness. Some vanilla confirms the sympathetic age; t22 delicate, complex and pretty sophisticated stuff; f21 long with firm, slightly oily mouthfeel and good malt-vanilla balance, even some late spice, spoiled only by the toffee-effect from the caramel; **b**22 malts like this are in danger of getting supermarkets a good name. **40%**. *Morrison's UK.*

UNSPECIFIED SINGLE MALTS (General)

Celtic Whisky Malt Scotch 12 Years Old (89) n21 some quality oak sits comfortably with the rich barley; **t**22 crisp, clean barley which develops in a honied direction; **f**23 more honey and then a gradual increase in spicy oak; **b**23 genuinely first-rate whisky of a Highland-meets-Perthshire style, massive complexity and balance; **40%** *from the Celtic Spirit Company – that's the Celtic race: not to be confused with football club. Although doesn't say so on the label, I can confirm this is a single malt.*

⋰ **Celtique Connexion 1990 Double Maturation Affinage En Fut De Sauternes** bott 03 **(87)** n22 delicate spices amid the barley; **t**23 mouthwatering and lively with a delicious washing of fruit over the firmer barley; **f**21 dries, bitter grape pips; quite unusual but dimmed slightly by toffee; **b**21 a clean malt with no shortage of charming flavour development. **43%**. *Celtic Whisky Compagnie.*

⋰ **Celtique Connexion 1990 Double Maturation Affinage Vin de Paille du Jura** bott 02 **(83)** n24 t19 f20 b20. Another rare example of whisky maturing in a French wine cask and living to tell the tale. The nose on this really does shine with glorious fruit clarity; the balance tends to wobble on the palate. Decent stuff, though, and well worth an investigation. **43%**. *Celtic Whisky Compagnie.*

The Classic Cask of The Millennium Aged 35 Years batch SW-202, dist 6/64, bott 9/99 **(87)** n22 t22 f22 b21. A distinctive and highly unusual malt, probably a Speysider, that has been swamped by one of the sweetest, silkiest sherry butts I've ever come across. One for the ladies. **40%**. *The Glenaden Distilling Co. 600 bottles.*

Cu Dhu (*see* Speyside Distillery)

Diners Club International Scotch Whisky 8 Years Malt (78) n18 t21 f19 b20. Lively, mouthwatering Speyside-style. **40%**. *Douglas Denham.*

Glen Shira (distillery, age unspecified) **(77)** n19 t21 f19 b18. A young, barely pubescent dram full of refreshing, uncomplicated but mouthwatering malt. Without the caramel, which guarantees a cream-toffee finish, it would have been a stormer. **40%**. *Exclusive to Asda UK.*

Glentromie 17 Years Old (distillery unspecified) **(68)** n19 t17 f16 b16. Charisma-free. **40%**. *Speyside Distillers. Not from own distillery.*

Harrod's Single Malt Aged 12 Years (78) n19 t21 f19 b19. Steady, untaxing game with a pleasant honied sheen to the finish. **40%**

Scotland Vatted Malts (also Pure Malts)

Like 2003, 2004 will probably not go down as a vintage year for the launching of great vatted malt. Even though, without question, it was again one of the most promising in living memory. But, sadly, that is not a surprise. Because if Vatted Malt Vintages are declared like Port Vintages, it is unlikely we will have had one since Noah was collecting wood.

What is it about vatted malt? Just why are good ones so hard to find?

I have my suspicions. Mainly it is because they tend to be cheaper than single malts, often bin ends of parcels of malts overlooked elsewhere – often with good reason – but perfect when thrown together to hit a designated market at the right price. In those cases quality takes a back seat ... and it shows.

Really, vatted malts should be very good indeed. Because, like blends, they should offer the drinker a complexity and balance that single malts cannot achieve alone. But often it seems that they miss the cut and thrust of grain whisky, that often misunderstood, even pilloried, whisky type. The result can be something dull and lifeless, a whisky desperate for a spark of inventiveness from somewhere.

Newcomers to whisky are often unsure just what a vatted malt is. Commonly it is marketed as a "Pure Malt". Labels that tend not to make a point that the whisky inside the bottle is a single malt are likely to say "Pure Malt". Which means, quite simply, that it is a whisky made from 100% malted barley, but not necessarily from the just a single distillery. For that reason any label offering "Pure Malt" has been included in the vatted malt section, for vatted means that it is malt from more than one distillery but containing no grain.

It has to be said, though, that since January 2002 the quality at the top end of the vatted malt spectrum has risen. Standing out from the mundane has been some pretty impressive bottlings with James Martin's Pure Malt 20 Years Old among the elite, though that went only in limited supply to Japan, and more commonly The Famous Grouse Vintage Malt 1992.

During 2004, Six Isles has begun to take on the legendary status last year's Bible suggested it might; Compass Box has launched its extraordinary Juveniles and the Jon, Mark and Robbo range has offered two sides of the same coin. Now it needs the bigger boys to turn their attention to this sector, to latch onto the promise of these relatively small batch bottlings. Who knows, 2005 might just be the year of the vatted malt.

Baxter's Malt (88) n*21* simple, clean, uncluttered fresh malt; t*22* beautiful mouth arrival, refreshing clean malt; f*23* outstanding development continuing on the same theme; b*22* no great age to this but it's all about classic, soft Speyside character. Lovely stuff. **40%**. *Gordon & MacPhail for Baxter's. Found in the famous soup company's shops on Speyside and at Aberdeen Airport.*

Baxter's 8 Years Old Malt (83) n*20* t*22* f*20* b*21*. Good weight and oil with some citrus on the malt. The oak adds a late dash of bitterness. **40%**. *Gordon & MacPhail for Baxter's. Found only in the Baxter's shops at Aberdeen Airport and at Fochabers, Speyside.*

Blackadder Smoking Islay cask 2002/01 **(86)** n*21* raw, young, windswept beaches; peat-reek from a nearby lumb etc. t*23* massive, clean, sweet peat, hardly any oak standing in the way; f*22* big spices and continued concentrated malt. The peat is everywhere but remains raw and unrefined; b*20* a pretty youngish Islay taking no prisoners. **55%. nc ncf sc** *(99% of one malt and 1% of something else added by the distillers to prevent it being sold as a self whisky).*

Blairmhor 8 Years Old (76) n*22* t*20* f*16* b*18*. The citrus notes suggest. Old Pulteney on the nose, but the finish is rather half-hearted. **40%**. *Inver House.*

Cardhu Speyside Pure Malt Aged 12 Years (88) n*22* superbly complex: no shortage of citrus and apple and pear notes to complement the deep malt, but there is also significant, almost dry, chalky oak – far more than the original Cardhu single malt – taking it off in a vaguely bourbony direction. Some spice buzz, too; t*23* much more punchy and spicy than its single malt predecessor with some weighty cocoa arriving early as the oak bites. The intensity and mouthfeel of the chewy, sweet malt is exceptional, the cleanliness awesome; f*21* the cocoa remains constant with a soft drying from the earlier sweet barley; a fraction too much oak at the death; b*22* this is a gloriously crafted vatted malt with the signature of Cardhu – sorry, I mean Cardow – clearly at the heart. On the downside there is just too much oak for such a delicate creature as this. And the description on the carton perhaps needs a little attention: "The whisky is distilled by the Spey ..." True if it were Cardhu in single malt form. But seeing as the whole point is that it isn't and there are lot of Speyside distilleries a long way from the Spey.... **40%**

Century of Malts (94) n*23* lots of malty snap and buzz, some intriguing apple-smoke tones, fresh and wonderfully complex; t*24* mindblowing complexity on arrival: Speysiders lead the pack but some wonderful strands of honey, smoke and oak guarantee imperious complexity; f23 long, busy malt still beautifully weighted and textured with the oak slowly bleeding into the picture; b24 tragically, a brand now discontinued: certainly the most complete vatted malt I have come across in my lifetime. Having malts from 100 distilleries is one thing, vatting them in harmony for near perfect weight and texture is something else. This was probably Colin Scott and his team's finest moment: an art form and treasure. By the way, the little book that comes with it is a work of genius, too ... **40%**. *Chivas.*

Clan Campbell 10 Years Old Vatted Malt (83) n20 t22 f20 b21. Fruitier, less feisty than the blend, as one might expect. But much less fun! Competent as drinking malt all the same. **40%**. *Chivas.*

⋰ **Compass Box Eleuthera** bottle identification L3350 **(85) n**21 a bit of an arm wrestle between oily peat and lighter malts; **t**22 the weighty peat makes a mouth-filling entrance and clutters the palate up slightly too early; **f**21 a little flat due to the oil; **b**21 enjoyable but clumsy by usual Compass Box standards. **46%**

Compass Box Eleuthera All Malt (first bottling with star compass points and orange/brown label, called "All Malt".) **(93) n**23 something herbal, some delicate citrus notes amid the outstanding barley and hiding oak. very clean, very different. The soft peat offers the perfect frame; **t**24 the immediate arrival on the palate is awesome with the flavours enveloping the mouth. It's all about texture and complexity rather than indiviual flavours: outstanding; **f**22 sweet at first, then a slow seeping of drying oak, couched by lingering smoke; **b**24 quite simply, one of the most complex and truly magnificent vatted malts of all time. A collector's piece. **46%. ncf nc.**

Compass Box Eleuthera Vatted Malt (second bottling (2003) with mauve central illustration, called "Vatted Malt".) **(87) n**22 peat is a little crisper, the barley dry and biscuity; **t**21 silky sweet arrival of peat then a fall-out of lighter, sharper, malty tones and vanilla; **f**22 very long, with beautiful intertwining of smoke, oak and barley; **b**22 a slightly smokier, oilier version. Delicious, but lacking that previous touch of genius. **46%. ncf nc.**

⋰ **Compass Box Juveniles (95) n**23 a sharp aroma of cat-nip, juniper, coriander all off-set by a smudge of honey; **t**23 exquisitely soft mouthfeel with acacia honey gaining ground on the stunning, velvet malt; **f**24 this one simply dissolves in the mouth: pure honey with the most intense and clean malt imaginable; **b**25 they've done it again!!! Almost an essay in delicate, sweet malt at its most complex. This is Scotch at its most erotic; a wand has been waved over these six casks. Simply fabulous. **44%**

⋰ **Compass Box Monster (89) n**22 the oily peat thuds unambiguously against the nose; **t**23 massive. The peat is sweet and oiliness keeps it crushed to the roof of the mouth; **f**22 drier now as some oak kicks in; **b**22 there has to be some Caol Ila in there somewhere amid all that oil. And may be Lagavulin for all the depth? Massive ... a monster!! **54.9%.** *Park Avenue, New York.*

Douglas MacNiven Islay Pure Malt 10 Years Old (82) n21 t21 f20 **b**20. Chunky, raw, green and young for its age but unmistakably from just one particular place in the world. **40%**. *Asda UK.*

⋰ **Dram House Age 12 Years** "Vatted from 12 Distilleries" **(86) n**20 fresh baked bread and a serious chunk of age; **t**22 arrives at full volume with the intense malt screaming to be heard amid the oak and caramel; **f**22 almost a grainy finale with lots of liquorice and coffee; **b**22 an almost perfect oiliness and barely perceptable smokiness helps see this big 'un over the big oak: session stuff of frightening moreishness. **46%. ncf.** *John Milroy.*

Dun Bheagan Pure Malt Aged 8 Years (81) n19 t22 f20 **b**20. Big, malty, sweet and very full flavoured. **43%. ncf.** *William Maxwell.*

The Famous Grouse Vintage Malt 1987 aged 12 Years (86) n21 bananas, grapes, oranges, figs: they are all there if you hunt for them, very clean and crystalline with a hint of peat; **t**22 teasing malt, lush fruit and soft smoke; **f**22 fruity, with soft oak and vanilla intermingling; **b**21 when this was released in 1999 you have no idea what a relief it was to find a well-mixed vatted malt. Re-visiting it for the first time in a couple of years, I can see why I was so pleased to see it. **40%**

The Famous Grouse Vintage Malt 1989 aged 12 Years (73) n19 t20 17 **b**17. A marked disappointment on the original '87. You get the feeling that extra sherry and perhaps caramel have combined to create something as hilly as a witch's chest. **40%**

The Famous Grouse Vintage Malt 1990 bottled 03 **(78)** n17 t21 **f**20 **b**20. Pity about the poor sherry nose. The mouth arrival is scrummy. **40%**

The Famous Grouse Vintage Malt 1992 bottled 02 **(89)** n21 complex: seems weighty at first but has plenty of air, too. Some crisp malt in there; **t**23 superb mouth arrival with a velvety floor of juicy malt. The fruitiness keeps in harmony. Overall, superbly mouthwatering; **f**22 touches of vanilla reveal some oak, but still it's the malt, with a little fizzing spice for company, that stars; **b**23 a joyously harmonious affair, boasting supreme complexity and confidence. A classic vintage and a classic vatting. **40%**

Fortnum & Mason Highland Malt 12 Years Old (74) n19 t20 f17 b18. A bland dram floored, it seems, by caramel and perhaps (though impossible to tell) sherry in tandem. **40%**. *UK*.

Glenalmond Highland Malt dist 94, bott 02 **(83)** n21 t21 f20 b21. Above-average vatted malt, cleverly using the relative youth of the barley to form refreshing waves around the mouth. Impressive. **40%**. *The Vintage Malt Whisky Co.*

⋰⋰ **Glen Cairie 12 Years Old Pure Malt (87)** n21 fresh, grassy, Speyside-esque; **t**23 perfectly structured, faultlessly simplistic barley; **f**21 a hint of vanilla and caramel; **b**22 it is exactly what it says on the tin: "pure". **43%**. *Red Lion Blending.*

Glencoe Aged 8 Years (*see* MacDonald's Glencoe)

⋰⋰ **Glen Crannog Pure Malt** (on back label calls itself Glen Crannog 5 Years Old) **(77)** n18 t21 f19 b19. A dusty nose, silky malt middle, gentle finish. Little discernible top dressing, though. **40%**. *T&A McClelland for Threshers*

⋰⋰ **Glen Drumm (78)** n18 t22 f19 b19. The nose slightly off-key but decent youthful barley freshness; the sweetness on the palate is as surprising as it is even. **43%**. *Langside Distillers.*

⋰⋰ **Glen Martin 5 Years Old Pure Highland Malt (84)** n20 t22 f21 **b**21. Youthful and by no means extravagant, there is still some wonderful custard-sweet, mildly oily-textured, nutty charm. Basic, but very attractive, indeed. **40%**. *For Sainsbury's, UK.*

Glen Nicol (80) n20 t20 f20 **b**20. An honest Joe of a malt: lots of lively character and straight as a die. **40%**. *Inver House.*

Glen Roger's Pure Malt Aged 8 Years Old Reserve (63) n18 t17 **f**13 **b**15. About as dead as a whisky gets. For French market.

Glen Rosa Pure Malt (83) n21 t22 f20 b20. Young, oily, fruity with massive Arran influence. Sweet, malty and easily drinkable. **40%**. *Isle of Arran.*

Glen Rosa Pure Malt 8 Years Old (81) n20 t22 f19 **b**20. Quite a bitter finish to the sweet malt. Quite light but chewy. **40%**. *Isle of Arran.*

⋰⋰ **Glensbury 21 Years Old Pure Malt (86)** n20 pear-drops and prune juice with a squirt of bourbon; **t**22 rich arrival of malt swiftly followed by fruit and spice; **f**22 the vanilla is controlled yet confident; **b**22 a highly unusual freshness to a Scotch so old and slightly bourbony. **40%**. *Red Lion Blending.*

Glenstone (71) n17 t19 f17 **b**18. Raw and full on. **40%**. *Kyndal.*

⋰⋰ **Hankey Bannister Pure Malt (87)** n23 unusually dexterous and uncluttered nose for a vatting; even a dose of honey amid the cleanest barley imaginable; **t**22 the mammoth intensity of the malt enjoys a rare balance; a slight oiliness clutters things a little; **f**20 soft vanilla and sawdust but again the barley controls the moment; a touch of toffee detracts from the magic; **b**22 impressive blending. **40%**. *Inver House.*

Hedges & Butler Special Pure Malt (76) n18 t19 f20 b19. Very evenly weighted and juicy. **40%**

Highland Fusilier 8 Years Old (78) n19 t20 f19 b20. Well-balanced and plenty of body. **40%**. *Gordon & MacPhail.*

∴ **Hogshead Pure Malt (73)** n18 t19 f18 b18. Ordinary and toffeed. **43%**. *Inverheath Ltd*

Inverarity Islay 10 Years Old (85) n22 laid-back, clean peat, gristy and dry; t21 woollen-textured and delicately peated; f21 quite chalky and dryish on one level, some peat offers something a little sweeter on another; b21 almost a teasing dram, so soft the flavours barely make it round the mouth. Something delightfully different. **40%**

∴ **Islay Connection 10 Years Old (86)** n21 young, gristy peat; t22 young and pungent for its age with the peat hitting the tastebuds at full speed; f22 there is a fresh malty sweetness to the death; the oak has no more than a bit part; b21 a well-made, faultlessly clean malt of unfulfilled promise that makes a virtue of its intense peatiness despite the lack of complexity. **40%**. *Celtic Whisky Circle.*

The Jacobite Highland Malt (84) n20 t21 f22 b21. A mouthwatering, fresh, effervescent and complex malt, especially towards the finish. **40%**. *Malt House Vintners.*

∴ **James MacArthur Pure Islay 1991 Aged 12 years (87)** n22 clean and uncomplicated, it seams a little younger than its years; t21 slightly too oily at first, the peat soon starts mending fences; f22 dries out so the peat is much more crisp and chewy; b22 a perfectly smoky little begger for peat freaks. **59.7%**

∴ **James Martin's Vintage 1984 (83)** n21 t20 f21 b21. An orangey number with pleasing toast-barley complexity. **43%**. *Glenmorangie plc.*

James Martin 8 Year Old Malt (87) n21 complex and quite toasty: drier and oakier than the average 8-y-o; t22 stylish mouthfeel, malty and a build-up of subtle sweet, citrus notes; f22 long, remains slightly chalky but the malts are inscrutable; b22 a discreet, thoughful vatting quite beautifully constructed. **40%**. *Glenmorangie for Oddbins UK.*

James Martin's Pure Malt 20 Years Old bott 02 **(89)** n22 honey and very soft smoke, sweetish but some pleasant oak, too; t23 big honey surge with the malt bubbling through in almost syrupy form but without the usual over sweetness from a similar texture: something to really savour; f22 dries slightly towards bitter chocolate with a dash of smoke wafting around for good measure; b22 what an extraordinary whisky: it poured like a liquor and, when tasted, offered the creamiest body I can ever remember coming across in nearly 30 years. Just amazing. A way above-average vatted malt with a touch of everything. **46%**. *Glenmorangie. 500 bottles Japan.*

Johnnie Walker Green Label 15 Years Old (92) n24 this is one of the best vatted noses on the market: superb complexity, relatively peatless but still boasting big weight amid some fresher Speyside notes; t23 bingo! Serious flavour explosion which leans towards malty sweetness with a gradual fade-in of drier oak; f22 now some oils arrive, plus a little mint suggesting good age; b23 this is easily one of the best vatted malts in the market, pretty sweet, too. **43%**

∴ **Jon, Mark and Robbo's The Rich Spicy One (85)** n19 a minor sulphur blemish doesn't overly detract from the busy, kitchen-condiment aroma; t23 a layer of semi-sweet malt is buried beneath weightier layers of fruit and hints of liquorice; f20 that slight flaw returns but the gentle pulse of the spice is endearing, as is the oaky dryness; b23 an intriguing, sherry-dripping dram that is exceptionally well balanced, suphur apart. Outstanding marketing: seems another of my ideas has bitten the dust while I'm busy writing books ...! Still, good luck to my old friend Dave (Robbo) Robinson who I am sure will produce a 90 from this with future editions. **40%**. *The Easy Drinking Whisky Company.*

⋰ **Jon, Mark and Robbo's The Smoky Peaty One (92)** n23 a faultlessly clean aroma where the reek enjoys a distinctive salty, coastal rock-pool edge; t22 again the peat is delicate yet coastal with a build-up of intense barley; f23 beautiful honey tones accompany the peat like a high phenol Highland Park; b24 genuinely high-class whisky where the peat is full-on yet allows impressive complexity and malt development. A malt for those who appreciate the better, more elegant things in life. **40%.** *The Easy Drinking Whisky Company.*

⋰ **Kelt Tour du Mond Very Rare Extra Old Pure Malt** 1995 Shipment **(93)** n24 freshly ground orange peel, covert nutmeg and profound salty-oaky tang; t23 beautifully weighted arrival, a background hint of smoke and spice that offers sweetness to the drier, even deeper, oak softened by vanilla caramel; f22 some sweetening custard on the lengthy deftly oaked finale; b24 the casks to this whisky spent a couple of months crossing the world by ship. And it shows: its sea legs have given it extraordinary balance.

Label 5 Pure Malt Matured for 12 Years (77) n20 t21 f17 b19. Competent and initially attractive. **40%.** First Blending Co.

The Living Cask (91) n22 spicy and lively; thick-textured malt and reasonable oak; t22 mouthwatering, sweet malt notes with a developing fruity edge and smoke; f24 remains chunky and intense and there are signs of the sweetness of the malt abating. Very soft signs of peat towards the outstanding and cocoa-laced finale; b23 just one of those drams you can chew forever. The complexity is awesome. **56%.** *Probably the most pointless tasting notes I'll ever write, as the whole point of the vatting is that it changes constantly as defined by George Saintsbury in his Notes On A Cellar Book of the 1920s. There he suggests topping up a cask of whisky on a solera basis, which is what they have been doing for a few years now at Loch Fyne Whiskies at Inveraray. Shifting sands, with very few bottlings the same, but fun anyway! This sample was drawn in June 2003.*

⋰ **Loch Dhup (86)** n22 a honeyed lead with soft smoke follow on; t22 excellent body with Caol Ila oil, but the emphasis on malt; f21 soft spices; b21 a charming vatting needing some attention on the finale strength, debatable. A special bottling solera vatted on the spot at Royal Mile Whisky in Bloomsbury, London, and blended by Duncan Ross, tasted by the store's more valued customers. You've heard of the Living Cask: this is the living bottle...

⋰ **Loch Fyne Whiskies Living Cask Volume 18 (84)** n20 t21 f22 b21. Some magical moments and a times almost bewildering complexity. But the hard backbone is just a little too straight and unyielding. A palate dazzler all the same with clever use of peat. **56%**

Lochinvar Pure Malt (84) n19 t22 f22 b21. A very good dram indeed showing no shortage of honey-smoke notes in the chorus. Rich, full-bodied and clearly one of the better ones to be found around Europe's supermarkets. *Roscow Greig (Somerfield) UK.*

⋰ **Lodhian Founders Choice First Edition Aged 10 Years (72)** n18 t19 f17 b18. Malty but bland. **40%.** For Lodhian Distillery, Sweden.

MacDonald's Glencoe Aged 8 Years (82) n20 t22 f20 b20. Mouthwatering in parts; lots of cereal, spice and kick. **58%. nc.** Ben Nevis Distillery.

Matisse Pure Malt Over 12 Years (73) n16 t21 f18 b18. Explosive on the palate, but too much caramel. **40%**

Old Elgin 8 Years Old (82) n21 t20 f21 b20. Lush, lengthy, honied and a little spicy. A good anytime, anywhere whisky. **40%.** Gordon & MacPhail.

Old Elgin 15 Years Old (71) n17 t19 f17 b18. A tad sulphury and off-key **40%.** Gordon & MacPhail.

Poit Dhubh 8 Bliadhna (81) n20 t22 f19 b20. Generously peated and rich in the middle but foiled by very un-Gaelic toffee. **43%.** Praban Na Linne. *Conduct their business, whenever possible, in Gaelic: bliadhna means "years old".*

Poit Dhubh 12 Bliadhna (82) n22 t21 f19 b20. Big, fruity and complex but rather bitter. **40%.** *Praban Na Linne.*

Poit Dhubh 12 Bliadhna Unchillfiltered (88) n23 oranges and juicy pears combine spectacularly wth a peat sub-stratum; t21 a mildly flat, toffeed arrival but then an eruption of smoky spices; f22 more spice, sweetening malt and then vanilla; b22 an exceptionally fine vatted malt with considerable attitude, complexity and personality to get over the low-key mouth arrival. Great stuff. **46%. ncf.** *Praban Na Linne.*

Poit Dhubh 21 Bliadhna (85) n22 fruity and spicy; t22 big, juicy malt arrival with spices and a touch of smoke; f20 rich toffee but some salty compromise; b21 a mouthwatering vatting with a distinctly coastal saltiness. **43%. ncf.** *Praban Na Linne.*

⚬ **The Pot Still 8 Years Old Pure Malt (88)** n22 clean, mildly honeyed and fresh; t23 a seriously beautiful palate arrival, silk-textured malt that builds into a fabulously spiced honey middle; f21 lengthy with just enough sweetness; b22 an enormously charming malt: the way vatted drams should be. **43.5%. ncf.** *Celtic Whisky Compagnie.*

Pride of Islay 12 Years Old (88) n22 real hospital antiseptic stuff here, oily, too; t22 comes to life with a soft upping of peaty intensity after some original fruity notes wear thin; f23 quite long and enjoys fine integration between peat and oak; b21 I love the gentle but firm nature of the peat with this one. Unusual as an Islay but then, as a vatted version, so it should be. **40%.** *Gordon & MacPhail.*

Pride of the Lowlands 12 Years Old (77) n20 t18 f20 b19. Lively and the character of a certain distillery shines clearly through. **40%.** *Gordon & MacPhail.*

Pride of Orkney 12 Years Old (72) n18 t19 f18 b17. A vatting from Orkney ... now I wonder which distilleries they used? As it happens, there is a very slight soapiness to this one. **40%.** *Gordon & MacPhail.*

Pride of Speyside 12 Years Old (87) n21 really deep malt, a touch of citrus and raw carrot! t22 beautiful mouthfeel. There is a sheen to the malt which intensifies as the oak encroaches; f22 stylish cocoa-touched finish: not the most complex, but elegant and shapely; b22 well if good ol' G&M can't get it right with a vatted Speysider, no-one can. A lovely dram. **40%.** *Gordon & MacPhail.*

Prince Lordon Old Malt (79) n21 t20 f19 b19. Clean, lively energetic malt, sharp grassy notes, refreshing on the nose, with enormous cream-toffee body and finish. **40%.** *VDB Spirit. A specially prepared kosher whisky, in which no sherry is used barrels are cleaned and so on. For US market.*

Royal Swan 10 Years Old Pure Malt (70) n18 t19 f16 b17. Fun at first, let down by dodgy finish. **40%.** *Quality Spirits International.*

Sainsbury's Malt Whisky Finished in Sherry Casks (69) n17 t20 f16 b16. Back to the drawing board on this one: balance is at a premium. Some better quality butts wouldn't go amiss. **40%.** *UK.*

Sainsbury's Pure Islay Malt Aged 10 Years (90) n23 oily, tarry, heavy ... and peaty; t23 outstanding oak and oil weight to guide the complex peat around the tastebuds; f22 softens, lots of vegetation; b22 you could not expect to find better from an own-label brand. One for Islay-philes to savour (except for evidence of caramel, which has docked points off the finish). Otherwise, pure Islay malt, indeed. **40%.** *UK.*

Safeway Islay Pure Malt 10 Years Old (94) n24 just stupendous salty, iodine peat character. The complexity is enormous; t23 gently oiled but otherwise a supreme mixture of gristy malt and a harder, firm barley juiciness; f23 about as long a finish as you could wish for with the gristiness continuing and at last some oak giving direction; b24 one of those stupendous drams that carries you back to the island wherever you may be sitting or standing at the time of drinking. Forget the fact this is from a supermarket, or is most probably vatted. This is Islay: an eye-wetting gem! Whisky you pray for. **40%.** *UK.*

Safeway Vatted Malt Aged 8 Years (70) n17 t18 f18 b17. Feinty and flawed on the nose but otherwise rich-textured and intensely malty. **40%.** *UK.*

Scottish Pride 12 Years Old Pure Malt (80) n20 t21 f19 b20. A lively, lovely and busy vatted malt of some character. **40%**

Sheep Dip (84) n19 t22 f22 b21. Young and sprightly like a new-born lamb, this enjoys a fresh, mouthwatering grassy style wth a touch of spice. Maligned by some, but to me a clever, accomplished vatting of alluring complexity. **40%**

The Six Isles Pure Island Malt Uisge Beatha (943) n24 fresh, alluring, sensuously smoked with an underlying intense barley charisma; t23 a gentle massaging of young peat malt never becomes overly sweet, beautifully oily and lush; f23 long, increasingly spicy: a glorious array of vanilla and barley; b24 Wow! For all the peat, the strength of the whisky is its masterful balance: never sweet, never dry. About as charming and charismatic a vatted malt as you are likely to find. Contains malt from Islay, Jura, Skye, Mull, Orkney and Arran. Together they make unquestionably the best standard, non-deluxe vatted malt I have found in my lifetime. **43%.** *William Maxwell.*

Stewarts Pure Malt (68) n16 t18 f17 b17. Loads of flavour but, for me, just doesn't gel **40%.** *Kyndal.*

Tambowie Highland Pure Malt (75) n18 t20 f19 b18. Don't think that this is the old Tambowie distillery come back to life. Just a vatted malt put together to bring the old name back to life? It's claimed that this is what they think the old distillery (built in 1885 – great year: that's when Millwall FC were founded) would have produced. My own feeling is that this is a degree too light in character. **40%.** *The Vintage Malt Whisky Co.*

Tambowie Highland Pure Malt 12 Years Old (73) n18 t18 f19 b18. Slightly fusty; has some bright fruity moments but fades too quickly. **40%.** *The Highlands & Islands Scotch Whisky Co.*

Tulchan Lodge 12 Year Old Speyside Malt (80) n19 t20 f21 b20. Pretty rich and builds up well; the toffee dictates at the last. **40%.** *Tulchan Estate.*

Vintner's Choice Highland Aged 10 Years (60) n18 t15 f13 b14. Staggeringly flat and unimpressive. **40%**

Vintner's Choice Speyside Aged 10 Years (73) n16 t19 f19 b19. Malty with some fruit. **40%**

Vintner's Choice Speyside Pure Malt Aged 10 years Finished in Port Wood dist 1991, bott Nov 2001 **(82)** n20 t22 f21 b19. Highly enjoyable, but lacking a little balance. **43%**

Waitrose Highland Malt Sherry Finished (80) n20 t21 f20 b19, Rich fruitcake with bite and spice to counter the softness of the sherry. **40%.** *Waitrose Stores UK.*

Waitrose Pure Highland Malt (78) n20 t21 f18 b19. Highly intense, delicious malt with some spice. *Waitrose Stores UK.*

Whisky Galore Pure Malt Aged 10 Years (60) n16 t16 f13 b15. Featureless. One to forget ... had there been anything to remember in the first place. **40%.** *Whisky Galore Ltd.*

Wm Morrison Islay Pure Malt Aged 10 Years (86) n21 delicate, moderately peated, seashores and that kind of stuff; t22 sweet with some pleasant vanilla notes to tone down the smoke, good malt firmness towards the middle; f21 quite light and clean then caramel toffee; b22 a very delicate and well-structured Islay for reflective moments. Doesn't paint the peat with a tar brush.

Wm Morrison Pure Malt Aged 8 Years ("A selection of Speyside malts") **(85)** n23 classically crisp and sharp malty notes; t22 a bristling array of malt and soft vanilla, absolutely deliciously tastebuds-tingling until...; f19 Aaaaarrrggghhhh!!!!! Bloody caramel spoils the party yet again; b21 this is really lovely young Speyside malt of the most mouthwatering variety. And then the caramel spreads toffee everywhere. Please stop spoiling otherwise really good whisky!!!!! **40%.** *UK.*

MYSTERY MALTS

"As We Get It" Aged 8 Years (78) n18 **t**20 **f**21 **b**19. Lovely, intense malt on a dais of rich oil, but the slightly overpowering oak influence on this bottling suggests we have something a lot older then "8". **59.4%.** *J.G Thomson (bottling no. L2018BB).*

Anchor Bay (74) n17 **t**20 **f**18 **b**19. Sweet overall, with a furry, bitter finish. **40%.** *Lombard.*

Blackadder Raw Cask Blairfindy (*see* Glenfarclas)

Pebble Beach (Speyside Distillation Area) **(79) n**18 **t**21 **f**20 **b**20. Fresh, clean malt but toffee-caramel dominates. **40%.** *Lombard.*

Golden Harvest (75) n19 **t**20 **f**18 **b**18. Another Lombard brand that looks promising but appears to be done to death by caramel. **40%.** *Lombard.*

Driftwood Highland Distillation Area (70) n18 **t**19 **f b**17. Flat; sinks without trace. **40%.** *Lombard.*

Tidal Ebb Islay Distillation Area (83) n21 **t**22 **f**20 **b**20. Some lovely peaty tones softened by light muscovado sugar. **40%.** *Lombard.*

Smoking Ember (81) n22 **t**20 **f**20 **b**19. The nose is glorious, fresh, straight from the malt kiln. But the full follow-through fails to materialise. **40%.** *Lombard.*

Spey Vintage 15 Years Old Highland Malt dist 86 **(74) n**17 **t**19 **f**19 **b**19. A malt that improves with familiarity and one for those with a fruity disposition. **40%.** *Alec Harvey Private Reserve. 18,645 bottles.*

Gordon & MacPhail Christmas Malt 10 Years Old bott 02 **(85) n**20 firm, crisp malt; **t**22 big and mouthwatering malt, grassy and firm; **f**21 big malt finale with some really classy oaky notes; **b**22 quality malt, worth drinking more than once a year. **40%**

Old St Andrews 5 Years Old Malt (in miniature bottle encased in plastic barrel) **(83) n**19 **t**22 **f**21 **b**21. A refreshing, mouthwatering dignified young dram of good stock. **40%.** *Rarely, in 30 years of opening whisky bottles, have I made such an ass of myself as with this one. The malt inside came as a welcome relief after the ordeal. If, like me, you spend an hour wondering how to get into the thing, here's a tip: the barrel holder is detachable. I will say no more.*

Old St Andrews 15 Years Old Malt (in miniature bottle encased in plastic barrel) **(81) n**20 **t**22 **f**19 **b**20. Malty and chewy with lots of vanilla and toffee. **40%.** *For barrel opening instructions, see above.*

Inverarity 10 Years Old (*see* Aultmore)

Inverarity Ancestral 14 Years Old (*see* Balmenach)

Scottish Grain

It's a bit weird, really. Many whisky lovers stay clear of blended Scotch, preferring instead single malts. The reason, I am often told, is that the grain included in a blend makes it rough and ready. Yet I wish I had a ten pound note for each time I have been told in the last year how much someone enjoys a single grain.

The ones that the connoisseurs die for are the older versions, special independent bottlings displaying great age. Yet only a few months back I was asked if I could include a young grain at a tasting to show what melt-in-the-mouth merchants these whiskies can be.

I wasn't given enough time to get the sample in, but I will show grains at tastings any day. Because, like single malts, grain distilleries produce whisky bearing their own style and signature. And, also, some display characteristics and a richness that can surprise and delight.

Most of the grains available in (usually specialist) whisky outlets are pretty elderly. Most are made from corn. Wheat was not introduced until later when prices dropped. And that helps give them either a Canadian or, depending on the freshness of the cask, an unmistakable bourbony style. So overtly Kentuckian can they be, I once playfully introduced an old single grain Scotch whisky into a bourbon tasting I was conducting and nobody spotted that it was the cuckoo in the nest ... until I revealed all at the end of the evening.

Light whiskies, including some Speysiders, tend to adopt this north American stance when the spirit has absorbed so much oak that the balance has been tipped. Grain whiskey is made from corn, particularly, to have that Canadian feel because the mouthfeel is so similar, too.

Younger grains may give a hint of oncoming bourbon-ness. But, rather, they tend to celebrate a softness in taste. Where many malts have a tendency to pulverise the taste-buds and announce their intent and character at the top of their voice, younger grains are content to stroke and whisper.

Scotch whisky companies have so far had a relaxed attitude to marketing their grains. William Grant has made some inroads with Black Barrel, though with nothing like the enthusiasm they unleash upon us their blends and malts. And Diageo are apparently content to see their Cameron Brig sell no further than its traditional hunting grounds, just north of Edinburgh, where the locals tend to prefer single grain to any other whisky. Hats off to Kyndal, though, for actually bringing out an impressive vintage version of their Invergordon.

The news for grain lovers has not been good this year with the closure of Dumbarton. I hope Allied, as a mark of respect for the doomed distillery, each year launch a special vintage of this crisp grain. Being a distillery that distilled from both wheat and corn, it would make a fascinating addition for whisky lovers to be able to try and spot the difference in style from the same age.

The tastings notes here for grains – both single and vatted – cover only a couple of pages. With Compass Box at the vanguard of launching the first vatted grain – their 2003 bottling being easily their best yet – expect this section to increase in size in forthcoming editions.

True, a whisky mass-produced by an enormous column still that would not be lost somewhere in a chemical plant, is not something the romantics like to dwell on. Especially when it is made not from golden, malted barley but from unmalted wheat or corn. Both are known to produce less flavour than barley.

But at last the message kicking in is that the reaction of this relatively lightweight spirit – and please, don't for one moment regard it as neutral, for it most certainly is not that – to oak can throw up some fascinating and often delicious possibilities.

Blenders have known that for a long time. The word is at last filtering through to more enlightened whisky connoisseurs the world over, some alerted or even seduced by the brilliance of the Cooley pure grain in Ireland.

Interest is growing. And people are willing to admit that they can enjoy an ancient Cambus or Caledonian. Even if it does go against the grain...

DISTILLERY LOCATOR

1 Invergordon   **A Aberdeen**
2 Cameronbridge   **B Dundee**
3 North British   **C Edinburgh**
4 Loch Lomond   **D Glasgow**
5 Dumbarton   Strathclyde
6 Girvan   Port Dundas

Key
△ **Major Cities**
○ Distilleries

Single Grain Scotch
ALLOA (see North of Scotland)

CALEDONIAN
Cadenhead's Caledonian Aged 31 Years dist Jan 63, bott Feb 94 **(88) n**21 extremely firm grain, rigid in character; **t**23 hints of sweet bourbon but really hard corn that thumps against the teeth. **f**21 dry, soft oak with echoing corn; **b**22 the last hurrah of a grain that obviously put a metal backbone into many a blend. **48.7%**

CAMBUS
Cadenhead's Cambus Aged 31 Years dist 63, bott 94 **(87) n**21 sweet, simple, bourbony; **t**23 rich, chewy, distinct corn and oily; **f**21 remains oily and full, some lovely lingering toasty oak; **b**22 an impressive grain that has taken the years in its stride and remained upbeat and full of character. **53.2%**

CAMERONBRIDGE
Cameron Brig db **(79) n**19 **t**21 **f**19 **b**20. Toffee on the light, sweet finish. **40%**
Peerless Cameronbridge 1978 cask 003, dist Aug 78, **(84) n**20 **t**23 **f**21 **b**20. Fat chewy and very Canadian in style. Excellent. **59.9%**. *Duncan Taylor & Co. Ltd.*

DUMBARTON
Cadenhead's Dumbarton Aged 32 Years dist Feb 62, bott Feb 94 **(85) n**21 genuinely soft and floral; **t**22 much more brittle here with teasing spices and lording corn; **f**21 dry toast and bitter marmalade; **b**21 amazingly firm grain with a lovely fruity edge. **49.9%**

GIRVAN
Black Barrel db **(82) n**20 **t**20 **f**22 **b**20. Dangerously drinkable, moreish grain boasting a soft, Canadian-style oakiness. Light, spicy fizz on the long finish. **40%**
Girvan 1964 db casks filled 30/4/64, bott 10/10/01 **(88) n**22 beautiful, rich corn notes: sweet, deep, yet clean and crystal clear despite age; **t**23 sweet, oily, bourbony, sensual. Brilliant mouthfeel! **f**21 lots of liquorice, oak and subtle vanilla; **b**22 a luscious, classical well-aged grain straight from the top drawer. **48%**. *1,200 bottles.*

INVERGORDON
Invergordon Single Grain db **(84) n**20 **t**21 **f**22 **b**21. High-quality, sweet, velvety grain: a fine representative of medium-aged stock from this distillery. **40%**
Invergordon Highland Grain The Stillman's Dram Distilled 1973 db **(88) n**21 sweet, soft and lush, heaps of toffee: really attractive; **t**23 firmer and fabulously spicy. Beautiful depth with storming oak richness; **f**22 chewy toffee, enormously rich; **b**22 brilliant grain whisky that puts many malts to shame.
Cadenhead's Invergordon Aged 13 Years (79) **n**20 **t**19 **f**20 **b**20. Very oily and soft, the subtle sweetness disguising the strength. **67.8%**
Peerless Invergordon 1965 cask 15539, dist Dec 65 36-y-o **(89) n**21 sweet corn and rich, telling oak; **t**23 sumptuous natural caramel combined with chewy corn: the sweetness is in perfect rhythm with the oak; **f**23 long, sweet and more of the same; **b**22 top of the range Canadian – for a Scotch! **51.8%**. *Duncan Taylor & Co.*

NORTH BRITISH
Adelphi North British 12 Years Old cask 41147, dist 90, bott 02 **(85) n**21 firm grain, soft oak; **t**22 amazingly sweet and rum-like; **f**21 the soft oak returns with some stunning oils; **b**21 a whisky for rum devotees. **67.5%**
⠿ **Adelphi North British 13 Years Old** dist 90 cask 52640 bott 03 **(87) n**22 lemon zest amid the corn; **t**22 stunningly sweet and deliciously oiled mouth

arrival; **f**21 a hint of spice but mainly vanilla; **b**22 faultlessly rich and chewy grain: fascinating that when compared with previous bottlings the scores are almost identical – 100/100 for consistency!! **63.5%**

Adelphi North British 13 Years Old cask 52640, **(87) n**21 soft, Canadian-style corn and oak: enticing; **t**21 delicious fat toffee with growing oak offering soft spice. Some fruit hangs around, too; **f**23 long, chewy with a hint of cocoa and increasing sweetness: stunning; **b**22 exemplary. **63.5%**

Scott's Selection North British 1974 bott 99 **(85) n**21 rich vanilla – not unlike a medium matured bourbon – deliciously sweet with the extra complexity of polished wooden floors and acacia honey; **t**22 dissolves in the mouth. It is vanilla and other delicate oaks all the way. Sweet, silky mouthfeel with the corn prominent, not unlike a superior Gibson's Canadian. Superb; **f**21 medium length and remains stubbornly sweet despite the oak trying to gather a hint of bitterness. Excepionally rich mouthfeel continues to the very last; **b**21 complexity may not be the name of the game here, but this aged grain shows what great spirit plus very good oak can produce over a quarter of a century. A minor classic. **53.1%**. *Robert Scott & Co.*

NORTH OF SCOTLAND

⋰∙ **Hart Brothers Alloa 1964** dist July 64 **(86) n**23 toasted marshmallows, natural vanilla and sweet Muscovado sugar all in a bourbony coating; **t**22 silky at first then a peppered spice attack as the oak rolls in; **f**20 although feeling a bit tired there is enough custardy vanilla to see it through; **b**21 like many ancient grains this has become delicious hybrid of half Canadian half bourbon strength unspecified (circa 44%) Sample tasted prior to bottling in July 04. Alloa grain was made at the North of Scotland distillery but tankered and filled into cask at their Dillichip Bond. Very rare stuff.

⋰∙ **Scott's Selection North of Scotland 1963** bott 98 **(88) n**22 buttery biscuits beneath a maizy, bourbony façade; **t**21 creamy textured, sweet vanilla and more light bourbony sweetness; **f**22 distant marzipan on the pillow-soft vanilla finale; **b**23 wonderfully yielding. **46.8%**

⋰∙ **Scott's Selection North of Scotland 1963** bott 99 **(82) n**20 **t**21 **f**21 **b**20. Enjoyably maizy and Canadian but lacks the usual disarming charm. **55%**

Scott's Selection North of Scotland 1963 bott 97 **(92) n**23 high-quality old bourbon: intense vanillas and natural caramels combine for a beautifully sweet, richly toffeed aroma. Fabulously well integrated spices and fruit add perfect complexity: damsons and dates about; **t**24 sweet and incredibly intense. Surprising viscosity for a grain that coats the mouth with pure demerara. The corn flits around in tandem with the cream-toffee oak: sensational and near flawless; **f**22 amazingly long, elements of dried vanilla and crushed pepper but it's all softly, softly and sexy; **b**23 if anyone thinks that grain whisky is inferior to malt, then grab hold of this. An appreciation and understanding of bourbon whisky would be advantageous but not essential. Much more of an ultra-fine bourbon than Scotch, but still one of the finest grains you'll ever find. Glorious. **46.8%**. *Robert Scott & Co.*

⋰∙ **Scott's Selection North of Scotland 1964** bott 03 **(90) n**22 buttery, sweet corn: slightly bourbony with a dash of Canadian; **t**23 extraordinary early sweetness that maintains balance and corn richness: the oak is a distant rumble; **f**22 Demerara sugar abounds, a touch of liquorice but the corn still blossoms even at the death; **b**23 is this really almost 40 years old? One hell of a cask for one hell of a whisky ... **43.6%**

⋰∙ **Scott's Selection North of Scotland 1971** bott 02 **(81) n**21 **t**21 **f**19 **b**20. Soft, sweet Canadian/bourbony notes are overpowered on the finale by an off-key bitterness. **49.9%**

Vatted Grain

Compass Box Hedonism (first bottling, large illustration, described as "Scotch Grain") **(86) n**_21_ clean, waxy, cream toffee, quite dusty, showing some age; **t**_22_ soft, silky grain then a quick surge of oak; **f**_22_ amazingly soft, sweet and lethargic. The oak returns apologetically; **b**_21_ its strength is its coyness. Canadian style.

⋯⋮⋯ **Compass Box Hedonism** bott 04 (bottle identification L4097) **(89) n**_22_ soft, circular vanilla with a spec of honey; **t**_22_ soft landing but enough chew in there to make it entertaining; **f**_23_ good length and spice; **b**_22_ grain again shown to its advantage. **43%**

Compass Box Hedonism Vatted Grain (second bottling, small central illustration, described as "Vatted Grain") **(87) n**_21_ crisp grain, a more clipped, fruity, mildly spiced chap; **t**_22_ much more forthcoming and intense grain carried along with more than a hint of upfront, oaky bourbon; **f**_22_ long, slightly oily with a build-up of sweet banana and vanilla. Dries beautifully; **b**_22_ really mouthfilling and intense. Canadian style. **43%. nc ncf.**

Compass Box Hedonism Vatted Grain (third bottling, same label as second bottling, but laser jet bottling code number L3 136) **(89) n**_22_ light cereals, perfectly placed between sweet and dry: clean, almost ethereal with just a hint of surprising bourbon-style oak for ballast; **t**_22_ enormously delicate with a soft, starchy beginning building up to something oilier and sweeter. Some serious lip-smacking spices evolve; **f**_22_ long, spicy and drying. There is much interplay between vanilla-oak and the grain; **b**_23_ this is the other side of the same Hedonism coin: really classy, but in this case light and spicy rather than the overtly sweeter, oilier, more velvety texture of the previous bottling. This one, though, wins hands down for eye-closing, contemplative complexity. **40%**

Scottish Blends

If it is time for re-evaluating any one whisky type then surely it has to be Blended Scotch. For it really is quite extraordinary how people the world over, with refined palates and a good knowledge of single malts, are so willing to dismiss blends without a thought.

Perhaps it is a form of malt snobbery: if you don't drink malts, then you are not a serious Scotch whisky connoisseur ... or so some people think. Perhaps it is the fact that something like 95 out of every 100 bottles of Scotch consumed is a blend that has brought about this rather too common cold-shouldering. Well, not in my books. In fact, perhaps the opposite is true. Until you get to grips with blends you may well be entitled to regard yourself knowledgeable in single malts, but not in Scotch as a whole. Blends should be the best that Scotland can offer, because with a blend you have the ability to create any degree of complexity. And surely balance and complexity are the cornerstones of any great whisky, irrespective of type.

Of course there are some pretty awful blends created simply as a commodity with little thought going into their structure – just young whiskies, sometimes consisting of stock that is of dubious quality and then coloured up to give some impression of age. Yes, you are more likely to find that among blends than malts and for this reason the poorest blends can be pretty nasty. And, yes, they contain grain. Too often, though, grain is regarded as a kind of whisky leper – not to be touched under any circumstances. Some writers dismiss grain as "neutral" and "cheap", thus putting into the minds of the uninitiated the perception of inferiority.

But there really is nothing inferior about blends. In fact, whilst researching *The Bible*, I have to say that my heart missed more than one beat usually when I received a sample of a blend I had never found before. Why? Well, with single malts each distillery produces a style that can be found within known parameters. With a blend, anything is possible. There are many dozens of styles of malts to choose from and they will react slightly differently with certain grains.

For that reason, perhaps, I have marked blends a little more strictly and tighter than I have single malts. Because blends, by definition, should offer more.

And they do not have to be of any great age to achieve greatness. Look at the brilliance of the likes of Royal Silk, Black Bottle, Bailie Nicol Jarvie, Teachers, Grants and others. Also, look at the diversity of style from crisp and light to peat dominant. Then you get others where age has also played an astonishing role, not least a 50-years-old, such as Royal Salute.

Just like malts, blends change in character from time to time as the availability of certain malts and grains dry up. The most unforgivable reason is because the marketing guys reckon it needs a bit of extra colour and precious high notes are lost to caramel or sherry. Subtlety and character are the keys for any great blend without fail. Usually they are found in abundance in Johnnie Walker Black Label. But for this edition of the *Whisky Bible* my last two samples displayed an unusual dullness. It is a whisky I have worshipped for a quarter of a century and I am certain it is simply a blip. An irritating one, and an aspect of whisky tasting that keeps you on your toes. Get tasting and let me know what you think.

The most exciting blends show bite, character and attitude. Silk and charm are to be appreciated. But after a long, hard day is there anything better than a blend that is young and confident enough to nip and nibble at your throat on its way down and then throw up an array of flavours and shapes to get your taste-buds round?

With Blended Scotch the range and possibilities are limitless. All it takes is for the drinker not just to use his or her nose and taste-buds. But also an open mind.

Scotland Blends

100 Pipers (67) n*17* t*17* f*16* b*17*. 100 Pipers: zero harmony. Young, less than pleasant grain. Was called 100 Pipers, then re-named Black Watch – now appears to be 100 Pipers again, though there is still a Black Watch. They keep changing the name but the same bloody awful whisky keeps appearing. **40%**. *Chivas.*

∴ **Aberdour Piper (83)** n*21* t*21* f*20* b*21*. For an economy bar whisky, this offers unusual depth with satisfyingly lucid crunchy grain, excellent bite and just the right addition of smoke. A real clean mouthful and an attractive and cleverly blended one at that. **40%**. *Haymon Distillers*

Acing Superior (76) n*18* t*22* f*18* b*18*. A really enjoyable and impressive 5-y-o-style blend with decent malt and sparkling grain, but let down for the purists by the colouring. **40%**

∴ **Aged Blend** (*see* Duncan Taylor Aged Blend)

Ailsa Craig (77) n*18* t*22* f*19* b*18*. The strangely anarchic, smoky yet mildly off-key nose for a blend is compensated by an extraordinary and quite delicious mouth arrival that heads in two distinctly different directions. The grain is hard and unyielding while the malt is oily and aided by sharp and intense barley and no little smoke. Hardly a blend: more of a delicious-tasting accident. Weird and, in part, wonderful. **40%**. *A Dewar Rattray.*

∴ **Alistair Graham Scotch Whisky (71)** n*17* t*19* f*18* b*17.* Spot the malt contest. Decent enough grain, though. **40%**. *For Sainsbury's, UK.*

The Andrew Usher Memorial Blend (92) n*23* beautifully firm grain which seems attached to succulent fruit. The malts are busy and spicy: a real blender's blend; t*24* explosive, mouth-enveloping stuff. The malts go hand-in-hand with the grain to create complex patterns all around the palate while the fruit ensures softness reigns; f*22* much lighter with toffee-vanilla gentleness against the foraging spice; b*23* one for the Andrew Usher hall of fame. The old man would have been proud of a blend that has it all. **49%**. *Kyndal.*

The Antiquary 12 Years Old (84) n*20* t*22* f*20* b*22*. There is some deliciously outstanding interplay between the fussy grain and the very rich malt. But the higher notes, especially on the nose, are clobbered by toffee: it's just too delicate a blend to take it. **40%**. *J & W Hardie.*

The Antiquary 21 Years Old (88) n*21* spicy with full malt and toffee to the fore; t*24* massive spice then thinning grain before a mega tsunami of honeyed malt crashes over the tastebuds: astonishing and very beautiful; f*21* soft, very old grains and peaty spices pick at the vanilla; b*22* this is a stylish blend that suggests that there is a lot of whisky much older than 21 in it. The mouth arrival borders on perfection.

Asda Finest Scotch (81) n*21* t*21* f*19* b*20*. A surprisingly complex, mouthwatering and well-balanced dram plucked off the supermarket shelf. The busy nose offers all you could ask of a young blend. Asda UK.

∴ **Asda Finest Old Scotch Aged 8 Years (79)** n*19* t*22* f*19* b*19*. A more than competent supermarket blend that positively shimmers on the tastebuds with a wondrous delivery of fresh, mouthwatering malt aided and abetted by crisp yet well aged grain. A sightly bitter finish, though. **40%**

Asyla (*see* Compass Box)

Auld Lang Syne (81) n*19* t*21* f*20* b*21*. A pretty good, clean blend that can barely be found these days. Easily spotted, though: thanks to a tone deaf packager in the Far East, the carton plays "Home, Home on the Range" when you open it rather than Burns' classic. **40%**. *Langs.*

Avonside (74) n*17* t*20* f*19* b*18*. Pleasant, but a little flat. **40%**. *Gordon & MacPhail.*

Avonside 8-years-old (81) n*18* t*21* f*22* b*20*. Beautifully honeyed: much more evidence of oak and age than on standard 8-y-o version. **57%**. *Gordon & MacPhail.*

The Bailie Nicol Jarvie (B.N.J) Over 6 Years Old. **(93)** n22 as fruity and mouthwatering as a riesling, but infinitely better. Green, grassy and youthful with almost perfect grain balance; t24 tarty and biting, the nose translates to palate with mouthwatering Speyside malt in harmony with exquisite flinty grain. It rarely gets better than this; f23 more grain here as the malt slowly wanders off and late oak adds to length with a brush of cocoa; b24 poetry in solution: a must-have blend for every cabinet. **40%.** *Nicol Anderson & Co. (Glenmorangie plc).*

Ballantine's Finest (83) n19 t20 f21 b23. A soft, deceptively complex light blend that grows in stature and charm as it develops on the palate. Superb grain charisma: great blending, lads! **40%.** *Allied.*

⸭ **Ballantine's Aged 12 Years (87)** n21 a steady-as-she-goes, grain-steered dram with hints of kumquat and buttered toast for extra effect; t22 lashings of cream-toffee punctuated by the occasionally exposed strata of Speyside-clean barley; f21 beautifully layered at first, with even the odd hint of something vaguely smoky. The toffee has too great a say, though; b23 the kind of old-fashioned, mildly moody blend Colonel Farquharson-Smythe (retired) might have recognised when relaxing at the 19th hole back in the early 50s. Too good for a squirt of Soda, mind. **40%** *Allied.*

Ballantine's Gold Seal 12 Years Old (88) n23 gently smoked with the most distant hints of very clean sherry: just beautiful; t21 the fruit ensures a rather too gentle entry onto the tastebuds, but excellent grain does some catching up to land a vanilla punch. The malt is lazy and relaxed; f22 some cocoa and rousing complex malty-oaky-smoky tones ensure a bitter-sweet ending; b22 very complex and alluring. **40%.** *Allied.*

Ballantine's Royal Blue 12 Years Old (90) n23 fabulous chalky-oak and big malt presence; t22 mouthwatering, fat, some dazzling citrus notes and then cocoa/coffee towards the spiced, complex middle; f22 sweetens with both malt and soft brown sugar The texture remains lush without ever being oily; b23 this blend has improved beyond recognition since I last tasted it: my hats off to the blender. This is for the Japanese market and, had I tasted this blind, I would have marked it down as a Japanese blend of the top order ... which is some compliment. **43%.** *Allied.*

Ballantine's 17 Years Old (96) n24 a floral lavender-mint combination balance with aplomb with the most intrinsic peat and grain: beguiling and wonderfully sexy; t25 this is it: balance, charm, guile, charisma ... the entire works in one voluptuous mouthful. First a sweet sheen coats the mouth then some grassy notes get you salivating before soft smoke provides the weight. Enormous with wave upon wave of intense barley sugar and peat but never heavy enough to snap a twig. This is masterful blending; f23 some oaks finally settle like sediment. Raisins and walnut complete the rich picture and spices add that extra dimension ... as if it was needed; b24 it's amazing that out of one lab comes two blends that give masterclass performances: Ballantine's 17 and Teachers. Both are outwardly weighty but reveal so much more that is gentle and complex. The point about this whisky is that you feel you never quite get to the bottom layer: labyrinthine liquid genius. **43%.** *Allied.*

Ballantine's 21 Years Old (81) n19 t20 f22 b20. A less than impressive sherry butt has made its way into this vatting and taken the edge off things slightly. The early finish remains impressive for its complexity with fabulously delicate peat weaving rich patterns, but the finale underlines the poor sherry. For the next edition expect this to be back in the high 80s/low 90s. **43%.** *Allied.*

Ballantine's 30 Years Old (91) n23 the nose is massaged by a creamy, ripe fruity, grapey and softly malt gem. Not a single sign of grain, except perhaps that cream; t23 this is too much ... now the tastebuds get the same treatment. The silky softness almost defies description; f22 mildly bitter as some grain bites, but the malt now compensates: high alcohol Horlicks; b23 I suppose the nature of the beast dictates that the style of a 30-y-o blend will move around a little: this really is very different..and superb! **43%**. *Allied.*

Ballantine's Limited (89) n*22* excellent clarity of fruit and barley; t*24* early grain and then a slow, complex delivery of malt surrounded by soft grape and the lightest coating of muscovado sugar; f*21* dryer with some bitter-almond and cocoa on the oak; b*22* a quality newcomer that is beautifully textured and quite fabulously constructed. **43%**. *Allied.*

Ballantine's Master's (84) n*21* t*22* f*20* b*21*. Excellent use of lively grain and chewy malt to counter something that towards the end especially is a little too soft and gentle. **40%**. *Allied.*

Bell's Exra Special (78) n*20* t*20* f*18* b*20*. The Bell's with no age statement. Decent arrival on palate with good biting grain to end what appears some decent Speyside maltiness through the middle. **40%**. *SA.*

Bell's Extra Special 8 Years Old (84) n*21* t*22* f*21* b*20*. A really sound and complex whisky with good weight and no shortage of style. Lovely spice on the finish. **40%**

Bell's 12 Years Old (90) n*22* new leather and a hint of honey; t*23* both grains and malts arrive in just about equal measures for very busy, complex start. Silky mouthfeel and some wonderful gently smoked spices; f*22* long and clean with vanilla dominating; b*23* absolutely quality blending, and pretty remarkable considering the mass scale on which it is achieved. No one style dominates, though it would be fair to say this is on the light side of medium in weight. **40%**

Bell's Islander (82) n*21* t*21* f*20* b*20*. A blend that has been discontinued a little while, though in 2003 I have spotted it in bars as far apart as Copenhagen and Oxfordshire. These later bottlings were softer than the first run with the added Talisker not showing to great effect. Chewy, but a little toffeed. **40%**

Ben Aigen (68) n*17* t*18* f*16* b*17*. Sweet caramel; bland and dusty. **40%**. *Gordon & MacPhail.*

Ben Alder (85) n*20* yielding and sweet; t*23* an absolute avalanche of complex fruit and barley flavours, stretched out by silky grain; f*21* sweet and rich with much toffee and spice; b*21* a delicious dram, especially with the massive mouth arrival. But not quite what it was at the moment. **40%**. *Gordon & MacPhail.*

Beneagles (67) n*17* t*18* f*16* b*16*. Flat and lifeless. 40%

❖ **Ben Roland Five Years Old (81)** n*19* t*21* f*20* b*21*. Caramel led, sweet, spicy and quietly complex. **40%**. *For Unwins, UK.*

Big Ben Special Reserve (80) n*19* t*22* f*19* b*20*. Solid young blend with that rush of grassy-Speysidey malt that hits the palate full on that I find irresistible. **40%**. *Angus Dundee.*

Big "T" (91) n*22* toasty and spicy, lively grain on a very clean malt bed: excellent; t*23* stupendous balance to the opening with both malt and grain making a bee-line for the tastebuds, complex and confrontational, with big spice kick; f*22* the grains move in with the vanilla but there is an exceptional sweet malt theme that stays to the end; b*24* this is my kind of whisky: busy, characterful, complex and charismatic. Available mainly in the Far East, but should be on the home and international stage. **40%**. *Tomatin Distillery Co.*

Black & White (79) n*18* t*20* f*21* b*20*. Fruity but just a tad musty with all the complexity on the finish. Much richer and less grain-dominated than a few years back. **40%**. *Diageo.*

Black Bottle (95) n*23* sizzling, jabbing grain versus heavyweight young peated malts: some match; t*24* the outcome on the palate is explosive: rampaging peaty malts put firmly in their place by crisp grain with a unique mouthfeel style, different even to Isle of Skye; f*25* softer, spent, sweet malts allow the more bitter cocoa-crusted grains to make a stand; b*23* a blend that has to be tasted to be believed: it is young yet enormous, raw yet sophisticated, wild, brazen and beautiful. Here's a tip for best drinking results: take big mouthful, then open and close mouth rapidly in exaggerated chewing action. The flavours that hit you will have you searching for a chair. And another glass ... **40%**

Black Bottle 10 Years Old (89) n22 so age-weightedly peaty it could be almost a single malt: the grains make little discernible impact; t23 soft, deft malt and firmer grain. The peat arrives after a short interval; f22 more vanilla and other oaky tones; b22 a stupendous malt of weight and poise, but possessing little of the all-round steaming, rampaging sexuality of the younger version. **40%**

Black Cock (78) n19 t20 f19 b20. Overtly grainy but a surprisingly malty mouthwatering quality makes for a half-decent blend. **40%**

⋰⋱ **Black Douglas (83)** n20 t20 f22 b21. Big, chewy, well weighted and fat. Pretty long, decently smoked nose and finale. **40%.** *Australia.*

Blackpool (73) n18 t19 f18 b18. Grain and sweet toffee. Easy going but never hits the bright lights. **40%.** *Invergordon.*

Black Prince (68) n16 t19 f17 b16. One rich flourish apart, way off target. **40%.** *Burn Stewart.*

Black Prince 12 Years Old (80) n19 t22 f19 b20. Soft and silky, there is good fruit and crisp grain. A spicy but toffeed finish. **43%** *Burn Stewart. A discontinued blend now: a collector's item if you see it.*

Black Top Finest De Luxe (77) n19 t21 f18 b19. Silky, sweet and rich, but a touch too much caramel dulls the complexity. **40%.** *Aberfoyle & Knight. South America.*

Black Watch (for tasting notes see 100 Pipers)

Blue Eagle (80) n18 t22 f20 b20. A big, booming arrival on the palate with fresh, intense malt that glistens and sparkles. *Edrington Group. Thailand.*

⋰⋱ **Blue Hanger 25 Years Old** bott 03 **(93)** n23 a silky sheen makes for the softest of nasal impacts; ripe grape and mango to the fore with a barley-sugar sub plot. Real fruit cake fodder; t24 lush arrival and then a slow unravelling of subtle spices; the fruitiness clings to the roof of the mouth as an obviously high malt percentage makes its mark; f22 some grain and oak are visible at last as a gradual thinning out of flavours begins; b24 an exceptional blend that offers a subtle bite to balance perfectly the lush intensity. The biter-sweet balance is exemplary. Brilliant. **45.6%. nc ncf.** *Berry Bros & Rudd.*

Bruce and Company Scotch Whisky (79) n19 t21 f20 b19. The minimalist label – "Scotch Whisky" in black on white – somehow perfectly summarises a minimalist dram. This, for all intents and purposes, is young grain whisky with a dash of malt – and I do mean a dash. And topped up with some colouring. Yet, it's sweet, has a rich mouthfeel, there are no off-notes and perfectly enjoyable – providing you are not on the hunt for complexity. **40%.** *Exclusive to Tesco UK.*

Buchanan's De-Luxe Aged 12 Years (85) n20 some deft smoke tries to trouble the rich fruits; t23 stunningly soft texture, enormously fruity with some firm grain through the middle and then spice. Great chewing whisky; f21 the spices continue and put life into the vanilla. Slightly bitter fade; b21 a lush blend with big presence. But I have met its alter ego, the odd bottling spoiled slightly by bad sherry influence. On its day, though, a very decent dram. **40%**

Buchanan's Special Reserve (93) n22 clean grape and quite floral; t24 sumptuous, ultra-lush mouth arrival with silky grain carrying with it clean sherry and sweet malt; f23 now the complexity really begins with some smoky spices digging into the fruit and oak; b24 one of those rare whiskies that makes you groan with satisfaction as it hits your tastebuds: certainly one of the most silky around offering nothing other than sheer, supremely engineered class. **40%**

Budgen's Finely Blended Scotch (75) n18 t20 f18 b19. A high-caramel but otherwise clean blend with a very enjoyable grain bite. **40%.** *Budgens Stores UK.*

Burn McKenzie (72) n18 t19 f18 b17. Some pretty firm grain is dealt with with caramel. Coking whisky, I believe, is the term. And rightfully unashamed of it. **40%.** *Burn Stewart.*

Campbeltown Loch (71) n*18* t*19* f*17* b*17*. More simplistic than of old. **40%.** *Springbank.*

Campbeltown Loch 25 Years Old (85) n*21* a massive injection of oak, almost too intense, but barley and fruit balances; t*22* quite massive, initially dry, oak which sweetens and develops into a honeyed barley beaut; f*21* the sweet barley sheen remains with vanillas softening things further; b*21* a supreme game of brinkmanship with the oak is won – just. *Springbank.*

Catto's Deluxe 12 Years Old (87) n*22* deftly done: fragile, honeyed malty notes with the promise of something Speysidey and mouthwatering; t*23* no disappointment: fresh malts bombard the tastebuds, then a gradual release of mouth-coating richer, oilier notes; f*21* sweet with coconut milk and firmer grains; b*21* a bolder and richer blend than the subtle version of a few years back. The stamp of class, though, is undeniable. **40%.** *Inver House.*

Catto's Rare Old Scottish Highland (89) n*22* fresh, sensual. The grains are brilliantly chosen to allow full malt impact; t*22* adorable formation of sweet Speyside malts just melt in with the lush grain; f*23* long and spicy and a touch of chalky oak adds to the balance; b*22* silky and rich, this is delicious everyday fare of considerable charm. A truly classic, crisp young malt that is way above its station. For confirmation, smell the honey on the empty glass. **43%.** *Inver House.*

Chivas Brothers 1801 (92) n*23* punchy oloroso: perhaps it is brittle from Glen Grant malt imitating Irish pot still, but this is so very much like a Jameson whiskey sherry cask; t*24* sweet, hard and brittle again. No-one will persuade me there aren't tons of sherried Glen Grant in this. Some salt seems to bolster the flavour explosion further; f*22* softer now as clean grain strikes but the spiced sherry is in close attendance; b*23* the kind of dram you just can't say no to. Quality. **50%.** *This, tragically, has now been lost to us and has evolved into Chivas "Revolve".*

Chivas Brothers Oldest and Finest (94) n*24* beguiling stuff of most untypical Chivas style: smoke and peat blending in with the fruit, nutmeg and allspice. The sherry influence is sublime; t*24* just flows on from where the nose left off. The sherry is clean and weighty and beautiful spices arrive to flit around the palate. The malt is big with a degree of smoke and the grains do what grains should do best: polish the malts and marry the styles. Absolutely breathtaking; f*22* long with smoke and a sound structure. The spices continue to sparkle and the fruit also gathers intensity; b*24* it breaks my heart to announce that the blend has been discontinued, though a search through specialist outlets should reveal the odd bottle or two lurking about. Make no mistake: this is testimony to the art of brilliant, sympathetic and intuitive blending. What we have here is a masterpiece. **43%**

Chivas Regal 12 Years Old (76) n*18* t*22* f*17* b*19*. The nose and finish are their usual drab selves, though this time there is a beautiful, if brief, Speyside sparkle to the early mouth arrival. The highest mark I have given this blend for some time ... which isn't saying much. **40%**

Chivas Regal 18 Years Old (82) n*19* t*23* f*19* b*21*. You get the feeling that there is a great blend trying to escape the smothering clutches of some so-so grain. The early Speyside malt mouthfeel is a delight. **40%**

Chivas Revolve (81) n*20* t*21* f*20* b*20*. A sherried dram that lacks complexity and direction. Not to be mentioned in the same breath as "1801", the blend it replaced. **40%**

Clan Campbell (88) n*21* an old-fashioned style: slightly raw big grain kick and bite with young Speysiders who also have a punch-up; t*23* the grains are side-tracked as the Speysiders go nuts: really, grassy and mouthwatering; f*22* long and malty; b*22* a blend that has changed dramatically, yet has somehow kept its family values. Much more bite than of old, yet the complexity and freshness on the palate has gone through the roof, while retaining its old-fashioned feel. A little stunner. **40%**

Clan Campbell Legendary Aged 18 Years (89) n22 accomplished oloroso notes are thinned by attractive grain-led vanilla: stylish stuff; t23 superb: a real outbreak of all things complex with soft grain at the centre but fruit heading from one malt to another and a very subtle smokiness from elsewhere; f22 more simple but the gentle vanilla and distant echo of spice is a tease; b22 greatly improved on recent years and now a dram of unquestionable distinction. **40%**

Clan MacGregor (88) n22 superb grains allow the lemon-fruity malt to ping around: clean, crisp and refreshing; t22 as mouthwatering as the nose suggests with first clean grain then a succession of fruity and increasingly sweet malty notes. Such a brilliant mouthful; f22 medium length with clever use of vanilla alongside very yielding grain; b22 a young blend that seems to have improved beyond recognition in recent years: maltier and perhaps a little older. A great everyday whisky of distinction. *Wm Grant's US.*

Clan MacGregor 12 Years Old (84) n21 t20 f22 b21. The suspicion is that the grains are a lot older than 12: there is a lot of bourbon-oaky character on the nose and on the mouth arrival. Great finish, but lacking the all-round fresh-faced charisma of the young MacGregor. *Wm Grant's US.*

Clan Roy (74) n18 t20 f18 b18. A clean, toffeed, blandish blend saved by a touch of spice towards the middle. **40%.** *Morrison Bowmore.*

⁖ **Classic Cask 15 Years Old** batch 401 **(91)** n20 slight marmalade with chunky, oaky vanilla; t22 tangled mouth arrival as the oak tries to impose itself but fails; settles towards the silky, malt middle with the first-class grains acting as a dais; f25 quite faultless finish that is just so long and explores quasi-bourbon haunts amid a beautifully sweet maltiness that is almost three dimensional in the dreamy semi-oily texture; for perfection's sake the grain also offers a little bite. For a blend, this is too good to be true; b24 from an ordinary nose, grows a quite extraordinary whisky. **43%.** *Red Lion Blending. 600 bottles.*

⁖ **Classic Cask 35 Years Old** batch 202 **(93)** n22 a curious mixture that gives itself just as much to glasses of sherry and bourbon as it does Scotch. Clean as a whistle, though; t23 a light-heavyweight that does not try to punch. The half-hearted jabs at the palate with chewy fruit and a sublimely textured grain; f24 slightly bitter finish balances well with the sweeter bout before; the very end is almost ancient rum-textured with a liquorice-coffee backbone sweetened with Demerara; b24 this is just so dangerous: open a bottle of this and it'll be gone before you know it. **43%.** *Red Lion Blending. 600 bottles.*

The Claymore (76) n17 t20 f19 b20. A much more tastebud-friendly blend than the old cut-and-thrust number of yore. Still can't say the nose does much for me but the developing fruitiness on the middle and finish is silky and complex. **40%.** *Kyndal.*

Cluny (85) n20 soft grain weathers the biting malt; t21 mouth-filling and big with the grain again doing its best to lighten the load. Soft vanilla arrives early; f22 very long with more malt, even a hint of something vaguely smoky and spicy, then toffee; b22 I do adore this kind of blend: slightly rough-edged, and every time you take a mouthful something slightly different happens. If I were to find fault, a touch too much caramel is evident at the very death. **40%.** *Kyndal.*

Compass Box Asyla (first bottling – large picture 43% abv) **(89)** n22 clean and simplistic, luxuriating in the effortless interlocking of soft malt and even softer grain; t23 suddenly comes alive on the palate with a fabulously textured malt thrust countered by silky grains; f22 delicate and so beautifully spiced, with a balancing dryness; b22 a really excellent first issue from whisky purist John Glaser that offers nothing but quality. **ncf.**

Compass Box Asyla (second bottling (2003) – small picture, fluted bottle 40% abv) **(93)** n23 charming complexity from the off with subtlety the key.

The barley is rich, the grain is yielding, the result is spellbinding; **t**23 simply to die for with layers of sparkling malt, toasted and honeyed but never overly sweet. The spice teases but no more; **f**23 only now do the grains lock on. Even so, the malt runs its course and spice, if anything, intensifies; **b**24 so sexy, you could almost make love to it. Unquestionably one of the best light blends on the market. **nc ncf**.

⠰⠰ **Compass Box Asyla** bottle identification L4097 **(92)** n22 like a trifle ... but without the sherry; **t**23 very clever strands of sugar-honey intertwine with both grassy malt and clean grain; **f**23 long and laid-back with no weight whatsoever but an erogenous caressing of the tastebuds with an almost covert flavour attack; **b**24 subliminal whisky that may wash over you unnoticed for the first two or three mouthfuls but then you wake up to what is happening to you: and that is pretty sexy stuff, believe me ... **40%**

Co-operative Group (CWS) Scotch Whisky (79) n19 t21 f20 b19. Young, mouth-filling, clean and quite juicy. Thoroughly decent. **40%.** *Co-op UK.*

Co-operative Group (CWS) Premium Scotch Whisky Five Years Old (73) n17 t21 f17 b18. Complex middle, but let down by poor cask selection. **40%.** *Co-op UK.*

Covent Garden 10 Years Old (88) n22 the style is classical and one of crystal clarity; **t**23 the marriage between those crisp, clean Speyside malts and refreshing grain is one of harmony and bliss: seems younger than its 10 years thanks to minimal oak interference; **f**21 which arrives towards the finish and dumbs down the rampaging complexity; **b**22 what an outstanding blend this is: pity – though no surprise – that the Cadenhead's shop in Covent Garden that sells it runs out so quickly. **40%** *Cadenhead's.UK.*

Crawford's 3 Star (78) n19 t20 f19 b20. A slightly more fragile thing than it once was with the grain a little firmer and the complexity levels upped. Very attractive. **40%.** *Kyndal.*

Crown Whisky Co. Very Rare Highland Special Reserve (74) n18 t19 f18 b19. A competent grainy blend with a hint of oak. **40%.** *Denmark only.*

⠰⠰ **Custer's Imported Scotch Whisky (81)** n19 t21 f20 b21. For an ultra cheaply here is surprising dexterity to this caramel-rich but otherwise clean and attractive dram. **40%.** *Pierre Charles, Europe.*

Cutty Sark (88) n23 light and floral with firm grain accentuating the malt; **t**22 big grain surge then a slow build-up of Speyside maltiness. Grassy and sharp throughout with a lovely Tamdhu-esque oiliness; **f**21 lots of vanilla and a thread of cocoa on the finale; **b**22 always been light, but virtually all peatiness has vanished of late. Even so, a real cracker of crispy grain. **40%**

Cutty Sark Aged 12 Years (82) n18 t22 f21 b21. A blemish on the nose, but an otherwise lovely, fresh blend showing more sherry than of old and excellent spices throughout. **40%**

Cutty Sark Aged 18 Years (93) n24 outstanding clean sherry influence, softly smoked and good oak, almost bourbony. Beautiful; **t**23 big, spicy and immensely chewy; **f**22 lots of cream toffee, and a hint of tiring oak, but the grain is really high quality and delicious; **b**24 absolutely stunning. The clever use of the grain is simply breathtaking. **43%**

Cutty Sark Aged 25 Years (90) n23 massive acacia honey and vanilla sing sweetly; **t**23 as intense as an old pot-still demerara with absolutely stunning mouthfeel and fruity richness; **f**22 long, with gathering spices and a hint of smoke. The grains are minute but exemplary and chocolate-coated; **b**22 heavy and honeyed, chewy and charming, the oak has a fraction too big a say but still quite delicious! **45.7%**

Cutty Sark Discovery (*see* Cutty Sark Aged 18 Years)
Cutty Sark Emerald (*see* Cutty Sark Aged 12 Years)

⠰⠰ **D Steven & Son (Wick) Ltd Finest 8 Years Old (80)** n20 t21 f19 b20. A solid, firm blend with satisfying smoke, bite and spice. Big grain finish. **40%**

Dewar's White Label (83) n21 **t**22 **f**19 **b**21. A decent, punchy, mildly biting blend where the grains are proud to show themselves and the malt makes enjoyable, soothing and sweetening noises. The toffee dims the sparkle somewhat, though. **40%.** *Curiously, White Label is now the possessor of a pale yellow one …*

Dewar's Ancestor Aged 12 Years (89) n22 clean, gently spiced but richly sherried nose; **t**23 curvaceous fruit blends superbly with crisp grains and teasing malt; **f**22 really gentle finish with vanilla, sherry and cold, milky coffee. The spices just take a ramble round the gob; **b**22 fabulous use of sherry cask as it is clean enough to allow an unusual degree of complexity. The unusual strength probably compensates for evaporation during the painfully slow pouring process … **43.5%**

Dewar's Special Reserve Aged 12 Years (91) n23 exceptionally well designed with the heavier smoke and fruit notes adding only a background noise to the slightly more three-dimensional grain and soft honey-malt; **t**23 big and mouthwatering with spices developing fast. Beautiful integration of the harder grains and a developing oakiness; **f**21 way too much toffee undoes some of the intricate complexity. The spices carry on unabated, though; **b**24 an unashamedly old-fashioned type of blended Scotch and closest to the traditional Dewar's style of pre-Second World War days. A seriously delicious transportation back in time to the days when blends were cherished. **43%**

⠶ **Dewar's 18 Years Old** db **(93) n**22 the oak from the grain leads the way on this with some soft malt and citrus fruit playing catch-up; surprisingly light and elegant for the colour; **t**24 the Dewar's signature of rigid complexity strikes from the off; a rock-hard wall of grain at first seems impenetrable then a fizzing, breathtaking and quite glittering array of malty-oaky tones of varying degrees of sweetness batter the grain into submission. Again some citrus bares its teeth in the middle; **f**23 there is a delicate cocoa dustiness to the malt that at last has broken free of the grain and fruit; **b**24 like all better blends, this is a whisky that needs re-visiting and listening to to get the best results. Handsome, distinguished and displaying almost immeasurable complexity. **43%**

⠶ **Dewar's Signature (93) n**23 distinctive and lucid despite some obvious age around. Very firm, almost crisp apples with sweeter malt softening the sharpness. The most subtle hint of something smoky ensures weight to the elegant, flighty complexity. One to take your time over and get to know; **t**24 an adorable attitude and edge to this one: the tastebuds are immediately pounded by jagged, busy spices; the grain is hard as nails with fabulous nip and bite and allows the truly mouthwatering malts to ricochet around the palate. Lusty and luscious, this is great stuff which gets even better as the cocoa-smoky middle emerges; **f**22 again the grains are confident enough to have their say, offering, amid clarity, a firm, cocoa-dusted hand that points to some serious age; the finale is at first slightly estery but at last unusually clean and clear; **b**24 a blend-drinker's blend that is uncompromising and not stinting on old-fashioned sophistication. Just love that spice kick and the biting boldness of the grains that hold their own amid some mouthwatering malt. This is serious whisky, of a style easily identified in the East by connoisseurs of Suntory's freshest and finest. An outstanding addition to the highest echelons of the blended Scotch. **43%**

Dew of Ben Nevis (76) n18 **t**19 **f**20 **b**19. Heavy duty stuff with a sweet finish. **40%.** *Ben Nevis Distillery.*

Dew of Ben Nevis Hector's Nectar (*see* Hector's Nectar)

Dew of Ben Nevis Millennium Blend (86) n20 weighty malt; **t**22 has that "married" feel, where the malts have combined to make a busy, impossible-to-describe whole; **f**22 back to the grains again: quite bitty and complex; **b**22 chunky and complex. **40%.** *Ben Nevis Distillery.*

Dew of Ben Nevis Special Reserve (81) n*19* t*20* f*22* b*20*. Very firm malt, sweet, full-bodied and punchy grain – even a hint of honey on the spicy finale. **40%**. Ben Nevis Distillery.

Dew of Ben Nevis Aged 12 Years (79) n*20* t*20* f*19* b*20*. Pretty straight down-the-line fare with some chunky malt but a flat finale. **40%**. Ben Nevis Distillery.

Dew of Ben Nevis Aged 21 Years (90) n*23* citrus 'n' salt; t*23* fabulous complexity wth illuminating malt showing sweetness to a salty depth and toasty oak; f*21* thins out towards vanilla and milky coffee, but with a little orange to lighten the load; b*23* a really lovely aged blend where the complexity is mind-blowing. Go get...!! **43%**. Ben Nevis Distillery.

Dimple 12 Years Old (83) n*21* t*20* f*21* b*21*. A puff of smoke adds a touch of clout to an otherwise light yet gently spiced and deliciously grained blend. **43%**

Dimple 15 Years Old (72) n*19* t*18* f*18* b*17*. Oh, dear: a real disappointment. Just never takes off or goes anywhere. **40%**

Diners Deluxe Old Scotch 12 Years Old (85) n*21* beautiful spices, intense, weighty malt, and firm grain; t*22* very big, oily and chewy malt arrival that offers immediate sweetness; f*21* an intriguing mixture of lingering smoke and cocoa-grain; b*21* genuinely classy stuff with attitude. **43%**. Douglas Denham for Diners Club.

Diners Supreme Old Scotch 21 Years Old (82) n*20* t*21* f*21* b*20*. A massive blend with no little bourbony-oaky style. **43%**. Douglas Denham for Diners Club.

The Dowans Hotel (88) n*21* soft, mildly smoked; t*22* more grain bite on the palate than the nose suggests; f*23* weighty and majestic: really quite sweet before some clever oak rolls in against the silky grain and bubbling peat; b*22* a seriously decent house blend of a style heavier than you might expect in a Speyside hotel. Worth a detour to find it if in that part of the world. **40%**. Inverarity Vaults for The Dowan's Hotel, Aberlour.

Duggans (76) n*17* t*20* f*19* b*20*. A young, high-grained blend which enjoys a short malty, spicy blast early on before settling for grainier, safer ground. **40%**. Morrison Bowmore.

⠿ **Duncan Taylor Aged Blend 35 Years Old** (Bourbon) **(81)** n*18* t*22* f*20* b*21*. Worn and weary but just enough honeyed touches to keep it impressive. **46%**.

⠿ **Duncan Taylor Aged Blend 35 Years Old** (Sherry) **(83)** n*20* t*19* f*23* b*21*. Exceptional chocolate honeycomb on the fruity finish. **43%**.

The Dundee (77) n*18* t*22* f*19* b*18*. Lots of upfront, grunting grain but the usual Angus Dundee superb mouth arrival. Caramel tucks away the finish, save for some lovely spice. **40%**. Angus Dundee.

Dunfife (75) n*18* t*20* f*19* b*18*. Refreshing and chewy. **40%**. William Maxwell.

Dunhill Old Master (87) n*20* rather caramelised, but some toasty maltiness thrives amid the well-balanced grains; t*22* rich, sweet, heather-honey malt then a middle like cream toffee candy; f*23* becomes even more interesting as the oak appears and spice, too: chewy and complex; b*22* sadly a discontinued blend available now only in more refined outlets in the USA and Japan until stocks run dry. Something wonderfully like "Quality Street" chocolates about this one: will be sadly missed when exhausted. **43%**

Dunhill Gentleman's Speyside Blend (89) n*22* excellently weighty, clean sherry; t*23* subtle honey amid the fruit. The grains are North Britishy-crisp and barley mouthwatering; f*21* vanilla and grape; b*23* I used to prefer Old Master, but as time has progressed I have come to appreciate Gentleman's for its deft charm. Perhaps it is because I am getting older and becoming a gentleman ... Sadly lost to us: available in tiny amounts only in Japan and USA. Someone should revive a wee classic like this. **43%**

EH10 (86) n22 almost too clean to be true: the grassiest of Speyside malt input plus bracing grain. One of the most subtle noses around; **t**23 as mouthwatering as the nose suggests; you can chew the fresh melting, malt while the grain offers something stiffer; **f**20 evidence of a little oaky age, but perhaps a little too light; **b**21 From the same charm school as Bailie Nicol Jarvie, but lacks finish. Otherwise delicious. **40%.** *Sainsbury UK (from Glenmorangie plc).*

The Famous Grouse (83) n21 **t**23 **f**19 **b**20. Remains sexy, elegant and refined with a stunning opening on the palate. But I can't help feeling that caramel has recently replaced some of the crisper notes, especially on the finish. **40%**

The Famous Grouse Cask Strength (87) n22 amazingly big, fresh clean sherry for a light blend: the grains cut into the fruit with precision and no little grace; **t**22 seriously fruity at first then a wave of malt and toffee. The grain reforms towards the middle; **f**21 quite soft with lots of toffee and vanilla; **b**22 a chewy, stylish dram that absorbs the strength easily. Again the toffee is a bit on the heavy side but the overall grain-malt balance is deft and delicious. **59.4%**

The Famous Grouse Gold Reserve Aged 12 Years (85) n19 honeycomb and oak make a sensuous pairing, but dulled by caramel; **t**23 just sensational. Honey and spice drip off the roof of the mouth. Some soft peat digs in with the oak; **f**21 lashing of vanilla and liquorice but again caramel dulls the picture; **b**22 a much more honeyed, richer and improved dram than of old. But the caramel could be cut considerably. **43%**

The Famous Grouse Islay Cask Finish (88) n21 beautifully weighted with kippery tones amid nipping grains; **t**22 a real chewy mouthful: sweet with lots of obvious malt; **f**23 more grain presence with vanilla drying out the sweeter barley. Remains smoky and very long; **b**22 if ever you wondered what a peaty Grouse would be like, here you go. What makes it work is the alluring softness of the smoke. Genuinely graceful for all its weight. **40%**

The Famous Grouse Port Wood Finish (75) n20 **t**20 **f**17 **b**18. A surprising hint of smoke, but otherwise fruity and flat. **40%**

Findlater's Finest (69) n17 **t**18 **f**17 **b**17. A furry, sticky palate; mildly rubbery. **40%.** *Kyndal.*

Findlater's Deluxe 15 Years Old (81) n21 **t**20 **f**20 **b**20. The fruity nose is followed by a chunky arrival on the palate where the malt is thick and chewy. Some coffee on the finale. Takes time to acclimatise to this style of blend, but worth every second. **40%.** *Kyndal.*

Findlater's Deluxe 18 Years Old (91) n22 a hint of dry Lübeck chocolate marzipan; **t**23 decent soft malt sprinkled with light muscovado sugar; **f**22 back to bitter almonds and bourbon amid the lush grain; **b**24 the cleanest, lightest yet most comfortably weighted of the Findlater clan by some margin; supremely balanced with a lush texture and lilting complexity. Some serious blending went into this one. **40%.** *Kyndal.*

Findlater's Deluxe 21 Years Old (89) n22 subtle sherry, clean with simmering spice just below the surface; **t**23 lazy and demure for a blend of such age: the malt does possess a certain countering brittleness to the softer grain; **f**21 vanilla and a hint of sultana and toffee fudge; **b**23 a pretty dreamy, end-of-day blend when you want your tastebuds featherdusted before retiring. **40%.** *Kyndal.*

Fortnum & Mason Choice Old 5 Year Old (83) n20 **t**21 **f**22 **b**20. Good, solid grain helps propel a decent percentage of malt to rich, gently spicy deeds. An impressive 5-y-o by any standards. **40%.** *UK.*

Fraser McDonald's (74) n16 **t**20 **f**19 **b**19. Attractive moments of lucid complexity between the big rubbery nose and the astonishingly sweet finale. Big stuff. Devotees of High Commissioner will know the style. **40%.** *A Bulloch.*

Frasers Supreme (77) n19 **t**19 **f**20 **b**19. A dash of smoke helps add weight. **40%.** *Gordon and MacPhail.*

∴ **"Frisky Whisky" Macho 60% (81) n**19 t20 f21 b21. Big, grainy caramel: a standard, mildly smoky blend apart from the warehouse strength delivery and excellent finish. Possibly the best label on the market, though. **60%.** John Milroy.

Gibson Glengarry (68) n16 t18 f17 b17. Tough going. **40%**

Glen Alba (75) n18 t19 f19 b19. Some young, sharp Speysidey notes, but pretty raw in places with the balance just failing to make the most of the mouthwatering properties. Even so, extra points for being such a clean dram. **40%.** Brand Development Ltd.

Glen Calder (71) n18 t19 f17 b17. Sweet; middle of the road. **40%.** Gordon & MacPhail.

Glen Catrine De Luxe (77) n17 t22 f19 b19. A dusty nose, but recovers for a rich, softly honeyed middle before caramel intervenes on the finish. **40%.** Glen Catrine.

Glen Crinan (72) n17 t19 f18 b18. Oily and full in places. **40%.** Edrington Group France.

Glen Crinan 12 Years Old (75) n17 t20 f19 b19. Maybe I'm being fanciful, but I'm sure I'm detecting Glenturret's hand in there somewhere. A little soapy at first, honey and spice later. **40%.** Edrington..

Glen Clova (70) n18 t18 f17 b17. Grain and caramel all the way. I'm sure there must be some malt in there somewhere, but the grain is clean and decent quality, at least. Ewen & Co for Oddbins UK.

Glendarroch Finest 15 Years Old (91) n21 very firm grain surrounded on all sides by peaty ancient malt and bourbony oak; **t**24 impressive mouthfeel and early spice arrival, then a glorious expansion of quite stunning malt of a richness that needs tasting for comprehension. You can lose yourself in this one for some time; **f**23 the grains bite back and are quite welcome to rescue you from a malty trance: you will appreciate it more if you wallow in the bourbony afterglow; **b**23 this is exceptionally high-quality blending and a marriage of malts and grains that were meant for each other. **43%.** William Gillies & Co.

Glen Dowan (80) n19 t21 f21 b19. Flinty and firm grain with excellent malt development. **40%.** J& G Grant.

Glen Dowan 21 Years Old (89) n21 fresh, coastal and lively; **t**22 a real live wire around the palate with big malt presence; **f**23 lovely spices and exceptional oak control: truly brilliant; **b**23 big, bold and a little salty. Delicious, especially the finale. Out of this world bitter-sweet balance. **43%.** J&G Grant Taiwan/Jap/Asia.

Glengarry (see Gibson Glengarry)

Glen Grigg (71) n16 t19 f18 b18. Young, heavy; subtlety at a premium. **40%.** Spar UK.

Glen Heather (90) n22 hard, unyielding and grain-heavy it may be but the ginger nut bite is engaging. Enticing, confident stuff with the faintest touch of peat; **t**23 fresh, young and mouthfilling. The grains remain brittle and reflect perfectly the Speysidey malts which ensure maximum salivation. Some really excellent spice. Exceptionally clean and crisply defined; **f**22 pretty long with a slight sweetening and softening towards the finale. Some late evidence of age; **b**23 a quite lovely and lively blend from the old school. Clean and distinctive with a marauding spiciness, this is a blend that takes me back 25 years in style. The colour suggests caramel should be lurking somewhere and it does show very briefly and causing virtually no damage at the death. But as a whole this is a throwback, a minor classic blend worthy of discovery. **40%** SH Jones at their shops in Banbury and elsewhere in the heart of England.

∴ **Glenmonarch (63) n**16 t17 f15 b15. Grim nose despite a inconclusive hint of peat; untidy mouth arrival while grain sweetens and then embitters for an awful finish. If there is malt in there I can't spot it other than possibly on the nose. And is it Scotch for sure? Doesn't say so on the label and

although it is heavily implied, I'd be surprised if it is. All horribly synthetic. **40%**.
Belarus Bottling Company

Glen Niven (79) n*20* t*19* f*20* b*20*. Way above average supermarket stuff: the nose shows superb grain qualities while the decent malt reveals itself in the finish. Overall, silky and complex. Rip out the OTT caramel and you would have a quality blend here. *Douglas MacNiven (Asda) UK*.

Glen Osprey (71) n*17* t*18* f*18* b*18*. A pageant of young grain that is generally pleasant enough, especially towards the finish. Beware, though. Another I tasted earlier in the year was off-key and seriously awful. **40%**. *Duncan MacBeth & Co.*

Glen Rosa (83) n*20* t*22* f*21* b*20*. Bit of a surprise package: purists will take a look at the colour and think "caramel". However, it never seriously materialises as a brilliant firm grain stars, bringing the best out of some clean, mouthwatering malt, Arran doubtless included. Seriously tasty, cracking old-fashioned stuff. **40%**. *Isle of Arran*.

Glen Rossie (80) n*20* t*20* f*20* b*20*. Grain-rich, sweet and soft. Limited variation, maximum simple charm. **40%**. *Morrison Bowmore*.

Glen Shira (79) n*20* t*21* f*19* b*19*. A young blend that shows delicious citrus-fruit qualities. **40%**. *Burn Stewart*.

Glenshire (69) n*17* t*18* f*17* b*17*. Clean, young and caramelised. **40%**. *William Maxwell*.

⸫ **Glen Stuart (79)** n*18* t*20* f*21* b*20*. Honest whisky despite the caramel with an excellent grain lead: good session stuff. **40%**. *For Unwins, UK*.

Glen Urquhart (82) n*20* t*21* f*20* b*21*. Gentle and mouthwatering with a touch of spice. **40%**. *Gordon & MacPhail*.

Glinne Parras (85) n*23* malt-rich and complex with evidence of some age and firm grain; t*23* wonderful oily-coated malt coats the mouth allowing rich cream toffee fudge to stick alongside something very obscurely smoked. The grains tingle pleasantly; f*19* flattens alarmingly and finds itself quickly spent; b*20* brilliant nose and mouth-start: the real enjoyment is all upfront. The finish could do with some attention. *Eaux de Vie*.

Glob Kitty (77) n*17* t*20* f*19* b*21*. Clean, firm-grained, light and biting. Good standard whisky. **40%**. *Lehar Aus.*

Golden Blend (88) n*21* a teasing aroma, one minute heavy the next of a fleeting grainy lightness: intriguing and attractive; t*22* honeyed and complex, major chewy sweet malt against melting grain; f*22* enters overdrive here, as the softness of the grain is stupendous. The malt has every chance to form a complex liaison with the gentle oak; b*23* a sound, sophisticated blend of excellent weight and evenness. At no time either bitter or sweet. **40%**. *Kyndal*.

Gordon Graham's Black Bottle (*see* Black Bottle)

The Gordon Highlanders (85) n*21* honey and ginger; t*22* pulses of grain rip through a sturdy malt wall; f*21* more honeycomb and fleeting spice; b*21* a seemingly light whisky but with a weighty middle of some aplomb. The arrival on the palate is almst brain-exploding: in many ways one of the most complex drams on the market. But I suspect a big caramel presence prevents this from being a genuine classic. Glorious, creamy, sweet and lip-smacking stuff. **40%**. *Wm Grant*.

The Grand Bark (84) n*22* t*22* f*20* b*20*. The nose and malty-spicy arrival on the palate are to die for. *Symposium International*.

The Grand Bark 21 Year Old (74) n*18* t*20* f*18* b*18*. The malt and grain just don't get on. **40%**. *Symposium International*.

Grand MacNish (89) n*22* young, feral and lively. Wild grain but shackled well by some raw malt which combines lavender and gorse for a wonderfully floral blend; t*23* I adore the way the grain and malt spark off each other. This is classic stuff; f*22* a rare display of Speyside grassiness late on in a blend: remains sweet and clean save for some late toffee; b*22* for those who prefer their whisky with character, eccentricity and attitude rather than water. **40%.** *MacDuff International.*

Grand MacNish 12 Years Old (81) n20 t21 f20 b20. Just about the softest grains you could ever wish for but the malts, though full and chewy, are just a little unbalanced. **40%.** *MacDuff International.*

Grand Old Parr Aged 12 Years (80) n21 t20 f19 b20. Uncompromising and rather unsophisticated, it lays the big flavours on with a trowel. Great fun, though. **43%**

Grant's (*see* William Grant)

Green Plaid (87) n22 buttered kippers and a sprinkling of sugar; t22 sweet, chewy, smoky malt is caressed by clean, yielding grain; f22 very long and sweet with minimum oak but surprising malt; b21 a touch of kindergarten smokiness does wonders for what appears to be a young dram. Really lovely stuff. And very old-fashioned. **40%.** *Inver House.*

Green Plaid 12 Years Old (85) n22 peated but deftly so, with really impressive grain softness; t21 early vanilla and toffee with a malty thrust towards the end; f21 medium length with the smoke re-forming; b21 a very subtle, almost whispering whisky. **40%.** *Inver House.*

Haig Gold Label (77) n19 t20 f19 b19. Easy going, clean but toffee rich. **40%**

Hamashkeh (79) n21 t21 f18 b19. A good old-fashioned blend with a delightful grain bite. Love it, but could do with dropping the caramel slightly for a crisper flavour. The only blended Scotch kosher whisky on the market. **40%.** *The Hamashkeh Co. (VDB Spirits Ltd). Specially prepared whisky, ensuring that the entire system is sherry-free, with barrels and even the bungs being thoroughly cleaned for use.*

Hankey Bannister (80) n20 t21 f20 b19. A mouthwateringly fresh yet toffeed young blend offering subtle spices. **40%.** *Inver House.*

Hankey Bannister 12 Year Old (77) n19 t21 f19 b18. Clean, sweet and syrupy. **40%.** *Inver House.*

Hankey Bannister 21 Year Old (85) n21 subtly spiced with some graceful malt; t22 busy, sweet and quite lush with good grain bite and clarity; f21 very soft oak, remains sweet, and a touch of spice; b21 a very easy-going dram with surprising excellent oaky control. **43%.** *Inver House.*

Harrods Finest Blended Aged 5 Years (83) n21 t21 f21 b20. Gives an impression of something older and wiser than five years in this one. Silky and old-fashioned in style, the grains have the leading edge and jag around the palate impressively. Too much toffee for this age, though: cut the caramel and you'd have something better still. Love it. **40%**

Hector's Nectar (84) n19 t22 f22 b21. A giant of a blend that takes no prisoners: young and pretty generous with the malt thrust, leaving complex grains for the biting finish. A good, rich, sweet session dram to be chewed and then the empty glass thrown in the fire!. **40%.** *Ben Nevis Distillers.*

Hedges & Butler Royal (75) n18 t20 f18 b19. Mouthwatering and crisp. **40%.** *Ian Macleod.*

Hedges & Butler Royal 5 Years Old (80) n17 t21 f21 b21. Try to ignore the pure caramel nose and finish: smoky, rich and beautifully weighted. **40%.** *Ian Macleod.*

Hedges & Butler Royal 15 Years Old (87) n21 heavy and fruity with real grainy bite; t22 no less weight: again the grain bites deep but there is a lot of viscous fruit to soften the impact; f22 long and chewy, delicious bitter-sweet finish; b22 bit of a throwback: not an uncommon style of blend before the Second World War. **43%**

Hedges & Butler 21 Years Old (91) n24 gently smoked and generously honeyed, this is an essay in subtlety and complexity; t23 mouth-filling, rich and lush, the grains then begin biting and nipping; f22 shows some silky ageing, offering a hint of top-order bourbon with lots of butter-toffee but also some caramel; **b**22 As a taster, just about impossible to spit out! Absolutely classic stuff. You cannot ask for more from an aged blend. Except the strength to be at 46% and to be non-filtered or coloured. **40%**. *Ian MacLeod*.

High Commissioner (74) **n**17 **t**21 **f**18 **b**18. A ubiquitous blend of spectacularly variable quality. This latest sample is mid-range with the usual rubbery nose, but the sweetness of the grain is a joy. Big stuff. **40%**. *A Bulloch*.

Highland Black Aged 8 Years (76) **n**20 **t**19 **f**18 **b**19. Cut the OTT caramel and you'd have a really decent blend. **40%**. *Alistair Graham Ltd (Aldi Stores)*.

Highland Choice (74) **n**17 **t**19 **f**20 **b**18. Soft, silky grain, sweet and attractive. **40%**. *Alistair Graham Ltd (Aldi Stores)*.

Highland Cross (89) **n**21 a very comfortable grain firmness; **t**22 mouthwatering malts arrive early and make a soft landing for the gathering grain; **f**22 there is a rich Speyside thread amid the oily grain; **b**24 This is a wonderful blend: deceptively complex and always refreshing. Love it! **40%**. *Edrington Group*.

Highland Dream 18 Years Old (87) **n**21 busy with the grain lively and enlivening; **t**23 brawny at first then a wonderful pell-mell of malty tones of varying intensity. Soft spice add further illustration; **f**21 a little toffee on the big grain-vanilla finish; **b**22 a handsome blend of the old school: my kind of relaxed session stuff. **43%**. *J & G Grant*.

Highland Earl (82) **n**20 **t**21 **f**21 **b**20. Rock-hard grain softened by caramel; the malt is pure Speyside. A little gem. **40%**. *Alistair Graham Ltd (Aldi Stores)*.

Highland Gold (80) **n**20 **t**19 **f**21 **b**20. A very clean if slightly oversweet blend boasting soft, yielding grain and even a hint of peat and age. Not at all bad. **40%**. *Australia*.

Highland Poacher (81) **n**18 **t**20 **f**22 **b**21. Young, grainy, mouthwatering. The nose and early arrival are odd, the development, though, is excellent and displaying early hints of smoke and delicious cocoa on finale. **40%** *Charlie Richards & Co*

Highland Queen (82) **n**20 **t**22 **f**20 **b**20. A clean, grassy, Speyside-led young blend, the crispness clipped by caramel. **43%**. *MacDonald & Muir*.

Highland Rose (83) **n**20 **t**22 **f**21 **b**20. Firm, high-quality blend with superb grains. Nothing withered about this one. I adore this style of whisky for everyday dramming. **40%**

Highland Stag (74) **n**17 **t**19 **f**20 **b**18. Grainy, biting, raw... but fun. **40%**. *R.N MacDonald. US.*

Highland Way (83) **n**20 **t**21 **f**22 **b**20. A lush, clean dram with a rich middle and brilliantly spiced finish. For a duty free blend, you can't go wrong. **40%**. *Highland Way Whisky Co.*

Highland Wolf (83) **n**19 **t**21 **f**22 **b**21 firm to crisp grain with impressive bite and spice. Good weight and late arrival of malt on finale. Well blended but let down a little by caramel. **40%** *Longman Distillers*

House of Campbell Finest (73) **n**18 **t**18 **f**19 **b**18. Very grainy and hard. **40%**. *Campbell Distillers.*

House of MacDuff Gold Rush Scotch Whisky (81) **n**20 **t**20 **f**21 **b**20. Clean, grain-laden and slight caramel. An acceptable and enjoyable blend, but is it whisky? This blend actually has tiny slivers of gold added and, strictly speaking, to be called whisky nothing outside caramel can be added ... time to pour yourself a glass and have a 24 carat debate. **40%**

House of Peers (88) **n**21 a soft wave of peat is the perfect go-between as grain and malt collide; **t**21 the marriage between delicious, biting grain and sweet malt is harmonious; **f**23 really goes into overdrive as that gentle smoke returns. Additional tingling grain helps make this a long, classical finish; **b**23 delicate smoke gives this attractive dram something extra to chew on. A really excellent example of how to make an outwardly light blend go a long way. **43%**. *Douglas Laing*.

Ian MacLeod's Isle of Skye (*see* Isle of Skye)

Immortal Memory (69) n17 t18 f17 b17. Easily forgotten. **40%**. *Gordon & MacPhail.*

Imperial Classic 12 Years Old (83) n20 t22 f21 b20. A two-toned dram that is hard as nails on one hand and yielding and succulent on another. Tasty stuff on both levels. **40%**. *Allied.*

The Inverarity (83) n19 t22 f20 b22. A beautifully rich blend which would be an absolute stunner if it dropped some caramel. **40%**. *Inverarity Vaults Ltd.*

Islay Hallmark (79) n21 t20 f18 b20. Not as complex as the days when it was Islay Legend, the finish in particular being rather dull, this blend still boasts a lovely nose and mouth entry. **40%**. *Morrison Bowmore.*

Islay Mist Aged 8 Years (85) n19 not entirely in harmony but for all the peat the grain does show well; t22 sweet, rich malt with plenty of peat on show; f22 chewy and fat; b22 excellent weight and freshness. Despite the youth, there is big character. **40%**. *MacDuff International.*

Islay Mist Premium Aged 17 Years (93) n23 one gets the feeling something very much older is lurking around: the gingery oakiness is big but kept in shape by the vastness of the peat. This is a balls-gripping blend you don't mess about with; t23 arms-behind-the-head, lean-back-and-close-the-eyes stuff. Meticulous citrus notes are bang in tune with the depth of rich, iodine-y peat. The grain is in evidence just lightening the load and offering vanilla oak; f23 the beautiful, lush, mildly oily texture continues. More citrus, especially lime, to combat the peat; b24 this is great, brave blending. I have compared it to one or two older samples of 17-y-o Islay Mist and this wins by several lengths. Brilliant. **43%**

Islay Mist Deluxe (82) n19 t22 f21 b20. For a blend, the grain is barely in evidence – texture apart – massacred under the weight of the fresh, young-ish peaty malt. Sweet, mildly citrussy chewy and lush. Great fun. **40%**. *MacDuff International.*

Isle of Skye 8 Years Old (93) n22 layers of peat dovetail with barley and solid grain while a wisp of honey sweetens things; t23 stunning. Magnificent fresh, oily peat pings round the palate, but leaves a smoky, toasty, oaky trail with a hint of marmalade fruitiness; f24 ridiculously long, remaining sweet and viscous with no shortage of oak and malt to bring the curtain down – eventually; b24 A textbook blend and an absolute must for any Islay-philes out there – in fact, a must for everybody! Your tastebuds are beaten up and caressed simultaneously. One of the most enormous yet brilliantly balanced whiskies in the world. **40%**. *Ian Macleod & Co.*

Isle of Skye 12 Years Old (91) n23 buttered kippers, big malt presence – even a hint of bourbon; t22 firm grain holds together the deft peat and intense vanilla; f23 one of the great blend finishes: smoky but allowing both oak and grain to shine for a sweetening finale; b23 This is a simmering blend of the very highest order: there is so much more beyond the peat. A real classic. **40%**. *Ian Macleod & Co.*

The Jacobite (76) n19 t20 f19 b18. A young, clean, no-nonsense, enjoyable blend with a big grain presence that puts the "bite" in Jacobite. **40%**. *Malt House Vintners.*

Jas Gordon Choice Highland Blend (77) n19 t20 f19 b19. Beautiful grains from an eight-year-old. **40%**. *Gordon & MacPhail.*

J&B Jet (88) n21 good, firm grain with a light Speyside shadow; t23 sublime mouth arrival with mouthwatering Speyside-esque malt leaping around the palate with enormous freshness, youth and energy; f21 mildly disappointing as some vague toffee notes dull the complexity, though gentle grainy-spice brightens the finale; b23 very much in the traditional J&B mould with some live-wire malt and grain keeping the tastebuds on their toes. **40%**

J&B Rare (90) n21 firm grain with a gentle Speyside edge; t22 mouthwatering and brittle, light yet stupendously rich as the malts fan out in all directions – other than a peaty one; f24 this is getting serious: the vanilla is spot on while shards of sharp malt and flinty grain rattle around the tastebuds; **b**23 for a while directly after the merger/takeover this blend went flat on us and I thought one of the great blends had been lost for good. Good news, folks, it's back! That wonderfully crisp Speyside freshness has been re-established and the blend is just like the old days. This is precious stuff: a bit of whisky heritage. Don't lose it again!!! **43%**

John Barr (75) n18 **t**20 **f**18 **b**19. A solid and honest blend with plenty of enjoyable fizz around the palate. 40%. *Kyndal.*

Johnnie Walker Black Label Aged 12 Years (89) n23 quite a thick malt presence but lighter grains and fruit, including grape, apple and tangerine lighten the load; **t**23 mouthfilling and chewy, deftly peated and boasting more lush grain; **f**21 more than normal fruit around, a bit on the sherry-ish side; **b**22 a beautifully weighted whisky but, even though scoring highly, nowhere near its best from this bottling. Normally there would be more smoke and complexity on the finish. This one has a heavier oily presence and a tad too much fruit. That said, this is still wonderful whisky: even off-form it still knocks most blends into a cocked hat. **43%**

Johnnie Walker Blue Label (87) n23 the covert peat is so deep it is almost drilled into the soft oak and fruit to form the stiffest of backbones to an otherwise sultry dram; **t**23 great complexity from the off with the grains hardly shy, offering a firm counter to the heathery malt; **f**19 terribly disappointing as it flattens out towards toffee treacle leaving only some spice to provide entertainment; **b**22 great nose and early dexterity but it is normally a lot better than this. **43%**

Johnnie Walker Gold Label (90) n23 strands of honey hold together some clean, firm grain and Speysidey grassiness and the most distant toll of peat: meticulous and refined; **t**23 spicy and sweet malt arrival on the palate with some much harder grains following on close behind; **f**21 relatively thin and bitter with the grains dominating to an unfair degree, though some peat smoke rumbles on to ensure weight and balance; **b**23 I have tasted any number of these since the very first bottling, and this is the first time it has out-scored Black Label – not least because it is so crisp, clean and beautifully defined. Also just slightly more peaty than most expressions which has guaranteed a superb balance. A blend-connoisseur's blend. **40%**

Johnnie Walker Premier (89) n22 leathery and waxy with distant hints of honey and peat; **t**23 big age on the malt, chewy nutty-toffee and quiet spices; **f**22 more peppery now with excellent oak amid the grain with toffee returning with some sweet coffee; **b**22 a luxurious blend with firm grain and big weight. A dram to take your time over. **43%**

Johnnie Walker Swing (79) n19 **t**22 **f**18 **b**20. Grainy, biting and explosive, this blend sets itself apart from the other JW brands but is ultimately too well toffeed for its own good. **43%**

Johnnie Walker Red Label (78) n19 **t**22 **f**18 **b**19. The salivating freshness on the palate is undermined by the heavy toffee which flattens what looked like developing into a slightly peaty finale. **40%**

John Player Special (89) n23 plenty of grassy fresh malt softens the grain. Genuinely wonderful and unfettered; **t**22 beautiful thirst-quenching fresh malt is lightened by good quality, clean grain; **f**22 clean, long, very soft vanilla but impressive malt; **b**22 Why can't more young blends be like this? Refreshing and mouthwatering, it positively basks in its youth. Of its type, utterly superb. **40%**. *Douglas Laing.*

John Player Special 12 Years Old (81) n20 **t**21 **f**20 **b**20. Solid and quite weighty, there are some teasing spices to go with the chewy malt. **43%**. *Douglas Laing.*

John Player Special 15 Years Old (88) n22 some serious age: big oak offers a bourbon style but doesn't interfere with the big apparent malt; **t**22 sweet, malt start then a burst of bourbony, oaky notes; f21 lots of vanilla and some signs of firm grain; b23 the age states 15 years: one gets the feeling something a little more grey-bearded than that is in there ... this is a busy and complex blend. **43%**. *Douglas Laing*

Kenmore Special Reserve (84) n19 t21 f22 b22. Beautifully easy going and soft. Some classic bite in there and no little complexity. A superb daily dram. **40%**. *Marks & Spencer UK.*

Kenmore Gold Special Reserve Deluxe Aged 10 Years (79) n18 t21 f20 b20. Rich, well malted with a little spice and grain-cocoa on the finish. Done down by too much caramel, though. **40%**. *Marks & Spencer UK.*

⋯ **King George IV (70)** n18 t18 f17 b17. Sweet but caramel dominated. **40%**. *John McEwan & Co.*

King of Scots (84) n20 t21 f21 b22. This is pretty raw whisky in places but what makes it a top-notch youngster is the superb balance. The grains dominate, but the malts really do make their weighty mark. Some good oiliness acts as a rich and tasty buffer. Great fun. **43%**. *Douglas Laing.*

King of Scots 12 Years Old (80) n19 t22 f19 b20. Some lovely oak involvement as well as rich malt and spice. But some toffee in there flattens the party somewhat. **43%**. *Douglas Laing.*

King of Scots 17 Years Old (87) n21 kumquats and a touch of honey; t23 early spices rendezvous with very firm grain: a serious mouthful; f21 slackens slightly in intensity but compensates in complexity. The oak is a little bitter but rich malt and vanilla compensate; b22 a beautifully aged blend. **43%**. *Douglas Laing.*

King of Scots 25 Years Old (90) n22 bourbon territory – age has given the nose a rare sheen: fruity and malty, too; t23 really excellent use of oak: acts as a counter to the sweet, silky grain enveloping the grapey malt; f23 long and richly textured with some bitter oaky tones but again the grain is absolutely outstanding; b22 supremely structured whisky with a most judicious and enterprising use of grain. The malts are clean and mouthwatering. A stunner. **40%**. *Douglas Laing.*

King Robert II (71) n17 t20 f17 b17. An otherwise honest, decent and mouthwatering blend spoiled somewhat by caramel. **40%**. *Ian MacLeod and Co.*

King's Pride (85) n20 slightly on the flat side; t23 fabulously complex mouth arrival, both malts and grains romping around the mouth with free expression. The grain is biting and fresh, the malt a grassy, mouthwatering mass with delicate, lightly smoked spices; f20 more slightly smoked malt, but gives ground a little to caramel; b22 take away some of the toffee effect and you have a really chewy, old-fashioned complex blend. **43%**. *Morrison Bowmore.*

⋯ **Kings Scotch (71)** n18 t19 f17 b17. Thin, with few surprises. **40%**. *The High Spirits Co.*

Kuchh Nai (81) n19 t22 f20 b20. Big, bold, spicy and immensely enjoyable. **40%**. *Kuchh Nai Marketing.*

Lancelot 12 Years Old (79) n18 t22 f20 b19. Powerful bitter oranges on the spiced finale. **40%**. *Edrington Korea.*

Lancelot 17 Years Old (74) n17 t20 f18 b19. Soft and honeyed. **40%**. *Edrington Korea.*

Langs Supreme Aged 5 Years (89) n23 diced apples and sultanas, some uglifruit in there, too. Hint of something spicy and the grain is soft and crisp in equal proportion. Supreme, indeed; t23 soft, yielding and mouthwatering young malts are reined in by hardening grains: a bloodless coup; f21 some spice and vanilla but a tad too much caramel; b22 this is perhaps an object lesson in how to balance malts and grains. Hopefully the new owners, Ian Macleod's, will cut the caramel and raise my markings even higher next year. **40%**. *Lang Bros.*

Langs Select Aged 12 Years (77) n21 t21 f17 b18. Frumpy and, for all the building spice, ultimately a little passionless. **40%**. *Lang Bros.*

Lauder's (72) n18 t19 f17 b18. Standard, caramel-rich fare. Delicious if short-lived mouth arrival, though. **40%. Macduff International.**

Lauder's 12 Year Old (85) n21 massively fruity: bananas and custard meet custard cream biscuits; t21 sweet with velvety grain. The malt offers weight and sparkle; f22 delicate vanilla and quite complex malts; b21 a really beautifully constructed blend offering finesse. **40%. MacDuff International.**

Lauder's 15 Year Old (86) n21 silky sherry influence; t23 really superb fruit-malt combo: about as rich-textured and velvety as you could wish for; f21 quite long and sweet with a delightful busy grain buzz; b21 oddly enough it needs the grain to inject complexity into a blend that is otherwise seamless. **43%. MacDuff International.**

Little Frog (84) n21 t22 f20 b21. A big, succulent Speysidey number with considerable charm. France only. **43%. William Maxwell for Société Dugas France.**

The Loch Fyne (85) n21 a silky aroma with some luxuriant grain and a hint of age; t22 again the grain shows first but then malt slowly flickers into life and with it some spice and butterscotch; f21 vanilla and a slight bitter-marmalade finale; b21 any peat about is now covertly operating within the spice. A good session dram, a little lighter than it once was. **40%. Loch Fyne Whiskies Inverary UK.**

Loch Lomond Single Blend (85) n21 smoky, sweet but firm; t22 big, oily, chewy. The grains just dissolve while the malt offers rigid resistance; f21 long, slightly rubbery as is the distillery trait but some vanilla to compensate; b21 a real heavyweight with a massive punch. A blend of malts and rains from the Loch Lomond distillery, including some crisp peaty stuff. Not exactly an exhibition of finesse, but real fun all the way. **40%**

Loch Ranza (two words, old all blue label) **(83)** n19 t22 f21 b21. A good, solid chewy blend of some panache. But a tad more bitter and toffeed than the present new bottling. **40%. Isle of Arran Distillers. Can still be commonly found in miniature form.**

Lochranza (all one word, cream and blue label) **(85)** n20 fresh grains, as one would desire from a blend, mingling with ease with a crisp maltiness; t22 lovely, firm mouthfeel, a hint of bitter orange then a wave of malt and caramel; f22 soft spices form a guard of honour around the outgoing sweet malt. The grain digs back in, but is softened by toffee-caramel; b21 for all its apparent lightness, a sturdy, classy blend fudged only by fudge, so to speak. **40%. Isle of Arran.**

Logan (83) n22 t22 f20 b19. Great nose and mouth arrival but vanishes towards the end, though it is not without a certain complexity. It seems like it's the end of Logan's run. It's been discontinued, I understand. Worth adding to a collection, though. **40%**

Long John (72) n17 t20 b17 f18. Grainy, fruity, lush but throat-gripping. **40%. Allied.**

McAndrews (68) n16 t18 f17 b17. A ubiquitous blend found in Britain's smaller off-licences and free houses. The caramel gives a nose not unlike a traditional Scottish west coast rum; on the palate young grains punch through the toffee-liquorice wall to offer something to bite on. **40%. Malt House Vintners.**

MacArthurs (80) n19 t22 f19 b20. Young, but a lot of quality malt is involved with very sympathetic grain. Silky. **40%. Inver House.**

⸬ **McCallum's Perfection (80)** n20 t21 f18 b21. Pretty competent and clean of no great age. Lovely malty sweetness combining with soft smoke for a full-bodied start and then finishing with firm grain. **40%. D & J Wallum, Australia.**

McGibbons (79) n19 t19 f21 b20. A pretty fat yet medium weighted blend that gathers momentum as the complexity builds. Good spicy finale. **43%. McGibbons.**

Mackinlay's (see Original Mackinlay)

MacLeod's Isle Of Skye (see Isle of Skye)

Mac Na Mara (88) n21 salt and soft fruits; t22 a jazzed-up combination of brittle malts, firm grain and flavour-enlivening salt, all on a slightly oily bed; f22 remains malty and complex; b23 a very impressive blend which I adore for its mildly rugged, macho character and superb complexity. **40%**. *Praban na Linne.*

Majestic Wine Fine Oak Cask Matured Scotch (78) n20 t20 f19 b19. Youthful, biting grain forms the backbone and much of the meat of this pretty tasty and easily drinkable dram. **40%**. *Majestic Wine UK.*

Major Parka (76) n16 t20 f21 b19. Poor nose, but refreshing grain on the palate. A light but solid and enjoyable blend. **40%**. *Lehar Austria.*

Marshal (72) n17 t19 f18 b18. Very decently spiced. The nose has enough caramel to be a rum. **40%**. *Wm Maxwell Ltd.*

Martins VVO (76) n19 t20 f18 b19. Pleasant, sweet, non-committal. **40%**. *MacDonald & Muir.*

Martins 20 Years Old (84) n19 t23 f21 b21. The rich, malty, deeply satisfying, complex middle just fails to deliver on the finish. Stained slightly by a minor sherry off-note. *MacDonald & Muir.*

Martins 30 Years Old (87) n22 clean, ripe sherry, grains very soft, mildly spiced; t22 silky, melt-in-the-mouth grain gives way to some sherry and sweet ginger; f22 soft vanilla and spices; b21 it's unlikely many drams are quite as laid-back as this. What it misses in complexity (where the 20-y-o wins hands down) it makes up for in succulent, sherried sloth. *MacDonald & Muir..*

Matisse Aged 12 Years (84) n21 t23 f19 b21. Big and voluptuous, but dies on the finish. **40%**

Matisse Aged 21 Years (63) n14 t17 f16 b16. Poor sherry influence. **40%**

Matisse Royal (81) n21 t20 f20 b20. Agreeable. Makes the most of some big grain. **40%**

Mitchell's 12 Years Old (91) n22 pounding sea-spray of Springbank offset by hard grain: clean yet brilliantly complex; t22 vigorous malt and quite stunning bitter-sweet banter; f23 too long to be true. Some oak drifts in but can't dislodge the salty grain. Something heavy (smoke or coffee?) at the very finish; b24 almost too complex and beautiful to be true. Magnificent. Should increase the strength. **43%**. *Springbank.*

Monster's Choice (69) n18 t19 f16 b16. Lots of liquorice and grain. **40%**. *Gordon & MacPhail.*

Muirheads (83) n19 t22 f21 b21 A beautifully compartmentalised dram that integrates superbly, if that makes sense. In other words, the nose is crisp grain but the flavours display big Speyside malt – mouthwatering and lush. With the aid of a fatty mouthfeel, the two meet on the finish: quality blending. Old fashioned and delicious. **40%**. *MacDonald & Muir.*

Northern Scot (76) n18 t20 f20 b18. Another young grainfest from Bruce and Co., and once more very serviceable, clean, devoid of any great complexity and enjoyable for its level – and greatly improved on how it was a few years back. Marred only by too much caramel: treat as a near-grain whisky and enjoy. **40%**. *Bruce and Co. for Tesco UK.*

Old Glen (81) n20 t21 f20 b20. The grain stars despite the 60% malt content. *V&S Sweden.*

⁂ **Old Glenn (78)** n20 t20 f19 b19. Young, clean, refreshing house whisky. **40%**

⁂ **Old Inverness (71)** n17 t18 f19 b17. Annoyingly cloying and heavy-handed in parts, but the spice on the finish does offer relief. **40%**. *J G Thompson & Co.*

⁂ **Old Masters Deluxe (78)** n17 t22 f19 b20. The odd blemish here and there doesn't detract from the rich-textured malt-rich sweetness that charms. **40%**. *James MacArthur.*

Old Mull (83) n22 t21 f20 b20. The nose offers fight and bite, but the body is lush and yielding. A real contradictory dram. **40%**. *Kyndal.*

Old Orkney "OO" 8 Years Old (79) n19 t21 f19 b20. A great improvemnet on the old "OO", with intense, delicious malt bouncing off the grain. Too much caramel, though. **40%**. *Gordon & MacPhail.*

Old Parr Superior (87) n23 this is great stuff: the sherry influence is clean and acts as little more than a foil for the crisp malt and light citrus; t22 surprisingly bitter mouth arrival but some bright malts lighten the load and sweeten things up; f20 quite dusty and dry with some late sherry re-surfacing with gentle grain having the very final word; b22 lighter than of old, but the clarity of taste is to be celebrated. **43%**

Old St Andrews 5 Years Old (77) n19 t21 f19 b18. Very soft, sweet, safe and friendly. Good middle with expansive texture. Caramel bowed. **40%**

Old St Andrews 8 Years Old (69) n16 t19 f17 b17. A flat, lifeless blend being phased out of existence. **40%**

Old St Andrews 12 Years Old (88) n21 fresh for age, clean, big malt and fine, clipped grain, distant hint of smoke; t23 outstanding Speyside-style clarity of malt, rich but never too sweet; f22 tapering finale with excellent vanilla; b22 an impressive newcomer for 2003. Loads of malt character thanks, ironically, to some excellent grain selection. Superb. **40%**. *Old St Andrews Japan.*

Old St Andrews Clubhouse (90) n22 clean as a whistle: both malts and grains are young but proudly so. A Speyside influence comes through loud and clear: mouthwatering; t23 the early arrival is identical to the nose: clear as the morning dew on the first green and no less grassy; f22 long with some grain gaining hold but bringing with it some soft vanillas; b23 a fair way to start any day. How I love young blends: fresh and lacking any sort of pretensions. It has quality enough. **40%**

Old St Andrews Golf Ball Miniatures (see Old St Andrews Clubhouse)

Old Smuggler (83) n19 t23 f20 b21. Transparently clear malt bounces off the grain like pebbles off a rock. Really flinty, crisp and deliciously fresh before some toffee arrives. **40%**. *Allied.*

⋅⋰⋅ **Old Spencer (73)** n18 t19 f18 b18. Attractive and clean but ultimately rather too sweet for its own good. **40%**. *Australia.*

The Original Mackinlay (74) n18 t20 f18 b18. This was my everyday whisky 20-odd years ago: today it is a much beefier version with, dare I say it, Fettercairn on the nose and follow-through. Tasty and weighty, but not quite the hard-grained dram I once cherished. Perhaps it should now be called The Not Quite Original Mackinlay. **40%**. *Kyndal.*

The Original Mackinlay 12 Years Old (80) n19 t21 f20 b20. Quite hefty with a spicy buzz and lingering complexity. **40%**. *Kyndal.*

Parkers (76) n17 t22 f19 b18. Flat, save for a busy early mouth rush of very decent complexity. **40%**. *Angus Dundee Ltd.*

Parkers 12 Years Old (81) n18 t19 f24 b20. Don't expect a mass market sop. Real bite to this, and for what it lacks in grace it makes up for with a finish of pure roast Brazilian coffee. Some real demerara rum style in there. **40%**. *Angus Dundee.*

Passport (80) n21 t22 f18 b19. Grainy and sharp malt at the start, but flattened by a toffee-caramel effect. Nothing like as grassy, sharp and intricate as it once was. **40%**. *Chivas.*

Peaty Craig (see Isle of Skye 8-y-o.) *From Tanner's, Shrewsbury, UK.*

Pinwinnie Royale (83) n19 t23 f20 b21. An absolutely classic, fresh young blend with crisp, rock-hard grain forming the frame on which the clean, mouthwatering malt hangs. Then a slow gathering of complex spices for good measure. Only a tad of caramel on the finish can be detected that lessens the all-round complexity and charm. **40%**. *Inver House.*

Pinwinnie Royale 12 Years Old (85) n*20* more apparent malt than its younger version with a touch of smoke thrown in to soften the grain. Some zingy citrus notes grab the attention; t*22* beautiful marriage between firm grain and rich malt; f*21* deliciously spiced; b*22* finely-textured and attractive throughout. **40%.** *Inver House.*

Politician Finest (89) n*21* pretty sharp grains softened by first-class crisp malt: light and flighty; t*22* really excellent used of clean young malt – probably the most of it Speyside - to refresh the tastebuds and make for a lip-smacking middle; f*23* excellent complexity here as the malt and grain battle it out. It's, literally, clean fun all the way; b*23* this is a terrific young blend. With its obvious reference to my favourite film of all time, Whisky Galore, it needed to be good – even go down well, if you pardon the pun – and hasn't disappointed in the slightest way. Stand up that blender and take a bow! **40%.** *Whisky Galore.*

Prince Albert De-Luxe Reserve (75) n*20* t*19* f*18* b*18*. Simple, sweet and silky. **40%.** *Red Lion Blending.*

Prince Charlie Special Reserve (71) n*17* t*18* f*19* b*17*. Not exactly my darling: young, sweet and shapeless, except at the end where the grains make a go of it. *Somerfield Stores UK.*

Prince Charlie Special Reserve 8 Years Old (78) n*18* t*19* f*21* b*20*. Takes a bit of getting used to, and investigating, thanks to the caramel. But underneath lies an enjoyable degree of complexity, especially at the chewy sweet-liquorice finish. Good grain-malt management. **40%.** *Somerfield Stores UK.*

⁙ **Prince Consort (78)** n*19* t*20* f*20* b*19*. Enjoyably honest, clean and pleasant if a little conservative. **40%**

⁙ **Prince of Wales Welsh Whisky (69)** n*17* t*18* f*17* b*17*. A syrupy aroma is compounded by an almost liqueurish body. Thin in true Scotch substance, probably because it claims to be Welsh but is really Scotch with herbs diffused in a process that took place in Wales. Interestingly, my "liqueur" tasting notes were written before I knew exactly what it was I was tasting, thus proving the point and confirming that, with these additives, this really isn't whisky at all. **40%**

The Queen's Seal (73) n*18* t*19* f*18* b*18*. Mildly dusty but decent Speyside input. **40%**. *Wm Maxwell Ltd.*

Real Mackenzie (80) n*17* t*21* f*20* b*22*. Gets off to a flyer on the palate with fabulous grain helping the young malts to go for it. Never the gentlest of drams; great to see it maintaining its raucous spirit. **40%.** *Kyndal.*

Red Seal 12 Years Old (82) n*21* t*21* f*19* b*21*. A mouthwatering blend that starts with a lovely grain kick. Overall balance is charming, but toffee numbs it down towards the finish. Still, a pretty good pub blend. **40%.** *Charles Wells UK.*

Robbie Dhu 12 Years Old (83) n*21* t*21* f*20* b*21*. Maintains its hallmark fruitiness but the usual soft peat is much reduced and silkiness has replaced complexity. This brand some years ago replaced the old Grant's 12-y-o. **40%.** *Wm Grant's.*

Robert Burns (78) n*19* t*20* f*19* b*20*. If Burns were alive today perhaps his tasting notes might be something like this. Ode to a blend: Och, wee shimmering noblest blen', tha most braken heart ye men', and this'n sets oot with grain so soft, til malt an' spice are heild aloft. **40%**. *Isle of Arran for the Robert Burns World Federation.*

⁙ **Robert Burns Superior 12 Years Old (88)** n*21* excellent, refreshing, tingling, early clarity to both grain and malt; t*23* mouth-tingling complexity is well weighted behind some very decent malts; no little fruit either; f*22* the oak on the grain wrestles with the malt but never gains the upper hand; b*22* a teasing blend that needs a second glass before it comes alive. **43%**. *Isle of Arran.*

⁙ **Robert Burns Superior 17 Years Old (73)** n*18* t*19* f*18* b*18*. An awkward, lumbering dram that lost its compass. **43%**. *Isle of Arran.*

❖ **Robert Burns Superior 21 Years Old (87)** n23 thick cut marmalade on salt-buttered, slightly singed toast; distant peat smoke binds in almost imperceptibly; t22 excellent richness and little stinting on the honey; a lovely buzz; f21 high coppery-malt presence; a delicious sheen rounds off the charm and some late grain bites wonderfully; b21 out of a very similar, impressive, pod to the 12-y-o. **43%. Isle of Arran.**

Robertson's of Pitlochry Rare Old Blended (82) n19 t21 f21 b21. Handsome grain bite with a late malty flourish. Classic light blend available only from Pitlochry's landmark whisky shop. **40%**

Rob Roy (88) n21 lots of malt activity but the grain is firm and biting; t23 the tastebuds are given a good going over with a really delightful array of malty tones ranging from fresh and grassy to subtly peated; f22 tends towards dry with vanilla, cocoa, some rising peat and toffee; b22 a profound whisky with big malt character and impressive complexity. A real no-nonsense, blend-drinker's dram. **40%. Morrison Bowmore.**

The Royal and Ancient (84) n19 t23 f21 b21. Sort the OTT caramel on the nose and you will have back one very good blend indeed. **40%. Cockburn & Campbell.**

The Royal & Ancient 28 Years malt content 50% **(95)** n24 enormously rich, floral, softly peated with stunning oak: a few molecules from perfection; t24 big malt arrival that just swamps the mouth with the enormity of its richness. Intense bitter-sweet barley along with something smoky, but honeyed enough to keep fabulous harmony; f23 signs of tiring oak, but forgivable. The malt is toasty, roasty, lightly peated and chewy. The grains, firm yet light, begin to glow as all else fades; b24 an incredible blend. The mouthfeel is spot on: the whole is a sheer masterpiece! **40%. Cockburn & Campbell.**

Royal Castle (51) n15 t14 f10 b12. Mustiness and caramel: genuinely unappealing. **40%. Arcus Norway.**

Royal Household (88) n22 a natural harmony between crisp grain and crisper malt, wonderfully refreshing and refined; t23 the translation onto the palate is spot on with a Speyside-style maltiness clipping alongside the rock-hard grain and a swirl of peat just about noticeable in the far distance; f21 taken down a peg by the late caramel; b22 this is a wonderfully sophisticated blend, far too delicate and high class to be able to support something as trade door as caramel. **43%. Diageo.**

Royal Salute 21 Years Old (93) n23 slightly smokier than of old which means there is even more depth, which hardly seems possible: just so silky and sensuous; t24 your tastebuds are caressed by grains that give themselves entirely to your desires, the malts provide the background music while vanilla-rich oak expresses maturity; f22 some gentle peats arrive towards the death as the malt takes a firmer grip; b24 just one of those whiskies you don't spit out – even when it is the 1,499th I have done for this book. Old blends are what Chivas do better than any other company and this comprehensively underlines why. **40%. Chivas.**

Royal Salute 50 Years Old distilled before 1953 **(95)** n24 extremely fine strands of bourbon with suet pudding and diced apples making way for more intense raisins as the whisky warms and oxidizes; just a shaving of something peaty plus some earthy farmyardy-zooey aromas. But its all rather fantastic and supremely balanced; t24 surprising peppery attack from the off with some very early smoke. But it's the mouthfeel that shines – no, glows! – enveloping and swamping every crevice with spiced fruit displaying exemplary composure. This is rich yet has enough bite and thrust to show shape and character. Astonishing for its age. Where the hell is the oak? Where are the cracks? Nature defying stuff; f22 only short to medium length but sweet and genuinely barley rich with perhaps a hint of silky grain. Crisp and almost too clean to be true; b25 a decade ago I tasted the Royal Salute 40 Years Old. It was probably the finest blend I had ever tasted. Now they have the 50-year-old. And it has ripped up and laughed at every rule in the book: finish apart, it has just got better and better. The most extraordinary thing here is the oak involvement. At 50 years you should be picking it out of your teeth. Not here. Instead, after its appearance on the wonderful nose, it all but vanished. Instead we are left to deal with an essay in balance. This is going for £6,000 a bottle. In reality a blended whisky showing this degree of balance and elan is truly priceless. **40%** *Seagram. 255 bottles*

Royal Silk Reserve (93) n22 classically light yet richly bodied under the clear, crisp ethereal grains. The freshly-cut-grass maltiness balances perfectly; t24 crystal clear grains dovetail with intense, mouthwatering and refreshingly sweet malt to create a perfect pitch while the middle is heavier and livelier than you might expect with the very faintest echo of peat; f24 delicate oils and wonderful grainy-vanilla ensures improbable length for something so light. Beautiful spices and traces of cocoa offer the last hurrah. Sheer bliss; b23 I named this the best newcomer of 2001 and it has just got better and better. A session blend for any time of the day, this just proves that you don't need piles of peat to create a blend of genuine stature. Possibly the best light blend on the market in 2003. A must-have. **40%.** *International Whisky Company.*

Safeway Finest (80) n20 t21 f19 b20 A clean, light grainy blend. Seriously impressive for a supermarket own label and delicate despite a gentle and cleverly balancing peat input. **40%.** *UK.*

Safeway Special Reserve Double Matured Aged 5 Years (73) n18 t19 f18 b18. Fruity, not unlike a Manor House cake. **40%.** *UK.*

Sainsbury's Scotch Whisky (72) n18 t19 f17 b18. A thick, heavy, bludgeoning blend. Sublety not quite the key here. **40%.** *UK.*

⸬ **Sainsbury's Finest Old Matured Aged 5 Years (72)** n19 t19 f17 b17. A comfortable dram until the caramel kicks in. **40%**

Sainsbury's Finest Old Matured Aged 12 Years (84) n20 t22 f21 b21. Great stuff: once past the caramel the honey blossoms in all directions. A hint of smoke does no harm, either. No shame in having this around the house. **40%.** *Sainsbury UK.*

Savoy Blended Scotch (75) n18 t20 f18 b19. A pleasant young malt lift in the early middle palate. **40%.** *Savoy Hotel UK.*

Scotch Brothers (70) n17 t19 f17 b17. Grainy, hard, biting and young. **40%.** *Russia.*

Scotch Blue 17 Years Old (78) n21 t20 f18 b19. Salty and biting complexity makes for impressive blend, but a little too sappy and caramelised. **40%.** *Korea.*

Scotch Blue Aged 21 Years (80) n21 t20 f19 b20. A pleasingly spiced, rich blend with agreeable chewability. **40%.** *Korea.*

Scots Club (72) n17 t19 f18 b18. Young, pleasant, basic fare. **40%.** *Kyndal.*

Scots Grey De Luxe (83) n19 t22 f21 b21 The toffeed nose is less than promising but the quality of their grain is outstanding with very impressive malt infusion. Chewy and desirable, despite the so-so aroma. **40%**

Scottish Collie (72) n18 t19 f17 b18. Starts promisingly but splutters at the finish. **40%.** *Quality Spirits Int.*

Scottish Collie Aged 12 Years (84) n22 t22 f19 b21 A well-constructed blend with fine character development let down by a slightly bitter finale. **43%.** *Quality Spirits Int.*

Scottish Glory (82) n19 t21 f20 b22. A very good standard blend with excellent grain bite but then a clean malty follow-through with some soft spices. **40%.** *Brands Development.*

Scottish Leader 12 Year Old (77) n19 t22 f18 b18. Fruity nose and lovely, complex mouth arrival but falters latterly. **40%.** *Burn Stewart.*

Scottish Leader 15 Year Old (87) n22 fabulous, supreme mixture of deep fruity tones, soft oak, rich barley and a wisp of smoke; t22 brilliant texture:

sweet with malt and plummy fruit and natural oak-caramel; f21 long, oily, chewy with lots of vanilla; b22 this is big stuff, sweet and yet gentle with it. **40%.** Burn Stewart.

Scottish Leader 22 Years Old (86) n23 mesmeric sherry influence: exceptional stuff; **t**22 rich grapey-sherry influence, big malt but very sweet; **f**21 fails to develop complexity save for a chocolate finale; **b**20 this is a lovely dram, but would be better if it wasn't quite so sweet. Much of its complexity is hidden. **40%.** Burn Stewart.

Scottish Leader Aged Over 25 Years (91) n24 charismatic peat offers the most sublime aroma you could imagine for a blend of this age. No off-notes whatsoever: what little grain can be detected stands firm and clean; **t**22 chewy, massively intense malt framed by succulent grain; **f**23 the peat returns, dovetailing with vanilla and lingering sweet barley; **b**22 a changed character from a few years back: heavier and fuller yet refusing to let age dim its innumerable qualities. A real belter of a blend. **40%.** Burn Stewart.

Scottish Leader Blue Seal (82) n21 **t**22 **f**19 **b**20. Impressive grain bite on the nose softened by rich malt. A fine dram by any standards. **40%.** Burn Stewart.

Scottish Leader Platinum (73) n19 **t**19 **f**18 **b**17. Rather bland. **40%.** Burn Stewart.

Scottish Leader Supreme (72) n17 **t**20 **f**18 **b**17. A variable dram these days: not a patch on when it had a sublime soft peating lurking about. That said, chewy, oily and pleasant with exceptional grain use. **40%.** Burn Stewart.

⋄⋄ **Scottish Prince Aged 19 Years (86) n**22 deep, sweet with high malt presence; **t**22 whoosh! A cascade of massive malt makes its mark with some grassy Speysiders leading the way; and rich grains just behind; **f**21 fades towards soft vanilla with some spectacular toasty notes followed by dry cocoa; **b**21 not a single off-note: nothing like as foppish as the Prince on the label. **40%.** Forbes Ross & Co Ltd.

⋄⋄ **Scottish Prince Aged 21 Years (86) n**20 no shortage of bourbon characteristics; enough vanilla for an ice-cream wafer **t**22 again the bourbon figures highly: some massively-aged grain dominates **f**23 the grain finally gets a foothold but the vanilla still holds fast **b**21 if I was a gambling man, I'd say there was a decent amount of ancient grain. No matter: this is stunning entertainment for the tastebuds. **43%** Forbes Ross and Co Ltd

Shieldaig The Classic Uisge Beatha (66) n15 **t**19 **f**16 **b**16. Thin and grainy. **40%.** William Maxwell and Son (Ian Macleod).

Shieldaig Collection Finest Old Uisge Beatha (see Shieldaig The Classic). William Maxwell and Son France.

⋄⋄ **Silver Barley (84) n**20 **t**22 **f**21 **b**21. Pre-pubescent even to the point of a slight new-makish quality. A blend, but no sign of the grain: just lots of invigorating, mouthwatering barley. Forget about mixers, one to start the day with. **40%.** John Milroy.

Something Special (84) n19 **t**23 **f**21 **b**21. An ordinary nose for Something Special but there is big, chewy compensation on the palate with what appears to be a solid phalanx of malt reinforcing the charming grains. A bit too toffeed on the finish, though. **40%.** Chivas.

Spar Finest (80) t20 **t**21 **f**19 **b**20. A standard blend, but of a superbly-balanced style I adore. The exquisite clean grains show nip and attitude – as they should – but there is sufficient malt for depth. Love to see the toffee effect go, though, and have it raw and refreshing. **40%.** UK.

The Spey Cast 12 Years Old (81) n18 **t**22 **f**21 **b**20. Lovely, complex, fruity dram. **40%.** Gordon & MacPhail.

Spey Royal (76) n18 **t**20 **f**19 **b**19. Quite a young blend with a big toffee effect but not without a delicious and lush early malt-grain explosion. **40%.** Diageo Thailand.

Standard Selection Aged 5 Years (92) n22 the rock-hard grain deflects the delicate smoke: uncompromising and enticing; **t**23 fabulous collection of fruity tones, balanced by an ever-increasing peat presence, brilliantly subtle with honey-barley; **f**23 the oak seems more than five years and softens the smoke; **b**24 a brilliant blend that appears a lot older than its five years: a stupendously stylish interpretation of peat with sweet barley. **40%.** *V&S Stockholm.*

Stewart's Cream of the Barley (71) n16 **t**19 **f**18 **b**18. Bubble-gum nose but a softer more malt-friendly and even complex mouth arrival than of old. **40%.** *Allied.*

Stewart's Finest (75) n17 **t**20 **f**19 **b**19. The nose is raw, the body sweet, curvaceous, toffeed and chewy. Annoyingly and dangerously drinkable. **40%.** *Kyndal.*

⠿ **Sullivan's Cove Premium Blend Scotch Whisky (69) n**16 **t**18 **f**17 **b**18. Sweet and fat on the palate with caramel and late grain bite. Shame about the nose. **40%.** *Tasmania Distillery Pty. Australia only.*

Swords (74) n18 **t**18 **f**20 **b**18. Big grain character with some cocoa and complexity on the oak-sculpted finish. Sturdy and unpretentious. **40%.** *Morrison Bowmore.*

The Talisman (87) n21 biting grain, but enticing and malt-encrusted, young and really attractive; **t**22 first-class mouth arrival with some Speyside-intense malt showing early before the grains regain a foothold; **f**21 lovely vanilla, the toffee is creamy and malt-rich; **b**23 a lively blend from the same stable as The Antiquary but shows much greater verve, vitality and fun. **40%**

Teacher's Highland Cream (95) n23 hard, brittle nose where both the grains and malts are sparking off each other. A distant, kippery peatiness drifts around in the background: not a blend you muck about with; **t**24 one of the best mouth arrivals of any whisky in the world. It has that magical, mercurial quality of combining lush malt with crisp grain and perhaps ever crisper malt carrying soft peat: a Russian doll of a delivery; **f**23 long vanilla tinged with smoke, a touch of toffee and the most gentle spices. Malt bobs around until the very end, sometimes lifting the heavier veil to display a grassy, mouthwatering alter ego; **b**25 if I had a pound for every time I've heard this whisky rubbished I could build a distillery. Frankly, Teacher's is one of the most consistent whiskies in the world and one of unyielding quality. Its greatest asset is its quiet assertiveness, its full body and yet an ability to reveal a feminine side. This is a whisky of spellbinding complexity and of a style that is an umbilical chord to our blending forefathers. One of my desert island whiskies. **40/43%.** *Allied.*

Te Bheag (84) n19 **t**22 **f**21 **b**22. Well balanced with good spice bite. **40%.** *Praban na Linne.*

Te Bheag's Connoisser's Blend (pronounced Chay Vegg) **(90) n**22 coastal and salty with some ascending soft peat; **t**23 superbly textured with a rich digestive-biscuit, slightly salty maltiness digging in. The grains offer a distant murmur; **f**22 soft peats nudge at the vanilla; **b**23 not quite as hardy on the tastebuds or peaty as previous bottlings, this still remains a quite stupendous and satisfying dram. **40%. ncf.** *Praban na Linne.*

Tesco Special Reserve (72) n18 **t**20 **f**17 **b**17. Quite weighty, but much of that towards the end is the way over the top caramel. Good early body feel and complexity, though. **40%.** *Tesco UK.*

Ubique (82) n20 **t**22 **f**21 **b**19. Fresh, mouthwatering with lots of Speyside character. A classy job. **40%**

Upper Ten (68) n17 **t**18 **f**17 **b**16. Makes a point of peat on the label, but fails to deliver balance. **40%.** *Arcus Norway.*

VAT 69 (86) n20 a noseful of young, nippy grain balanced with grassy malt and a hint of toffee; **t**22 brilliant arrival of complex and superbly balanced young grains and malts; **f**21 pretty long, with the oak and grain having the lion's share of the character; **b**23 exemplary young blend: fresh, clean and mouthwatering. This, to me, offers the kind of balance and style that encapsulates a light blend. No problems with water and even ice on the hottest days. **43%**. *Wm Sanderson/Diageo.*

∴ **Waiting Thirty Three Years** (*see* The Whisky House)

Waitrose Scotch Whisky (80) **n**19 **t**20 **f**21 **b**20. Clean, firm-grained and stylish. Excellent bite. **40%**

∴ **Waitrose Premium Scotch Ei8ht Years Old** (86) **n**20 excellent, tight grain chipping contentedly at the breezy malt despite the caramel; **t**23 starts firmly with the crisp grain then blossoms into a malt-edged middle that sweetens succulently to counter the pounding spices; **f**22 remains firms and true with some raisin and cocoa and a touch of caramel at the death; **b**21 thoroughly enjoyable dramming reduced in stature by caramel. **43%**

∴ **Waitrose Premium Scotch Whi12ky Years Old** (82) **n**20 **t**21 **f**21 **b**20. The outstanding design, like the "Ei8ht" year old, is likely to appeal to a new generation of whisky lovers. The whisky itself is silky and citrussy and hits a delicious peak with nuts and coffee-toffee. **43%**

Walker and Scott Finest (82) **n**20 **t**21 **f**20 **b**21. Rock-hard and brittle grain gives a clean shape for the malts to develop around. High grain content, but a Speyside grassiness is quite delicious as is the mildly citrussy nose; marks docked only for late toffee. Impressive and old-fashioned. **40%**. *Sam Smith's UK.*

The Watsonian Club Whisky (77) **n**19 **t**20 **f**19 **b**19. A soft, sweet, clean blend with a dry finish. **40%**

∴ **The Whisky House 33 Years Old 1969** (92) **n**23 some serious age here, but the integrity of the malt never wavers. The grain is barely discernible except maybe that bourbony background; **t**24 a series of explosions, controlled and uncontrolled, offer pace and thrust to the mouth arrival: the delivery and diversity of flavours is fast and complex. Again there is a slick bourbony edge, not to mention some very distant smoke amid the Demerera sweetness; **f**22 more spices as the vanilla bites deep; **b**23 a very unusual blend of no little antiquity. Perfect for bourbon-loving Scotch drinkers. Its overall finesse, however, is unambiguous. **50.5%**. *The Whisky House, Belgium.*

White Horse (92) **n**23 beautifully smoky: big weight with the grains shrinking by comparison; **t**24 magnificently rounded at first then wave upon wave of varying characteristics ranging from clean, fresh malt to heavier, smoky notes with even room for a little vanilla and sultana; **f**22 long, vanilla-rich with some light peat still drifting around; **b**23 this is one of the greatest young blends on the market: only the oiliness presented by, probably, Caol Ila, takes it out of a mark in the mid-90s. When Lagavulin was used there was a cleaner, crisper feel. But I am nit-picking: it is not entirely unknown for me to have a less than harmonious reltionship with some of the world's bigger distillers. But if I were Holmes, I would doff my deerstalker to this masterpiece of a blend; as it is one even he would fail to fathom and one that proves that greatness is not achieved by the age of the whisky but the understanding and feel for how the elements combine and interact. Proof, were it needed, that even among the big boys there are still quality blenders around who know how to make a pulse race. **43%**. *Diageo.*

Whyte & Mackay (80) **n**20 **t**19 **f**21 **b**20. Not a nose or body for the faint-hearted: big and blustery. A surprisingly tamed Fettercairn seems to be at the core, surrounded by dates and walnuts in a rich fruitcake frame with no shortage of lightly molassed sugar. Very distinctive and bold. **40%**

Whyte & MacKay 12 Years Old (84) **n**21 **t**21 **f**20 **b**22. Beautifully wallowing grain offers little shelter to some rollicking malty notes: curiously light yet weighty – totally intriguing. **40%**. *Kyndal.*

Whyte & Mackay 15 Years Old (89) **n**22 moist dates and walnut cake:yummy; **t**23 more fruitcake and some honey and mango; **f**22 the grains dig in and team up with some rubbery malt for a dryish finish; **b**22 a once-great blend that, sadly, is no longer mixed. Can still be found at some specialist outlets around the globe. A sad loss: a really great blend. **43%.** *Kyndal.*

Whyte & Mackay 15 Years Old Select Reserve (86) n21 wonderfully subtle fruit, dates and soft peat; t23 beautifully textured malt with soft grain on a hard grain field: genuine complexity here; f21 plenty of vanilla brushed with toffee; **b**21 a really neat blend with slightly more toffee effect than the old version. **40%**

Whyte & Mackay 18 Years Old (89) n22 dried dates moistened by sultanas: the malt hangs firm; t23 voluptuous and silky, sweet grain and malt marriage made in heaven; f22 simplifies and reverts back to the dates again; **b**22 a stylish, tamed brute of a blend. A whisky as expansive as its creator. But a whole lot sexier. **40%.** *Kyndal.*

Whyte & Mackay 21 Years Old (85) n20 slightly nibbled at by some vaguely off-sherry notes but this is compensated for by an exhilarating display of low-flying citrus notes; t22 the mouth luxuriates with that silky, "married" feeling you get with W&M blends; f21 nutty, points docked for the return of that mild flaw again, but it's nothing too serious; **b**22 this blend is so well married it wears slippers and smokes a pipe. **43%.** *Kyndal.*

Whyte & Mackay 30 Years Old (93) n24 flawless fruit, amazingly intense clean malt and the softest of vanilla-laden grain, all entwined with a waft of light smoke; t22 a very fresh sherry feel dominates at first, then behind that arrives a procession of muted malty notes; f23 so soft and gentle you could wash a baby in it. Probably the result of W&M's marrying process, the subtlety is quite astonishing. Some treacle toffee on the very finish is still outflanked by some gathering spice; **b**24 there is no evidence of a tired cask here at all: the tastebuds are entirely engulfed by something enormous and deeply satisfying. **40%.** *Kyndal.*

Whyte & Mackay High Strength (87) n18 rubbery, the weak link; t22 beautifully sweet with lashings of lightly molassed sugar forming the bridge between the soft grain and harder, more rigid malts; f24 long and caressing, massively intense with hints of liquorice and malt concentrate. One of the best finishes of any blend on the market: positively sensual; **b**23 only the poor nose prevents this from being one of the greatest blends of them all. It has enormous character and confidence and flavours attack the tastebuds from all angles. Damn it: forget the nose, just go for it and enjoy something a little special. **52.5%.** *Kyndal.*

William Grant's 100 US Proof Superior Strength (91) n23 sublime chocolate lime nose, decent oak; t23 big mouth arrival, lush and fruity with the excellent extra grain bite you might expect at this strength; f22 back to chocolate again with a soft fruit fade; **b**23 a fruitier drop now than it was in previous years but no less supremely constructed. **50%** *(100 US proof).*

William Grant's Ale Cask Reserve (88) n20 old, peculiar aroma of spilt beer: pretty malty to say the least; t23 enormous complexity with myriad malt notes varying from sweet and chewy to bitter and biting; f22 quite long with some toffee and hops(??) Yes, I really think so; **b**23 a real fun blend that is just jam-packed with jagged malty notes. The hops were around more on earlier bottlings, but watch out for them. Nothing pint-sized about this: this is a big blend and very true in flavour/shape to the original. **40%**

⠿ **William Grant's 12 Years Old Bourbon Cask Reserve (89)** n22 a hard nose until warmed, then the malts blossom with sweeter balance; t23 delicate wafer dissolving in the mouth; the oak arrives quite early but behaves impeccably; padded out further by teasing smoke; f22 only towards the finish can the grain really be picked out, being one of a number of chewy layers; lovely cup cake death; **b**22 clever weight, but not one for the crash, bang, wallop merchants. **40%**

William Grant's 15 Year Old (70) n17 t20 f16 b17. Crushed mercilessly by caramel. No pulse whatsoever. **40%**

∵ **William Grant's 18 Years Old Port Cask Reserve (86)** n22 (apologies in advance, but ...) bluebells in a dank, earthy, north-facing garden enlivened by beautifully fresh fruit; t23 it would probably not be possible to make the landing on the palate any softer: a mixture of firm and soft grain play their part in keeping the complexity going; f20 lengthy, but flattened rather by a prolonged toffee effect; b21 doesn't quite unravel the way you might wish or expect. **40%**

William Grant's Classic Reserve 18 Years Old (93) n24 salty, aroma of crashing waves on a beach, seaweed, yet no more than a hint of peat. Grains are crisp and biting but the malt blunts them: sensational; t23 big fruit kick-off followed by wave upon wave of breaking malt. The complexity, especially with the arrival of the peat, is nothing short of mind-boggling; f23 long, fruity and still softly peated. The grains offer gentle oak and a drifting sweetness; b23 few whiskies maintain such high levels of complexity from nose to finish. A true classic. **40%**

William Grant's 21 Year Old (96) n24 the sea crashing into the most glorious sherry butts imaginable. Salt and fruit in abundance, smoke is there too but shy, the malt and grains are almost in a passionate embrace and the sweet saltiness is almost erotic; t25 telling fresh oloroso makes a great backdrop for the astounding passion play to unfold on the tastebuds. Mouthfeel and weight: perfect, complexity: perfect, sherry input: perfect, malt presence: perfect, grain input: perfect; f23 more oak makes itself known, to a slightly bitter degree. Despite that, the fruit remains juicy and the malt chewy; b24 whisky is all about balance and complexity. In my lifetime I have encountered probably a handful that come close to this. This, quite simply, is a blend of a quality rarely achieved. **40%**

William Grant's 25 Years Old (90) n23 extremely clean and telling oloroso: butts of the highest standard, but they reduce the complexity somewhat; t24 the fruit is ripe and grain offers lush softness for the malts to thrive. The complexity is massive and the tongue is working overtime against the roof of the mouth to get to grips with the gentle enormity of the blend; f21 spicy and oak-dried; b22 another peach of a blend. There is no other family of blends that comes close to touching the all-round brilliance of Grant's (the boring 15-y-o apart!). **40%**

William Grant's Family Reserve (94) n25 this, to me, is the perfect nose to any blend: harmonious and faultless. There is absolutely everything here in just-so proportions: a bit of snap and bite from the grain, teasing sweet malts, the faintest hint of peat for medium weight, strands of oak for dryness, fruit for lustre. Even Ardbeg doesn't pluck my strings like this glass of genius can; t23 exceptionally firm grain helps balance the rich, multi-layered malty tones. The sub-plot of burnt raisins and peek-a-boo peat adds further to the intrigue and complexity (if it doesn't bubble and nip around the mouth you have a rare sub-standard bottling); f22 a hint of caramel can be detected amid returning grains and soft cocoa tones: just so clean and complex; b24 there are those puzzled by my obvious love affair with blended whisky – both Scotch and Japanese – at a time when malts are all the rage. But take a glass of this and carefully nurture and savour it for the best part of half an hour and you may begin to see why I believe this to be the finest art form of whisky. For my money, this brand – brilliantly kept in tip-top shape by probably the world's most naturally gifted blender – is the closest thing to the blends of old and, considering it is pretty ubiquitous, it defies the odds for quality. It is a dram with which you can start the day and end it: one to keep you going at low points in between, or to celebrate the victories. It is the daily dram that has everything. **40%**

William Grant's Sherry Cask Reserve (84) n23 t20 f21 b20. The nose is one almost of juicy blackcurrants tinged with malt and oak. Outstanding.

The follow-up, though clean and almost velvety, doesn't quite hit those same heights. **40%**

William Lawson's Finest (83) n*19* t*21* f*21* b*22*. Not only has the label become more colourful, but so, too, has the whisky. However that has not interfered with the joyous old-fashioned grainy bite. A complex and busy blend from the old charm school. **40%**

William Lawson's Scottish Gold Aged 12 Years (88) n*22* soft yet weighty with dulcet citrus, fruity notes; t*23* crisp grains interlink superbly with very clean grape and some sweet malt; f*22* a smattering of cocoa aids the spices towards a drying finish after the sweetish build-up; b*21* don't get me wrong here: this is very, very good whisky. But once it was great. Something, I suspect some very good quality sherry butts, has intervened and what it gives with one hand it takes with the other ... in this case, complexity. For years Lawson's 12 was the best example of the combined wizardry of clean grain, unpeated barley and good bourbon cask that you could find anywhere in the world: a last-request dram before the firing squad. Today it is still excellent, but just another sherried blend. What's that saying about if it's not being broke...? **40%**

❖ **William Lawson's 21 Years Old (90)** n*23* soft apple-cinnamon overture with deft malt; t*24* the grain arrives early and is clean and precise; the malt forms an alliance with softer grains while the crisper ones cuts like a knife through the palate; f*21* the malt falls away quickly leaving clean grain; b*22* the stunningly complex nose and first minute on the palate is a hard act to follow – too hard for the finale. Only a small tinker away from being an absolute must-have-at-all-costs classic. **40%**

William Lawson's Founder's Reserve Aged 18 Years (95) n*24* a sublime marriage of fresh marmalade and something delicately smoked. The grain is firm and offers a crystal clarity. The whole thing is stunning; t*24* yes, it's a Lawson's and there really is something peaty on this – I am stunned. Again, just like the nose there is an almost erotic unravelling of the layers: first fruity notes, then vanilla-coffee grain then this final unbuttoning to reveal naked peat caressed by honey-toasted malt; f*23* long vanilla notes with soft, smoky spice: the finish is short-ish ... probably all the excitement; b*24* sensual and seductive, this quite extraordinary dram was just what I needed after the relative disappointment of Lawson's 12. The best branded whisky I have tasted for the first time while writing this book. – and this is dram number 1,604. This whisky is a real turn-on. I could be enticed to see the etching on the back of the bottle any time... **43%**

William Peel Founder's Premium Aged 7 Years (77) n*18* t*20* f*20* b*19*. A decent, solid blend. **40%**. *France*.

Windsor Premier Aged 12 Years (90) n*23* absolutely first-class for the age: a celebration of balance and charm with just enough fruit to soften the grain and marauding malt; t*23* fresh, sweet, immensely barley-rich with engaging oak and a chocolatey-smoky-honeyed depth, excellent grain coating; f*21* heaps of vanilla, dries attractively; b*23* one hell of a blend. Outwardly simple, but enormous complexity lurks everywhere. Brilliant. **40%**

Windsor Prestige Aged 17 Years (87) n*22* honeycomb and soft grain; t*23* enormously malt-rich but thins rapidly as some grains tuck in; f*20* remains a bit thin as the vanilla arrives. Some late fruit arrives; b*22* at the strength it is bottled, it's like having a Jaguar and putting a Mini engine in it. I have also tasted one of these that was not up to scratch, especially on the nose. But I'm sure that was a freak. **40%**

Wm Morrison Finest Scotch (68) n*17* t*18* f*16* b*17*. Way too overstacked with caramel. Supermarket fodder. *UK*.

MISCELLANEOUS

∴ **Jaburn & Co Pure Grain & Malt Spirit (53)** n14 t13 f13 b13. Tastes like neutral grain and caramel to me. Some shop keepers, I hear, are selling it as whisky though this is not claimed on the label. Trust me: it isn't. **37.5%.** *Jaburn & Co, Denmark.*

∴ **House of Westend Blended Whisky (67)** n17 t18 f16 b16. No more than OK if you are being generous; some tobacco-dirty notes around. Doesn't mention country of origin anywhere on the label. **40%.** *Bernkasteler Burghof, Germany.*

∴ **Shepherd's Export Finest Blend (46)** n5 t16 f12 b13. A dreadful, ill-defined grain-spirit nose is softened on the palate by an early mega-sweet kick. The finish is thin and eventually bitter. Feeble stuff. **37.2%** "A superb blend of Imported Scotch Malt whiskies and Distilled N.Z. grain spirit", claims the label which originally gives the strength as 40%, but has been over-written. Also, the grain, I was told, was from the USA. *Southern Grain Spirit, NZ.*

Irish Whiskey

Is it just irony? One of those strange twists of fate? But a few years back the name Jameson was hardly synonymous with the new wave of appreciation sweeping over Irish whiskey.

People had at last discovered the brutal glory of Pot Still. They were wallowing in the outrageous magnificence and cunning of Bushmill's triple-wood 16 years old. They were taking Ireland's very own favourite, Power's, to their hearts. They were marvelling at Cooley's peated malts. They were being soothed by the velvet embrace of Blackbush. And, dare I say, trying to get to grips with the complexity of a Knappogue. Standard Jameson – not to be confused with the honeyed Gold and that essay in sherry, the 1780 – was for the true Irish whiskey lover not very high on the list of names to be encountered and conquered.

But the tasting carried out for this guide succeeded only in confirming something that a few dozen glasses of assorted Irish over the last year had suggested to me. And that was while some trusty brands were going backwards, that plodding old workhorse Jameson had turned into a thoroughbred. And what was more it had moved up on the blind side of the others and was leading by a nose ...

It was only a decade ago that I regarded the standard Jameson a bit of a sham Irish. It was characterless quaffing fuel, with every last trace of Irishness wrung out of it. Today, among Irish blends, it stands almost aloof. It has not only embraced Irishness but now it radiates it. The Pot Still level has risen dramatically, the casks have been clean and uncluttered and the result is the most lucid and erudite of all Ireland's ambassadors. And that is saying something ... Which means that other stalwarts are letting the side down. Well it is extraordinary that, while marked highly, neither Green Spot nor Redbreast have hit my awards list. Every year for the last decade they would have done, but the samples tasted here were just a little flatter than before, a trait I had first noticed late in 2002. And as for Power's ... something is still not right there at all, at all. And I have pretty strong suspicions regarding the culprit. Watch future editions closely to see if they return to their traditional status.

One of the major developments in Irish whiskey has seen the retirement

of Barry Walsh whose name in the country's distilling folklore with be stamped as indelibly as his grandfather's name, Maurice Walsh, has been in Irish literature. His place has been taken by Bushmills stalwart of stocks Billy Leighton. Maybe because of Barry's imminent retirement it has been a relatively quiet twelve months on the Irish distillers front. Apart, that is, from Jameson 18 being deservedly well received in America and Bushmills bringing out a series of single casks for select markets.

Soon after the other big Irish news – the merger of Great Spirits of the USA and Clontarf of Ireland to create Castle Brands – Knappogue 1994 was finally released, a year or so older than its previous vintages but with the use this time of second and third fill bourbon barrels as well as first. For this reason it is more delicately coloured than the younger '93 vintage. And, if I say so myself, a lot more complex and sophisticated. Only modesty prevents me from saying it is the best new Irish of the year....

Irish Whiskey Terms

For those of you new to Irish whiskey, or confused by the terms used, here's a simple guide to understanding the variations in Irish whiskey.

Pure Pot Still: The indigenous whiskey of Ireland. Pure Pot Still is a term used for over 130 years for a whiskey made in copper pots from a mixture of malted and unmalted barley. Once this way of making whiskey was known also to the Lowlands of Scotland, where it has long died out, and was used by distillers as a way of avoiding paying tax on malt. The flavour is entirely different from a whiskey made exclusively from malted barley, which has an all-round softer flavour and texture. Once, it was made all over Ireland, the big Dublin distilleries particularly proud exponents of the artform. But after the withering of the industry and a century of continuous closures, Pure Pot Still today is made at one last outpost: the Midleton distillery near Cork. Cooley distillery confusingly call some of their single malt Pure Pot Still. Technically, because of the fact it is made in a copper pot, it is. But in the spirit and tradition of Irish whiskey it most certainly is not.

Single Malt: Just like Scotland, Ireland makes malt whiskey using double and triple distillation. Cooley use two stills, Bushmills and Midleton, make triple-distilled malt, though the latter has never been bottled as a single malt whiskey and instead is used in blends.

Single Grain: Amazingly no single grain whiskey was bottled in Ireland until I designed the three Clontarf whiskies and persuaded the brand owners, very much against their wishes, to include a single grain Irish. It has taken Ireland by storm. Because the Cooley grain used is as yielding yet flavoursome as any around, Cooley have a hot back, though, and their own Greenore now outpoints it.

Blended: Theoretically this could have a much wider range of styles than even Scotland. Some of Cooley's whiskey found its way into one or two Irish Distillers brands after the latter bought stocks during the aborted take-over. But these days Cooley blend from Cooley whiskies and Irish Distillers use only their own. So there is no Pure Pot Still from Midleton, mixed with peated malt from Cooley, with two types of grain to counter the flavour meltdown. Even so, blends produced from Midleton can be among the most complex on earth, especially as they have been experimenting in including whiskeys matured in virgin oak casks. But the likes of Jameson Gold or Jameson 18 are far removed from the Cooley blends, consisting of malt and grain made at the same plant and which can be variations on a theme, some much more tuneful than others. But Cooley cannot be criticised for this practice. Not only do they offer some impressive blends, but they are doing no different from Irish Distillers, who boast the extraordinary Black Bush – made up simply from a single grain from Midleton and a single malt from Bushmills. And, it has to be said, that no harm is being done, either, by Irish Distillers having their hands on the best sherry butts I have seen sourced from Jerez in the last ten years by the Scotch, Japanese and Irish whisky industries combined.

Pure Pot Still
JAMESON
John Jameson Academy bottled by M D Daly & Sons, Academy Street, Cork. **(92) n**23 **t**23 **f**22 **b**24. Living history – a bottled time machine. Jameson pot still at its very finest preserved with stunning freshness from its heyday. A once-in-a-lifetime treat. This single bottle produced from the old, now lost, Jameson distillery in Dublin dates probably from the early 1950s. It is found only at the Lidsay House Restaurant in London's Soho. No strength stated.

MIDLETON (old distillery)
Midleton 25-y-o Pot Still db **(92) n**24 astonishing aroma: fabulously fruity and fresh despite its great age. Even so, there is a wonderful oaky-vanilla depth that not only displays age but actually highlights the richness of the unmalted barley. A lovely toffee sweetness hangs over the proceedings and an unmistakable hint of bourbon-character has begun to win through, softened by a Canadian-style vanilla lightness – yet always unmistakably and uniquely Irish! Excellent complexity throughout; **t**24 a tantalising, lively palate-buster from the off with an oily sweetness immediately clinging to the roof of the mouth. An astonishing and most delicate spiciness balances superbly against the stark crispness of the mouth-watering, rye-ish unmalted barley; **f**21 only medium length but with a big, dark chocolate depth, a rich echo of the aged oak; **b**23 a really enormous whiskey that is in the truest classic Irish style. The un-malted barley really does make the tastebuds hum and the oak has added fabulous depth. Interesting when tasted against an American rye – the closeness of the character is there to be experienced, but also the differences. A subtle mature whiskey of unquestionable quality. Superb. **43%**

Midleton 30-y-o Pot Still db **(85) n**19 heavier, more deeply brooding with some honey and oily, crushed pine nuts. A molassed sugar sweetness is also evident. An oaky, substantial, well-balanced aroma, but with great age in evidence; **t**22 immediately mouth-watering, grassy and spicy. Beautifully sweet and malty but it's the almost bitter un-malted grain which gains the upper hand and is soothed by the deep and fabulously balanced oak; **f**22 clean and slightly oily with a build-up of vanilla and malt, very crisp and firm, almost hard; **b**22 a typically brittle, crunchy Irish pot still where the un-malted grains have a telling say. The oak has travelled as far as it can without having an adverse effect. A chewy whiskey which revels in its bitter-sweet balance. An impressively tasty and fascinating insight into yesteryear. **45%**

⋯∷⋯ **Midleton 1973 Pure Pot Still** db **(95) n**24 forget about adding water: get this up to full body temp and see the layers of honeyed barley appear between elegant flakes of oak. Hints of citrus and ripe pear. Lovely and just so pure pot still; **t**24 lush, multi-layered delivery of the sweetest malt tempered by an iron grip of mouthwatering barley and vanilla; **f**23 almost a bourbony feel to the finish with the oak having a big say, but still cannot overcome the rigidity of the barley; **b**24 the enormous character of true Irish pot still whiskey (a mixture of malted and unmalted barley) appears to absorb age better than most other grain spirits. This one is in its element. But drink at full strength and at body temp (it is pretty closed when cool) for the most startling – and memorable effects. I have no idea how much this costs. But if you can find one and afford it ... then buy it!!

MIDLETON (new distillery)
Green Spot (92) t23 mouthwatering and fresh on one level, honey and menthol on another; **t**23 crisp, mouthwatering with a fabulous honey burst, alarmingly sensuous; **f**23 faint coffee intertwines with the pot still. The thumbprint thread of honey remains; **b**23 has remained in this honey state for a

few years now, once previously a bit sharper. Soft yet complex throughout. Unquestionably one of the world's greatest branded whiskies. **40%.** *Irish Distillers for Mitchell & Son, Dublin.*

Jameson 15 Years Old (89) n24 the raisiny, deftly honeyed brittle pot still eventually dominates the spice. Brooding stuff and very old fashioned; t23 Jameson Gold-like shafts of honey pierce the oaky, barley rich intensity. Outstanding bittersweet shape, but just tending towards the sweeter side of things; f20 docked marks for the surprising brevity of the finale, though some cocoa makes a guest appearance; b22 finish apart, this is sensational stuff of a style universally unique to Ireland, the Midleton Distillery in particular. **40%.** *Irish Distillers. A limited edition to mark the year 2000.*

Redbreast 12 Years Old (90) n23 an unhurried display of ripe fruits which, together with the sharpness of the pot still, reminds me of a firm, pure rye, only this is a tad spicier; t23 more lazy spice, though not before the shock waves of complex, mouthwatering barley notes on a field of clean sherry; f22 lingering fruity toffee-sherry; b22 remains an all-Ireland great institution and one of the few pure pot-still whiskeys still around. Amazing to think this was a dead duck until my book Jim Murray's Irish Whiskey Almanac was released in 1994 when the brand was due to be withdrawn. The only change in the whiskey over those near 10 years is that the sherry today is a fraction lighter, the heavy effect once being similar to that found in the equally glorious Jameson 1780. Not to be confused with the rare blend Redbreast Blend (see Irish Blends) **40%.** *Irish Distillers.*

OLD COMBER

Old Comber 30 Years Old Pure Pot Still (88) n23 t24 f20 b21. A classic example of a whiskey spending a few summers too many in wood: increasing age doesn't equal excellence. That said, always very drinkable and early on positively sparkles with a stunning mouthfeel. Out of respect for the old I have made the markings for taste cover the first seven or eight seconds ... **40%**

TULLAMORE

Cadenhead's Tullamore 38 Years Old dist 52, bott 91 **(63)** n16 t16 f15 b16. A collector's whiskey that, if unwisely opened, reveals an essay in oak.

Cadenhead's Tullamore 41 Years Old dist 49, bott 91 **(89)** n22 t22 f22 b23. One of those rare whiskies which has incorporated excess oak and converted it into something quite stupendous. A great testament to the Tullamore distillery, and one I opened a bottle of at a tasting in Germany not so long ago. Outstandingly beautiful. **65.4%. nc ncf sc.**

Cadenhead's Tullamore 42 Years Old dist 48, bott 91 **(72)** n18 t19 f17 b18. Drinkable despite big oak dominance, but on its last legs. **65.3%. nc ncf sc.**

Knappogue Castle 1951 bott 87 **(93)** n23 a heady mix of over-ripe – almost black – banana and big oak. A blend of molasses and demerara sugar mixed with honey, ripe greengages and pepper ... almost rum-like; t24 big and booming. Rich start, attractively oily and mouthwatering. The unmalted barley and even oats show well while the middle provides plenty of estery Jamaican pot-still rum; f22 long, hard and brittle – as to be expected from an Irish of this genre. Bourbon-style vanilla with chewy liquorice. An estery, vaguely honeyed finale; b24 highly individualistic. Another year in cask might have tipped this over the edge. We are talking brinkmanship here with a truly awesome display of flavour profile here ranging from traditional Irish pot to bourbon via Jamaican pot-still rum. A whiskey of mind-boggling duplicity, tricking the tastebuds into one sensation and then meandering off on a different tangent altogether. About as complex and beguiling as a straight Irish whiskey ever gets. **40%.** *Great Spirits.*

Single Malt
COOLEY

Connemara db **(82)** n*22* t*21* f*19* b*20*. Delicate, almost apologetic peat; quite flinty and hard on the nose; sweet, gristy malt with the peat at first coming out to play and making a feeble, begrudging appearance. Not the same old smoky Connemara we have come to know and love. **40%**

Connemara Cask Strength db **(88)** n*22* buttered kippers, oily, gentle smoke; t*23* sweet and sweetens further as the peat makes a dignified entrance with lovely chewy malt: exceptionally creamy and lush; f*21* a threat of spice never quite materialises, but the vanilla is clean and dry; b*22* not one of those big, blistering Connemaras where you could stand a spoon in the peat reek, but rather a more subtle and sophisticated Irish requiring time to explore. **58.5%**

⠿ **Connemara 12 Years Old** db **(91)** n*23* vivid, gristy peat for all the age; t*23* sweet, buttery arrival with the peat gathering pace and soft spices dig in with the oak; f*23* long, a hint of toffee then back to lengthy spice; b*22* not perhaps the most complex Irish of all time, but effective and beautifully made. **40%**

Locke's Malt 8 Years Old db **(76)** n*20* t*20* f*18* b*18*. Not unpeated Cooley at its best by any means: other expressions of this brand have been far nearer the mark. Pleasant citrus on the nose and chewy malt on the mouth arrival, but rather wan after that. **40%**

The Tyrconnell db **(89)** n*22* oranges and cedar, clean malt and courteous oak; t*23* blemish free, so clean and mouthwatering but with a hint of something almost salty; f*21* pretty long with the malt continuing to buzz around the palate. The vanilla also begins to show well; b*23* this is easily the best Tyrconnell yet. Enormous thought and work has gone into the cask selection. **40%**

The Tyrconnell (Limited Edition) (84) n*19* t*21* f*22* b*22*. Lots of lovely citrus on nose and palate, but goes curiously flat at point of entry. Even so, lots of charm and sophistication, especially on the finish, even when all cylinders aren't used. **40%.** *Cooley. 5000 bottles. Confusingly, the label says "Single Malt" and "Pure Pot Still". This is a single malt.*

Avoca (76) n*19* t*20* f*18* b*19*. Chewy and sweet at first but turns bitter as the grain and oak bite. **40%.** *Cooley for Aldi.*

Cadenhead's Cooley 10 Years Old dist 92, bott 03/03 **(84)** n*21* t*22* f*20* b*21*. Cooley in its malty splendour with some delicate peat hanging around. Just a bit raw around the edges, though. **59.8%**

⠿ **Clonmel (78)** n*19* t*22* f*18* b*19*. Starts beautifully, brightly but dies under a welter of toffee blows. Won a Gold Medal in Brussels, apparently ... amazing: shows you what a lifetime of drinking Cognac does to some people ... Claims to be "Pure Pot Still". It isn't (in Irish terms): it's malt. **40%.** *Celtic Whisky Compagnie.*

⠿ **Clonmel Peated Aged 8 Years (86)** n*22* bone-hard peated malt with unusually limited sweetness; t*23* after a soft, malty start the peat starts kicking up a fuss, filling the mouth with smoke and hickory; f*20* the smoke is extinguished by caramel; b*21* take the toffee away and you would have one hell of an Irish. Claims to be "Pure Pot Still". It isn't (in Irish terms): it's malt. **40%.** *Celtic Whisky Compagnie.*

Clontarf Single Malt (85) n*20* citrus and coal smoke; t*22* clean, busy, toasted if slightly toffeed malt: elegant and lip-smacking; f*21* fades for a while but returns with vanilla and spices; b*22* a malt I created as a consultant blender in the late 90s which is of a similar style to the blueprint I drew up. Very drinkable indeed ... but I would say that. **40%**

⠿ **Glen Dimplex (88)** n*23* solid malt with a hint of honey; charming, blemish-free; t*22* gentle development of the malts over simple dusty vanilla; f*21* quite dry, spiced and a little toffeed; b*22* overall, clean and classically Cooley. **40%.** *Cooley.*

James MacArthur 1992 Peated Irish Single Malt (85) n*21* Irish Arbroath smokies, sweet at first then something oilier and oakier coming through; t*22* full texture holding together soft molassed sugar, hints of liquorice and full-bodied peat; f*21* long with the smoke drifting happily until some drier oaky tones begin to develop into cocoa powder; b*21* surprising that at this young age a few aged cracks are noticeable amid the beauty. **61%**

⁖ **Jon, Mark and Robbo's The Smooth Sweeter One Irish Malt (89)** n*22* a dry, oak-rich vanilla aroma with barley, dried pine nuts and distant honey-bourbon to balance; t*23* much more fresh and mouthwatering than the nose suggests with a thick dollop of honey for the main theme: pretty young, almost embryonic, whiskey; f*22* decent spice, nut oils and then more vanilla and late cocoa-caramel; b*22* seriously enjoyable whiskey for all its youth, especially for those with a sweet tooth. **40%.** *Easy Drinking Whisky Co.*

Knappogue Castle 1990 (91) n*22* t*23* f*22* b*24*. For a light whiskey this shows enormous complexity and depth. Genuine balance from nose to finish; refreshing and dangerously more-ish. Entirely from bourbon cask and personally selected and vatted by a certain Jim Murray. **40%. nc.** *Great Spirits.*

Knappogue Castle 1991 (90) n*22* t*23* f*22* b*23*. Offers rare complexity for such a youthful malt especially in the subtle battles that rage on the palate between sweet and dry, malt and oak and so on. The spiciness is a great foil for the malt. Each cask picked and vatted by the author. **40%. nc.** *Great Spirits.*

Knappogue Castle 1992 (94) n*23* heavy oil and rich with a hint of spice, enormously intense with a vague stratum of honey. Big and well structured, strengthened by the massive depth of malt; t*23* big oily arrival on the palate ensures a biscuity maltiness and a slightly molassed sweetness clings to the roof of the mouth. Lush, chewy and deep with a subtle bitter-sweet balance. Delicate peppers make for a teasing but controlled middle; f*24* the lingering spice tends to play peek-a-boo with the oily, almost unbelievably intense maltiness. At the death dries fabulously to show surprising age; b*24* a different Knappogue altogether from the delicate, ultra-refined type. This expression positively revels in its handsome ruggedness and muscular body: a surprisingly bruising yet complex malt that always remains balanced and fresh – the alter-ego of the '90 and '91 vintages. I mean, as the guy who put this whiskey together, what do you expect? But it's not bad if I say so myself and was voted the USA's No. 1 Spirit. Virtually all vanished, but worth getting a bottle if you can find it (I don't receive a penny – I was paid as a consultant!). **40%. nc.** *Great Spirits.*

Knappogue Castle 1993 (see under Bushmills)

Limerick Cooley Aged 9 Years cask 10839, dist 91, bott 00 **(83)** n*19* t*22* f*20* b*22*. Typical Cooley: heaps of delightfully intense malt with a slight bitterness as the oak progresses. **67.3%.** *Adelphi under their green, Irish flag of Limerick Distillery.*

⁖ **Magilligan (88)** n*22* slightly waxy and honeyed: Cooley at its softest; t*23* beautiful arrival of highly intense, spotlessly clean malt. The sweetness level is near perfect; f*21* some spices develop but fade quickly; b*22* a genuinely decent cask of Cooley at its maltiest. **43%.** *Ian MacLeod.*

⁖ **Magilligan 8 Years Old Peated (82)** n*21* t*22* f*19* b*20*. Very lightly peated by Cooley standards; sweet throughout but the finish is disappointingly dim. **43%.** *Ian MacLeod.*

⁖ **Magilligan Vintage 1991 Sherry Finish (79)** n*22* t*19* f*19* b*19*. The rare experience of a Cooley in sherry butt. This one doesn't quite hang together, though. **46%.** *Ian MacLeod.*

⁖ **Merry's Single Malt (83)** n*20* t*22* f*20* b*21*. Ultra-clean barley rich nose is found on the early palate. The finish is flat, though. **40%**

Sainsbury's Irish Single Malt (87) n*22* clean, slightly citrussy; t*22* beautifully fresh and crisp with a wonderful spreading of an almost gristy maltiness; **f**21 vanilla, oak and a little prickle; **b**22 refreshingly crisp and clean. A thoroughly good malt. **40%. UK.**

Scotch Malt Whiskey Society Irish Malt Cask 117.1 Aged 12 Years (Cooley unpeated – unstated) dist Nov 89, bott Jun 02 **(83)** **n**18 **t**22 **f**22 **b**21. Typically early Cooley make: off-key aroma but a veritable malt bomb to follow. **49.5%**

Scotch Malt Whiskey Society Irish Malt Cask Aged 13 Years (Cooley unpeated – unstated) 117.2 **(85)** **n**19 mildly dusty, biting nose, but powerful malt to compensate; **t**23 that malt arrives with a vengeance on the palate then mildly austere and mean the barley feel intensifies to the exclusion of all else; **f**22 barley sugar and soft vanilla; **b**21 a closed kind of Cooley that almost implodes into its barley-rich core. **48.3%. nc ncf sc.**

Scotch Malt Whiskey Society Irish Malt 118.1 Aged 9 Years (Cooley peated – unstated) dist Aug 92, bott Jun 02 **(91)** **n**23 oily kippers, salt and vanilla; **t**24 sweet, clean peat which fades to reveal an orangey-malty middle of some magnitude; **f**22 perhaps over-sweet barley amid lingering smoke; **b**22 a minor classic here, certainly one of the best Cooley malts in bottled form. This is beautifully made whiskey by any standards. **58.2%**

Scotch Malt Whiskey Society Irish Malt 118.2 Aged 10 Years (Cooley peated – unstated) **(91)** **n**21 pretty low, oily phenols intermix with some vanilla notes to present something strangely and attractively earthy and floral; **t**24 sweet and silky with nip and bite, the smoke forms a friendly, protective carpet for interplay to develop; **f**23 the peat is now pretty confident and thick, the initial sweetness is fading and some oak plays gently with the phenols; **b**23 exceptionally attractive, well-made malt with a stunning peat personality. **56.6%. nc ncf sc.**

Shanagarry (76) **n**19 **t**20 **f**18 **b**19. Pleasant, but lacks depth. **40%.** For Intermarche France. Note: Label says "Pure Pot Still". But it is single malt.

⚬⚬ **Shannahan's (92)** **n**23 beautifully young, fresh and zesty: this distillery's best style; **t**22 refreshing, clean barley that tries to be little else; **f**24 excellent late complexity as some first-class soft vanilla appears; more citrus cleans the palate; **b**23 Cooley natural and unplugged: quite adorable. **40%**

Slieve na Gcloc (84) **n**21 **t**20 **f**22 **b**21. No, I wasn't drunk when I typed the name. And I was sober enough to detect a slight feinty note that reappears towards the death. Until then, curiously thin. A pleasant cocoa and peat malt, but one not quite gelling as it perhaps might. **40%.** For Oddbins.

Waitrose Irish Single Malt (83) **n**20 **t**22 **f**20 **b**21. Pulsating sweet malt: clean as an Irish whistle and beautifully mouthwatering. Really impressive. With the slightly flat finale I suspect it has caramel: without it, it would be better still. **40%.** UK.

OLD BUSHMILLS

Bushmills 10 Years Old (82) **n**22 **t**21 **f**19 **b**20. A beefed-up, sherried number compared to a few years back; attractive but in need of finding some complexity from somewhere. **40%.** Irish Distillers

Bushmills 12 Years Old Distillery Reserve (84) **n**20 **t**22 **f**21 **b**21. Quality malt that boasts a complex middle. A decent dram for quiet reflection. **40%**

Bushmills 16 Years Old Triple Wood (93) **n**23 a basket of ripe fruit, with apples, pomegranates and grapes to the fore. Just so delicate! **t**24 seismic waves of spicy fruit, juicy and salivating in effect; **f**22 vanilla and a sprinkling of cocoa represents the moderate oak presence; **b**24 this has become the leader of the Bushmills tribe. Few whiskies can maintain this degree of sophistication. Love it! **40%**

Bushmills 21 Year Old (74) **n**19 **t**19 **f**18 **b**18. Full-flavoured yet strangely off-key: never quite gels. **40%**

The Old Bushmills Distillery Single Cask Rum Barrel 1988 db cask no. 14355 **(88)** **n**21 a sharp, punchy addition to the soft malt, but impossible to pinpoint exactly what. Lively nose prickle with some Demerara-style weight; **t**22 spicy and hawkish from the start while a bitter-chocolate shadow forms early on; **f**23 quietens and sweetens slightly, the malt has a very sweet edge and a distant touch of liquorice adds an oaky feel; **b**22 I do a lot of work with rum, but it is quite impossible to distinguish just what sort of spirit had been in the cask before the whiskey. At a guess – though mainly from the nose I'd say Demerara. A real mouthful, with only an extra sweet dimension revealing a rummy connection. Quite lovely, though. **53.8%** *for La Maison Du Whisky. Fr.*

⠿ **The Old Bushmills Distillery Single Cask Bourbon Barrel 1989** db cask no 8139 **(88) n**21 fruity, but otherwise languid with some dry, solid age apparent; **t**23 mouthwatering malt that really allows the barley to shine; **f**22 long and revelling in its fresh barley richness; some very late, papery and dry oak at the death; **b**22 Old Bushmills really springing a surprise with its depth for the age. **56.5%.** *USA.*

⠿ **The Old Bushmills Distillery Single Cask Bourbon Barrel 1989** db cask no 8140 **(84) n**20 dry, clean and slightly closed; **t**22 as above except a small injection of citrus; **f**21 peppery and warming; some extra cocoa on the finale; **b**21 quite a fiery number, closed early on but with excellent cocoa finale. **56.5%.** *USA.*

⠿ **The Old Bushmills Distillery Single Cask Bourbon Barrel 1989** db cask no 8141 **(88) n**20 dry; soft barley; **t**23 pure Bushmills in all its chalky yet oaky barley richness: distinctive and delightful with a bit of a nip; **f**23 seriously impressive on the barley front with better balanced cocoa; **b**22 the only one of the three bourbon casks to scream "Old Bushmills" at you for its unique style. **56.5%.** *USA.*

⠿ **The Old Bushmills Distillery Single Cask Rum Barrel 1989** db cask no 7110 **(81) n**21 **t**20 **f**20 **b**20. Big, biting and hot but some serious malt. **53.7%.** *USA.*

⠿ **The Old Bushmills Distillery Single Cask Rum Barrel 1989** db cask no 7112 **(84) n**20 **t**21 **f**22 **b**21. Sweet and attractively simple with excellent late malt. **53.7%.** *USA.*

⠿ **The Old Bushmills Distillery Single Cask Rum Barrel 1989** db cask no 7122 **(77) n**18 **t**19 **f**21 **b**19. Hot and refuses to hang together although the finale is a late delight. **53.7%.** *USA.*

⠿ **The Old Bushmills Distillery Single Cask Sherry Butt 1989** db cask no 7428 **(79) n**19 **t**20 **f**20 **b**20. Rich and malty in parts but hot and just not quite gelling. **53.7%**

⠿ **The Old Bushmills Distillery Single Cask Sherry Butt 1989** db cask no 7429 **(90) n**22 passion fruit among the citrus. Sensual and gentle; **t**22 gets into a malty stride from go then a slow burning sherry fuse; **f**23 delightful finish that is long, vanilla-rich but with the most subtle interwoven fruit and barley and natural caramel; **b**23 charismatic, charming, self-confident and supremely elegant. **53.7%.** *USA.*

⠿ **The Old Bushmills Distillery Single Cask Sherry Butt 1989** db cask no 7430 **(91) n**21 slightly sweaty armpit but a good malt recovery **t**23 sweet, enormously malty for a sherry-influenced dram **f**24 mildly salty, with many layers of sweet malt and spice that go on almost endlessly **b**23 this is a massively complex and striking Bushmills well worth finding: casks 7429 and 7430 could be almost twins...!! **53.7%** *USA*

⠿ **Bushmill's Millenium Malt Selected for The Bushmills Inn** db dist 1975 cask no 179 **(88) n**23 quite dry with a lazy, white pepper bite doing its best to shield some delicate, almost disintegrating apple-ish fruit. A touch of bees wax offers a sweet roundness. Overall: intricate, delicate and ultra-complex with no shortage of sawdust oakiness. Bourbon notes evident as the glass warms; **t**22 an enormous up-front malt showing much greater kick than the strength suggests. Surprisingly fat and full bodied for a Bushmills; again there are distant rumbles of fruit amid the gathering oak; **f**20 There is a bitter sub-stratum that over-emphasises the age, though rich cocoa notes parry the blow. The waxiness returns at the very end and with it some vague hints of blood orange; **b**23 it has taken 25 years to mature this one and it needs just as long to get to the bottom of it. A sophisticated if mildly creaking whiskey to take your time over and then marvel at. **43%.** *Exclusive to the Bushmills Inn, Bushmills.*

The Old Bushmills Distillery Single Cask Distiller's Reserve Bourbon Barrel 1990 db cask no. 4650 **(91) n**20 quite harsh oak at first but settles as the malt slips into gear; hints of marshmallows; **t**24 profound citrus character with melting barley, a sensational marriage all the more harmonious for some striking spice; **f**23 medium length but a continuation of the fruity, mouthwatering mêlée of before. Soft vanillas see this classic Irish out; **b**24 don't be put off by the non-committal nose: the arrival on the palate is a thing of beauty and legend. A Bushmills you will never forget. **54.4%** *for La Maison Du Whisky. Fr.*

Knappogue Castle 1990 (see Cooley)

Knappogue Castle 1991 (see Cooley)

Knappogue Castle 1992 (see Cooley)

Knappogue Castle 1993 (91) n22 an uplifting, lively nose, lightly malty and grassy and exceptionally clean; **b**22 intense malt vies for supremacy with a surge of controlled spice. The dominant cloves are well contained and are met with mouthwatering sweetness that is rather brittle yet fresh – like warm toffee-apple; **f**23 soft spice suffuses with natural cream-toffee sweetness, gentle with a tantalising hint of cocoa and toast. Lush, oily and exceptionally long on the finish; **b**24 this is a malt of exceptional character and charisma. It is almost squeaky clean but proudly contains enormous depth and intensity. The chocolate finish is an absolute delight. Quite different and darker than any previous Knappogue but not dwarfed in stature to any of the previous three vintages. Created by yours truly. **40%. nc.** *Great Spirits.*

⠿ **Knappogue Castle 1994 (95) n**24 teasingly delicate and complex: first with a mouthwatering intertwining of fresh cut grass enlivened by hints of zesty lemon, then a mild floral tone. The sharpness is not blunted even by soft oaky vanilla. The whole is crisp, clean and vivid: a Bushmills nose that will leave you gasping; **t**24 soft, malty arrival at first which is delicately sweet, then an on-rush of lively barley notes flood around the tastebuds. The oak ties in with the natural zestiness to help form a wonderful bitter-sweet feel to the proceedings; **f**23 barley and oak remain in harmony as soft spices add extra warmth; unbelievably clean despite the subtle cocoa notes indicating advancing years. A shy oiliness keeps the sweeter notes locked to the roof of the mouth. Some late natural toffee/butterscotch dulls the brittleness of the barley; **b**24 the blender, I can tell you with uncanny insight, aimed at re-creating the delicate, complex feel of the K92 and this has been achieved with something to spare. Now the big question for him is: how the bloody hell does he improve on this? Perhaps by plugging the small gap between vatting and bottling where the extra time in the cask saw a minor degree of toffee develop, docking the brand by a point. But this remains the most sophisticated Knappogue of them all not least because of the extra depth. And the one of which I am most proud as there are 150 ex-bourbon casks here and not a single peep of an off-note. **40%.** *Castle Brands.*

Single Grain
COOLEY

Clontarf (black label) **(86) n**21 hard and crisp and enticing; **t**22 rigid grain again, this time softened by gentle oak and toffee; **f**21 lazy spices tack onto the oak. The toffee dies more quickly than expected; **b**22 when I created this whiskey some years back as a consultant I was putting on to the market the first-known pure Irish grain whiskey ... against the wishes of the Clontarf Company. But it has been an enormous success, not least because of Cooley's consistently high quality of grain. This is a bit more caramel-rich than in my day, but still a very, very drinkable drop. **40%.** *Clontarf Irish Whiskey Co.*

Greenore 8 Years Old db **(89) n**23 soft, sweet corn, delicious hints of bourbon; **t**22 rich, soft oils, melt-in-the-mouth grain and just a hint of barley for good measure; **f**22 crisps up as the oak returns; **b**22 just a lovely grain whiskey from one of the world's finest grain distilleries. **40%.**

Blended

Ballygeary (80) n20 **t**21 **f**20 **b**19. Fresh and mouthwatering with an impressive malty thrust. Decent oak, too. **40%.** *Cooley for Malt House Vintners.*

Black Bush (see Bushmills Black Bush)

Brennan's (86) n21 malty and pleasantly sweet and fruity despite some oakiness adding weight; **t**22 big, lush malt kick softened and thinned by grain while oak adds some excellent spice; **f**21 pretty long, oaky yet never loses balance; **b**22 a very well put together blend with impressive malt magnitude. **40%.** *Cooley for Shaw Ross USA.*

Buena Vista old stock (74) n17 **t**20 **f**18 **b**19. Muscovado sugar and soft vanilla. **40%.** *Irish Distillers, San Francisco, USA only.*

Buena Vista new stock (74) n17 **t**19 **f**19 **b**19. A softer, lusher dram than the original bottling with bigger toffee input. Qualitywise, on a par. **40%.** *Cooley, San Francisco, USA only.*

Bushmills Black Bush (91) n24 amazingly spicy – a bit like the old 1608 – with clean but lively sherry and freshish malt. This is one crackerjack nose; **t**23 stunning: the sweetness is exemplary as it sits snugly between the enormity of the fruit and the clarity of the malt. Somewhere in there is a raisiny sheen; **f**21 dropped points for a toffee-caramel finale, which undermines some of the complexity. Even so, the sherry remains lip-smacking and the spices behave themselves; **b**23 the quality of the sherry used boggles the mind. Remains a true classic. My word, though, what I would do to see a 46% non-coloured, non-chill filtered version. **40%.** *Irish Distillers.*

Bushmills Original (79) n19 **t**20 **f**19 **b**21. A light blend that has improved dramatically in recent years. The aroma is of Fox's Biscuits Party Rings, as is the finish topped with some toffee and chocolate. **40%.** *Irish Distillers.*

Bushmills 1608 (88) n22 massive surge of fruit and malt all intermingling with light spices with hardly any grain evidence; **t**23 pure silk: the sherry holds the foreground allowing spices to build up from the rear; **f**22 at last a little grain appears, accentuating the sherry; **b**21 a beautiful Irish that on the evidence of this bottling has turned away from big and spicy to a more velvety sherry number. *Irish Distillers.* **40%**

Cassidy's (77) n19 **t**20 **f**19 **b**19. Uncomplicated and refreshing. **40%.** *Cooley for Marks & Spencer UK.*

Castelgy (81) n20 **t**20 **f**20 **b**21. Strange name, familiar blend style from Cooley. This one does have a little extra fruit from somewhere on the nose and excellent young malt grip on the finish. **40%.** *Cooley for Lidl.*

Clancey's (82) n20 **t**21 **f**21 **b**20. A curiously sweet and nutty affair, not unlike Nutella. Fabulous grain use. **40%.** *Cooley for Wm Morrison UK.*

Clontarf Reserve (gold label) **(83) n**20 **t**22 **f**20 **b**21. Big, complex chewy blend with some detailed and delicious grain and vanilla involvement. A whiskey I created some years back, but I don't quite remember the toffee influence being quite this telling on the finish. Very sound whiskey, still, though. **40%.** *Clontarf Irish Whiskey Company.*

Coleraine (74) n18 **t**21 **f**18 **b**17. Another improved offering than compared to recent years: less firebrand and more sweet and sultry. Still lacks any real complexity although the mouth arrival is much, much more fulfilling than it once was. **40%**. *Irish Distillers.*

Crested Ten (see Jameson Crested Ten)

Dunphys (68) n16 t18 f17 b17. Hard-as-nails blend: rigid grain allows little other development. At least what appears a little pot still does give an Irish feel to it. **40%**. *Irish Distillers IR.*

Delaney's (71) n18 t19 f16 b18. Half decent, but lacking finish or depth. **40%**. *From Cooley for Co-operative Group.*

Finnegan (75) n19 t19 f18 b19. A simple blend with good malt showing. **40%**

Golden Irish (93) n24 firm yet deeply complex with fabulous malt/grain texture. Text-book stuff; t22 voluptuous, silky, ultra malty and fresh; f23 long, with gathering grains and sublime vanilla; b24 a stunning, brilliantly balanced blend that groans with mouthwatering complexity. **40%**. *Cooley Distillers for Dunne's Stores IR.*

Jameson (95) n23 crisp pot still bounces off some firm and clean grain. Fresh sherry offers a softer dimension; t24 melt-in-the-mouth sherry is the prelude to brilliant pot-still sharpness. A real mouthful that you can suck and chew at the same time with some real bite in there; f24 vanilla, fruit and some prickly spice; b24 from a pretty boring bit-of-a- nothing whiskey to a sheer classic in the space of a decade: not bad going. The inclusion of extra pot still is one thing; getting the balance as fine as this is something else. Truly magnificent: this is the current Irish masterpiece. As classically Irish as someone called Seamus O'Crimmins. **40%**. *Irish Distillers.*

Jameson 12 Years Old (89) n22 first sturdy sherry and crisp grain then a clean but understated pot-still clarity; t23 fresh, first-fill sherry offers a velvety contrast to the prickly barley and oak combination: sensuously bitter-sweet; f21 very light with the sherry now carried on the back of the grain; b23 a clean, flighty blend with superb use of spices. The sherry and pot still both appear light in character and the balance is charming. **40%**

Jameson 15 (see under Pot Still section)

Jameson 18 Years Old first batch JJ18-1 db **(92)** n23 vigorous and vivid pot still with no little shortage of honey, lovely oak only softens rather than adds weight; t24 this is Irish blended to its complex best: chewey, corny oils counter the sparkling unmalted barley which is firm and crisp; gentle hints of very fine bourbon; f22 soft cocoa tones work well with the persistent oil but the pot still continues to guarantee high notes to the very last. Wonderful spices flourish throughout; b23 this is using pot still with enormous imagination and sympathy. A really top range Irish tht celebrates its roots and reminiscent of the first-ever bottlings of Jameson Gold. **40%** *Irish Distillers*

Jameson 18 Years Old second batch JJ18-2 db **(76)** n19 t20 f18 b19. Some barley and honey does poke out through the cream toffee, but it's all relatively blandish by standards set by the first stupendous bottling. **40%** *Irish Distillers*

Jameson 18 Years Old third batch JJ18-3 db **(89)** n21 soft honey permeates some light sherry tones and more rigid pot still, some hints of bourbon; t23 mouthwatering start and then a lift off of big spice. The pot still is pounding and relentless, the grain firm and the malt sweet. Excellent complexity; f22 the honey returns while the pot still begins to tighten and harden. A grapey sub-plot attempts to soften the punches but with only limited success; b23 this is big Irish with attitude. Much closer to the first bottling, it cuts down on the honey slightly and offers a more bourbony character. That said, the pot still guarantees this as uniquely Irish. The spices amaze. Beautiful stuff. **40%** *Bottled at 75cl especially for launch into American market but will be available at 70cl elsewhere.*

⠶ **Jameson 18 Years Old Fourth Batch (83)** n21 t21 f20 b21. Very pleasant but limited degree of sparkle: the age is evident, as is the toffee. **40%**. *Irish Distillers.*

⠆⠆ **Jameson 18 Years Old Fifth Batch (89)** n22 some enlivening pot still moments; very deep and fruity; t23 really delightful meeting between friendly pot still, oaky spice and fruit; f22 some toffee seeps in but the slight liquorice depth compensates slightly as the age really begins to sing ballads of yesteryear; b22 great to see this charming blend back on track; understated to the point of shyness. **40%.** *Irish Distillers.*

Jameson 1780 Matured 12 Years (94) n23 lush and confident, spicy and warming: there is a prevailing oloroso undercurrent head on against some sharp pot still; t24 a whiskey that fills the mouth with thick, bitter-sweet sherry, then the unmistakable delights of old pot still coupled with a short but effective fly-past of spice. The pot still dominates – towards the middle after the early sherry lead; f23 pretty long with neither pot still nor sherry showing any signs of wanting to leave; b24 this blend has now been discontinued and if you should see one hanging around an old off licence grab it with both hands. The 12-y-o that has taken its place appears to be using as much sherry, but it appears to be a lighter style, as is the pot still. The 1780 was the last commercial link with the old Irish whiskies I fell in love with in the early 70s. A colossus of an Irish, of a sherry type now entirely lost which couldn't come from any other country in the world. **40%.** *Irish Distillers.*

Jameson Crested Ten (88) n23 the enormity of the pot still is awesome: lovely sherry-ginger balance; t23 amazingly clean sherry then traces of malt and vanilla; f19 too much toffee but some decent malt helps compensate; b23 a beautifully balanced whiskey let down only by the weak finish. **40%.** *Irish Distillers.*

Jameson Distillery Reserve (available at Jameson, Dublin) **(74)** n20 t20 f17 b17. Starts well but becomes flatter than the Irish Midlands. Nothing like as good as previous bottlings I have tasted. Just a one-off, I am sure. **40%.** *Irish Distillers Dublin.*

Jameson Distillery Reserve (available at Midleton – see Midleton Distillery Reserve)

Jameson Gold (94) n24 layered elements of soft honey and subtle, mildly bourbony oak criss-crossing the crisp pot still; t24 honey and barley all the way, wonderfully rich and silky, cocoa shows early too with a fruit chocolate character; f22 some age apparent towards the bitter-sweet finale, as is butterscotch; b24 if you don't enjoy this, then you just don't get what Irish whiskey is all about. Vattings vary from bottling to bottling, but this is quite representative and falls comfortably within its colourful spectrum. **40%.** *Irish Distillers.*

Hewitts (87) n22 big, intense, heavy malt-rich with some clean fruity-grapey notes in the background. Dark cherries and chocolate complete the mix; t22 intriguingly deep, packed with even more grapey fruitiness. The malt clings to the mouth in tandem with crisp grain, though the body is curiously oily and full; f20 custard creams and dry, thinner grain with just a late hint of malt; b23 a lovely blend that somehow manages to be light, medium and heavy at various stages. **40%** *Irish Distillers. The only blend from Midleton using exclusively malt and grain and no pot still (mixture of malted and unmalted barley).*

Inishowen (73) n18 t20 f17 b18. Someone's stolen the peat and replaced it with cream toffee. **40%.** *Cooley.*

Kilbeggan (76) n19 t20 f18 b19. Fruity in part but the bite is sharp and attractively relentless. **40%.** *Cooley.*

Locke's (73) n18 t20 f17 b18. Big malt through the middle, but it all just fizzles out. **40%.** *Cooley.*

⠆⠆ **Merry's Special Reserve (75)** n20 t19 f18 b18. Dull. **40%**

Midleton Distillery Reserve (85) n22 punchy barley; t22 rich, intense barley with some mouthwatering fruit and spices; f20 vanilla-toffee; b21 a whiskey which, for all its muscovado sweetness offers some memorable barley moments. **40%.** *Irish Distillers Midleton Distillery only. Was once bottled as*

Jameson Distillery Reserve exclusive to Midleton. Changes character slightly with each new vatting. This one is some departure.

Midleton Very Rare 1984 (70) n19 t18 f17 b16. Disappointing with little backbone or balance. **40%**. *Irish Distillers*.

Midleton Very Rare 1985 (77) n20 t20 f18 b19. Medium-bodied and oily, this is a big improvement on the initial vintage. **40%**. *Irish Distillers*.

Midleton Very Rare 1986 (79) n21 t20 f18 b20. A very malty Midleton richer in character than previous vintages. **40%**. *Irish Distillers*.

Midleton Very Rare 1987 (77) n20 t19 f19 b19. Quite oaky at first until a late surge of excellent pot still. **40%**. *Irish Distillers*.

Midleton Very Rare 1988 (86) n23 integrated rock-hard pot still and softer vanilla. Touches of honey and mint add to the complex equation; t21 the first MVR to offer immediate Irishness; busy and attractively muddled; f21 a late chalky dryness counters a building malty sweetness; b21 a landmark MVR as it is the first vintage to celebrate the Irish pot-still style. **40%**

Midleton Very Rare 1989 (87) n22 citrussy and spicy, the malt is hard-chiselled into the overall chararacter: some formidable pot still, too; t22 very vivid pot still which follows the firm grain; f22 the hard, brittle unmalted barley makes itself heard: you could break your teeth on it; b21 a real mouthful but has lost balance to achieve the effect. **40%**. *Irish Distillers*.

Midleton Very Rare 1990 (93) n23 carrying on from where the '89 left off. The pot still doesn't drill itself so far into your sinuses, perhaps: more of a firm massage; t23 solid pot still again. There is a pattern now: pot still first, sweeter, maltier notes second, pleasant grains third and somewhere, imperceptibly, warming spices fill in the gaps; f24 long and Redbreast-like in character. Spices seep from the bourbon casks; b23 astounding whiskey: one of the vintages every true Irish whiskey lover should hunt for. **40%**. *Irish Distillers*.

Midleton Very Rare 1991 (76) n19 t20 f19 b18. After the Lord Mayor's Show, relatively dull and uninspiring. **40%**. *Irish Distillers*.

Midleton Very Rare 1992 (84) n20 t20 f23 b21. Superb finish with outstanding use of feisty grain. **40%**. *Irish Distillers*.

Midleton Very Rare 1993 (88) n21 pot still with sub plots of honey and pepper; t22 the pot still makes use of the dry hardness of the grain; f23 beautiful elevation of the pot still towards something more complex and sharp balancing superbly with malt and bourbony-oak texture; b22 big, brash and beautiful – the perfect way to celebrate the 10th-ever bottling of MVR. **40%**. *Irish Distillers*.

Midleton Very Rare 1994 (87) n22 pot-still characteristics not unlike the '93 but with extra honey and ginger; t22 the honeyed theme continues with malt arriving in a lush sweetness; f21 oily and a spurt of sharper, harder pot still; b22 another different style of MVR, one of amazing lushness. **40%**. *Irish Distillers*.

Midleton Very Rare 1995 (90) n23 big pot still with fleeting honey; t24 enormous! Bitter, sweet and tart all together for a chewable battle of apple and barley. Brilliant; b21 some caramel calms proceedings, but Java coffee goes a little way to restoring complexity; b22 they don't come much bigger than this. Prepare a knife and fork to battle through this one. Fabulous. **40%**. *Irish Distillers*.

Midleton Very Rare 1996 (82) n21 t22 f19 b20. The grains lead a soft course, hardened by subtle pot still. Just missing a beat on the finish, though. **40%**

Midleton Very Rare 1997 (83) n22 t21 f19 b21. The piercing pot still fruitiness of the nose is met by a countering grain of rare softness on the palate. Just dies on the finish when you want it to make a little speech. Very drinkable. **40%**. *Irish Distillers*.

Midleton Very Rare 1999 (89) n21 malt and toffee: as sleepy as a night-time drink; t23 stupendous grain, soft enough to absorb some pounding malt; f22 spices arrive as the blend hardens and some pot still finally battles its way through the swampy grain; **b**23 one of the maltiest Midletons of all time: a superb blend. **40%.** *Irish Distillers.*

Midleton Very Rare 2000 (85) n22 citrus and new-mown straw; **t**21 so soft it barely troubles the tastebuds. Some harder unmalted barley makes itself heard; **f**21 toffee and bitter cocoa, but still very soft mouthfeel; **b**21 an extraordinary departure even by Midleton's eclectic standards. The pot still is like a distant church spire in an hypnotic Fen landscape. **40%.** *Irish Distillers.*

Midleton Very Rare 2001 (79) n21 **t**20 **f**18 **b**20. Extremely light but the finish is slightly on the bitter side. **40%.** *Irish Distillers.*

Midleton Very Rare 2002 (79) n20 **t**22 **f**18 **b**19 The nose is rather subdued and the finish is likewise toffee-quiet and shy. There are some fabulous middle moments, some of flashing genius, when the pot still and grain combine for a spicy kick, but the finish really is lacklustre and disappointing. **40%.** *Irish Distillers*

⋯⋯ **Midleton Very Rare 2003 (84) n**22 **t**22 **f**19 **b**21. Beautifully fruity on both nose and palate (even some orange blossom on aroma). But the delicious spicy richness that is in mid launch on the tastebuds is cut short by caramel on the middle and finish. A crying shame, but the best Midleton for a year or two. **40%.** *Irish Distillers.*

Millar's Special Reserve (87) n21 attractive grains lighten and interact with the clean malt: we have complexity here; **t**22 big malt arrival then a wonderful development of spice tinged with muscovado sugar; **f**22 vanilla and even more malt with the grains pulsing in the background; **b**22 this is a complex dram from Cooley that needs time to understand it. Delicious, so it is. **40%.** *Cooley.*

O'Brien's (77) n18 **t**20 **f**19 **b**20. Big grain shape with softening grains. **40%.** *Somerfield UK.*

O'Hara (80) n20 **t**21 **f**19 **b**20. A genuinely fine blend from Cooley. **40%.** *For Millar's.*

Old Dublin (73) n17 **t**20 **f**17 **b**19. A clean blend that rarely troubles the inner tastebuds. Sweet with no pretensions of grandeur whatsoever. **40%.** *Irish Distillers.*

Old Kilkenny (86) n21 really biting pot still and grain ... on an own-label blend?! **t**22 mouthwatering rich pot still and then diffusing grain; **f**21 not even the toffee from the caramel can ruin the richness of the grain; **b**22 a real shock to the system. Traditional pot still character in an own-label product, and real quality stuff to boot. However, gather up as many of the labels as you can that tell you it's triple distilled. Cooley are likely to take over the blend from Irish Distillers later in 2003 so the biting barley character will be lost for a softer malt-based blend. In this form a collectable one for Irish whiskey lovers worldwide. **40%.** *Asda UK.*

Old Midleton Distillery Blended Whiskey 1967 35 Years Old (92) n24 a really cut-glass clean, pot still character and, although sharp, soft marmalady grain lightens the experience: some honey wanders from the emptied glass; **t**23 rock-hard barley chips at the tastebuds, wonderfully fruity and mouthwatering. The grain offers something much sweeter and softer: two separate tales being told simultaneously; **f**22 mainly clean grain with soft vanilla drifting in. The barley does offer some late sharpness and some late bitter almond reminds you of the enormity of the age; **b**23 this is a real one-off bottling of a quite unique Irish whiskey (actually coming from the old Midleton distillery, surely that should be "whisky"?). Apparently this one cask was filled in 1967 from a mixture of Midleton pure pot still and Midleton grain. After all this time, no-one knows why. But it was rescued by enthusiasts David Radcliffe and Sukhinder Singh and bottled for their respective businesses. I'm delighted to report (unlike Sukhinder's soon-to-become legendary Dunglass) that this is a little stunner. **41.1%** www.potstill.com and www.thewhiskeyexchange.com

Paddy (68) n16 **t**19 **f**16 **b**17. Good old Paddy: I knew it wouldn't let me down. While other lesser Irish whiskies have improved, Paddy has steadfastly refused to budge: dusty, cloyingly sweet and shapeless. Like an ugly duckling, I'm almost becoming fond of it. Hang on a minute, I'll have another taste: no, actually I'm not. About as unclassicallly Irish as someone called Pedro Manchovitz. **40%.** *Irish Distillers.*

Powers (87) n22 rugged pot still, but not quite as butch as it once was; **t**24 brilliant mouth arrival, one of the best in all Ireland: the pot still shrieks and attacks every available tastebud. Too short-lived, though; **f**20 the ending, once the final traces of pot have vanished, is long and dull, save for some lovely spice. Sweet beyond recognition with toffee and ... toffee; **b**21 is it coincidence that as Jameson has become more pot-still accentuated, Power's – once the very last bastion of grizzled pot-still blend – has become cissified? If they cut the colouring many of the problems will disappear, I feel. But at the moment it is a pale – or should I say dark? – shadow of its once magnificent self. **40%.** *Irish Distillers.*

Powers 12 Years Old (77) n21 **t**20 **f**18 **b**18. Disappointing: surely should be seeing more out of this baby? **40%.** *Irish Distillers.*

Redbreast Blend (88) n23 some genuinely telling pot-still hardness sparks like a flint off the no less unyielding grain. Just love this; **t**23 very sweet and soft, the grain carrying a massive amount of vanilla. Barley offers some riches, as does spice; **f**20 a climbdown from the confrontational beginnings, but pretty delicious all the same; **b**22 really impressed with this one-off bottling for Dillons the Irish wine merchants. Must try and get another bottle before they all vanish. **40%.** *Irish Distillers for Dillone IR (not to be confused with Redbreast 12-y-o Pure Pot Still).*

Safeway Irish Whiskey (86) n21 stupendous, top-quality grain rarely seen in supermarket own-label brands marrying comfortably with some sharp, fresh malt; **t**22 the oiliest Irish I have come across for a while: any silkier and this will have been distilled in Macclesfield! But the freshness of the malt is superb and telling; **f**22 stunning vanilla delivery and soft malt; **b**21 a brilliant own-label brand but ... arrrrgggghhhh!!! This is where I get militant: please don't confuse the words pot still on an Irish whiskey label with traditional Irish Pot Still of malted and unmalted barley. This is a superb blend of grain and single malt. **40%.** *Cooley for Safeway UK.*

Tesco Special Reserve Irish Whiskey (87) n21 belligerent malt, young but well directed, spices the more docile grain; **t**23 the malts are stupendously juicy and have no problems punching their way entirely through the rich, clean grain; **f**21 really it's the grains that have the day here, but such is their superb quality, no problem; **b**22 delicious! Underlines the fact that Cooley produces one of the world's best grain whiskies and a very sharp, decent malt. **40%.** *Cooley for Tesco UK.*

✑ **Tir No Nog (78) n**20 **t**21 **f**18 **b**19. Chewy and pleasant but lots of overactive toffee. **40%.** *Cooley.*

Tullamore Dew (75) n18 **t**20 **f**18 **b**19. Less than inspiring, maybe. But it has picked up on the pot still in recent years. Less throat-ripping, more balance. There is hope yet. **40%.** *Irish Distillers for Campbell and Cochrane.*

Tullamore Dew 12 Years Old (81) n21 **t**21 **f**20 **b**19. Enjoyable citrussy, pot-still tones criss-cross from the nose to the toffeed, Canadian finale. **40%.** *Irish Distillers for Campbell & Cochrane.*

Tullamore Dew Heritage (79) n20 **t**22 **f**19 **b**18. Fat and lush, the mouthwatering action is upfront on the tastebuds before the long toffeed, mildly spiced finale. **40%.** *Irish Distillers for Campbell & Cochrane.*

Waitrose Irish Whiskey (77) n20 **t**19 **f**20 **b**18. Very sweet but the grain is stupendous. **40%.** *UK.*

✑ **The Wild Geese (79) n**20 **t**22 **f**18 **b**19. Easy drinking and pleasant late spice but not enough gravity for the caramel. **40%.** *Cooley for Avalon.*

Wm Morrison (see Clancey's)

American Whisky

Bourbon has long ruled the roost in America. It has had an almost clear run since Prohibition encumbered upon Americans a lighter palate and rye began to fall from grace in favour of its cornier cousin. But now rye is making a comeback, with interest growing internationally for this most full-flavoured of spirits. At least one distillery is looking at increasing the number of mashes they produce each year, and with good reason. It is beginning to slowly creep into new markets the world over, often stunning whiskey lovers who discover it for the first time. Already Sazerac Rye is being regarded by some converts as the Holy Grail of rye. It's a hard one to argue against.

Rye, though, is not alone in adding diversity to the American whisky scene. The last decade has seen the birth of five malt distilleries – four making from barley, the other two from rye. Only one has yet to bottle, the Triple Eight Distillery in Nantucket, Massachusetts, whose single malts are currently maturing away in former Jim Beam barrels. The oldest has now reached four years of age and plans are already afoot to begin filling into sherry butts.

Some 3,000 miles away in California, St. Georges have again bottled at 3-years-old, their Lot 4 being far and away the best expression yet. But now America really does have its own single malt region ... and that is found further north up the coast at Portland, Oregon. When I visited there a few years back I came across the Clear Creek Distillery, which once again produced another quite breathtaking edition of their beautifully peated Macarthy's. But not that far away in the same town, it appears I had overlooked a second distillery, Edgefield. Their make has been improving year on year and I will be rectifying my gross oversight by returning to Portland to carry out some tastings in the town where I will be holding up the produce of both distilleries to comparison with some of Scotland's finest. Those assembled will soon discover that their local malt is more than a match.

It is even on a par with the very best of the extraordinary malted rye brilliance of Old Potrero. The Anchor Distillery in San Francisco has continued to bring out "essays" of the mouthwatering, above-weight punching giant that has set American whiskey distilling alight in recent years and, like Macarthy's, has earned a place among the world's elite whiskies.

So small-batch American single malt is in good shape at the moment. Which it has to be to catch the attention of drinkers in a country that has so many first-class ryes and bourbons to choose from. I have long held the belief that America today makes the best quality whisky in the world and the exercise of tasting most of what is on offer has confirmed that.

Whisky would not be whiskey and I wouldn't be me if I didn't find an exception to that rule. And that comes in the form of what was one of the great blended whiskeys in the world: Seagram 7 Crown. For years I have championed its cause and if you ever spot me at Chicago Airport or somewhere else in the United States reading or writing in a bar you are likely to find a glass of the stuff by my side. Usually it ranks in the low to mid-90s in my rating system. Not this time: it didn't even hit the 90 mark. Usually a bold, rye-fest of a beast, the sample I received was still deliciously drinkable. But it had lost that cutting edge, it shone where once it sparkled. I detected a slight rye reduction, but enough to change its shape. Some institutions are above tampering with. Seagram 7 Crown is one.

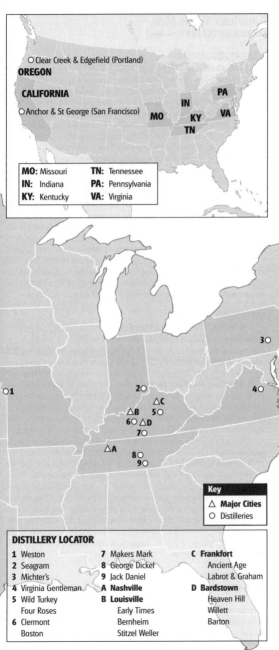

MO:	Missouri	TN:	Tennessee
IN:	Indiana	PA:	Pennsylvania
KY:	Kentucky	VA:	Virginia

Key
△ **Major Cities**
○ **Distilleries**

DISTILLERY LOCATOR

1	Weston	7	Makers Mark	C	**Frankfort**
2	Seagram	8	George Dickel		Ancient Age
3	Michter's	9	Jack Daniel		Labrot & Graham
4	Virginia Gentleman	A	**Nashville**	D	**Bardstown**
5	Wild Turkey	B	**Louisville**		Heaven Hill
	Four Roses		Early Times		Willett
6	Clermont		Bernheim		Barton
	Boston		Stitzel Weller		

American Single Malt
ANCHOR DISTILLERY (see Rye)

CLEAR CREEK DISTILLERY
McCarthy's Oregon Single Malt Aged 3 Years db **(94)** n*24* just a hint of fusel oil, but – hey – who cares? The nose is astounding, incredibly delicate peat combined with an almost industrial oiliness, similar to that my old dad brought home with him each night from the machine shop. Distillers just can't buy an aroma like this; t*23* this is too good to be true: the malt and peat melt into the mouth with startling complexity and the sweetness is beautifully disguised behind soft oak; f*23* very long, soft oils drifting around the palate with peat which fluctuates between big and deft; b*24* this is a dram I could drink any day ... and would if I had the supplies. And, although I may be stoned to death for saying so, the closest whisk(e)y I have come across is how Ardbeg was 20 years ago – but it's a fact. Not as good, admittedly, but some of the similarities are spine-tingling. This is landmark American whiskey and one of extraordinary quality.

⠿ **McCarthy's Oregon Single Malt Aged 3 Years** bottling No. 4 **(93)** n*24* massively oily and pungent peat: no quarter given or asked t*23* astonishing bitter-sweet balance with the peat, usually sweet, offering a firm dryness that sits well with the oak and much sweeter strands of barley f*22* the oiliness still clings to the roof of the mouth and the barley continues to offer a mouth watering depth b*24* if was tasting this blind, I would say this is one of the best Caol Ilas I had come across for quite a few years: the oiliness is up on the last bottling and has probably lost a degree of complexity because of it. But this is still a whiskey you pin gold medals to. Fabulous and just about faultless. **40%**

EDGEFIELD DISTILLERY
⠿ **Edgefield Distillery Hogshead** db bott 11 Mar 02 **(87)** n*22* clean, fruity malt with a distinct oaky buzz; t*23* the malt has a distinctive rigidity that is mouth watering and enormously rich; almost a rye character to the firm fruitiness; f*20* softens through caramelisation; b*22* for a first attempt from a new distillery that began life in only 1998, this really is an extraordinary achievement. **46 (92 proof).**

⠿ **Edgefield Distillery Hogshead** db bott 25 Apr 02 **(90)** n*23* a more than vague bourbony character acts as a weighty foil to the powerful malt; fruity and spicy, cinnamon in particular. Again, a rye-style fruitiness is noticeable; t*23* unrefined Demerara and molasses ad a sugary edge to the toasty, roasty malt; big and distinctly intense; f*21* a degree of a caramel again dulls the malt; b*23* this is seriously complex whisky from a distillery that has set about creating a quite unique and specific character. Quite superb. **46% (92 proof).**

⠿ **Edgefield Distillery Hogshead** db bott 4 Sep 03 **(93)** n*24* drier, yet still "rye"-fruity and spiced with banana and vanilla; t*24* if this were bourbon, I would be celebrating the "small grain" texture. A curious rye character threads through the rich barley; some hints of honey towards the middle; f*22* a touch of toffee flattens some of the higher notes but there is still an enormous vanilla-barley battle to enjoy; b*23* it really takes some believing that a distillery, at its third attempt, has come up with something quite this brilliant. I'm not sure where the caramel is coming from: either natural or added, but without it, it would be phenomenal. **46% (92 proof).**

ST GEORGE DISTILLERY
St George Single Malt Aged 3 Years db **(75)** n*17* t*19* f*20* b*19*. Without doubt the fruitiest whisk(e)y I have tasted in nearly 30 years of sampling the stuff. The nose in particular is some kind of raspberry or similar fruit, more eau de vie than whiskey. That said, this is beautifully distilled and clean with a wonderful bite near the finish: it is just that the malt has been lost along the way. **43%**

St George Single Malt Aged 3 Years Lot 2 db **(82)** n*19* t*21* f*21* b*21*. Much better. The fruit still clings to the nose, but this time malt rings loud and clear round the tastebuds and there is superb interaction with the oak. Once more, supremely made and, once that fruit is lost, we will have an absolutely top-rank malt on our hands. **43%**

⇝ **St George Lot 3** db **(82)** n*20* t*20* f*21* b*21*. Another fruitfest from St George that again shows excellent clarity, but has wandered off the malty path. Quite pithy in places and always enjoyable. **43%**

⇝ **St George Lot 4** db **(87)** n*23* for some reason there is a beguiling drift of rye, apple and cinnamon, but – at last!!! – it is the richness of the malt that really takes off; t*20* drier than any other St George, with a slow evolution of malt against some flakey, oaky tones; f*22* remains dry but the slight bitterness is perfectly received by barley and busy spices; b*22* Eureka! Them thar pesky Californians have gone and struck themselves malt. Not fool's malt, but the pure stuff, yessiree!!! Just took four years of copper panning. **43%**

Bourbon

Bourbon confuses people. Often they don't even realise it is a whiskey, a situation not helped by leading British pub chains, such as Wetherspoon, whose bar menus list "whiskey" and "bourbon" in separate sections. And if I see the liqueur Southern Comfort listed as a bourbon one more time I may not be responsible for my actions.

Bourbon is a whiskey. It is made from grain and matured in oak, so really it can't be much else. To be legally called bourbon it must have been made with a minimum of 51% corn and matured in virgin oak casks for a minimum of two years. Oh, and no colouring can be added other than that which comes naturally from the barrel.

Where it does differ, from, say Scotch, is that the straight whiskey from the distillery may be called by something other than that distillery name. Indeed, the distillery may change its name which has happened to two this year already and two others in the last three or four. So, to make things easy and reference as quick as possible, I shall list the distilleries first and then their products in alphabetical order.

BARTON

Located close to downtown Bardstown, Barton specialises in young, inexpensive bourbons for the US market. At their best Barton whiskeys possess a unique bite and crispness that helps create impressive complexity ... and the firm rye character does little harm, either. With the loss of the Heaven Hill distillery and closure of other plants since World War II, Barton is now the last distilling outpost in a town once famed for bourbon production and now the home of the industry's museum.

BUFFALO TRACE

For too long the venerable whiskeys of the Ancient Age distillery were known only by Kentuckians and bourbon connoisseurs across the United States. Owners Sazerac, though, have slowly given the ruggedly handsome old place at Leestown, on the outskirts of Frankfort, a really big spruce up. No more so than with the name itself, which was changed from Ancient Age to Buffalo Trace to attract a younger, more international market. For those not in the know, a Buffalo Trace is a track made by herds of buffalo; and this distillery sits by the banks of the Kentucky River, where buffalo made their regular crossing. To add a little confusion, Japanese distillers Takara Shuru own the Blantons brand, perhaps the most internationally recognised of all the distillery's top-of-the-range products. Buffalo Trace is now finding more and more markets globally and it is no surprise to us who have long admired the distillery's make that it is receiving a warm welcome wherever it goes. Irritatingly, years of slight underproduction means that growth of all Buffalo Trace whiskies will, at least for a little while, be at walking pace rather than a stampede.

BROWN-FORMAN

Until April 2002, the Brown-Forman distillery in Shively, Louisville, was better known as Early Times. Perhaps having that distinctly non-21st century feel to it, like Ancient Age, it was a name that had to go. Mind you, it has taken Brown-Forman 62 years to put their name on the place, having bought it in 1940 when it was known as the Old Kentucky Distillery ... even though it had been standing only five years. Three major brands are distilled here: Old Forester, Early Times and Woodford Reserve. Early Times was the odd one out for being distilled with a higher corn and lower rye content; Woodford Reserve was the odd one out for having its barrels matured at Labrot & Graham; and Early Times was the odd one out for having some of its make being matured in second-hand barrels to make American whisk(e)y as opposed to Bourbon.

FOUR ROSES

For years the beautiful Four Roses distillery in Lawrenceburg was protected under the mighty umbrella of Seagram. Today it is owned by Japanese distillers Kirin, who perhaps have a greater desire for the lightest of all Kentucky's bourbons to hit a wider audience. For a while, Four Roses as a bourbon vanished off the US radar altogether, but now is back. Unlike most of the other distilleries, Four Roses does not own an enormous number of brands, concentrating on those that carry its distinctive name. However there is a move towards the single barrel market that should be watched carefully – and explored whenever possible.

HEAVEN HILL

If you buy a bourbon anywhere in the world that is mildly quirky in appearance or name, or that is own-label, the probabilities are that the whiskey contained therein originates from Heaven Hill. Exactly where it will have been distilled is another matter. In 1996 the original, stupendous Heaven Hill distillery was consumed by fire and for a while the stills at Early Times were rented to work on a beer made from the original Heaven Hill recipe. Now their whisky is made at the state-of-the-art Bernheim distillery in Louisville, a good distance away in style and miles to the original Heaven Hill distillery in Bardstown. On top of that, the company had to buy in surplus bourbon stocks from elsewhere to replace some of the 90,000 barrels destroyed in the inferno. The possibility of the old distillery being rebuilt is still a twinkling in the eyes of some. And not without good reason. From seven years onwards HH is bourbon you overlook at your peril, but when reaching 12 years the original Bardstown Heaven Hill bourbon ranks among the world's greatest whiskies.

JIM BEAM

Two distilleries serve Jim Beam. The last time I really had a good look – a few years back I admit – the lesser known (in fact virtually unknown) distillery at Boston Clermont was making the most characterful bourbon. Amongst bourbons freely available around the world these days, Jim Beam Black, a rich and chewy individual ranks among the best ... and usually costing little more than the standard and much more famous White Label version despite having a few extra years in the wood. Even standard Jim Beam is showing a touch more attitude these days. But pride of place, for me, in the entire Jim Beam portfolio is the astonishing Jim Beam Rye. Its distinctive mustard-yellow label is enough to get connoisseurs salivating at 50 yards and any liquor store outside the United States having it on their shelves makes them a very serious and knowledgeable whisky outlet indeed.

LABROT & GRAHAM

A picture postcard distillery that has recently been rescued from little more than a pile of rubble to be far the most attractive distillery on the American continent. It is remarkable not least for triple distilling its bourbon using old-fashioned pot stills, not unlike those once found four miles along Glenns Creek at the now dead Old Crow distillery. Distilling was re-introduced at Labrot & Graham as recently as 1996 and now its make is in a bottle for the first time. I never quite believed the predictions that it would be a perfect fit for the Woodford Reserve that was launched from the richest barrels of Old Forester they could find, despite originally sharing the same generously ryed mashbill. Instead we have the Woodford Reserve Four Grain which is, as John Cleese might say, something completely different. And no less delicious. There had been talk about re-naming the distillery Woodford Reserve, but so far wiser counsel has prevailed.

MAKER'S MARK

A small and attractive distillery located in stunning country at Loretto, making it Kentucky's southern-most distillery. Also probably the most stable and consistent of all bourbons quite capable at times of being nothing short of sublime. From using a wheat rather than rye recipe, the small copper stills make a full bodied bourbon that matures majestically and, to date, I cannot remember being let down by a bottle yet. Seemingly being the inventors of plastic-wax seals – red for the standard brand, gold and black for older, smaller batch versions – this style of closure has been much imitated in recent years and has a lot to answer for. For a time it was one of the unlikely stars of the Australian soap *Neighbours*: a bottle of Maker's Mark would be seen most days behind the left shoulder of pub landlord Lou Carpenter. Despite its neck level failing to plunge in about three years, one day it suddenly vanished. Obviously a member of the cast had discovered its myriad charms. Despite its weighty body, Maker's Mark is a classic anytime anywhere bourbon. Even in Australia.

WILD TURKEY

For me, a world heritage whisky, if there is such a thing. Both for its whiskey and for the distillery which is perched precariously it seems on a cliff with a sheer drop of 259 feet into the Kentucky River. The whiskey is no less dramatic, especially when it has passed eight years of age. Like Buffalo Trace it ranks in my top three of world distilleries for the extraordinary magnitude of its bourbon. For some time my preferred Wild Turkey was the Rare Breed which simply rejoiced in its honeyed richness and complexity, even though batches could vary from time to time. Today the distillery has a new Champion, the Wild Turkey Russell Reserve, a 10 Year Old named after distillery manager Jimmy Russell (a true master distiller if ever there was one), who will soon be retiring after more than 40 years at the plant. Jimmy prefers to see his whiskeys bottled at 101 proof (50.5% abv) and this is no exception. At younger years Wild Turkey can be ordinary and even the 8-year-old these days is outshone by similar whiskeys its age from around Kentucky. But it is part of the right of passage for every whisky connoisseur to get to grips with Wild Turkey in its most exulted state.

Bourbon

1492 Bourbon (see Heaven Hill 80 Proof)

American Star (86) n21 enormous small-grain character; **t**22 big and roasty yet with plenty of sweet corn to balance out, lovely rye follow-through; **f**21 some hints of cocoa amid the vanilla and fruity grains; **b**22 a seriously good rye-recipe bourbon with enormous full-bodied and fruity character. Sweet and lingering. **40% (80 proof).** *Bernkasteler Germany.*

Ancient Age (75) n18 **t**19 **f**19 **b**19. Light, pleasant but half cooked. **40% (80 proof).**

Ancient Ancient Age 10 Star (89) n22 lavender and soft rye amid the rich corn; **t**23 complex small grain, centring around the rye, but also slightly nutty with some raisiny fruits; **f**22 oak comes steaming in to gently dry the broadening corn. Spices begin to bite; **b**22 what we have here is a bourbon that knows how to offer complexity: a thinking man's bourbon. Much better than it once was. **45% (90 proof).**

Ancient Ancient Age 10 Years Old (94) n23 superb oak richness with the corn floating around and the rye biting and nipping; **t**24 Kentucky heaven: this is bourbon as it should be. The small grains just play around offering a fruitiness of under-ripened greengages and the sweet nuttiness of sunflower seeds, bristling with complexity; **f**23 remains long and playful: the rye is a fraction bitter and cocoa adds to the dryness, but the corn offers all the sweetness required; **b**24 this is my everyday drinking whiskey when back home in Kentucky. A tiny fraction heavier now than previously, I actually prefer it when they choose barrels from the bottom of the warehouse to make the complexity even more nerve-tingling. Then, usually, it scores around 95. But you really can't complain about this: find me a Scotch of the same price or age to match its complexity and I'll show you a British whisky magazine publisher not in it just for the money. **43% (86 proof).**

Anderson Club (see Heaven Hill Aged 6 Years 90 Proof)

Aristocrat (see Heaven Hill 80 Proof)

Baker's Aged 7 Years batch B-85-001 **(88) n**22 excellent rye bite to the very firm and sweet nose. Fabulously fruity: mature plums and slightly over-ripe banana star; **t**23 again the rye kicks off early and allows a slightly bitter and prickly, softly spiced middle to ensure this is a characterful, multi-layered bourbon that follows a deliciously unique agenda; **f**21 massively complex follow-through, with quite enormous and beautiful cocoa notes; **b**22 a chocoholic's bourbon if ever there was one. Changed shape slightly in the last few years with a bigger rye firmness. Tasty, armchair stuff. **53.5% (107 proof).** Jim Beam.

Baker's Aged 7 Years batch B-90-001 **(85) n**21 soft, corn dominant, vanilla-rich with sexy rye sub-plot; **t**22 clean corn with a chewy toffee-apple middle; **f**21 extremely soft and undemanding despite some late small grain; **b**21 not quite in the same league as the bigger batch 85, but pretty timeless, enjoyable stuff. **53.5% (107 proof).** Jim Beam.

Barclay's Bourbon (79) n20 **t**21 **f**18 **b**20. Economical in development, there is still enough rye and nutty oiliness to keep the tastebuds amused. Little sparkle on the finish. **40% (80 proof)**

Basil Hayden's (77) n21 **t**19 **f**18 **b**19. Some attractive rye riches, but overall disappointingly thin and lacking in depth. **40% (80 proof).** Jim Beam.

Benchmark (see McAfee's Benchmark)

⠿ **Black Jack (86) n**23 massively firm with a rye dominated wall carrying with it some good age; **t**22 a wonderful intertwining of firm grain and ultra-soft corn. The oils give much to chew on; **f**20 rather too relaxed with now the oil dominating like a straight corn whiskey. Strange; **b**21 what starts as a ryefest loses power dramatically, though the outcome remains tasty. **37%.** Australia.

Blanton's (89) n20 relatively raw, grainy, hot and unwieldy for a Blanton; **t**23 goes into honeyed overdrive with a superb rye-based back-up; **f**23 bitter, slightly fruity rye and some major oak incursions, but still the honey continues; **b**23 forget the nose: once on the palate you are entering honeyed bliss. **42.5% (93 proof).** Buffalo Trace.

⠿ **Blanton's Gold Edition** barrel no 12 w/house H rick 35 dumped 16 Oct 03 **(91) n**22 a fraction closed for Blanton's but spice enough to show it's ticking; **t**24 a velvety coating of sweetcorn with a tingling layer of rye and leathery liquorice; the elan is spellbinding; **f**22 remains sweet with lashings of natural toffee; **b**23 seamless. **51.5% (103 proof).** Buffalo Trace.

Blanton's Gold Edition barrel no. 226 w/house H Rick 32 dumped 12 March 02 **(93) n**23 stunning rye and small grains hammering into the oak; **t**24 beautiful, silky arrival of honeyed oak and lush, busy grains; **f**22 more vanilla, chills out ... or would do if a massive spice surge didn't want to have the last word; **b**24 brilliant complexity: top-order bourbon. Grab any bottle you spot. **51.5% (103 proof).** *Buffalo Trace.*

Blanton's Barrel no. 239 w/house H Rick 49 dumped 21 Oct 02 **(91)** n*23* bourbon concentrate, and absolutely stunning, complex bourbon at that, with big age and heavy, sweet oak; t*23* dry, mouth-puckering oak sweetens as the juicy corn arrives. A beautiful shimmer of honey, but kept in check by peppery spice; f*22* sweet corn forms a juicy interlude before the softer, saner vanillas return; b*23* massive whiskey, and not because of the natural strength. Age and nature have had a big input here. The results are enormous and breathtakingly enjoyable. **67.7% (135.2 proof).** *Buffalo Trace.*

⸬ **Blanton's Gold Edition** barrel no 241 w/house H dumped 1 May 03 **(89)** n*23* marmalade, honeycomb, polished leather and a wisp of rye; t*23* a zillion little flavour explosions erupt around the palate offering hints of ginger amid the Demerara oak and sweet corn; f*21* dries quickly with some deft liquorice; b*22* my first whiskey of a new tasting day: the sun is shining, the birds are singing and my tastebuds are being made love to. What a wonderful world ... **51.5% (103 proof).** *Buffalo Trace.*

⸬ **Blanton's Silver Edition** barrel no 53 w/house H rick 8 dumped 22 Apr 02 **(94)** n*24* near faultless: the oak is offering a chocolate-orangey lead while a small, busy gaggle of rye notes try to persuade you they offer the fruitier route; t*23* mouth-enveloping with a lovely corn-oiliness but the explosion of rye and oak-induced spices is simply orgasmic; f*23* after the eruption, a dignified and incredibly long powering down of hundreds of waves of flavour, ending in a creamy, natural toffee sweetness; b*24* almost beyond words. **49% (98 proof).** *Buffalo Trace.*

⸬ **Blanton's Silver Edition** barrel no 118 w/house H rick 27 dumped 12 Jun 03 **(83)** n*22* t*22* f*20* b*21*. Genteel and refined with the accent on corn and some waspish rye spice. **49% (98 proof).** *Buffalo Trace.*

⸬ **Blanton's Single Barrel** barrel no 69 w/house H rick 55 dumped 19 Jan 04 **(91)** n*23* a riot of small grains with distant marmalade; sweet ripe plums, too; t*22* simmering bitter-sweet corn-rye battle with rich banana and custard middle; f*23* quite intense with a liquorice, bitter coffee surge; b*23* goes down a treat: one to swallow and never spit. **46.5% (93 proof).** *Buffalo Trace.*

⸬ **Blanton's Single Barrel** barrel no 240 w/house H rick 49 dumped 21 Oct 02 **(93)** n*23* the rye says hi; t*23* small-grain lead with lots of little skirmishes allowing a superb corn-rye battle to develop; f*24* lovely oak control with soft cocoa add depth; the flavour waves keep on exploding as they hit home; b*23* sheer quality throughout. **67.3% (134.3 proof).** *Buffalo Trace.*

Blanton's Single Barrel barrel no. 520 w/house H Rick 55 dumped 23 Aug 01 **(89)** n*22* superb oak of quite perfect weight; t*23* big and oily mouthfeel, a toffeed middle that you can chew indefinitely; f*22* soft vanilla and a touch of marmalade and spice; b*22* simply a quality bourbon. **46.5%.** *Buffalo Trace.*

⸬ **Blanton's Special Reserve** barrel no 76 w/house H rick 16 dumped 3 Mar 03 **(83)** n*21* t*21* f*20* b*21*. A steady sort of fellow that is mid-range in all its attributes. **40% (80 proof).** *Buffalo Trace.*

⸬ **Blanton's Special Reserve** barrel no 102 w/house H rick 49 dumped 6 Aug 02 **(85)** n*23* Seville oranges, some chalky oak, fresh-baked corn bread with lots of natural vanilla and caramel; t*21* surprisingly dry middle after an early gridlock of pulsating, mouthwatering rye amid the corn; f*20* vanilla; b*22* decent and subtly complex, but the nose promises more than is delivered. **40% (80 proof).** *Buffalo Trace.*

Blanton's Special Reserve barrel no. 180 w/house H Rick 10 dumped 6 Aug 02 **(79)** n*20* t*21* f*19* b*19*. Pleasant, but surprisingly flat for Blanton's. **40% (80 proof).** *Buffalo Trace.*

⸬ **Blanton's Straight From the Barrel** barrel no 109 w/house H rick 27 dumped 29 May 03 **(89)** n*23* like sticking your head in a barrel: warming top rye notes mingle with passion fruit and toasty oak; **t**22 for all the power the corn-rich message is simple and seductive; **f**22 despite the sweetness the small grains dig in bitterly; **b**22 another great cask from a great distillery. **64.9% (129.8 proof).** *Buffalo Trace.*

Blue Grass State (77) n19 **t**19 **f**20 **b**19. Clean, good toast and vanilla. **40% (80 proof).** *Somerfield UK.*

Bowman's Bourbon (81) n20 **t**20 **f**21 **b**20. A very decent, well-balanced, softly spiced and rich young-to-medium-age bourbon originating from Heaven Hill. A fine everyday shot. **40% (80 proof).** *A Smith Bowman.*

Booker's 7 Yrs 3 Months batch C92-I-15 **(92) n**24 a stunningly integrated aroma: fresh rye and almost green corn in perfect harmony with dry toasty oak and sweet chestnuts; **t**23 corn and sweetened cocoa in equal measures, slightly lush but the rye pops up to make a very complex middle; **f**22 remains sweet but with fade-out of the constituent flavours as graceful as the setting sun; **b**24 of the batches I have come across over the years, the finest yet, not just because of the extra sweetness, but the complexity required to keep that sweetness at bay. Brilliant. **63.25% (126.5 proof).**

Booker's 7 Years 4 Months batch no. C90-D-11 **(88) n**22 burnt raisins and heavy sweet corn; **t**23 incredibly sweet: the sweet corn is thick enough to stand a spoon in, velvety and chewy; **f**21 decent liquorice as the oak kicks in; **b**22 clever Booker Beam: he's picked a different style, but kept the quality bang on course. This really is a treat for corn whiskey lovers! **63.25% (126.5 poof).** *Jim Beam.*

Booker's 8 Years 8 Months batch no. C87-D-21 **(86) n**22 light and quite malty, almost dank hessian amid some growing rye; **t**23 corn much more prominent, then a hugely satisfying surge of honey and spice: delicious; **f**20 slightly flat compared to the excellent build-up. Some decent rye lingers, though; **b**21 a rich bourbon that varies in style from batch to batch. This one has a better than average middle with no shortage of rye, but is let down in the final stages. **62.45% (124.9 proof).** *Jim Beam.*

Bourbon Falls (see Heaven Hill 86 Proof)

Bourbon Royal (see Heaven Hill 80 Proof)

Buffalo Trace (94) n23 sharp rye screams above the complex corn, citrus and oak: seriously absorbing; **t**24 stupendous, softly oiled mouthfeel with the corn absorbing some prickly rye and spice; **f**23 sweet, remains oily with some cream toffee. The small grains re-emerge for a last battle with the corn; **b**24 I simply adore this whiskey: the weight is just about perfect as is the corn-oak, bitter-sweet harmony. The small grains add great colour and complexity. A whiskey gem of the world. **45%. (90 proof).**

Bulleit Bourbon Frontier Whiskey (88) n22 light and teasing: mallows roasting on an open fire plus pine nuts and vanilla. Honest, folks; **t**22 the faintest dry oak start vanishes within seconds for a rich follow-through of sweet chestnut, a busy complexity of malted barley and rye and then spice; **f**22 mildly oily, softly honeycombed and chocolatey for a chewy, bitter-sweet finale. Like all that's gone before, exceptionally well balanced and satisfying; **b**22 absolutely excellent from first to last, an essay in balance and control: I doubt if any frontier whiskey of Boone's day was half as good as this. **45% (90 proof).**

Cabin Hill (see Heaven Hill 80 Proof)

Champion (see Heaven Hill 80 Proof)

Chapin & Gore (see Heaven Hill 80 Proof)

Chapin & Gore 86 Proof (see Heaven Hill 86 Proof)

Chesapeake (see Heaven Hill 80 Proof)

Chillie Gone Crazy (see Heaven Hill 80 Proof)

Classic Cask Bourbon Aged 17 Years Distilled 1983 batch GL-106 bott 00 **(87) n**21 an oily, roasty aroma, full of mocha, a sliver of liquorice and some excellent small grains with the rye having greater say than the delicate malt. Superb grip on the nose; t21 a classic explosion of sweet, oily liquorice and simmering spice. The middle becomes a simple mixture of toffee and dried dates; f23 medium length vanilla with a hint of hickory, honey and nuts on the finale; b22 a beautiful bourbon that shows no sign of fade whatsoever. Simplistic towards the middle and finish but the journey there is sensational. **45.4% (90.8 proof).** *The Classic Cask Co. Bardstown. 600 bottles.*

Classic Cask Bourbon Aged 17 Years Distilled 1985 batch GL-108 bott 02 **(86)** n20 for the big colour and age, this is light and minty with extra emphasis on the corn; t22 beautifully delicate with a fine sharp rye kick against the much sweeter corn and oak; f22 soft, gracious exit, the vanilla taking the lead with liquorice following tamely behind. Some lovely late roast notes and a little sap emphasise the age; b22 talk about gentle giants – really charming bourbon that looks like it wishes to bludgeon you, but instead sings lullabies. **45.4% (90.8 proof).** *The Classic Cask Co. Bardstown. 600 bottles.*

Colonel Lee (69) n17 t17 f18 b17. Grim stuff. **40%.** Barton.

Colonel's Pride (see Heaven Hill 80 Proof)

∴ **Cougar (93)** n24 biting, rip-roaring, rabid rye offering astonishing crispness and finesse on the corn. One of the all-time great rye-rich bourbon aromas; t23 massive rye makes for a crisp, fruity and mouth-watering arrival. The corn eventually softens the impact and ensures sweetness; f23 much more well-behaved with vanilla and corn now leading the way but the rye just continues to salivate the palate; b23 one of the most characterful, purposeful bourbons you could imagine. This Illinois cracker is one of the best-kept secrets in the bourbon world. **37%.** *Australia.*

Daniel Stewart Aged 8 Years (88) n22 rich, leathery and pipe-tobacco-sweet but underneath a second stratum of young grain: unusual; t22 brilliantly spiced yet sweet corn forms an oily-textured middle; f22 lots of blistering small grain and spice; b22 a very sweet yet complex bourbon of light-to-medium weight. **45% (90 proof).** *Heaven Hill.*

Daniel Stewart Aged 12 Years (95) n24 floral, honey and outstanding clean oak and corn: a classy act; t24 heather, honey, hints of citrus and then some serious oak, but always sweetened by the rich corn. The rye offers a spicy and even more complex background; f23 such a delicate fade: the sweetness falls over aeons, the oak gathering density at the same rate. But the rye continues its merry tune; b24 it is pretty obvious that the original old Heaven Hill peaks at 12: it always has in the time I have known it. Awesome, spellbinding bottlings like this place it amongst the world's elite. **53.5% (107 proof).** *Heaven Hill.*

Dierberg's (see Heaven Hill 80 Proof)

Distiller's Pride (see Heaven Hill 80 Proof)

Don & Ben's (see Evan Williams Aged 7 Years 86 Proof)

Dowling Deluxe Aged 8 Years 100 Proof (84) n21 t22 f20 b21. Simplistically sweet and oaky. **50% (100 proof).** *Heaven Hill.*

Eagle Rare Single Barrel Bourbon 10 Years Old (89) n23 big: touches of honey add to the peek-a-boo rye and distant demerara; t23 initial sweet arrival of rye, then chewy oak and corn, followed by peppery, toffee attack; f21 very long, remaining on the vanilla-caramel theme; b22 a delight. *Buffalo Trace.*

Eagle Rare 10 Years Old (78) n21 t20 f18 b19. Lush, big and chewy toffee but very limited complexity. Decent whiskey, but I never seem to get on with this one as I do with other Buffalo Trace bourbons, either for one reason or another. Strange. **50.5% (101 proof).** *Buffalo Trace.*

Eagle Rare 17 Years Old (94) n24 fabulous combination of roasted almonds and pecan pie, all topped with brown sugar, stewed apples and the faintest dash of honeycomb. Brilliant – almost a template for how aged bourbon should be; t23 lighter, cleaner initial mouthfeel than would be expected and the cranking up of rich, leathery, liquoricy, slightly phenolic oak notes takes a little time; f23 plateaus out with lots of demerara sweetness, a drying vanilla and toffee. Spices begin to rise towards the finale like a phoenix from the ashes: big but manageable; **b**24 the nose is wondrous, the taste is lighter, but only marginally less awesome, though the spice on the finish is a masterstroke. Such a consistent, reliable whiskey over the years. One of the all-time great bourbons. **45% (90 proof).** *Buffalo Trace.*

Early Times (brown label) (80) n19 **t**21 **f**20 **b**20. A very light but well-made bourbon. Clean, with hints of cinnamon and citrus. Quite refreshing. **40%. (80 proof).**

Early Times (yellow label) (83) n20 **t**21 **f**21 **b**21. A heavier, more vanilla-rich bourbon that offers a consistent, delicate, sweet theme throughout with butterscotch on the finish. **40% (80 proof).**

Echo Spring (see Heaven Hill 80 Proof)

Elijah Craig 12 Years Old (96) n24 gentle lavender and violets merge into a rye-oak soup. As heavy as it seems, it just floats around the glass, and as dry as the oak appears, the inherent mildly honeyed sweetness offers the perfect riposte: fabulous; **t**24 now the honey is so much more apparent, but some rye-weathered spice keeps it under control; **f**23 long, spiced cream toffee, but doesn't even begin to soften or undermine the enormous depth to this whiskey; **b**25 this whiskey is all about contrast and balance, power and subtlety. It is a world masterpiece, the kind of whiskey that makes you glad to be alive. My heartfelt praise and thanks to the boys at HH for keeping this one of the world's most consistently astounding treats. **47% (94 proof).** *Heaven Hill.*

Elijah Craig 18 Years Old Single Barrel barrel no. 821 barrelled on 22 Oct 82 **(81) n**19 **t**22 **f**19 **b**21. Surprisingly low key with little on the nose but picking up for a burnt honey finish, though the finish is a bit on the tired side. **45% (90 proof).** *Heaven Hill.*

Elijah Craig 18 Years Old Single Barrel barrel no. 495 barrelled on 18 Nov 82 **(88) n**22 vanilla and milky coffee. The rye shows well; **t**22 beautiful sweet corn in tandem with some big oak notes; **f**22 small grains to the rescue as the oak fails to gain control. Really delicious, complex stuff; **b**22 breaks all the rules: how can a bourbon survive this number of Kentucky summers and come out sweet as a nut? **45% (90 proof).** *Heaven Hill.*

Elmer T Lee Single Barrel (88) n22 distinct citrus and light corn-rich notes; **t**23 sweet corn again with hints of banana and rye; **f**21 a very settled, toffeed finale with a hint of spicy rebellion; **b**22 a more delicate and less rye-infested bottling than some. Really delicious. **45% (90 proof).** *Buffalo Trace.*

Evan Williams (see Heaven Hill 80 Proof)

Evan Williams 100 Proof (see Heaven Hill 100 Proof)

Evan Williams Aged 7 Years (83) n22 **t**21 **f**20 **b**20. Sweet, corn-rich with caramel on the middle and a dry, oaky finish. **43%.** *Heaven Hill.*

Evan Williams 15 Years (90) n23 heavy duty age, but enough sweetness to absorb the oaky impact; **t**22 too thick to drink through a straw, with again the oak dominance thwarted by amazingly active corn. The spices buzz blissfully; **f**22 liquorice and demerara sugar head-to-head; **b**23 there is no way that a bourbon carrying this amount of oak should be enjoyable. But it is much more than that: a grizzly arm-wrestle in which you come out a smiling victor. Macho stuff ... and magnificent. **50.5% (101 proof).** *Heaven Hill.*

Evan Williams 23 Years Old (86) n22 the oak is creaking a bit with a hint of sap on the aroma, but a thread of sweetness keeps it together; **t**22 massive mouth arrival with enough small grain to offer complexity enough to drive off the oak, even time for some orangey notes to arrive; **f**21 soft vanilla and a build-up of sweetish corn; **b**22 hats off to this bourbon. It defies nature by surviving this amount of time in the barrel: the original richness of the spirit must have played a significant start. This is some beast and, by the second glassful, a bit of a beauty, too. **53.5% (107 proof).** *Heaven Hill.*

Evan Williams 1783 (see Heaven Hill 10 Years 86 Proof)
Evan Williams Old (see Heaven Hill 100 Proof)
Evan Williams Vintage 1989 Single Barrel (87) n22 heavy-ish oak thinned by soft lime: a gentle giant; **t**22 enormous corn dominance and then a chewy layer of toffee; **f**21 incredibly soft with the small grains rising without anger; **b**22 for all the early puff, one of the more gentle single-barrel expressions from Kentucky. **43.3% (86.6% proof).** *Heaven Hill.*

Evan Williams Vintage 1990 Single Barrel (91) n23 a stunning herbal start blossoms into a ginger-honey sweetness. The small grains are lively, with the malt and rye becoming a fruity and citrussy one; **t**23 a fresh and clean start allows the corn to develop beautifully before the rye takes hold. Brilliant bitter-sweet balance and complexity that dances around the palate; **f**22 medium length only, but the quality is outstanding with a new layer of fresh rye on soft corn bringing the curtain down; **b**23 a bourbon that celebrates the part rye and malt notes can play against the more neutral background of corn. At times, almost too complex to be true. **43.3% (86.6 proof).** *Heaven Hill.*

Evan Williams Vintage 1993 Single Barrel (89) n22 busy citrus battling with fresh and fruity rye; **t**22 delicate small grains dominate at first, then a wave of oak followed by sweet corn; **f**22 pretty long and quite dry with some chalky oak enlivened by returning rye and liquorice; **b**23 a steady, sexy, delicate bourbon that is a lot more complex than it initially seems. **43.3% (86.6%).**

Ezra Brooks (79) n19 **t**20 **f**20 **b**20. A light-to-medium weight bourbon with a standard nose but offering good sweet liquorice on the rich finish. **45%**

Fighting Cock Aged 6 Years (84) n22 **t**22 **f**20 **b**20. Brilliant nose of old, waxy wooden floors and a really battling palate arrival of almost fruity corn. Quite hot. **51.5% (103 proof).** *Heaven Hill.*

Four Roses (84) n22 **t**21 **f**20 **b**21. A sweet and charming bourbon that is light and sophisticated but always pulls up short of being a world beater. Now that the distillery is on its own I expect this perennial under-achiever to go through the roof quality-wise. The stocks are there, as the single-barrel expressions illustrate, and as I have seen over the years when inspecting the warehouses. Keep your eyes peeled and tastebuds at the ready. Four Roses is likely to become a thorn in their competitors' sides. **40% (80 proof).**

Four Roses Single Barrel barrel 2-13-926, bott 22 Oct 99 **(89) n**23 small grains to the fore with a lovely malt-rye interplay – certainly more rye apparent on this batch than normal, fittingly delicate and floral; **t**22 denser on the palate, surprisingly heavy. It all hangs on the rye base, but fans out with roasty, burnt raisins, a hint of coffee and burnt fudge. Unbelievably chewy; **f**22 more of the same, though the fade-out is slow, roasty and tantalising; **b**22 the best bottled sample from this distillery I'd tasted at the time. **43% (86 proof).**

Four Roses Single Barrel barrel 2-1093E, bott 7 Dec 00 **(90) n**23 just so delicate with the rye making a proud stand against equally crisp corn. Hedgerow flowers with a touch of honey; **t**22 initially much sweeter than the nose suggests, hints of molasses sugar doubling with the rich corn; **f**22 lovely arrival of oak doesn't quite bother the general sweetness; **b**23 pips the previous bottling thanks to stupendous rye involvement. A benchmark whiskey for the distillery. **43% (86 proof).**

Four Roses Single Barrel Reserve (80) n22 **t**21 **f**18 **b**19. Starts promisingly and the rye gives good weight but fades alarmingly. This is now a discontinued line but the odd bottle can still be seen in specialist outlets the world over. **43% (86 proof).**

Gentleman Earl (see Heaven Hill 80 Proof)

George T Stagg (97) n25 I cannot really find a fault here: the oak is big enough to add a herbal almost medicinal quality, which on its own could be a downer were it not for the extraordinary, just about perfect, counter provided by sharp, juicy rye fruitiness and sweetening corn. Stick your nose in this – but only after you have warmed it to body temperature and you have about 15–20 minutes to spare. Really, tasting notes are pointless in some ways: look for it and you will find it there. This in some way redefines complexity; **t**24 the enormity of the age and strength at first wrinkles and shrivels the palate, but when your eyes have stopped watering and you can focus, you will see you're in Eden. The splendour of the rye leads the way, with a soft oily body forming from which much more succulent corn springs. The oak is a vaguely bitter pulse somewhere in the background. In the midst of this a buttery, small-grain anthem is played over and over again; **f**23 much quieter by comparison but the fruits remain and now a natural, caramelised corn sweetens the building, coffeed oak; **b**25 I have tried this with water at varying strengths, but to get the best out of this bourbon you must be brave. Take at full strength, but only in very small amounts. Such is the enormity of this whiskey it will soon spread around the palate offering its full service. Along with a certain Ardbeg, this George T Stagg is without any shadow of a doubt one of the two best whiskies it has ever been my luck and privilege to taste in nearly 30 years. **68.8% (137.6 proof).** Buffalo Trace.

⸭ **Gold Country Aged 8 Years (88) n**22 marzipan and marmalade; **t**22 the most teasing criss-crossing soft, sweet vanilla and firmer grains; never more than a gentle caress; **f**21 soft as a marshmallow and as roasted at the end as a toasted one; **b**23 exceptionally delicate for its age and colour. Take your time to discover this most subtle of bourbons. **40% (80 proof).** France, Denmark.

Gold Label (see Heaven Hill 80 Proof)

Hancock's Reserve Single Barrel (83) n21 **t**21 **f**20 **b**21. A tad butyric but still employs enough sweet liquorice charm to make for a very decent whiskey. **44.45% (88.9 proof).**

Heaven Hill 80 Proof (75) n18 **t**20 **f**18 **b**19. Green, young and lively; no shortage of flavour for all its tender years. **40% (80 proof).** Comes with gold, blue, green and white labels.

Heaven Hill 86 Proof (83) n20 **t**22 **f**20 **b**21. Probably the maltiest bourbon I have tasted in 29 years of savouring the stuff: barley springs out at you from all directions. Fresh, juicy and mouthwatering: delicious and a real surprise package. **43% (86 proof).**

Heaven Hill 100 Proof (78) n19 **t**20 **f**19 **b**20. There is lots of rye and toffee here. **50% (100 proof).**

Heaven Hill Aged 6 Years 80 Proof (88) n22 green corn but lively rye; **t**22 lots of fresh rye and massive spice sparkle; **f**22 hints of sweet liquorice as the oak says, "hello"; the corn remains youthful and a fun antidote to the oak; **b**22 this is wonderful, sophisticated whiskey: the jump from five to six years is a chasm. **40% (80 proof).**

Heaven Hill Aged 6 Years 90 Proof (88) n22 pine alongside the fresh rye; **t**23 brilliant rye and barley complexity swamped by a wave of sweet corn: unbelievably tasty; **f**21 soft oak with hints of liquorice and demerara sugar; **b**22 weighty bourbon with excellent small-grain complexity. **45% (90 proof).**

Heaven Hill Aged 6 Years 100 Proof (85) n20 flattish, toffeed; **t**22 big oak kick takes the breath away; **f**22 some spice and shy rye, flattens slightly as the toffee returns; **b**21 tasty, but a bit of a lazy one, this. Natural, caramel-dependent and short of oomph. **45% (90 proof).**

Heaven Hill Aged 10 Years 86 Proof (86) n21 attractive weight with hickory and liquorice combining; the vanilla is sweet, the grains subdued except for some dogged rye; **t**21 spicy, chewy kick off with a firm rye development; softly oiled and slowly gathers sweetness; **f**22 quite long and the building grain offers great complexity and balance; **b**22 takes a little time to get going but a sophisticated number in some ways showing greater age than expected with the whole being better than the parts. **43% (86 proof).**

Heaven Hill Ultra Deluxe (see Heaven Hill 80 Proof)

Heaven Hill Ultra Deluxe 5 Years (76) n20 t19 f18 b19. In a bit of a toffeed trough here, halfway between the juicy, lively 4-y-o and the more, small-grain pounding, oak-heavy 6-y-o. **40% (80 proof).**

Heaven Hill Ultra DeLuxe 6 Years (see Heaven Hill Aged 6 Years 90 Proof)

Henry McKenna (see Heaven Hill Aged 6 Years 80 Proof)

Henry McKenna Single Barrel Aged 10 Years Bottled in Bond barrel no. 208 barrelled on 1 May 92 (91) n23 no prisoners here at all: minty toothpaste after a marmalade breakfast then black coffee with muscovado sugar and spice ... phew! t23 chewy with enormous oak presence from the first moment. The spice is magnificent; f22 back to Jamaican Blue Mountain coffee, reasonably heavy roast with a fluttering of cocoa and more brown sugar; b23 knife and fork bourbon with stupendous character and presence. A sublime selection. For grown-ups only. **50% (100 proof).**

Jacob's Well batch B-0230-JW459 (84) n22 t20 f21 b21. Still seen around from time to time (though pretty rarely), this small-batch bourbon concentrates on a lavender delicacy and subtle sweetness. **42% (84 proof).** *Jim Beam.*

Jefferson's Reserve 15 Year Old batch no. 2 (94) n24 this is to die for: gently oiled, which means the rye and corn stick to the nose, the sweetness and sharp fruit in equal measure; t24 brilliant corn/rye entry on the palate then a shimmering honey. Great age, but always elegant and refined while the complexity dazzles; f22 very soft landing with vanilla and rye to the fore. The complexity remains superb; b24 a great whiskey: simple as that. **45.1% (90.2 proof).**

Jim Beam (85) n21 charmingly floral with a soft rye undercurrent; t21 sweet corn arrival then soft oaky-vanilla notes; f22 hints of soft liquorice and then much drier mouthwatering vaguely malty tones; b21 this whiskey has improved enormously in recent years. Still light and easy going, there appears to be an element of extra age, weight and complexity. **40% (80 proof).**

Jim Beam Black (90) n23 big and bruising, there is weighty oil and liquorice; t23 beautifully sweet, manuka honey and then liquorice, candy and rich rye; f22 soft vanilla and liquorice; b22 I just so love this bourbon. The closest in style to a Jack Daniel's because of a mildly lumbering gait. Any time, any day whiskey of the very top order. **43% (86 proof).**

Jim Porter (see Heaven Hill 80 Proof)

John Hamilton (see Heaven Hill 80 Proof)

J T S Brown (see Heaven Hill 80 Proof)

J T S Brown 86 Proof (see Heaven Hill 86 Proof)

J T S Brown 100 Proof (see Heaven Hill 100 Proof)

J T S Brown 6 Years 80 Proof (see Heaven Hill Aged 6 Years 80 Proof)

J T S Brown 6 Years 100 Proof (see Heaven Hill Aged 6 Years 100 Proof)

J T S Brown 8 Years (see Old Heaven Hill Very Rare Aged 8 Years 86 Proof)

J T S Brown 10 Years (see Heaven Hill 10 Years 86 Proof)

J W Dant (see Heaven Hill 80 Proof)

J W Dant (see Heaven Hill 100 Proof)

J W Kent (see Heaven Hill 80 Proof)

Kentucky Beau (see Heaven Hill 80 Proof)

Kentucky Crown Aged 8 Years (88) n22 pipe-tobacco-sweet, sensual; t22 there is a layer of oily, sweet corn before spices arrive; f22 sweet vanilla and corn; b22 a charmingly sweet yet spicy bourbon. **45% (90 proof).** *Germany.*

Kentucky Crown Very Rare Aged 16 Years (87) n22 distinct kumquat and over-ripe pears, really excellent oak; t23 sweet, oily corn followed by liquorice and citrus: big, threatening yet mouthwatering; f20 levels out with a tad too much natural caramel; b22 a mildly abrupt toffeed end just when it was getting good. **53.5% (107 proof).** *Germany.*

Kentucky deLuxe (see Heaven Hill 80 Proof)

Kentucky deLuxe 86 Proof (see Heaven Hill 86 Proof)

Kentucky Gentleman (89) n23 improbable small-grains complexity for a whiskey so young; **t**23 lots of rye charging around the palate and malt adds something sweet and weighty. The corn imposes itself gently; **f**21 quietens and becomes a little bitter; **b**22 this was always a little belter for its age, but this is the best I have tasted yet. The small-grain quality is unimpeachable. Delicious. **40% (80 proof).** *Barton.*

Kentucky Gold (see Heaven Hill 80 Proof)

Kentucky Spirit Single Barrel barrel 10 warehouse A, rick 51, bott 9 May 02 **(89) n**23 very dry despite the subtle oranges and burnt honey; **t**23 explodes on entry: punchy, rye-based spices and then big toffee-liquorice, genuinely spectacular early middle; **f**21 very dry, the oak offering toasty vanilla; **b**22 this is big bourbon but the complexity is lost towards the finish as the oak kicks in. **50.5% (101 proof).**

Kentucky Tavern (86) n22 some age and weight amid the rye-led small grains; **t**22 mouthwatering, fresh and very busy; **f**21 a touch of liquorice; **b**21 typical fare from Barton distillery: for Scotch drinkers, their whiskey is the equivalent of young Speyside malt, refreshing and mouthwatering. This is no exception. **40% (80 proof).** *Barton.*

Kentucky Supreme (see Old Heaven Hill Very Rare Aged 8 Years 80 Proof)

Kentucky Vintage batch 02-38, dist 22 Feb 94, bott 9 Mar 02 **(83) n**21 **t**22 **f**20 **b**20. Pretty hefty in places, sweet with some citrus fruit. **45% (90 proof)**

Knob Creek Aged 9 Years (90) n24 marmalade on slightly burnt toast, beautiful, sweet fruit, mainly pears, and then a dash of soft rye and an edge of saltiness, some honey as a side-dish; **t**22 softly spiced, oaky, busy start; then a powerful delivery of natural toffee. A playfully biting, tastebud-nipping character tries to add momentum; **f**22 chocolate toffee balances out the vanilla and ensures a dry, slightly oily and long finish; **b**22 the best aroma from the JBB Small Batch selection; softer on the tastebuds than previous bottlings, but still a power player. **50% (100 proof).** *Jim Beam.*

Lone Oak Aged 12 Long Years (89) n23 really sexy oak involvement with the small grains making some noise and good, controlled age; **t**24 astonishingly silky mouth arrival with some very oily and sweet corn being countered superbly by bitter oak. Honeydew melon and muscovado sugar offer the counterbalance while the small grains go wild; **f**20 heaps of toffee, then a quick fade; **b**22 the short, simple finish is a bit of a surprise package in one of the silkiest bourbons on the market shelf. **50.5% (101 proof).** *Germany.*

McAfee's Benchmark (79) n20 **t**21 **f**19 **b**19. Light, young and corn-rich. **40% (80 proof).** *Buffalo Trace.*

McAfee's Benchmark 8 Years Old (83) n21 **t**21 **f**20 **b**21. Fruity, mouthwatering and refreshing. **40% (80 proof).** *Buffalo Trace.*

McScrooge's (see Heaven Hill 80 Proof)

Maker's Mark (Red Wax Seal) (black on buff label) **(89) n**23 wispy aroma with delightful strands of exotic fruit and honey. The old fruitcake is still there, but these days the complexity and balance are nothing short of stunning. Beguiling oak adds to the overall feeling of class; **t**23 lush, pleasingly deep and quite malty. A firm nuttiness adds extra oily, chewability to the toffee and liquorice; **f**21 perhaps drier than of old with signs of a little extra age. Caramel toffee continues its interplay with the oak to guarantee a bitter-sweet edge; **b**22 an old faithful of a bourbon. Never lets you down and being from the wheaty school always shows good oak balance. **45% (90 proof).**

Maker's Mark (Black Wax Seal) (gold on black label) **(93) n**23 thick, charred notes, deep, mildly waxy, hints of cordite; **t**24 oily and immediately mouthfilling with a quite stupendous soft honey, grainy sweetness that balances almost to perfection with the toasty, liquorice-caramel, burnt sugar deeper tones. A pepperiness is on a wavelength almost too subtle to be heard. This is cerebral drinking; f22 much less taxing on the tastebuds with a more toffeed departure. Vanilla and other well-ordered oaky tones are also present and correct; b24 simply outstanding bourbon with the most clever weight ratio. A whiskey that demands solitude and the ability to listen. The story it tells is worth hearing again and again. **47.5% (95 proof).**

Mark Twain (see Heaven Hill 80 Proof)

Mark Twain Aged 12 Years 100 Proof (88) n22 the obvious oak remains light and corny; **t**22 hard rye and fruity, the sweetness is well camouflaged; **f**22 slightly burnt toast, very roasty; **b**22 a well-disciplined bourbon that looks at one point as though the oak has taken too firm a grip but the complexity never ends. **50% (100 proof).** *Heaven Hill.*

Martin Mills (see Heaven Hill 80 Proof)

Mattingly & Moore (see Heaven Hill 80 Proof)

May's (see Heaven Hill 80 Proof)

❖ **Medley (85) n**18 a little murky and nondescript; **t**23 surprising small grain surge; enormously busy palate with the rye really digging deep; **f**22 remains gentle and pulsing with rye and barley; very late, delicious cocoa on finish; **b**22 intimate small grains make this an unusual and sophisticated experience. **40% (80 proof).**

Mellow Bourbon (see Heaven Hill 80 Proof)

Military Special (see Heaven Hill 80 Proof)

Mound City (see Heaven Hill 80 Proof)

Noah's Mill batch 02-71, dist 2 Jul 87, bott 1 Nov 02 **(91) n**23 stunning small grain, the rye in particular starring; **t**23 excellent transfer from nose to palate with busy grains pounding the tastebuds; **f**21 takes a breather as some corn and oak give a softer landing; **b**24 this is one of Kentucky's most complex whiskies by far. Small grains, big heart. **57.15% (114.3 proof).**

No Face (see Heaven Hill 80 Proof)

No Face 86 Proof (see Heaven Hill 86 Proof)

Old 1889 (see Heaven Hill 80 Proof)

Old 1889 Aged 10 Years 86 Proof (85) n22 mango has somehow slipped into the equation here: one of the fruitiest Heaven Hill numbers I've ever known; **t**20 really light with the corn glowing on the palate; **f**22 the small grains offer a nutty dimension to the gentle corn; **b**21 quite different HH from what I usually see. This is much more light and delicate with less of the usual richness those old big copper stills guaranteed. A real one-off. **43% (86 proof).** *Heaven Hill.*

❖ **Old Bardstown Aged 6 Years (83) n**19 **t**21 **f**22 **b**21. A thin nose compensated for by decent rye-based small grain on entertaining finale. **40% (80 proof).**

❖ **Old Bardstown Aged 10 Years Estate Bottled (95) n**24 syrup; heavy duty molten liquorice! lovely rye sub-strata with even a hint of lavender. Some kumquats and burnt raisin complete the dreamy ultra-complex intro; **t**24 sit down and take a thumping: like chewing chocolate fudge except each and every tasebud is caked in a beautifully oiled, all-consuming liquor from heaven (hill?); **f**23 lighter oils allow the small grains to display their soft, surprisingly mouthwatering charms; some surprising late oranges; **b**24 this is what great bourbon is all about. An absolute masterpiece from the old school and, tragically, also probably from a now lost distillery. Go get!! **50.5% (101 proof).**

Old Charter 8 Years Old (77) n19 **t**19 **f**20 **b**19. A simple, sweet, toffeed bourbon with limited complexity. On this evidence, not quite what it once was. **40% (80 proof).**

Old Charter 10 Years Old (82) n21 **t**21 **f**20 **b**20. Sweet corn but fails to develop on the rich start. **43% (86 proof).**

Old Charter 12 Years Old (87) n22 some dazzling oak but always enough room for the small grains to flourish; t23 small-grain arrival on palate; genuinely complex with a spicy kick all the way; f20 surprising amount of natural toffee flattens it a little; b22 until that toffee arrives this is a deliciously complex dram. Well worth an investigation. **45% (90 proof).**

Old Charter Proprietor Reserve 13 Years Old (89) n23 kumquats and lemon peel, marmalade on light toast; t22 fruity from the word go then a wave of corn and very soft rye; f21 gentle vanillas; b23 what an enormously delicate bourbon for such great age. Graceful and charming. **45% (90 proof).**

Old Fitzgerald (79) n18 t20 f21 b20. One of the sweetest bourbons around: the nose does it no favours but a chewy toffee fightback. **43% (86 proof).**

Old Fitzgerald Very Special 12 Years Old (80) n18 t23 f20 b19. Warming spice paves the way for a crashing wave of corn and oak. But that excellent middle apart, something is curiously lacking. **45% (90 proof).**

Old Fitzgerald's 1849 8 Years (90) n21 ethereal corn and wheat; t23 lush and sweet arrival with a mixture of sugar and honey on the corn: the wheat fizzes around the roof of the mouth; f23 remains sweet with a late citrus surge and then drier vanilla tones; b23 light yet big. The sweetness is enormous but avoids going OTT thanks to excellent oak balance. A delight and the best of the Old Fitz range by a country mile. **45% (90 proof).**

Old Forester (89) n22 an explosion of small grains pepper the nose, hints of marmalade; t23 chunky and deep with liquorice-toffee but it's the softly spiced apple and pear juiciness that wins the day; f22 the liqorice factor increases as oak makes a stand; b22 if anyone asks me to show them a classic rye-rich bourbon where the small grains really count, as often as not I'll show them this. **43% (86 proof).** *Brown-Forman.*

Old Forester Birthday Bourbon Vintage 1989 (94) n22 big fruit only partially masked by telling oak; t24 superb: absolutely perfect weight on the palate with soft oil, but a cauldron of frothing small grains. The rye input is extraordinary but completely under control. Toffee apple provides the extra sweet juiciness but balances things perfectly; f24 one of the longest controlled finishes not just in bourbon but any whiskey. Those small grains just simmer away, nibbling playfully at the tastebuds, the sweetness level varying with the depth of the oak. Pulsating and rhythmic, it just seems to go on forever; b24 a bourbon for toffs and swells. Sheer class, offering complexity on a silver platter: a bourbon connoisseur's bourbon if ever there was one. Unquestionably one of the bourbons of the decade. **47.5% (95 proof).** *Brown-Forman.*

Old Forester Birthday Bourbon Vintage 1990 (90) n23 apples and cinnamon, over-ripe figs, a fraction smoky and rye-rich; t23 delicate vanilla arrives early, then a wave of rye and yet more powering oak. Pretty dry; f22 sweetens with corn, then the dry oak returns; b22 seriously delicate and sophisticated bourbon. **44.5% (89 proof).** *Brown-Forman.*

Old Forester Birthday Bourbon Vintage 1990 95 Proof (91) n22 compressed, heavyweight oak and rye; t23 chewy and molassed, the small grains punch delicious holes through the spicy morass; f23 long, lingering, spiced at first, then trailing off towards a dry, burnt toast, cold black coffee finale; b23 not for the squeamish: there is enormous complexity, but laid on with a trowel. **47.5% (95 proof).** *Brown-Forman.*

Old Forester 100 Proof (89) n23 beautifully weighted clementine, hickory and coffee: a real nose full; t22 cream toffee sweetens out with fat corn and a sprinkling of molassed sugar. The rye thuds in alongside some glittering spice; f22 the spice just continues its tingling journey around the palate, soft toffee and vanilla offering a softer finish than predicted; b22 as ever, very high quality bourbon from one of Kentucky's most consistent distilleries. **50% (100 proof).** *Brown-Forman.*

Old Heaven Hill (see Heaven Hill 80 Proof)

Old Heaven Hill 100 Proof (see Heaven Hill 100 Proof)

Old Heaven Hill Very Rare Aged 8 Years 80 Proof (82) n*20* t*21* f*21* b*20*. Unusually citrussy for this distillery: lemon and lime knitting with green corn. Amazingly youthful for its age. **40% (80 proof).**

Old Heaven Hill Very Rare Aged 8 Years 86 Proof (86) n*22* lording oak offers honey to the corn; t*22* two-tiered: very light corn battles the more compelex small grain and growing oak; f*21* more small grains and soft vanilla; b*21* intriguing bourbon with greater maturity than the 80 proof version: delightful in its own right, but just on the edge of something significant, you feel. **43% (86 proof).**

Old Heaven Hill Very Rare Aged 10 Years 80 Proof (84) n*21* t*21* f*21* b*21*. Very soft, sweet corn-laden and even. **40% (80 proof).**

Old Heaven Hill Very Rare Aged 10 Years 86 Proof (see Heaven Hill 10 Years 86 Proof)

Old Heaven Hill Very Rare Aged 10 Years 100 Proof (93) n*23* heavier and rich, fruitcake style. Really beautiful and subtle but telling rye involvement; t*24* weighty and just so spectacularly rich. Really is prize-winning heavy British fruitcake with raisins and cherries to chew on before a lovely walnut oiliness arrives, followed by corn concentrate; f*23* the lull after the storm, but the birds sing sweetly because the rye re-appears for a gentle but wonderfully complex finale; b*23* this is astonishing bourbon, the type that makes you glad to be in the know. Brilliant. **50% (100 proof).**

Old Heaven Hill Aged 15 Years 100 Proof (86) n*21* thinnish for its age; t*22* biting grain with a surge of sweet corn; f*22* remains sweet with the oak keeping its distance until very late on; b*21* for all the whiskey's colour, this doesn't have much of a 15-years-old's normal belligerent attitude. This is sweet and flighty and a little oily, too. Most un-Heaven Hill. **50% (80 proof).**

⁙ **Old Joe Aged 12 Years Bottled in Bond** (distilled at DSP KY 39) **(91)** n*21* perhaps sluggish at first but some biting corn and oak make amends before the rye really takes off; t*24* beautiful radiance of sweet, rich corn backed by deep rye. Lots of copper influence here: amazingly rich yet firm and solid; f*23* still bites deep but the rye/oak/coffee/burnt raisin union is strong and long; b*24* an absolutely top-notch bourbon, beyond the nose, of the very old school that just exudes class and charisma. **50% (100 proof).**

Old Kentucky Amber Aged 10 Years (87) n*22* soft, sweet toffee apple; t*21* very gentle arrival with some nipping grain and sweet corn, but some toffeed oak dominates; f*22* there is a clever build-up in complexity with the small grains beginning to really delight; b*22* a chilled-out, relaxed bourbon at first finally gets the rye to talk. **45% (90 proof).** *Germany.*

Old Kentucky No. 88 Brand Aged 13 Years (92) n*22* excellent rye nip and oak weight, great balance; t*24* mouthwatering, fresh and fruity despite the great age: the corn is sharp but a malty character fights through. The complexity is awesome; f*23* slightly smoky in style with vanilla and figs; b*23* stunning whiskey of classic proportions: hard to find, but grab a bottle if you can. **47% (94 proof).** *Germany.*

⁙ **Old Rip 12 Years Old (93)** n*22* heavily molassed, kumquats and grapes; t*24* shimmering over-ripe tomatoes with red liquorice candy; lots of rye spice prickles about; f*23* much more sensual now with sweet corn mash fading out with some vanilla and bitter-sweet chocolate; b*24* for a 12-y-o the colour is sensationally dark: must have spent a lifetime in the highest ricks: textbook bitter-sweet balance. **52.5% (105 proof).**

Old Rip Van Winkle 10 Years Old 90 Proof (88) n*23* chocolate marzipan and corn; t*22* sweet, slightly oily and demerara sugar; f*21* spicy vanilla; b*22* really well balanced and weighty whiskey. **45% (90 proof).**

Old Rip Van Winkle 10 Years Old 90.4 Proof (85) n*21* vanilla; t*22* spicy, chewy rye; f*21* spice and vanilla plus some sweet corn; b*21* light-bodied but packing a spicy punch. **45.2% (90.4 proof).**

Old Rip Van Winkle 10 Years Old 107 Proof (86) n21 biting rye; **t**22 more rye from the off, but quite hot; decent corn oil sweetens things; **f**21 vanilla and cocoa; **b**22 a hotter than average bottling and it has nothing to do with the alcohol! **53.5% (1-7 proof).**

Old Rip Van Winkle 12 Years Old (89) n21 light and fruity, figs and distant liquorice; **t**23 juicy, a hint of malt at first, grass and grapes and then harder rye and soft corn: deliciously complex; **f**22 liquorice and some gritty rye; **b**23 wonderful balance and drive to this bourbon: for something so outwardly light, the flavours just keep on coming. **45.2% (90.4 proof).**

Old Rip Van Winkle 15 Years Old (88) n22 attractive banana-sandwich aroma, topped by some unusual smokiness; **t**21 fragile, uncluttered, corny; **f**22 the small grains begin to bite and show great complexity; **b**23 one of those bourbons where the sum is better than the parts. Really superb balancing act and holds back the years supremely. **45% (90 proof).**

Old Rip Van Winkle 15 Years Old (93) n24 intense honey-nut and corn, like breakfast cereal in which you could happily bury your nose; **t**23 biting corn forms the bitter-sweet, slightly oily background with some oak arriving early, but adds only depth and something else to chew on; **f**23 enormously complex: again the corn leads the way but the honey returns with some cocoa and a bit of mouth prickle keeps the tastebuds occupied further; **b**23 this is a cracker. It always was. It was once a wheated bourbon, and still could be because rye doesn't make any kind of telling contribution here. A classic for sure. **53.5% (107 proof).**

Old Weller Antique 7 Years In Wood (86) n22 kumquats, tangerines and crushed walnuts: could be Santa's stocking! **t**22 syrupy liquorice-toffee sweetness then drier oak; **f**21 lazy spices mingle with toffee; **b**21 a heavyweight wheated bourbon that's a bit lethargic but thoroughly entertaining. **53.5% (107 proof).** *See also Weller and WL Weller for other members of the same "family".*

Original Barrel Bourbon Aged 12 Years (see Daniel Stewart Aged 12 Years)

Pappy Van Winkle 20 Years Old (78) n21 **t**20 **f**18 **b**19. Nothing like as bone-crushingly dry as some previous bottlings, but this still has way too much oak for me. There are some honeycomb moments on the nose and early arrival, but after that the balance is lost. **45.2% (90.4 proof).**

Pennypacker (87) n22 rye-rich small grains bury themselves deeply into the fruit and oak; **t**22 a firm, brittle mouthfeel, again with the rye showing brightly; **f**21 lots of honeyed vanilla and hazelnuts amid the vanilla; **b**22 the PR blurb from the importers that came with this bottle said the whiskey is three years old. It's a lot older than that, I can assure you. Seriously well made bourbon with big small-grain presence and decent age. **40% (80 proof).** Borco Hamburg.

Pure Kentucky XO batch 02-19, dist 14 Nov 89, bott 8 Feb 02 **(88) n**22 seriously impressive small-grain complexity, pretty light and enlightening despite age; **t**23 masses of honey, hickory and demerara sugar, the balance coming from drier oak; **f**21 plateaues out; **b**22 really firm, confident, well-aged whiskey. **53.5% (107 proof)**

⟜ **Real McCoy (82) n**21 **t**20 **f**21 **b**20. Some early rye and liquorice fails to give this oily bourbon the firm backbone it needs or a conclusive direction. Attractive and mildly spiced but a little frustrating. **37%.** *Australia.*

Rebecca (see Heaven Hill 10 Years 86 Proof)

Rebel Yell (86) n22 strawberries and corn, beautifully fruity and rich; **t**21 still fruity, more strawberry – plus melon this time – then a slow assimilation of oak and some oily corn; **f**21 an oaky layer dries the palate; **b**22 my word: this brand has moved on some. The fiery, spicy peppery attack has vanished entirely and the citrus notes have been replaced by softer strawberries, but stays true to its fruity style. Lovely wheated stuff. **40% (80 proof).**

Ridgemont Reserve 1792 (90) n22 small grains abound with rye and vanilla passionately embraced; a lovely waft of acacia honey offers the balance; t23 subtle delivery of rich small grains again, this time on a bed of Muscovado sugar; f22 a gathering of oaky spices with weighty honeycomb, liquorice and hickory confirming the age; b23 quality bourbon from a distillery that rarely allows its spirit to age this far. The result is a sophisticated bourbon exuding a rye-rich charisma and the most subtle of sweet themes. **46.85% (93.7 proof).** *Barton Brands.*

Rock Hill Farms (89) n21 thin, but honeyed; t22 slightly hot at first with developing sweet corn; f24 slowly awakens and the small grains go wild: the rye kicks in to give a hard fruit edge, a hint of malt but the sweet corn and oak combining is superb; b22 rock by name, rock by nature: a very hard whiskey which rewards patient study handsomely. **50% (100 proof).** *Buffalo Trace.*

Rowan's Creek batch 02-72, dist 26 Feb 85, bott 5 Nov 02 **(78)** n21 t20 f18 b19. Loads of honey and liquorice, but way too heavily oaked. **50% (100 proof)**

Safeway Bourbon (77) n18 t19 f20 b20. Exceptionally light and lemon-zesty. As refreshing a bourbon as you are likely to find in the UK. **40% (80 proof).** *UK.*

Sainsbury's Kentucky Bourbon Three Years Old (71) n18 t18 f17 b18. Pleasant, sweet but too young to have gathered a personality. The bland, caramel finish is rather old. **40% (80 proof).** *Sainsbury's, UK.*

Sam Clay (see Heaven Hill Aged 6 Years 80 Proof)

Sam Clay 8 Years (see Old Heaven Hill Very Rare Aged 8 Years 80 Proof)

Sam Sykes (see Heaven Hill 80 Proof)

Samuels 1844 (see Heaven Hill Aged 6 Years 101 Proof)

Seven Hills (see Evan Williams Aged 7 Years 86 Proof)

Scotch Malt Whisky Society Heaven Hill Aged 12 Years 1992 (94) n24 use this as a template for what a truly great bourbon nose should look like; t22 I have rarely tasted bourbon at this strength outside a Kentucky warehouse or my lab. Only Stagg and the odd Blantons gets close to this in intensity, but its takes a little while for the bourbon to settle: when it does the corn character really does go nuts; f24 only at the death does the rye begin to gain ground and with it comes a stunning degree of depth and complexity. The oiliness is first-rate and it's bitter-sweet liquorice all the way; b24 textbook bourbon with old Heaven Hill at its optimum age. Some members of the SMWS quit because of this bourbon bottling, I am told. Their loss. More to go round for true whiskey lovers of all denominations. **66.8% (133.6 proof). nc ncf sc.**

Smokey Jim (85) n21 excellent small-grain complexity; t22 rich, full arrival on the palate; brilliant mouthfeel; f21 back to a dark, juicy, fruity rye character towards the end; b21 genuinely complex and satisfying everyday bourbon. Excellent. **40% (80 proof).**

Ten High (70) n17 t18 f17 b18. Light, clean and untaxing. Good for mixing. **40% (80 proof).** *Barton.*

Tesco Old Kentucky (78) n19 t20 f19 b20. Young, sweet, very clean with a hint of hickory. **40% (80 proof).**

Thedford Colonial Style Batch No 001 **(93)** n24 whoa boy!!! Enormous and gratifying. Big age with coffee and vanilla thumping home, but kept in check by old orangey fruitiness. Immense; t22 back to normality after the big alcohol bite, bringing in softer vanilla and small grains; f24 feather-soft finish with lovely oils and deep, dark mocca; an absolute joy; b23 not an easy whiskey to find, but find it you must. It is a tame monster. Last seen at The Vintage House, Soho, London. **46.3% (92.6 proof).** *Josiah Thedford and Sons, Louisville.*

Tom Moore (83) n21 t20 f22 b20. The rye on the nose pops up at regular intervals on the palate, but overall this is a really deft, undemanding whiskey yet offering above-average complexity. **40% (80 proof).** *Barton.*

Tom Sims (see Heaven Hill Aged 6 Years 80 Proof)

T W Samuels (see Heaven Hill 80 Proof)

T W Samuels (see Heaven Hill 86 Proof)

T W Samuels 100 Proof (see Heaven Hill 100 Proof)

T W Samuels 6 Years 90 Proof (see Heaven Hill Aged 6 Years 90 Proof)

Red Eye Aged 6 Years (86) n21 spot-on rye involvement: very complex; t22 honeyed and chewy; f21 lovely vanilla climb-down, with the grains having as big a say as the oak; b22 a bourbon of attractive complexity and weight. **45% (90 proof).** *Bardstown.*

Van Winkle Special Reserve (82) n19 t22 f20 b21. Subdued nose, then a sweet, almost molassed explosion before a quick fade. Good early oak, though. **45.2% (90.4 proof).**

Very Old Barton Aged 6 Years (88) n22 green and lively with the rye really getting in amongst the powering corn. Green tea is also about; t22 brittle small grains melt into the sweetening corn: a touch oily; f22 remains sweet despite the onset of some drying oak; b22 it's a bit like sweetened green tea in alcohol with a strong rye kick-back. Unique as a style amongst bourbons and wholly enjoyable. **40% (80 proof).** *Barton.*

Vintage Bourbon 1976 bott 7 Mar 01 **(94)** n23 light muscovado sugar sprinkled over rye and even a touch of malt, the oak very relaxed; t24 stunning mouthfeel, gently oiled with a slow arrival of sweet corn and then a fruitier rye: again the oak is delicate and sympathetic; f23 gentle spices and a build-up of honey; b24 this barrel must have sat on the bottom level of a warehouse somewhere for it to be this unscathed and beautifully rounded after a quarter of a century of Kentucky sunshine. A freaky and fantastic bourbon you must find at all costs. **43% (86 proof).**

Vintage Bourbon 1980 bott 26 Oct, 00 **(90)** n22 surprisingly green corn and greener rye: enormous fresh grain despite weighty oak; t22 wonderul medium-sweet mouthfilling, corn, a hint of tangerine and apple; f23 now it gets heavy with big rye kicking in with the liquorice oak; b23 outstanding whiskey offering different levels of complexity and enjoyment. A little classic. **43% (86 proof).**

Vintage Bourbon 1983 bott 10 Nov 00 **(87)** n22 mint, mango and liquorice; t22 enormous rye depth and bite; f21 softer vanilla; b22 very good weight and balance to a quite complex if a little oaky bourbon. **43% (86 proof).**

Virgin Bourbon Aged 7 Years 101 Proof (88) n22 very gentle oak with distant and intriguing hints of rice paper and pine; t23 vaguely honeyed with lots of liquorice-toffee; f21 dries with rye-tingling spices; b22 seriously complex, big and lip-smacking. We are talking serious bourbon, here. **50.5% (101 proof).** *Heaven Hill.*

Virgin Bourbon Aged 15 Years 101 Proof (89) n23 chunky oak, liquorice and a touch of lemon; t22 dry, crushing oak with just enough corn and demerara sweetness to keep on course; b22 small grains take control while the oak lifts slightly to leave a soft vanilla; b22 a drier version than some 15-y-o but substantial and stupendous all the same. **50.5% (101 proof).** *Heaven Hill.*

Walker & Scott Bourbon (84) n23 t20 f20 b21. A delightful pub bourbon of good age and impressive complexity. The nose in particular is an orgy of superb small grain. **40%.** *Samuel Smith UK.*

Weller Centennial 10 Years Old (85) n23 soft fruit, citrus and freshly shelled peas: a delight; t21 very dry start with a soft oak kick and spices: very warming; f20 enormous natural toffee sweetens it at the finish; b21 as gentle as a cruise on the old Kentucky river. **50% (100 proof).**

Weller 12 Years Old (90) n23 oak is the star here, and at several levels, offering heavier liquorice notes and soft vanilla. Mint and apple also get in on the act; t23 sublime corn attack but the oak gives it a bitter edge: this is enormously intense stuff; f21 back to that toffee again: sweet and creamy and seeing off the oak; b23 immensely deep and satisfying with a magnificent chewability. **45% (90 proof).**

Westridge (see Heaven Hill 80 Proof)

Wild Turkey (80) n20 t19 f21 b20. An improvement in recent years: the orangey nose is striking and impressive while the palate is thin. The finish toffees up for a rich finale. **40% (80 proof).**

Wild Turkey Aged 8 Years (86) n21 spicy orange with salt; t22 corn dominant but lovely coffee; f21 dry vanilla and other oaky notes, the spice returns; b22 not quite such a pressure cooker bourbon as a decade ago, subtlety replacing flavour power. **50.5% (101 proof).**

Wild Turkey Russell's Reserve Aged 10 Years (96) n23 stunning rye-citrus combo pans out to reveal a mint and oak-encrusted, leathery corn sweetness; t24 seriously mega for its age, not so much in the firm cocoa-oak but the utter enormity of the small-grain depth. Once more all paths lead to clean and chewy corn; f24 gentle, minty spices cool the mouth; b25 this is dream-time whiskey, entirely befitting the name of my close friend and mentor Jimmy Russell. This is a controlled explosion of complexity, the constant light sweetness overseeing those darker, brooding passages. Only Yoichi in Japan offers a stated 10-y-o whisky which can stand shoulder to shoulder with this, though not always. Entirely flawless whiskey. **50.5% (101 proof).**

Wild Turkey Aged 12 Years (90) n22 peaches and cream, topped with demerara sugar, beautiful nutty fruitcake; t22 pretty sweet on the uptake with that sugary quality bursting forward, and estery like an old Jamaican rum; f23 liquorice and corn interweave beautifully; b23 this is great whiskey, perhaps not the most complex from this stable but the effect is uplifting. **50.5% (101 proof).**

Wild Turkey Rare Breed batch W-T-02-91 **(94)** n24 gorgeous honey threading its way through diced dates, old leather and rye with a teasing sprinkling of spice: magnificent; t24 massively intense launch, waxy honeycomb with fabulously controlled demerara sweetness and an edge of rye; f22 long, lightly liquoriced toffee with the honey hanging on, as does the rye and a soft build-up of cocoa; t24 a big bourbon with the proportions being generous and almost perfectly proportioned. The classiest of class acts. **55% (110 proof).**

Wild Turkey Rare Breed batch W-T-01-99 **(89)** n23 toffee and nuts with big corn thrust; t22 sweet, soft, with building rye and spice; f22 spicy with liquorice and hints of honey; b22 compared to previous Rare Breeds this is relatively sweet and simple. Still beautiful, though. **54.2% (108.4 proof).**

W L Weller Special Reserve 7 Years Old (84) n21 t22 f20 b21 A bigger whiskey than of old with lots of orangey tones on the nose and a lush, sweet and peppery body. **45% (90 proof).** *For other members of the Weller "family" see also Old Weller and Weller.*

Woodford Reserve Distiller's Select (88) n22 some striking levels of light and heavy oak glued together by firm corn; the rye offers the excitement; t22 some sweetened coffee notes hit the tastebuds running; heavy muscovado sugar takes on the rye; f22 vanilla heavy at first then a hint of liquorice candy; b22 great balance: a whiskey with pretensions of being light but seems to fail at every turn. Busy, chewy and rye-enhanced. **45.2% (90.4 proof).** *Brown-Forman.*

Woodford Reserve Four Grain (90) n20 highly unusual with a different nose to any other bourbon I know: very light liquorice, kind of Old Forester but without the intensity, and extraordinary floral tones; t24 big and rambling with a quite massive flavour explosion. The small grains are working overtime to provide a deep spicy-fruit texture to the oak. The liquorice comes through, but so does the rye by the spadeful and much softer oilier corn notes. Sensational; f23 calms down, though it takes its time: very rarely have I experienced the small grains in a bourbon working with such complexity: the oak barely gets a look in; b23 what a supreme bourbon. The nose is a bit confusing, but once it hits the tastebuds it has one thing on its mind: to blow you away. I shall ensure a bottle of this is always somewhere near my desk in future ... that's if they ever release it!! **47.2% (94.4 proof).** *Brown-Forman.*

Woodford Reserve Personal Selection (83) n21 t21 f20 b21. Heaps of toffee character, which tends by definition to make for a soft ride but at the expense of the complexity which is a byword of Woodford Reserve. Delightful in its own right with lovely rye-spice sub-plot, but the brilliance of Four Grain and Distillers' Select tends to spoil you a little. **45.2% (90.4 proof).** *Brown-Forman.*

Wm Morrison Old Kentucky Special No. 1 Brand (76) n18 t20 f19 b19. A very decent cooking bourbon with some weight, spice and natural toffee. A genuine chewing bourbon. **40% (80 proof).** *Wm Morrison UK. Ignore the back label nattering on about three years and blended and all that rubbish. This is a straight bourbon.*

⠿ **Woodstock (86)** n23 brittle, rye-encrusted frame around which Big stuff; t22 an oily bag of tricks which is decidedly rye rich despite the toffeed corn; f21 lovely complexity towards the finale as the oil spreads first the rye and then much softer corn. Subtle spices abound as does an attractive buttery note; b20 a lazy bourbon towards the very end that does its best not to impress despite the early sharp rye presence. Still a charmer, though. **37%.** *Australia.*

Yellow Rose of Texas (see Heaven Hill 80 Proof)

Yellow Rose of Texas 8 Years (see Old Heaven Hill Very Rare Aged 8 Years 86 proof)

Tennessee Whiskey
GEORGE DICKEL

George Dickel Aged 10 Years Distilled in or Before 1986 (71) n17 t19 f17 b18. The only Dickel I have seen being sold either on a shelf or bar in the last 12 months. And my least favourite. Weirdly musty and out of alignment. Dickel is usually a lot, lot better than this load of tat. **43% (86 proof).**

JACK DANIEL

Gentleman Jack Rare Tennessee Whiskey (79) n19 t21 f20 b19. One of America's cleanest whiskeys, sweet and improbably light. An affront to hardened Jack drinkers, a blessing for those with a sweet tooth. **40% (80 proof).** *Brown-Forman.*

Jack Daniel's (Green Label) (84) n20 t21 f22 b21. A light but lively little gem of a whiskey. Starts as a shrinking violet, finishes as a roaring lion with nimble spices ripping into the developing liquorice. A superb session whiskey. **40% (80 proof).** *Brown-Forman.*

Jack Daniel's Old No. 7 Brand (Black Label) (87) n21 thick, oily, smoky, dense, corn syrupy ... it's Jack Daniel; t23 sweet, fat, chewy, various types of burnt notes: tofffee, toast etc. etc; f21 quite a sweet, fat and toffeed finale; b22 a quite unique whiskey at which many American whiskey connoisseurs turn up their noses. I always think it's worth the occasional visit; you can't beat roughing it a little. **43% (86 proof).** *Brown-Forman.*

Jack Daniel's Single Barrel (88) n22 more fruit on this than most Jacks, still plenty of liquorice and burnt toast; t22 spicy and immediately warming: some real kick to this with the blows softened by the sweetness of the corn and the surrounding thick oils; f22 very consistent with the sweetness fading, despite some rye input, then oak starting to make a stand; b22 a characterful, rich whiskey, with plenty of corn sweetness and some excellent spice. **40% (80 proof).** *Brown-Forman.*

VIRGINIA BOURBON

Virginia Gentleman 80 (cream, sepia and red label) **(84)** n20 t22 f21 b21. A very light bourbon with a distinctive, easy-going sweet corn effect then spicy, mildly bitter oak and cocoa. **40% (80 proof).** *A Smith Bowman.*

Virginia Gentleman 90 (coloured label) **(89)** n21 the leathery oak has much more to say than the corn, but it's all done in whispers; t23 charming entry onto the palate with, first, chewy oak then more teasing rye and a dash of honey here and there; **f**22 the small grains really come out to play, accompanied by spices, superb mouthfeel with excellent drying towards the very end; **b**23 you know, forget about this being the only Virginia whiskey. Romance apart, this is one hell of a whiskey where complexity is the foundation stone. Marvellous stuff. **45% (90 proof).** *A Smith Bowman.*

Corn Whiskey

Dixie Dew Kentucky Straight Corn Whiskey (89) n22 some very decent oak and vanilla to add to the dryish corn, complex by corn whiskey standards; **t**22 wonderfully balanced, starting dry and oaky then the corn building up with the sweetness; **f**22 long even with a dash of spice – much improved than in recent years; **b**23 brilliant whiskey that should have a far wider market. **50% (100 proof).** *Heaven Hill.*

J W Corn 100 Straight Corn Whiskey (87) n21 oily and rich with some much drier oak present; **t**22 thumping early oak offsets the sweet corn which fails to quite take off; **f**22 really spicy and big; **b**22 this has the biggest oak character on the market at the moment, which means a drier style and no shortage of spice. **50% (100 proof).** *Heaven Hill.*

Mellow Corn (85) n21 slight cooking oil aroma, but the oak adds a delicate spice; **t**22 full-bodied and textured, the oils helping the corn to stick to the roof of the mouth while a softly spiced sweetness develops; **f**21 sweet and chewy like a Barbadian rum; **b**21 I first drank this brand back in 1974 and I can safely say that I've never encountered it, or any other whisk(e)y, with an oilier texture: if you don't like the whiskey, you could always fry your eggs in it. Seriously delicious, though! **50%** *Medley Company. (Heaven Hill).*

Rye; Single Malt Rye
ANCHOR DISTILLERY

Old Potrero Single Malt Whiskey Aged One Year Essay 6-RW-ARM-3-A "a distilled spirit produced from rye malt mash aged ... in new uncharred oak barrels". In barrel 18 Apr 96, bott 8 Jan 98 **(86) n**18 a hint of feinty oil can be detected over the sharp rye but the worst of this burns off as it warms in the glass to reveal stupendous honey; **t**23 enormous presence, oily as one would expect, but the build-up over ever-sweetening fruit is astonishing; **f**23 the oils have burnt off early and now we are left with soft vanilla and a rye residue: it is sublime, even for something so young; **b**22 here we have a collector's item: a slightly flawed Old Potrero – a bit like finding an English stamp with the queen's head missing. These were early days in the company's distilling life and the middle cut is a little too wide affecting the nose ... but hey: they wanted to create a rye people would recognise 200 years ago, and this would be exactly it! But the other side of the same coin is that those oils give fabulous extra richness to the body. Still a beaut! **62.3% (124.6 proof).** *814 bottles.*

Old Potrero Single Malt Whiskey Aged One Year Essay 7-RW-ARM-5 "a distilled spirit produced from rye malt mash... aged... in new uncharred oak barrels". In barrel 3 June 97, bott 25 May 99 **(88) n**20 oily, wide middle cut allows the rye a full, bitter-sweet run and lovely trademark honey shadow follows the rye wherever it goes; **t**23 very soft arrival on the palate, despite the strength, with gentle honey dovetailing with the much sharper, fruitier rye. The oil on the palate is a masterstroke as it clings to the roof of the mouth and won't let go; **f**22 amazing degree of vanilla for a year-old barrel but it's there with hints of orange; **b**23 this is just such expressive whiskey: I adore the extra oil and richness it brings. Something different but certainly not diffident. **61.75% (123.3 proof).** *2,175 Bottles.*

Old Potrero Single Malt Whiskey Aged Two Years Essay 7-RW-ARM-6 "a distilled spirit produced from rye malt mash ... aged ... in new and used uncharred oak barrels". In barrel 31 Dec 97, bott 14 Jul 00 **(92)** n22 the extra year has introduced spice and a little dryness, bitter orange and biting rye; t24 sensational mouth arrival: the rye simply explodes on impact scattering rock-hard fruity debris around the palate. The honey takes time to arrive, but does so on the back of some mouthwatering grainy notes – extraordinary; f23 long and lusty with the rye still holding court. Citrus notes rise and fall, the rye fades and re-emerges, the brilliance is a constant; b23 in July 1900 this was the best two-year-old bottled whiskey the world had ever seen. **62.1% (124.2 proof).** *3,448 bottles.*

Old Potrero Single Malt Whiskey Aged Two Years Essay 8-RW-ARM-7A/8A "a distilled spirit produced from rye malt mash ... aged ... in new and used uncharred oak barrels". In barrel 9 Dec 98, bott 20 Apr 01 **(85)** n21 spiced-up citrus, very grain with some sweetening toffee; t22 the toffee remains a constant but the rye pricks enough with its accompanying oil to give plenty to chew on; f21 constant: more of before, but with less rye bite and settling for a more bitter edge; b21 the complexity levels are down on this one thanks mainly to the rich vein of toffee than runs naggingly through the whiskey. **62.2% (124.4 proof).**

Old Potrero Single Malt Straight Rye Whiskey Aged Three Years Essay 5-RW-ARM-2-A (93) n24 textbook stuff: liquorice-embossed rye, hard as nails, but caresses the senses. You beauty! t24 big, uncompromising, bold and fruity. Just so sweet with hints of honey and demerara, but the firmness of the rye is the spine to it all and cocoa provides a perfect counterweight; f22 slightly toffeed with rich oaky-vanilla but all the time the rye peppers the tastebuds; b23 this is what makes rye whiskey, for me, the most enjoyable style in the world. Brazen and bedazzling. **62.6% (125.2 proof).** *1,880 bottles.*

Old Potrero Single Malt Straight Rye Whiskey Aged Three Years Essay 8-RW-ARM-8-A (94) in barrel date 9 Dec 98, bott 19 Apr 02 n23 much drier and subtle. The rye is relatively closed, but open enough to get you salivating; t25 nothing closed about the rye now as it erupts from the first mouthful. Brilliant fruit (wild cherries)-honey balance, as good as any rye currently on the market. Faultless and fabulous, the candy sweetness is kept in check by the impervious rye. One of the greatest whiskey-tasting experiences money can buy; f23 much softer and well behaved now, going back to the comparative serenity of the nose. A hint of toffee-vanilla towards the finish; b23 when you open a bottle of this, you go for the long haul: this is no splash of water or coke job, and forget the ice. This, for its age and style, is the most unique whiskey in the world: expect to be thrown a few times before you learn to ride it. A very dear friend and colleague of mine is quoted as saying that the Old Potrero ryes are "the most noteworthy development in American whiskey in living memory." I kind of know what he means but cannot begin to agree. I was playing and coaching soccer in Maryland when they were still making rye there and I remember the deep sadness I felt when I was notified of the closure of the last distillery in the state where it more or less all began. And the shock and dismay at the news that Old Crow, Old Taylor and Old Grand-dad distilleries were all being closed to devastate bourbon-making in the Frankfort area. And never will I forget the tears I shed as Heaven Hill burned and the joy as I watched, stone by stone, Labrot & Graham rise from a pile of charming rubble (and the play area for my son and me) into Kentucky's one and only pot-still distillery. Rather, back in 1998 I wrote of Old Potrero in my book *Classic Bourbon Tennessee and Rye*, "This is the most exciting taste in world whiskey at the moment. The youngest classic of them all." Five years on every word still rings true.

⋯ **Old Potrero Single Malt Straight Rye Essay 10-SRW-ARM-A** db **(93)** n22 despite the lower strength there is no shortage of he-man aromas; the slight feintiness takes a tad longer to burn off but it's a harmless, earthy flaw compensated by a bewildering array of overmatured fruity notes seasoned by soft linseed, a vague herbal note and a dollop of manuka honey. One of the heaviest OP noses yet; **t24** you need about five minutes to sort your way through this one: the rye is the first note apparent and then it breaks off into three or four different directions, each with a varied flavour code: part of the rye contains cocoa and is dry and deliciously chocolaty while another faction takes the route to Demerara with a softly estered rum beat to it. As a compliment to this a rye and honeyed thread weaves its way around the palate. Finally the rye also links up with a sawdusty vanilla effect, which passes for oak; **f23** impossible to tell where the middle ends and the finish starts: this is top shelf whiskey for adults and ones who know how to make the most of the finish of their mouthful: just sit back, eyes closed and listen to spellbinding, bitter-sweet tales of rye and honey; **b24** I know some of you will be beating your breasts and wailing: OP's down from teeth-dissolving barrel proof to a sissified 45% abv. The reason, I have been told, is that barmen have a big problem when trying to mix at cask strength. I understand the problem, but it is one easily overcome: drink it straight … **45% (90 proof).**

Rye; Straight Rye

Classic Cask Straight Rye Aged 15 Years Distilled 1984 batch RW 101, bott 99 **(88)** **n23**: a voluptuous overture of spring flowers and under-ripe fruit. Quite brittle and clean with a surprising malt undertone; **t23** the hardness of the rye arrives early and spreads sensuously around the mouth, painting an oily, spicy glow: mouthwatering and dangerously moreish; **f21** somewhat tired with the oak suppressing the sweeter rye notes; **b21** shows excellent balance early on but diminishes in style and complexity as the oak gathers and the age shows. Very enjoyable, nonetheless. **45% (90 proof).** *Classic Cask Co. Bardstown.*

Classic Cask Straight Rye Aged 15 Years Distilled 1986 batch RW 103, bott 01 **(75)** **n20** **t20** **f17** **b18**. Pleasant and soft, but disappointingly missing the usual complexity and intensity one expects from a rye. **45% (90 proof).** *Classic Cask Co. Bardstown.*

∴ **Fleischmann's Straight Rye (93)** **n23** a wonderful confusion of rock hard rye and softer, fruitier notes: uncluttered by too great age, it is unambiguously rye; **t24** clean arrival, soft fruits and then gradual scaling up of the firmness of the rye: just so magically mouth watering and warming at the same time; **f22** hard, chunky rye softened by vanilla and orange marmalade; **b24** it is hard to believe that a whisky as classically simple and elegant as this, and so true to its genre, comes in a plastic bottle. You don't have to pay through the nose for magnificent whisky. **40%.** *Fleischmann Distilling Co (Barton).*

Jim Beam Rye (93) **n24** lemon zest, mint and lavender: a stunning bag of tricks; **t24** early rye broadside followed by some tender fruit and oak. This battle between rock-hard rigidity and gentle fruit is astonishing; **f22** long and flinty with cocoa rounding things off; **b23** almost certainly the most entertaining and consistent whiskey in the entire Jim Beam armoury. A classic without doubt.

Old Rip Van Winkle 12 Years Old Time Rye (90) **n23** two-toned rye, both chunky and light and flitting: seriously attractive; **t23** big crunchy, brittle rye kick from the very first moment, really beautifully fruity; **f22** remains bitter and crisp at first but then softens as natural oaky-caramels appear; **b22** a profound, fruity, refreshing and old-fashioned rye that's hard to find. **45% (90 proof).** *Mac Y Denmark.*

Old Rip Van Winkle 13 Years Old Family Reserve Rye (91) **n23** big and belligerent, the rye forms a fruity, rock-hard crust; **t24** vroom … !! Off she goes on a massive ryefest. Brilliant bitter-sweet grain stomps with hob-nailed boots around the palate, both fresh yet well aged. Everything is a contradiction –

so complex; **f***21* quietens down alarmingly as the caramel kicks in which sweetens it a little while some bitter coffee/rye notes still chatter in the background; **b***23* an alarmingly complex whiskey that seems to make the rules up as it goes along. Anarchic and adorable. **47.8% (95.6 proof).**

Old Rip Van Winkle 15 Years Old (1985) Family Reserve Rye (91) **n***22* minty, firm oak but the rye does show good, fruity shape; **t***23* brilliant rye ruggedness, really hard at first but showing a feminine, fruity side: an intriguing mixture of molasses and demerara sugar sees off the oak; **f***23* that sweetness lasts the course, allowing the rye open season on the tastebuds; **b***23* a supremely improbable rye that has managed to retain a zesty freshness over 15 summers. Brilliant. **50% (100 proof).**

Old Rip Van Winkle 15 Years Old (79) **n***22* **t***20* **f***18* **b***19*. Spicy rye, but the oak cuts deep on the nose while to taste mildly sappy but some rye does leak out of the oakiness. This is for the guy who buttonholed me at a tasting I gave in Zurich in 2002 and wanted to know about a Van Winkle 15-y-o rye he had recently tasted in a bar over 100 proof which had been there for some time and he felt was out of condition. Dug this out of my library: this bottling dates to around 1994/95. Seems to fit the bill: amazed it is still around. **53.5% (107 proof).**

Pikesville Supreme Straight Rye (87) **n***23* a curious and delicious mixture of traditional British scrumpy cider and new car interior: this is traditional straight rye at its freshest and fruitiest; **t***21* much lighter arrival than the nose suggests, even a hint of corn in there. The fruit slowly starts to return, but only after a sprinkling of brown sugar then a thumping measure of rye; **f***21* that usual Heaven Hill rye bitterness on the ending plus some caramel-vanilla to sweeten things a little; **b***22* not quite as in your face with the rye as was once the case. **40% (80 proof).** *Heaven Hill.*

Rittenhouse Straight Rye (85) **n***21* the rye is barely awake but offers soft fruit amid the toffee-vanilla; **t***21* clean and sweet, the rye takes a little time to make its mark but eventually does so to add warming spices: all very subdued, though; **f***21* bitter-sweet with accent on the bitter, pretty oily; **b***22* this, the only rye in America I'm aware of spelt "Whisky" rather than "whiskey", has always been the least rye-pronounced. But this bottling makes a virtue of it. **40% (80 proof).** *Heaven Hill.*

Rittenhouse Straight Rye 100 Proof Bottled in Bond (86) **n***21* the extra alcohol still does little to rouse the rye from its slumbers; **t***22* much earlier rye thrust, subsides as the body sweetens, then reappears; **f***21* more oily and clingy to the palate with a late, slightly burned toasty finish; **b***22* a weighty guy. **50% (100 proof).** *Heaven Hill.*

Sazerac Rye 18 Years Old (96) **n***25* traditonal straight rye doesn't come more complex, confident or clean than this: there is a hard grainy edge, but it is softened by over-ripe juicy cherry and blackberries. Subtle and sophisticated; **t***24* the brittle quality of the rye shows to full effect here, but there is a softness – a tad oily – which also beguiles. Fruity and improbably flavoursome: close your eyes and wallow; **f***23* takes a little rest as the toffee makes a mark, but such is the intensity of the rye and oak that waves of spices and fruit continue to break against the tastebuds; **b***24* I remember being given my first sample of this: it was in the lab at Buffalo Trace before it went into bottle and a legendary brand was born. I was standing at the time ... I had to sit down. I wondered what it would be like to sample away from the romance of the beautiful distillery where the casks were laying ... well, now you know. I was presented with the first-ever bottle of Sazerac Rye as a token of thanks for my help in identifying its qualities and (some hope) weaknesses. I trust the person who stole it out of my bag while I was giving a tasting in New York appreciated it as much as I. If he/she still has it, I would be grateful if it is returned, care of my publishers, no questions asked. And one final thing: my late father was born in 1916. This is the 1,916th whiskey I have tasted for this book. Need I say more? **45% (90 proof).**

Wild Turkey Kentucky Straight Rye (88) n21 very gentle rye on a decent oak base; **t**23 the extra strength helps propel the lush rye forward, but it remains sweet and refrains from nipping and biting ... at first; **f**22 nips and bites and becomes more bitter; **b**22 an improved rye with much better integrated rye fruitiness than of old. **50.5% (101 proof).**

MICHTERS DISTILLERY

·⁘· **Overholt "1810" Sour Mash Straight Rye Whiskey (91) n**23 allow a minute or two to oxidize then breath in sweet rye, primroses and ginger bread, and a fair chunk of oak, too; **t**23 just fabulously explosive: the oak is pretty big but cannot undermine the intensity of the rye. The spice sizzles and spits at you like a Cumberland sausage; **f**22 very hard rye chisels at the taste buds; some cocoa for good, bitter yet balanced effect; **b**23 I have been hearing reports that this truly classic Old Timer, complete in 4/5 quart bottles, can still be dug up in back-wood liquor stores. This, the very last of the true Pennsylvanian rye, is Klondike stuff. **46.5% abv (93 proof)**. *A Overholt & Co, Pennsylvania.*

Kentucky Whiskey

Early Times Kentucky Whiskey (71) n17 t18 f18 **b**.18 Lightweight and thin, the corn tends to go it alone with a touch of toffee to prop it up. **40% (80 proof)**. *Brown-Forman.*

American Whiskey Blend

Seagram's 7 Crown (89) n23 rich with heavy vanilla and rye; **t**22 complex grain and oak battle: the softness of the neutral grain acts as the perfect foil for the crisper rye; **f**22 silky, sweet, soft corn and vanilla; **b**22 this is beautiful whiskey, but on this evidence not a patch on the rye-infested giant it has been for the last couple of decades. The rye level seems to have been reduced and I trust that this is just a rogue batch. Still a little mouthwatering stunner for sure, but it was much better the way it was: semi-wild and flavour-explosive. Like that it was an American institution – something too rare and precious to be tampered with ... **40% (80 proof).**

Japanese Whisky

Sadly, if you want to discover Japanese whisky you must still go to Japan. Of the 148 Japanese whiskies I have tasted for this book, only a handful are available in markets outside the nation in which they were distilled or blended. This is very frustrating when you see that many of the distilleries are nowhere near on full production and some are either silent or closed.

Part of the problem has been the Japanese custom of refusing to trade with their rivals. Therefore a Japanese whisky, if not made completely from home-distilled spirit, will instead contain a percentage of Scotch rather than whisky from fellow Japanese distillers.

This, ultimately, is doing the industry no favours at all. The practice is partly down to the traditional work ethics of company loyalty and an inherent, and these days false, belief that Scotch whisky is automatically better than Japanese. Back in the late 1990s I planted the first seeds in trying to get rival distillers to discuss with each other the possibility of exchanging whiskies to ensure that their distilleries worked more economically.

In the meantime word is getting round that Japanese whisky is worth finding. Indeed, there is so much interest in these little-known brands (outside Japan that is) that I have even given an all-Japanese whisky tasting in Holland.

Two leading lights are getting whisky drinkers switched on to just what oriental delights we are missing: the malts of Yoichi and Hakushu. Both make whiskies that rank unquestionably among the very finest in the world, though Yoichi – the brilliance of which I'm proud to have first brought to the world's attention in 1997 – these days has to be a little more careful with their use of sherry. Less than a handful of Scotch distilleries, though, can match their and Hakushu's supremely complex makes.

As if stirred by the recent success and fame of Yoichi, other distillers in Japan have begun looking at bringing out single cask bottlings and I hope to have reviews of a number of them for the 2005 edition. However, they can be hard to find for the whisky drinker – even in Japan. Some sell out almost as soon as they are released.

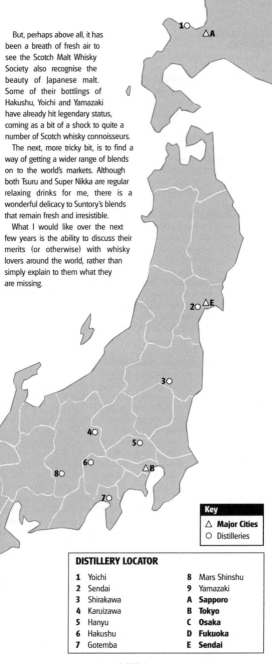

But, perhaps above all, it has been a breath of fresh air to see the Scotch Malt Whisky Society also recognise the beauty of Japanese malt. Some of their bottlings of Hakushu, Yoichi and Yamazaki have already hit legendary status, coming as a bit of a shock to quite a number of Scotch whisky connoisseurs.

The next, more tricky bit, is to find a way of getting a wider range of blends on to the world's markets. Although both Tsuru and Super Nikka are regular relaxing drinks for me, there is a wonderful delicacy to Suntory's blends that remain fresh and irresistible.

What I would like over the next few years is the ability to discuss their merits (or otherwise) with whisky lovers around the world, rather than simply explain to them what they are missing.

Key

△ **Major Cities**
○ Distilleries

DISTILLERY LOCATOR

1	Yoichi	**8**	Mars Shinshu
2	Sendai	**9**	Yamazaki
3	Shirakawa	**A**	**Sapporo**
4	Karuizawa	**B**	**Tokyo**
5	Hanyu	**C**	**Osaka**
6	Hakushu	**D**	**Fukuoka**
7	Gotemba	**E**	**Sendai**

Single Malts
CHICHIBU

Golden Horse Chichibu db **(80)** n*19* t*21* f*20* b*20*. Light, toasty and delicate yet the oak is prominent throughout. Good balancing sweet malt, though. **43%.** *Toa.*

Golden Horse Chichibu 10 Years Old Single Malt db **(82)** n*19* t*22* f*21* b*20*. Developing citrus notes lighten the weight as the oak and sweet malt go head to head. **43%.** *Toa.*

Chichibu 14 Years Old Single Malt db **(89)** n*20* tangerine peel and rice: two years older than the 12-y-o, that hint of bourbon has now become a statement; t*23* brilliantly eclectic arrival on the palate with no organisation at all to the flurry of malt and bourbony oak and tangerine-fruity spices that are whizzing around; f*23* pretty long with firm vanilla and a distinctive oiliness. Something approaching a whiff of smoke adds some extra ballast to the oak; b*23* we are talking mega, in-your-face taste explosions here. A malt with a bourbony attitude that is unquestionably superb. **57%.** *Toa.*

FUJI GOTEMBA, 1973. Kirin Distillers.

⬙ **The Fuji Gotemba 15 Years Old** db **(92)** n*21* diced nuts, especially pistachio with vanilla and a sprinkling of sugar; t*23* mouth watering from the start with a sensational development of sweet malt; f*24* plateaus out with textbook spices binding sweet malt and dry oak. The length is exemplary; b*24* quality malt of great poise. **43%.** *Kirin.*

⬙ **The Fuji Gotemba 18 Years Old** db **(81)** n*20* t*19* f*21* b*21*. Jelly-baby fruitiness, complete with powdered sugar. Big, big age apparent. **43%.** *Kirin.*

Fuji Gotemba 20th Anniversary Pure Malt db **(84)** n*21* t*20* f*22* b*21*. The nose is a lovely mixture of fruit and mixed oak; the body has a delightful sheen and more fruit with the malt. Handsome stuff. **40%.** *Kirin.*

HAKUSHU, 1973. Suntory.

Hakushu 1984 db **(95)** n*22* delicate banana and malt with a gentle fly-past of peat. The oak is unbowed but sympathetic; t*25* staggeringly beautiful: wave upon wave of astonishing complexity crashes against the tastebuds. The malt is intense but there is plenty of room for oak in varying guises to arrive, make eloquent speeches and retire. The intensity of spice is spot on – perfect; f*24* long, more spice and greater malt intensity as the oak fades. Only the softest hints of smoke; mouthwatering to the last as mild coffee appears; b*24* a masterpiece malt of quite sublime complexity and balance. The sort of experience that gives a meaning to life, the universe and everything ... **61%**

Hakushu 1988 db **(92)** n*21* overtly peaty and dense, pleasant but lacking usual Hakushu complexity; t*24* mouthwatering start with massively lively malt and fresh peating hanging on to its coat-tails. Some amazing heather–honey moments that have no right to be there; the peat intensifies then lightens; f*23* lots of rich peat and then intense vanilla; crisp and abrupt at the finale with late bitter chocolate; b*24* like all great whiskies this is one that gangs up on you in a way you are not expecting: the limited complexity on the nose is more than compensated for elsewhere. Superb. If this were an Islay malt the world would be drooling over it. **61%**

Suntory Pure Malt Hakushu Aged 10 Years db **(89)** n*23* exemplary grassiness, fresh malt: mouthwatering and refreshes the senses; t*24* spot-on, top-of-the-range malt. The freshness and integrity of the barley is beyond belief: thirst-quenching whisky of the highest order; f*20* becomes rather toffeed and less well defined. A subtle display of spice compensates; b*22* beautifully crafted whisky that's fresh and rewarding. **40%.** *The name Hakushu appears in small writing on the front label.*

Suntory Pure Malt Hakushu Aged 12 Years bott 2002 db **(95)** n*23* fresh clean malt with the vaguest hint of peat imaginable, but such is the clarity of the nose it can be spotted; **t**24 just wonderful crispness to the mouthwatering barley, gristy and fresh with a building of stupendous peaty spices; **f**24 beautifully refined with some oak just offering extra chewability; **b**24 this is one of the best distillery-bottled whiskies since the turn of the new millennium. Simply magnificent. **43%**

Suntory Pure Malt Aged 12 Years (no bottling date) db **(84) n**20 **t**23 **f**20 **b**21. Deliciously malty with no little fruit, but the finish is disappointingly flat save for some welcome spices. **43%**

Suntory Pure Malt Hakushu 15 Years Old Cask Strength db **(92) n**21 curiously muted: one assumes it is a fruit-oak influence that is keeping the higher barley notes at bay; **t**24 gets back into the old Hakushu groove with a truly stunning display of mouthwatering malt in all its regalia: honeycomb too. Somehow manages to be big and chewy and light and flighty all at the same time; **f**23 good length, toasted honey, marmalade and spices; **b**24 if only the nose had been right, this would have been one of the truly great whiskies. The enormity on the palate is something you are unlikely to forget for a long time while the balance between barley, honey and oak is extraordinary. **56%**

Suntory Pure Malt Hakushu Aged 20 Years db **(94) n**23 fresh, mildly grapey fruit combined with subtle waves of peat; **t**24 the peat is now less subtle: wave upon wave of it bringing with it flotsam of drifting oak and then a very sharp malt tang; **f**23 long, sweet spice but the oak forms a chunky alliance with the firm peat. The bitter-sweet compexity almost defies belief; **b**24 a hard-to-find malt, but find it you must. Yet another huge nail in the coffin of those who purport Japanese whisky to be automatically inferior to Scotch. **56%**

Scotch Malt Whisky Society Cask 120.1 Aged 21 Years (93) n23 fruit and nuts sprinkled with fresh malt, very muesli in style, fresh oak, clean yet astonishingly complex; **t**23 voluptuous mouthfeel, the barley is intense and so mouthwatering. Some lovely nip and bite adds extra complexity; **f**22 slightly shot but clean and enormously malty; **b**25 a malt of genuine class and integrity. The entire balance of the whisky is flawless. **60%**

Scotch Malt Whisky Society Cask 120.2 Aged 14 Years (92) n23 no more than a dusting of peat over soft cocoa, sensuous and teasing, like fingers running down your spine, barely touching the skin; **t**23 a firm, biting malt again uncloaks its peat slowly and with more than a degree of eroticism; **f**22 a slight bourbony-oaky sweetness intervenes on the keyhole peat show; **b**24 do you drink this whisky or make love to it? I'm not altogether sure. One of the few whiskies I recommend with water ... in the form of a cold shower! **62%. nc ncf sc.**

KARUIZAWA, 1955. Mercian.

⌐ **Karuizawa 1972 Aged 31 Years** db cask 5530 **(78) n**19 **t**18 **f**21 **b**20. Oaky and hot with just a bit too much age.

⌐ **Karuizawa 1973 Aged 30 Years** db cask 6249 **(84) n**20 **t**21 **f**22 **b**21. Sweet barley and very silky oaky vanilla. Plucked from the cask just in time.

⌐ **Karuizawa 1974 Aged 29 Years** db cask 6115 **(91) n**23 brilliant complexity: juicy dates and figs wrapped around a theme of richly oaked barley; **t**22 much sweeter arrival on the nose with burnt fudge and toast arriving for the middle; **f**23 slightly salty, the barley seems both sweet and roasty. Soft liquorice makes this one you can chew for hours; **b**23 an exhibition of bitter-sweet enormity.

⌐ **Karuizawa 1975 Aged 28** Years db cask 4066 **(85) n**20 salty, coastal; thick oak; **t**21 early malt sweetness is blasted away by a red-hot follow-through; **f**23 much more relaxed late middle and finish with they honey thread soothing the singed taste buds; **b**21 loud at first, it sings sweet lullabies at the death. Always complex.

⋙ **Karuizawa 1976 Aged 27 Years** db cask 6949 **(83)** n19 t20 f23 b21.
Big, mouthfilling but just a touch too much oak among the honey.

⋙ **Karuizawa 1977 Aged 26 Years** db cask 7614 **(74)** n17 t20 f19 b18.
Some decent sweetness but doesn't quite work.

⋙ **Karuizawa 1978 Aged 25 Years** db cask 2368 **(87)** n21 seaweedy
and shoreline, but without the peat; t20 almost violent arrival of searing sherry
and vicious oak: hang on to your chair; f23 calms down stupendously with soft
smoky peat to be found in the many strata of clean fruit and barley; b23 extra
dry sherry, biting, salty and with a big coastal tang.

⋙ **Karuizawa 1979 Aged 24 Years** db cask 8835 **(94)** n23 much more
fruit than is usual for this distillery with apples and fresh pear; lots of barley
survives despite the age; t23 the barley is drinking in gentle honey and cocoa-
enriched oak; f24 marvellously long with teasing, toasted caramelised oak
adding a glorious repost to the rich, Demerara-sweetened barley; b24 one of
those rare casks that appears to have had a magic wand waved at it and stardust
sprinkled liberally. Simply magnificent.

⋙ **Karuizawa 1980 Aged 23 Years** db cask 7614 **(89)** n22 solid age but
the softness of the toffee-apple and barley sugar is first class; attractive bourbony
notes develop; t21 gripping, wild and hot at first, then a series of soothing waves
of malt and liquorice; f24 peppery and estery; the honey-malt mouthfeel is long,
lush and fabulous; b22 a classy Japanese malt that relishes the battle against
advancing oak.

⋙ **Karuizawa 1981 Aged 22 Years** db cask 8280 **(73)** n17 t19 f19 b18.
Sharp redcurrants but too obvious off-notes abound.

⋙ **Karuizawa 1982 Aged 21 Years** db cask 8527 **(85)** n21 a forest full of
honey bees; t21 deep honey and toasted fudge; the middle erupts with strangely
enjoyable sap; f22 gentle malt with a pinch of moscavado sugar and liquorice; b21
a mature whisky showing some sag but just hanging onto its sexy, alluring figure.

⋙ **Karuizawa 1983 Aged 20 Years** db cask 8609 **(88)** n20 slightly
estery; chocolate honeycomb and a slice of pine; t24 estery, rich enormous
copper presence; f22 medium length with elegant wisps of honey and toffee;
b22 tasted blind you would bet your own grandmother that this was pot still
Jamaican rum. And one probably older than your gran ...

⋙ **Karuizawa 1984 Aged 19 Years** db cask 2563 **(78)** n17 t20 f21 b20.
Some quality touches of grape against smoky grist, and the mild peat is a redeeming
and unexpected surprise, but what a shame that minor sulphury blemish.

⋙ **Karuizawa 1985 Aged 18 Years** db cask 6885 **(90)** n22 honey as a
side dish on butterscotch tart; t22 mouth filling, oilier than usual with sumptuous
malt and oak; f23 wonderful tones of butterscotch sweetened over the
broadening oak. Just a slight sprinkling of cocoa; b23 whisky that celebrates its
middle age with a show of complex intensity.

⋙ **Karuizawa 1986 Aged 17 Years** db cask 8170 **(94)** n23 full-frontal,
naked sherry. And spicy, too; t23 massive, almost uncontrollable sherry-malt
explosion; dried dates and vanilla concentrate form an unlikely but delicious
alliance; f24 long, fruity with hidden spices; the malt ducks in and out playfully;
b24 find a faultless sherry butt and place in it a whisky of the very finest quality
and complexity. This is the result.

⋙ **Karuizawa 1987 Aged 16 Years** db cask 8694 **(93)** n23 amazingly
soft malt with just a touch of far-away, background smoke; t23 brilliant malt
arrival: the barley sings from every direction; f24 surprising lack of development
as the oak remains shy and the barley rules unhindered; just the faintest wisp of
smoke here and there; b23 almost like a malt-shake in its barley intensity. No
complaints here, though.

⋙ **Karuizawa 1988 Aged 15 Years** db cask 691 **(88)** n20 malty banana
and custard; t22 drying oak at first and then the most teasing build-up of honey

imaginable; **f**23 this creeping effect continues with a crescendo of acacia honey and green-grassy barley in total control of the oak; **b**23 quite fabulous whisky that exudes confidence and charisma.

⁘ **Karuizawa 1989 Aged 14 Years** db cask 2941 **(91) n**22 soaring fruity notes interlock beautifully with soft bourbon; **t**23 hard, metallic arrival at first then a fabulous deployment of sugared fruits on a bed of chewy oak; **f**23 big vanilla, subtle spices and a very late waft of smoke; **b**23 there would be quite a number of Scottish distilleries who would pray to produce a malt this simplistically stylish.

⁘ **Karuizawa 1990 Aged 13 Years** db cask 7905 **(85) n**19 surprisingly flat despite the malt; **t**21 velvet mouth arrival then a kick of clean barley; **f**23 long, malt-rich and beautifully layered; **b**22 deliciously mouth-watering yet firm and unyielding barley is stand-offish towards the oak. The finish is awesomely rich. The texture is excellent.

⁘ **Karuizawa 1991 Aged 12 Years** db cask 8294 **(87) n**22 beautifully fresh and gristy; **t**22 big delivery of clean malt which sweetens; **f**22 a simple barley-vanilla tail with some soft brown sugar; **b**21 charming, well proportioned but not overly taxing.

Karuizawa Pure Malt 15 Years (76) n17 **t**21 **f**20 **b**18. Some vague sulphur notes on the sherry do no favours for what appears to be an otherwise top-quality malt. (Earlier bottlings have been around the 87–88 mark, with the fruit, though clean, not being quite in balance but made up for by an astonishing silkiness with roast chestnut puree and malt). **40%**

Karuizawa Pure Malt Aged 17 Years (90) n20 bourbony, big oak and pounding fruit; **t**24 enormous stuff: the link between malt and fruit is almost without definition; **f**23 amazingly long and silky. Natural vanilla melts in with the almost concentrated malt; **b**23 brilliant whisky beautifully made and majestically matured. Neither sweetness nor dryness dominates, always the mark of a quality dram. **40%**

KOMAGATAKE

Komagatake 10 Years Old Single Malt db **(78) n**19 **t**20 **f**19 **b**20. A very simple, malty whisky that's chewy and clean with a slight hint of toffee. **40%**. *Mars.*

SENDAI, 1969. Nikka.

⁘ **"Miyagikyou" 10 Years Old** db batch 18C10D **(88) n**22 teasing layers of peat amid ripe fruit; **t**20 just a little jumbled at first but the fruitiness, figs especially, makes an impact; **f**23 now it really does go onto another plane as the peat returns to offer waves of the most gentle smokiness. Quite brilliant; **b**23 by far and away the most deft and complex Sendai seen on the market. **45%**

⁘ **"Miyagikyou" 15 Years Old** db batch 20C44C **(84) n**20 **t**21 **f**22 **b**21. Very typically Sendai: light body and limited weight even with all the fruit. Clean and gathers in overall enjoyability, though. **45%**

Sendai 12 Years Old (code 06C40C) db **(83) n**17 **t**22 **f**23 **b**21. To put it politely, the nose is pretty ordinary; but what goes on afterwards is relative bliss with a wonderful, oily, fruity resonance. For those thinking in Scotch terms, this is very Speysidey with the malt intense and chewy. **45%**. *Nikka.*

⁘ **Sendai Miyagikyou Nikka Single Cask Malt Whisky 1986** db dist 16 May 86 bott, 5 Dec 03 **(88) n**22 stewed prunes and oranges; the first rumbles of bourbon and smoke wafting around for extra weight; **t**20 big fruit kick but a little out of sync; **f**24 a super nova of a kick back with peat appearing as if from nowhere and the big, booming, bourbony notes and sweetness at the end offering dozens of waves of complexity. A touch of cocoa rounds it off magnificently; **b**22 little to do with balance, everything about effect. **63.2%**

⁘ **Sendai Miyagikyou Nikka Single Cask Malt Whisky 1992** db dist 22 Apr 92, bott 5 Dec 03 **(84) n**19 **t**20 **f**24 **b**21. Very strange whisky: I would never have recognised this as Sendai. I don't know if they have used local oak on this but the fruity, off-balance nose and early taste is compensated by an orgy of mouth-watering, softly smoked barley that sends the taste buds into ecstasy. A distinct, at times erratic, whisky that may horrify the purists but really has some perzaz and simply cannot be ignored. **55.3%**

SHIRAKAWA

Shirakawa 32 Years Old Single Malt (94) n23 ripe mango meets a riper, rye-encrusted bourbon. We are talking a major aroma here; **t**24 the most intense malt you'll ever find explodes and drools all over your tastebuds. To make the flavour bigger still, the oak adds a punchy bourbon quality. Beautiful oils coat the roof of the mouth to amplify the performance; **f**23 long, sweet and malty. Some fruitiness does arrive but it is the oak-malt combination that just knocks you out; **b**24 just how big can an unpeated malt whisky get? The kind of malt that leaves you in awe, even when you thought you had seen and tasted them all. **55%.** *Takara.*

YAMAZAKI, 1923. Suntory.

Yamazaki 1991 db **(88) n**21 bourbony and light with a substratum of soft malt; **t**23 astonishing unfurling of mouthwatering malt tones that spreads over the mouth revealing a subtle hint of smoke and beautifully graceful oak; **f**22 long, lashings of cocoa powder and again soft barley hand-in-hand with gentle oak; **b**22 closed when cold, improves dramatically when warmed on the hand. But the mouth arrival really does deserve a medal. **61%**

Yamazaki 1993 db **(87) n**23 smoky and clean; gristy and Port Ellen-ish with a bit of extra exotic oak; **t**23 sweet, spicy, vaguely Islay-ish start with the peats developing but not at the expense of dense malt. The oak is refined and there is something unusually coastal for a non-Scottish peated malt; **f**20 rather hard, closed and brittle. Metallic malt scrapes against rock-like peat; **b**21 a real surprise package. At times quite Islay-ish in style – Port Ellen in particular – but the finish is more realistic. A really delicious experience nonetheless.

Suntory Pure Malt Yamazaki 10 Years Old db **(79) n**20 **t**21 **f**19 **b**19. Almost unnatural fruitiness, as though wild fruit yeast spores have been at work. Malty and sweet, nonetheless. **40%**

Suntory Pure Malt Yamazaki 25 Years Old db **(91) n**23 quite intoxicating marriage between grapey fruitiness and rich oak: supremely spiced and balanced with a wave of pure bourbon following through; **t**23 big, big oloroso character then an entrancing molassed, burnt raisin, malty richness; **f**22 subtle spices, poppy seed with some late bitter oak; **b**23 being matured in Japan, the 25 years doesn't have quite the same value as Scotland. So perhaps in some ways this can lay claim to be one of the most enormously aged, oak-laden whiskies that has somehow kept its grace and star quality. **43%**

Suntory Pure Malt Yamazaki Cask Strength db **(88) n**22 very light, flimsy weight but the malty grassiness impresses; **t**23 absolutely pure Yamazaki in concentrate: refreshing malt that sweetens and fattens; **f**21 a light, toffeed finale without the complexity of either the nose or early palate; **b**22 a malt of indisputably high quality. **56%**

Scotch Malt Whisky Society Cask 119.1 Aged 22 Years (81) n20 **t**22 **f**20 **b**19. Enormous amounts of natural toffee from the bourbony oak. Missing some complexity but the overall experience is pretty rewarding. **51%. nc ncf sc.**

Scotch Malt Whisky Society Cask 119.4 Aged 10 Years (92) n22 young, thumping peat, very clean and curiously non-coastal in style; **t**24 a peat explosion of almost unbelievable intensity. Nothing quite like this the world over (now) as the intense barley sweetness is both gristy and mashy; **f**24 a long, long, long finale as it takes a while for all that peat to disperse. It does so with both elegance and eloquence with the melt-in-the-mouth malt simply knocking you out; **b**22 not many marks for balance here, as it's pretty one-sided. But anyone missing out on this experience will kick themselves. Perhaps it should be renamed Banzai! **58%**

YOICHI, 1934. Nikka.

Hokkaido 12 Years Old db **(87) n**23 a mixed bag of citrus and oak, really very beautifully balanced; **t**22 very firm malt and crisp-textured, even the fruit is hard; **f**21 very light with crisp barley and drying vanilla; **b**21 full-flavoured malt with absolutely zero yield. Just ricochets around the palate. **43%**. *Nikka.*

Nikka Single Cask Malt Whisky 10 Years Old dist 14/12/88, bott 14/12/98 db **(93) n**23 big oak influence: bourbony in character with ripe plums, too. One assumes local oak has been used; **t**24 seriously big bourbon character: massively sweet, rich deep barley and the lightest rumble of peat; **f**22 gentle, oily with some molassed sugar on the rolling smoke; **b**24 this is a seriously big whisky for the serious whisky drinker. Amazingly high-quality malt where the wood plays the dominant role but leaves space enough for malt development. **62.2%**. *Nikka. From the Yoichi distillery.*

⠂⠒⠂ **Yoichi 10 Years Old** db batch 14116A **(75) n**19 **t**19 **f**18 **b**19. Proof that sulphur can detract even from a great like Yoichi. **45%**

Yoichi 10 Years Old (code 14B22 new "Yoichi" distillery label) db **(88) n**18 fruity but sulphur blemish then fine malt notes maintain the shape; **t**23 very hard, biting malt: firm in style, almost like a blended whisky, but some fruit softens the impact; **f**23 a build-up of gentle, peaty spices all the more remarkable for there having been little sign of smoke on the nose or early palate; **b**24 typical Yoichi. Even when it shows a flaw it recovers to an unbelievable degree: like a champion ice skater who falls at the first leap and then dances on as if nothing happened. Keeps you guessing to the very last about what is to happen next. Fabulous verve and complexity. **45%**. *Nikka.*

Yoichi 10 Years Old (code 12I32 old Hokkaido "Yoichi" distillery label) db **(91) n**22 the peat brushes the nose like a feather on skin: just so delicate; **t**23 immediate flinty malt, amazingly hard and tooth-cracking then softened slowly by a salty, peaty edge; **f**23 peaty, delicate and now as soft, thanks to vanilla, as it was previously uncompromisingly hard. Some toffee and coffee aid the finale; **b**23 yet another teasing, unpredictable dram from Yoichi. **43%**. *Nikka.*

Yoichi 10 Years Old (code 14H62A old Hokkaido "Yoichi" distillery label) db **(91) n**23 big malt but it is the delicate quality of the peat that is most remarkable. Oak is present, but this is almost too clean to be true; **t**23 sweet and soft, then that Yoichi trademark gradual build-up of peat; **f**22 hard and brittle despite the softness of the peat, long and chewy with a hint of liquorice and honey; **b**23 the crispness and bite of this whisky makes it almost blend-like in style – which goes to underline the complexity. **43%**. *Nikka.*

Yoichi 10 Years Old (code 14H62B old Hokkaido "Yoichi" distillery label) db **(89) n**23 fruity, oranges, a sprinkling of peat and fresh malt; **t**21 enormously malty with the peat arriving late; **f**22 soft vanilla and more grapey fruit then the peats come into their own; **b**23 soft and delicate with beautifully chewy peat throughout. **43%**. *Nikka.*

Yoichi 10 Years Old (code 24G48C old Hokkaido "Yoichi" distillery label) db **(93) n**23 for an aroma carrying smoke this is almost austere: but this is an illusion. Some crisp malty, softly peated notes give it a delicate depth and massive sophistication; **t**23 enormous malt, absolutely brimming with lusty barley. Refreshing and mouthwatering, yet all the time that soft peat is present; **f**24 a quite brilliant marriage between rich barley and soft oak. No more than the slightest hint of very distant smoke; **b**23 a Yoichi in its "Old Speyside" phase, with just a waft of peat-reek to add some ballast to the enormous, clean malt. The fade is nothing short of fabulous. A Japanese version of Ardmore: whisky for grown-ups. **43%**. *Nikka*.

Yoichi 10 Years Old (code 24H18C old Hokkaido "Yoichi" distillery label) db **(89) n**20 firm, very lightly peated malt with softening vanilla, fruity; **t**23 honeyed and much sweeter than the nose suggests, mouthfilling and oily; **f**23 gentle peppers mix with the barley but the sweetness pervades on the very long, mildly peated finish; **b**23 another bottle of understated genius. **43%**. *Nikka*.

Yoichi 12 Years Old (code 06C14 new Yoichi label with distillery drawing) db **(91) n**21 spicy fresh oloroso; **t**24 big, clean sultana-fruit with a gathering intensity of ripe dates and sweet, gently smoked malt; **f**22 dies slightly, but the dates remain, as does the smoke. The oak kicks in with a late bitter finale; **b**24 absolutely magnificent malt with a no-holds-barred intensity of fruit and malt. **45%**. *Nikka*.

Yoichi 12 Years Old (code 16J32 new Yoichi label with distillery drawing) db **(87) n**20 clean fruit and soft oak; **t**22 massive malt and toffee, almost like a night drink; **f**23 major complexity kicks in with some incredibly juicy fruity notes marrying into a ripping malt theme; **b**22 a pretty light Yoichi almost devoid of peat. After getting over a toffee-led lull the malt comes to life with impressive results. **45%**. *Yoichi*.

Yoichi 15 Years Old (code 10J44 old green back label) db **(94) n**23 roast chestnuts plus salty, soft peat and dried dates: awesome complexity; **t**24 the dates have moistened, the peat positively glows, having been seasoned with salt, the fruitiness is full but in perfect proportion; **f**23 for the enormity of the nose and mouth arrival, the soft peated spices offer a charming sophistication to the intense barley. The fruit remains yielding and the oak no less soft and accommodating; **b**24 the kind of whisky that propels a distillery into super league status. A classic. **45%**. *Nikka*.

Yoichi 15 Years Old (code 06C10 new buff-coloured back label) db **(90) n**22 nutty, intense clean malt with just a light dusting of peat. The fruits are light and plummy; **t**22 very clean malt, almost gristy in its delicate nature. The peat no more than tickles the tastebuds. A weak grapejuice sweetness offers further complexity; **f**23 amazingly delicate, a beautiful combination of barley and vanilla. The peat remains playful and wonderfully balanced; **b**23 this is a succulent malt of enormous complexity. Typical Yoichi. **45%**. *Nikka*.

Yoichi 20 Years Old db **(95) n**23 magnificently intense oloroso (a tiny fleck of sulphur burns off in about 10 minutes when warmed), the background malt oak-laden; **t**23 again it's oloroso that leads the way, apparently too intensely at first but quickly settling to allow some stupendous spices to unravel and create balance. Fabulous bitter-sweet harmony; **f**25 Okay, guys, help me out here. Spot the fault. I can't. The fruit is now spotlessly clean and displaying a grapey complexity, the spices are warming but not entirely engulfing, the oak is firm and adds no more than a hint of dryness and at last the malt comes into full play to offer both mouthwatering barley and something slightly smoky. If you can pick a defect, let me know; **b**24 I don't know how much they charge for this stuff but either alone or with mates get some for one hell of an experience. What makes it all the more remarkable is that there is a slight sulphury note on the nose: once you taste the stuff that becomes of little consequence. **52%**. *Nikka*.

⋯∷⋯ **Yoichi Nikka Single Cask Malt Whisky 15 Years Old** dist 30 Apr 85, bott 24 Jul 00 **(91) n**23 awesome sherry with the spiced malt hanging on to thick, winey, leathery coat-tails; **t**23 the immediate arrival of salty sherry is simply too much. It takes a while for the malt to make a terrified entrance; when it does there is an almost immediate balance as the fruitiness drifts towards a salty, toasted malty, oaky middle; **f**22 long, salty with soft liquorice and; **b**23 at first it seems far, far too much of a sherried thing. It takes further investigation and a lot of bravery to get to the bottom of one of the most extraordinary sherry casks to come out of Japan in the last five or six years. **58.7%**

⋙ **Yoichi Nikka Single Cask Malt Whisky 1990** db dist 4 Aug 90, bott 17 Oct 03 **(84) n**21 **t**20 **f**22 **b**21. Most probably a dry sherry cask set the tone for this: astringent by Yoichi standards and although the finish offers a complex vanilla and liquorice counter, this isn't an Hokkaido great. **60.8%**

⋙ **Yoichi Nikka Single Cask Malt Whisky 1991** db dist 25 Feb 91, bott 12 Dec 03 **(95) n**24 there appears to be no shortage of pears and grapes, yet the pride of place goes to a mouth-watering, stunning gristiness made all the more vivid thanks to maltiness that is distantly elegant and fleeting as a formationed-flock of geese flying overhead; **t**24 faultless sherry with not a chip to its sheen begins mouth-puckeringly pungently and then heads off to a much sweeter malt theme, with that elegant peat fanfared on the nose gathering in wonderful intensity; **f**23 long with juicy dates, sprinkling of cappuccino and, of course, that extraordinary peat; **b**24 it was because I managed to taste many casks like this while tramping through Yoichi's warehouses over the years that I declared the distillery in the world's top six. Taste this, then e-mail me to disagree. **64.5%**

Scotch Malt Whisky Society Cask 116.1 Aged 16 Years (94) n24 a style of Yoichi I know so well and so adore: half bourbon-oaky character, half proud malt. The intensity and complexity is nothing short of brilliant; **t**23 a perfect match to the nose: sweet bourbony tones, then oak-extracted toffee intensified by stunning malt; **f**23 long, rich, chewy, mildly spiced and clean as a whistle; **b**24 brilliantly made malt in total harmony with its oaky confines. If this were Scotch, it would be about 30-y-o in style; if it were bourbon, it would be from Frankfort. Need I say more? **56.6%. nc ncf sc.**

Scotch Malt Whisky Society Cask 116.2 (91) n22 big and bourbony, sweet malt and oak infusing to form a marmalade fruitiness; **t**23 some age on this, with again some major bourbon-style sweetness lifting from the vanillins. The malt follows later, clean, intense and chewy; **f**23 and so it goes on: more of the same, wave upon wave as if in a loop; **b**23 totally top rate. This is where single malt meets bourbon in style. The battle is long and bloody and only one winner emerges: the person lucky enough to be drinking it.

Scotch Malt Whisky Society Cask 116.3 Aged 11 Years (84) n22 **t**21 **f**20 **b**21. Chewy, bourbon-caramel character with decent spice on the finish. Perhaps lacks the usual Yoichi complexity, though. **60.6%. nc ncf sc.**

Scotch Malt Whisky Society Cask 116.4 Aged 13 Years (88) n23 east meets west: ol' West Virginia, that is. Massive bourbony kick before the amazingly complex and light malty notes filter through. Intriguingly delicious; **t**22 some citrus tones fleetingly come to life before rich oak and richer malt take command; **f**21 bitter-sweet and drying before a mildly molassed sugary oakiness wins through; **b**22 a pretty challenging whisky to Scotch malt lovers, as the style is very Japanese. It allows a bourbony-oaky incursion so far before setting down its limits. Will that incursion have gone too far for some purists, I wonder? **64.9%. nc ncf sc.**

Unspecified Malts

⋙ **"Hokuto" Suntory Pure Malt Aged 12 Years (93) n**22 trademark delicate lightness; fleeting barley chased by soft vanilla; **t**24 melt-in-the-mouth malt arrival; hints of honey work well with the loftier barley and earthier oak; **f**23 honey on toast with just a little toffee; **b**24 another example of Suntory at its most feminine: just so seductive and beautiful. Although a malt, think Lawson's 12-y-o of a decade ago and you have the picture. **40%**

Nikka Whisky From the Barrel (89) n20 carries some weight; good age and subtle malty sugars; **t**23 exemplary mouthfeel: delightful oils and nipping spices but the malt remains clean and very sweet; **f**22 some dryer oakiness but the malt keeps its balancing sweetness; **b**24 a whisky that requires a bit of time and concentration to get the best out of. You will discover something big and exceptionally well balanced. **51.4%**. *Nikka*.

Vatted Malts

All Malt (86) n22 delicate yet intensely malty: a bit like it says on the bottle, in fact! Those who drink Scotch will recognise the style as Speyside in its grassy, mouthwatering tones and as clean and clear on the nose as a crystal spring. When warmed, some smoke appears (aromatically, I mean!); **t**21 fresh and then sharply intense, with a fleeting hardness more associated with unmalted barley. Brilliantly mouthwatering and chewy with a slow unravelling of distant peatiness; **f**21 late arrival of drier vanilla, oaky tones and Java coffee: long and delicious; **b**22 the best example by a mile of an almost unique style of vatted whisky: both malt and "grain" are distilled from entirely malted barley, identical to Kasauli malt whisky in India. Stupendous grace and balance. **40%**. *Nikka*.

Malt Club (77) n18 t20 f18 b21. Young in character with attractive vitality from the moment it crunches the tastebuds. Really lovely balance throughout. **40%**. *Nikka*.

Mars Maltage Pure Malt 8 Years Old (84) n20 t21 f21 b22. A very level, intense, clean malt with no peaks or troughs, just a steady variance in the degree of sweetness and oak input. Impossible not to have a second glass of. **43%**. *Mars*.

Pure Malt Black batch 02C58A **(95)** n24 an exquisitely crafted nose: studied peat in luxuriant yet deft proportions nestling amid some honeyed malt and oak. The balance between sweet and dry is faultless. There is neither a single off-note nor a ripple of disharmony. The kind of nose you can sink your head into and simply disappear; **t**23 for all the evident peat, this is medium-weighted, the subtlety encased in a gentle cloak of oil; **f**23 long, silky, fabulously weighted peat running a sweet course through some surging malt and liquorice tones with a bit of salt in there for zip; **b**25 well, if anyone can show me a better-balanced whisky than this you know where to get hold of me. You open a bottle of this at your peril: best to do so in the company of friends. Either way, it will be empty before the night is over. **43%**. *Nikka*.

Pure Malt Red batch 02C30B **(86)** n21 firm vanilla gives an oaky lead to this one; **t**21 light and malty with the vanilla again coming up fast: light-bodied otherwise with a dash of honey; **f**22 bang on course in character with the oak sticking gently to its task while the malt weaves tasty patterns on the tastebuds; **b**22 a light malt that appears heavier than it actually is with an almost imperceptible oiliness. **43%**. Nikka.

Pure Malt White batch 02C30C **(92)** n23 massive, Islay-style peat with a fresh sea kick thanks to brine amid the barley; **t**24 again, the peat-reek hangs firmly on the tastebuds from the word go, the sweetness of the barley tempered by some drying oaky notes suggesting reasonable age. Lots of subtle oils bind the complexity; **f**22 liquorice and salt combine to create a powerful malty-oak combo. An oily, kippery smokiness continues to the very end; **b**23 a big peaty number displaying the most subtle of hands. **43%**. *Nikka*.

Pure Malt White batch 06J26 **(91)** n22 soft peat interrupted by gentle oak; **t**23 biting, nippy malt offering a degree of orangey-citrus fruit amid the building smoke; **f**22 sweet vanilla and light smoke that dries towards a salty, tangy, liquorice finish; **b**24 a sweet malt, but one with such deft use of peat and oak that one never really notices. Real class. **43%**. *Nikka*.

Southern Alps Pure Malt (93) n24 bananas and freshly peeled lemon skin: one of the world's most refreshing and exhilarating whisky noses; **t**2t crisp youngish malts, as one might suspect from the nose, mouthwatering and as a clean as an Alpine stream; **f**22 some vanilla development and a late slightly creamy flourish but finished with a substantial and startling malty rally boasting a very discreet sweetness; **b**24 this is a bottle I have only to look at to start salivating. Sadly, though, I drink sparingly from it as it is a hard whisky to find, even in Japan. Fresh, clean and totally stunning, the term "pure malt" could not be more apposite. Fabulous whisky: a very personal favourite. **40%.** *Suntory.*

Super Nikka Vatted Pure Malt (76) n20 **t**19 **f**19 **b**18. Decent and chewy but something doesn't quite click with this one. **55.5%.** *Nikka.*

Taketsuru Pure Malt 12 Years Old (80) n19 **t**22 **f**19 **b**20. For its age, heavier than a sumo wrestler. But perhaps a little more agile over the tastebuds. Lovely silkiness impresses, but lots of toffee. **40%.** *Nikka.*

Taketsuru Pure Malt 17 Years Old (89) n21 firm oak, but compromises sufficiently to allow several layers of malt to battle through with a touch of peat-coffee; **t**22 massive: a toasted, honeyed front gives way to really intense and complex malt notes; **f**23 superb. Some late marmalade arrives from somewhere: the toast is slightly burnt but the waves of malty complexity are endless; **b**23 not a whisky for the squeamish. This is big stuff – about as big as it gets without peat or rye. No bar shelf or whisky club should be without one. **43%.** *Nikka.*

Taketsuru Pure Malt 21 Years Old (88) n22 middle-aged bourbon with a heavy, vaguely honeyed malt presence; **t**21 the oak remains quite fresh and chewy. Again, the malt is massive; **f**22 sweet, oily and more honey arrives; **b**23 a much more civilised and gracious offering than the 17-y-o: there is certainly nothing linear about the character development from Taketsuru 12 to 21 inclusive. Serious whisky for the serious whisky drinker. **43%.** *Nikka.*

Zen (84) n19 **t**22 **f**22 **b**21. A sweet, gristy malt that is light and clean. **40%.** *Suntory.*

Japanese Single Grain

⠶ **Nikka Single Cask Coffey Grain Whisky 1991** db dist 1 Oct 91, bott 12 May 03 **(93) n**22 a mountainous forest of oak rather deliciously sweetened by what appears to be corn and simmering, boiled rhubarb. Strands of bourbon; **t**24 brilliant mouth arrival with a perfect bitter-sweet radiance of corn and oak. There is a turbulent lushness as vanilla concentrate yet a deftness to the touch as the grain and oak intermingles for the softer middle; **f**23 the oak has a more bitter say but it is still a decidedly tactile experience; **b**24 I have tasted much Japanese straight grain over the years but this is the first time in bottled form for public consumption. And Nikka have exceeded themselves. Forget the word "grain" and its inferior connotations. This is a monster whisky from the bourbon family you are unlikely ever to forget. Use the first couple of mouthfuls for a marker: once you get the idea, life will never quite be the same again. Track down…and be consumed. **61.9%**

Blends

Ajiwai Kakubin (*see* Kakubin Ajiwai)

Amber (75) n18 **t**20 **f**18 **b**19. Similar in style to "Old" but with more toffee caramel. A silky experience. **40%.** *Mars.*

Black Nikka (72) n17 **t**20 **f**17 **b**18. Big grain presence and decent middle; carries a caramel tang. **37%.** *Nikka.*

Black Nikka Special (70) n16 **t**20 **f**17 **b**17. Simliar to ordinary Black Nikka, except weighed down by extra caramel **42%.** *Nikka.*

Black Nikka Aged 8 Years (82) n20 **t**21 **f**21 **b**20. Beautifully bourbony, especially on the nose. Lush, silky and great fun. Love it! **40%.** *Nikka.*

The Blend of Nikka (90) n21 a dry, oaky buzz infiltrates some firm grain and sweeter malt; **t**23 brilliant! Absolutely outstanding explosion of clean grassy malts thudding into the tastebuds with confidence and precision: mouthwatering and breath-catching; **f**22 delightful grain bite to follow the malt; **b**24 an adorable blend that makes you sit up and take notice of every enormous mouthful. Classy, complex, charismatic and brilliantly balanced. **45%.** *Nikka.*

Boston Club (Brown Label) **(73) n**17 **t**20 **f**18 **b**18. "More Boston Strangler than Boston Club", I wrote somewhere on tasting this some years back. Certainly they have sorted out the dreadful finish on the old bottling, and this is pleasant enough, but devoid of any challenge thanks possibly to caramel although the spice does. **40%.** *Kirin.*

Boston Club (70) n16 t19 f18 b17. Less opaque than the Brown Label, lighter in body with a fraction less toffee-caramel **37%.** *Kirin.*

Crescent (82) n19 t22 f20 b21. Fresh, grassy, lightweight malt dominates. A spot of the old caramel toffee, perhaps? Without it, this would be a stunner. **43%.** *Kirin.*

Diamond Whisky (73) n17 t20 f18 b18. Another blend where complexity takes second place to caramel though it does have some sweet, attractive moments. **43%.** *Nikka.*

Emblem (76) n18 t20 f18 b20. Richly textured bend with a deliciously clean and salivating malt character. **40%.** *Kirin.*

Evermore (90) n22 big age, salt and outstanding malt to counter the oak; t23 more massive oak wrapped in a bourbony sweetness with glorious malts and a salty, spicy tang; f22 long, sweet malt and crisp grains: plenty to chew on and savour; b23 top-grade, well-aged blended whisky with fabulous depth and complexity that never loses its sweet edge despite the oak. 40%. *Kirin.*

Gold & Gold (83) n21 t22 f20 b20. Some lovely, crisp malty moments set against firm grain and softened by honey. Something to get your teeth into, but perhaps a touch too much toffee. **43%.** *Nikka.*

Golden Horse Bosyuu (80) n20 t21 f19 b20. Soft grain melts beautifully in the mouth. **40%.** *Toa.*

Golden Horse Busyuu Deluxe (93) n22 some decent signs of age with some classy oak alongside smoke: sexy stuff; t24 fruity profile simply because it is so fresh: massive malt presence, some of it peaty, bananas and under-ripe grapes; f23 clean malt and some sharpish grain with a touch of bite, continuing to tantalise the tastebuds for a long time; b24 whoever blended this has a genuine feel for whisky: a classic in its own right and one of astonishing complexity and textbook balance. **43%.** *Toa. To celebrate the year 2000.*

Golden Horse Grand (78) n19 t21 f19 b19. Decent malt, sweet and a little chalky. **39%.** *Toa.*

Hibiki (82) n20 t19 f23 b20. The grains here are fresh, forceful and merciless, the malts bouncing off them meekly. Lovely cocoa finale. A blend that brings a tear to the eye. Hard stuff – perfect after a hard day! Love it! **43%.** *Suntory.*

Hibiki 17 Years Old (74) n17 t20 f19 b18. Hmmm, an odd cask or two got into this one I think. The fruity effect has gone OTT and we have quite a syrupy sweetness which doesn't quite fit with sharp finish. Not the usual house style at all. I suspect the next bottling will be a lot better. **43%.** *Suntory.*

Hibiki 21 Years Old (93) n24 fruitier notes of cherry and sherry with a triumphal triumvirate of intense malt, the subtlest of pure smoke and leathery oak combining for maximum, stupendous complexity, also a dash of kumquats; t22 fat and oily, like the nose hinting slightly at bourbon but the grains thin the middle out sufficiently to let the malt, mildly peaty and otherwise, through; f23 long and intense with more lightly orchestrated smoke and lashings of late, grapey fruit and a build-up of first, sweet malts, then a drier, spicier oak; b24 when people refer to Yoichi as the exception that proves the rule about Japanese whisky, I tend to point them in the direction of this. If I close my eyes and taste this, cherry blossom really does form in my mind's eye. Yet this is a classic whisky in any language or any culture. **43%.** *Suntory.*

Hibiki 30 Years Old (87) n21 curious mix of peat and bourbon; t22 sweet, fat oak: bourbon all the way; f22 the glorious rich-textured sweetness continues forever; b22 Kentuckians would really go for this one: the smoke might confuse them a little, though. Pretty unique the world over. **43%.** *Suntory.*

Hi Nikka Whisky (68) n16 t18 f17 b17. Very light but lots of caramel character. A good mixer. **39%.** *Nikka.*

Imperial (81) n20 t22 f19 b20. Flinty, hard grain softened by malt and vanilla but toffee dulled. **43%.** *Suntory.*

Kakubin (80) n19 t21 f20 b20. A beautifully constructed, fresh, bright and mouthwatering blend. Refreshing and so dangerously moreish! **40%.** *Suntory.*

Kakubin Ajiwai (82) n20 t21 f20 b21. Usual Kakubin hard grain and mouthwatering malt, with this time a hint of warming stem ginger. **40%.** *Suntory.*

Kakubin New (90) n21 gritty grain with very hard malt to accompany it; **t**24 stunning mouth arrival with heaps of mouthwatering young malt and then soft grain and oil. Brilliant stuff; **f**21 some beautiful cocoa notes round off the blend perfectly; **b**24 seriously divine blending: a refreshing dram of the top order. **40%.** *Suntory.*

Kingsland (81) n21 t22 f17 b21. An ultra-lively and mouthwatering blend with a short, dry finish. Overall, quite impressive, refreshing and moreish. *Nikka.*

Master's Blend Aged 10 Years (87) n21 integrated fruit and flinty malt; **t**23 mouthwatering and massively fruity, very sweet, light muscovado sugar and malt; **f**22 trails off towards vanilla; **b**21 chewy, big and satisfying. **40%.** *Mercian/Karuizawa.*

New Kakubin Suntory (*see* Kakubin New)

New Shirokaku (74) n18 t19 f19 b18. Grain-heavy, hard and toffeed. **40%.** *Suntory.*

The Nikka Whisky Aged 34 Years blended and bottled in 99 **(93) n**23 bourbony and rich: over-ripe cherries and wet tobacco with chunks of moist Melton Mowbray fruitcake. The oak, for all its weight, remains charming; **t**23 big and fruity and then a surge of oak, perhaps mildly over-aged, but still intact and firm, excellent waxy sweetness through the middle; **f**24 wonderfully spicy and mouth-filling. Excellent oily texture guarantees a good malt presence as the oak dries and takes final control; **b**23 a Japanese whisky of antiquity that has not only survived many passing years, but has actually achieved something of stature and sophistication. Over time I have come to appreciate this whisky immensely. It is among the world's greatest blends, no question. **43%.** *Nikka.*

Oak Master (78) n19 t20 f19 b20. Foraging malts on the nose and palate counter a big grain surge. Decent, silky whisky, though a little on the bitter side. **37%.** *Mercian.*

Ocean Luckey (70) n17 t18 f17 b18. Grainy, chalky and pretty weightless. **37%.** *Mercian.*

Ocean Whisky Special Old (83) n20 t21 f21 b21. Deliciously rich malt is absorbed effortlessly into melt-in-the-mouth grain. Good blending. **40%**

Old (77) n18 t20 f20 b19. Light, sweet, chewy. Good, clean session whisky. **43%.** *Mars.*

Old Halley (71) n18 t19 f17 b17. Flat, not unpleasant but toffee-reliant. **37%.** *Toa.*

Red (75) n17 t19 f20 b19. On the thin side: the grains are to the fore and aft but there is good late spicy bite amid the toffee. **39%.** *Suntory.*

Robert Brown (74) n19 t20 f17 b18. What a pity! Too much toffee has overshadowed some lovely spice. **40%.** *Kirin.*

Royal 12 Years Old (89) n22 chalky and dry, but malt and oranges add character; **t**23 fabulously complex arrival on the palate with some grainy nip countered by sparkling malt and a hint of smoke; **f**21 the grains and oak carry on as the spice builds; **b**23 a splendidly blended whisky with complexity being the main theme. Beautiful stuff. **43%.** *Suntory.*

Royal 15 Years Old (91) n23 kumquats and lime give a fruity start to an immensely malty aroma; **t**23 the grain kicks off early bringing with it some oak, then an immediate malt explosion with a spicy drop-out, lashings of clean, juicy fruit; **f**22 the grain rules OK. But the oaky vanilla is a joy; **b**23 this is outstanding blended whisky. **43%**. *Suntory.*

Special Reserve 10 Years Old (94) n23 magnificent approach of rich fruit buttressed by firm, clear grain. Some further fruity spices reveal some age is evident; **t**24 complex from the off with a tidal tsunami of malt crashing over the tastebuds. The grain holds firm and supports some budding fruit; **f**23 a touch of something peaty and pliable begins to take shape with some wonderful malty spices coating the mouth; **b**24 a beguiling whisky of near faultless complexity. Blending at its peak. **43%**. *Suntory.*

∴ **Suntory Hibiki 17 Years Old (88) n**20 a weighty, lumbering assembly of big, almost bourbony oak and macho malt. Sumo stuff; **t**22 the grains absolutely go into overdrive on immediate mouth arrival before a wonderful gathering of eclectic barley notes take off into every direction; grain tries to get involved but is shoe-horned out; **f**23 beautiful spices and some impressive grain-inspired coffee notes dovetail with the thick malt; **b**23 this is a massive whisky, but not just because of the strength. The crescendo is glass-shattering, only elements of toffee towards the late middle and finish prevents the explosion. **50.5%. ncf.**

Suntory Old (89) n19 dusty and fruity. Attractive nip and balance; **t**24 mouthwatering from the off with a rich array of chewy, clean fresh malt: textbook standard, complete with bite; **f**23 subtle oak on the grain offers texture alongside the silky malt; **b**23 this is a blend that seems to offer both old and new whiskies something of genuine class. The nose is average, but from then on this is about as sure-footed a blending as you will find. A gem. **43%**. *Suntory.*

Suntory Old Mild and Smooth (84) n19 **t**22 **f**21 **b**22. Chirpy and lively around the palate, the grains soften the crisp malts wonderfully. **40%**

Suntory Old Rich and Mellow (89) n20 very lightly smoked with healthy maltiness; **t**23 complex, fat and chewy, no shortage of deep malty tones, including a touch of smoke; **f**23 sweeter malts see off the grain, excellent spices; **b**23 a pretty malt-rich blend with the grains offering a fat base. Impressive blending. **43%**

Super Nikka (93) n23 excellent crisp, grassy malt base bounces off firm grain. A distant hint of peat, maybe, offers a little weighty extra; **t**23 an immediate starburst of rich, mouthwatering and entirely uncompromising malt that almost over-runs the tastebuds; **f**23 soft, fabulously intrinsic peaty notes from the Yoichi School give brilliant length and depth. But the cocoa notes from the oak-wrapped grain also offer untold riches; **b**24 a very, very fine blend which makes no apology whatsoever for the peaty complexity of Yoichi malt. The grain really is melt-in-the mouth stuff. A better sample, this, for having kicked out some – though not all – of the totally unnecessary caramel of old. Now it's pretty classy stuff. However, Nikka being Nikka you might find the occasional bottling that is entirely devoid of peat, more honeyed and lighter in style (21-22-23-23 Total 89 – no less a quality turn, obviously). Either way, an absolutely brilliant day-to-day, anytime, any place dram. One of the true 24-carat, super nova commonplace blends not just in Japan, but in the world. **43%**. *Nikka.*

Torys (77) n19 **t**20 **f**19 **b**19. Lots of toffee in the middle and at the end of this one. The grain used is top class and chewy. **37%**. *Suntory.*

Torys Whisky Square (80) n19 **t**20 **f**21 **b**20. At first glance very similar to Torys, but very close scrutiny reveals slightly more "new loaf" nose and a better, spicier and less toffeed finish. **37%**. *Suntory.*

Tsuru (93) n23 apples, cedar, crushed pine nuts, blood oranges and soft malt, all rather chalky and soft – and unusually peatless for Nikka; **t**24 fantastic grain bite bringing with it a mouthwateringly clean and fresh attack of sweet and lip-smacking malt; **f**22 a continuation of untaxing soft malts and gathering oak, a slight "Malteser" candy quality to it, and then some late sultana fruitiness; **b**24 gentle and beautifully structured, genuinely mouthwatering, more-ish and effortlessly noble. If they had the confidence to cut the caramel, this would be even higher up the charts as one of the great blends of the world. As it is, in my house we pass the ceramic Tsuru bottle as one does the ship's decanter. And it empties very quickly. **43%. Nikka.**

The Whisky (88) n22 fresh barley sugar and oaky, bourbony tones; **t**22 good weight and hard barley rigidity against the softer grains; **f**21 quite simplistic with soft vanilla; **b**23 a really rich, confident and well-balanced dram. **43%.** *Suntory.*

White (75) n20 **t**19 **f**18 **b**18. After a classically nippy nose, proves disappointingly bland. **40%.** *Suntory.*

Za (79) n19 **t**21 **f**19 **b**20. Some lively boisterous grain offers a suet-pudding chewiness. A little bitter on the finish. **40%.** *Suntory.*

Canadian Whisky

It is becoming hard to believe that Canadian was once a giant among the world whisky nations. Dotted all over its enormous land large distilleries pumped out thousands upon thousands of gallons of spirit that after years in barrel became a clean, gentle whisky.

It was cool to be seen drinking Canadian in cocktail bars on both sides of the pond. Now, sadly, Canadian whisky barely raises a beat on the pulse of the average whisky lover. It would not be beyond argument to now call Canadian the forgotten whisky empire with column inches devoted to it measured now in millimetres. It is an entirely sad, almost heartbreaking, state of affairs though hopefully not an irreversible one. The finest Canadian, for me, is still a whisky to be cherished and admired. But outside North America it can be painfully hard to find.

The last year was the first in which not one Canadian whisky was included in the 70-odd tastings I conducted around the world. Each time I suggested adding one to the whisky line up, the organisers declined not least because they claimed that the whiskies were almost impossible to find in their country. In the next year I shall make an effort to try and do something about that unacceptable statistic. But it would be great to hear from the distillers of a move to promote their finer products and that there is confidence matched by budgets to remind the world of just what a treat they are missing.

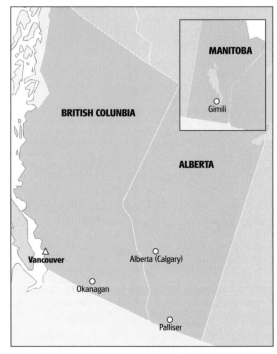

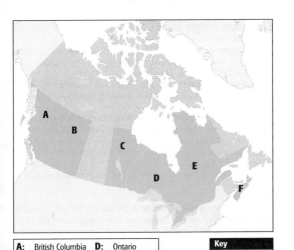

A:	British Columbia	D:	Ontario
B:	Alberta	E:	Quebec
C:	Manitoba	F:	Nova Scotia

Key
△ Major Cities
○ Distilleries

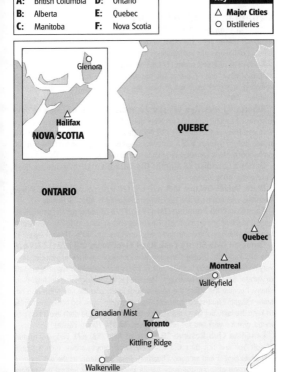

Canadian Single Malt
GLENORA

Glen Breton db **(81)** n*19* t*21* f*20* b*21*. Enormously sweet malt, in almost concentrated form with a tantalising whiff of smoke hanging around; mildly spiced and slightly oily, soapy finale. **43%**

⠿ **Glen Breton Rare** db **(80)** n*18* t*21* f*20* b*21*. The caramel nose is a bit soapy but the buttery, sweet malt, with its vanilla fizz, makes for a very pleasant experience. **43%**

⠿ **Glenora 1990 Aged 14 Years Single Cask** db **(89)** n*22* firm malt but with a distinctive bourbony (or very old Canadian) weight and some attractive natural toffee; t*23* massive malt arrival on the palate buoyed with that dense fudge-caramel; f*22* the oak is distinctive and almost Kentuckian; the malt is profound and the chewy weight is excellent; b*22* by far and away the best Glenora yet bottled. And good to see the distillery use its actual name. **43%**

OKANAGAN

⠿ **Long Wood 8 Years Old Malt** db **(74)** n*19* t*20* f*17* b*18*. There are no discernable off notes and a pleasant liquorice-spice prevails. But the true life has been strangled out if it by caramel. A tragedy, in whisky terms, as this is very rare malt from a lost distillery. **40%**. *Germany.*

Canadian Blended Whisky

Alberta Premium (89) n*23* so brittle, just one tap should crack it into a thousand pieces, yet it still offers enormous floral complexity; t*23* an indecent amount of flavours hits the tastebuds running, the grains are chewy and busy – this is hard as nails and superb! f*21* the downside as toffee takes over, sweet and soft; b*22* what I would give to see this whisky in the bottle without a drop of colouring: the complexity would blow the mind. As it is, just settle for mere brilliance. **40%**

Alberta Springs Rye Whisky 10 Years Old (86) n*23* signs of some crispness: beautiful fruit amid excellent oak; t*21* gentle grains melt into a toffeed softness, fruity and full-bodied; f*20* the toffee envelops the finale but some oak makes its way through; b*22* a softer, considerably less rye-rugged Canadian. Still an honour to drink Canadian rye that is just that. **40%**

Barton's Canadian 36 Months Old (78) n*19* t*20* f*19* b*20*. Sweet, toffeed, easy-going. **40%**. *Barton.*

Black Velvet DeLuxe (80) n*20* t*20* f*20* b*20*. Consistent, clean, toffeed Canadian with rich body and decent fizz on the finish. **40%**. *Schenley.*

Canadian Club Premium (78) n*19* t*20* f*19* b*20*. Lovely nip and pinch on the nose and some bite on the finish. Enlivening and, in parts, lush. The most visible Canadian whisky in the world, and pretty consistent, too. **40%**. *Hiram Walker.*

Canadian Club Sherry Cask Aged Eight Years (76) n*22* t*17* f*19* b*18*. The problem with putting Canadian whisky into what here appears to be a very high-quality sherry fresh-fill cask or two is that the spirit is naturally too light to withstand the grapey onslaught. The result is less whisky but more high-proof sherry. I admire the effort; the nose is quite lovely and the late finish also has some delightful fruit-spice moments. But the middle is just too one-dimensional. I'd keep the faith, but some tinkering is needed here. If you don't like it first time round, give it a year and see what happens. **41.3%**. *Hiram Walker.*

Canadian Club Reserve 10 Years of Age (88) n*21* intriguing mixture of soft fruit and rich corn; t*23* delicately sweet mouth arrival, then a slightly oily development and an almost heathery, floral complexity as the oak appears; f*22* beautiful play-out: the oaky vanilla dries attractively against the sweeter corn; b*22* this is great blending: a whisky sympathetic to the idea of balance and poise. An everyday dram of distinction. **40%**. *Hiram Walker.*

Canadian Club Premium Classic Aged 12 Years (86) n22 pretty chunky cream toffee; t22 more toffee but the corn is quite voluptuous and gentle spices hover; f21 curious bitter-sweet affair with the oak quite pronounced; b21 a busy Canadian which fails to match the Reserve's all round-charm and guile. No shortage of character, though. **40%**. *Hiram Walker*.

Canadian Host (74) n19 t18 f19 b18. Sweet, light, weirdly fruity. **40%**. *Barton*.

Canadian Mist (74) n19 t18 f19 b18. One of those helium-light blends with lots of sweet fruitiness. Lots of vanilla. **40%**. *Brown-Forman*.

Canadian Supreme (74) n18 t19 f19 b18. A light, banana-ry blend that is young but extremely fruity. **40%**

Corby's Canadian 36 Months Old (85) n20 subtle variants of vanilla; t21 sweetcorn to start, oils up and then fills the mouth; f22 develops into something almost sawdusty. Impressive complexity for one so young; b22 always attractive with fine bitter-sweet balance and I love the late spice kick-back. **40%** *Barton. Interesting label: as a keen ornithologist, I had no idea there were parrots in Canada. Must be related to the Norwegian Blue.*

Crown Royal (93) n23 seriously big rye offers a hard and fruity edge to the soft corn and oak; t24 rock-hard and crisp mouth arrival thanks to the early rye, softens for the corn and then the rye sends some fruity shockwaves around the palate; f22 bitter and booming: big controlled oak finale on gentle oil; b24 this has definitely changed in the last seven or eight years, as all blends must. It has a slightly larger rye dependency than of old but the mouthwatering effect is sublime. An international great. **40%**

Crown Royal Limited Edition (91) n24 floral tones to the fore as the rye shows its hand with a wonderful and perfectly matched hint of citrus, too; t23 hard at first, then softens as the corn gets a grip; f21 a touch bitter and dry at first but becomes fruity and complex as the small grain re-emerges; b23 delicious whisky which shows great sleight of hand in dealing with some powerful rye. Depending on the bottling, this vies alongside Crown Royal for sheer élan. **40%**

Crown Royal Special Reserve (88) n23 great subtlety: various small grains – you could swear barley was in there somewhere – gang together to offer a nose worth five minutes of anyone's time; t23 firm rye impact and then a rich development of sweet corn; f20 lots of vanilla but disappointingly flat with too much toffee at the death; b22 re-introduce some life back into the finale and you'd have a classic on your hands. Quite brilliant until the finish. **40%**

Forty Creek Barrel Select (new bottling) **(84)** n23 t19 f21 b21. Beautifully made clean whisky which appears to have a big fruit input, sherry-cask in style. The nose offers a delicious apricot jam and, though it goes a bit fat and confused on mouth entry, it re-forms to complete a fruit and nut finish unique in the whisky world. Very different and really worth finding. **40%**

Forty Creek Barrel Select (old bottling) **(79)** n20 t20 f19 b20. A well-made but curiously dry whisky despite some fruity edges. **40%**. *Kittling Ridge*.

Forty Creek Three Grain (84) n20 t20 f22 b22. Dry with a very attractive evolution of complex grain notes, coupled with decent oak. I have found the odd bottling that has been a touch feinty on the nose, but that hasn't affected its performance on the palate. **40%**. *Kittling Ridge*.

Gibson's Finest Aged 12 Years (86) n23 great aroma, brilliant balance between firm oak and even firmer corn; t22 lush mouthfeel, medium sweet with dry oak; f19 toffee kicks in and dulls things down way too much; b22 an otherwise great whisky spoiled by caramel. Nothing like the whisky it was. **40%**

Gibson's Finest Rare Aged 18 Years (93) n23 serious oak here, but the oily intensity of the corn balances out perfectly; t24 honey and corn combine wonderfully, drier oak notes act only as a counterweight; f23 long with less honey now, more demerara sugar brushed over the corn, with the oak continuing to offer a drier backdrop; **b**23 this is like one of those honied cereals you always have to have a second bowl of. It takes Canadian whisky into a new dimension. Truly brilliant. **40%**

Gibson's Finest Sterling Edition (88) n23 gentle, almost green corn and good oak, natural and unblemished; **t**21 oily and sweet, mildly hot then a wonderful delivery of molten corn; **f**22 a delicate, softly oaked finish with the spices reforming for a second attack; **b**22 a refreshing Canadian whisky in that I detect very little caramel interference. Great stuff! **40%**

Golden Wedding (see Schenley Golden Wedding)

Gooderham & Worts Ltd (90) n23 excellent trilogy of fresh corn, soft rye and something fruity; **t**23 a supremely weighted and deliciously sweet start bursts from the off. Not as much rye as I remember, though, as I was involved in the blending development of this brand; **f**22 lots of rich corn and deep oaky vanilla. Pure Canadian on a golden platter; **b**22 sensational Canadian, though on this bottling the rye input has been taken down a peg or two, which is a shame. Even so, a real stunner for its genre. **45%**

Hamilton (77) n18 **t**20 **f**20 **b**19. Young grains are kept on the leash to offer very sweet toffee. Very well made and easy-going. **40%**

Hiram Walker Special Old Rye Whisky (86) n22 clean corn with hints of oak and toffee; **t**21 superb bitter-sweet arrival; **f**22 some corn oil develops and vanilla frames the busy grain involvement; **b**21 a rich, solidly constructed, sweet whisky with some excellent late grain development. Good old-fashioned Canadian. **40%**

Lot No. 40 (93) n24 one of the most magnificent and rarest noses in the world: malted rye. Hints of spearmint chewing gum, kumquats, boiled sugar candy, all enveloped in that unique rye fruitiness; **t**24 brittle and hard at first then soft rye-powered fruit arrives, slightly peppery towards the middle, heavy roast cocoa and soft rye oil; **f**23 decent oak presence and some straggling fruity rye notes; **b**23 this is great whisky, irrespective of whichever country it came from. As for a Canadian, this is true rye whisky, one with which I was very proud to be associated in the early blending days. Elegant stuff. **43%**

McGuinness Silk Tassel (78) n19 **t**20 **f**19 **b**20. As silky as the name suggests: fruity, bitter orange and spice. **40%**

McMaster's (80) n19 **t**20 **f**21 **b**20. Velvet-textured and buttered sweet corn. Dangerously easy-to-drink session whisky. **40%.** Barton.

Northern Light (82) n20 **t**21 **f**20 **b**21. A young, natural, unpretentious Canadian grain blend with a good, clean character and first-class bite. Very attractive. **40%.** Barton.

Pike Creek finished in port barrels **(87) n**21 curious amalgam of corn and fresh wine; **t**23 soft, silky mouthfeel and then a whoosh of sweetness; **f**21 some spices prosper as the port makes a stand, genuinely fruity at first then becoming a little more bitter as the oak arrives; **b**22 much more complexity now than from the first bottlings. A Canadian of genuine style and character. **40%.** Allied.

Royal Reserve (85) n21 lots of lively corn ... and even a hint of rye; **t**21 clean, chewy, oily corn with decent oak presence; **f**22 really takes off as almost imperceptible rye gives a subtle deeper, richer edge; **b**21 a lovely Canadian which doesn't suffer from too much fruit interference and actually appears to have some discernible rye in the blend. **60%.** Corby.

Safeway Canadian Rye Whisky (75) n18 **t**18 **f**20 **b**19. A reasonable, clean, sweet if uninspiring Canadian. **40%.** UK.

Seagram's 83 Canadian Whisky (68) n18 **t**17 **f**16 **b**17. Caramel-dominated these days. **40%.** The "83" refers to 1883, not a 1983 vintage, and certainly nots its rating ...

Seagram's Five Star Rye Whisky (77) n19 **t**19 **f**20 **b**19. Corn-dominated despite the name. Enjoyable tail-off. **40%**

Seagram's VO (94) n24 the wonderfully weighted rye input offers lavender and violets, the oak input is quite beautiful: delicate and sexy; **t**23 corn oil softens the arrival and then a swathe of grainy-corny notes hits you head-on; **f**23 rye returns to declare open season on the tastebuds; **b**24 brilliant whisky not afraid to take on its rye roots. I guess the rye is malted and comes from Lawrenceburg, Indiana: I may be wrong ... it has been a few years since I was in the old Seagram lab, while they have had to take on the losing of stocks from the old Waterloo and LaSalle distilleries. And my blender mate there has retired. But such is the richness and complexity of this blend someone is still doing a supreme job there and understands what makes rye tick. If you don't have a bottle of this, then you don't possess a true, traditional Canadian. **40%**

Schenley Golden Wedding (83) n20 **t**21 **f**21 **b**21. Beautifully silky textured and rich. Great distillate used here which is both prickly and luxurious. Lovely stuff. **40%**

Schenley OFC Aged 8 Years (93) n24 brilliant nose: awesome complexity here as the grains tease around the vanilla. Perfectly weighted; **t**23 again, outstanding balance on the sweetness as you chew at the grain and lick at the thin sugary coating; **f**23 soft spices, vanilla and traces of late honey; **b**23 some re-writing of history here: the label says "Original Fine Canadian" under OFC. Actually, I'm pretty convinced it originally meant Old Fire Copper. I can think of other things OFC stand for, perhaps not suitable for this book, but I will settle instead for Outstandingly Flavoured Creation, for this remains one of Canada's top three finest traditional blends, one which comes back at you with each mouthful with greater and greater complexity. **40%**

Silk Tassel (see McGuinness Silk Tassel)

Tangle Ridge Aged 10 Years (67) n17 **t**17 **f**16 **b**17. One of the worst Canadians I have tasted in years: something sweet and unpleasant has been added. The mouthfeel and effect are dreadful, the nose isn't much better. Considering this is based on rye whisky, you could almost cry. Still see it in specialist outlets from time to time: one to avoid. **40%**

Tesco Canadian Whisky (75) n18 **t**18 **f**20 **b**19. As close as makes no difference to Safeway own label. **40%.** *UK.*

Wiser's De Luxe (86) n21 youngish: banana and soft vanilla teams with rich corn; **t**21 immediate soft spice but the corn dominates; **f**22 teasing vanilla and corn weave complex patterns; **b**22 one of the most dangerously quaffable drams you'll find in Canada. All the better for having minimal fruit interference. **40%.** *Hiram Walker.*

Wiser's De Luxe 10 Years Old (93) n23 a blueprint for Canadian noses: firm and hard-grained then, below the surface, soft, subtly sweetening vanilla. Clean and brittle; **t**23 big grain push that's hard and biting then gently yielding as the corn sweetens and fattens; **f**23 long and buttery with the cleanest, most gentle and softly sweetened corn imaginable. Hints of rye ping around the tastebuds at the death: you'll have no doubt why this is one of my regular whiskies when I'm working in Canada; **b**24 feeling this whisky come alive on the palate is like watching the dawn break: slow, sometimes imperceptible, but when it's over you feel you have experienced a timeless, simple beauty. **40%.** *Hiram Walker.*

Wiser's Special Blend (72) n18 **t**19 **f**17 **b**18. A pretty cramped blend with little expression. **40%**

European Whisky

Europe is getting bigger and more diverse ... and I don't just mean thanks the recent enlargement of the EU. In whisky terms distilling has not only expanded and embraced new cultures, but to a degree has become a little more refined.

It is a continent where distillers appear impressed by single malt and other whisky traditions, but are determined to go about things in their own, idiosyncratic way. In last year's Bible I told you about the quite brilliant, and entirely unique oat whisky from Austria's Oswald Weidenauer. Now, from France, is a massively flavoured dram made from Buckwheat – or Black Wheat as they call it there. Eddu Silver from Distillerie des Menhirs offered the first nose from a whisky sample sent to me in several years that completely confused me entirely. It nosed like a rye-style whisky yet clearly wasn't a rye and, equally, reminded me of spirits I had tasted in Japan. For good reason, it transpired, as buckwheat is used there.

Naturally, the biggest Eurosceptics come from the UK, where I have listened to arguments among people in the trade there that these whiskies are a poor relation to Scotch. And certain critics' marks I have seen given for these whiskies tend also to treat them as if by the same rules as, say, a Speyside malt.

Of course they could not be any more different. It is like comparing Pure Irish Pot Still to an Irish single malt or straight rye to a straight bourbon. Comparisons are pointless: they are a different species of whisky and should be enjoyed and treated that way. Therefore, in the marks I give the points are dropped only if they are poorly made or matured, or suffer by comparison to previous bottlings from the same distillery or region, or if vital balance is lacking. It is not because they don't taste like Scotch ...

In the same way, it would be pointless comparing a Buffalo Trace against the German Hessicher Whiskey, another fabulous breakthrough during the last year. Because in February 2004 was launched a genuinely pulse-racing addition to the European whisky lexicon with the continent's first specially produced bourbon-style whisky made from 56% corn and the remainder of the mashbill split equally between rye and malted barley. It is a treat of a whisky, as good as anything offered by German whisky distillers.

Just two weeks later came another newcomer: Welsh whisky. This had been the most successfully hyped of all the new whiskies to enter the marketplace and we were not to be let down as it made the most impressive start to any new European bottling I can ever remember. And busy: between March 1st and June 1st there had been five different bottlings to help quench the demand.

Within a few years a fruity drop of Cornish whisky will also be making its way into the market place. A Belgium malt has already been bottled, though it cannot yet be called whisky because it is not three years of age; Mackmyra of Sweden, meanwhile, are holding back the launch of their range of maturing whiskies.

It is hard to believe that the next twelve months will be quite such an eventful one in Europe, although you never know. It is not unknown for distillers across that continent to make small batches of whisky and release it only if they are satisfied with its outcome. For that reason any package arriving at my tasting lab with a European postmark heads the queue for opening. In the last year French buckwheat whisky and German "bourbon" arrived and conquered, plus the best drop yet was despatched from the only malt distillery on wheels, Switzerland's Swissky. Together they helped create what might well be regarded upon in the not too distant future as a classic, a liquid golden year for European whisky.

The big question is: just what is coming next?

AUSTRIA
HAIDER

❖❖ **J H Feinster Roggenwhisky L4/00** db **(88) n**22 fabulously pungent in that unique Haider style: both floral and fruity at the same time and in equal measure with a dollop of manuka honey for extra kerpow; **t**23 soft mouth arrival, a quiet punch-up between spices and then an oily smattering of rye; **f**21 quite hard but always chewy rye and oak; **b**22 this is a highly unusual, in your face, whisky which takes some acclimatising to: once you get the picture it's fun all the way. **41%**

❖❖ **J H Feinster Roggenwhisky Fassstarke L4/99** db **(88) n**21 a distinctively herbal rye style with minimum fruit; **t**22 mouthfilling and sweetened by almost molassed rye; **f**23 the rye hangs round but only to keep the oak development under control; unrefined sugar softens the final blows; **b**22 something of a bruising whisky where the aggressive rye fist-fights all comers ... and wins. **54%**

❖❖ **J H Roggen-Malzwhisky Reserve Nougat L17/99** db **(75) n**18 t18 f20 b19. Sharp, hot and hard as nails. **43%**

J H Feinster Roggenwhisky L21/98 (81) n18 t20 f22 b21. Very sweet with excellent oak weight and even rye distribution. Lovely spice v demerara at the finale. **41%**

J H Feinster Roggenwhisky Fassstarke L42/97 (91) n20 sharp, hard and flinty. The grains really kick hard here; **t**24 brilliant weight on the mouth and then a series of slow spicy explosions, each unleashing clear, chewy rye on the palate: a pyrotechnical display of rye at near enough perfection; **f**24 superb chocolate adds sublime balance to the fruity rye and bitter oranges; **b**23 look at this from any angle and you have a minor masterpiece on your hands: quite sublime. **54%**

J H Gersten-Malzwhisky L10/99 db **(80) n**19 t21 f19 b21. Slightly chalky with a tad more oak interference than it needs. That said, the malt is gristy, chewy and clean with a slight buzz of spice. Impressive. **41%**

J H Gersten-Malzwhisky L10/99 Fassstarke db **(83) n**20 t21 f21 b21. Holds together better on the nose at a fuller strength plus an extra hint of honey on the finish. More compact and not far off delicious. **54%**

J H Gersten-Malzwhisky Karamell L66/98 db **(74) n**16 t19 f20 b19. An off-beam nose – well it was a very early barrel – is rescued to a degree by a sweet malt surge towards the death. **41%**

J H Gersten-Malzwhisky Karamell L66/98 Fassstarke db **(77) n**16 t21 f20 b20. Much more early intense malt offers a sugared coating at the start and a hint of liquorice on the finale. A big difference. **55%**

J H Roggen-Malzwhisky L20/98 db **(90) n**22 intense, sweet rye and clean, spicy, fruit; **t**23 outstanding clarity of crisp, hard rye that sweetens by the second, quite plummy and juicy; **f**22 the bitterness returns – and then some – and dry pounding oaky tones add a late chalkiness. Hints of honey lurk in the background; **b**23 simply excellent and quite classic rye whisky. Congratulations to all concerned for a delicious job well done. **41%**

J H Roggen-Malzwhisky Fassstarke L6/98 db **(88) n**20 surprisingly closed nose; **t**25 high octane, faultlessly clean rye that completely hammers the palate with a welter of fruity, cherry-laden punches. Clean, chewy and breathtaking: man, this is rye whisky!!!! **f**21 just like the nose, flattens alarmingly; **b**22 if it could be like the arrival on the palate from nose to finish, we'd have a world classic! **55%**

J H Roggen-Malzwhisky Nougat L3/99 db **(74) n**17 t19 f19 b19. The rye has been flattened into submission. **41%**

J H Gersten-Malzwhisky Nougat L3/99 Fassstarke db **(78) n**17 t20 f21 b20. The rye sparkles much more here than at the lower strength, especially on the long finish. **50%**

WELDENAUER DISTILLERY

Waldviestler Hafer Whisky 1998 db **(79)** n20 t21 f18 b20. An oily, assertive whisky that, while sweet, shows signs of a bitterness and imbalance despite the enormous fruitiness on the nose. That said, the oats do come through loud and clear and make quite a porridge, if a slightly salted one. **42%**

Waldviestler Hafer Whisky 1999 db **(89)** n23 oat-crunchies breakfast cereal combined with soft honey and a sprinkling of sugar: amazingly clean yet so much going on; t21 initially hard on the palate then it softens as a grainy sweetness spreads across the roof of the mouth, excellent texture; f22 pure oats: just so pure and clean, you could almost chew it: remarkable; b23 this is unique whisky and as such deserves time in the glass to oxidise and warm. Once you become accustomed to the taste, the complexity is spellbinding. **42%**

Waldviestler Hafer Whisky 2000 db **(94)** n23 some delicate spices link beautifully with oak 'n' oats; t24 sumptuous, just about perfectly weighted with the most sublime oil involvement, then that unique oaty quality that is sweetish, but softly so, yet with a drying mealiness; f24 long, really intense oat character which dries in the most delicious manner of any whisky I have ever encountered! b23 this was the best new whisky worldwide of 2002. Totally unique in character, flawless in distillation and awesome in subtlety. **42%**

∵ **Waldviestler Hafer Whisky** (with 2004 silber medaille sticker on neck) db **(89)** n21 sharp and punchy nose; a salted porridge character; t23 so much sweeter than the nose with the most astonishing take-off of tart oat, with a countering subtle, milky sweetness that fills the palate; f22 still sharp and bitters slightly; a vaguely rye-like fruitiness hovers around a bit; b23 brilliant, though not quite the all-round grace of the last uniquely oaty bottling; but still your taste buds know they've been hafered ... **42%**. *Bottled Nov 03, though not stated.*

WOLFRAM ORTNER DESTILLERIE

∵ **Nock-Land Pure Malt 2000** db **(77)** n18 t20 f19 b20. Intense, sweet malt and spices combine with a mild tobacco effect for a curious, distinctive but decent dram. **48%**

BELGIUM
DISTILLERIE LAMBICOOL

∵ **Belgium Pure Malt** db **(81)** n19 t19 f22 b21. This is a new make and therefore not strictly whisky. The distillers are marketing this in order to fund their whisky-making venture, a wise move not least because the rich, superbly textured finish overcomes the hesitant tobacco-smoke start for a rewarding and impressive finale; and there is even lavender on the nose of the empty glass. Well worth finding a bottle to help support a promising cause. **40%**

BULGARIA

12 Years Finest Bulgarian db **(81)** n19 t21 f21 b20. Some whisky! Takes no prisoners with an onslaught of what appears to be fresh European oak: more like a 35–40-year-old Scotch. Chewy, sweet with a big liquorice finish. Some decent malt does makes it through and shows at the end. Beautifully textured, clean and obviously well made. Very drinkable whisky indeed, but not for the lily-livered. **43%**

FRANCE
Single Malt
DISTILLERIE WARENGHEM

Armorik db **(63)** n15 t18 f14 b16. Too feinty and what appears to be caramel dependent. Some of the fat, oiliness is pleasant for a while, but a long way to go on the learning curve here. **40%**

DISTILLERIE DES MENHIRS

❖ **Eddu Silver** db **(91)** n *21* slight tobacco yet clean enough to allow the grain a big fruity entrance; t *24* an outstanding arrival of something sweet and simmering; a unique mouthwatering character appears half rye half barley yet something deliciously different again; the salivating sweetness that builds is surprising and has a distinct Demerara sugar feel to it; f *22* quite a deep and lengthy final chapter with the clean, boiled apple fruitiness balancing comfortably with subtle oak. Some bitterness digs in but is dealt with by pulsating grain; b *24* the best whisky to come out of France by some considerable distance. This is distilled from Buckwheat, the kind of thing the Japanese are tempted to work with on their own indigenous spirits. The massive flavour profile will win appreciation from anyone who enjoys a no-holds-barred rye. **40%**

Blended

Whisky Breton (80) n *19* t *20* f *21* b *20*. An altogether better effort; malty and assertively drinkable with attractive, firm, chewy grains and a late, lingering sweetness. A lively, characterful and creditable blend. **40%**

GERMANY
BLAUE MAUS

❖ **Blaue Maus Single Malt** Fass Nr 2 dist 8/92, bott 3/04 db **(83)** n *20* t *21* f *22* b *20*. The nose offers childhood memories of damp washing through a mangler; the malt is intense and satisfying but altogether an unusually bitter offering. **40%**

Blaue Maus Single Malt Whisky Fassstarke 2, dist 8/93, bott 9/02 db **(84)** n *19* t *22* f *21* b *22*. This is more of a man than a maus: big, oily, heavy-weighted deep molassed sweetness. Lovely spices, too. Really well balanced and a better nose would catapult it into the top bracket. **40%**

Glen Mouse Pure Malt Whisky Fassstarke 2, dist 8/86, bott 1/98 db **(81)** n *20* t *19* f *21* b *21*. Exceptionally clean distillate with massive oak richness. **40%**

❖ **Krottentaler Single Malt** Fass Nr 2 dist 7/94, bott 3/04 db **(87)** n *21* fresh-baked fruitcake; t *23* quite an impressive arrival of legions of burnt raisins sweetened with toffee; f *22* sweet with lingering oak and barley; b *21* caramel cuts out some complexity but also the bitterness: a very big whisky. **40%**

Krottentaler Single Malt Whisky Fassstarke 1, dist 6/94, bott 7/02 db **(77)** n *16* t *21* f *21* b *19*. On the feinty side but, as ever, the result is a big whisky with chewy sweet oils and intense malt. Once over the nose, it's a lovely journey. **40%**

Mouse db **(92)** n *22* rich, big vanilla and thick malt: a touch of distant honey to a nose more akin to bourbon than malt; t *24* sensational: the mouthfeel is near perfect with just the right amount of subtle sweetness leaking into the big oak; f *23* more bitter as the tannins mount, roast Java coffee; b *23* this is an outstanding whisky that any bourbon lover will cross a few countries for. And you will have to: this is malt kept in a small barrel at the distillery bar at Egolsheim/Neuses. You cannot get it anywhere else. Strength unknown.

❖ **Piraten Pur Malt Whisky** Fass Nr 1 dist 8/95, bott 1/04 db **(84)** n *20* t *21* f *22* b *21*. As chewy as a mouth of tobacco and Bristol-fashion on the superbly honeyed if somewhat toffeed finale. Whimsically, the first-ever whisky I know of to come with its own leather eye-patch: just as well you don't need your sight to enjoy this. Do ye all knock it back at once ... **40%**

❖ **Schwarzer Pirat Single Malt** Fass Nr 1 dist 7/94, bott 3/04 db **(86)** n *19* a tad feinty but some bourbony oak compensates; t *22* lots of bitter-sweet skirmishes; torched raisins; f *23* excellent spice and buzz adds to the toffee-apple finale; b *22* similar in many ways to Krottentaler (bott 04) except that there is less toffee and the complexity has risen accordingly. **40%**

Schwarzer Pirat Single Malt Whisky Fassstarke 3, dist 7/94, bott 9/02 db **(77)** n*17* t*20* f*20* b*20*. Again the nose is hard going but this is compensated for by a sweet, spicy, charismatic malt on the palate. **40%**

⠿ **Spinnaker Single Malt** Fass nr 2 dist 7/93, bott 1/04 db **(85)** n*19* malty and containing that distinct Blau Maus character; t*22* beautifully mouthfilling, delicately sweet malt with not a single blemish; f*22* much more intense with something smoky adding to the already thickening body; b*22* seriously enjoyable, intense malt whisky. **40%**

Spinnaker Single Malt Whisky Fassstarke 3, dist 9/93, bott 9/02 db **(82)** n*19* t*22* f*21* b*20*. Superbly made malt, delicate in its weight and possessing a light muscovado sugar sweetness the entire voyage. Just a little heavy on the nose to be a ship-shape great whisky, but I could drink this one any time any place. Especially Germany ... **40%**

GRUELS

Schwabischer Whisky Single Grain db **(80)** n*19* t*21* f*19* b*21*. Full credit for an excellent first attempt. The nose is good if a tad off-key and the dying embers a little bitter. But the intense oily, rich, sweet, buttery middle is a delight. Familiarity breeds anything but contempt with this characterful whisky. **43%**

⠿ **Schwabischer Whisky Single Grain 1991** db dist Feb 91 **(84)** n*20* t*22* f*21* b*21*. Nutty-toffee nose translates into a firm, mouth watering whisky of some finesse that loses out at the finish with that toffee again. **43%**

BRENNEREI HOEHLER

⠿ **Hessicher Whiskey** db dist 17 Feb 01 bott 17 Feb 04 **(91)** n*23* A diamond hard nose, the sparkle offered by a clever malt-oaky sweetness, the rigidity by the unforgiving rye: lovely stuff; t*22* stunning arrival of rye that does a comprehensive hatchet job on the tastebuds as it gets into stride. The corn offers a more neutral sweetness; f*23* remains hard at the core but there is a toffee sweetness lurking and some latent spice b*23* one of the real perks of the job is the sheer diversity: here we have a superbly made bourbon style German whiskey with roughly 56/22/22 recipe of corn/rye/malted barley. And it has been distilled to a very high standard. It doesn't taste exactly like bourbon, nor is it like malt. But it is entirely delicious. Go and find it. **42%**

SLYRS

⠿ **Slyrs Bavarian Single Malt 2001** db **(79)** n*18* t*19* f*22* b*20*. Different fingerprints here from previous bottlings with the nose offering curious bacon pizza and the palate shimmering with distant honey on the excellent malty finish. **43%**

Slyrs Bavarian Single Malt 1999 db **(84)** n*20* t*21* f*22* b*21*. A very competently made malt whisky that celebrates its clean simplicity. The nose is vanilla-bound but on the palate it takes off slowly, first clearing a soft oak hurdle and then really letting the malt go into overdrive. Thoroughly enjoyable, high-quality quaffing whisky that will need to be made in greater amounts if they keep up this standard. **43%**

SONNEN SCHEIN

⠿ **Sonnen Schein Sherry Wood Finish 1989** db bott 00 **(57)** n*14* t*17* f*12* b*14*. Oddly enough, the sherry appears to accentuate the dreadful tobacco smoke character to this. The finish really does hurt. **43%**

Sonnen Schein Single Malt Whisky 1989 bott 00 db **(69)** n*17* t*17* f*18* b*17.* Very unusual stale tobacco aroma and possibly (I am guessing as a lifelong non-smoker) taste. A whisky that tastes slightly better second time round, though not by much. Room for improvement here, I think. **43%**

POLAND
LIEBONA GIORA
Dark Whisky (77) n19 t19 f20 b19. Lots of grain character with perhaps a tad too much toffee, but the texture is alluring and appealing and finishes well with decent oak and lustre. **40%**

SPAIN
Blended
DYC (81) n20 t21 f19 b21. Thin and grainy in parts but the bite is attractive and assertive while the malt comfortably holds its own. **40%**

SWITZERLAND
BRENNEREI-ZENTRUM BAUERNHOF
⠿ **Swissky** db **(91)** n23 young, clean, fresh malt which sparkles with a hint of apple: one of the best noses on the European scene; t23 stunningly clean arrival and then the most delicate of malty displays that all hinges around a juicy youth to the barley. The sweetness is controlled, refined and evenly distributed; a soft oiliness helps to lubricate the tastebuds; f22 no less soft and simple with the oak offering the kind of weight that can barely be detected; b23 while retaining a distinct character, this is the cleanest, most refreshing malt yet to come from mainland Europe. Hats off to Edi Bieri for this work of art. Moving stuff. **42%**

Swissky (label shows boxed drawing of pot still) db **(84)** n19 t22 f21 b22. Only the most distant hint of feintiness takes away from the beauty of this rich malt. The oils are sublime, as usual from this distillery, and the malt is sweet and chewy. If anything, I am marking down. **42%**

Swissky (label shows man working a pot still) db **(83)** n20 t21 f21 b21. A thinnish, clean malt at first with some decent oak depth to bolster the copper-rich finale. **42%**

Swissky '00 Selection db **(89)** n21 intense, clean malt tinged with hints of citrus and hazelnut; t23 stunning mouth arrival: the texture is near enough perfect and the development of the sweet malt is a delight; f22 soft vanilla works well with the light oil and generous malt, praline on the finale; b23 what a fabulous whisky! The texture is to die for and the malty-nutty complexity is extraordinary. Probably a nation's finest whisky yet. **42%**

LES VIGNETTES
⠿ **Glen Vignettes "Abred" Peated Swhisky Pur Malt** db **(89)** n22 wonderfully delicate peat; a beautifully gristy nose and although there is a background noise, it is easily ignored; t23 awesome delivery with top-rate bitter-sweet edge as the peat yodels without an off-note in the background; f22 dryish vanilla and sweet peat; b22 fabulous whisky from a distillery that finds peat to its liking and suiting its style: no coastal notes here – hardly surprising ...! – but just great virtuosity with the smoke. **45%**

⠿ **Glen Vignettes "Annouim" Initial Swhisky Pur Malt** db **(85)** n19 initial celery, more malt as it warms; t22 much richer than the nose, sweeter and cleaner: impressive, in fact; f22 toffee and barley; b22 the odd distilling anonymously cannot disguise a top-grade malt of easy drinking. **45%**

⠿ **Glen Vignettes "Gwenwed" Syrah Cask Swhisky Pur Malt** db **(74)** n17 t20 f18 b19. A lush, big-impact malt weighed down by caramel and that distinctive celery-spicy distilling character. **45%**

TURKEY
Ankara Turk Viskisi (80) n20 t20 f19 b21. Soft and gentle despite the clear grain with soft delicate oak on the finish. Quite beautifully balanced: a genuinely charming whisky to be taken seriously. **43%**

WALES

⸭ **Penderyn** db cask nos 5–99 **(91)** n23 raisins on the nose, light playful malt and then a backdrop of sweet wine; t23 absolutely staggering arrival on the palate of malt landing with almost snowflake delicateness. Immediately a second movement, this time of bitter-sweet fruit, blood orange included, sweeps down over the startled tastebuds. Astonishing stuff; f22 slightly bitter and tart towards the finish and two variants of oak begin to dive into the melee; b23 it was my pleasure and privilege to be the first person from outside the company to discuss and analyse the beauty of this whisky at its spectacular official launch on St David's Day 2004. I told them they were tasting not just an historic malt whisky, but one that deserved the highest praise in its own right. Re-tasting it again for the Bible, I stand by every word. **46%**

⸭ **Penderyn** db bott code 04/02 **(89)** n22 a sharp freshness from the Madeira casks is very apparent; there is a boiled sweet fruitiness also while the malt is ethereal; t22 big malt weight defies the nose, clean yet pleasantly cluttered; f22 the fruit returns here for a surprisingly chunky contest with thick malt; b23 exceptional balance and charisma for a whisky so young. **46%**

⸭ **Penderyn** db bott code 04/03 **(86)** n21 the lightest aroma yet with pencil-thin malt just pricking through the fruity veil; t21 the arrival of the Madeira out-manoeuvres the malt and kicks up some spice in the process; f22 happier with itself as the fruit and malt find common ground, chewy with soft oils and the very first, surprising, signs of cocoa; b22 not quite so well integrated as the previous bottlings, though cask choice was probably limited by now. Even so, still a gentle joy, especially for its tender years. **46%**

⸭ **Penderyn** db bott code 04/04 **(90)** n23 much better with the Madeira offering a rich, raisiny cushion on the nose, a teasing bite which is sweetened by bourbon; t23 deeply satisfying fruit that has stunning depth to its controlled, demerara sweetness; f21 light, fruit-free with cocoa finale; b23 the old Welsh magic has returned. Brilliant! **46%**

⸭ **Penderyn Cask Strength First Release** db **(86)** n21 almost a hint of juniper amid the clean malt; t21 thin fruit and warming; some liquorice and botanical tones again with a distinct Genevre style; f22 still that juniper thread is apparent, buzzed by malts; really very mouthwatering and curiously satisfying finale; b22 a very different Penderyn that should seduce the gin and tonic merchants: oddly delicious. **61.8%**

⸭ **The Penderyn Millenium Cask 2000** db **(90)** n22 delicate soft-bourbon oaky tones, which is not what you expect from a three-year-old whisky; the fruit is soft yet somehow champions the clean malt; t22 warming, massively malt at first and then big vanilla and a mouthwatering grape and lychee fruit cocktail; f23 just so long with loads of natural toffee vanilla perfectly at home with the concentrated malt and layered fruitiness; b23 this is one very complex whisky offering style and first-class integrity. A dilemma for those who own this historic whisky: luckily you can taste the miniature while keeping the full bottle for posterity. Or should that be the other way round? **61.6%**

World Whiskies

I have long said that whisky can be made just about anywhere in the world; that it is not writ large in stone that it is the inalienable right for just Scotland, Ireland, Kentucky and Canada to have it all to themselves. And so, it seems, it is increasingly being proved.

Perhaps only sandy deserts and fields of ironstone can prevent its make physically and Islam culturally, though even that has not been a barrier to malt whisky being distilled in both Pakistan and Turkey. While not even the world's highest mountains or jungle can prevent the spread of barley and pot.

Outside of North America and Europe, the whisky's traditional nesting sites, you can head in any direction and find it being made. South America may be well known for its rum, but in the south of Brazil, an area populated by Italian and German settlers many generations back, malt whisky is thriving. In even more lush and tropical climes it can now also be found, with Thailand leading the way.

Japan has long represented Asia with distinction and whisky-making there is in such an advanced state and to such a high standard the *Whisky Bible* has given it its own section. But while neighbouring South Korea has ended its malt distilling venture, further east, and at a very unlikely altitude, Nepal has forged a small industry to team up, geographically, with fellow malt distillers India and Pakistan.

And Africa is also represented. There has long been a tradition of blending Scotch malt with South African grain. Last year I mentioned that I had heard of a South African single malt. Well now I can report that I have tracked it down: Three Ships Ten Years old from the James Sedgwick Distillery, a pleasant enough offering without uprooting trees. Hopefully I will have visited it by the time the 2006 edition is inside your pocket and been able to file a feature for the website. A continent's one and only distillery is well worth discovering.

This section is shorter than I originally planned. The reason is simple: rather than use old, outdated tasting notes, my aim has been to gather fresh samples, preferably by visiting or re-visiting these far off distilleries.

One new whisky-making region is due immediate study: Australia. From a distance of 12,000 miles, the waters around Australia's distilleries appear to be muddied. Quality appears to range from the very good to extremely poor. And during the back end of 2004 I managed to discover this first hand when I visited three Tasmanian distilleries and Bakery Hill in Melbourne.

Certainly green shots are beginning to sprout at the Tasmania Distillery which has now moved its operation away from its Hobart harbour site to an out of town one close to the airport. The first bottlings of that had been so bad that it will take some time and convincing for those who have already tasted it to go back to it again. However, having been to the warehouse – and currently tasting samples from every single cask they have on site – I can report that it is only a matter of time before those first offerings will be little more than distant – though horrific – memories. Keep your eyes on www.whiskybible.com and you will discover when it will be safe to put your head above the parapet.

It may still be a year or two before Whisky Tasmania's malt is ripe enough for bottling, though they have now made some heavily peated spirit which will give them vatting options in three or four years time.

Away from Tasmania there is malt distilling – and further plans to distil – all over Australia. On that has already made it into the shops is from Booie Range, which like Sullivan's Cove suffers from a frighteningly unattractive nose, but unlike early bottlings of the Hobart whisky regroups and recovers significantly on the palate.

The remaining casks of Wilson's malt from New Zealand are disappearing fast and when in New Zealand last year I discovered the stills from there were not just making rum in Fiji but whisky as well. We are all aware of the delights of island whisky ... just what a Pacific Island whisky will be like though? I can feel another journey coming on ....

Which leaves Antarctica as the only continent not making whisky, though what some of those scientists get up to for months on end no one knows. Still, effluent might be a problem there, though it should make the perfect whisky with ice ...

AUSTRALIA
BAKERY HILL DISTILLERY, 1999. Operating

Bakery Hill Classic Malt cask No. 08, bott 04, db **(91) n**22 florid, highly intense malt with a speckle of feint and peat; **t**23 beautifully salivating and rich with the intensity of the sweet malt leaping off the scales; **f**23 mega cocoa, long and wonderfully structured wind-down; **b**23 this has moved on massively from the first test bottlings of a year ago. The slight feints burn off on the nose quickly and we are left with something copper and malt rich and very special from Australia's finest distillery. **46%**

Bakery Hill Classic Malt Cask Strength db **(87) n**22 astonishingly clean with gooseberries attached to the malt; **t**22 young malt rips through the tastebuds and settles comfortably with an oily landing; **f**22 big cocoa thrust seems to be the hallmark of the distillery; **b**21 relatively youthful and for all its malty razzmatazz would benefit with a touch more oak. **65%**

Bakery Hill Double Wood cask No. 0508, bott 04, db **(80) n**19 **t**19 **f**21 **b**21. The introduction of the French oak serves only to add a certain fruity astringency to an otherwise clean and attractive dram. **46%**

Bakery Hill Peated Malt cask No. 12, bott 04, db **(90) n**22 soft peat harmonises with intense malt, deftly weighted and oozing class; **t**23 there is teasing gentleness to the smoke that borders on eroticism, the sweetness is refined and layered with oak piling in the riches; **f**22 thins out a little towards the dry finale; **b**23 for sureness of touch at such young age, this is quite an amazing malt. For those who prefer their peat brushed on rather than glued. **46%**

Bakery Hill Peated Malt Cask Strength cask No. 14, bott 04 (aged 4 years), db **(94) n**24 kippery aroma with a dash of lemon on the side; **t**23 a real mouthful of subtle, pulsating peats which have to battle through the sweet malt; young but has such extraordinary depth and charisma; **f**24 goes into overdrive, fabulously long with layer upon layer of encrusted peat that clings limpet-like to the roof of the mouth; **b**23 show this to anyone and tell them it not an Islay: they will never believe you. The phenol levels here are quite stunning, but so too is the excellence of distillation. I found this cask in Bakery Hill's warehouse last year and swooned, even queried its origins – so distillery Dave Baker bottled it! The good news is that I have tasted a cask or two similar to this at the distillery: there is more of this kind of brilliance to come over the years! **65%**

BOOIE RANGE DISTILLERY

Booie Range Single Malt db **(72) n**14 **t**20 **f**19 **b**19. Mounts the hurdle of the wildly off-key nose impressively with a distinct, mouth watering barley richness to the palate that really does blossom even on the finish. **40%**

TASMAN DISTILLERY

Great Outback Rare Old Australian Single Malt (92) n24 I could stick my nose in a glass of this all day. This is sensational: more a question of what we don't have here! The malt is clean, beautifully defined and dovetails with refined, orangey-citrus notes. The oak is near perfection adding only a degree of tempered weight. I don't detect peat, but there is some compensating Blue Mountain coffee; **t**24 just so beautifully textured with countless waves of clean, rich malt neither too sweet nor too dry. This is faultless distillate; **f**21 lightens considerably with the oak vanilla dominating; **b**23 What can you say? An Australian whisky distillery makes a malt to grace the world's stage. But you can't find it outside of Australia. This will have to be rectified. Strength not known

LARK DISTILLERY

Lark Distillery Single Malt Single Cask Bottled April 01 db **(88)** **n**22 apples and cinnamon: other peppery spices dig in to the oily malt; **t**22 massively malty, clean and fruity with a powdery oak offering further complexity; oily and fat; **f**22 beautifully spiced and delicate with fluttering malty tones caressing the palate; **b**22 this is lovely whisky, superbly made and offering both guile and charisma. Congratulations: Australia has entered the ranks of serious whisky distilling nations. **40%**

Lark Distillery Single Malt Single Cask Bottled Sep 02 db **(82)** **n**18 **t**22 **f**21 **b**21. A touch feinty but the malt is intense and recovers superbly on the palate for a genuinely delicious dram. Certainly one of the maltiest bottlings you'll find worldwide, almost Cardhu-like. **40%**

Lark Distillery Single Malt Single Cask Bottled Jan 03 db **(83)** **n**19 **t**21 **f**22 **b**21. Again big malt intensity but the body is thinner, the finish, as the malts begin to show their complexity, is brilliant. A superb dram with a slight nose blemish. **40%**

⋯⋯ **Lark Distillery Single Malt Whisky** Sept 03 db **(79)** **n**18 mildly feinty, though some very delicate peat sweetens and enriches. No shortage of complexity and weight; **t**21 well oiled with big barley middle. Fills the mouth where delicate hints of peat first spreads then offers a peppery theme; really excellent early sweetness which endures; **f**20 pounding malt, big and oily which continues to fill the mouth until some oak makes a late, drying appearance; **b**20 this has to be the Jekyll and Hyde of malt whisky. Taste it direct from the bottle and the feints trouble you. Allow it to breath in the glass for an hour and burn off the oils and you are left with a superbly peated malt of great character. Patience is certainly a virtue with this one. (My marks are an average between the two).

Lark Distillery Single Malt 2nd Release October 1999 (78) **n**17 **t**21 **f**20 **b**20. Mildly feinty and fruity, it does offer a mouthwatering malty theme which is realised on the palate. A dram best served if a small proportion is put into a smallish bottle and kept warm overnight. This will burn off some of the feints and you are left with a very drinkable Aussie malt. **40%**

SMALL CONCERN DISTILLERY

⋯⋯ **Cradle Mountain Pure Tasmanian Malt (87)** **n**21 curiously vivid bourbon character; sweet vanilla with hints of tangerine and hazelnut. Really very, very attractive; **t**22 an almost perfect translation onto the palate: gloriously sweet and gently nutty. The mouthfeel and body is firm and oily at the same time, the barley sparkles as the oak fades. Exceptionally subtle, clean and well made; **f**21 pretty long with some cocoa offering a praline effect; **b**23 a knock-out malt from a sadly now lost distillery in Tasmania. Faultlessly clean stuff with lots of new oak character but sufficient body to guarantee complexity. **43%**

Vatted Malt

⋯⋯ **Cradle Mountain** db **(77)** **n**19 **t**21 **f**18 **b**19. Doesn't quite gel for me, though it has some delicious malty moments. **46%**. *This is a vatting of Aussie malt from Cradle Mountain and Springbank single malt scotch.*

∴ **Cradle Mountain Double** db **(88)** n*20* no shortage of fruit with tangerines and diced green apples to the fore; t*23* in your face malt of almost awesome intensity. Lashings of clean barley, grassy notes showing both age and youth; f*23* lingers at first, then the Cradle Mountain signature of fruit and nuts descends. Also the cocoa is back with some serious oak present but always in control; b*22* this appears to be a different vatting to the 46% with greater Tasmanian whisky evident – although it isn't! Much more poise and zest and no shortage of charisma. Brilliant stuff. **54.4%.** *This is a vatting of Aussie malt from Cradle Mountain and single malt scotch from Springbank.*

TASMANIA DISTILLERY

Old Hobart db **(69)** n*16* t*19* f*17* b*17.* The nose still has some way to go before it can be accepted as a mainstream malt, though there is something more than a little coastal about it this time. However, the arrival on the palate is another matter and I must say I kind of enjoyed its big, oily and increasingly sweet maltiness and crushed sunflower seed nuttiness towards the end. Green (and yellow) shoots are growing. The whisky is unquestionably getting better. **60%**

∴ **Old Hobart** db **(78)** n*18* t*20* f*21* b*19.* Ground-breaking stuff. The first-ever truly drinkable whisky from the Tasmania Distillery. An impressive double whammy of virgin oak and fresh Australian port wood manages to overpower the usual ugly aroma that offers little more than a minor blemish. Some bite and spice on the finish guarantees complexity to a fruity procession. **60%.** *(2003 bottling).*

∴ **Sullivan's Cove** db **(61)** n*13* t*15* f*17* b*16.* Some malt but typically grim, oily and dirty; awesomely weird. **40%.** *(2003 bottling). Australia.*

Sullivan's Cove Classic (capped with a black seal) db **(64)** n*15* t*16* f*17* b*16.* A feinty dram, off-key and in need of a good tidy-up, though much better and cleaner than the gold seal. As this is a distillery's first attempt, I would rather encourage than fire off shells at a soft target. My advice is always to buy a bottle and see how a new distillery evolves. Again, the whisky can be improved dramatically by heating the glass in your hand to burn off the excess oils. **40%**

Sullivan's Cove Classic (capped with a gold seal) db **(58)** n*12* t*15* f*16* b*15.* Feinty with a weird aroma of rotting vegetables on top. Some malt gurgles through, but it's not a pleasant experience. The gold cap and seal at the top was used only by the founders of the distillery and therefore represents the first-ever bottlings from Sullivan's Cove. **40%**

WHISKY TASMANIA

Based in Burnie, have yet to bottle.

BRAZIL
HEUBLEIN DISTILLERY

Durfee Hall Malt Whisky **(81)** n*18* t*22* f*20* b*21.* Superbly made whisky; the intensity of the malt is beautifully layered without ever becoming too sweet. Very light bodied and immaculately clean. Good whisky by any standards. **43%**

UNION DISTILLERY

Barrilete (72) n*18* t*19* f*18* b*17.* Nothing particularly wrong with it technically; it just lacks vitality. Thin but extremely malt intense. **39.1%**

Blended

∴ **Green Valley Special Reserve** batch 07/01 **(70)** n*16* t*19* f*17* b*18.* A softly oiled, gently bitter-sweet blend with a half meaty, half boiled sweet nose. An unusual whisky experience. **38.1%.** *Muraro & Cia.*

∵∴ **Natu Nobilis** batch 277929A **(81)** n19 t21 f20 b21. The grain is sympathetic and soft; the malt is shy but makes telling, complex interceptions. Very easy and enjoyable dramming. **39%.** *Seagram do Brasil.*

∵∴ **Malte Barrilete Blended Whisky** batch 001/03 **(76)** n18 t20 f19 b19. This brand has picked up a distinctive apple-fruitiness in recent years and some extra oak, too. **39.1%.** *Union Distillery.*

∵∴ **O Monge** batch 02/02 **(69)** n17 t18 f17 b17. Poor nose but it recovers with a malty mouth arrival but the thinness of the grain does few favours. **38.5%.** *Union Distillery.*

∵∴ **Pitt's (84)** n21 t20 f22 b21. The pits it certainly aint!! A beautifully malted blend where the barley tries to dominate the exceptionally flinty grain whenever possible. Due to be launched later in 2004, this will be the best Brazil has to offer – though some fine tuning can probably improve the nose and middle even further and up the complexity significantly. I hope, when I visit the distillery early in 2005, I will be able to persuade them to offer a single malt: on this evidence it should, like Pitt's, be an enjoyable experience and perfect company for any World Cup finals. **40%.** *Busnello Distillery.*

INDIA
AMRUT DISTILLERY

∵∴ **Amrut Single Malt** db B.No.01 25-2-04 **(82)** n20 t22 f19 b21. The press picked this up and made a point of saying that experts can't tell between this and top Scottish malt. Interesting. Certainly this can be easily mistaken for an old Scotch single malt, though not a top one. That said, this is enjoyable stuff especially when considering the Indian distiller's perennial problem of overcoming the fierce temperatures that make maturation such a nightmare. With Amrut there is profound oak on both the nose and finish, giving the impression of a Speyside at about 35 or 36 years. That, usually, isn't always good. However, the sweet richness of the malt on the palate is a joy, with a boundless energy that pulses through to the prickly, oaky finish. Solid, honest whisky (with a non-scotch flourish at the finish) that would, after a black coffee, follow the finest Chicken Korma. (If you want to know more about Indian whisky, find the chapter on the distilleries I visited there in *Jim Murray's Complete Book of Whisky*). **40%. ncf.**

NEW ZEALAND
WILSON DISTILLERY

Milford Aged 10 Years Limited Edition dist 91 bott Aug 02 batch no. F9/0/08 **(89)** n22 mildly minty, dry oak suppressing slightly the barley-sugar sweetness; gentle peat adds lovely depth; t23 rich, clean malt then that superb, trademark Wilson distillery fizz accompanying that delicate smoke; f21 softer oaky notes but some brittle peat offers some length to an otherwise abrupt finish; b23 charming yet always busy on the palate. **43%** *New Zealand Malt Whisky Co. 5573 bottles.*

Milford Aged 12 Years Limited Edition dist 90 bott Oct 02 batch no. E50/0 **(88)** n22 firm, crisp barley; the oak is dry despite a faint burbony character; a slight shake of black pepper; t24 beautifully mouth-watering and rich, the malt is stunningly intense and its usual ultra-clean self. A little bite and fizz towards the middle; f20 quite light, short and a touch thin; b22 the mouth arrival and barley lift-off is the stuff of New Zealand whisky legend; only the closed finish prevents this being a major classic. Excellent whisky. **43%** *New Zealand Malt Whisky Co. 2840 bottles.*

Lammerlaw Aged 12 Years Peated Malt Sherry Cask Finishing (85) n22 softly and delightfully peated: gentle malt and oak with a thread of honey; t19 abrasive and uneven at first then a surge of lightly honied malt leads to a decent oaky-malty middle; f23 now the peat kicks in for a sensuous finale. Sweetens brilliantly on the light but chewy finish. Great complexity; b21 gets over the hurdle of the rough start to finish how it began on the nose: wonderfully! **50%. nc ncf.** *From Wilson Distillery, though it says Willowbank on the label.*

Cadenhead's Lammerlaw 10 Years Old (88) n*22* big, fresh malt with a drying, chalky oak influence; t*23* mouthwatering, clean, juicy malt. A touch of salt seasons it and the complexity is further aided by warming spices and the most subtle hints of citrus; f*21* back to that drying, chalky oak; b*22* seriously sensuous and complex malt from a tragically lost distillery. Pure New Zealand, but Speyside in style, and puts a good number of Speysiders to shame with its balance and complexity. **48.2%**

Meenan's Lammerlaw 12 Years Old (90) n*23* beautifully honeyed, with lavender and a very distant rumble of peat: the oak suggests something older; t*23* an outstanding delivery of soft, fruity malts, a layer of sweet honey and some oak and distant smoke; f*21* heaps of vanilla and soft spice and a gradual build-up of something peaty; b*23* this is a genuinely complex, beautifully made malt where the oak makes a wonderful divergence. A classic from any continent. **50%.** *Available only in New Zealand.*

Blended

⠿ **Kiwi Whisky (37)** n*2* t*12* f*11* b*12*. Strewth! I mean, what can you say? Perhaps the first whisky containing single malt offering virtually no nose at all and the flavour appears to be grain neutral spirit plus lashings of caramel and (so I am told) some Lammerlaw single malt. The word bland has been redefined. As has whisky. **40%.** *Ever-Rising Enterprises, NZ, for the Asian market.*

⠿ **Wilson's Superior Blend (89)** n*22* stupendously clean and malt rich. Imperiously mouthwatering and enticing; t*23* brilliant, almost dazzling clean malt arrival sharpened even further with mildly though distant crisp grain. One of the world's maltiest, most salivating blends, perhaps a touch simplistic but the charm of the malt endures while the ultra-delicate oak offers a teasing weight; f*21* loses marks only because of a caramel-induced toffee arrival, but still the malt and grain are in perfect sync while the drying oak offers balance; b*23* apparently has a mixed reception in its native New Zealand but I fail to see why: this is unambiguously outstanding blended whisky. On the nose you expect a mouthwatering mouthful and it delivers with aplomb. Despite this being a lower priced blend it is, intriguingly, a marriage of 60% original bottled 10-y-o Lammerlaw and 40% old Wilson's blend, explaining the high malt apparent. Dangerous and delicious and would be better still at a fuller strength...and with less caramel. **37.5%.** *Continental Wines and Spirits, NZ.*

SOUTH AFRICA
Single malt
JAMES SEDGWICK DISTILLERY

⠿ **Three Ships 10 Years Old Single Malt** db **(81)** n*20* t*20* f*21* b*20*. Distinctive with crushed digestive biscuit on the nose and a complex array of fruity, oaky tones on the palate. The malt is very light, though. **43%**

Blended

Harrier (77) n*17* t*20* f*21* b*19*. Perfumy and sweet; very easy to drink soft grain. **43%.** *South African/Scotch Whisky.*

Knights (77) n*16* t*21* f*20* b*20*. Spot-on grain: a sumptuous blend with genuinely impressive and high-quality bite and balance. **43%.** *South African/Scotch Whisky.*

Three Ships sample B, **(87)** n*21* thin, hard grain offset by softer, Islay (Bowmore-ish style) smoke. Delicate and attractive; t*22* again it's grain first to show, then a slow evolution of malt with peat drifting in as the spices arrive; f*22* excellent sweet-dry balance with toffee taking out the top notes; b*22* seriously drinkable blended whisky offering excellent balance. Has improved beyond recognition in recent years: now the pride of the fleet. **43%.** *South African/ Scotch Whisky.*

whiskybible.com

Let Jim Murray keep you in touch with what's going on around the world's whiskies

www.whiskybible.com

Jim will be regularly updating the site, filing reports about distilleries in his multi-award-winning prose from Scotland to Scandinavia, from Austria to Australia. If a new whisky distillery pops up somewhere in the world be sure that Jim Murray will be paying it a visit....

Also look out for details of new whiskies to be launched in 2005 and find out how to get his exclusive review and ratings of the bottlings.

The site will include an international guide to which distilleries welcome visitors, contact numbers for whisky clubs and organisations, liquor stores offering a choice of over 250 whiskies and lots, lots more.

In fact, **www.whiskybible.com** will have all the things we wanted to put in Jim Murray's Whisky Bible but just didn't have the room.

Keep in touch with Jim Murray. The most passionate and independent voice in world whisky.

Slàinte

I t seems that you can't have a Bible without a whole lot of begetting. And without all those listed below – a cast of thousands for the 2004 edition which now seems like millions (and few others besides whose details I have again mislaid amid the chaos) – this 2005 Bible would never have been begot at all. Special thanks, as usual, to **Martin Corteel, Darren Jordan and David Ballheimer at Mission Control**; to Soren Norgaard for providing my additional tasting lab in Denmark; to Takeshi Mogi for help keeping me on the ball in Japan and Claudia Hamm likewise in Europe. Heroes all.

Esben Andersen; Paul Aston; David Baker; Liselle Barnsley; Rachel Barrie; Jim Beveridge; Edi Bieri; Borat; Etienne Bouillon; Neil Boyd; David Brisset; Karen Brown; Kim Brown; Andy Burns; Bill Caldwell; Jenny Cantrell; Tina Carey; Chris Carlsson; Alex Carnie; Mark Carpenter; Candy Charters; Julie Christian; Ricky Christie; Georgie Crawford; Andy Crook; Rick Connolly; Andy Cook; Paula Cormack; Andy Cornwall; Silvia Corrieri; Isabel Coughlan; James Cowan; David Cox; Ronnie Cox; Fergal Crean; Andrew Currie; Bob Dalgarno; Craig Daniels; Martin Dawson; Jürgen Deibel; Alex Delaloye; Gordon Doctor; Ed Dodson; Jean Donnay; Lucy Drake; Jonathan Driver; Colin Dunn; Lucy Egerton; Carsten Ehrlich; Duncan Elphick; Richard Evans; Roy Evans; Alex Fitch; Robert Fleischmann; Mary Forest; Angela Forsgren D'Orazio; Tim French; Emma Gill; Fiona Gittus; Richard Gordon; Ed Graham; George Grant; Lynn Grant; Donald R Greeter; Christian Gruel; David Hallgarten; Archie Hamilton; Andy Hart; Donald Hart; Julian Haswell; Michael Heals; CJ Hellie; Lincon Henderson; Irene Hemmings; Robert Hicks; Vincent Hill; Aaron Hillman; Sandy Hislop; Sarah-Jane Hodson; Karl-Holger Hoehler; Mark Hunt; Ford Hussain; Ily Jaffa; Richard Joynson; Naofumi Kamaguchi; Larry Kass; Jaclyn Kelly; Daniel Kissling; Dennis Klindrup; Mana Kondo; Lex Kraaijeveld; Libby Lafferty; Fred Laing; Stuart Laing; Bill Lark; Walter Lecocq; Patricia Lee; Anne Marie Le Lay; Guy Le Lay; Billy Leighton; Darren Leitch; Jim Long; Martin Long; Linda Love; Bill Lumsden; Antony McCallum-Caron; Steve MCarthy; Stuart MacDuff; Lynne McEwan; Sarah McGhee; Helen McGinn; Doug McIvor; Lorne McKillop; Kirsty McLeod; Fred McMillan; Janice McMillan; Steven McNeil; Patrick Maguire; Elaine Masson; Norman Mathison; David Maxwell-Scott; Lee Medoff; Clare Meikle; Jon Metcalf; Rick Mew; Robbie Millar; Jack Milroy; Tatsuya Minagawa; Euan Mitchell; Matthew Mitchell; Jürgen Moeller; Takeshi Mogi; Daniela Dal Molin; Rainer Mönks; Les Morgan; Chris Morris; Mary Morton; Gordon Motion; Arthur Motley; Malcolm Mullin; Alison Murray; Andrew Murray; Charles Murray; David Murray; James Murray; Shin Natsuyama; Marc Neilly; Margaret Nicol; Micke Nilsson; Sir Iain Noble; Edel Nørgaard; Johannes Nørgaard; Lis Nørgaard; Søren Nørgaard; Barbara Ortner; Wolfram Ortner; Lucy Pritchard; Richard Paterson; Rupert Patrick; Plamen Petroff; Dave Phelan; Simon Pointon; Warren Preston; Annie Pugh; David Radcliffe; John Ramsey; Alan Reid; Geraldine Roche; Colin Ross; Duncan Ross; Jim Rutledge; Christine Sandys; Charlie Saunders; Leander Schadler; Gerd Schmerschneider; Mick Secor; Tammy Secor; Tara Serafini; Catherine Service; Euan Shand; Sukhinder Singh; Emanuel Solinsky; Sue Stamps; Florian Stetter; Tamsin Stevens; David Stewart; Kathleen Stirling; Kaj Stovring; Derek Strange; Noel Sweeney; Graham Taylor; Jo Terry; Jens Tholstrup; Corinna Thompson; Stuart Thompson; Terry Threlfall; Hamish Torrie; Sarah True; Robin Tucek; Ben Upjohn; Ian Urquhart; Johan Venter; Kenneth Vernon; Billy Walker; Jamie Walker; Karen Walker; Leesa Walker; Barry Walsh; Susan Webster; Oswald Weidenauer; Jan H Westcott; Jack Wiebers; Lars-Göran Wiebers; Alex Williams; Lisa Wilson; Arthur Winning; Lance Winters; Graham Wright.